Lecture Notes
in Business Information Processing   **381**

Series Editors

Wil van der Aalst
RWTH Aachen University, Aachen, Germany
John Mylopoulos
University of Trento, Trento, Italy
Michael Rosemann
Queensland University of Technology, Brisbane, QLD, Australia
Michael J. Shaw
University of Illinois, Urbana-Champaign, IL, USA
Clemens Szyperski
Microsoft Research, Redmond, WA, USA

T0212125

Marinos Themistocleous ·
Maria Papadaki (Eds.)

Information Systems

16th European, Mediterranean,
and Middle Eastern Conference, EMCIS 2019
Dubai, United Arab Emirates, December 9–10, 2019
Proceedings

 Springer

Editors
Marinos Themistocleous (iD)
University of Nicosia
Nicosia, Cyprus

Maria Papadaki
British University in Dubai
Dubai, United Arab Emirates

ISSN 1865-1348   ISSN 1865-1356   (electronic)
Lecture Notes in Business Information Processing
ISBN 978-3-030-44321-4   ISBN 978-3-030-44322-1   (eBook)
https://doi.org/10.1007/978-3-030-44322-1

This Springer imprint is published by the registered company Springer Nature Switzerland AG
The registered company address is: Gewerbestrasse 11, 6330 Cham, Switzerland

Preface

The European, Mediterranean, and Middle Eastern Conference on Information Systems (EMCIS) is an annual research event addressing the discipline of Information Systems (IS) from a regional as well as global perspective. EMCIS has successfully helped bring together researchers from around the world in a friendly atmosphere, conducive to the free exchange of innovative ideas. EMCIS is one of the premier conferences in Europe and the Middle Eastern region for IS academics and professionals, covering technical, organizational, business, and social issues in the application of information technology. EMCIS is dedicated to the definition and establishment of IS as a discipline of high impact for IS professionals and practitioners. EMCIS focuses on approaches that facilitate the identification of innovative research of significant relevance to the IS discipline following sound research methodologies that lead to results of measurable impact.

This year, we received 138 papers from 39 countries from all continents and 46 of them were accepted with an overall acceptance rate of 33.3%. Unlike previous years, EMCIS 2019 did not accept any short papers. All papers were submitted through the easyacademia.org online review system. Track chairs assigned reviewers and the papers were sent for double-blind review. The papers were reviewed either by members of the Conference Committee or by external reviewers. Track chairs submitted 9 papers and each of these papers was reviewed by a member of the EMCIS Executive Committee and one member of the International Committee. The conference chairs submitted 3 papers in total which were reviewed by two senior external reviewers each. Overall, 48 papers were accepted for EMCIS 2019 as full papers submitted to the following tracks:

- Big Data and Analytics (7 accepted papers)
- Blockchain Technology and Applications (3 accepted papers)
- Cloud Computing (2 accepted papers)
- Digital Services and Social Media (3 accepted papers)
- e-Government (4 accepted papers)
- Enterprise Information Systems (4 accepted papers)
- Health-Care Information Systems (3 accepted papers)
- Information Systems Security and Information Privacy Protection (4 accepted papers)
- Innovative Research Projects (4 accepted papers)
- IT Governance (5 accepted papers)
- Management and Organizational Issues in Information Systems (7 accepted papers)

The papers were accepted for their theoretical and practical excellence as well as the promising results they presented. We hope that the readers will find the papers interesting and we are open for a constructive discussion that will improve the body of knowledge in the field of IS.

December 2019   Marinos Themistocleous
                                                        Maria Papadaki

Organization

Conference Chairs

Maria Papadaki	The British University in Dubai, UAE
Marinos Themistocleous	University of Nicosia, Cyprus
Muhammad Mustafa Kamal	Coventry University, UK

Conference Executive Committee

Vincenzo Morabito (Program Chair)	Bocconi University, Italy
Paulo da Cunha (Program Chair)	Coimbra University, Portugal
Gianluigi Viscusi (Public Relations Chair)	École polytechnique fédérale de Lausanne, Switzerland

International Committee

Heinz Roland Weistroffer	Virginia Commonwealth University, USA
Piotr Soja	Cracow University of Economics, Poland
Peter Love	Curtin University, Australia
Gail Corbitt	California State University, USA
Miguel Mira da Silva	University of Lisbon, Portugal
Vishanth Weerakkody	University of Bradford, UK
Lasse Berntzen	Buskerud and Vestfold University College, Norway
Marijn Janssen	Delft University of Technology, The Netherlands
Stanisław Wrycza	University of Gdansk, Poland
Kamel Ghorab	Alhosn University, UAE
Angelika Kokkinaki	University of Nicosia, Cyprus
Celina M. Olszak	University of Economics in Katowice, Poland
Flora Malamateniou	University of Piraeus, Greece
Soulla Louca	University of Nicosia, Cyprus
Andriana Prentza	University of Piraeus, Greece
Inas Ezz	Sadat Academy for Management Sciences (SAMS), Egypt
Klitos Christodoulou	University of Nicosia, Cyprus
Ibrahim Osman	American University of Beirut, Lebanon
Przemysław Lech	University of Gdańsk, Poland
Euripidis N. Loukis	University of the Aegean, Greece
Mariusz Grabowski	Cracow University of Economics, Poland
Elias Iosif	University of Nicosia, Cyprus
Małgorzata Pańkowska	University of Economics in Katowice, Poland

Catarina Ferreira da Silva	Université Claude Bernard Lyon 1, France
Aggeliki Tsohou	Ionian University, Greece
Paweł Wołoszyn	Cracow University of Economics, Poland
Sofiane Tebboune	Manchester Metropolitan University, UK
Fletcher Glancy	Miami University, USA
Aurelio Ravarini	Universitario Carlo Cattaneo, Italy
Wafi Al-Karaghouli	Brunel University, UK
Ricardo Jimenes Peris	Universidad Politécnica de Madrid (UPM), Spain
Federico Pigni	Grenoble École de Management, France
Paulo Henrique de Souza Bermejo	Universidade Federal de Lavras, Brazil
May Seitanidi	University of Kent, UK
Sevgi Özkan	Middle East Technical University, Turkey
Demosthenis Kyriazis	University of Piraeus, Greece
Karim Al-Yafi	Qatar University, Qatar
Manar Abu Talib	Zayed University, UAE
Alan Serrano	Brunel University, UK
Steve Jones	Conwy County Borough, UK
Tillal Eldabi	Ahlia University, Bahrain
Carsten Brockmann	Capgemini SE, Germany
Ella Kolkowska	Örebro University, Sweden
Grażyna Paliwoda-Pękosz	Cracow University of Economics, Poland
Heidi Gautschi	IMD Lausanne, Switzerland
Janusz Stal	Cracow University of Economics, Poland
Koumaditis Konstantinos	Aarhus University, Denmark
Chinello Francesco	Aarhus University, Denmark
Pacchierotti Claudio	University of Rennes, France
Milena Krumova	Technical University of Sofia, Bulgaria

Contents

Cloud Computing

Digital Services and Social Media

E-Government

Enterprise Systems

HealthCare Information Systems

Information Systems Security and Information Privacy Protection

Innovative Research Projects

IT Governance

Management and Organizational Issues in Information Systems

Big Data and Analytics

A Practice Based Exploration on Electric Mobility as a Service in Smart Cities

Bokolo Anthony Jr.[(✉)] and Sobah Abbas Petersen

Department of Computer Science,
Norwegian University of Science and Technology,
NTNU, 7491 Trondheim, Norway
{anthony.j.bokolo,sobah.a.petersen}@ntnu.no

Abstract. With increase in urban residents and CO_2 emission from vehicles, there is need to deploy smart electric mobility services termed as Electric Mobility as a Service (eMaaS) facilitated by innovations in Information Communication Technology (ICT) to mitigate environmental issues, improve social inclusion, and enhance economic growth. However, citizens and stakeholders are faced with issues related to acquiring appropriate information needed to make decisions which impacts their wellbeing and natural environment due to heterogenous data being generated from various sources. Therefore, this study adopts Enterprise Architecture (EA) and integrates Application Programming Interfaces (APIs) to improve interoperability for acquisition, processing, retaining, and dissemination of mobility relevant data. Secondary data from the literature and ArchiMate modeling tool was utilized to model eMaaS case to verify the feasibility of EA to improve city transport services. Findings from ArchiMate reveal that EA provides a theoretical and practical approach that supports mobility services in smart cities.

Keywords: Smart cities · Smart mobility · Electric mobility · Big data · Enterprise architecture · ArchiMate modeling language

1 Introduction

Presently, more than half of the world's citizens resides in cities and urban environments are facing challenges in areas such as in congested transport infrastructure, energy effectiveness, climate change, and environmental pollution [1]. Accordingly, the transportation sector is under pressure to reduce reliance on traditional combustion engine vehicles which releases CO_2 emissions that pollutes the environment and are utilizing Electric Vehicles (EVs) which are characterized as being lowly polluting, energy efficient, and noiseless [2]. Thus, the transition towards Electric Mobility as a Service (eMaaS) is believed to improve sustainable transportation in smart cities as it facilitates the reduction of carbon dioxide emissions [3]. eMaaS in smart cities comprises of deployment of fleets of EVs such as electric bicycles, electric cars, and segways to support collaborative sharing [4].

Furthermore, cities are faced with issues relates to silos which hinders smart services due to lack of interoperability and openness to produce value-added services

© Springer Nature Switzerland AG 2020
M. Themistocleous and M. Papadaki (Eds.): EMCIS 2019, LNBIP 381, pp. 3–17, 2020.
https://doi.org/10.1007/978-3-030-44322-1_1

across multiple platforms. Thus, there is need for interoperable standards to foster development of open ecosystems and expose the commercial potential of mobility data [5], where interoperability refers to the ability of different devices to communicate with each other and exchange information. Moreover, processing and visualizing mobility related data is not straightforward due to heterogenous data being generated from different sources such as position of EVs, routing, EV usage, EV parking stations, charging stations locations, EV battery status, and city transport data, etc. [6]. Such challenge entails deployment of innovative Information Communication Technology (ICT) solutions, such as Application Programming Interface (API) capable of enabling interoperability and providing access to processed and stored data needed to deliver information on mobility related services [7]. Thus, API serves as data adapters integrated for establishing connections to different mobility platforms, external databases, and real-time streaming data [8].

In addition, researchers such as Sánchez et al. [9] suggested developing architecture to address eMaaS requirements for the actualization of smart electric mobility (e-mobility) services. The authors mentioned that architecture supports the deployment of applications that access heterogeneous data produced from different sources in an open and standardized approach. Respectively, Enterprise Architecture (EA) is adopted in this study to provide information on the current as-is structure of mobility services thus serving as an informational foundation for making decisions for transportation development. Likewise, EA provide a medium to develop and envision to-be conditions for mobility planning [10]. EA provides a holistic scope and offers aggregate and broad view of the entire corporation comprising of business processes, organizational structure, strategic aspects, software and data, and IT infrastructure.

Besides, EA provide systematic support for transformation and is driven by IT and/or business-oriented application based on citizens and stakeholders' concerns [11]. Respectively, this study presents EA approach that integrates API for improving interoperability and handling e-mobility related data which is key enabler for improving transportation operation in providing collaborative, flexible, and efficient e-mobility service to citizens in cities. The structure of the paper is as follows Sect. 2 is literature review. Section 3 is application of EA in eMaaS, Sect. 4 is the results. Section 5 is discussion and implications lastly Sect. 6 is the conclusion, limitations, and future directions.

2   Literature Review

2.1   eMaaS and Big Data in Smart Cities

Clearly the topic on smart mobility is gaining importance globally due to significant increase in number of cars within cities which causes pollution issues and serious threat to citizens quality of life [12]. Thus, there is need to employ sustainable mobility such as electric vehicles (for example electric bicycles, electric cars, segways, etc.), which comprises of infrastructure for e-mobility and IT system towards EV fleet management [2] as seen in Fig. 1. This is because fossil fuel vehicles used in transportation are a significant contributor to CO_2 emission, and are considered as one of the main hindrances to sustainable development.

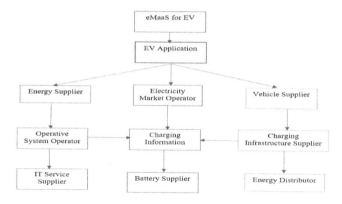

Fig. 1. Value chain of IT and electric players

Figure 1 depicts the value chain of IT and electric system working together to facilitate eMaaS for EVs which are perceived as an important contributor in the reductions of greenhouse gas production and are one of the most prospective solutions for decarbonization of urban transportation [12]. Hence, in smart cities EVs play a major role in urban transportation in decreasing carbon dioxide emission. But, for EVs to be used there is need to depict the entire e-mobility chain to citizens in a flexible and resourceful manner. Accordingly, in cities eMaaS utilizes different categories of data such as public data (schedules, routes, road conditions, etc.), business data (fees, ticket information, charging stations), and private data (user preferences, user targets, citizens profiles) [6].

These data are generated in volume, velocity, variety, and veracity and processing these data into actionable and valuable insights and making it open for mobility application usage is an issue that has not fully been addressed in the literature. Although, few studies have examined big data in mobility domain, they are mostly concerned with addressing functional requirements and designs of mobility services [3]. Hence, there is need to develop flexible and efficient big data processing platform between data sources and mobility applications.

2.2 API for Data Interoperability

Currently, smart mobility solutions are transforming data to services for citizens, stakeholders and city transport operators. Thus, integrating open and private data, static, open, and real-time data from different sources and there are issues related to aggregating, exploiting, and re-conciliating of data to facilitate eMaaS orchestration [7]. Furthermore, eMaaS provides standardized services that utilize heterogeneous data sources such as available transport data, real-time data regarding vehicles, ticketing pricing, etc. to provide customized mobility services to citizens, as well as to stakeholders for monitoring and planning [4]. eMaaS concept provides access to new markets for data services creating prospects for additional profits and market growth [6]. Likewise, eMaaS utilize data which is to be shared among citizens and stakeholders, such as geographical data providers, city administration, public transport providers, EV charging station providers etc. [13].

Clearly, there is a need for an approach such as API that would facilitate sharing and usage of such data thereby orchestrating open data interoperability [12]. API acts as a gateway, enabling smart mobility applications to access specific data seamlessly using Extensible Markup Language (XML) or other formats such as JavaScript Object Notation (JSON) [14]. Additionally, API uses Representational State Transfer (REST) protocol over HTTP using JSON in integrating several different data sources to retrieve raw data from a data source in its native format (XML, JSON, comma- separated values (CSV) or others) to provide mobility data [3]. API helps mobility service providers open-up data and offers the ability to collect data from diverse sources and make the data available and searchable. Thus, in this study API is integrated as a technology that supports interoperability of variety of data and protocols across diverse devices to support eMaaS in smart city.

2.3 Background of Enterprise Architecture

According to Chen et al. [15] an enterprise refers to one or more organizations sharing a definite objectives, goals, and mission to offer an output such as a service or product. Architecture models constitute the fundamental of an approach and serve the purpose of making the complexities of the real world manageable and understandable to humans [16]. Presently, cities are increasingly using IT not only to underpin existing mobility services but also to develop new opportunities that creates new source of competitive advantage. Thus, to improve transportation services cities must deploy IT related service. Likewise, mobility service providers need to tactically manage IT to strategically mange business operations. Accordingly, there is needs for integrating a standardized model such as enterprise architecture that holistically represent all component within e-mobility services, with the use of schematics and graphics to depict how parts of the components are interrelated.

The concept of EA was proposed by John Zachman in 1987 based on architecture in civil to be extended in enterprises to decrease complexity of developing Information Systems (ISs) [17]. Thus, EA is a structure for aligning IT and business within enterprise and aims to provide appropriate ISs based on business demands [16]. EA provides a well-developed, systematic approach to align corporations and their utilization of technology to offer alignment across mobility operations and design [11]. Many establishments adopt EA as part of their IT planning and management activities for strategic prioritization and alignment in guiding their decisions towards improving bottom line impact and managing innovative changes [16]. Moreover, EA describes the components that make up the complete system and offers a blueprint from which the system can be deployed [15], it entails the essential structure of an organization and facilitates transformation by providing a holistic perspective regarding as-is and as to-be processes and structures. It promotes integration and consistency across infrastructure, process, application, and information, for improved business performance, thereby lessens organizations complexity via reuse and sharing of components and standardizations [11].

EA can be applied in mobility domain to ideally help stakeholders to efficiently plan, communicate document, analyze, and design IT and business-related issues by providing decision support for stakeholders providing information for mobility service providers [16]. Moreover, EA provide systematic support to mobility transformation and change that affects both IT and business structures providing an aggregate and broad structure of the entire eMaaS operation driven citizens and stakeholders' concerns [18]. Furthermore, EA is suitable to be applied in eMaaS as it aids to envision, lead, plan, design, and manage transportation operations in current, transitionary, and future conditions within smart cities. It describes the e-mobility services in terms of structure, strategy, information flows, physical instantiations, and business process [11]. It improves the performance and quality of mobility processes and improves productivity across the city by integrating data sources. The blueprints designed by EA provide a basis for modelling and optimizing e-mobility services enabling mobility service providers to decrease complexity by outlining the operating principles and technical standards for guiding mobility operations [17].

2.4   Related Works

A few studies have investigated e-mobility services in smart cities, among these studies Ruohomaa and Salminen [19] researched on MaaS in relation to industry 4.0 approach. The authors focused on addressing main area of development to understand the opportunities and issues related to e-city bike services and how produced data could be utilized to improve city mobility services. Furthermore, Bellini et al. [20] designed an architecture for data ingestion and analytics in the context of mobility and transport integrated services grounded on ontology and tools for data aggregation and service creation in smart cities. Experiment was carried out to test the approach in a city. Besides, Kamargianni and Matyas [6] developed a business ecosystem for MaaS. The researchers depicted the actors and their respective roles in MaaS and provided a holistic method for MaaS concept development and identified the eMaaS areas that needed to be explored. Data was collected using interviews based on focus groups.

Similarly, Melis et al. [4] proposed a crowdsensing service-oriented architecture for smart mobility and demonstrated the implementation of microservice paradigm to actualize mobility services system. The authors utilized microservice to expose and orchestrate data service. Also, Brand et al. [21] designed an architecture for achieving interoperability of e-mobility. The architecture was developed based on The Open Group Architecture Framework (TOGAF) for enterprise architecture and it aimed to provides adequate integration of electricity system to support the charge process based on data from market parties. The authors adopted qualitative method and collected data using structured interviews to validate their approach. Likewise, Kuehl et al. [22] designed a service-oriented business model for e-mobility. Their research aimed to gain improved understanding of existing e-mobility services and provide an approach that is simple yet comprehensive and convenient to describe e-mobility services.

Moreover, Tcholtchev et al. [23] designed a mobility data cloud that provide a framework for collecting, aggregating, processing, and analysis of mobility data generated from numerous sources. The authors utilized various data to facilitate collaborative sharing of mobility resources such as EVs, charging stations, etc. A prototype was presented to evaluate their approach based on trials method. Additionally, Abdelkafi et al. [24] proposed an innovative business model to create value for e-mobility. The proposed approach enabled the categorization and adoption of business model patterns, identified via the integration of different dimensions to be adapted to fit into the domain of e-mobility. Likewise, Tcholtchev et al. [12] explored the integration of open data, network providers, and cloud services to improve e- mobility in smart cities. The researchers designed a distributed architecture for the provision of mobility data cloud in achieving EV sharing via a cloud-based system for data handling.

Additionally, Mäkelä and Pirhonen [25] proposed a business model to improve value creation of electric mobility in complex private service system. The researchers demonstrated how the model can be used as an analysis tool to understand and describe value creation complexity of e-mobility in developing industry. Action research method was employed using case study to collect data from nine e-mobility firms. The reviewed studies applied data to improve mobility services of EVs and non-EVs towards reducing pollution by supporting collaborative mobility sharing services. Although, architectures were proposed in the literature, there are fewer studies that adopted EA approach and APIs to improve interoperability of eMaaS apart from Brand et al. [21]. Nevertheless, the authors are more concerned about improving EV changing and enhancing energy markets. Thus, this study adds to the body of knowledge by presenting the application EA and integration of API for data interoperability in enhancing eMaaS in smart cities.

3   Application of EA in eMaaS

This study adopts enterprise architecture approach and presented an architecture to promote eMaaS in smart cities. The architecture is developed in prior study [26] based on TOGAF standard analogous to previous study Brand et al. [21]. Accordingly, Fig. 2 depicts the architecture which comprises of seven layers.

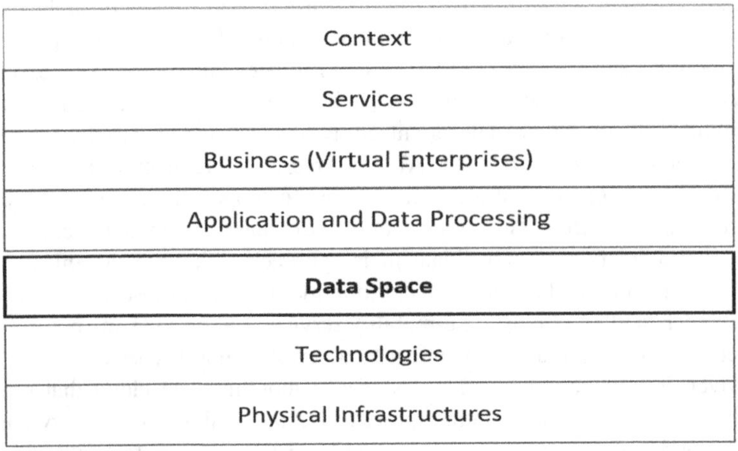

| Context |
| Services |
| Business (Virtual Enterprises) |
| Application and Data Processing |
| **Data Space** |
| Technologies |
| Physical Infrastructures |

Fig. 2. Architecture for data interoperability of eMaaS

Figure 2 shows the architecture which comprises of context, service, business, application, data space, technologies, and physical infrastructures layers. Thus, each of the layers are discussed below;

3.1 Context Layer

This layer mainly entails the drivers, priorities, and important characteristics in delivering effective eMaaS to citizens and stakeholders. The context layer entails requirements that relates to stakeholders' concerns, wants, and associated drivers/enablers that improve quality of life [27]. Hence, this layer specifies the scope, goals, etc. related to citizens and stakeholders' necessities as regards to urban mobility. Accordingly, the context layer specifies the aims to be attained which in this study involves achieving an interoperable data oriented eMaaS.

3.2 Service Layer

This layer aims to effectively deploy specified outputs and competently achieving specified key performance goals [28]. In this research services are provided by trusted parties such as municipalities, EV provider, mobility service provider, payment company, etc. that facilitates eMaaS in smart cities. Moreover, this layer is linked to the application layers via business layer through HTTP protocols [3]. Therefore, this layer comprises of various smart services that are part of the mobility operations.

3.3 Business Layer

This layer includes enterprises or establishments involved in city mobility service such as municipality, city transport company, payment firm, EV rental company, energy company, etc. [21]. Accordingly, this layer encompasses virtual enterprises that collaborate towards providing e-mobility services to citizens to support transportation in smart city. The business layer depicts the flow of co-ordination of enterprise and business procedures deployed across each firm [27]. Besides, the business layer aligns each enterprise's daily routine with IT to provide business centric view for mobility operations.

3.4 Application and Data Processing Layer

The applications and data processing layer provide a set of APIs and systems to manage and post-process data coming from data space layers. This layer addresses interoperability among heterogenous data sources from different technologies and devices [10]. This layer allows remote access to e-mobility services via set of tools to users to access and visualize data coming from the physical infrastructures layer [26]. This layer also provides mobile applications and web portal to address the mobility needs and requirements of citizens and stakeholders via request/response and publish/subscribe protocols, exposing mobility data via RESTful API [9]. Further, this layer aids stakeholders to deploy existing tools to develop new application for improving mobility services to satisfy contextual information needs of citizens [29].

3.5   Data Space Layer

This layer mainly involves the retaining, exchange, publishing of processed data via application layer [26]. The data space provides massive data storage for historical, online, and real-time datasets to support e-mobility applications. It is responsible for managing, storing and providing access to wide range of retained data and data sources towards providing valuable insights [29]. It exposes mobility service via APIs to access data in several formats for querying and discovering data sources that facilitates seamless data access by application layer [21]. These data sources include physical devices, sensors, energy meters, public data, weather, transport, city transport data, etc. These data sources are compiled and stored as datasets in data space layer to provide citizens with mobility services that intensively depend on these data [9].

3.6   Technology Layer

The technology layer offers infrastructure needed to run applications, comprising of hardware, system software, and communication hardware [26]. Besides, this layer comprises of temporal storage, managing, and handling of big data by ensuring that acquired data are cleansed to confirm the quality of data. Thus, a context-aware component is introduced to filter out unrelated data and to implement quality check and data harmonization [3]. Moreover, the technology layer entails big data infrastructures needed to process, historical, online and real-time data [21]. Furthermore, this layer provides mechanisms to efficiently clean, analyze, and transform these large sets of diverse data simultaneously by executing batch processing of static and online data, and stream processing of real-time data [20].

3.7   Physical Infrastructures Layer

This layer comprises the production of real-time data from various sources such as physical devices, sensors, energy meters, EVs, etc. [20]. In terms of e-mobility, this layer is the core of architecture as its specifically designed for accessing and transmitting data coming from physical and IoT devices based on different protocols such as Message Queuing Telemetry Transport (MQTT) using subscribe and publish communication [3]. Thus, this layer entails meters and sensors that collects real-time data of EVs within the city to perform demand-supply mobility fleet management. Similarly, this layer enables interoperability across heterogeneous sources, both software and hardware via MQTT protocol [20]. Also, this layer deploys wired and wireless technologies such as IEEE 802.15.4, ZigBee and Bluetooth, LoRaWAN, etc. are employed for to facilitate remote communications through the Internet [9].

4   Results

This section depicts meta-model evaluation of the eMaaS case in ArchiMate, where metamodels are the fundamentals of EA and they describe the essential IT and business artefacts. They provide high level common language and precise view of the structure and dependencies between pertinent sectors of the organization [16]. Additionally, metamodels provides an approach that makes the complexities of the real world manageable and understandable to humans ideally supporting stakeholders of establishments to efficiently communicate, plan, document, and design IT and business associated issues.

In this study ArchiMate is used for designing metamodels in validating the presented architecture (see Fig. 2) for eMaaS transport scenario towards EV usage in smart city. ArchiMate is an independent and open modeling language for EA. In addition, ArchiMate is a useful tool to model applications, business processes, and technology towards supporting collaboration on enterprise level. ArchiMate supports design modelling languages for IT solutions and business processes. ArchiMate was developed based on TOGAF to offer a generic and integrated model that enable communication and decision making across domains such as in smart cities [30].

It provides uniform illustrations for diagrams that describe EA, thus offering a graphical language for the representation of EA over time in relation to motivation (context), business, application, and technology layer [15]. In this study to conceptualize the eMaaS scenario, services, data space, physical infrastructures layer are included as an extension to ArchiMate. Moreover, we opted for the ArchiMate language as it a widely accepted open standard for modeling EA and it fits well with the TOGAF standard that was employed to conceptualize our EA (see Fig. 2). According, Fig. 3 depicts the meta-model for eMaaS operation for EV in smart city modelled in ArchiMate to evaluate the feasibility of each of the architecture layers.

The meta-model presented in Fig. 3 provides a good overview of how APIs and EA can support eMaaS, where each elements of the model were identified from the literature (see Sect. 2.4). The attaining of smart mobility through ICT lies in the usage of data from different sources and processing into valuable information delivered via application to offer services, consumed by citizens and stakeholders. This includes the collection of huge heterogenous amounts of data from the physical infrastructures layer, the aggregation and processing of historical, online, and real- time data in technology layer, and storage and usage of data to provide useful mobility information.

Therefore, in the physical infrastructures layer heterogenous real-time data is transmitted from surveillance cameras, traffic sensors, EVs, charging stations, buildings, metering devices, etc. via Bluetooth, ZigBee, Wi-Fi, WLAN communication protocols to the technology layer [31]. Next historical, online, and real-time mobility data are processed in the technologies layer which is the central processing component for data computation. This layer also comprises of data pre- processor, rules engine, message queue, data filter, Hadoop, and storage. Data pre- processing involves mobility data normalization which plays a critical role in dealing with different data parameters scaling the data to a specific small and accurate range. To normalize the gathered data, the Min-Max technique is employed as it is widely used technique to scale up and properly transform data values. Moreover, Message Queue (MQ) method is adopted which is based on defined rules utilized to store generated mobility data in a suitable format in MQ which offers a mechanism that positions and avoids delay and halt of processing. The MQ technique is deployed when it receives M message at t time which is sent accordingly as a filtered data to be processed by Hadoop which first stores the huge datasets in distributed format.

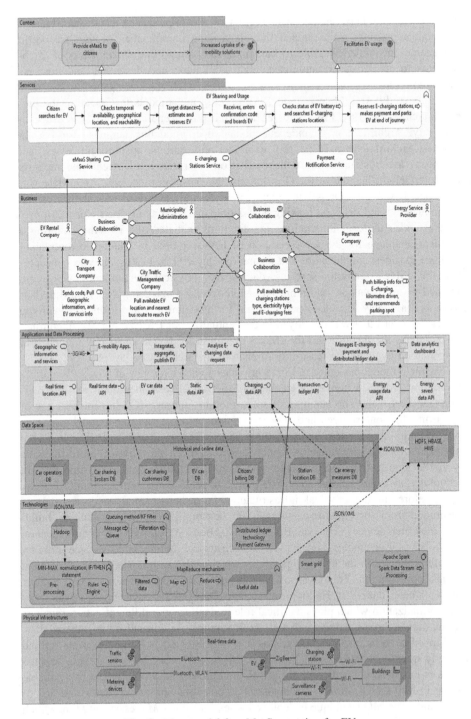

Fig. 3. Meta-model for eMaaS operation for EV

Next, data filtration is employed to filter the data and remove noise using Kalman Filter (KF) to speed up the data processing and separate the valuable and noisy data. Furthermore, Hadoop employs MapReduce technique for processing filtered mobility data. MapReduce employs mapping of filtered mobility data that are transformed to another set of mobility data. Then, the reduce process merges mobility data produced which results in some values that are reduced in size. Hadoop is employed to analyze online and historical data for offline/static processing. Therefore, to process real-time data Apache spark is integrated. Spark is a batch in-memory computing technique that perform micro-batch procession through Spark-streaming. Besides, spark is an open source program aimed at speeding up and mining meaningful information quickly for decision making. As compared to Hadoop MapReduce, Spark offers an efficient alternative as it provides faster performance and is suitable for real-time and online applications processing.

In the data space layer, for storage of the processed mobility data Hadoop Distributed File Service (HDFS) is employed as it is distributed, supplementing the MapReduce processing on smaller subsets of larger data cluster which supports the scalability demand of mobility data processing. Moreover, HBASE is employed to improve processing speed on Hadoop as it improves the fault tolerance and usability and provides real-time read/write lookups. Likewise, HIVE is integrated as it supports managing and querying of mobility data that is saved on the Hadoop cluster. Thus, HIVE is used for querying since SQL cannot be utilized to query, hence HiveQL is used to query mobility data on Hadoop cluster to support eMaaS in smart cities. Furthermore, the data space layer consists of distributed ledger technology payment gateway and smart grid which transmits energy and data from and to EVs, charging stations and buildings. In the data space layer processed data are stored in HDFS which comprises of HBASE and HIVE connected to other external data sources (car operators, car sharing brokers, car sharing customers, EV car, citizen/billing, station location, and car energy measures database).

Furthermore, in the application and data processing layer, sources of data related to mobility is accessed by citizens and stakeholders via RESTful APIs (real time location, real time data, EV car data, static data, charging data, transaction ledger, energy usage data, and saved energy data API) which resides in the application layer that provides a common standardized platform for utilization of mobility related data that are represented in JSON or XML format. Additionally, application and data processing layer comprise of e-mobility applications and data analytics dashboard that makes use of Geographic information and services data as well as application process (integrating, aggregating, publishing EV charging data, analyzing e-charging data request, and managing e-charging payment, and distributed ledger data).

Next, the business layer depicts the virtual enterprises (EV rental company, city transport company, municipality administration, city traffic management company, payment company, and energy service provider) that collaborates to provide mobility related services (sends code, pull geographic information, and EV services info, pull available EV location and nearest bus route to reach EV, and pull available e-charging stations type, electricity type, and E-charging fees, and push billing info for e-charging, kilometer driven, and recommends parking spot). Similarly, the service layer entails business collaborating to provides services such as eMaaS sharing service, e-charging stations service, and payment notification service for improving EV sharing and usage which helps to achieve eMaaS goals (provide eMaaS to citizens and facilitates EV usage) and target (increased uptake of e-mobility solutions) in making cities smarter.

5   Discussion and Implications

Over the years there have been development towards e-mobility mainly in the emergence of EVs that enable decrease of carbon dioxide emissions, improves collaborative e-bicycles, e-cars, and segways sharing, and management of EV fleets in urban environment [4]. Improving transport services and data management is just the first step towards realizing smart cities [32]. But processing and using big data into valuable and usage insights for various mobility applications is an issue [3]. Likewise, accessing and usage of such mobility data is also challenging due to interoperability issue. In this paper we presented an approach to realize eMaaS for handling mobility data by adopting EA and APIs to improve interoperability for management of mobility relevant data that enables collaborative e-mobility services for citizens in an efficient and flexible manner.

Furthermore, the presented EA for eMaaS provides access to open data via APIs that provide interoperable data formats. As recommended by Kamargianni and Matyas [6] the architecture provides an ecosystem composed new data markets for transport services by creating opportunities for additional incomes and market growth. Moreover, findings from ArchiMate modelling reveal that the presented EA approach for eMaaS provides standardized services which flexibly and efficiently integrates heterogeneous data sources, such as available historical, online, and real-time transport data regarding EVs and transport infrastructures to provide customized mobility information to citizens, as well as monitoring and planning tools to policy- makers.

Implications from this study provides innovative services for citizens and e-mobility operators in managing and providing solutions to integrate and produce support for interoperability towards sustainable transport systems. The presented EA for eMaaS provides integrated data via API for decision support towards decreasing public costs of mobility, streamlining use of mobility application, providing information for supporting connected citizens/drivers manipulating data, and defining solutions for improving interoperability within data sources. Findings, from ArchiMate modelling provides abstract model that facilitates eMaaS replication and interoperability of data solutions to facilitate data processing towards enhancing data processing performance, while enabling intelligent decisions to produce insights within e-mobility context.

Finally, this paper provides a solid case for data integration in smart mobility, and presents a Meta-model (see Fig. 3) of how this could work in practice. As such, it addresses an issue that is highly relevant in switching to a green society, and could provide valuable input to cities and car sharing companies, as well as opening up avenues of future research.

6 Conclusion, Limitations, and Future Directions

The electrification of transportation has been prioritized in several European countries such as Norway, Finland, The Netherlands, United Kingdom, etc. To improve mobility operations in smart cities there is need for an infrastructure that provides distributed storage and processing of huge volumes and variety of mobility related data, generated at high velocity, without performance issues, and provides value-added services to achieve sustainable transportation services. Therefore, this study presented an architecture based on APIs that stores, processes, analyse and provides interoperable data to improve e-mobility services within smart city environment. ArchiMate modelling tool was employed to validate the feasibility of the presented architecture for eMaaS. Findings suggest that the architecture enables sharing and consumption of mobility data thereby managing transport data as openly available mobility data to improve EV sharing in smart cities.

Irrespective of the contribution, this study is faced with few limitations. First, empirical data was not collected to statistical test the architecture. Secondly, this study is more concerned with EVs sharing linked to mobility scenario only. Third, although this study discusses a mobility ecosystem with electric vehicles, electric bikes, Segways, etc. this paper is more focused on electrical vehicles only. Future works will involve collecting data from experts in transport companies located in Norway to statistically test the presented eMaaS EA. Additionally, EA will be extended to other urban services such as smart energy service. Also, the usage of other mobility means such as electric bikes, Segways, etc. will be further explored as the research progresses. Besides, experiments from big data analytics of eMaaS will be are presented in future using simulations where the developed architecture is to be deployed in a virtual mobility environment and tested to extract some pertinent evaluation in order to measure the feasible of the proposed approach as related to parameters such as time and cost (money). Future direction may also involve exploring the approximation as regards to time and money to be involved in implementing the proposed approach in a real-world scenario as a project.

Acknowledgements. This publication is a part of the +CityxChange smart city project under the Smart Cities and Communities topic that is funded by the European Union's Horizon 2020 Research and Innovation Programme under Grant Agreement No. 824260. The authors gratefully acknowledge the support of the project partners; Trondheim Municipality, Powel AS, TrønderEnergi AS, FourC AS, IOTA, and the participants of work packages 1 and 2 as well as the whole project team.

References

1. Anthony Jr., B., Majid, M.A., Romli, A.: A trivial approach for achieving smart city: a way forward towards a sustainable society. In: NCC, pp. 1–6 (2018)
2. Dijk, M., Orsato, R.J., Kemp, R.: The emergence of an electric mobility trajectory. Energ. Policy **52**, 135–145 (2013)

3. Cheng, B., Longo, S., Cirillo, F., Bauer, M., Kovacs, E.: Building a big data platform for smart cities: experience and lessons from Santander. In: International Congress on Big Data, pp. 592–599 (2015)
4. Melis, A., Mirri, S., Prandi, C., Prandini, M., Salomoni, P., Callegati, F.: Crowdsensing for smart mobility through a service-oriented architecture. In: IEEE International Smart Cities Conference, pp. 1–2 (2016)
5. Kubler, S., Robert, J., Hefnawy, A., Främling, K., Cherifi, C., Bouras, A.: Open IoT ecosystem for sporting event management. IEEE Access 5, 7064–7079 (2017)
6. Kamargianni, M., Matyas, M.: The business ecosystem of mobility-as-a-service. In: Transportation Research Board, vol. 96 (2017)
7. Nesi, P., Badii, C., Bellini, P., Cenni, D., Martelli, G., Paolucci, M.: Km4City smart city API: an integrated support for mobility services. In: SMARTCOMP, pp. 1–8 (2016)
8. Chaturvedi, K., Kolbe, T.H.: InterSensor service: establishing interoperability over heterogeneous sensor observations and platforms for smart cities. In: ISC2, pp. 1–8 (2018)
9. Sánchez, L., Elicegui, I., Cuesta, J., Muñoz, L., Lanza, J.: Integration of utilities infrastructures in a future internet enabled smart city framework. Sensors 13(11), 14438–14465 (2013)
10. Aier, S., Gleichauf, B., Saat, J., Winter, R.: Complexity Levels of Representing Dynamics in EA Planning. In: Albani, A., Barjis, J., Dietz, Jan L.G. (eds.) CIAO!/EOMAS-2009. LNBIP, vol. 34, pp. 55–69. Springer, Heidelberg (2009). https://doi.org/10.1007/978-3-642-01915-9_5
11. O'Brien, C.: Enterprise Architecture Management: Insights in the digital context. Innovation Value Institute, pp. 1–11 (2018)
12. Tcholtchev, N., Farid, L., Marienfeld, F., Schieferdecker, I., Dittwald, B., Lapi, E.: On the interplay of open data, cloud services and network providers towards electric mobility in smart cities. In: 37th Annual IEEE Conference on Local Computer Networks-Workshops, pp. 860–867 (2012)
13. Schleicher, J.M., Vögler, M., Inzinger, C., Dustdar, S.: Modeling and management of usage-aware distributed datasets for global smart city application ecosystems. PeerJ Comput. Sci. 3, e115 (2017)
14. Raetzsch, C., Pereira, G., Vestergaard, L.S., Brynskov, M.: Weaving seams with data: conceptualizing city APIs as elements of infrastructures. Big Data Soc. 6(1), 1–14 (2019)
15. Chen, D., Doumeingts, G., Vernadat, F.: Architectures for enterprise integration and interoperability: past, present and future. Comput. Ind. 59(7), 647–659 (2008)
16. Lagerström, R., Franke, U., Johnson, P., Ullberg, J.: A method for creating enterprise architecture metamodels: applied to systems modifiability. Int. J. Comput. Sci. Appl. 6(5), 89–120 (2009)
17. Rouhani, B.D., Mahrin, M.N., Nikpay, F., Nikfard, P.: A comparison enterprise architecture implementation methodologies. In: International Conference on Informatics and Creative Multimedia, pp. 1–6 (2013)
18. Saat, J., Aier, S., Gleichauf, B.: Assessing the complexity of dynamics in enterprise architecture planning-lessons from chaos theory. In: AMCIS Proceedings, pp. 1–8 (2009)
19. Ruohomaa, H.J., Salminen, V.K.: Mobility as a service in smart cities-new concept for smart mobility in Industry 4.0 framework. In: ISPIM Conference Proceedings, pp. 1–12 (2019)
20. Bellini, P., Nesi, P., Paolucci, M., Zaza, I.: Smart city architecture for data ingestion and analytics: processes and solutions. In: IEEE Fourth International Conference on Big Data Computing Service and Applications, pp. 137–144 (2018)
21. Brand, A., Iacob, M.-E., van Sinderen, Marten J.: Interoperability architecture for electric mobility. In: van Sinderen, M., Chapurlat, V. (eds.) IWEI 2015. LNBIP, vol. 213, pp. 126–140. Springer, Heidelberg (2015). https://doi.org/10.1007/978-3-662-47157-9_12

22. Kuehl, N., Walk, J., Stryja, C., Satzger, G.: Towards a service-oriented business model framework for e-mobility. In: European Battery, Hybrid and Fuel Cell Electric Vehicle Congress, pp. 1–9 (2015)

23. Tcholtchev, N., et al.: The concept of a mobility data cloud: design, implementation and trials. In: 38th International Computer Software and Applications Conference Workshops, pp. 192–198 (2014)

24. Abdelkafi, N., Makhotin, S., Posselt, T.: Business model innovations for electric mobility—what can be learned from existing business model patterns? Int. J. Innov. Manag. **17**(01), 1–41 (2013)

25. Mäkelä, O., Pirhonen, V.: The business model as a tool of improving value creation in complex private service system-case: value network of electric mobility. In: 21st International RESER Conference (2011)

26. Petersen, S.A., Pourzolfaghar, Z., Alloush, I., Ahlers, D., Krogstie, J., Helfert, M.: Value-added services, virtual enterprises and data spaces inspired enterprise architecture for smart cities. In: 20th Working Conference on Virtual Enterprises (2019)

27. Abu-Matar, M., Davies, J.: Data driven reference architecture for smart city ecosystems. SmartWorld/SCALCOM/UIC/ATC/CBDCom/IOP/SCI, pp. 1–7 (2017)

28. Winter, R., Fischer, R.: Essential layers, artifacts, and dependencies of enterprise architecture. In: EDOCW, p. 30 (2006)

29. Anthony Jr., B., Majid, M.A., Romli, A.: Green information technology system practice for sustainable collaborative enterprise: a structural literature review. Int. J. Sustainable Soc. **9** (3), 242–272 (2017)

30. Pittl, B., Bork, D.: Modeling digital enterprise ecosystems with Archimate: a mobility provision case study. ICServ 2017. LNCS, vol. 10371, pp. 178–189. Springer, Cham (2017). https://doi.org/10.1007/978-3-319-61240-9_17

31. Anthony Jr., B., Abbas Petersen, S., Ahlers, D., Krogstie, J.: API deployment for big data management towards sustainable energy presumption in smart cities-a layered architecture perspective. Int. J. Sustainable Energy **39**, 1–27 (2019)

32. Ahlers, D., Wienhofen, L.W.M., Petersen, S.A., Anvaari, M.: A smart city ecosystem enabling open innovation. In: Lüke, K.-H., Eichler, G., Erfurth, C., Fahrnberger, G. (eds.) I4CS 2019. CCIS, vol. 1041, pp. 109–122. Springer, Cham (2019). https://doi.org/10.1007/978-3-030-22482-0_9

An Experimental Comparison of Machine Learning Classification Algorithms for Breast Cancer Diagnosis

Markos Marios Kaklamanis[1(✉)], Michael E. Filippakis[1],
Marios Touloupos[1,2], and Klitos Christodoulou[2]

[1] Department of Digital Systems, University of Piraeus, Piraeus, Greece
mmkaklamanis@hotmail.com, {mfilip,mtouloup}@unipi.gr
[2] Institute for the Future, University of Nicosia, Nicosia, Cyprus
{touloupos.m,christodoulou.kl}@unic.ac.cy

Abstract. In this paper four machine learning algorithms are compared in order to predict if a cell nucleus is benign or malignant using the Breast Cancer Wisconsin (Diagnostic) Data Set. The algorithms are K-Nearest Neighbours, Classification and Regression Trees (CART), Naïve Bayes and Support Vector Machines with Radial Basis Function Kernel. Data visualization and Pre- Processing using PCA will help in the understanding and the preparation of the dataset for the training phase while parameter tuning will determine the optimal parameter for every model using R as programming language. Also, 10-fold Cross Validation is used as a resampling method after comparing it with Bootstrapping, as it is the most efficient out of the two. In the end, our comparison shows that the machine learning model that marked the highest Accuracy is the one that is trained using K Nearest Neighbours. Nowadays, one of the most common forms of cancer among women is breast cancer with more than one million cases and nearly 600,000 deaths occurring worldwide annually [1]. It is the second leading cause of death among women and thus it must be detected at an early stage in order not to become fatal [2]. Thus, the importance of diagnosing if a biopsied cell is benign or malignant is vital. However, this process is quite complicated as it involves several stages of gathering and analysing samples with many variables, making the final diagnosis a demanding and timely procedure. The rapid growth of Artificial Intelligence and Machine learning and their implementation in Medicine give us a new perspective in the way we process and analyse medical data. Medical experts can use Data Mining techniques and improve their decision making by extracting useful information from massive amounts of data.

Keywords: Data mining · Breast cancer · Classification · Diagnosis · Machine learning

1 Introduction

The Wisconsin Diagnosis Breast Cancer (WDBC) dataset is publicly available at UCI (Machine Learning Repository) and was created by Dr. William H. Wolberg, W. Nick Street and Olvi L. Mangasarian at the University of Wisconsin Hospital at Madison,

© Springer Nature Switzerland AG 2020
M. Themistocleous and M. Papadaki (Eds.): EMCIS 2019, LNBIP 381, pp. 18–30, 2020.
https://doi.org/10.1007/978-3-030-44322-1_2

Wisconsin, USA. It includes 569 samples of cancer biopsies, each one with 32 attributes. [3] Except the id and diagnosis columns, all the other are numeric laboratory measurements of digitized cells nuclei characterized with ten attributes. Each attribute has a column with a mean, standard error and worst value. The attributes are Radius, Texture, Perimeter, Area, Smoothness, Compactness, Concavity, Concave points, Symmetry, and Fractal dimension. These features are computed from a digitized image of a fine needle aspirate (FNA) of a breast mass. They describe characteristics of the cell nuclei present in the image.

The use of classification systems in medical diagnosis is becoming more and more popular. The evaluation and collection of data from the patients and the analysis from experts are the key factors for a successful diagnosis. However, with the implementation of artificial intelligence in this field, new classification techniques have a big contribution in both minimizing potential errors done by inexperienced personnel and examining medical data in shorter time and more detailed.

In this paper we are going to implement four classification algorithms, k-Nearest Neighbours, Support Vector Machines with Radial basis function kernel, Classification and Regression Trees (CART) and Naïve Bayes. The first three are non-parametric which means they use a flexible number of parameters that often grows as they learn from more data. They are computationally slower but make fewer assumptions about the data. The last one, Naïve Bayes is considered a parametric algorithm which means it has a fixed number of parameters. Is computationally faster but makes stronger assumptions about the data, thus, performing well if the assumptions turn out to be correct or performing badly if the assumptions are wrong.

These algorithms were selected because they combine attributes that cope with the complexities of our dataset, as WBCD has a relatively small sample size, with thirty attributes and no missing values. K-Nearest Neighbours and Support Vector machines are good choices as they perform better in small sample size datasets than in larger ones where the computational cost becomes higher and the performance drops. Also, KNN benefits from the lack of missing values as it does not handle them effectively but also because we have only one parameter to tune in order to optimize it [14, 17]. However, the fact that we have high dimensional data might be a problem and a dimensionality reduction technique might be a good choice to implement. On the other hand, SVMs and Naïve Bayes do not face the same problem with high dimensional data, with the first one having also the kernel trick, which with the use of the appropriate kernel function is able to solve complex problems [10]. We are going to use the Gaussian or Radial basis function kernel. Except from performing well in high dimensional space, Naïve Bayes is very fast and effective, requires a small amount of data for training and perform well with noisy and missing data [14, 15]. However, it is affected if there are many correlated features in the data, a problem that CART handles effectively as it identifies the most important variables and eliminate the non-significant ones and thus, not needing a feature selection step. Finally, all the algorithms above exceed in binary classification problems such ours.

There are many papers that have analysed and developed many models and solutions around this dataset. In this study, we are going to perform parameter tuning for every one of the four algorithms we stated earlier in order to evaluate their performance. The performance metrics we used are Prediction Accuracy and Kappa statistic [14].

For the parameter tuning we will perform grid search where the parameter value that will score the highest accuracy will be chosen. If we have two tuning parameters, we will try pairs of these parameters and the one with the best accuracy will be chosen. To improve generalization ability, we will try grid search with two different methods, Bootstrapping and 10-fold Cross Validation [14]. The one with the best output will be implemented. In order to deal with some issues that might affect the performance of our models like high dimensionality and correlated features we will perform Principal Component Analysis.

2   Related Work on Breast Cancer Diagnosis

Salama et al. [4] provided a comparison among different classification algorithms such as Naïve Bayes, Instance based KNN (IBK), Sequential Minimal Optimization (SMO), J48 decision tree and Multi-Layer Perceptron on three different datasets using WEKA data mining tool. In WDBC data set the results show that the classification using SMO only or using fusion of SMO and IBK or SMO and MLP is superior in comparison to the other classifiers.

Padmavathi [5] performed a comparative study on WBC dataset for breast cancer prediction using RBF and MLP along with the logistic regression. The logistic regression was performed using logistic regression in SPSS package and MLP and RBF were constructed using MATLAB software. It was observed that neural networks took slightly higher time than logistic regression, but the sensitivity and specificity of both neural network models had a better predictive power over logistic regression. When comparing MLP and RBF neural network models, it was found that RBF had good predictive capabilities and also time taken by RBF was less than MLP. Zand [6] tested C4.5, Naïve Bayes and the back-propagated ANN on SEER breast cancer data set in order to find the most suitable one for predicting cancer survivability rate using WEKA toolkit for his experimentation. The ANN and C4.5 decision tree has comparable performances. The calculated Accuracy is 86.5% and 86.7% respectively with C4.5 having less computation time.

Delen et al. [7], compared two popular data mining techniques, ANN and C5 Decision Trees along with Logistic Regression for breast cancer survival analysis using the SEER data set. The results showed that C5 decision tree had the highest performance with 93.6% accuracy while ANNs were second with 91.2% accuracy and the Logistic Regression last with 89.2% accuracy.

Dumitru [8] applied the Naive Bayes classifier to the Wisconsin Prognostic Breast Cancer (WPBC) dataset, containing a number of 198 patients and a binary decision class: non-recurrent-events having 151 instances and recurrent-events having 47 instances. The main performance measure of the classifier was accuracy, which was about 74.24%, in compliance with the performance of other wellknown machine learning techniques.

You et al. [9] provided a comparative analysis on the utilized potential classification tools (back-propagation neural network, linear programming, Bayesian network and support vector machine) on the problem by using the WDBC dataset from the UCI machine learning repository which consisted of numeric cellular shape features extracted from pre-processed Fine Needle Aspiration biopsy image of cell slides. Here Naïve Bayes classifier gave an accuracy of 89.55%.

Akay [10] applied SVM with feature selection to diagnose the breast cancer. For training and testing phase the WDBC dataset was used. More specifically, the proposed method produced the highest classification accuracies (99.51%, 99.02% and 98.53% for 80–20% of training-test partition, 70–30% of training-test partition and 50–50% of training-test partition respectively) for a subset that carried five features. Also, other measures such as the sensitivity, specificity, confusion matrix, negative predictive value and positive predictive value and ROC curves were used to show the performance of SVM with feature selection.

Ravi Kumar et al. [11] presented a comparison among the different Data mining classifiers on the database of breast cancer Wisconsin Breast Cancer (WBC), by using classification accuracy. The aim was to establish an accurate classification model for Breast Cancer Prediction, in order to make full use of the invaluable information in clinical data, especially which is usually ignored by most of the existing methods when they aim for high prediction accuracies. The dataset is divided into training set with 499 and test set with 200 patients. In this experiment, they compared six classification techniques in Weka software and comparison results show that Support Vector Machine (SVM) has higher prediction accuracy than those methods. Different methods for breast cancer detection are explored and their accuracies are compared.

Kharya et al. [12] developed a probabilistic breast cancer prediction system using Naive Bayes Classifiers which can be used in making expert decision with highest accuracy. The system may be implemented in remote areas like countryside or rural regions, to imitate like human diagnostic expertise for treatment of cancer disease. The aim of this work was to design a Graphical User Interface to enter the patient screening record and detect the probability of having Breast cancer disease in women in her future using Naive Bayes Classifiers, a Probabilistic Classifier. The prediction is performed from mining data from WPBC dataset. Further from the experimental results it has been found that Naive Bayes Classifiers is providing improved accuracy with low computational effort and very high speed. The accuracy was found to be 93%.

3 Data Pre-processing

3.1 Data Distribution

Firstly, we want to explore and visualize relationships between the different attributes within the breast cancer dataset using R studio and its packages. We start by removing irrelevant features and then check the class distribution among the dataset. Although the class distribution is imbalanced with 62.74% for Benign and 37.26% for Malignant (Table 1), it is not so much to worry for a possible rebalancing of our dataset. Because data are distributed in a wide range, features were standardized, so they have a mean of '0' and a standard deviation of '1'.

Table 1. Frequencies percentage

Frequencies percentage	Number of instances	Percentage
Benign	357	62.74165
Malignant	212	37.25835

3.2   Correlation Matrix

In this correlation Matrix below (Fig. 1), correlations between attributes are displayed in dark color. Color intensity and the size of the circle are proportional to the correlation coefficients. For example, radius_mean with perimeter_mean and area_mean is strongly correlated, but area_mean with fractal_dimension _mean is not.

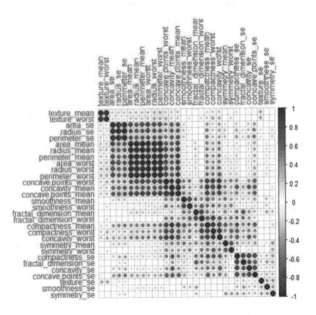

Fig. 1. Correlation matrix

3.3   Principal Component Analysis

With Principal Component Analysis our aim is to extract the most relevant features of the data, or the variables which seem to influence the most our dependent variable [18]. Using PCA we transform the current features into a new set of orthogonal (uncorrelated) features (principle components), with each new one being a composite of all the original features of the dataset. Then, the performance of each of the new variables is evaluated and the one that has the best performance on the dataset is determined. In the end, PCA returns the new variables that have the strongest correlation with the dependent variable [18]. In the Table 2 and Fig. 2 below we can see the variance of each of the synthetic features generated by PCA. It depicts the influence each synthetic feature provides towards our dependent variable.

Table 2. Importance of principal components

Principal components	Standard deviation	Proportion of variance	Cumulative proportion
PCA 1	3.6444	0.4427	0.4447
PCA 2	2.3857	0.1897	0.6324
PCA 3	1.6786	0.0939	0.7263
PCA 4	1.4073	0.0660	0.7923
PCA 5	1.2840	0.0549	0.8473
PCA 6	1.0988	0.0402	0.8875
PCA 7	0.8217	0.0225	0.9101
PCA 8	0.6903	0.0158	0.9259
PCA 9	0.6457	0.0139	0.9399
PCA 10	0.5921	0.0116	0.9515

We can see that the 63.24% of our variance is explained by the first two components. We need 10 principal components to explain more than 95% of our variance and 17 to explain more than 99% out of 30. After data pre-processing, it is time to split our dataset in two separate sets, one training set for training our classification algorithms and one validation for testing the performance of our trained algorithms on unseen data. The Split Ratio will be 0.7 for the training set and 0.3 for the test set because three out of four are non-parametric (KNN, SVM, CART), thus, they require a lot more training data to estimate the mapping function.

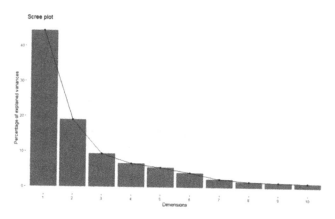

Fig. 2. Barplot of variance explained by principal components

4 Machine Learning Algorithms

4.1 CART (Classification and Regression Trees)

The first classification algorithm we are going to use is the Classification and Regression Trees (CART). Classification and Regression Trees or CART for short is a term introduced by Leo Breiman [13] to refer to Decision Tree algorithms that can be used for classification or regression predictive modelling problems. This algorithm creates binary trees and as a result, from every node always emerge two branches. As an attribute selection method for splitting the tree uses the Gini index and as a pruning method, the Error-Complexity pruning which first generates a sequence of trees pruned by different amounts and then it picks one of them by checking how many classification errors each of them made with a different dataset [17]. For CART, cp (Complexity Parameter) is the one parameter we can tune. The complexity parameter (cp) is used to control the size of the decision tree and to select the optimal tree size. If the cost of adding another variable to the decision tree from the current node is above the value of cp, then tree building does not continue. We will test cp values between 0.01 and 0.10 by 0.01 (Table 3).

Table 3. Grid search results for optimal parameter (CART)

Resampling	Cp	Accuracy	Kappa
10-fold Cross Validation	0.01	0.9396795	0.8719438
Bootstrap	0.01	0.9156959	0.8186547

From the table above we can see that for Cp = 0.01 with 10fold Cross Validation we score the highest Accuracy (93.96%) and Kappa value (87.19%) in our training set. The next step is to see how well our model generalizes in unseen data tuning our parameter Cp = 0.01. After running our model on the validation set, we can see below that the Accuracy of our final model is 91.23%, lower by 2.73% from our prediction based on the training data.

4.2   K-Nearest Neighbours

The next algorithm we are going to use is k-Nearest neighbours. It falls under lazy learning, because there is no explicit training phase before classification [17]. Instead, any attempts to generalize or abstract the data is made upon classification. It is named like this because it uses information about a data's point k nearest neighbour to classify unlabelled data. It starts by choosing k, a variable that refers to the number of nearest neighbours that are going to be used. Then we need a training dataset with observations that are classified, as labelled by a nominal variable. For every unlabelled observation in the test dataset, k-NN identifies k observations in the training data that are more similar to each other. Finally, the unlabelled test observation is assigned to the class that has most of the k nearest neighbour. A critical aspect of the k-NN algorithm is choosing an appropriate k value, as it determines the performance of the model significantly. [14]. A large k value reduces the impact of variance caused by noise but can bias the learner, and as a result, we can miss small but important patterns. On the other hand, choosing a very small k makes the influence of outliers bigger in the classification process. However, smaller values, in general, give us the ability to choose more complex decision boundaries that fit better our training data. The difficulty is to find

Table 4. Confusion matrix for CART

Prediction	Benign	Malignant
Benign	98	9
Malignant	6	58
Accuracy	0.9123	
Kappa	0.8145	

what decision boundary (straight line or curved) better represents the concept that must be learned. For KNN, k (Number of Neighbours) is the parameter we can tune. We will test k values between 1 and 20 (Tables 4 and 5).

Table 5. Grid search results for optimal parameter (KNN)

Resampling	K	Accuracy	Kappa
10-fold Cross Validation	3	0.9673077	0.9285430
Bootstrap	11	0.9540315	0.8997692

From the table above we can see that for k = 3 with 10-fold Cross Validation we score the highest Accuracy (96.73%) and Kappa value (92.85%) in our training set. The next step is to see how well our model generalizes in unseen data tuning our parameter k = 3. After running our model on the validation set, we can see that the Accuracy of our final model is 96.49%, lower by 0.24% from our prediction based on the training data (Table 6).

Table 6. Confusion matrix for KNN

Prediction	Benign	Malignant
Benign	106	1
Malignant	5	59
Accuracy	0.9649	
Kappa	0.9241	

4.3   Naïve Bayes

The Naïve Bayes algorithm describes a simple method to apply Bayes theorem to classification problems [17]. Although it is not the only machine learning method that utilizes Bayesian methods, it is the most common one. It is named as such because it makes some naïve assumptions about the data. In particular, Naïve Bayes assumes that all the features in the dataset are equally important and independent [14, 15]. These assumptions are rarely true in most real-world problems. However, in most cases, when these assumptions are violated, Naïve Bayes performs well. This is true even in extreme cases where strong dependencies are found among features. For Naïve Bayes, fL (Laplace Correction) and adjust (Bandwidth Adjustment) are the two parameters we can tune. Laplace smoother or correction is a simple trick to avoid zero probabilities It adds a small number to each of the counts in the frequencies for each feature, which ensures that each feature has a nonzero probability of occurring for each class. We can assume that our training set is so large that adding one to each count that we need would only make a negligible difference in the estimated probabilities yet would avoid the case of zero probability values (Table 7).

Table 7. Grid search results for optimal parameters (Naïve Bayes)

Resampling	Adjust	fL	Accuracy	Kappa
10-fold Cross Validation	1.5	0.5	0.8972436	0.7783919
Bootstrap	1.5	0.5	0.8918576	0.7667068

From the table above we can see that for fL = 0.5 and Bandwidth adjustment = 1.5 with 10-fold Cross Validation we score the highest Accuracy (89.72%) and Kappa value (77.83%) in our training set. The next step is to see how well our model generalizes in unseen data tuning our parameters fL = 0.5 and adjust = 1.5. The next step is to see how well our model generalizes in unseen data. After running our model on the validation set, we can see that the Accuracy of our final model is 88.30%, lower by 1.42% from our prediction based on the training data (Table 8).

Table 8. Confusion matrix for KNN

Prediction	Benign	Malignant
Benign	101	6
Malignant	14	50
Accuracy	0.8830	
Kappa	0.7439	

4.4   SVM (Radial Basis Function Kernel)

Support Vector Machines (SVM) is a machine learning technique used for classification tasks. The way they work is by identifying the optimal decision boundary that separates data points from different groups (or classes), and then predicts the class of new observations based on this separation boundary [10]. Depending on the situations, the different groups might be separable by a linear straight line or by a non-linear boundary line. Support vector machine methods can handle both linear and non-linear class boundaries [14]. These methods can be used for both binary and multi-class classification problems. Although in real life data the separation boundary is generally non-linear, the SVM algorithm performs a non-linear classification using what is called the kernel trick. The most commonly used kernel transformations are polynomial kernel and radial kernel. Classical techniques utilizing radial basis functions employ some method of determining a subset of centres. Typically, a method of clustering is first employed to select a subset of centres. An attractive feature of the SVM is that this selection is implicit, with each support vectors contributing one local Gaussian function, centred at that data point [14, 16]. For Support Vector Machines with Radial Basis Function Kernel, Sigma (smoothing term) and C (cost constraint) are the two parameters we can tune with caret. Sigma is defined in a Gaussian distribution as the standard deviation. For a larger Sigma the decision boundary tends to be flexible and smooth. It tends to make wrong classification while predicting but avoids overfitting. For a smaller Sigma, the decision boundary tends to be strict and sharp, but also it tends to overfit. Cost constraint or C refers to the penalty for misclassifying a data point. When C is small the misclassification cost is low ('soft margin'). However, when C is large the misclassification cost is high and the classifier tends to avoid misclassifying data, leading though to overfitting ('hard margin'). We will test a range of values for C and Sigma between 1 and 5 and 0.025 and 0.10 respectively (Table 9).

Table 9. Grid search results for optimal parameters (SVM with Radial Basis function kernel)

Resampling	Adjust	fL	Accuracy	Kappa
10-fold Cross Validation	1.25	5	0.9673718	0.9288801
Bootstrap	1.25	2	0.9548192	0.9021220

From the table above we can see that for Sigma = 0.25 and C = 5 with 10-fold Cross Validation we score the highest Accuracy (96.73%) and Kappa value (92.88%) in our training set. The next step is to see how well our model generalizes in unseen data tuning our parameters Sigma = 0.25 and C = 5. After running our model on the test set, we can see that the Accuracy of our final model is 95.32%, lower by 1.41% from our prediction based on the training data (Table 10).

Table 10. Confusion matrix for SVM with radial Basis function kernel

Prediction	Benign	Malignant
Benign	105	2
Malignant	6	58
Accuracy	0.9535	
Kappa	0.8988	

Overall, most of our algorithms performed well in terms of Accuracy with the worst being Naïve Bayes and CART with 89.72% and 93.96% respectively. These algorithms Kappa value was also low with 0.7783 and 0.8719. On the other hand, KNN and SVM with Radial Basis function Kernel marked the highest Accuracy estimation with 96.73% with Kappa values of 0.9285 and 0.9288 respectively.

5   Results and Discussion

In our final step, we are going to check how well our algorithms performed on test data, compare them and choose the best one. Looking at Fig. 3 and Table 11, most of our estimations were optimistic as the final Accuracies were slightly lower.

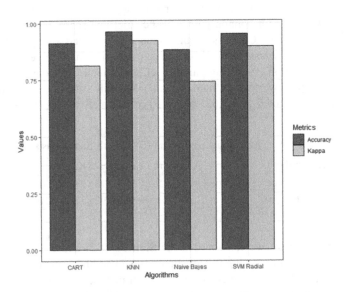

Fig. 3. Barplot of accuracy and Kappa values for the validation set

Table 11. Model comparison based on the validation set

Algorithms	Accuracy	Kappa
CART	0.9123	0.8145
KNN	0.9649	0.9241
Naïve Bayes	0.8830	0.7439
SVM with radial basis function kernel	0.9532	0.8988

The biggest difference between Accuracy based on the training and test data results was demonstrated by CART with a drop of 2.73%. Also, Naive Bayes and SVM with Radial Kernel Accuracy on test data was 88.30% and 95.32%, lower by 1.42% and 1.41% respectively, while KNN's fell slightly (0.24%) from 96.73% to 96.49%. Overall, KNN performed better in the test data, reaching an Accuracy of 96.49% with Naïve Bayes having the worst one with 88.30%. Some of the reasons of these results are because KNN performs better when training data is larger than the number of features, like our case with the WBCD dataset. In the opposite scenario, SVM with radial function kernel outperforms KNN. Also, by implementing PCA we reduced the dimensionality of our data, favouring KNN over Naïve Bayes and SVM with RBF kernel which scale better in high dimensions than KNN.

6 Conclusions

We considered the problem of predicting breast cancer diagnosis using different machine learning techniques, optimizing their hyperparameters and implementing 10-fold Cross Validation and Bootstrapping. Our analysis was focused on tuning our models' parameters in the most efficient way and comparing different classification techniques under the same resampling conditions using caret package and R as programming language. The results showed that 10-fold Cross Validation was the best resampling method in this case and K-Nearest Neighbours the algorithm with the highest Accuracy at 96.73% and 96.49% on training and validation data accordingly.

7 Future Work

Currently, Machine Learning models are still in the testing and experimentation phase for cancer diagnosis. As datasets are getting larger, more complex and of higher quality, more accurate models are being developed. This paper presents one way out of many to analyse this dataset focusing on the optimal parameter selection with two different resampling methods. Other feature selection techniques (RFE), machine learning techniques (LDA, ANNs, Logistic Regression) and metrics (ROC curve) can be used and build even more accurate prediction models.

References

1. Lyon IAfRoC: World Cancer report. International Agency for Research on Cancer Press, pp. 188–193 (2003)
2. U.S. Cancer Statistics Working Group. United States Cancer Statistics: 1999–2008 Incidence and Mortality Web-based Report. Atlanta (GA): Department of Health and Human Services, Centers for Disease Control and Prevention, and National Cancer Institute (2012)
3. Wolberg, W.H., Street, W.N., Mangasarian, O.L.: Breast Cancer Wisconsin (Diagnostic) data Set, UCI Machine Learning Repository
4. Salama, G.I., Abdelhalim, M.B., Zeid, M.A.: Breast cancer diagnosis on three different datasets using multiclassifiers. Int. J. Comput. Inf. Technol. (2277 – 0764), **01**(01) (2012)
5. Padmavati, J.: A comparative study on breast cancer prediction using RBF and MLP. Int. J. Sci. Eng. Res. **2**(1), 14–18 (2011)
6. Zand, H.K.K.: A comparative survey on data mining techniques for breast cancer diagnosis and prediction. Indian J. Fundam. Appl. Life Sci. **5**(S1), 4330–4339 (2015). ISSN 2231–6345
7. Delen, D., Walker, G., Kadam, A.: Predicting breast cancer survivability: a comparison of three data mining methods. Artif. Intell. Med. **34**, 113–127 (2005)
8. Dumitru, D.: Prediction of recurrent events in breast cancer using the Naive Bayesian classification. Ann. Univ. Craiova Math. Comput. Sci. Ser. **36**(2), 92–96 (2009)
9. You, H., Rumbe, G.: Comparative study of classification techniques on breast cancer FNA biopsy data Int. J. Artif. Intell. Interact. Multimedia **1**(3), 6–13 (2010)
10. Akay, M.F.: Support vector machines combined with feature selection for breast cancer diagnosis. Expert Syst. with Appl. **36**, 3240–3247 (2009)

11. Ravi Kumar, G., Ramachandra, G.A., Nagamani, K.: An efficient prediction of breast cancer data using data mining techniques. Int. J. Innov. Eng. Technol. (IJIET) **2**(4), 139 (2013)
12. Kharya, S., Agrawal, S., Soni, S.: Naïve Bayes classifiers: probabilistic detection model for breast cancer. Int. J. Comput. Appl. **92**(10), 26–31 (2014)
13. Timofeev, R.: Classification and Regression Trees (CART) Theory and Applications | Errors and Residuals | Statistical Classification (2004). Scribd. https://www.scribd.com/document/256433144/Classification-andRegression-Trees-CART-Theory-and-Applications. Accessed 2 Nov 2018
14. Lantz, B.: Machine Learning with R. 2nd edn., pp. 65–87, 89–124, 225–231, 239–247, 293–311, 315–324. Packt Publishing, Birmingham (n.d.)
15. Barber, D.: Bayesian Reasoning and Machine Learning, pp. 203–213. Cambridge University Press, New York (2012)
16. Gunn, S.R.: Support Vector Machines for Classification and Regression (1998)
17. Mitchell, T.M.: Machine Learning, pp 52–75, 156–177, 230–244. McGraw-Hill Science/Engineering/Math, New York, 1 March 1997
18. Jolliffe, I.T.: Principal Component Analysis, 2nd edn., pp. 10–29, 111–127. Springer, New York (2002). https://doi.org/10.1007/b98835

Taking Complexity into Account: A Structured Literature Review on Multi-component Systems in the Context of Predictive Maintenance

Milot Gashi[1(✉)] and Stefan Thalmann[2]

[1] Pro2Future, Graz, Austria
`milot.gashi@pro2future.at`
[2] Business Analytics and Data Science Center, University of Graz, Graz, Austria
`stefan.thalmann@uni-graz.at`

Abstract. One of the most prominent use cases of a digitized industry is predictive maintenance. Advances in sensor and data technology enable continuous condition monitoring, thus, extending the opportunities for predictive maintenance. However, so far, most approaches stick to a simplistic paradigm viewing industrial systems as a single-component system (SCS), assuming independence or partially neglecting interdependencies between components. However, in practice, multiple components are coupled which interact with each other; thus, leading to a multi-component system (MCS) view. Implementing the MCS is challenging, but promises many advantages for predictive maintenance. We conduct a structured literature review to investigate the current state of research about MCS and how this can be transferred to data-driven predictive maintenance. We investigate the characteristics of MCS, the promises in contrast to SCS, the challenges of its implementation, and current application areas. Finally, we discuss future work on MCS in the context of predictive maintenance.

Keywords: Predictive maintenance · Multi-component systems · RUL · Stochastic dependence

1 Introduction

One of the most prominent use cases discussed in the context of digitization of industry or Industry 4.0 is predictive maintenance [20]. Various data-driven approaches for predictive maintenance in different industrial application settings can be found [32, 35, 40, 41]. This increasing interest from practice and science has three major reasons. First, maintenance is always a relevant topic and has huge influence on the production costs, quality, and reliability [6]. Second, the information basis increased due to the growing availability of cheap and powerful sensor technology [35, 44]. And finally, huge advances in data processing capabilities and the new rise of artificial intelligence (AI) offer new opportunities to build predictive models [45].

As a result, predictive maintenance was promoted in many industry sectors [29]. Despite the advancements in this field, current approaches predominantly rely on

M. Themistocleous and M. Papadaki (Eds.): EMCIS 2019, LNBIP 381, pp. 31–44, 2020.
https://doi.org/10.1007/978-3-030-44322-1_3

the paradigm of a SCS for their predictive maintenance models, rather than MCS [12–14, 19]. The most important reason to stick to SCS is the complexity of the system level maintenance modeling and limited algorithmic and computational power in the past [12–14]. Thus, SCS models and approaches are applied to complex systems composed of multiple subsystems ignoring their interdependencies. So far, the results are acceptable, but in practice, these assumptions are not reasonable as more precise results could not be achieved [13, 14].

AI based models realize good results for stable production processes for which good experience-based data sets are available. This is however changing as a result of mass customization, more complex production processes, and shorter product life cycles in digitized manufacturing [42]. Consequently, the production lines and their configuration change more frequently, or many different variants of one machine can be found in practice. Hence, data sets for one of those variants is small in most cases and not enough for training traditional models (small data challenge) [46]. Additionally, shorter product life cycles demand faster learning and a switch from experienced based models to data driven models. All these challenges and limitations lead to the need for new approaches which handle all these aspects properly. MCS seem promising in this regard.

MCS models and approaches are rarely used in predictive maintenance, but generally used in other research fields, such as corrective maintenance and preventive maintenance. However, the complexity of manufacturing systems, requires reliable condition monitoring, thus, various sensors are embedded within these systems for providing condition monitoring. This data can be used to predict the system health encouraging the need for state-of-the-art predictive maintenance approaches. Hence, this sounds promising to analyze the literature in these fields and to transfer the insights to data driven predictive maintenance for MCS.

The aim of this paper is to investigate the state of research on how MCS models and approaches can be used in the context of predictive maintenance. The goal is to identify promising solutions and their characteristics, advances in contrast to SCS, application areas and lastly, the challenges for their implementation. The next section provides an overview of the background with regard to MCS. In Sect. 3, the methodology used to conduct a literature review is introduced. Section 4 describes the results. Finally, conclusions are made defining the outlines for possible future work.

2 Background

2.1 Multi Component Systems

MCS are more complex than SCS as they consider a higher degree of complexity and dynamic behavior of the environment. MCS models represent a variety of components, regarding both life span and purpose, and also represent interactions between sub-components. An MCS is defined as a system which consists of multiple components, and these components strongly interact with each other [4, 8, 15, 17]. Therefore, dependencies among system components are assumed and can be modelled. Moreover, an MCS is often described as a complex system [15] which consist of multiple interacting sub-components [7]. Also, a complex system is defined as a system, which consist of multiple components and the reliability dependency between system and components' may not be completely known [35]. Furthermore, the term MCS is mostly used as interchangeably to refer to both the system, which consists of multiple assets or engineering assets consisting of multiple components [5]. Figure 1 shows an example of an MCS – a welding device which is composed of several components such as cooling unit or hosepack. In the MCS now, interdependencies between these sub- components can be modeled and considered for analytical tasks. In the related work focusing on MCS, the interdependencies are classified into three key categories: stochastic, economic, and structural interdependencies [2, 6].

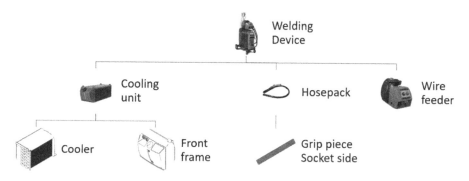

Fig. 1. Multi-layer MCS structure based on hierarchical structure.

Stochastic interdependencies between multiple components are present within the system; when the deterioration process of one or multiple component is affected from the deterioration state of other components [2, 8, 11, 19]. Moreover, the deterioration process of a component depends not only on the current state of the system and on the operation conditions of the system but also on the current state of other components which it is interacting with. For example, an old worn out component which interacts with new components, will potentially accelerate the wear rate of a new one, which in turn might have the same effect on the already worn up component [17].

Economic dependencies represent the cost relationships between components. The assumption is that the maintenance of a group of components at once lead to different costs than applying separate maintenance for each component [2, 11, 19]. In literature, two types of economic dependencies exist. The first type is noted as positive economic dependence, which provide that the joint maintenance costs for a group of components lead to cheaper costs, compared to performed maintenance on components separately. The second type is known as negative economic dependence, which in contrast provides that the joint maintenance costs of a group of components leads to higher costs than performing maintenance individually [2, 6].

Structural dependencies mean that multiple components within a system are structurally dependent [2, 3, 11, 19]. In other words, the components structurally form a part within the MCS. Whereby a failure implies actions, such as disassembly, on the other components too. For example, while replacing a component, it indirectly forces other components to be dismantled or replaced as well.

However, in the latest trend, the possibility of the fourth type of interdependencies, i.e., the resource dependence has been considered. Resource interdependence is focused on describing or modeling the dependency between a component or group of components and spare parts or even a limited number of maintenance workers [19].

2.2 Predictive Maintenance

Maintenance in industrial setting or manufacturing equipment is essential to guarantee higher quality, productivity, sustainability, and safe working environment [20]. Traditional approaches, e.g. time-based maintenance or condition-based maintenance usually perform maintenance based on the current state of devices. Time-based maintenance ensures that maintenance is performed at regular basis based on predefined time-interval [2, 6]. Condition-based maintenance uses the data gathered through multiple sensors, which are assembled within the equipment for providing condition monitoring [6].

Predictive maintenance is gaining a lot of attention in the last decade, due to the availability of condition monitoring data [35]. The aim of predictive maintenance is to identify the optimal time for maintenance and thus also in a proactive way. Implementing effective prediction offers a variety of benefits including increase of system reliability, machine availability, production performance, sustainability, system safety, maintenance effectiveness and decrease maintenance costs, number of accidents, and downtime machinery. Predictive maintenance is also defined as condition-based maintenance followed by a prediction, which uses the knowledge derived from the analysis of crucial parameters regarding the degradation of the device [20]. In most cases, the aim of prediction is to estimate Remaining Useful Life (RUL) and its confidence intervals [20].

Existing approaches rely on the SCS metaphor so far. Statistical or AI approaches are applied without considering the interdependencies of the subcomponents explicitly. However, the complexity of current manufacturing processes is increasing tremendously. On the one hand the number of components and the interactions between these components are increasing. Also, cheap sensors, powerful algorithms, increased bandwidth and ever-growing storage capacity increase the available data basis significantly. As a result of digitization and mass customization, the variability with regard to the components is increasing sharply. Usually, the number of similar product variants is large, but the data set for one specific variant is small [3]. Hence, the challenge is to transfer the insights and models from one variant to another. Traditional approaches considering only the SCS which conveniently lack to handle this particular challenge and the general requirements resulting from digitization of industry. Therefore, predictive maintenance for MCS is gaining more attention in the last years, aiming for more realistic solutions, which are applicable in real complex use cases [35].

3   Methodology

We conducted our structured literature review about MCS in the context of predictive maintenance based on Webster and Watson [31]. The literature review is conducted focusing on the period 2008 to 2019 as shown in Table 1. In order to perform the forward and backward search, Google scholar is used. Within this process 19 relevant keyword combinations suitable for the review were identified and applied to 11 Journals and 1 Conference. These journals and the conference are selected, since the MCS topic is a key focus and they have great impact factor. The search is performed with restriction to title, abstract and author-specified keywords.

Table 1. Review Matrix for data-driven solution for MCS. In the x-axis relevant keywords are listed. On the top of the table each journal/conference is represented as distinct column.

Keywords combinations / Journals and Conferences	Computers in Industry	International Journal of Advanced Manufacturing Technology	Computers & Industrial Engineering	Reliability engineering & systems safety	Journal of Intelligent Manufacturing	Journal of Manufacturing Systems	Industrial Management and Data Systems	Expert Systems with Applications	Mechanical Systems and Signal Processing	IEEE Transactions on Reliability	European Journal of Operational Research	Prognostics and Health Management, PHM, International Conference on	SUM
multi-compont + diagnosis	0	0	0	0	0	0	0	0	0	0	0	3	3
MCS + imperfect	0	2	2	3	0	1	1	0	0	0	0	0	9
MCS + failure	1	6	5	16	1	1	0	0	0	6	6	0	42
MCS + prognostics	1	0	0	4	0	1	0	0	0	0	0	0	6
MCS + diagnostic	0	0	0	0	1	1	1	0	0	0	0	0	3
MCS + information	0	0	0	7	2	0	0	0	0	0	1	0	10
MCS + data uncertainty	0	0	0	1	0	0	0	0	0	0	0	0	1
MCS + Condition Monitoring	0	0	1	2	0	0	0	0	0	0	1	0	4
MCS + predictive maintenance	0	0	0	3	0	0	0	0	0	1	0	0	4
MCS + conditions	0	4	2	1	0	0	0	1	0	0	0	0	8
MCS + degradation	0	2	2	9	1	1	0	0	0	3	1	0	19
MCS + deterioration	0	0	2	4	0	0	0	1	0	0	1	0	8
MCS + Stochastic	0	1	2	9	0	2	1	0	0	0	2	0	17
MCS + CBM	1	0	3	8	1	1	0	0	0	1	3	0	18
Multi unit system + condition monitoring	0	1	0	1	0	0	0	0	0	1	0	0	3
CBM + Stochastic dependence	0	0	1	3	0	1	0	0	0	0	0	0	5
Multi components + complex system	0	1	2	7	0	0	0	1	0	0	3	0	14
Complex systems + prediction	1	6	2	11	1	0	0	17	5	1	1	0	45
Complex systems + degradation	2	3	2	11	0	0	1	6	4	5	0	0	34
Keywords: 19 / SUM:	6	26	26	100	7	9	4	26	9	18	19	3	253
UNIQUES	4	18	11	46	4	2	2	21	6	10	6	3	133

To identify the most relevant papers, an abstract and conclusion scan is performed to the 133 distinct papers identified before. All papers that focus on providing data driven approaches to maintenance, such as preventive maintenance, time-based maintenance, condition-based maintenance, or predictive maintenance for MCS, or complex system are considered as relevant. Finally, 30 papers are selected as relevant.

Thus, 14 additional papers are identified in a backward and forward search according to Webster and Watson. Consequently, 44 papers are chosen and analyzed in detail, providing a good overview about the current research state with regard to data driven solution for MCS. In the last step, the identified papers are scrutinized in detail using the qualitative content analysis [43]. Here, some works are dropped after careful analysis, because the focus of these papers did not exactly fit the goal of this literature review, and as a result, the analysis of 31 papers is provided in the next section.

4 Results

4.1 Characteristics of MCS

MCS models provide the option to describe a system in much more detail, thus, providing a more detailed but also more complex description of reality. In the following we will present these core characteristics of MCS models we found in our structured literature review.

In the literature, dependencies between components within an MCS model are well described. These dependencies can be classified into four groups: stochastic, structural, economic, and resource-based dependence [19].

The *stochastic dependence* describes the effect of the health-state of one specific component towards all other related components [2, 8, 11, 30]. The main advantage of considering stochastic dependencies is a higher accuracy while estimating or predicting RUL and reliability of the system, sub-system or components. Moreover, this will provide a valuable basis to reduce overall costs, while performing cost optimization approaches. The challenge is to collect sufficient data to detect and then model stochastic dependencies.

The *structural dependence* focuses on the structural dependence between coupled components within a system. In this case, replacement of a component requires dismantling or replacement of other components. In literature, structure dependencies are clustered into two groups: technical dependence, where technical point of view is considered, and performance dependence where performance point of view is investigated. Modeling structural dependence, accordingly, strongly improves maintenance cost [2].

Managing maintenance actions is not a pure technical approach, economic aspects like costs or benefits are crucial as well and they are represented in the *economic dependence*. Economic dependence shows the impact on the costs, while considering maintenance to related components instead of applying maintenance only to the failed/worn out components. Combining maintenance on multiple components, could either increase costs, heading to negative economic dependence, or decrease them, leading to positive economic dependence. The key advantage of modeling economic dependence is obviously the improvement on maintenance costs [2, 6].

Lastly, the *resource dependence* is focused on the relationship between components and needed resources (e.g., spare parts, human resources) to perform maintenance [1]. Typically, the following resource categories have been investigated in literature: maintenance workers, tool parts, spare parts, transport, and budget. Maintenance scheduling can be properly achieved, granted that the needed resources are available. First and foremost, organizing the needed resources accordingly, helps to improve sustainability and overall maintenance costs. In general, dependencies between components for SCS are ignored (as shown in Table 2), thus, reducing the complexity while modeling the systems, but missing important aspects which are present in practice.

Table 2. MCS characteristics in comparison with SCS.

Characteristics	SCS	MCS	Advantages
Economic dependence	No	Yes	Cost optimization
Structural dependence	No	Yes	Cost optimization
Stochastic dependence	No	Yes	Reliability, Accuracy, Cost optimization
Resource dependence	No	Yes	Availability, Sustainability
Interaction with human beings and environment	No	Yes	Reliability, Accuracy
Variability of components	Yes	Yes	Reliability, Accuracy
Stochastic reliability structure	Yes (only deterministic structure)	Yes	Reliability, Accuracy

Moreover, interaction of components with humans and their environments increases the complexity further [16]. Considering these interactions, could possibly help to improve system reliability, and fault or wear out prediction/detection accuracy. This aspect is difficult to model, because of the unpredictable nature of human behavior and the complex application context. Therefore, this aspect was not considered regarding both SCS and MCS as shown in Table 2.

Another important characteristic of MCS, is the variability between components. Usually, a system consists of a number of components, which are different regarding key characteristics, such as life span. These characteristics are important when estimating the RUL, since the prediction accuracy within this aspect is essential. Moreover, modeling this aspect properly, could also help to improve system reliability.

In the reviewed papers, the reliability structure of an SCS is often assumed to be deterministic, rather than stochastic [33, 35]. Further, the stochastic reliability structure (shown in Table 2) is another important characteristic of MCSs. However, in practice, complex MCS meets high uncertainty in the system reliability structure. Furthermore, a capability to recognize and model this characteristic can be a big advantage, when handling use cases in industrial practice.

4.2   Decision Support for Maintenance of MCS

Predicting the RUL for a system requires understanding of how the degradation process of system evolves over time and accurate estimation of the deterioration state. Modelling the degradation process for MCS requires modeling of MCS characteristics, such as interdependencies to provide reasonable estimation and prediction. Therefore, in the last decade, this topic has gained more research interest [38].

Predicting the RUL consist of two key parts, known as diagnostics and prognostics (see Table 3). On the one hand, diagnostics aims to identify the need for modeling the interactions between components. On the other hand, prognostics focus more on modelling the interactions, while predicting the RUL of components, or the whole system. In the following, we will discuss the results of various works with focus in both diagnostics and prognostics for MCS. In particular, the deterioration relationship between components and the advantages of interdependencies between components, the application area, and the methods used to model interdependencies are discussed.

In literature, researchers stated the need for monitoring and modelling interactions between MCS components in fault identification and maintenance support. Assaf et al. [17, 36] introduced approaches on fault detection with a focus on the stochastic interdependencies between components. Moreover, all these works focus on 1-1 mutual deterioration relationship between components within an MCS. Results are evaluated using both a Gearbox testing platform and a numerical example. For this purpose, methods such as Short Time Fourier Transform (SFTF) for time frequency domain analysis was introduced [17, 36]. The main advantage of using this method is that, it can denoise signals, which contain data from different components (mixed nature of the signal), thus, providing high accuracy on extracting components health indicators. Assaf et al. [36] shows that using unsupervised methods such as Gaussian Mixture Models, the health indicators can be extracted automatically and in an accurate way.

In the analyzed literature, the focus has not been only on diagnostics, but also on RUL estimation for MCS. In this case, Xu et al. [39], proposes a state discretization technique based on change point detection algorithm to model state-rate stochastic interdependences between components. The main advantage of this method is that it can handle multiple change point problems for multivariate time series with different levels of dependences. The evaluation is performed using a simple Gearbox platform which consists of two components. Furthermore, only a 1-1 mutual deterioration relationship between components is considered.

Bian et al. [33] proposes an approach in which stochastic interdependences between components are modeled as continuous-time stochastic, and the degradation interactions as change points in signals using a change point algorithm based on Schwarz's criterion [34]. This enables the option to deal with linear degradation data, and discrete type degradation rate interaction. This approach considers only 1-1 and 1-M (M > 1 and represents number of components) interactions between components.

Lee et al. [35], introduced a predictive maintenance framework for MCS based on discrete time Markov chain models for modeling deterioration processes of components and BN used to model the reliability structure of the system. The key advantage of using this approach is that it can properly handle the uncertainties and component reliability. The author did not provide explicitly the information regarding the deterioration relationship within this work. Yet, using BN to model and predict the reliability structure of the system provides enough evidence, that only 1-1 and 1-M deterioration interdependencies between components are considered.

The literature focused on RUL estimation for MCS in real use cases, such as Turbofan Engines and Civil Aerospace turbine [37, 38], stochastic interdependencies are modeled using Bayesian hierarchical models. The key advantage behind this approach is that it can handle both high uncertainty and non-linear degradation data. By definition, the introduction of Bayesian-based models shows that the 1-M relationship is handled accordingly.

Table 3. Result's overview of the research works with focus on modeling RUL.

Paper	Method	Deterioration relationship	Application area	Advantages	Focus of the approach
[17]	STFT	1-1 mutual interaction	Gearbox testing platform/numerical example	Mixed nature of the signals, high accuracy on extracting component health Indicators	Diagnostics
[36]	STFT and Gaussian Mixture Models			Automatically and accurately extract components health indicators	
[39]	State discretization technique based on change point detection algorithm		Gearbox	Multiple change point problems for multivariate time series with different levels of dependences	Prognostics
[33]	Change point detection and Bavesian framework	1-1 and 1-M	Simulation study	Linear degradation data and discrete type degradation rate interaction	
[35]	Markov chains and Bavesian network (BN)			Uncertainties and component reliability	
[37]	Bayesian hierarchical Model		Civil aerospace gas turbine	High uncertainty and non-linear degradation data	
[38]	Ratio has ed change point detection and hierarchical Bayesian model				
[5]	Multiple linear regression and Gaussian Process Regression		Industrial cold bos in a petrochemical plant	Multivariate time series data and relationship between variables, which is not explicitly defined	

Rasmekomen et al. [5], models state-rate degradation between components using a regression-based approach and is evaluated using a two-component real use case of industrial cold box in a petrochemical plant. The approach followed within this work, consisting of two key steps. In the first step, the deterioration behavior of each component explicitly is modeled using a multivariate linear regression model. Next, the Gaussian process regression is used to model the interdependencies between components. Within this work, 1-1 and 1-M deterioration relationship was studied.

In general, the focus in this research area is more into use cases of simple MCS (two components system), or simulation studies, rather than on real use cases of complex MCS, which consist of multiple components, and various complex interdependencies are present.

4.3   Improve Decision Quality

Reliability and cost optimization in the context of predictive maintenance for industrial settings are of central interest. Therefore, the key focus in our selected papers was primarily on improving maintenance quality, but also on precise and accurate prediction of fault events or RUL. In the considered papers, on the one hand, the focus is primary on finding the optimal time for decision support. On the other hand, various papers focus not only on improving the maintenance timing [3, 6, 8], but also on the required type of maintenance [2, 21, 22]. Hence, in this section, we will introduce several works and their application highlighting these aspects.

In our review we found solutions with a focus on improving decision quality by only estimating the optimal time to perform maintenance. These solutions take the advantages by modeling only economic dependencies, or together with structural or stochastic dependencies. Laggoune et al. [3], proposes an opportunistic replacement policy for MCS over hydrogen compressor in an oil refinery is introduced. The introduced opportunistic policy considers the economic dependence between components. Moreover, in this work, the small data challenge was successfully handled by considering the bootstrap and Weibull technique.

Niu et al. [8], introduces an approach, which estimates the optimal maintenance time for components within a braking system of rail vehicles was proposed. The nonparametric modeling was applied on the component level, and later this model is used to find the global optimization on the system level. Nguyen et al. [6], introduces a decision-making process considering multi-level details for MCS. This approach provides high quality decision regarding the optimal time for maintenance by considering stochastic, structural, and economic dependencies. Do et al. [12], introduces a model for a Gearbox system which aims for optimal maintenance time for a two-component system considering stochastic and economic dependencies. In this case, it has been shown that the state dependence between components is important and it has a significant impact of 29.3% on the cost. Kammoun et al. [10], introduced a new approach based on data mining to optimize selective maintenance for MCS. This approach aims to find the optimal maintenance time by considering economic dependencies. This solution is suitable, if only maintenance data are available and sensor data are missing. Van Horenbeek er al. [27] introduced a new approach, which considers stochastic, structural, and economic dependencies to provide optimal maintenance time by considering short-term information, such as component degradation, into maintenance planning. We found several papers, which consider only economic, or altogether with stochastic, or structural dependence between the components and aim to improve decision quality by taking into account only optimal maintenance time [9, 11, 13, 14, 18, 24–26, 28, 32].

The introduction of stochastic dependencies while aiming for optimal timing of maintenance is complex. Rasmekomen et al. [5] introduced an optimization of condition-based maintenance policy for MCS considering state-rate interactions. This works shows that the decision quality could be improved by considering the stochastic interdependencies between components. Feng et al. [4] provides a novel approach based on stochastic dependencies in which one dominant/independent component and "n" statistically dependent components are used to optimize the maintenance timing.

In our selected papers, we found various works with focus on improving the quality of decision support, which do not restrict their focus only on optimal time, but also consider the required maintenance type, or the relevant sparse parts. For instance, Verbert et al. [21], proposed a new approach for railway network case, which represent a typical MCS. In this work, the economic and structural dependencies are investigated and modeled providing significant impact on decision quality. Furthermore, this approach provides decision support by considering both the optimal time, and the required type of maintenance. Another approach for improving the decision quality for high pressure in casting machine was introduced in [22]. Besides the optimal time for maintenance, also the required relevant maintenance action is provided. Nguyen et al. [2] proposes a joint optimization of optimal maintenance time and required spare parts using the advantage of prognostic information and economic dependency. Moreover, the structural importance together with predictive reliability is considered to improve the decision-making process. Duan et al. [23], introduces a new approach considering the economic dependencies for feed system of a machine tool. The aim was to improve the decision quality by introducing both the optimal time and maintenance type. This approach is suitable for MCS with multiple identical components.

Summarized, the focus of the papers on improving decision quality for MCS is more focused on estimation of optimal time. However, there are various papers, which alongside optimal time, also focus on other aspects, such as maintenance type, or the relevant spare parts. Furthermore, several solutions are either evaluated against simple MCS, usually consisting of two or three components, or the approaches are evaluated using simulation studies, rather than real life use cases.

5   Conclusion and Future Work

In this paper, we investigated the application of MCS models and approaches in the context of predictive maintenance. Our review identified different interdependencies and their application settings. Our review provides an overview of already existing approaches and can be used to select suitable approaches. The review also showed that MCS are superior to SCS in terms of prediction quality and decision quality. Additionally, MCS provide advanced decision perspectives which are useful in the context of predictive maintenance. To our best knowledge, the M-M relationship of stochastic interdependencies were not considered in the current works and is an aspect which requires more attention from the research community.

Our literature review also showed that research on MCS in the context of predictive maintenance is in an early stage. Most MCS presented in the investigated papers are simple, i.e., having 2–5 subcomponents and they are evaluated in simulation scenarios. Thus, the work on MCS in the context of predictive maintenance can be considered as mostly theoretical and more research on the implementation and application of MCS in practice is needed. This can be also considered as the promising direction for future research.

Second, researchers frequently mention that data collection and modelling of interdependencies between MCS components is a complex task. However, so far, no approaches helping deciders in this process can be found until now. Hence, studies, frameworks, guidelines supporting this modelling effort seem very useful and are considered as a further avenue for future research.

Third, most authors highlight the advanced decision support features of MCS models, but literature lacks work on representations or interfaces so far. However, to evaluate this in practice, suitable approaches are needed. This is especially true as maintenance workers also expect a certain level of explainability before they trust and accept MCS solutions. Hence, to push the acceptance of MCS in industrial practice more research on the presentation of MCS recommendations is needed.

Acknowledgments. This research work is done by Pro2Future. Pro2Future is funded within the Austrian COMET Program-Competence Centers for Excellent Technologies- under the auspices of the Austrian Federal Ministry of Transport, Innovation and Technology, the Austrian Federal Ministry for Digital and Economic Affairs and of the Provinces of Upper Austria and Styria. COMET is managed by the Austrian Research Promotion Agency FFG.

References

1. Keizer, M.C.A.O., Flapper, S.D.P., Teunter, R.H.: Condition-based maintenance policies for systems with multiple dependent components: a review. Eur. J. Oper. Res. **261**(2), 405–420 (2017)
2. Nguyen, K.-A., Do, P., Grall, A.: Joint predictive maintenance and inventory strategy for multi-component systems using Birnbaum's structural importance. Reliab. Eng. Syst. Saf. **168**, 249–261 (2017)
3. Laggoune, R., Chateauneuf, A., Aissani, D.: Impact of few failure data on the opportunistic replacement policy for multi-component systems. Reliab. Eng. Syst. Saf. **95**(2), 108–119 (2010)
4. Feng, Q., Jiang, L., Coit, D.W.: Reliability analysis and condition-based maintenance of systems with dependent degrading components based on thermodynamic physics-of-failure. Int. J. Adv. Manuf. Technol. **86**(1-4), 913–923 (2016)
5. Rasmekomen, N., Parlikad, A.K.: Condition-based maintenance of multi-component systems with degradation state-rate interactions. Reliab. Eng. Syst. Saf. **148**, 1–10 (2016)
6. Nguyen, K.-A., Do, P., Grall, A.: Multi-level predictive maintenance for multi-component systems. Reliab. Eng. Syst. Saf. **144**, 83–94 (2015)
7. Jamshidi, M.: Systems of Systems Engineering: Principles and Applications. CRC Press, Boca Raton (2008)
8. Niu, G., Jiang, J.: Prognostic control-enhanced maintenance optimization for multi-component systems. Reliab. Eng. Syst. Saf. **168**, 218–226 (2017)
9. Cheng, G.Q., Zhou, B.H., Li, L.: Joint optimization of lot sizing and condition-based maintenance for multi-component production systems. Comput. Ind. Eng. **110**, 538–549 (2017)
10. Kammoun, M.A., Rezg, N.: Toward the optimal selective maintenance for multi-component systems using observed failure: applied to the FMS study case. Int. J. Adv. Manuf. Technol. **96**(1–4), 1093–1107 (2018)
11. Huynh, K.T., Barros, A., Bérenguer, C.: Multi-level decision-making for the predictive maintenance of k-out-of-n: F deteriorating systems. IEEE Trans. Reliab. **64**(1), 94–117 (2014)

12. Do, P., Assaf, R., Scarf, P., Iung, B.: Modelling and application of condition-based maintenance for a two-component system with stochastic and economic dependencies. Reliab. Eng. Syst. Saf. **182**, 86–97 (2019)
13. Li, H., Deloux, E., Dieulle, L.: A condition-based maintenance policy for multi-component systems with Lévy copulas dependence. Reliab. Eng. Syst. Saf. **149**, 44–55 (2016)
14. Zhou, X., Huang, K., Xi, L., Lee, J.: Preventive maintenance modeling for multi- component systems with considering stochastic failures and disassembly sequence. Reliab. Eng. Syst. Saf. **142**, 231–237 (2015)
15. Bektas, O., Jones, J.A., Sankararaman, S., Roychoudhury, I., Goebel, K.: A neural network filtering approach for similarity-based remaining useful life estimation. Int. J. Adv. Manuf. Technol. **101**(1-4), 87–103 (2019)
16. Desforges, X., Diévart, M., Archimède, B.: A prognostic function for complex systems to support production and maintenance co-operative planning based on an extension of object-oriented Bayesian networks. Comput. Ind. **86**, 34–51 (2017)
17. Assaf, R., Do, P., Scarf, P., Nefti-Meziani, S.: Diagnosis for systems with multi- component wear interactions. In: 2017 IEEE International Conference on Prognostics and Health Management (ICPHM). IEEE, pp. 96–102 (2017)
18. Shi, H., Zeng, J.: Real-time prediction of remaining useful life and preventive opportunistic maintenance strategy for multi-component systems considering stochastic dependence. Comput. Ind. Eng. **93**, 192–204 (2016)
19. Alaswad, S., Xiang, Y.: A review on condition-based maintenance optimization models for stochastically deteriorating system. Reliab. Eng. Syst. Saf. **157**, 54–63 (2017)
20. Schmidt, B., Wang, L.: Predictive maintenance: literature review and future trends. Int. Conf. Flex. Autom. Intell. Manuf. (FAIM) **1**, 232–239 (2015)
21. Verbert, K., De Schutter, B., Babuška, R.: Timely condition-based maintenance planning for multi-component systems. Reliab. Eng. Syst. Saf. **159**, 310–321 (2017)
22. Tambe, P.P., Mohite, S., Kulkarni, M.S.: Optimisation of opportunistic maintenance of a multi-component system considering the effect of failures on quality and production schedule: a case study. Int. J. Adv. Manuf. Technol. **69**(5-8), 1743–1756 (2013)
23. Duan, C., Deng, C., Wang, B.: Optimal multi-level condition-based maintenance policy for multi-unit systems under economic dependence. Int. J. Adv. Manuf. Technol. **91**(9-12), 4299–4312 (2017)
24. De Jonge, B., Klingenberg, W., Teunter, R., Tinga, T.: Reducing costs by clustering maintenance activities for multiple critical units. Reliab. Eng. Syst. Saf. **145**, 93–103 (2016)
25. Bouvard, K., Artus, S., Bérenguer, C., Cocquempot, V.: Condition-based dynamic maintenance operations planning & grouping. application to commercial heavy vehicles. Reliab. Eng. Syst. Saf. **96**(6), 601–610 (2011)
26. Martinod, R.M., Bistorin, O., Castañeda, L.F., Rezg, N.: Maintenance policy optimisation for multi-component systems considering degradation of components and imperfect maintenance actions. Comput. Ind. Eng. **124**, 100–112 (2018)
27. Van Horenbeek, A., Pintelon, L.: A dynamic predictive maintenance policy for complex multi-component systems. Reliab. Eng. Syst. Saf. **120**, 39–50 (2013)
28. Zhu, W., Fouladirad, M., Bérenguer, C.: A multi-level maintenance policy for a multi-component and multifailure mode system with two independent failure modes. Reliab. Eng. Syst. Saf. **153**, 50–63 (2016)
29. Selcuk, S.: Predictive maintenance, its implementation and latest trends. Proc. Inst. Mech. Eng. Part B: J. Eng. Manuf. **231**(9), 1670–1679 (2017)
30. Bian, L., Gebraeel, N.: Stochastic framework for partially degradation systems with continuous component degradation-rate-interactions. Naval Res. Logist. (NRL) **61**(4), 286–303 (2014)

31. Webster, J., Watson, R.T.: Analyzing the past to prepare for the future: writing a literature review. MIS Q. **26**(2), xiii–xxiii (2002)
32. Hu, J., Zhang, L., Liang, W.: Opportunistic predictive maintenance for complex multi-component systems based on DBN-HAZOP model. Process Saf. Environ. Prot. **90**(5), 376–388 (2012)
33. Bian, L., Gebraeel, N.: Stochastic modeling and real-time prognostics for multi- component systems with degradation rate interactions. IIE Trans. **46**(5), 470–482 (2014)
34. Schwarz, G.: Estimating the dimension of a model. Anna. Stat. **6**(2), 461–464 (1978)
35. Lee, D., Pan, R.: Predictive maintenance of complex system with multi-level reliability structure. Int. J. Prod. Res. **55**(16), 4785–4801 (2017)
36. Assaf, R., Nefti-Meziani, S., Scarf, P.: Unsupervised learning for improving fault detection in complex systems. In: 2017 IEEE International Conference on Advanced Intelligent Mechatronics (AIM), pp. 1058–1064. IEEE (2017)
37. Zaidan, M.A., Harrison, R.F., Mills, A.R., Fleming, P.J.: Bayesian hierarchical models for aerospace gas turbine engine prognostics. Expert Syst. Appl. **42**(1), 539–553 (2015)
38. Zaidan, M.A., Relan, R., Mills, A.R., Harrison, R.F.: Prognostics of gas turbine engine: an integrated approach. Expert Syst. Appl. **42**(22), 8472–8483 (2015)
39. Xu, M., Jin, X., Kamarthi, S., Noor-E-Alam, M.: A failure-dependency modeling and state discretization approach for condition-based maintenance optimization of multi-component systems. J. Manuf. Syst. **47**, 141–152 (2018)
40. Canizo, M., et al.: Real-time predictive maintenance for wind turbines using big data frameworks. In: 2017 IEEE International Conference on Prognostics and Health Management (ICPHM), pp. 70–77. IEEE (2017)
41. Baptista, M., et al.: Forecasting fault events for predictive maintenance using data- driven techniques and ARMA modeling. Comput. Ind. Eng. **115**, 41–53 (2018)
42. Lasi, H., Fettke, P., Kemper, H.G., Feld, T., Hoffmann, M.: Industry 4.0. Bus. Inf. Syst. Eng. **6**(4), 239–242 (2014)
43. Mayring, P.: Qualitative content analysis. A Companion Qual. Res. **1**, 159–176 (2004)
44. Sun, Q., Ye, Z.-S., Chen, N.: Optimal inspection and replacement policies for multi-unit systems subject to degradation. IEEE Trans. Reliab. **67**(1), 401–413 (2017)
45. Makridakis, S.: The forthcoming Artificial Intelligence (AI) revolution: Its impact on society and firms. Futures **90**, 46–60 (2017)
46. Thalmann, S., Gursch, H.G., Suschnigg, J., Gashi, M., Ennsbrunner, H., Fuchs, A.K., Schreck, T., et al.: Cognitive decision support for industrial product life cycles: a position paper. In: COGNITIVE 2019: The Eleventh International Conference on Advanced Cognitive Technologies and Applications, IARIA, pp. 3–9 (2019)

Smiling Earth - Raising Citizens' Awareness on Environmental Sustainability

Sobah Abbas Petersen[1(✉)], Idar Petersen[2], and Peter Ahcin[2]

[1] Department of Computer Science,
Norwegian University of Science and Technology, Trondheim, Norway
sap@ntnu.no
[2] SINTEF Energy, Trondheim, Norway
{Idar.Petersen,Peter.Ahcin}@sintef.no

Abstract. This paper describes the design and implementation of a mobile app, Smiling Earth, to support citizens to contribute to climate change by being aware of their carbon footprint and making changes in their daily energy consumption and transportation. One of the main aims of this work is to explore the ways in which ICT could help raise awareness and educate citizens about their actions and their consequences on the environment. The Smiling Earth app is designed to visualise data about citizens' activities and to motivate citizens to change their behavior to reduce their CO_2 emissions by adopting a healthier lifestyle. The app takes a broader perspective of CO_2 emissions, bringing together the transport and energy sectors. The design process and a preliminary evaluation of Smiling Earth is presented in the paper. This work has been conducted as a part of the EU H2020 DESENT project.

Keywords: CO_2 emissions · Green transportation · Behavior change · Mobile app · Carbon footprint · ICT and sustainability

1 Introduction

Global warming is one of the biggest and most urgent issues facing the world today. Transportation, electricity consumption and domestic heating are responsible for a large part of greenhouse gas emissions, which contribute to climate change. A survey from Statistics Norway [1] shows that on average, 50% of the Norwegian household's incomes are spent on housing, energy and transportation and one of the biggest contributors to Carbon Dioxide (CO_2) emissions is transportation [2]. Savings can be made with better energy and transportation management, and in Norway, transport is the sector where most emissions cuts will be made in the near future [3]. While physical activity such as walking or cycling for short trips are possibilities, many still choose to drive to work to save time and for flexibility [2], or out of habit [4]. The main motivations for the work presented in this paper is to explore the use of ICT to motivate citizens to reduce their carbon footprint by changing their behavior. More specifically, to switch from driving internal combustion-based vehicles to less carbon intensive means of transport to those that emit less CO_2, such as electrical vehicles (EV), cycling or walking, which increase their physical activities too. We believe that this is a

M. Themistocleous and M. Papadaki (Eds.): EMCIS 2019, LNBIP 381, pp. 45–57, 2020.
https://doi.org/10.1007/978-3-030-44322-1_4

relevant step towards taking action to combat climate change and its impacts and for responsible and sustainable societies, in line with the United Nations' Sustainable Development Goals (SDG). One of the areas in which ICT could contribute towards achieving the SDGs is to help citizens perceive them not as isolated, single goals detached from their daily lives; rather as goals they will contribute to as a part of their daily lives and activities. Indeed technologies are most effective when they help people to achieve the goals they have already decided upon [5].

In the European project, DESENT [6], the affordances of mobile smart phones and their pervasiveness are explored for precisely this. A mobile app, Smiling Earth, is designed to (i) increase citizens' awareness about their CO_2 emissions through visualising data about their daily activities; and (ii) motivate citizens to change their behavior to reduce their CO_2 emissions by adopting a healthier lifestyle. Smiling Earth takes a broader perspective of CO_2 emissions, bringing together the transport and energy sectors as well as the lifestyle (e.g. transportation modes) of individuals.

The aims of this paper are to describe a gamified mobile app, Smiling Earth, designed to create awareness about carbon footprints and affect individuals' behavior change towards more sustainable choices and actions in their daily lives. The overall research question addressed is the paper is: Can the combination of energy and transport data and individual energy consumption in terms of CO_2 emissions motivate people to manage energy better and reduce CO_2 emissions?

The rest of this paper is organised as follows: Sect. 2 describes the DESENT project; Sect. 3 provides an overview of the related work; Sect. 4 describes the behavior change model that guides the design; Sect. 5 describes the design process; Sect. 6 describes the Smiling Earth app; Sect. 7 describes the evaluations and provide an overview of the main results; Sect. 8 reflects on the results of the evaluations and Sect. 9 concludes the paper and provides a brief overview of the future work.

2 DESENT Project

The success of smart city development needs integrated solutions about energy, transport, service and governance with the full involvement of multiple stakeholders, such as governments, public and private enterprises and citizens. The European H2020 project, DESENT, focuses on providing a smart decision support tool for urban energy and transport, by developing innovative approaches and utilizing cutting-edge technologies using co-creation. The consortium which integrates municipalities, universities, research institutes, enterprises and private companies from three European countries (Austria, The Netherlands and Norway), tackles the various challenges by implementing the innovative solutions in demo cities. DESENT will support smart decision making for policy makers and personalised services for citizens.

One of the focus areas of DESENT is to use the energy and transportation data to motivate citizens to change their mobility habits through ICT. Energy companies and grid owners are a part of the consortium, who will use this data and take the initiative to drive the behavior change of their current and potential customers.

3   Related Work

Games and gamified applications have been used to motivate and engage users and to raise their awareness about energy consumption. Several examples have focused on the energy consumption aspects. For example, a competition-based game, *The Kukui Cup*, motivates university students in Hawaii to change their energy consumption behavior in their dorms [7]. Students' real-world activities, such as switching off lights when they leave the room, are displayed in a virtual setting, using a website. A social, multi-player game for improving home energy related behavior, *Power House*, supports people minimize the energy consumption by their families [8]. Another application that promotes the reduction of CO_2 for individuals and families is *EcoIsland*, by using individual psychological incentives and social incentives as well as learning-related features, such as self-reporting [9, 10]. *Ducky* supports an eco-friendly lifestyle and quantifies, visualises and communicates everyday climate activities of individuals and communities to increase citizens' knowledge and awareness about their CO_2 emissions [11].

A pervasive persuasive mobile application designed for tracking green transportation choices, *UbiGreen*, tracks an individual's transport options, e.g. carpooling and walking, and provides feedback using a metaphor from nature as the "wall paper" for the mobile app [2]. Based on the choices, the metaphor changes; one of the metaphors was a polar bear on an iceberg where the iceberg increases in size if the individual makes greener transportation choices [12]. Another gamified app that focuses on urban mobility is the MUV app developed to encourage people to adopt sustainable mobility modes in the awareness of their potential role as agents of urban livability [13, 14].

Metaphors from nature seem to be a powerful means of raising users' awareness and creating an emotional attachment; the metaphor of a tree and a bear on an iceberg were used in *UbiGreen*, while *EcoIsland* used an island and the sea level as a metaphor.

4   Behaviour Change

Designs to affect behavior change require an understanding of how humans adopt or change behaviors. We have based our work on the Transtheoretical Model of Behaviour Change (TTM), developed in the health sector [15]. TTM posits that behaviour change progresses through six stages of change. The first stage is *Precontemplation* stage when the individuals do not consider changing their behaviour, which could be due to a lack of awareness of the consequences of their behaviour. The second stage is *Contemplation*, when individuals are intending to change, but not immediately, and are more aware of the change benefits. At this stage, the individual is interested and perhaps may explore possibilities to change their behaviour, but is not ready to make a commitment to change. The third stage is *Preparation*, when the individual has decided to change behaviour and intends to take action in the near future. During the fourth stage, *Action*, a change is observable and the individual works hard to keep their new behavior. During this stage, it is important for individuals to get support for keeping up their new behavior by through helping relationships or contingency management support. During the fifth stage, *Maintenance*: keeping the behaviour is easier, but individuals may be tempted to go back to their previous behavior. The sixth stage is *Termination*, when there is no more risk for individuals to go back to their previous behaviour.

TTM provides a conceptual framework for our design to support behavior change and aligns with how we aim to support behavior change through our Smiling Earth app. The first stage is to inform users to raise awareness and then to educate and persuade them to decide to change their behavior. Thus, our current design and evaluation of Smiling Earth has focused on these stages.

5   Design Process

The design process was influenced by the setting for the project. The user group for the Smiling Earth are the general citizens and electricity consumers in urban areas. Since the project consortium included energy companies and we had easy access to them, we chose to work closely with them to leverage on their knowledge of their customers. We also believe that their support for Smiling Earth will promote the app among the end users; i.e. the citizens. The energy company was represented mostly by both technical support and the business people. In addition to the energy company, the design and development team included researchers with engineering, ICT and economics backgrounds.

A participatory design approach was followed with close interactions with the energy company, who played the roles of an important stakeholder, an end user as well as an expert. Their enthusiasm and availability enabled us to conduct several formative evaluations and design iterations, using sketches and the rapid prototyping tool Proto.io[1]. An agile design and development process was adopted, which is illustrated in Fig. 1

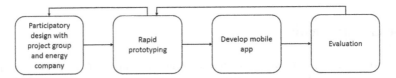

Fig. 1. Design and evaluation process

6   Description of Smiling Earth

The central concepts that influence the design of Smiling Earth were CO_2 emissions, health benefits, environmental impact and economic profit. The Graphical User Interface (GUI) for the main page is designed to reflect these concepts and draw the user's attention to the concept of CO_2 emissions and how that affect the world we live in; see Fig. 2. We have used the earth as a metaphor, which is placed in the centre of the screen. This metaphor is used to create an emotional attachment [12] and to show

---

[1] https://proto.io/.

the impact of a high carbon footprint (global warning) which may be caused by the user's actions. The main screen, the dashboard for the app, shown in Fig. 2 ((a) and (b)), shows the daily values of CO_2 emissions from transportation and domestic heating. The circular indicator informs the user about the current value of CO_2 emissions in kg of CO_2. The number indicated in the circle is the daily value. The circular progress bar for each circular indicator shows the user's value relative to the maximum allowed level of emissions; i.e. the target for the user must be less than this maximum amount. The daily goal for the CO_2 limit is 4 kg CO_2 for the carbon footprint. The screen shots in Fig. 2 show three possible states (out of five); (a) shows a very happy earth due to low emissions w.r.t. the maximum level; (b) shows a happy face, but less happy than (a) as the CO_2 emissions are reaching close to the maximum; (d) shows a very dismal picture of the earth due to a high level of emission, far above the maximum level.

The colour code that is used in the GUI are blue for values that are related to housing (such as the household heating and electricity consumption) and green, which is related to transportation, such as walking, cycling or EVs.

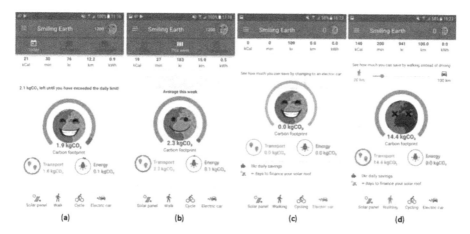

Fig. 2. Smiling Earth concept and GUI

Fig. 2 in (c) and (d) show estimations of CO_2 values, when the user selects a transportation or heating mode. The symbols on the bottom of the screen are "estimation buttons" which are for solar panels, walking, cycling and an electrical vehicle, from left to right. By clicking on the "estimation buttons", the relevant values will be displayed. For example, in Fig. 2(c), the estimated CO_2 emission by selecting an electrical vehicle is shown as 0.0 kg. On the other hand, the estimation for walking while either sometimes driving a combustion engine vehicle or using conventional heating means could lead to a higher CO_2 emission as shown in (d). These values are based on statistical data [16] and analyses conducted by SINTEF Energy and the DESENT partners.

A menu on the top left of the screen enables users to see their CO_2 emissions and other values such as calories burnt and money saved, over the previous week, month or year. The visualisation of CO_2 emissions for a week and for a month are shown in Fig. 3. The red horizontal line marks the maximum limit; i.e. users are encouraged to keep their total CO_2 emissions below that level. The blue and green colour coding is used to indicate the emissions due to household actions or transportation actions; e.g. Figure 3(a) shows that 5 kg of CO_2 out of the total of 8 kg, were from household activities. Bar graphs are used to visualise the data for a week while the continuous graph shown in (b) seemed a better visualisation of the data for a longer time period such as a month or a year.

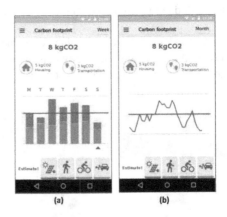

Fig. 3. Smiling Earth - CO_2 emission data visualization

6.1   System Architecture and Data Sources

The focus of this paper is on the mobile app and the mobile interface design as this is one of the critical elements in supporting behavior change. However, creating synergy among energy related data and transport or mobility data and the data on the user's behavior through the mobile device are not trivial problems. These are distributed data sources, which required a software architecture that supported distributed databases and computed data across these sources. An overview of the architecture of the system is illustrated in Fig. 4. The mobile app stores user data captured by the mobile device, such as activity type and level, and obtains calculations of CO_2 and calories from a server. The server is linked to a number of distributed data sources, which provide real time and historical information that are relevant for the services offered by the mobile app.

Two approaches were used to calculate the carbon footprint and costs related to the energy consumption. In the first phase of development, users provided a monthly value of their electricity consumption. A typical yearly energy consumption profile was then calibrated to fit this value. In the second development phase, the app estimated the

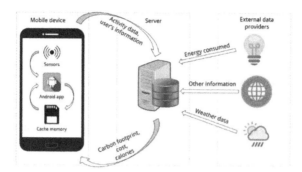

Fig. 4. Smiling Earth system architecture

heating needs of the user based on the outside temperature. The electricity consumption profile was calibrated with smart meter values or from the Elhub[2]– a central unit to manage electricity consumption data in Norway.

Solar installation outputs are, similarly, estimated based on standard profiles or if available for the specific location, actual real time data will be used in future. The carbon footprint and costs from driving were estimated on user provided data for fuel consumption and a conversion value of $2348gCO_2e/L$ [17] and the distance travelled captured by the mobile device. The fixed costs of the vehicle are estimated using the value and age of the vehicle and standard value depreciation factors.

7   Evaluation

Using a participatory approach, formative evaluations of the design have been conducted with business and technical people from the energy company. The focus of these evaluations were the concept and overall design and the GUI. Questionnaires were used to obtain systematic feedback. The main parts of the evaluations were focused group discussions and therefore the emphasis was on the dialogue, interaction and feedback from the participants. Screenshots of the design were presented with brief explanations, followed by discussions and a questionnaire. The questionnaire was designed with focus on the concepts and usability in focus. The feedback and input from the workshops were used to improve the concept and the design.

The participants liked the earth metaphor, monitoring their carbon footprint and seeing their carbon footprint history. The main feedback and suggestions for improvements include the colours used for the estimation of values and consideration of the values that were shown on each screen so as to minimize the cognitive load on a user to remember information across the different screens. One concern was the quality of the data that is displayed and the correctness of the estimations as this was important for the users to trust the data and the app, which is an important issue for citizens using

---

[2] https://elhub.no/.

the app. The overall feedback was very positive and constructive, and provided input for the next iterations of the design.

This paper reports the results of the final evaluation of the prototype described in Sect. 6. The final questionnaire was designed to evaluate the general concept, usability, motivations and behaviour change of the users through using Smiling Earth. The evaluation was conducted by observations, a post-intervention questionnaire and semiformal interviews. There were five participants who were university students and owned Android devices; four with IT background. The participants were asked to install Smiling Earth on their mobile devices and use it for 8 days. The questionnaire consisted of forty-six statements where the users were asked to agree or disagree, based on a Likert scale: 0: Strongly disagree, 1: Disagree, 2: Neither agree or disagree, 3: Agree and 4: Strongly agree.

An evaluation of all the elements included in the questionnaire is beyond the scope of this paper. In the following subsections, we will present the results for the statements that were related to the concepts of Smiling Earth related to behaviour change, and the potential of acceptance of Smiling Earth, based on the Technology Acceptance Model (TAM) [18].

7.1 Evaluation of Behaviour Change

The questions Q1–Q7 in the questionnaire addressed the support for behaviour change in Smiling Earth. The responses to these statements are shown in Table 1.

Table 1. Statements related to behaviour change

Questions	Related to behaviour change and concept
Q1	During the test period, I chose a different transportation means than I normally use to achieve better results in the app
Q2	I was surprised by how much my daily activities were affecting the environment
Q3	Viewing the data visualised in the app made me want to make some changes to reduce my emissions
Q4	I would tell people I know about the app so that they also become aware of their impact on the environment
Q5	After using the app, I am considering buying an electric car or solar panels in the future, to reduce my emissions
Q6	The app motivated me to change my behavior to a more sustainable one
Q7	My concern for the environment has increased after using the app

The responses to the statements related to behaviour change are shown in Fig. 5. The responses to Q1 is not surprising as the participants, who were students, did not own a car and used the bus or cycled or walked. The low scores for Q5 and Q2 could be partly explained by the result for Q1; particularly Q5 as the investment in an EV or solar panels were not something that the students were planning at the time of the evaluation. The responses to Q3 and Q7 suggest that the users' concerns for the environment were not increased after using the app. Through the interviews, it appears that they were aware of the climate problem and want to do something about it. They want to engage others, and the positive responses to Q4 indicate that. Although the results were not very positive, the interviews indicated that the users' knowledge about CO_2 emissions were improved and the awareness among them about the impacts of their everyday activities on the environment was increased.

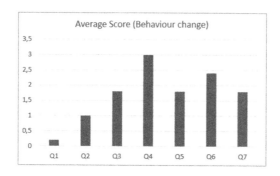

Fig. 5. Smiling Earth Evaluation – Support for behaviour change

7.2   Evaluation of Potential Acceptance

The prototype of Smiling Earth is a proof of concept and it is hard to establish or envisage the impact of the app through the evaluations. TAM considers the ease of use and perceived usefulness of a system as two most important determinants of the actual use of a system. It claims that if an app is perceived easy to use, it will be perceived as useful, and thus the intention to use the app will increase. We have applied TAM as a part of the evaluations, using a set of statements, which are shown in Table 2. The TAM model and how the statements in the questionnaire relate to TAM are shown in Fig. 6.

Table 2. Statements related to TAM

Questions	Related to behaviour change and concept
Q16	I find the link between energy, carbon footprint, activity, and expenses motivating
Q38	I find the visualization of last week's historical data useful
Q41	I find it useful to have a defined daily limit for the carbon footprint in the app
Q24	I think I would use this app frequently
Q46	Do you think you would like to use this app?
Q26	I think the app was easy to use

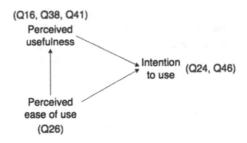

Fig. 6. Smiling Earth Evaluation – Technology Acceptance Model

The responses to the statements related to TAM are shown in Fig. 7. The participants perceive that Smiling Earth is useful (Q16, Q38 and Q41) and that it is easy to use (Q26). However, the scores for statements to indicate intent to use are lower, although they are positive.

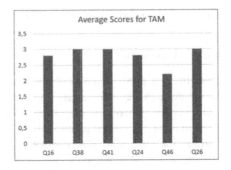

Fig. 7. Smiling Earth – TAM, Perceived usefulness, ease of use and intent

8 Reflections

The concept of linking energy consumption and transport medium was initially difficult to understand for some of the users. Furthermore, the threshold of relating energy consumption data to one's own carbon footprint and contribution to the CO_2 emissions was high. The evaluation results from TAM indicate that, in general, users perceived Smiling Earth to be useful and intended to use the app. The scores for intention to use was less, which could be explained by the comments from users that they did not like the Smiling Earth app running on their mobile devices constantly, perhaps due to privacy concerns. The issue of trusting the data that is provided was raised also by some of the users. Indeed, this is an important factor in the design, in particular, from progressing beyond the Contemplation stage to the Preparation stage in the TTM behaviour change model. Furthermore, participants expressed that Smiling Earth contained new terminology and concepts, and that it was crucial that these concepts were thoroughly explained to get people to use the app.

The formative evaluations indicated that the concept of the Smiling Earth app was interesting and understandable for the users (details of this part of the evaluations are available from [19]). The results for the statements related to motivation indicated a positive score, while the participants were indifferent to the statement that Smiling Earth raised curiosity about energy and environment. The feedback from the interviews indicate that users would like Smiling Earth to include social aspects such as a community of users and ranking or competitions among them. Further exploration of the relationship between motivation and curiosity [20] will be done and the social game mechanics [21] to support these will be considered.

The results indicating behaviour change due to the use of Smiling Earth, such as the later stages in the TTM model, were not convincing. This is perhaps due to the fact that the user group was students who used an environment friendly transport mode already. The main feedback from the evaluations indicated that the concepts were interesting and motivating. One of the main feedback from the evaluations was that the concepts were complex, in particular, linking one's own everyday actions to kilograms of CO_2 and this requires some careful thoughts around the user interface and how to communicate this to the users in an interesting and engaging way.

The overall results look positive and convincing enough to continue developing the concept and the Smiling Earth app and the evaluations have provided valuable feedback to enhance as well as simplify the app.

9   Conclusion and Future Work

This paper describes a mobile app, Smiling Earth, designed to create awareness about carbon footprints and affect individuals' behavior change towards more sustainable actions in their daily lives. The overall research question addressed is the paper is: Can the combination of energy and transport data and individual energy consumption in terms of CO_2 emissions motivate people to manage energy better and reduce CO_2 emissions? A prototype was developed through iterative design and formative evaluation cycles with an energy company and researchers. A behaviour change model, TTM, was used as a conceptual framework to support behavior change. The results show that Smiling Earth supports the early stages of TTM, by contributing to raising the awareness of users and motivating them to learn more about how their daily activities could impact the environment through CO_2 emissions.

The results from the evaluations of the prototype show that the concept of Smiling Earth is interesting and understandable for the users and that it motivates users to change their behaviour to environmentally sustainable habits. However, work remains to get users to actively use Smiling Earth and sustain behaviours that emit less CO_2.

The future plans for this work include further development of the concept and prototype based on the users' feedback and enhancing capabilities such as the social aspects, user communities and enhancing the gamification aspects for intrinsic motivation and raising the users' curiosity to support behaviour change. We also plan to conduct more evaluations with other user groups; e.g. car owners.

Acknowledgements. This work has been funded by the Norwegian Research Council and the European Union's H2020 research and innovation programme, under the grant agreement No. 857160. Smiling Earth was implemented and evaluated by 2 MSc, Celine Minh and Ragnhild Larsen, and a summer student at NTNU. The authors would like to thank NTE and the participants of the workshops for their valuable contributions.

References

1. Statistics Norway: Survey of consumer expenditure 2012 (2017). https://www.ssb.no/en/inntekt-og-forbruk/statistikker/fbu. Accessed 26 June 2017
2. Froehlich, J., et al.: UbiGreen: investigating a mobile tool for tracking and supporting green transportation habits. In: CHI 2009, pp. 1043–1052. ACM (2009)
3. Granell, C., et al.: Future internet technologies for environmental applications. J. Environ. Model. Softw. **78**, 1–15 (2016)
4. Nyblom, Å., Eriksson, E.: Time is of essence - changing the horizon of travel planning. In: 2nd International Conference on ICT for Sustainability (ICT4S 2014). Atlantis Press (2014)
5. Fogg, B.J.: Persuasive Technology: Using Computers to Change What We Think and Do. Morgan Kaufmann Publishers, San Francisco (2003)
6. DESENT: Smart decision support system for urban energy and transportation (2016). www.jpi-urbaneurope.eu/desent. Accessed 14 Nov 2019
7. Brewer, R.S., et al.: Lights off. Game on. The Kukui cup: a dorm energy competition. In: CHI 2011, Vancouver, BC, Canada (2011)
8. Reeves, B., Cummings, J.J., Anderson, D.: Leveraging the engagement of games to change energy behavior. In: CHI 2011, Vancouver, BC, Canada (2011)
9. Shiraishi, M., et al.: Using individual, social and economic persuasion techniques to reduce CO_2 emissions in a family setting. In: Persuasive 2009, Claremont, California, USA (2009)
10. Takayama, C., Lehdonvirta, V.: EcoIsland: a system for persuading users to reduce CO_2 emissions. In: Workshop on Pervasive Persuasive Technology and Environmental Sustainability, pp. 73–76 (2008)
11. Glogovac, B., et al.: Ducky: an online engagement platform for climate communication. In: Nordic CHI 2016 (2016)
12. Dillahunt, T., et al.: Motivating environmentally sustainable behavior changes with a virtual polar bear. In: Foth, M., et al. (ed.) Workshop on Pervasive Persuasive Technology and Environmental Sustainability, pp. 18–22 (2008)
13. Caroleo, B., et al.: Measuring the change towards more sustainable mobility: MUV impact evaluation approach. Systems **7**, 30 (2019)
14. Di Dio, S., Lissandrello, E., Schillaci, D., Caroleo, B., Vesco, A., D'Hespeel, I.: MUV: a game to encourage sustainable mobility habits. In: Gentile, M., Allegra, M., Söbke, H. (eds.) GALA 2018. LNCS, vol. 11385, pp. 60–70. Springer, Cham (2019). https://doi.org/10.1007/978-3-030-11548-7_6
15. Prochaska, J.O., Velicer, W.F.: The transtheoretical model of health behavior change. Am. J. Health Promot. **12**(1), 38–48 (1997)
16. Statistics Norway: Emissions of greenhouse gases, 1990–2015, final figures. https://www.ssb.no/en/natur-og-miljo/statistikker/klimagassn/aar-endelige/2016-12-13?fane=tabell&sort=nummer&tabell=287212. Accessed 28 June 2017
17. Greenhouse Gas Emissions from a Typical Passenger Vehicle: Office of Transportation and Air Quality, EPA (2014)

18. Davis, F.D.: Perceived usefulness, perceived ease of use, and user acceptance of information technology. MIS Q. **13**(3), 319–339 (1989)
19. Minh, C.: Mobile app: integrated financial, energy and transport services. Department of Computer Science, Norwegian University of Science and Technology, Norway, p. 123 (2017)
20. Gómez Maureira, M.A., Kniestedt, I.: Games that make curious: an exploratory survey into digital games that invoke curiosity. In: Clua, E., Roque, L., Lugmayr, A., Tuomi, P. (eds.) ICEC 2018. LNCS, vol. 11112, pp. 76–89. Springer, Cham (2018). https://doi.org/10.1007/978-3-319-99426-0_7
21. Oliveira, M., Petersen, S.: The choice of serious games and gamification. In: Ma, M., Oliveira, M.F., Baalsrud Hauge, J. (eds.) SGDA 2014. LNCS, vol. 8778, pp. 213–223. Springer, Cham (2014). https://doi.org/10.1007/978-3-319-11623-5_18

Knowledge and Human Development Authority in Dubai (KHDA) Open Data: What Do Researchers Want?

Hani AlGhanem[1(✉)], Akram Mustafa[2], and Sherief Abdallah[1]

[1] Computer Science, The British University in Dubai, Dubai, UAE
Hanismg@hotmail.com, sherief.abdallah@buid.ac.ae
[2] Computer Science, James Cook University, Townsville, Australia
Akram.mohdmustafa@my.jcu.edu.au

Abstract. Government open data is a booster for government performance, transparency, and innovation. The purpose of this study to investigate how researchers use Dubai open data on Dubai Pulse platform, Using Dubai open data for Knowledge and Human Development Authority in Dubai (KHDA) shows was not covered by academic researchers. To find the reasons behind that, a systematic review were conducted for all published papers and academic researchs in the period of 2015 until 2019. 68 articles were identified, but only 38 articels passed the including/excluding criteria, and considered within this study. The majority of researchers focus mainly on detailed students' datasets. on the other hand the published KHDA open dataset provide many usefull datasets but it's not including detailed students datasets; a gap between the required datasets by researchers and what KHDA open dataset provide is found. Therefore, to bridge the gap and improve researches in educational domain, KHDA needs to provide more students' details that supports machine-readable format to become useful and usable for researchers.

Keywords: Open data · Dubai pulse platform · Dubai open data · KHDA

1 Introduction

Data is the main factor in the information technology revolution [31]. Jetzek, Avital, Bjorn-Andersen, Kulk and Van Loenen emphasize on increasing of open data provided by the governments as it provides transparency for government performance and it is considered a booster for the Information technology industry, in addition to participation and collaboration between public and private sectors which leads to the creation of new businesses and services [31, 34]. Open data can cover various areas, including transportation, crime and security, municipality, and education. Ceolin *et al.* states that it is not allowed to expose private data due to open data sensitivity, so it is usually preprocessed or aggregated to hide personal information [17]. Furthermore, Okamoto explains that open government data is used to develop government performance and the local community [41]. Salloum explains that any open data analysis and mining needs to be pre-processed in a way to be readable by humans and machines [44].

© Springer Nature Switzerland AG 2020
M. Themistocleous and M. Papadaki (Eds.): EMCIS 2019, LNBIP 381, pp. 58–70, 2020.
https://doi.org/10.1007/978-3-030-44322-1_5

Open data comes as essential for governments to improve innovation, performance, market and financial systems, and transparency. It is standard for stable governments to have a dedicated institute to manage the entire government's open data, as open data has a straight affect on citizens by providing the best standard of living, covering health, education, housing, entertainment, and happiness [54]. Davies asserts the importance of having open data leads to more government transparency [18].

In 2015 Dubai regulated open data law by his Highness Sheikh Mohammed Bin Rashid Al Maktoum, the vice president and prime minister of the United Arab Emirates (UAE), and ruler of the Emirate of Dubai. Later the Dubai government launched a governmental institute called Dubai Pulse, which responsible for managing all open data for the Dubai government. Dubai Pulse manages many entities, including KHDA and many other governmental institutes [55].

2   Literature Review

Kulk and Van Loenen summarizes the opinions of thirty experts in the open data definition. It concludes that open data should comply with nine rules, which are complete, primary, timely, accessible, machine-processable, non-discriminatory, non-proprietary, license-free, and reviewable [34]. Bonina figures out the definition of open data as "A piece of content or data is open if anyone is free to use, reuse, and redistribute it" [15].

Braunschweig et al. clarify that open data can be published from each government institute or can be gathered and formed by one government entity that is dedicated to managing the open data for all government institutes in centralized and standardized format. These data sets can be integrated, explored and analyzed to generate an aggregated format using diagrams or other formats [16]. The analysis process can be done manually or using some software tools depending on the dataset complexity. Also there are many other ways that can be used to analysis open data, Dwyer et al. uses standard filtering and grouping to generate charts and visual results [21], while Lee et al. and Van Poucke et al. use machine learning algorithms to analyze open data [36], [50]. On the other hand, Folmer et al. and Lnenicka use linked open data [24, 37].

Although Martin et al. doubt the ability to calculate the number of benefits and the return on investment of open data, as there is much optimistic calculation considering only a few factors [39]. Jetzek, Avital and Bjorn-Andersen express that the government's open data in the European Union were improving the countries' economy with billions of EUR [31], this also supported by Bonina, as it highlights the importance of open data and provides new opportunities in the information technology domain, which leads to economical growth. Also, it increases the values provided through the analysis of open data by interacting between the public, private sectors, and citizens [15].

3 Research Methodology

Folmer expresses that even there are a lot of published open data sets by governments, but indicators show low usefulness of open data sets [24]. Davies categories the users of open data into four categories, first, is the private sector, second, is other government institutes, third, is academic institutes and researchers, and forth are volunteers. Many ways and techniques can be used to deal with open data [18]. As this study focus on researchers' requirements from open data, the following questions were formulated.

(1) Is KHDA's open data useful for academic researchers?
(2) Why is KHDA's open data used/not used in the researches?
(3) Is KHDA's data useful?
(4) Can the provided KHDA data be analyzed?

The answers to all these questions are essential because they give a clear understanding of the usefulness of KHDA's data. Knowing the reasons that help or hinder researchers in using it, which leads to knowing what is required in order to provide better data format and better dataset to be presented in Dubai Pulse by KHDA.

3.1 Proposed Methodology

To find if there is a gap between KHDA open data provided and what researchers are looking for, a comparison method was used in order to address the variation. Figure 1 below shows the steps required to find the gap and the reasons behind it. A systematic review for all published academic papers having the following keywords "School Dubai", "KHDA", and "Dubai education" from the period of 2015 until 2019; as this is the period when Dubai open data were published online. The collected papers were filtered out to eliminate any duplication or unrelated papers to Dubai education, While the remaining papers were used in this study.

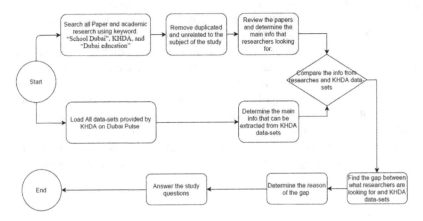

Fig. 1. Proposed methodology workflow

In parallel, the lower path of Fig. 1 shows the steps of downloading all KHDA's datasets, then determines the educational information and that can be extracted from KHDA's dataset. Then a comparison is conducted to find the difference and the gap between the upper path and lower path. Further analysis finds the reasons behind the gap; the final step is to answer the research questions and address the critical findings.

3.2   Researchers Requirements

By searching specifically for published papers and research dissertations or thesis related to schools and open data using the following keywords "Dubai education," "KHDA," "School Dubai." A screening method applied to determine the source of these studies and how it uses open data in the research area. The search filters only the articles from 2015 and after, as open data were officially launched in Dubai in 2015. 68 papers were collected and downloaded, only 38 papers were passed filter criteria, there are 38 papers published having varieties of the sources of data including Questionnaires/Surveys with 27 research studies using it, Case Study Analysis with 7 research studies using it, Interviews/focus groups with 13 research studies using it, and Observation/Document or Report Analysis/screening with 23 research studies using it, but none of them depend on the open data of Dubai pulse.

3.3   KHDA Dataset

There are many Datasets provided by KHDA on Dubai Pulse platform, which include general information about schools and education centers as:

(1) Free zone higher education programs institute, (contains 705 records).
(2) Free zone higher education institute, (contains 39 records).
(3) Private training institutes courses and activities (contain 52,209 records).
(4) Private schools enrolment and training capacity, which comes as separated five datasets to covers education years from 2012–2013 to 2016–2017, with a total of 838 records.

3.4   KHDA Data Processing and Analysis

In this study, the datasets downloaded as comma-separated values (CSV) files. Files were opened on Microsoft excel as the first step to have precise data. The Arabic language column was removed to analyse the English format data within the files.

The first dataset comes from in Ti_Educationcentercourses.csv and converts into Excel format Ti_Educationcentercourses.xlsx, Arabic columns gets removed from the sheet "course," and "parentactivityar." a pivot table and aggregate functions get used to extract statistical facts about the most popular Parent activity, activity, and courses.

Table 1 shows that the majority of courses comes under Professional and Management Development Training with total of 32,298 courses, but the next parent activity comes as Technical and Occupational Skills Training with 6,548 courses, and this shows a big gap between first two courses parent activities with total difference of 25,750 courses, so the difference is 3.9 times of the Technical and Occupational Skills Training courses.

Table 1. List of Parent Activities ordered by number of course

Parent Activity	Number of Courses
Professional and Management Development Training	32298
Technical and Occupational Skills Training	6548
Computer Training	5508
Language Training	2478
Fine Arts Training	1879
Education Support Services	1876
Child Skills Development Training	1260
Tutoring Services	360

The second dataset comes as two files which are related to each other, the first file Hep_Programs and Hep_Search, which presents higher education programs and higher education institute in free zones. To process these two CSV files, first, they get converted into Excel files and then get imported into SQL Server. PLSQL used to make inner joining between two tables, to link two tables, and to extract data from both tables as one dataset result. There are some issues with the provided data. Based on retrieval for latitude and longitude fields, a script generates to be used by the Google Maps Platform to help in building a heat map.

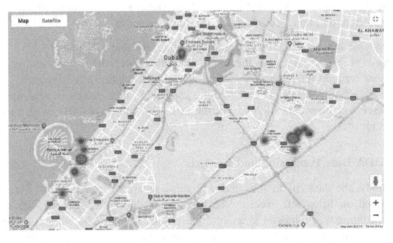

Fig. 2. Heat map of center location using Google maps platform.

Figure 2 shows the heat map of center locations, which is clustered into three central locations of Dubai. Dubai pulse also provides a map view for its datasets but showing the data differently. While investigating the data, some columns came with inconsistent data. The column of "accredited by professional body" shows different formats as

(1) Some data have comma-separated values "AMBA, EQUIS, AACSB." (2) Some data have semicolon-separated values "AACSB; CAA." (3) Some data have with mix separators command and & values "EQUIS, AACB & AMBA's." (4) Some data have "and" separators "EASA and GCAA." (5) Some data have the same values with different writing as "CAA, "Commission for Academic Accreditation (CAA)," and "CAA" (with space).

The Third dataset is for the historical data of schools rating by KHDA, in addition to other information related to a school ID, curriculum, grades, location, and school type. The historical data covers the period from 2012 to 2016.

A different approach is used with this dataset in order to predict a school's rating. Rapid miner studio tool used to build the model, using K-NN algorithm Weighted item-based KNN with cosine/Pearson similarity. Data preparation is required to convert the provided human-readable format into a machine-readable format.

The first step is to read the prepared dataset from an excel sheet and setting the required fields that are needed to be considered in building the model using "select attribute" control. Then data is split into two parts, the first part contains 90% of the dataset that will be used by "Item K-NN" control to train the model, while the other part that contains 10% of the dataset will be used by "apply model" control to predict the result of the rating value of schools. The last step of the process is to check the performance and the accuracy of applying the K-NN algorithm using Performance (Rating Prediction). This control calculates root mean square error (RMSE), mean absolute error (MAE) and normalized mean absolute error (NMAE), the experiment results are 1.224 for RMSE, and 0.873 for MAE, 0.218 NMAE.

4   Results and Discussion

By investigating the numbers published in papers related to "open data" in the period from year 2000 to 2018 (as the current year 2019 excluded as its not finished yet), using Google scholar search engine with specifying advanced search to search papers with "open data" and by choosing return articles dated between 2000 and 2018. Also, two other options were removed from search criteria, which are "include patents" and "include citations". The results per year explained in Fig. 3 below.

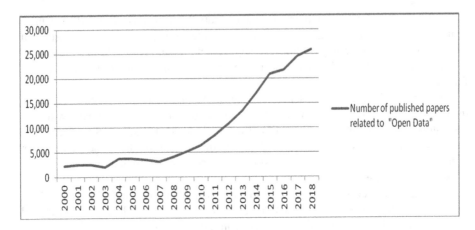

Fig. 3. The number of published papers related to "open data."

Figure 3 shows clearly the great attention and interest in open data increasing with time. During the period from 2000 until 2009 there was a small increase over the years, with an average of 297 published papers increased every year, after that in 2010 it shows significant increase and the number of published paper of open data increased dramatically to achieve around 25,900 published papers with an average of 1,951 published papers increased every year. Martin, addressed that the government's interest is increasing in open data throughout the years in many areas, including transportation, security, and the economy as it supports the concept of open governments, which requires significant efforts to be done by government's institutes to expand this concept and increase the benefits of using it. Some challenges are hindering open data from being used, or it hinders the re-use of open data from getting the maximum benefit of it. These challenges categorized as (1) Governance challenges, (2) Economic challenges, (3) Legal framework, (4) Data related challenges, (5) Metadata, (6) Access to open data, (7) User and re-users skills [39].

A further analysis conducted to determine what information researchers are looking for, the below matrix classifies each research paper into seven classifications as (1) School/facilities, (2) Curriculums/Programs, (3) Students, (4) Parents, (5) Health/special need, (6) Policies and (7) Teachers/Management.

The summary of Table 2 shows that the majority of researchers are looking for students' data. A total number of 23 pieces of research focuses on students' information, and 12 pieces of research on Curriculums/Programs info and 10 pieces of research focus on Health/special need, 9 pieces of research on education policies, 8 pieces of research on Teachers/Management, 2 pieces of research on Parents, and 1 research on school facility.

Table 2. Matrix of main info that researchers are looking.

Keywords	Reference	School/ Facilities	Curriculums/ Programs	Students	Parents	Health/ Special needs	Policies	Teachers/ Management
Dubai education	[32]	Yes						
Dubai education	[33]		Yes	Yes				
Dubai education	[26]			Yes	Yes	Yes		
Dubai education	[23]		Yes				Yes	
Dubai education	[9]		Yes	Yes				
Dubai education	[49]		Yes					Yes
Dubai education	[22]			Yes		Yes		
KHDA	[1]		Yes				Yes	
School Dubai	[46]			Yes		Yes		
School Dubai	[28]			Yes		Yes		
School Dubai	[48]			Yes		Yes		
School Dubai	[30]			Yes			Yes	
School Dubai	[3]			Yes		Yes		
School Dubai	[2]			Yes		Yes		
School Dubai	[5]			Yes				
School Dubai	[35]		Yes	Yes				
School Dubai	[40]			Yes		Yes		
School Dubai	[11]						Yes	
School Dubai	[25]			Yes		Yes		
School Dubai	[19]				Yes			
School Dubai	[60]		Yes	Yes				
School Dubai	[47]						Yes	Yes
School Dubai	[14							Yes
School Dubai	[43]		Yes					
School Dubai	[45]			Yes				
School Dubai	[52]			Yes			Yes	
School Dubai	[10]			Yes			Yes	Yes
School Dubai	[29]		Yes					
School Dubai	[8]							Yes
School Dubai	[42]			Yes		Yes		
School Dubai	[6]			Yes				
School Dubai	[4]		Yes	Yes				
School Dubai	[51]		Yes	Yes				
School Dubai	[7]		Yes				Yes	
School Dubai	[13]							Yes
School Dubai	[27]			Yes				
School Dubai	[38]						Yes	Yes
School Dubai	[12]							Yes
Total		1	12	23	2	10	9	8

Table 3 below summarizes the comparison between what KHDA provided of Datasets and what researches were looking for.

Table 3. Matrix table shows provided/Required Info and KHDA Dataset and Researchers.

#	Provided/Required info	Provided by KHDA	Researchers looking for
1	Free zone higher education programs institute	Yes	No
2	Free zone higher education institute	Yes	No
3	Private training institutes courses and activities	Yes	No
4	Private schools enrolment and training capacity	Yes	No
5	School/facilities	No	Yes
6	Schools Curriculums/Programs	Yes	Yes
7	Students	No	Yes
8	Parents	No	Yes
9	Health/special need	No	Yes
10	Education/school policies	No	Yes
11	Teachers/Management	No	Yes

As shown in Table 3, there is a gap between what KHDA provides and what researches are looking for, as from 11 areas of information investigated, only "Schools Curriculums/Programs" was the common area. This leads to another question if Schools Curriculums/Programs area of information is a common area, then why researches do not use it. So further investigation has been made to check what kind of curriculums and programs information is provided, the result shows the KHDA provides a very high level of data, as it is just determining what curriculum have provided for each school, while researchers drill down to the detailed level of the programs and how it affects students. KHDA provides even the information domain, but researchers are looking for details about the program that is not provided by KHDA's open dataset. So we conclude that the data provided by KHDA is not matching what researchers were looking for to build their study in schools education fields. This answers the first and second questions of this study.

Based on Sect. 3.4 related to KHDA data processing, it shows clearly that KHDA open dataset can provide useful datasets and information about schools, programs, courses, curriculums, education centers, geographic, and other info. As dataset analyzes and processes, much useful information extracted.

Data processing and analysis focus on how to go through the provided datasets from, read it, modify it in order to become machine-readable. Also, many analysis techniques and methods were used, including excel, aggregate, SQL/PLSQL, machine learning, Rapid Miner. Analysis Results were presented in many formats, including tabular forms, charts, cross matrix, maps, predicted table, so this answer the third and fourth research questions positively as KHDA Datasets on Dubai pulse platform can be analyzed and provide a piece of useful information.

5   Conclusion

Open data considered essential for governments in order to maintain transparency and to provide a chance for the private sector to come up with new products or to improve the services. Therefore, researches related to open data increased dramatically year by year during the last decade. In this study, an overview about one area of Dubai Pulse and focus on open data related to KHDA, by screening all published papers related to "School Dubai," "KHDA", and "Dubai education" keywords since 2015. Although results show that none of the published papers used the KHDA's open data, the analysis of the KHDA open dataset shows useful data about Dubai educational system in general.

Nevertheless, as most researchers are looking for students' details datasets, which are not provided by KHDA so far, so this study came to highlight the need to reconsider the published KHDA's open dataset to meet the researcher's requirements, which will improve studies in the education field. So KHDA needs to consider publishing data related to students, curriculums/programs information, health/special needs, education policies, teachers/management, parents, and school facilities. Finally, KHDA's open data should be manipulated to become machine-readable.

References

1. Al Ahmad, A.: The impact of the KHDA policy on teaching Arabic as a first language: an exploratory study among selected schools in Dubai (Doctoral dissertation, The British University in Dubai (BUiD)) (2018)
2. Al Behandy, N.S., et al.: Epidemiological Profile and Clinical Characteristics of the Childhood Asthma Among School Students in Dubai, UAE (2015)
3. Al Faisal, W.: Childhood disability among students population in Dubai, school-based screening strategy, Dubai, UAE, 2016. Int. J. Ped. Neo Heal. **1**, 1–13 (2016)
4. Al Herbawi, D.A.: The effectiveness of Brain Gym® exercises on improving students' performance in classes of middle school boys in private schools in Dubai, UAE (Ethnographic Study Conducted at the American International School. Dubai, UAE) (Doctoral dissertation, The British University in Dubai (BUiD)) (2018)
5. Al Mashhadani, S.S., Al Khoory, T., Saleh, N., Fargali, K., Mathew, R., Al Qasem, N.: National survey of the oral health status of school children in Dubai, UAE. EC Dental Sci. **8**, 48–58 (2017)
6. Al-Raheal, F.I.: The impact of teaching extended thinking: a study on high school students' comprehension skills in a private school in Dubai (Doctoral dissertation, The British University in Dubai (BUiD)) (2018)
7. Abdelsalam, A.M.: The use of streaming as a differentiated strategy in middle school mathematics classes: a case study of a private American-curriculum school in Dubai (Doctoral dissertation, The British University in Dubai (BUiD)) (2018)
8. Albasha, W.: Teachers' perspective on engaged teaching: study from an American curriculum elementary school in Dubai (Doctoral dissertation, The British University in Dubai (BUiD)) (2018)
9. Alghawi, M.A.: Needs assessment of gifted education programmes in Dubai; an investigative case study of governmental primary schools (Doctoral dissertation, The British University in Dubai (BUiD)) (2016)

10. Alkutich, M.: Examining the impact of school inspection on teaching and learning; Dubai private schools as a case study (Doctoral dissertation, The British University in Dubai (BUiD)) (2015)

11. Alkutich, M., Abukari, A.X.: Examining the benefit of school inspection on teaching and learning: a case study of Dubai private schools. Teach. Learn. 9(5), (2018)

12. Almarzouqi, A.: Toward professionalising teaching in the UAE: An investigation of emirati public secondary school teachers' understanding of their profession in Dubai (Doctoral dissertation, The british University in Dubai (BUiD)) (2015)

13. Ayouby, E., Mahmoud, S.: Perceptions of the change of the school teacher's role in the United Arab Emirates (UAE) an investigation of teachers' views from eight schools in Dubai and Sharjah (Doctoral dissertation, The British University in Dubai (BUiD)) (2016)

14. Bdeir, R.: Teacher effectiveness: a case study using value-added method to measure teacher effectiveness in one UK curriculum school in Dubai (Doctoral dissertation, The British University in Dubai (BUiD)) (2015)

15. Bonina, C.M.: New business models and the value of open data: definitions, challenges and opportunities. NEMODE–3K Small Grants Call (2013)

16. Braunschweig, K., Eberius, J., Thiele, M., Lehner, W.: The state of open data. Limits of current open data platforms (2012)

17. Ceolin, D., et al.: Reliability analyses of open government data (2013)

18. Davies, T.: Open data, democracy and public sector reform. A look at open government data use from data. gov. uk. (2010)

19. Dickson, M., Kadbey, H., Mcminn, M.: Correlating beliefs and classroom practices of public school science teachers in Abu Dhabi, UAE. J. Turk. Sci. Educ. 13(3), 161–172 (2016)

20. Doukas, C., Goudas, T., Fischer, S., Mierswa, I., Chatziioannou, A., Maglogiannis, I.: An open data mining framework for the analysis of medical images: application on obstructive nephropathy microscopy images. In: 2010 Annual International Conference of the IEEE Engineering in Medicine and Biology, pp. 4108–4111 (2010)

21. Dwyer, R.G., Brooking, C., Brimblecombe, W., Campbell, H.A., Hunter, J., Watts, M., Franklin, C.E.: An open Web-based system for the analysis and sharing of animal tracking data. Anim. Biotelemetry 3(1), 1 (2015)

22. El Hariry, Y.: Attitudes of parents of children with special educational needs and disabilities towards diagnosis and intervention in Dubai and its implication on education (Doctoral dissertation, The British University in Dubai (BUiD)) (2017)

23. Farrugia, C.: Legtimacy of cross-border higher education policy: a comparative case study of Dubai and Ras Al Khaimah. State University of New York at Albany (2016)

24. Folmer, E., Beek, W., Rietveld, L., Ronzhin, S., Geerling, R., den Haan, D.: Enhancing the usefulness of open governmental data with linked data viewing techniques. In: Proceedings of the 52nd Hawaii International Conference on System Sciences (2019)

25. Ghanim, M., Dash, N., Abdullah, B., Issa, H., Albarazi, R., Al Saheli, Z.: Knowledge and practice of personal hygiene among primary school students in Sharjah-UAE. J. Health Sci. 6(5), 67–73 (2016)

26. Ganesh, S.: Inclusive education-perception of parents of students with special needs in segregated settings in Dubai (Doctoral dissertation, The British University in Dubai (BUiD)) (2017)

27. Hadayat, N.: Impact of a cognitively modified instruction on vocabulary acquisition of second language users of grade 2: a study conducted in a private American school in Dubai (Doctoral dissertation, The British University in Dubai (BUiD)) (2016)

28. Hussain, H.Y., Al Attar, F., Makhlouf, M., Ahmed, A., Jaffar, M., Dafalla, E., Mahdy, N., Wasfy, A.: A study of overweight and obesity among secondary school students in Dubai: prevalence and associated factors. Int. J. Prev. Med. Res. 1(3), 153–160 (2015)

29. Huzefa, F.: Investigating best curriculum, instruction and assessment practices in exemplary British schools in UAE (Doctoral dissertation, The British University in Dubai (BUiD)) (2016)
30. Ibrahim, A., Mahmoud, S.: Principals' communication styles and school performance in Al Ain government schools, UAE. Int. J. Res. Stud. Educ. 6(1), 29–46 (2017)
31. Jetzek, T., Avital, M., Bjorn-Andersen, N.: The value of open government data: a strategic analysis framework. In: SIG eGovernment pre-ICIS Workshop, Orlando (2012)
32. Kavitha, H., Kumar, R.S.: An overview of school libraries with special reference to the schools affiliated with central board of secondary education in Dubai. Int. J. Adv. Res. Manage. Soc. Sci. 6(3), 44–49 (2017)
33. Kshatriya, S., Keränen, K.: Building a Case of Diverse Knowledge Transfer in Higher Education between Finland and Dubai to Facilitate Sustainable 21st Century Learning and Better Engagement of Emirati Students (2017)
34. Kulk, S., Van Loenen, B.: Brave new open data world? Int. J. Spatial Data Infrastruct. Res. 7, 196–206 (2012)
35. Lata, M.K., Dubey, R.: The Effects of Hill Training To Improve the Speed, Acceleration and Stride Rate among Under 17 Athletics Trainee Indian High School Dubai
36. Lee, J., Park, G.L., Han, Y., Yoo, S.: Big data analysis for an electric vehicle charging infrastructure using open data and software. In: Proceedings of the Eighth International Conference on Future Energy Systems, pp. 252–253, May 2017
37. Lnenicka, M.: An in-depth analysis of open data portals as an emerging public e-service. Int. J. Soc. Educ. Econ. Manage. Eng. 9(2), 589–599 (2015)
38. Mahdy, N.H.: The impact of leadership styles on teachers' professional development: a study of a private school in Dubai (Doctoral dissertation, The British University in Dubai (BUiD)) (2016)
39. Martin, S., Foulonneau, M., Turki, S., Ihadjadene, M.: Risk analysis to overcome barriers to open data. Electron. J. E-Govern. 11(1), 348 (2013)
40. Master, K.M., Kaur, C.P., Narasimhan, A., Mizrab, N., Ali, M., Shaik, R.B.: Impact of electronic gadgets on psychological behavior of middle school children in UAE. Uni Emirates Arab. Gulf Med. J. 5(S2), S54–S60 (2016)
41. Okamoto, K.: What is being done with open government data? An exploratory analysis of public uses of New York City open data. Webology 13(1), 1 (2016)
42. Panzer, A.L.H.: A study of the awareness, identification, diagnosis and management of Auditory Processing Disorder in children and its impact within a Dubai based private primary school (Doctoral dissertation, The British University in Dubai (BUiD)) (2017)
43. Saleh, H.A.: A Study of the effectiveness of the next generation science standards implementation at a private US curriculum school in Dubai, UAE (Doctoral dissertation, The British University in Dubai (BUiD)) (2018)
44. Salloum, S.A., Mhamdi, C., Al-Emran, M., Shaalan, K.: Analysis and classification of Arabic Newspapers' Facebook pages using text mining techniques. Int. J. Inf. Technol. Lang. Stud. 1(2), 8–17 (2017)
45. Shakky, P.E.: Is emotional intelligence an indicator of academic achievement for elementary school students in Dubai? (Doctoral dissertation, The British University in Dubai (BUiD)) (2017)
46. Shirali, A., Huijsmans, W.M., Sottocornola, M.: Letter to the editor: genetic editing of secretory pathway of penicillium chrysogenum after observation of increased secretory rates in an increased stress environment (Microgravity) a research proposal by high school students in Dubai. Fine Focus 4(2), 163–169 (2018)

47. Tabassum, A.: Transforming school: role of school leadership in managing educational change–a case study of an American school in Dubai (Doctoral dissertation, The British University in Dubai (BUiD)) (2018)
48. Taryam, M.O., Al Abadi, K., Hussein, H., Al Faisal, W., Alam, M.W., AlBehandy, N.: Visual Impairments and Eye Morbidities among School-Age Children (5 to 18 Years Old) Qualitative Assessment in Dubai, UAE (2016)
49. Van Niekerk, B.: Is an IEP a useful tool to deliver inclusive education? a survey of general and special educators' perception of the IEP usefulness within an inclusive private primary school in Dubai (Doctoral dissertation, The British University in Dubai (BUiD)) (2016)
50. Van Poucke, S., Zhang, Z., Schmitz, M., Vukicevic, M., Vander Laenen, M., Celi, L.A., De Deyne, C.: Scalable predictive analysis in critically ill patients using a visual open data analysis platform. PLoS ONE 11(1), e0145791 (2016)
51. Younes, M.I.: The impact of CLIL on Arabic, English and content learning of Arab high school students in the UAE (Doctoral dissertation) (2016)
52. Zamani, Z.: The effect of servant leadership on students' engagement in social studies class: analyzing perception of middle school students in Dubai (2018)
53. Zeleti, F.A., Ojo, A., Curry, E.: Emerging business models for the open data industry: characterization and analysis. In: Proceedings of the 15th Annual International Conference on Digital Government Research, pp. 215–226 (2014)
54. Dyson, L. (ed.): Beyond Transparency: Open Data and the Future of Civic Innovation. Code for America Press, Los Angeles (2013)
55. Oren, E., Kotoulas, S., Anadiotis, G., Siebes, R.M., ten Teije, A.C.M., van Harmelen, F.A. H.: Marvin: A platform for large-scale analysis of Semantic Web data (2009)
56. بدبي. المفتوحة البيانات قانون يصدر راشد بن محمد. https://www.emaratalyoum.com/local-section/other/2015-10-17-1.831307. Accessed 18 May 2019 (2015)

An Immersive Web Visualization Platform for a Big Data Context in Bosch's Industry 4.0 Movement

João Rebelo$^{(\boxtimes)}$ ⓘ, Carina Andrade ⓘ, Carlos Costa ⓘ,
and Maribel Y. Santos ⓘ

Department of Information Systems, University of Minho, Guimarães, Portugal
`a74636@alunos.uminho.pt`,
`{carina.andrade,carlos.costa,maribel}@dsi.uminho.pt`

Abstract. Motivated by challenges that emerged from Complex Event Processing (CEP) in Big Data contexts, an Intelligent Event Broker (IEB) was previously proposed as a CEP system built on flexible and scalable Big Data technologies and techniques, being already applied to Industry 4.0 scenarios. A key feature of the IEB lies in an effective visualization system for meta-monitorization and management. An analysis of previous scientific and technical literature has shown scarcity of proposals or development of such mechanisms. This paper proposes a Web Visualization Platform for managing and monitoring an IEB system based on novel approaches that include interactive exploration techniques, tridimensional visualizations and mixed-reality environments. Being mainly targeted towards Industry 4.0, this paper presents a demonstration case at Bosch Car Multimedia Portugal. Results indicate that significant value can be obtained when the visualization system is applied to decision support scenarios within organizations foreseeing event processing, Big Data, and Industry 4.0 projects.

Keywords: Big Data Visualization · Immersive Analytics · Complex Event Processing

1 Introduction

As the Industry 4.0 movement emerges and popularizes, organizations are trying to make use of the data produced inside and outside of their facilities to improve their business processes and, consequently, to achieve better results and increase their business value. Considering this movement and the related technological evolution, machines or other devices used in organizations are already producing data in realtime and enabling its processing immediately after the occurrence of various events. With stream processing, data produced by Internet of Things (IoT) devices will be useful for organizations by delivering value in a short time frame and by providing insights about the status of the organization's processes and environment.

However, having data is not synonymous of organizational improvement. In fact, having several data sources with different formats or data being produced at different

M. Themistocleous and M. Papadaki (Eds.): EMCIS 2019, LNBIP 381, pp. 71–84, 2020.
https://doi.org/10.1007/978-3-030-44322-1_6

velocities can bring chaos to the organization. To avoid this chaos, a system that enables event processing in real-time is crucial to improve the organizations' daily operations, considering that, nowadays, data variety, volume, and velocity are key aspects of event processing. In this context, an Intelligent Event Broker (IEB) system was proposed in [1], serving as a guide for the implementation of Complex Event Processing (CEP) systems in Big Data contexts. In the logical and technological architecture of the system, besides the components related to the data collection, processing, and aggregation, it was considered a Mapping and Drill-down component for monitoring the evolution of the IEB. With this component, the chaos that can result from deploying such systems at scale can be minimized using innovative and immersive visualization components, both generically and idealized for Industry 4.0 scenarios. This work is focused on the proposal, demonstration and validation of the immersive visualization system.

The relevance of this type of visualization system in the Big Data era and its proposed system architecture are explained further in this paper. The roles of the system components are also explained, as well as their function within key areas of the IEB deployment context. The proposed visualization system is followed by a demonstration case in the production lines of Bosch Car Multimedia Portugal, an organization currently aligned with the Industry 4.0 movement.

This document is structured as follows. Section 2 presents a brief introduction to the IEB and the related challenge that motivates this work, as well as an identification of challenges regarding data visualization in Big Data and their relevance to the challenge of this paper. Section 3 presents the architecture for the Web Visualization Platform proposed in this work. Section 4 presents the demonstration case at Bosch Car Multimedia Portugal. Finally, Sect. 5 presents the conclusions for this work and some prospects of future work.

2   Conceptual Background

2.1   Intelligent Event Broker (IEB)

The IEB proposal consists of a CEP system specially designed for Big Data contexts, having the goal of providing an event processing-oriented architecture to the age of high data volume, variety and velocity. Its system architecture combines a typical CEP-based architecture with flexible and scalable Big Data technologies and techniques [1]. Such a typical CEP architecture comprises three principal areas: a collection of *source systems*, an intermediate processing unit and a collection of *destination systems*. In the IEB, *Source Systems* can be any relevant physical devices or virtual data sources such as IoT Gateways, APIs, databases, Hive tables or HDFS files. Similarly, *Destinations Systems*, can also be relevant physical devices, data stores or relevant business applications, such as E-Mail, SMS or analytical dashboards.

The broker component itself is IEB's area dedicated to event collection, event processing, event aggregation, rules verification, application of machine learning models, and execution of triggers. (i) The *Producers* component is designed to standardize the collection of events using Kafka (kafka.apache.org/), a distributed streaming platform. Here, events are serialized into the form of broker beans representing the business entities. Then, they follow their path to be published in a Kafka topic that is stored in a cluster of Kafka brokers. (ii) The *event processor* (Kafka consumers embedded into Spark applications) subscribes Kafka topics and is always listening for new events, regardless of frequency. (iii) This component is also responsible for the runtime translation of *rules* that are defined in Drools (drools.org), a *rules engine* technology. These rules reflect the business requirements and can be classified as *strategical, tactical,* and *operational*. (iv) Complementary data arriving from any *source system* can be used to bring additional insights to the business requirements that are being evaluated. (v) The *triggers* component is related to the *rules engine*, and it is responsible for the connection to the *destination systems,* performing actions due to the application of the rules. (vi) The *event aggregator* component is responsible for the data aggregation. Druid (druid.io) is the suggested technology to perform the aggregations and to store them for the calculation of *Key Performance Indicators* (KPIs), since it is a columnar storage system already explored and considered as being able to aggregate huge amounts of event data with sub-second response times [2, 3]. (vii) The *predictors & recommenders* component is considered as being relevant in this type of system, ensuring the possibility of introducing *machine learning* capabilities into event processing systems. This component considers the existence of a *lake of machine learning models* that were previously trained and that are applied to events according to what is defined in the rules.

Considering the expected constant increase in data and complexity resulting from the system behavior throughout its daily activities when deployed in contexts like Industry 4.0, smart cities, agriculture, among many others, the IEB system architecture additionally proposes the introduction of a *Mapping & Drill-down System,* parallel to the main broker component. This system's goal is to allow the constant and longterm monitoring of the IEB, even in greatly complex scenarios. To achieve this component, the IEB proposes the implementation of a *Graph Database* whose data model is based on meta-data from the IEB with the mapping of all its existing components, their relationships, and instantiations. This will serve as the data source for a *Web Visualization Platform,* which constitutes the challenge of this paper.

As the architecture of the IEB was already instantiated with a demonstration case at Bosch Car Multimedia Portugal, using event data from its Active Lot Release system, this paper's demonstration case will expand the previous one, using the same data.

2.2 Data Visualization in Big Data and Its Relevance to the IEB

Although there are still many challenges related to the Big Data characteristics, the value of analyzing Big Data is widely recognized in the scientific community [2]. The main differences between Big Data Analytics and traditional statistical analytics are related to the data volume, its high dimensionality, complexity, and data variety, as well as the noise, errors, or other problems found in the data. However, more data is not synonymous of better information or better decisions, being necessary to find new ways for visualizing Big Data and face the identified challenges [3].

Regarding the challenges directly related with visualization in Big Data contexts, Gorodov e Gubarev [4] mention: (i) the visual noise created by the data volume available for analysis; (ii) limitations of the presentation devices (e.g., screens dimensions) and of the user's physical perception; (iii) the information loss due to aggregations performed for dealing with the data volume; (iv) increased hardware needs to compute dynamic visualizations; and, (v) high rate of changes when the visualizations are connected to dynamic data sources. The work of Agrawal et al. [5] agrees with those challenges, also associating them with the needed scalability to migrate from the traditional visualizations to the visualizations in the Big Data era: (i) scalability of the perception (limitations related to the user's perception and to the visualization devices); (ii) real-time scalability (challenges related to the visualizations' changes due to the vast amount of data that arrives at the system in real-time); and, (iii) scalability of the interaction (limitations related to the interaction response time due to the high latency of the visualization mechanisms).

Some strategies to deal with these challenges come from novel Big Data systems that are designed with such issues in mind (like the IEB); from new conceptual strategies to visualization; and from innovative technologies and devices. Conceptually, both previously mentioned authors refer to choosing the right type of representations for the data, sampling, filtering or parallelization as examples of such strategies. The most innovative trend of research, both conceptual and technological, is Immersive Analytics. This topic is dedicated to the exploration of new interaction and presentation technologies for decision support [6] as well as the study of the potential of virtual and augmented reality technologies, the use of large touchscreen displays, or even the use of multisensory infrastructures offering a more immersive experience to users [6, 7]. Some examples for the practical use of these techniques may be: (i) the use of immersive technologies for the collaborative analysis of multidimensional data [8]; (ii) the use of virtual reality technologies and platforms for scientific data visualization [9]; and, (iii) the creation of *In situ* visualizations using augmented reality [10].

Another relevant consideration is the growing trend of using Web development for the creation of data visualizations [11]. This new trend takes advantage of the evolution of Web programming languages to implement dynamic, responsive, and interactive data visualizations [12]. Solutions such as D3.js (d3js.org/), ECharts (echartsjs.com), or the Data-Driven Guides [13] are examples of different Web-based approaches for the current challenges of Big Data visualization as well as the adoption of native Mixed Reality capabilities and performance improvements on modern browsers that brought the Immersive Analytics concept to the Web [14].

In this context, and as already highlighted in the introduction, the need for a system like the IEB arises from the technological evolution and the Industry 4.0 movement, which are transforming the factories far beyond what we once knew. However, it is required that such a system (and its data) can be easily and (semi)-autonomously managed and monitored. This vision for the management and monitoring of a unified system using innovative and immersive visualization techniques was not yet identified in any related work. In fact, the only work that mentions the use of dashboards in a system that aims to integrate CEP and Big Data concepts was the work of [15]. However, in this specific case, the dashboards are not being used for the management and monitoring of such system, nor do they have the level of innovation and functionality presented here. For this reason, to the best of our knowledge, this work can be significantly useful for advancing the state of the art regarding data visualization for the (meta) management and monitoring of CEP systems in the Big Data era.

3   Architecture of the Web Visualization Platform

Motivated by the previously mentioned challenges that affect the long-term, real-time, continuous monitoring and management of an IEB deployed in production environments, a Web Visualization Platform based on novel and immersive technologies and techniques is instantiated as a Web-based system architecture, proposed to fulfill the previously described role of *Mapping and Drill-down System* of the IEB. The presented approach for this IEB component considers a previously defined and developed Graph Database (out of the scope of this paper) and the here proposed Web Visualization Platform composed by an API layer and a Web Application layer.

The API layer leverages the connection between the Web application and the graph database. Due to the high variety of technological options, the development of this component should be based on the use-case, available human and business resources and complexity of the infrastructure. Options for the development of this layer can vary between the simple usage of native database REST APIs or prebuilt drivers, like the Neo4j Bolt Driver for JavaScript (git.io/JeoJ5), directly in the application code for easier direct queries (at the expense of harder maintainability); or the development of more robust solutions based on a custom REST or GraphQL (graphql.org) API, that would allow for separation of functions and roles between layers, abstracting the data model and structure from the frontend and even allowing the integration of future additional data sources, like monitoring data from specific component software whose data might be relevant but not applicable or suitable to the graph database's data model.

The Web Application layer described below is divided in four fundamental areas of visualization, where relevant conceptual visualization components are proposed. Further demonstration and validation of those components are presented in Sect. 4. The four main areas are presented in the following subsections. Figure 1 presents the conceptual architecture of the Web Visualization Platform with the previously described layers and proposed components within the context of the *Mapping & Drill-down System*.

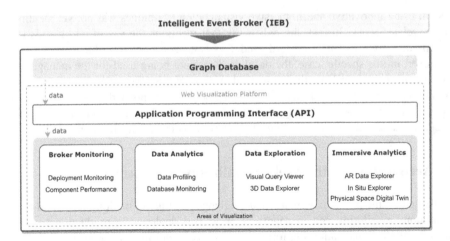

Fig. 1. Conceptual architecture of the proposed Mapping & Drill-Down System.

3.1 Broker Monitoring

The goal of components in this area is to provide continuous monitoring of the IEB infrastructure in production-ready environments. As detailed in Sect. 2, a typical IEB deployment includes several individual *software* solutions that often come with built-in monitoring metrics and mechanisms. Similarly, deploying the IEB in production will demand a local or remote hardware infrastructure whose monitoring can be critical, especially as the complexity of the IEB grows over time. Two components are here proposed:

- The Deployment Monitoring is a component to monitor the deployment infrastructure that houses an IEB instance, particularly detailing relevant information regarding resource usage of both hardware and software. Development of this component should be based on logs, metrics and rules gathered from sources such as system metrics (e.g. CPU usage, memory use, disk space usage, etc.) or, in cases of remote/cloud-based deployment, through connections to built-in or personalized monitoring and telemetry services, as available in solutions like Amazon Cloud-Watch or Azure Monitor;

- In turn, the Component Performance is a component dedicated to monitoring the internal performance of the software from broker components (e.g. Apache Spark, Apache Kafka, etc.). Such an analysis guarantees detailed monitoring of both broker and individual component performance, allowing for possible detection of system bottlenecks or business-related anomalies. Development of this component can be achieved via custom metrics, addition checkpoints in the broker architecture codebase and/or through native metrics and tools preconfigured in the component's software.

3.2 Data Analytics

Components in this area are related to the graph database and its data structure. Interactive graphical representations and editable temporal overviews from data gathered and stored granularly over time should allow long-term monitoring of both the data model and database technology. Conceptually, two different components are proposed.

The Data Profiling component aims to provide a holistic view over data based on statistical analysis and informational summaries of relevant parts of the dataset. This should allow for tasks such as continued assessing of data quality, identification of patterns, and pure metadata analysis.

Additionally, a Database Monitoring component is proposed to make use of metrics, logging, and other analytics mechanisms provided by the chosen database technology to continuously monitor its performance in matters such as of transaction information, storage usage, or query performance.

3.3 Data Exploration

Exploration components are meant to offer new and customized approaches to traditional visualization strategies in desktop and touch-enabled devices. By leveraging the naturally understandable visual properties of graphs and its relationships between nodes, two conceptual components are proposed:

The Visual Query Viewer as a component intends to provide an interactive, query-based, visual approach to graph exploration, bridging the gap for non-technical users not proficient in the relevant query language(s) by allowing the dynamic visual selection of nodes and relations that, on the background, translate the actions into proper language-specific queries and return the proper results in a familiar, easily interpretable fashion.

The 3D Data Explorer component devises a tridimensional representation of the graph structure that represents the data, using volume and a third interactable axis to provide a step further in data exploration. Even using traditional interaction techniques in desktop and mobile devices, such a component allows a more immersive, interactive, and deeper analysis than the possibilities offered by simple 2-dimensional non-volumetric representations of a graph.

3.4 Immersive Analytics

These innovative components provide novel approaches for visualization, presentation, and interaction, by leveraging mixed-reality environments and techniques, resulting in an enhanced solution to the challenges provided by the related context. Three innovative components are here proposed.

An AR Data Explorer component aims to bring the 3D Data Explorer component one step further by allowing the exploration of the graph database in an augmented reality environment which results in an even deeper immersive exploration environment and its application in newer visualization formats (like a Head-Mounted Display) and interaction techniques (like voice and gesture-recognition).

The *In Situ* Explorer, given the industry-bound theme of the project, is proposed as a way to present virtually generated information on top of location-specific physical components, providing an augmented reality experience that offers live and on-site relevant information, alerts, or status changes to the user.

Finally, a Physical Space Digital Twin is proposed as a Virtual Reality enabled facsimile of the factory plant that allows the user to remotely explore it as if he/she is present on-site, providing a real-time link to production performance and factory component monitoring.

Flexible, extensible, and diverse solutions from the vast ecosystem that is modern Web development allow for a wide range of different options when implementing a practical demonstration of the proposed architecture and its components, both in the open source and propriety software domains. The goal of this proposal is to leverage both mature and innovative software solutions for the Web to deliver next-generation visualization experiences for the end-user, as it will be presented in the following demonstration case. However, within the proposed architecture, the use of different software stacks and technological components is not only possible but highly incentivized, as long as those efforts better suit the use case and the organization.

4 Demonstration Case at Bosch Car Multimedia Portugal

A demonstration case for the proposed system was developed at Bosch Car Multimedia Portugal by adding a fully functional *Mapping and Drill-down* component to the work previously started by [1]. Connecting to the previously existing Neo4j database, arises the development of an Express.JS (expressjs.com) multipage Web application, serving EJS-based views on the client-side, supported by custom JavaScript logic and imported libraries/frameworks. Relevant general features of the Web application include: (i) encrypted and secure HTTPS and BOLT (Neo4j's own communication protocol) connections by implementing SSL certificates; and (ii) platform/environment abstraction by containerizing the application using Docker, allowing for ease of development, testing, and deployment in a secure, remote, and cloud-based infrastructure.

To demonstrate the design simplicity, the flexibility of the development, and the variety of development options proposed in the architecture, the demonstration case is mostly based on open source libraries, frameworks, and solutions. The Web application features a design language that follows Bosch's brand guidelines achieved through the development of a custom Bootstrap 4 (getbootstrap.com) theme customized using Sass. This demonstration case focused mainly on the most interactive and immersive features of the proposed architecture, having the following components been the most extensible developed and tested.

4.1   Visual Query Viewer

This component is based on a design and implementation modification of PopotoJS (popotojs.com), an open source JavaScript library built over D3js. The library connects to the Neo4j database via secure REST API connection and automatically manages the interaction and communication between the database and the application.

The *Visual Query Viewer* component features three main interactive sections: Graph, Query, and Results. The *graph* is the main section that presents the graph database's taxonomy (based on Neo4j labels) and an SVG-based interactive navigation of the graph that allows technical and non-technical users to query the database using actions like selecting/deselecting a value, adding/removing relationships between nodes, and using logic gates. The *query* section presents a text-based approach to the user queries, both using a natural language approach (starting with "I'm looking for...") but also showing the correspondent Cypher query (Neo4j's query language) that composes the current visualization. Lastly, the *Results* section presents a custom-designed view of the query results matching the current state of the interactive graph query. In the IEB context, the *Visual Query Viewer* component allows the exploration of the data available in the graph database, which reflects the data model of the IEB itself. Using this component, the instantiations of the several IEB components can be explored in an easy and intuitive way. In Fig. 2 this component can be seen in action within the general application layout and design. As an example, the figure shows the relationships around the instantiation of "ALR Producer" as a *Producer* component of the IEB. Related *broker bean* and *event producer* component instantiations are shown as the user progressively drills-down the information, tracking the cycle of an event through the system.

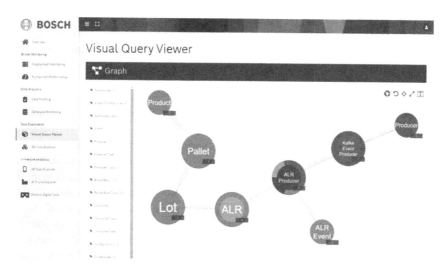

Fig. 2. Visual Query Viewer component

4.2   3D Data Explorer

The *3D Graph Explorer* component leverages an open source 3D Force-Directed Graph Web component (git.io/fjywM) allowing for the tridimensional rendering of a graph data structure using an interactive force-directed layout. Using the official Neo4j JavaScript driver, the 3D Graph Explorer implements a customized implementation of the 3D Force-Directed Graph library backed by data retrieved from the Neo4j database. Other features of this component include real-time WIMP (Windows, Icons, Menus, and Pointer) and post-WIMP based interaction with the graph and live structure updates, including the addition of labels representing the relationship between nodes, arrows to indicate the directionality of these relationships, and label-based color-coded nodes.

4.3   AR Data Explorer

Following the approach from the 3D Graph Explorer, this component leverages a fork of the same 3D Force-Directed Graph Web component specifically tuned to work as an A-Frame component (git.io/JeoJy). A-Frame (aframe.io) is an open source Web framework for building Virtual Reality experiences on the Web by registering components with a declarative and extensible structure using HTML-like semantics. Having the graph visualization within an immersive and positionally-tracked environment, the *AR Data Explorer* component becomes an Augmented Reality experience by introducing 8th Wall Web (8thwall.com/web), an Augmented Reality platform for the mobile Web that uses only Web standards to implement a proprietary Simultaneous Localization and Mapping (SLAM) engine, 6-Degrees of Freedom (6DoF) Tracking, Surface Estimation, Image Tracking, and other features for the real-time AR on the Web. 8th Wall Web, being the only proprietary software in the demonstration case, can expand and integrate multiple 3D JavaScript frameworks, including A-Frame.

Other open-source solutions, namely ARjs (git.io/Je4Vp) were tested and considered. However, although capable, ARjs is a limited library that works only for marker-based applications and does not feature the advanced tracking and positional capabilities of 8th Wall Web that allow for markerless experiences. Extra features and conveniences like an extensible API, built-in event handling methods, high quality documentation, and multiple easily available channels for help and support are also advantages of 8th Wall Web.

For the demonstration case, the AR Data Explorer (Fig. 3) is comprised of an 8th Wall Web markerless/world-tracking SLAM based scene that superimposes the 3D force-graph over the tracked real-world captured by the users' camera-device. The custom user interface allows for the repositioning of the graph in the scene, allowing for adjustments based on the user's environment and supports touch-enabled interactions for selection, resizing, and rotation as real-time interaction in an AR environment. Furthermore, considering the ubiquity of the Web in Internet-enabled devices, the demonstration case features a custom post-WIMP based method of voice interaction.

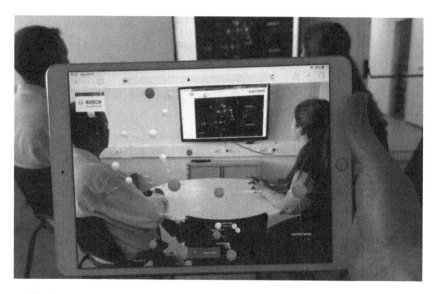

Fig. 3. 3D Graph Explorer and AR Data Explorer demoed at a Bosch meeting.

Inspired by popular current digital assistants, the component features a demonstration of the implementation of the open source library Artyom.js (sdkcarlos.github. io/sites/artyom.html), a convenient wrapper of the recent *speechSynthesis* and *WebkitSpeechRecognition* APIs that allowed for the introduction of hands-free interaction by using voice detection and voice commands to control and alter the augmented reality scene. Voice-based interaction, especially continuous mode-based solutions (which Artyom.js supports), allows for the usage of the system in Head-Mounted Displays that may not feature (or require) hand-based input controls.

The AR Data Explorer, demonstrated in Fig. 3, allows for a deeper, closer, and more immersive interaction with the graph database, supporting even a large scale expansion. In this context a user can figuratively insert himself inside the graph and interactively explore its information as it surrounds him. This constitutes an intuitive and interesting way of data exploration, for example in teamwork environments such as brainstorming sessions, problem-solving discussions or sprint planning meetings.

4.4 *In Situ* Explorer

By considering the layout of Bosch's newest factory at Bosch Car Multimedia Portugal in Braga and its production lines, the *In situ Explorer* component (Fig. 4) features an innovative approach to Augmented Reality on the Web, by leveraging both the markerless capabilities and the recently developed Image Target (marker based) capabilities of 8th Wall Web for a novel approach to a large scale tracking solution on an industrial setting. Image-based markers are used for starting the application and setting the virtual world in the correct positions over the real-world setting, while SLAM-based smart recentering allows for the user to move over greater distances within the scene while avoiding significant drift of the virtual environment.

Fig. 4. ALR Live Explorer component at the Bosch Car Multimedia Portugal facilities.

As demonstrated in Fig. 4, the *In situ Explorer* tracks the position of factory machines and components, and presents relevant information on-site overlaid on top of the correspondent component, providing immersive and attention-grabbing access to real-time, animated, and easy to understand critical information on the factory floor to the relevant users. In this specific case, we can see a Bosch production line presenting different types of machines (e.g., inspection machines and insertion machines). In one of the insertion machines, a label with relevant information can be seen above it, showing the component rejection and productivity percentage at that moment. For a better understanding of the presented data, a green ball is shown representing a positive situation for the overall machine status. With this type of interaction with the production lines, the production control can be done in an easy way, with just-in-time actions.

This demonstration case has allowed to test how the system would function on a real use-case scenario. As intended, the developed interfaces allowed for an interactive, immersive exploration of the mapped IEB components and instantiations. The also allowed the leveraging of component representations as an intuitive graph for easy drill-down of data. Additionally, as shown in the figures, the developed case was presented at Bosch Car Multimedia Portugal facilities and shown to relevant professional and stakeholders, both from the factory and from the IEB development team, from which positive feedback was received on this proof-of-concept.

5 Conclusion and Future Work

This paper shares the proposal for the design and implementation of a Web Visualization Platform for a Big Data/CEP system, motivated by current needs in the Industry 4.0 movement and challenges in the Big Data visualization realm. Since the system proposed in this work is being developed as a part of an IEB, a contextualization of the IEB architecture was carried out to share the motivation for the system and its design details. The exploration of the challenges of data visualization in Big Data contexts, as well as the directions found in the literature review to surpass them were analyzed. As a contribution to the state of the art, this paper presents and fully explains a proposed architecture for meta-monitorization and management of the IEB, by dividing it in key areas where innovative, immersive techniques are leveraged to create next-generation visualizations on the web as conceptual components. Moreover, a demonstration case at Bosch Car Multimedia Portugal is presented to validate the proposed architecture and to present an example of a possible technological and logical approach to the development of the entire *Mapping & Drill-down System* component of the IEB.

The key take-away for future work is related to the significant potential for further improvement and expansion, besides the users' formal assessment. Conceptually, future component proposal could be made to leverage the yet to be developed *Machine Learning* capabilities of the IEB in order to make the system more proactive; and real-time collaborative capabilities could be added to existing and future components to harness the advantages of having human resources working as a team in data exploration. Technologically, upcoming Web paradigms like the proposed mixed-reality Web standard API WebXR (immersiveweb.github.io/webxr) and WebAssembly (webassembly.org) code will further facilitate the conceptualization and development of widely available immersive visual experiences on the Web that do not suffer from the performance bottlenecks found in the current pure JavaScript based solutions. As varied organizations develop and provide better backend infrastructures and more mature data models, it is hoped that this proposal can pave the way for the development of newer, highly performant and deeply immersive visualizations, not only for the IEB but for many other business and Big Data challenges.

Acknowledgements. This work has been supported by national funds through FCT – Fundação para a Ciência e Tecnologia within the Project Scope: UID/CEC/00319/2019 and the Doctoral scholarship PD/BDE/135101/2017 and by European Structural and Investment Funds in the FEDER component, through the Operational Competitiveness and Internationalization Programme (COMPETE 2020) [Project nº 039479; Funding Reference: POCI-01-0247-FEDER-039479]. Authors acknowledge the Virtual and Augmented Reality work of Ana Dias, André Domingues, Maria Cardoso, Rui Faria and Vanessa Ferreira, the Bosch Car Multimedia and the 8thWall team that supported our work during the development phase.

References

1. Andrade, C., Correia, J., Costa, C., Santos, M.Y.: Intelligent event broker: a complex event processing system in big data contexts. In: AMCIS 2019 Proceedings, Cancún, Mexico (2019)
2. Pyne, S., Rao, B.L.S.P., Rao, S.B. (eds.): Big Data Analytics. Springer, New Delhi (2016). https://doi.org/10.1007/978-81-322-3628-3
3. Tsai, C.-W., Lai, C.-F., Chao, H.-C., Vasilakos, A.V.: Big data analytics: a survey. J. Big Data **2** (2015). https://doi.org/10.1186/s40537-015-0030-3

4. Gorodov, E.Y., Gubarev, V.V.: Analytical Review of Data Visualization Methods in Application to Big Data. https://doi.org/10.1155/2013/969458, https://www.hindawi.com/journals/jece/2013/969458/. Accessed 15 Dec 2018

5. Agrawal, R., Kadadi, A., Dai, X., Andres, F.: Challenges and opportunities with big data visualization. In: Proceedings of the 7th International Conference on Management of Computational and Collective Intelligence in Digital EcoSystems - MEDES 2015, Caraguatatuba, Brazil, pp. 169–173. ACM Press (2015). https://doi.org/10.1145/2857218.2857256

6. Chandler, T., et al.: Immersive analytics. In: 2015 Big Data Visual Analytics (BDVA), Hobart, Australia, pp. 1–8. IEEE (2015). https://doi.org/10.1109/BDVA.2015.7314296

7. Sicat, R., et al.: DXR: a toolkit for building immersive data visualizations. IEEE Trans. Visual Comput. Graphics 25, 715–725 (2019). https://doi.org/10.1109/TVCG.2018.2865152

8. Butscher, S., Hubenschmid, S., Müller, J., Fuchs, J., Reiterer, H.: Clusters, trends, and outliers: how immersive technologies can facilitate the collaborative analysis of multidimensional data. In: Proceedings of the 2018 CHI Conference on Human Factors in Computing Systems - CHI 2018, Montreal QC, Canada, pp. 1–12. ACM Press (2018). https://doi.org/10.1145/3173574.3173664

9. Donalek, C., et al.: Immersive and collaborative data visualization using virtual reality platforms. In: 2014 IEEE International Conference on Big Data (Big Data), pp. 609–614 (2014). https://doi.org/10.1109/BigData.2014.7004282

10. ElSayed, N.A.M., Thomas, B.H., Marriott, K., Piantadosi, J., Smith, R.T.: Situated analytics: demonstrating immersive analytical tools with augmented reality. J. Visual Lang. Comput. 36, 13–23 (2016). https://doi.org/10.1016/j.jvlc.2016.07.006

11. Mei, H., Ma, Y., Wei, Y., Chen, W.: The design space of construction tools for information visualization: a survey. J. Visual Lang. Comput. 44, 120–132 (2018). https://doi.org/10.1016/j.jvlc.2017.10.001

12. Shahzad, F., Sheltami, T.R., Shakshuki, E.M., Shaikh, O.: A review of latest web tools and libraries for state-of-the-art visualization. Procedia Comput. Sci. 98, 100–106 (2016). https://doi.org/10.1016/j.procs.2016.09.017

13. Kim, N.W., et al.: Data-driven guides: supporting expressive design for information graphics. IEEE Trans. Visual Comput. Graphics 23, 491–500 (2017). https://doi.org/10.1109/TVCG.2016.2598620

14. Butcher, P.W.S., Ritsos, P.D.: Building immersive data visualizations for the web. In: 2017 International Conference on Cyberworlds (CW), Chester, pp. 142–145. IEEE (2017). https://doi.org/10.1109/CW.2017.11

15. Flouris, I., et al.: FERARI: a prototype for complex event processing over streaming multi-cloud platforms. In: Proceedings of the 2016 International Conference on Management of Data, New York, NY, USA, pp. 2093–2096. ACM (2016). https://doi.org/10.1145/2882903.2899395

A Data Modelling Method for Big Data Warehouses

Marta Nogueira$^{(\boxtimes)}$, João Galvão, and Maribel Y. Santos

ALGORITMI Research Centre, University of Minho, Guimarães, Portugal
a74931@alunos.uminho.pt,
{joao.galvao,maribel}@dsi.uminho.pt

Abstract. Current increases on the data characteristics that define the advent of Big Data have led to a novel area of research, by updating (or even replacing) traditional Data Warehousing solutions into the age of large volumes of fast and diverse data. Although relevant, such endeavors have failed to provide complete and general design and implementations approaches. A recent work has however proposed a general-purpose, integrated, detailed and thoroughly evaluated approach for the design and implementation of Big Data Warehouses. From that, this work proposes, demonstrates and validates a method for modelling Big Data Warehouses, based on a set of sequential rules that aim to semi-automatically translate a traditional relational data model into the proposed Big Data Warehouse model. Positive results have shown how such method can empower the scientific and organizational domains in their efforts to more easily migrate from common traditional Data Warehouses into Big Data Warehousing solutions.

Keywords: Big Data Modelling · Big Data Warehousing · Data engineering

1 Introduction

With the popularization of Big Data and its applicability in a world with constantly higher volume, variety and velocity of data, the scientific community started to give more attention to Big Data Warehouses (BDWs) and the need for changes in the traditional Data Warehousing (DWing) context, due to its growing limitations. Research in this topic, however, has been quite scarce due to the novelty of the topic. Existing conceptual studies have not been successful in developing a general approach on how to design and implement those BDWs and have mostly been focused on unstructured approaches and use-case, technology-driven solutions.

The work of Santos and Costa [1] presents a proposal with a structured approach, including several models and methods for the design and implementation of BDW. It integrates both batch and streaming data, and includes mechanisms for the collection, storage, processing and analysis of Big Data. One of Santos and Costa's Big Data Warehousing (SC-BDWing) key considerations is a novel method to model the data structures to be stored in an indexed storage component with batch and streaming data.

The work presented in this paper addresses the data modeling approach proposed by SC-BDWing, proposing a set of sequential rules for transforming a traditional relational data model into one of the patterns of the design and implementation of BDWs.

M. Themistocleous and M. Papadaki (Eds.): EMCIS 2019, LNBIP 381, pp. 85–98, 2020.
https://doi.org/10.1007/978-3-030-44322-1_7

This paper is structured as follows. Section 2 presents conceptual background that briefly overviews the scientific contributions of BDWing and Big Data Modelling and summarizes the SC-BDWing approach. Section 3 presents the proposed method and the rules applied over the data model of a popular data-centric benchmark (as an explanatory example). Section 4 validates the method by applying it to different benchmarking examples previously used by SC-BDWing. As such, the validation of the method compares the results of the demonstration cases with the results of the original authors. Lastly, Sect. 5 summarizes the contributions of this work and includes considerations for future work.

2   Related Work

2.1   (Big) Data Warehousing and (Big) Data Modelling

Nowadays, the volume and variety of data became the characteristics that challenge the processing of traditional Data Warehouses (DWs). Data is no longer centralized on OLTP (Online Transaction Processing) systems, because it is highly distributed with different structures and an exponential growth rate [2]. Higher volumes of data, advanced analytics and real-time needs make BDWs substantially different from traditional DWs in several key aspects [3, 4]. Furthermore, due to the unique challenges they face, BDWs must address new characteristics such as distributed and parallel storage and processing; scalability; flexible storage for structured and unstructured data and support for both batch and streaming (real-time) data [5, 6].

A specific challenge of BDWing systems lies in the role of data modelling. In BDWs, data structures must be based on new logical models that are more flexible than traditional relational models, where the dimensional data model was usually used [7]. In these Big Data contexts, the schema of data can lack proper structure (or not exist at all) and can change over time according to both infrastructural capabilities, like storage systems, and logical considerations, as business requirements [8]. As such, a data model in the era of Big Data needs to guarantee that all analytical needs are properly met [9].

One of the main challenges on this subject is that current models and methods for the design of BDWs lack validation and do not offer structured general-purpose approaches. This is worsened by: (i) the considerable quantity of competing Big Data technologies whose capabilities often overlap; (ii) use-case driven approaches to BDWing; and, (iii) disregarding Data Modelling as a main concern, despite the claims that ignoring decades of architectural best practices would be a mistake.

Two major strategies can be used to implement BDWs. This first is *"lift and shift"*, where traditional DWs are augmented to be able to answer these novel challenges by leveraging Big Data techniques (e.g. real-time processing) and technologies (e.g. NoSQL and Hadoop), frequently adapted to specific use-cases [11]. Several works and vendors have prioritized this strategy, with approaches such as: proposing strategies to add near real-time capabilities to the DW [12], highlighting the need to explore the Hadoop ecosystem, specifically SQL-on-Hadoop solutions like Hive, for several roles of the DW [13], or proposing changes to the data model, as shown by efforts to convert relational DW schemas into NoSQL databases [14] and multidimensional data models into tabular data models [15]. The second strategy, *"rip and replace"*, consists on a full replacement of the DW with state-of-the-art Big Data techniques and technologies [16, 17]. This strategy is predicted to become more common [16, 17], as recent research has shown that non-structured practices and guidelines are not sufficient, highlighting the need for properly evaluated models and methods to design and build BDWs [10, 18, 19].

As shown in this subsection, the scientific and technical space seems ripe for the introduction of coherent, complete, general and detailed solutions for the design and implementation of BDWs. The SC-BDWing approach is now presented.

2.2 A Novel Approach to the Design and Implementation of BDWing Systems

From the previously cited ambiguity and lack of general approaches for the design and implementation of BDwing, the work of [1], devised such an approach, based on the *"rip and replace"* strategy, here named SC-BDWing, for short.

The SC-BDWing proposal consists of a general-purpose, complete solution that focus both on the physical layer (technological infrastructure) and on the logical layer (data models, data flows and interoperability). The proposed approach includes a set of artifacts (two methods and two models) with suitable mechanisms for collecting, storing, processing and analyzing both structured, semi-structured and unstructured data that thoroughly suit BDWing use-cases. Those artifacts are as follows. A model of logical components and data flows that describes how different components (e.g. for storage, processing, analytics, privacy, etc.) should be considered in the system and how they interact; a method that details the collection, preparation and enrichment of both batch and streaming data; and, a model of the technological infrastructure that suggests tested alternatives for the implementation of the complete system and how to deploy it in both cloud and on-site environments.

The fourth and last artifact is a method for BDWs data modelling which is of primary relevance to the work presented in this paper. The data modelling method includes specific data structures denominated as *analytical objects, complementary analytical objects* and *date, time* and *spatial objects*. An *analytical object* is an independent subject and is a highly denormalized and autonomous structure that can answer queries without the constant need to join other objects. An object is considered a *complementary analytical object* if its *granularity key* is included in an *analytical object*, which means that this object is tightly coupled with that *analytical object*, complementing it (in a more traditional context, Sales could be considered an *analytical object* and Customer a *comlementary analytical object*). An adequate practice would be to include several temporal attributes (*date, time objects*) that complement the *analytical objects* and the use of *spatial objects*. These objects are significantly useful for standardizing temporal and spatial attributes across the *analytical objects*. Other data structures or components of those data structures are present in the general data model. For a complete overview of SC-BDWing approach, please refer to [1].

The results and demonstration cases of their work have shown the capability of the SC-BDWing approach to be applied in several relevant contexts, both traditional scenarios such as retail, finance and industry, and emergent use cases such as Smart

Cities. Effectively, an organized and cohesive guide on how to design and implement BDWs has been produced, empowering researchers and developers with an easily applicable and adaptable way of supporting analytics in Big Data environments.

Given the lack of contributions for standard data modelling in BDWs and how the very relevant traditional DWing approaches can be enhanced in the Big Data era, this paper shows how the method of SC-BDWing can be extended to help practitioners and the scientific communities in the transition from those limited traditional solutions into a BDWing context.

3   A Data Modelling Method for Big Data Warehousing

Considering the relevance of data denormalization and by leveraging the structured approach to data modelling for BDWs proposed in [1], the work presented in this paper includes the proposal of a semi-automatic method for BDWs modelling composed by seven rules. These devised rules need to be executed sequentially and repeatedly until no changes in an overall execution occur. This allow for the transformation of a traditional relational data model into a data model for BDWing. All data models and examples here presented use Entity-Relationship Diagrams (ERD) as they offer an easy and understandable way to present both traditional DWing and BDwing concepts.

The proposed method includes seven rules, all presented below. The step by step process of applying each rule was devised in several flowcharts that provide a schematic representation of the logical reasoning behind each rule, making it not only easier to understand and read but also enriching the approach by providing a starting point for future works, like translating the rules into programming code. These flowcharts are available on a GitHub repository (https://github.com/A74931/dm-bdwing).

To facilitate the presentation of the method and to better clarify the process, the data model of the popular TPC-H Benchmark [20] (Fig. 1) is used as demonstration (demo) case. This benchmark models a business environment as a general industrial setting which must manage, sell or distribute a product on a global market, representing a quite common use case for traditional DWing scenarios.

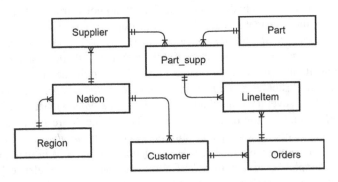

Fig. 1. TPC-H data model (version 2.18.0). Adapted from [20]

R1: Proposing objects of the type *Date*, *Time* and *Spatial* Object

The first rule consists on verifying the need for temporal and/or spatial attributes and in the proposal of the corresponding *date object and time object,* and the *spatial object.* In the SC-BDWing approach, including temporal and/or spatial attributes inside *analytical objects* could severely increase the needed storage space and compromise the stability and performance of the BDW. In this sense, there are advantages in the proposal of considerably small and individual *date, time* and *spatial objects* that will not affect the performance of the BDW. This also gives more flexibility to the temporal granularity of the objects and standardizes spatial attributes across *analytical objects.*

Figure 2 shows the result of applying R1 to the demo data model. The "Nation" and "Region" entities are classified as *spatial objects* (highlighted in grey). The "LineItem" and "Orders" entities include several *date* attributes, suggesting the creation and classification of a *date object* (highlighted in green).

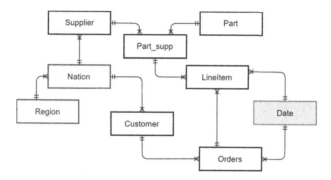

Fig. 2. TPC-H data model after applying R1. (Color figure online)

R2: Proposing objects of type *Analytical Object*

The second rule consists in classifying objects as *analytical objects*. These objects allow the analysis of the business processes by several perspectives, like analyzing

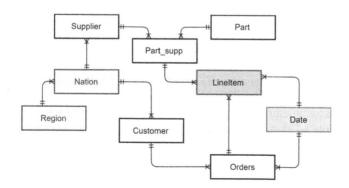

Fig. 3. TPC-H data model after applying R2. (Color figure online)

Sales by Customer or by Product. The identification of these objects is done by looking into the entities in the relational data model that only have relationships with other entities of the types M:M (many-to-many) or M:1 (many-to-one). Figure 3 shows the result of applying R2 to the demo data model. As all relationships from "LineItem" to other entities are of type M:1, it is classified as an *analytical object* (highlighted in red).

R3: Proposing Denormalized Objects

The third rule emerges to verify the cases were different entities can be integrated to form a denormalized object. The aim is to enhance the performance of the BDW by avoiding many joins between objects when processing the data. The identification of this type of object is done by looking into the Foreign Keys (FKs) of the entities, such as the number of FKs between two entities A and B must comply with the following condition, meaning that the entities can be denormalized if the sum of the FKs of the pair A-B is higher or equal than three, and if A or B have only one FK:

$$\sum FK(A+B) \geq 3 \text{ AND } (FK(A) = 1 \text{ OR } FK(B) = 1).$$

Figure 4 shows the result of applying R3 to the demo data model. In this case, the "Customer" entity was denormalized into the "Orders" entity and the "Supplier" entity was denormalized into the "Part_supp" entity (highlighted in purple).

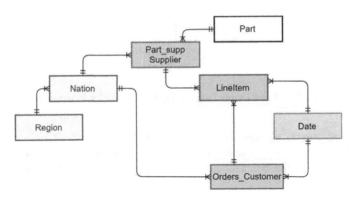

Fig. 4. TPC-H data model after applying R3. (Color figure online)

R4: Proposing Multiple Denormalized Objects

The fourth rule looks for the denormalization of entities that are usually involved in the normalization (in a relational schema) of M:M relationships. This means that in the BDW the several entities will be integrated avoiding unnecessary joins between objects. Whenever an entity integrates more than one FK, the proposal of objects that integrate multiple relationships can be done by verifying the following condition:

```
SELECT Count Distinct (FK_1, FK_2,...) = 1
```

If the condition is matched, the several entities are denormalized into the entity according to the foreign key. Figure 5 shows two examples derived from the demo TPC-H example. In example (a), the condition is verified for "PartKey" and "SupplierKey", as both are FKs and are also used as Primary Key (PK) of the entity. Example (b) presents a similar pattern but the rule never applies for the FKs, as the pair "CustomerKey" and "DateKey" can be found with the same values in several "Orders".

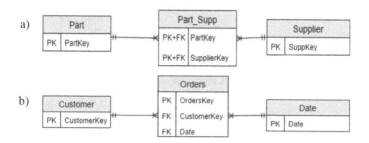

Fig. 5. Examples of objects with multiples relationships.

R5: Proposing Standardized Objects

The fifth rule aims to verify the existence of standardized objects. As such, the rule searches for entities that satisfy two conditions: having low cardinality and having only relationships of types 1:M or 1:1 with other entities. For all the entities that verify the two conditions, a manual verification of the several cases is made. As the identification of standardized objects has a strong dependency of the specific business context, a manual verification is suggested to ensure that no entities of significant analytical were denormalized. This verification should be made by an expert in both the data model and the underlying context (business model) and considered as a critical deciding factor of whether an object is a standardized object, or not. Afterwards, Sect. 4.1 will present an example of *standardized objects.*

R6: Proposing Autonomous Objects

The sixth rule proposes the denormalization of autonomous sets of entities, which in the context of this work are objects that have an independent existence and that cannot be denormalized into other objects. As such, this rule looks for objects that only have one relationship of type 1:M or 1:1 with other entities. At this stage of the proposed method, relationships between the entity and the *date, time* and *spatial objects* are excluded from the verification. This means that if an entity has two relationships, one that matches the condition of R6 and another one to those special objects, this entity should still be considered and denormalized as an autonomous object.

Figure 6 shows the demo data model after applying R6. As the entity "Region" only has a relationship of 1:M with "Nation" and the entity "Part" only has a relationship of 1:M with "Part_supp Supplier", both were integrated into an autonomous object (highlighted in purple).

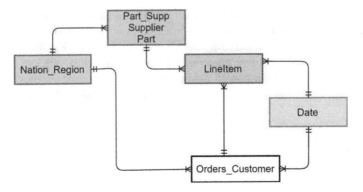

Fig. 6. TPC-H data model after applying R6. (Color figure online)

R7: Proposing objects of type *Complementary Analytical Object*
The seventh rule proposes the classification of the objects obtained by the application of the previous rules as *complementary analytical objects*. This rule verifies if an object has at least one relationship of M:M or M:1 and at least one relationship of 1:M or 1:1. If this condition matches, the object is classified as a *complementary analytical object*. If this condition fails, a second condition is verified to see if the object only has relationships of 1:M and 1:1, and if it has high cardinality. Figure 7 shows the demo data model after applying R7. After verifying these conditions, the objects "Orders_Customer" and "Part_Supplier", named from the integration of Part-Supp, Supplier and Part, were classified *as complementary analytical objects* (highlighted in blue).

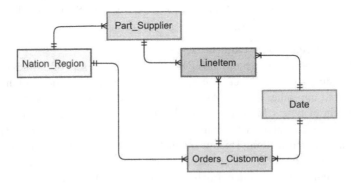

Fig. 7. TPC-H data model after applying R7. (Color figure online)

4 Demonstration and Evaluation

4.1 Method Demonstration

A demonstration of the proposed method is devised by applying it to the data model of the popular TPC-DS Benchmark [21]. This benchmark models a business environment of a large retail company that manages, sells and distributes products nation-wide both in local stores and over the Internet. As such, this represents a common use-case with considerable complexity, as it models several business processes including sales, returns, promotions, customers, items and warehouse. Figure 8a presents the original data model, based on a relational schema. The proposed flowcharts were used for helping in the application of the method. The proposed rule set was applied twice. As no changes were verified in the second iteration, the final data model was concluded, as presented in Fig. 8b. The highlights from the process are as follows:

- R1: object "Date" is identified and classified as *date object;* object "Time" is identified and classified as *time object;* objects "Customer_demo", "Customer_add" and "Household_demo" are verified and classified as *spatial objects;*
- R2: entities "Web_sales", "Catalog_sales", "Store_sales", "Web_returns", "Catalog_returns" and "Store_returns" are classified as *analytical objects;*
- R3 and R4: no entity in the data model verified these rules;
- R5: entities "Ship-mode" and "Reason" matched the condition, however, in the manual verification, only "Ship_mode" was classified as a standardized object, as it was considered that "Reason" does not make sense as a standardized object in this business context;
- In R6: entity "Income_band" is denormalized into "Household_demo";
- In R7: entities "Catalog_page", "Web_site", "Web_page", "Call-center", "Promotion", "Customer" and "Inventory" are classified as complementary analytical objects. Although the entities "Item" and "Store" did not fulfill the first condition, they verified the second condition and, therefore, are classified as complementary analytical objects as well.

After running all the rules, the entities "Warehouse" and "Reason" did not fulfill any rule of the method, which leave them unclassified.

In summary, after the application of the proposed method the following classifications were made: 3 denormalized objects ("Ship_mode", "Web_site" and "Income_band"), 6 *analytical objects*, 10 *complementary analytical objects*, 1 *date object*, 1 *time object* and 3 *spatial objects*. It should be noted that to simplify the presented data model, objects "Customer_demo", "Customer_add" and "Household_demo" were grouped inside a rectangle because they share the same relationships with other objects.

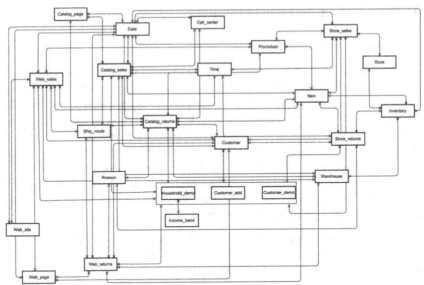

a)   Original data model. Adapted from [18].

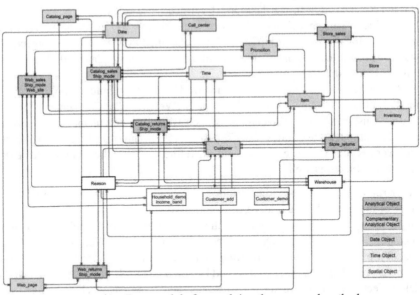

b)   Data model after applying the proposed method.

Fig. 8. TPC-DS data model

4.2 Method Evaluation

In this section, the resulting TPC-DS data model after applying the proposed method, will be compared with the proposed by SC-BDWing, a data model manually defined. Both data models are presented in Fig. 9.

The data model proposed by SC-BDWing includes 2 *analytical objects*, 5 *complementary analytical objects*, 1 *date object* and 1 *time object*. In its turn, the data model obtained by applying the proposed approach includes 6 *analytical objects*, 8 *complementary analytical objects*, 1 *date object*, 1 *time object* and 1 *spatial object*.

Comparing the results of the two data models there are noteworthy differences in the number of *analytical objects*, *complementary analytical objects* and *spatial objects*. In the case of *analytical objects*, the original authors consider that the best approach involves the denormalization of the objects "store_sales", "catalog_sales" and "web_sales" and "store_returns", "catalog_returns" and "web_returns" into two general objects, "sale" and "return", respectively.

Their modelling approach considered the objects "store", "call_center", "catalog_page" and "web_page" as descriptive families of Sales, which were here classified as *complementary analytical objects*. This difference is justified by the way on how authors interpret the relevance of such objects to the organization. In the work described in this paper, the method makes no semantic or context specific judgements. Nevertheless, a data engineer can improve the obtained model by leveraging other constructs and guidelines from the SC-BDWing data modelling method.

Additionally, in the SC-BDWing approach, spatial objects are not mandatory and, for that reason, that object was not considered. However, the authors mention that the inclusion of the spatial object is possible, pointing to the result obtained in this work.

The different results between both data models are mainly because the first considered a very specific, drilled-down, and summarized approach to the data model considering several use case contexts, the characteristics of data and the queries to be answered. The result of this work, which is method-based, provides a more general and global approach to a data model that only takes into consideration data modelling guidelines and the good practices defined in the authors' methodology.

In short, the resulting data models are not mutually exclusive. As expected, a (semi)-automated approach to data modelling can only ensure a proper way of translating the traditional mindset on data modelling to a mindset that makes sense in BDWing. As a good principle inherited from DWing, background knowledge on the specific modelling context, technological optimizations, business needs, adequate objects and attributes for analysis should always be taken into consideration. Even so, the proposed method is successful in achieving a first, global version of the data model, helping practitioners building a first draft of a BDW model.

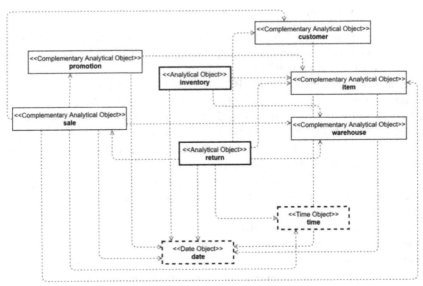

a)   Data model by SC-BDWing approach. Adapted from [1]

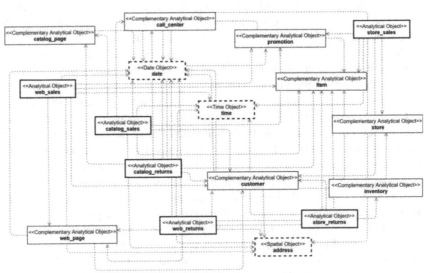

b)   Data model after applying the proposed method

Fig. 9. TPC-DS data model - Evaluation

5   Conclusions

This paper proposed a method for the semi-automatic identification of data models for BDWing, allowing its application in multiples contexts, such as traditional areas and emergent ones (e.g. Smart Cities). This approach is of major relevance to the scientific community and to practitioners as it facilitates the transition from common traditional Data Warehouses to the era of Big Data.

The proposed method includes of seven sequential rules which are thoroughly explained, demonstrated and validated with relevant examples based on common real use cases. For each rule, a step-by-step flowchart is provided to facilitate the modelling process. When compared with a fully manual example, the proposed work offers a general resulting model that complies with the conceptual principles of the methodological background and that works best as a first modeling effort that should then be validated and optimized by an use case expert or data engineering.

For future work, the method will be extended and enriched to address all the constructs included in the SC-BDWing approach. This should be possible through an iterative improvement process that could include the creation of new rules, properly evaluated and validated by relevant examples in different key business scenarios of Big Data. Additionally, it is aimed to further discuss and analyze the "semi" aspect of the semi-automatic method, as an effort to develop the proposed method as computer code, achieving a fully automated process.

Acknowledgements. This work is supported by FCT – *Fundação para a Ciência e Tecnologia* within the Project Scope: UID/CEC/00319/2019, the Doctoral scholarship PD/BDE/135100/ 2017 and European Structural and Investment Funds in the FEDER component, through the Operational Competitiveness and Internationalization Programme (COMPETE 2020) [Project nº 039479; Funding Reference: POCI-01-0247-FEDER-039479].

References

1. Santos, M.Y., Costa, C.: Big Data: Concepts, Warehousing and Analytics, FCA - Editora de Informática (2019)
2. Tria, F.D., Lefons, E., Tangorra, F.: Design process for big data warehouses. In: 2014 International Conference on Data Science and Advanced Analytics (DSAA), pp. 512–518 (2014)
3. Krishnan, K.: Data Warehousing in the Age of Big Data. Newnes, Boston (2013)
4. Tria, F.D., Lefons, E., Tangorra, F.: Big data warehouse automatic design methodology. Big Data Manage. Technol. Appl. 115–149 (2014). https://doi.org/10.4018/978-1-4666-4699-5. ch006
5. Goss, R.G., Veeramuthu, K.: Heading towards big data building a better data ware-house for more data, more speed, and more users. In: ASMC 2013 SEMI Advanced Semiconductor Manufacturing Conference, Saratoga Springs, NY, pp. 220–225. IEEE (2013)
6. Mohanty, S., Jagadeesh, M., Srivatsa, H.: Big Data Imperatives: Enterprise Big Data Warehouse, BI Implementations and Analytics. 1st edn. http://dl.acm.org/cita-tion.cfm?id= 2517701
7. Kimball, R., Ross, M.: The Data Warehouse Toolkit: The Definitive Guide to Dimen-sional Modeling. Wiley, Hoboken (2013)
8. Santos, M.Y., Costa, C., Galvão, J., Andrade, C., Pastor, O., Marcén, A.C.: Enhancing big data warehousing for efficient, integrated and advanced analytics: visionary paper. In: Cappiello, C., Ruiz, M. (eds.) Information Systems Engineering in Responsible Information Systems. Lecture Notes in Business Information Processing, vol. 350, pp. 215–226. Springer, Cham (2019). https://doi.org/10.1007/978-3-030-21297-1_19

9. Santos, M.Y., Costa, C.: Data models in NoSQL databases for big data contexts. In: Tan, Y., Shi, Y. (eds.) Data Mining and Big Data, pp. 475–485. Springer, Cham (2016). https://doi.org/10.1007/978-3-319-40973-3_48

10. Costa, C., Santos, M.Y.: Evaluating several design patterns and trends in big data warehousing systems. In: Krogstie, J., Reijers, H.A. (eds.) CAiSE 2018. LNCS, vol. 10816, pp. 459–473. Springer, Cham (2018). https://doi.org/10.1007/978-3-319-91563-0_28

11. Clegg, D.: Evolving data warehouse and BI architectures: the big data challenge. TDWI Bus. Intell. J. **20**, 19–24 (2015)

12. Golab, L., Johnson, T.: Data stream warehousing. In: 2014 IEEE 30th International Conference on Data Engineering, pp. 1290–1293 (2014)

13. Das, T., Mohapatro, A.: A study on big data integration with data warehouse. Int. J. Comput. Trends Technol. **9**, 188–192 (2014)

14. Yangui, R., Nabli, A., Gargouri, F.: Automatic transformation of data warehouse schema to NoSQL data base: comparative study. Procedia Comput. Sci. **96**, 255–264 (2016). https://doi.org/10.1016/j.procs.2016.08.138

15. Santos, M.Y., Costa, C.: Data warehousing in big data: from multidimensional to tabular data models. In: Proceedings of the Ninth International C* Conference on Computer Science & Software Engineering - C3S2E 2016, Porto, Portugal, pp. 51–60. ACM Press (2016)

16. Russom, P.: Evolving Data Warehouse Architectures in the Age of Big Data, The Data Warehouse Institute (2014)

17. Russom, P.: Data Warehouse Modernization in the Age of Big Data Analytics, The Data Warehouse Institute (2016)

18. Costa, E., Costa, C., Santos, M.Y.: Efficient big data modelling and organization for hadoop Hive-based data warehouses. In: Themistocleous, M., Morabito, V. (eds.) EMCIS 2017. LNBIP, vol. 299, pp. 3–16. Springer, Cham (2017). https://doi.org/10.1007/978-3-319-65930-5_1

19. Vieira, A.A.C., Pedro, L., Santos, M.Y., Fernandes, J.M., Dias, L.S.: Data requirements elicitation in big data warehousing. In: Themistocleous, M., Rupino da Cunha, P. (eds.) EMCIS 2018. LNBIP, vol. 341, pp. 106–113. Springer, Cham (2019). https://doi.org/10.1007/978-3-030-11395-7_10

20. TPC-H: TPC BenchmarkTM H Standard Specification Revision 2.18.0 (2018). http://www.tpc.org/tpc_documents_current_versions/pdf/tpc-h_v2.18.0.pdf

21. TPC-DS: TPC BenchmarkTM DS - Standard Specification, Version 2.11.0 (2019). http://www.tpc.org/tpc_documents_current_versions/pdf/tpc-ds_v2.11.0.pdf

Block Chain Technology and Applications

Towards a Better Understanding of the Value of Blockchains in Supply Chain Management

Michael Lustenberger[✉], Florian Spychiger, and Sasa Malesevic

Zurich University of Applied Sciences, Winterthur, Switzerland
{luse,spyc,malv}@zhaw.ch

Abstract. Whether or not blockchain technology adds value to supply chains is a highly controversial topic. It has been lauded as the technology that brings transparency and efficiency to supply chains. However, others find this view overly optimistic. In this paper, we aim to add more insight into the issue by applying an action design research approach. We develop and evaluate two artifacts in collaboration with companies and use the results to conclude how blockchain technology can help overcome issues in the current supply chain information flow. It shows that blockchains can provide a shared trust base and a common standard that allows for increased information exchange between supply chain partners. Based on our findings, we propose a research agenda for studying blockchain technology with a stronger focus on governance mechanism and transparency issues.

Keywords: Blockchain · Supply chain · Information flow · Governance · Transparency

1 Introduction

Supply chain management (SCM) explores inter-organizational relationships and the coordination of processes and activities between organizations to improve their performance [1]. Despite the term "supply chain", such relationships are, in reality, non-linear and have a complex network structure [2]. Based on extensive research, there is strong evidence that enhanced coordination and integration within such supply chain networks positively correlates with higher performance by all network members [3, 4]. A particularly important enabler for tight coordination among supply chain partners is the network-wide integration of the information flow [5, 6].

In recent years, blockchain has emerged as a new technology with the potential to integrate and improve the information flow along supply chains significantly [7, 8]. The identified benefits of this technology in SCM are manifold and include enhanced identity management for assets and individuals [9], the avoidance of inefficient intermediaries [10], increased product traceability [11], and an immutable, secure audit trail [12]. However, as blockchain is a new phenomenon, the benefits of this new technology in SCM is the subject of much discussion among theorists as well as practitioners [13–15]. Although some large companies such as Kühne + Nagel [16] and Carrefour [17]

© Springer Nature Switzerland AG 2020
M. Themistocleous and M. Papadaki (Eds.): EMCIS 2019, LNBIP 381, pp. 101–112, 2020.
https://doi.org/10.1007/978-3-030-44322-1_8

have started to experiment with blockchain-based applications in their supply chains, there remains a lack of understanding about how blockchain technology can help overcome issues in the current supply chain information flow in practice (see [18]).

To gain greater insight into this topic and to understand better the value of blockchains for SCM, we developed two blockchain-based artifacts for a food label and a pharma supply chain of two companies to address the following research question:

Can blockchain technology help overcome issues in the current information flow for supply chain networks?

The contributions of this study are two-fold. First, we present the experience gained from two practice use cases. Second, based on the outcome of the two real-world cases, we derive a research agenda for further studies about the value of blockchain for supply chain networks.

The remainder of the paper is structured as follows: In the *related work* section, we review the existing literature to elaborate on issues in the current information flow for supply chain networks as well as on blockchain technology and its applications in supply chains. In the next section, *research method*, we describe our research design. In *results*, we introduce the two case studies by formulating the problem and presenting insights generated by the implementation of the two artifacts, while in the *discussion*, we reflect on the findings and formalize what we have learned. Finally, in the *conclusion*, we summarize our results.

2   Related Work

2.1   Issues in the Current Supply Chain Information Flow

The advent of new information system technologies has greatly facilitated the exchange of information in supply chains [5, 19]. Nevertheless, the new technological possibilities are not exhausted, and many companies are less involved than one would expect [20]. Supply chain players need to acquire information technology (IT) skills to utilize the full potential of these new systems successfully [21]. At the same time, a mutual willingness to share information requires trust between supply chain partners [22]. However, supply chain networks are shaped by power and information asymmetries [23] as well as diverging interests [5]. Research shows that the more hierarchic and centralized the structure, the more difficult it is to establish that necessary trust [24]. As a result, many companies are still not willing to share data with their supply chain partners [25]. Without shared standards and a basis of trust, supply chain networks suffer from several issues in their information flows [5, 22]. First, there is an insufficient exchange of information among supply chain partners. As a result, upstream or downstream visibility is limited, and the tracing of goods within the supply chain is complicated. Second, no unique data truth exists in the supply chain, which makes auditing a tedious task. Third, if company information systems are not integrated, processes involving several parties are hard to automate. Fourth, the lack of connectedness leads to the inclusion of countless intermediaries functioning solely as information brokers.

2.2 Blockchains

The blockchain is an emergent technology initially developed for the digital cash system Bitcoin [26]. Subsequently, the technology has been further developed to register and transact any digital asset as well as to store "smart contracts" and to carry out processes in a distributed manner when all predefined conditions have been fulfilled [27, 28]. These second-generation blockchains can be understood as a "general-purpose programmable infrastructure with a public ledger that records the computational results" [29, p. 244], and they offer four essential qualities that are extremely valuable for applications in SCM [29, 30]:

(1) Immutability: Once the data is stored on a blockchain ledger, entries cannot be altered due to a cryptographic hash chain.
(2) Transparency: Since each participant stores a copy of the ledger locally, every transaction history is visible.
(3) Decentralization: Participants agree on a single truth using a consensus mechanism. No central authority is needed.
(4) Process automation: Smart contracts can be deployed to automate secure business processes involving several parties.

This immutable, transparent, and autonomous peer-to-peer processing and storing of data is based on the decentralized structure of blockchains. By decentralizing all protocols and functions, blockchains avoid the need for a central authority to operate and develop the network system. This shift from a centralized to a decentralized (IT) system implies a change from trusting in a single network owner to trusting in the shared protocols of the blockchain network. Therefore, it seems plausible from a theoretical perspective to assume that the lack of trust, traditional power structures, and information asymmetries in supply chains mentioned above might be overcome by the introduction of decentralized blockchain-based IT systems. Moreover, by creating a shared IT infrastructure based on mutual trust, it should – theoretically at least – be possible to address current supply chain issues such as visibility, auditability, automation, and intermediaries.

2.3 Blockchain Application in SCM

There has been a lot of research in the area of SCM and blockchain, mainly discussing the optimization of supply chains through blockchain technology. Research has been most active in the fields of supply chain finance, information flow, and supply chain traceability, where the last accounts for more than 40% of total research [31].

An attempt to review the literature on applications systematically suggests five use case clusters of blockchain-based applications in SCM [32]: visibility, integrity, orchestration, virtualization, and finance. The review concludes that, currently, the main focus of blockchain-based applications is tracing goods and automating supply chain operations. The authors of another review suggest extended visibility and traceability, supply chain digitalization and disintermediation, improved data security, and smart contracts as being the value generators of blockchain technology for SCM [33]. They also suggest that the pharmaceutical and food industries are the most promising sectors for implementation.

In another recent study, the impact of blockchain technology in agriculture and food supply chains was investigated [34]. Most projects focus on food safety and integrity, as well as better supervision and support for small farmers. Although some benefits of using blockchain technology in food supply chains seem apparent – such as tackling unfair pricing, facilitating trade, and monitoring social and environmental responsibility – there are also specific issues. First, blockchain is not sufficiently accessible to all the participants in a network; second, the permanent tracking of goods might raise privacy concerns; and third, blockchain technology is not yet mature enough for utilization in daily operations.

A review of the current research regarding blockchain applications and the biomedical domain shows that scientific literature focuses mainly on integration, integrity, and access control of health records [35]. The authors of the review state that the field is still not well explored and note that within the scope of their investigation, only one study presented a real-world scenario. The implementation process of blockchain projects faces numerous challenges, and network adoption is only possible if a critical mass of stakeholder engagement can be achieved [36]. The lack of standards and governance models [36], as well as incentivization misalignments, represent the most significant issues [37], reported also in the normative literature [38, 39].

To overcome such challenges, [40] proposes an implementation strategy, where only a small number of participants adopt blockchain technology and demonstrate its value by using real-life examples. However, due to a lack of successful real-life implementations, the evidence provided in the literature for the theoretically claimed benefits and issues of blockchain applications in supply chains remains untested and needs to be explored practically.

3   Research Method

In order to understand the impact of blockchain technology on supply chain networks, we applied an action design research (ADR) method [41]. ADR allows for the design of an IT artifact embedded in an organizational context. The issues and the proposed solution addressed in this study call for close collaboration with industry requiring continuous examination of the specific organizational setting by intervening and evaluating [41].

Any further insight gained should contribute not only to academic discussion but also highlight relevant, practical recommendations for companies attempting to apply blockchain technologies to their supply chain network. In our research design, we followed the four stages of the ADR approach (see Fig. 1).

In the problem formulation stage, we gathered knowledge on the state-of-the-art as well as issues in the current information flow of supply chains through an extensive literature review [42] by applying the keywords (and combinations thereof) "blockchain", "supply chain management", "supply chain", and "literature review" on several online data portals (Google Scholar, ResearchGate, ScienceDirect). We sent invitations

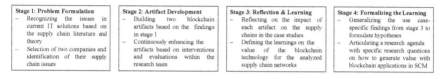

Stage 1: Problem Formulation	Stage 2: Artifact Development	Stage 3: Reflection & Learning	Stage 4: Formalizing the Learning
– Recognizing the issues in current IT solutions based on the supply chain literature and theory – Selection of two companies and identification of their supply chain issues	– Building two blockchain artifacts based on the findings in stage 1 – Continuously enhancing the artifacts based on interventions and evaluations within the research team	– Reflecting on the impact of each artifact on the supply chains in the case studies – Defining the learnings on the value of the blockchain technology for the analyzed supply chain networks	– Generalizing the use case-specific findings from stage 3 to formulate hypotheses – Articulating a research agenda with specific research questions on how to generate value with blockchain applications in SCM

Fig. 1. The research design includes four adapted stages based on the ADR approach.

to 800 companies located in Switzerland and selected two of them based on their responses. The two companies chosen operate in the food and pharmaceutical industries respectively, the sectors – according to [33] – most relevant for blockchain applications in SCM. In February 2018, we conducted semi-structured interviews [43] with the two companies to understand better the current problems in their respective supply chain information flow. Between February and May 2018, in the artifact development stage, we developed two different blockchain-based artifacts to address the issues from the previous stage. This process was supported by the entire research team as well as the companies involved. In the reflection & learning stage, the artifacts were evaluated by the independent blockchain expert group from the Swiss Alliance for Data-Intensive Services on 26 June 2018. This provided a clearer understanding of the value of blockchain technology for the supply chain information flows analyzed. In the final *formalizing the learning* stage, we generalized our case-specific findings.

4   Results

4.1   Problem Formulation

The first company is a multinational producer of pharmaceuticals and a market leader in a highly competitive environment which requires the continuous optimization of processes. Its current supply chain reaches multiple countries all over the world. During the production process, materials have to go through many different stages until an finished product is forthcoming.

If the company wants to conduct a proper analysis of the production process, quick access to information about material flows along the entire supply chain is required. Furthermore, each entity creates data which must be communicated to the next party.

In the company's supply chain, the communication process between two adjacent parties is ordinarily efficient, and the flow of data is present. However, a problem occurs when information from an entity further upstream or downstream is required.

Moreover, the process of tracing the finished product back to its origin poses a significant challenge if an integrated information system does not offer the required transparency. In the highly regulated medical sector, especially, it is mandatory for a company to provide full documentation about the origin and quality of their products. Due to the missing information exchange beyond directly adjacent supply chain players, it is hard to fulfill the regulatory requirements since most of the documentation process is still paper-based and distributed among different systems and operators.

The second company analyzed in this study is an association acting as a food label for numerous regional producers of dairy and meat products. For a label which gives consumers not only the assurance of legal compliance but also of regionally produced, high-quality products, it is crucial to safeguard their credibility. For this reason, independent certification authorities regularly audit each partner to guarantee the label's certified food supply chain. Because of the complexity of this process, several problems in the information flow arise. First, it is difficult to trace a finished meat product back to a specific animal as the identification system is not yet foolproof. Second, to track the entire process, all partners in the food supply chain need to store relevant documentation (often paper-based) for the disclosure of selected product histories on request. This makes the auditing process time-consuming as information is scattered among many supply chain members. Third, coordination of the entire verification process is problematic because each player might use a different database and there is no shared system implying that an auditor has to visit each production site in person every second year to certify the label's requirements. A fourth issue is that owing to a lack of transparency on product level, only supply chain members are certified and not the actual products themselves.

4.2 Artifact Development

The pharma artifact implements a private blockchain-based application built on Hyperledger Fabric whose architecture is shown in Fig. 2. The selection of a private blockchain was an essential criterion for the multinational company to maintain full control over access and development of the system as well as to allow for private transactions between its network members. In the application, a predefined membership service manages access rights to a shared information system for all supply chain partners. Once all network partners have access to the system, each step in the supply chain needs to be communicated and validated through the blockchain network. Raw material suppliers register their materials in the blockchain which then can be transferred by transportation companies to the manufacturers. Each manufacturer selects the raw materials required and registers its manufactured products as new assets on the blockchain. Once registered, these new products can be transferred again to the next supply chain partner, who again selects the required materials and registers its newly manufactured products on the blockchain. Ultimately, every stage from raw material supply to finished product is recorded on the blockchain. A regulator or client is, therefore, able to trace the entire history of a product along the supply chain using one system.

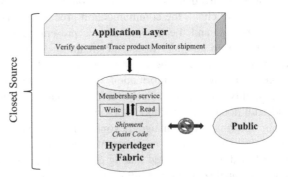

Fig. 2. Architecture of the pharma artifact based on Hyperledger Fabric. Everything is secure and only accessible by authorized members.

In addition to monitoring the flow of tangible goods, the artifact has two further benefits. First, by storing a cryptographic hash of essential documents on the block-chain, users can verify the authenticity of certificates, batch documents, or invoices in a tamper-proof environment. Second, by connecting a Raspberry Pi 3 to the artifact, it is possible to record temperature during transportation and to send the data via mobile communication to the blockchain. Based on the immutable chain codes (smart con-tracts), shipment conditions can be continuously monitored, and if, for example, a temperature deviates from a predefined range, the application sends an automatic e-mail alert to the shipper and the consignee.

In contrast to the pharma company, full transparency and less system control were no issue for the small, regional food label. Their network incorporates many small heterogeneous players with non-standardized databases. The label artifact consists, therefore, of a blockchain-based platform that gives everyone in the supply chain network (from the consumer or small farmer to large enterprises) easy access to a documentation system. As shown in Fig. 3, the artifact is based on Ethereum, where each partner can use an asset registry contract that creates a new smart contract for each asset (e.g., a cow). This creates an immutable entry for every asset in the system which can be mapped to existing identification systems, e.g., earmarks. Once registered on the blockchain, ownership of the smart contract (asset) can be transferred only by the current owner to a new owner. In this way, the ownership history of the asset is recorded and can be traced. Once the asset arrives at a production site (e.g., the butcher), it can be further processed into new assets (e.g., steaks) by the new asset owner. For that purpose, the "parent" smart contract creates new "child" assets which, in turn, can be further processed along the supply chain. This processing is equipped with different control mechanisms enforced by the "parent" smart contract; for example, only the owner is allowed to process an asset, and a newly created asset may not have a higher weight than its parent. Such mechanisms allow for plausibility checks along the supply chain. Finally, end-consumers in the supermarket have the option of scanning a QR-code to access the entire supply chain history of their purchase.

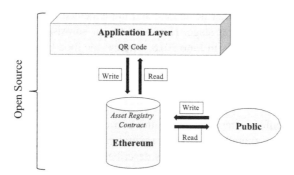

Fig. 3. The label artifact allows everyone to access the asset registry contract stored on the publicly accessible Ethereum blockchain.

5 Discussion

5.1 Reflection and Learning

Based on the development and implementation of blockchain-based artifacts in the two supply chains, we suggest that blockchain technology can provide an effective way to improve on multiple issues.

First, it can tackle the lack of visibility. Specifically, it increases visibility within the supply chain and allows companies to exchange information across the entire network. Further, due to the facilitated exchange of information and the digitization of paper-based processes, there should be an overall increase in the efficiency of daily operations. Second, it improves the auditability of all kind of supply chain processes. In economic sectors confronted with high-quality standards and many legal regulations, it is crucial to offer an immutable audit trail of information. Blockchain-based document verification creates the basis for an efficient, detailed, digital auditing process. This suggests a further opportunity for the label supply chain; it is now possible to create audit trails (and therefore certificates) at product level rather than only at the producer level. Third, blockchain technology allows smart contracts to monitor and enforce agreements between supply chain partners autonomously, for example, by imposing penalties in the case of deviation from a predefined temperature range during transportation. Fourth, based on our observations, we believe that disintermediation is possible. The products from both companies in our study rely on external certification authorities to be checked and verified. By using a blockchain, it is possible to reduce this dependency on external auditors thanks to a shared data system giving authorities and consumers direct access to an immutable audit trail.

Besides the potential for overcoming the identified supply chain issues, our artifacts also revealed some technical limitations. In the publicly accessible Ethereum blockchain, transaction fees can be quite substantial although throughput is rather low. The private Hyperledger Fabric platform improves on this by using a different consensus mechanism resulting in fast transactions and no fees. Due to these technical issues as well as the economic possibilities of the two companies, we were confident that the pharma artifact could be further developed and implemented in the daily operations of the pharma network at a later stage. However, to our surprise, the pharma company abandoned the project entirely in June 2018, whereas the food label association showed interest in developing the artifact further.

5.2 Formalizing the Learning

Even though the different reactions from the two companies were difficult to understand initially, we eventually arrived at several new research hypotheses. First, to materialize the advantages of blockchains described in the previous section, it is not sufficient simply to implement the technology, since the technology *per se* enables only a technological infrastructure. To exploit the full potential of blockchain-based networks, the governance aspects of these decentralized systems [12], as well as standards [36] and incentive structure [37], play a significant role. A shared information system requires a specific set of rules about how to develop the system, who has what rights, and how to integrate new members. The development and implementation of such decentralized blockchain governance are much more difficult in a strongly centralistic and hierarchic supply chain with a high degree of asymmetric power and interest distribution. In contrast, a decentralized network structure – such as the supply chain of the food label association – with flat hierarchies and symmetric interest distribution represents a promising initial situation for the successful creation of a governance structure for a shared blockchain system.

Second, the supply chain needs to share a strategic interest to increase its transparency and auditability; the entire business model of the food label association relies on these characteristics. By contrast, a trade-off between efficient information exchange and privacy prevails in many other businesses. As long as companies fear losing out if they disclose information, greater transparency in supply chains will be hard to achieve. Based on these two hypotheses, we propose a research agenda for future studies.

Whereas the normative literature suggests some research directions for blockchain governance [39], our research agenda is clearly motivated by two practical applications. First and most importantly, further studies should focus on governance mechanisms in blockchain-based applications and networks. How can decentralized systems be coordinated? What are the structural prerequisite for successful blockchain implementation? Second, in most industries, transparency is viewed more as a threat than an asset. It would be interesting to investigate further the "business model" for transparency in traditional companies. How can current business models be modified so that transparency and collaboration become worthwhile goals? What is needed from a business perspective for companies to be willing to invest in the potential benefits of blockchain applications? Third, even though we worked with companies and observed practical applications, it is still necessary to see other such systems operating in real-world situations. Further studies of operational applications are needed to incorporate additional factors from practice into the analysis to understand better the circumstances under which a blockchain-based supply chain application can be successfully implemented.

6   Conclusion

In this paper, we have studied the application of blockchain technology in SCM using two developed artifacts. In doing so, we contributed to the literature in two ways:

First, our artifacts show that, depending on the specific application, blockchain technology can overcome supply chain issues such as visibility, auditability, automation, and intermediaries. Common to all blockchain-based applications is an acceleration of digitization due to the need for a shared and trusted IT infrastructure in the supply chain network. These findings have enabled us to answer our research question ("Can blockchain technology help overcome issues in the current information flow for supply chain networks?") in the affirmative.

Second, as a result of our artifacts, we could see that blockchains are only beneficial if they are implemented in a supply chain which has already a decentralized organization, and a business strategy that supports transparency and auditability. Without that premise, it is a challenge to tackle the incentive and governance issues arising from blockchain technology. In our case, only the food label supply chain already offers the prerequisite decentralized structure with the result that only this case will be developed further.

Consequently, we expand on the normative literature and propose a research agenda motivated by two real-world use cases for studying blockchain technology in SCM with a stronger focus on governance mechanism and transparency issues in blockchain-based networks and applications. Additionally, more real-world implementations of blockchain-based supply chain solutions need to be studied to create further insight into where and when this new technology can be successfully implemented.

References

1. Cooper, M.C.: Supply chain management: more than a new name for logistics. Int. J. Logist. Manage. **8**(1), 1–14 (1997). https://doi.org/10.1108/09574099710805556
2. Choi, T.Y., Kim, Y.: Structural embeddedness and supplier management: a network perspective. J. Supply Chain Manage. **44**(4), 5–13 (2008). https://doi.org/10.1111/j.1745-493X.2008.00069.x
3. Frohlich, M.T., Westbrook, R.: Arcs of integration: an international study of supply chain strategies. J. Oper. Manage. **19**(2), 185–200 (2001). https://doi.org/10.1016/S0272-6963(00)00055-3
4. Ataseven, C., Nair, A.: Assessment of supply chain integration and performance relationships: a meta-analytic investigation of the literature. Int. J. Prod. Econ. **185**, 252–265 (2017). https://doi.org/10.1016/j.ijpe.2017.01.007
5. Lee, H.L., Whang, S.: Information sharing in a supply chain. Int. J. Manuf. Technol. Manage. **1**(1), 79 (2000). https://doi.org/10.1504/IJMTM.2000.001329
6. Vanpoucke, E., Vereecke, A., Muylle, S.: Leveraging the impact of supply chain integration through information technology. Int. J. Oper. Prod. Manage. **37**(4), 510–530 (2017). https://doi.org/10.1108/IJOPM-07-2015-0441
7. Gunasekaran, A., Ngai, E.W.: Information systems in supply chain integration and management. Eur. J. Oper. Res. **159**(2), 269–295 (2004). https://doi.org/10.1016/j.ejor.2003.08.016
8. Casey, M.J., Wong, P.: Global Supply Chains Are About to Get Better, Thanks to Blockchain (2017). https://hbr.org/2017/03/global-supply-chains-are-about-to-get-better-thanks-to-blockchain
9. Mainelli, M.: Blockchain Will Help Us Prove Our Identities in a Digital World (2017). https://hbr.org/2017/03/blockchain-will-help-us-prove-our-identities-in-a-digital-world
10. Koetsier, J.: Blockchain Beyond Bitcoin: How Blockchain Will Transform Business in 3 to Years (2017). https://www.inc.com/john-koetsier/how-blockchain-will-transform-business-in-3-to-5-years.html
11. O'Marah, K.: Blockchain: Enormous Potential Demands Your Attention (2017). https://www.sup-plychaindigital.com/technology/blockchain-enormous-potential-demands-your-attention
12. Kshetri, N.: Blockchain's roles in meeting key supply chain management objectives. Int. J. Inf. Manage. **39**, 80–89 (2018). https://doi.org/10.1016/j.ijin-fomgt.2017.12.005

13. Alicke, K., Davies, A., Leopoldseder, M., Niemeyer, A.: Blockchain technology for supply chains - a must or a maybe? (2017). https://www.mckinsey.com/business-functions/operations/our-insights/blockchain-technology-for-supply-chainsa-must-or-a-maybe
14. Wüst, K., Gervais, A.: Do you need a Blockchain? In: 2018 Crypto Valley Conference on Blockchain Technology (CVCBT), pp. 45–54. IEEE (2018)
15. Queiroz, M.M., Teles, R., Bonilla, S.H.: Blockchain and supply chain management integration: a systematic review of the literature. Supply Chain Manage. Int. J. (2019). https://doi.org/10.1108/SCM-03-2018-0143
16. Schmidt, A.: Kuehne + Nagel deploys blockchain technology for VGM Portal (2018). https://news-room.kuehne-nagel.com/kuehne–nagel-deploys-blockchain-technology-for-vgm-portal/
17. Thomasson, E.: Carrefour says blockchain tracking boosting sales of some products (2019). https://www.reuters.com/article/us-carrefour-blockchain-idUSKCN1T42A5
18. Petersen, M., Hackius, N., von See, B.: Mapping the sea of opportunities: blockchain in supply chain and logistics. IT Inf. Technol. **60**(5–6), 263–271 (2018). https://doi.org/10.1515/itit-2017-0031
19. Tapscott, D., Tapscott, A.: Blockchain Revolution: How the Technology Behind Bitcoin is Changing Money, Business, and the World. Portfolio/Penguin, New York (2016)
20. Deflorin, P., Hauser, C., Scherrer-Rathje, M.: Schweizer Unternehmen sehen Digitalisierung als Chance. Die Volkswirtschaft **88**(5), 58–61 (2015)
21. Liu, H., Wei, S., Ke, W., Wei, K.K., Hua, Z.: The configuration between supply chain integration and information technology competency: a resource orchestration perspective. J. Oper. Manage. **44**(1), 13–29 (2016). https://doi.org/10.1016/j.jom.2016.03.009
22. Fawcett, S.E., Osterhaus, P., Magnan, G.M., Brau, J.C., McCarter, M.W.: Information sharing and supply chain performance: the role of connectivity and willingness. Supply Chain Manage. Int. J. **12**(5), 358–368 (2007). https://doi.org/10.1108/13598540710776935
23. Cox, A.: The art of the possible: relationship management in power regimes and supply chains. Supply Chain Manage. Int. J. **9**(5), 346–356 (2004). https://doi.org/10.1108/13598540410560739
24. Capaldo, A., Giannoccaro, I.: How does trust affect performance in the supply chain? The moderating role of interdependence. Int. J. Prod. Econ. **166**, 36–49 (2015). https://doi.org/10.1016/j.ijpe.2015.04.008
25. Özer, Ö., Zheng, Y.: Establishing trust and trustworthiness for supply chain information sharing. In: Ha, A.Y., Tang, C.S. (eds.) Handbook of Information Exchange in Supply Chain Management, pp. 287–312. Springer, Cham (2017). https://doi.org/10.1007/978-3-319-32441-8_14
26. Nakamoto, S.: Bitcoin: a peer-to-peer electronic cash system (2008)
27. Wood, G.: Ethereum: a secure decentralised generalised transaction ledger. Ethereum project yellow paper, vol. 151, pp. 1–32 (2014)
28. Cachin, C.: Architecture of the hyperledger blockchain fabric. In: Workshop on Distributed Cryptocurrencies and Consensus Ledgers, p. 4 (2016)
29. Xu, X., et al.: A taxonomy of blockchain-based systems for architecture design. In: 2017 IEEE International Conference on Software Architecture (ICSA), Gothenburg, Sweden, pp. 243–252. IEEE (2017). https://doi.org/10.1109/ICSA.2017.33
30. Voshmgir, S.: Blockchains, Smart Contracts und das Dezentrale Web, pp. 17–35. Technologiestiftung, Berlin (2016)
31. Tribis, Y., et al.: Supply chain management based on blockchain: a systematic mapping study. In: MATEC Web of Conferences, vol. 200 (2018). https://doi.org/10.1051/matecconf/201820000020. article number 00020

32. Blossey, G., Eisenhardt, J., Hahn, G.: Blockchain technology in supply chain management: an application perspective. Presented at the Hawaii International Conference on System Sciences (2019). https://doi.org/10.24251/HICSS.2019.824

33. Wang, Y., Han, J.H., Beynon-Davies, P.: Understanding blockchain technology for future supply chains: a systematic literature review and research agenda. Supply Chain Manage. Int. J. **24**(1), 62–84 (2019). https://doi.org/10.1108/SCM-03-2018-0148

34. Kamilaris, A., Fonts, A., Prenafeta-Boldú, F.C.: The rise of blockchain technology in agriculture and food supply chains. Trends Food Sci. Technol. **91**, 640–652 (2019). https://doi.org/10.1016/j.tifs.2019.07.034

35. Drosatos, G., Kaldoudi, E.: Blockchain applications in the biomedical domain: a scoping review. Comput. Struct. Biotechnol. J. **17**, 229–240 (2019). https://doi.org/10.1016/j.csbj.2019.01.010

36. Dobrovnik, M., Herold, D., Fürst, E., Kummer, S.: Blockchain for and in logistics: what to adopt and where to start. Logistics **2**, 18 (2018). https://doi.org/10.3390/logistics2030018

37. Sternberg, H., Baruffaldi, G.: Chains in chains – logic and challenges of blockchains in supply chains. In: 51st Hawaii International Conference on System Sciences, pp. 3936–3943 (2018)

38. Piscini, E.: Why 2017 is Blockchain's Make or Break Year (2017). https://www.coindesk.com/why-2017-is-blockchains-make-or-break-year

39. Beck, R., Müller-Bloch, C., King, J.L.: Governance in the blockchain economy: a framework and research agenda. J. Assoc. Inf. Syst. **19**(10), 1020–1034 (2018)

40. Sulkowski, A.J.: Blockchain, business supply chains, sustainability, and law: the future of governance, legal frameworks, and lawyers? Delaware J. Corp. Law **43**(2), 303–345 (2019). https://doi.org/10.2139/ssrn.3205452

41. Sein, M.K., Henfridsson, O., Purao, S., Rossi, M., Lindgren, R.: Action design research. MIS Q. **35**(1), 37–56 (2011). https://doi.org/10.2307/23043488

42. Vom Brocke, J., Simons, A., Niehaves, B., Riemer, K., Plattfaut, R., Cleven, A.: Reconstructing the giant: on the importance of rigour in documenting the literature search process. In: ECIS, pp. 2206–2217 (2009)

43. Myers, M.D., Newman, M.: The qualitative interview in IS research: examining the craft. Inf. Organ. **17**(1), 2–26 (2007). https://doi.org/10.1016/j.infoandorg.2006.11.001

Users' Knowledge and Motivation on Using Cryptocurrency

Omar Alqaryouti[1(✉)] , Nur Siyam[1] , Zainab Alkashri[1] ,
and Khaled Shaalan[1,2]

[1] The British University in Dubai, Dubai, United Arab Emirates
omar.alqaryouti@gmail.com, nur.siyam@gmail.com,
zainabalkashri@gmail.com, khaled.shaalan@buid.ac.ae
[2] School of Informatics, University of Edinburgh, Edinburgh, UK

Abstract. Cryptocurrency is a decentralized digital currency stored in an online form that does not fall under governments and banks control. This study aimed at understanding users' knowledge and their motivation on using cryptocurrency through structured interviews. Data was gathered through in- person interviews with three participants (n = 3). The analysis of the interviews indicated that (1) most participants have a clear understanding of cryptocurrency nature, albite some misconceptions, (2) most participants were able to explain technical aspects of cryptocurrency such as mining and market cap, (3) main uses of cryptocurrency according to participants were investment and currency, (4) perceived benefits of cryptocurrency are decentralization, security, anonymity, ease of use, and low fees, (5) perceived disadvantages were cryptocurrency not being recognized everywhere. Finally, (6) all participants planned to continue using cryptocurrency in the future. Although the number of participants was small, this research can be considered as a pilot study for future research aiming at understanding cryptocurrency users' behaviour.

Keywords: Cryptocurrency · Bitcoin · Cryptocurrency Users' Knowledge · Technology Acceptance Model (TAM) · Cryptocurrency Risks · Cryptocurrency Benefits

1   Introduction

Nowadays, cryptocurrency domain is attracting a lot of interest. Cryptocurrency is a decentralized digital currency stored in an online form that does not fall under governments and banks control, which was proposed in an attempt to replace the fiat currency. In 1983, Chaum had proposed the electronic cash [1]. However, this proposal was not implemented as it required the adoption from banks. In 2009, the first cryptocurrency was suggested, called bitcoin, which depended on the mass work of a distributed peer-to-peer network to maintain and record all of the transactions in a public ledger [2–4]. Through peer-to-peer network, the transactions occur without any central repository. Bitcoin is a virtual currency; in its network the nodes are anonymous. Creating new cryptocurrencies, also known as Cryptocurrency Mining, is the process where users present their computing power for payments verification and recording in the public ledger [5].

© Springer Nature Switzerland AG 2020
M. Themistocleous and M. Papadaki (Eds.): EMCIS 2019, LNBIP 381, pp. 113–122, 2020.
https://doi.org/10.1007/978-3-030-44322-1_9

Blockchain is the underlying technology for cryptocurrencies. Blockchain technology is an ingenious framework that can potentially transform transactions and change completely the interaction mechanism in doing business. These transactions are known as blocks, hence the name blockchains. Blockchain enables the transactions recording through a distributed database structure in a protected and secured ledger using the hashing power. Therefore, the transactions are permanent, unchangeable and anonymous [6]. Just like any other currency market, the cryptocurrency value changes and can be affected by the economy and policy changes. Cryptocurrencies are saved in the blocks. Each transaction is recorded in a block with an associated encrypted permanent time stamp and distributed across the blockchain through the publicly distributed and decentralized ledger. All transaction details are saved in a block from A to Z, containing all the information, making the system trustworthy to other users [7].

As illustrated in Fig. 1, using digital currencies have lots of benefits. These incorporate nonattendance of a focal authority, unknown participants, fast settlement of transactions and minimized transaction fees that empower micropayments [3]. Digital currencies have been plagued by the double spending problem (DSP), which intends using the same unit for money many times. The data on drive is the representation of money; yet, this information could be replicated when transferring the proprietorship. This issue is solved by bitcoin when the participants agree on the public ledger of the history of movements of money that occurs between the users. Many biased people can agree on improper histories in order to take the control over the systems, so the agreement on public ledger is not secure enough. Bitcoin avoids this by requiring

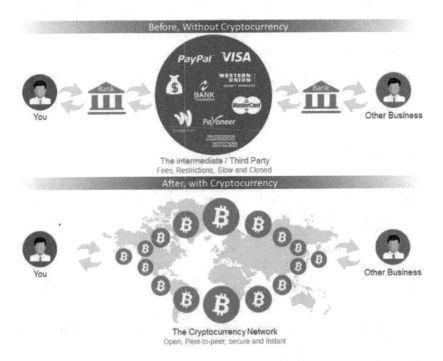

Fig. 1. Traditional versus Cryptocurrency

individuals to fix computational issues to record on the blockchain [4]. When there is no adopter to the process, the bitcoin will get almost zero transactions, since there is no method to move money between the accounts. By taking off all the identifying signs and resembling participants by transactions the privacy will exist [8]. Cryptocurrencies solve the DSP, uncover cheating out of public avouch, has a near-zero transaction fees, and has the ability with the public authentications to detect frauds [8].

Cryptocurrency mining is an important element in the cryptocurrency network which is available to the public [5]. Miners are the individuals who collect the blocks while mining is the process of resolving the computational problem. The process of mining requires electricity, heating, and bandwidth. Miners are paid off for their work by bitcoins. The aim of mining is to create new bitcoins to run them into the currency. Special hardware is required for the mining process. Hashes are used to identify the amount of individual computations that would happen in a minute. The aggravator bitcoin system needs cumulative computational control added substance about all of mining labour worker around the globe [4].

Marketing Capitalization (Market Cap) is a popular standard for traditional securities, having sole inferences in crypto. As such, market cap in most of cases is made of multiplying the quantity of the prominent stock shares by the price of the current one. When a coin has 100 tokens prominent and exchanging for $10 a coin, it will have a market cap of $1000. Habitually, financial system of measurements and proportions analyses the stocks and bonds. But there are no financial statements published by the crypto. The top five cryptocurrencies include: Bitcoin which is the first at $94 billion, Ethereum which is the second-biggest, at $32 billion, Ripple at $10 billion, Bitcoin cash at $5 billion, and Litecoin at $3 billion [9].

A transaction is a message that is sent by someone in order to transfer money. The elements of the basic transaction are: numbers of bitcoins to send, the address of the receiver of bitcoins, and a private key used for signing in and verifying the transaction. The addresses cannot be used again in bitcoin. Coinbase, BitPay, and Bitstamp are examples of online bitcoin sites to help in managing bitcoin wallets and making the conversions into fiat currencies easier [4]. Mining is not the only way to gain bitcoins. Exchanging can happen between the bitcoins and national currencies, or even in between the products and services. A free 'wallet' software is available to allow participants to use their cryptocurrencies [5]. A 'wallet' keeps the users updated with every move through their accounts. Moreover, private and public keys are stored in the wallet [10].

The importance of this study comes from the notion that cryptocurrencies are not yet regulated by governments and users are vulnerable to theft and fraud. Thus, users' knowledge of cryptocurrencies dynamics and the associated benefits and risks of using it are of utmost importance to protect them.

This study aims to answer the following questions regarding users' knowledge of Cryptocurrency an its perceived usefulness:

1. What is the users' knowledge of Cryptocurrency?
2. What is the perceived usefulness of using Cryptocurrency?

2 Literature Review

As bitcoin first appeared in 2009, many researches were carried concerning cryptocurrency and blockchain. However, the patterns of cryptocurrency usage and the ways blockchain characteristics impacts users' trust is still understudied [11].

Many preceding studies that aimed at understanding the patterns of cryptocurrency usage studied the ways people get to know about bitcoin, and what is their perception about it. Consequently, with the advanced technical streams of research, researchers are keener on studying cryptocurrency users characteristics and motivation [3]. For instance, Maurer et al. [12] formed an anthropological view of cryptocurrency users, opposing the notion that cryptocurrency will be capable of addressing regulations, privacy and equity issues. Bohr and Bashir [13] studied the culture of cryptocurrency users, finding that some demographic features affected the usage patterns of cryptocurrency. Similarly, Yelowitz and Wilson [14] found that users who were interested in cryptocurrency usage were also interested in computer programming or illegal activities.

Christopher [15] studied the reasons behind cryptocurrency use. Speculation, algorithmic trust, spending power and money laundering were four reasons that motivated the people to use cryptocurrency. Christopher argues that spending power in cryptocurrency is related to the deflation concept. When the supply of new bitcoins decreases, the worth of spending power will increase. Similarly, Khairuddin et al. [16] found that the factors that impact user's motivation are: a role in monetary revolution and user empowerment and perception of real value.

Gao et al. [4] pointed out that some users misunderstood the real functions of Bitcoin. The study also found similar results as in Christopher [15] and Khairuddin et al. [16] regarding user motivation. Glaser et al. [17] differed from the others, as he drew attention to the specific use of cryptocurrency in exchanging currency. He found that the new users and the informed ones exchanged fiat currency to digital currency for speculating payments.

3 Theoretical Background

We use the technology acceptance model (TAM) framework to analyse the aspects of the technology acceptance process in the case of cryptocurrency. TAM, which was first developed by Davis in 1989 [18], is considered an important tool to understand the process of technology adoption. Even though situations particulars affect the experimental support of the model, it remains a useful tool to understand the factors that impact technology adoption or rejection [19]. According to TAM, the two basic principles that speculate the adoption of a particular technology are perceived ease of use and perceived usefulness by the user. Perceived ease of use can be defined as the extent to which the user believes that using a particular technology will be effortless. This also includes user's perceived knowledge on how to operate or use that technology. On the other hand, perceived usefulness can be defined as the user's belief on how the intended technology will impact his/her job performance [20].

In this research, we are concerned with two specific factors from the TAM model; user's knowledge on cryptocurrency, and therefore its perceived ease of use, and user's motivation for using cryptocurrency, and hence, its perceived usefulness. Figure 2 shows how user's knowledge and motivation impact perceived ease of use and usefulness respectively.

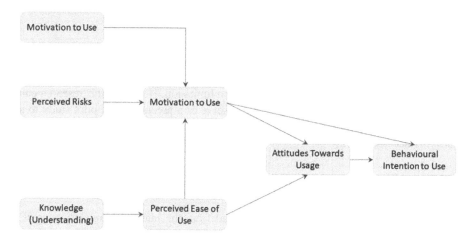

Fig. 2. User's knowledge and motivation impact perceived ease of use and usefulness

4   Methodology

This study follows a case study approach that employs qualitative data using interviews to gain insights on users' knowledge regarding cryptocurrency and their perceived usefulness. Case studies are best suited for exploratory and descriptive research. Moreover, case studies can be used to examine the reasons behind a particular phenomenon in its real-life context after formulating a theoretical background [21].

Data was gathered through in-person interviews with three participants (N = 3). Purposeful sampling was used since this study is concerned about frequent cryptocurrency users [22]. All participants were males, Arabs, and lived and worked in the United Arab Emirates. We refer to each participant as (Participant A, B, and C) to maintain anonymity. Table 1 shows the demographic information of the study participants.

Interview questions aimed at exploring users' knowledge on cryptocurrency aspects such as cryptocurrency mining, market cap, and wallet. Interview procedures were prewritten to insure consistency among all interviews. Each interview lasted about 20 min. Interviews were held and recorded after obtaining participants consents. The recordings were later transcribed and used for data coding using a computer assisted qualitative analysis program. Personal data was removed from transcripts to ensure participants confidentiality and preservation of privacy rights [23]. Transcripts were first thoroughly read to gain general insights on emerging themes. Interview data was then classified into codes that were predetermined by the research questions and sub-codes that emerged from the interviews.

Table 1. Participants demographic data

Participant	Age	Nationality	Education	Occupation	Years using cryptocurrency
Participant A	38	Soudanes	Computer Engineering	Business Intelligence Specialist	1.5
Participant B	40	Egyptian	Computer Science	Technology Architect Business	2
Participant C	32	Palestinian	Industrial Engineering	Improvement Analyst	2

The sample size of this study is considered a limitation. However, this research can be used as an exploratory case study that can serve as a precursor or a pilot study to a large-scale project. Exploratory case studies aim at identifying whether further investigation is necessary [22].

5 Analysis of Findings

This section presents the findings that emerged from the interviews regarding users' knowledge of cryptocurrency and their motivation to use it.

First, participants were asked to describe what cryptocurrency means. All the participants displayed a general understanding of the concept. Their answers varied between cryptocurrency being and encrypted currency and a blockchain token. For example, participant C said cryptocurrency is "*a digital currency used to monetize block chain transactions*". However, none of the participants were able to explain the cryptocurrency protocol or to verify the legitimacy of it. When asked about cryptocurrency mining, participants were able to give detailed answers. For example, participants B and C pointed out that mining involves solving algorithmic equations that solve a "hash" problem. Whoever solves this algorithm first, becomes the owner of that block. Moreover, participants B and C stated that mining is a way of validating blockchain transactions. Participants A and C maintained that mining requires a state-of-the art machines and a lot of energy power. Participants were also able to explain the meaning of market cap and how it is associated with the stability of cryptocurrency value, as participant C states "*The higher the market cap indicates cryptocurrency stability and trading volume*". Finally, all participants defined the cryptocurrency wallet as a digital wallet that can store your crypto assets. Participant B added that the wallet should be secured and connected to the currency blockchain. Participant C further elaborated by listing some types of wallets, "*There are many types of wallets such as online, like instant web-based wallets, and offline like Cold Storage USB from Nano ledger, and algorithm-based wallets among others*". Figure 3 shows the codes that emerged from the "User Understanding" theme.

When asked about the uses of cryptocurrency, all users said that it can be used for e-commerce or as an investment. For example, participant A said "*I have decided to invest some amount to make some profit*". Participant B said "*It can be used for trading and ecommerce websites for replacing currencies*". Participant A added that cryptocurrency can be used for currency exchange, "*I can buy and sell digital currencies online*". Figure 4 shows the emerging codes from the "Cryptocurrency Uses" theme.

All participants believed that cryptocurrency has a lot of benefits. For example, all participants considered the decentralization of cryptocurrency as one of the most important characteristics, "*banks are not involved in the transactions since it is peer to peer transactions with no middle party*". Participants A and B said cryptocurrency transactions are secured and anonymous. They also pointed out that it is easy to use. Participants B and C also considered fast transactions as a benefit, "*It saves my time because of its flexibility*". Lastly, participant B maintained that cryptocurrency gives you full control over your account, in addition to the low fees it requires. Figure 5 shows the emerging codes from the "Cryptocurrency Benefits" theme. On the other hand, participant B pointed out that one disadvantage of using cryptocurrency is that it is not recognized everywhere yet.

Lastly, all participants were positive when asked whether they intend on continuing using cryptocurrency in the future, "*Yes of course. The crypto currency is the future of the currency because it allows the individual to easily control and transfer their wealth without high bank fees or government control*".

Fig. 3. Emerging codes for "User Understanding" theme

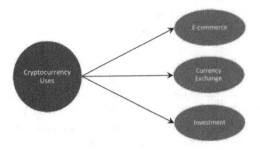

Fig. 4. Emerging codes for "Cryptocurrencies Uses" theme

6 Discussion

This section provides a discussion of the findings, which can be summarized as follows: (1) most participants have a clear understanding of cryptocurrency nature, albite some misconceptions, (2) most participants were able to explain technical aspects of cryptocurrency such as mining and market cap, (3) uses of cryptocurrency according to participants were investment and currency, (4) perceived benefits of cryptocurrency are decentralization, security, anonymity, ease of use, and low fees, (5) perceived disadvantages were cryptocurrency not being recognized everywhere, and (6) all participants planned to continue using cryptocurrency in the future.

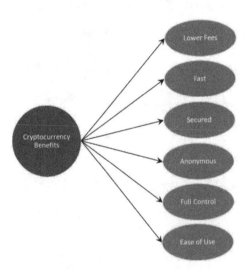

Fig. 5. Emerging codes for "Cryptocurrencies Benefits" theme

Even though participants were confident about their understanding of cryptocurrency, they were not able to explain the mechanism of its transfer protocol. However, this did not affect their ability to use cryptocurrency regularly, as both a currency and investment, which coincides with previous studies [4]. Moreover, participants were able to demonstrate technical understanding of cryptocurrency mining, wallet and market cap.

However, the participants had several misconceptions regarding security and privacy issues of cryptocurrency. Participants perception of having control over the transactions resulted in them being unconcerned about their privacy when using cryptocurrency. However, it has been proven that transactions are not fully anonymous. For instance, wallet clustering and network traffic are methods that can be used to track transactions on the blockchain. Moreover, there are no security procedures built into cryptocurrency protocol that prevent fraud or wrong transactions, which are the main characteristics of credit and debit cards [24]. Our participants were unaware of these issues, despite many examples of cryptocurrency fraud circulating in the media. Participants were right regarding the advantage of using cryptocurrency without having a third -party that may store personal information. However, anonymity may play as a double-faced sword as illegal transactions and theft might be easy to perform.

Even though the participants stated they will continue using cryptocurrency, one major disadvantage that bothered them was its low adoption rate. This problem is due to cryptocurrency failing to fit the needs of the general population [4]. Credits cards are easily used for online transactions, and cash is accepted everywhere. So even though cryptocurrency have some advantages over other payment methods such as its low fees and decentralization, it is still not fit for day-to-day transactions.

7   Conclusion

This paper aimed at studying users' perceptions on cryptocurrency uses. It also aimed at exploring the perceived benefits and risks on using cryptocurrency. Even though the number of participants was small (n = 3), this research can be considered as a pilot study for future research aiming at understanding cryptocurrency users' behaviour. As for any new technology, future research can consider investigating the reasons people choose to adopt or not to adopt cryptocurrencies. If cryptocurrency will become a widely used form of payment, it is critical to ensure that its users are aware of the privacy and security issues involved with the use of such method.

References

1. Chaum, D.: Blind signatures for untraceable payments. In: Chaum, D., Rivest, Ronald L., Sherman, Alan T. (eds.) Advances in Cryptology, pp. 199–203. Springer, Boston (1983). https://doi.org/10.1007/978-1-4757-0602-4_18
2. Nakamoto, S.: Bitcoin: A peer-to-peer electronic cash system (2008). http://bitcoin.org/bitcoin.pdf
3. Kazerani, A., Rosati, D., Lesser, B.: Determining the usability of bitcoin for beginners using change tip and coinbase. In: Proceedings of the 35th ACM International Conference on the Design of Communication, New York, NY, USA, pp. 5:1–5:5 (2017)

4. Gao, X., Clark, G.D., Lindqvist, J.: Of two minds, multiple addresses, and one ledger: characterizing opinions, knowledge, and perceptions of bitcoin across users and non-users. In: Proceedings of the 2016 CHI Conference on Human Factors in Computing Systems, New York, NY, USA, pp. 1656–1668 (2016)
5. Hayes, A.S.: Cryptocurrency value formation: an empirical study leading to a cost of production model for valuing bitcoin. Telematics Inform. **34**(7), 1308–1321 (2017)
6. Alqaryouti, O., Shaalan, K.: Trade facilitation framework for E-commerce platforms using blockchain. Int. J. Bus. Inf. Syst. (in press)
7. Gainsbury, S.M., Blaszczynski, A.: How blockchain and cryptocurrency technology could revolutionize online gambling. Gaming Law Rev. **21**(7), 482–492 (2017)
8. Van Alstyne, M.: Why bitcoin has value. Commun. ACM **57**(5), 30–32 (2014)
9. Coinist: Understanding Cryptocurrency Market Cap (2019). https://www.coinist.io/cryptocurrency-market-cap/. Accessed 06 Nov 2019
10. Blockgeeks: Cryptocurrency Wallet Guide: A Step-By-Step Tutorial. Blockgeeks, 27 February 2017. https://blockgeeks.com/guides/cryptocurrency-wallet-guide/. Accessed 06 Nov 2019
11. Sas, C., Khairuddin, I.E.: Design for trust: an exploration of the challenges and opportunities of bitcoin users. In: Proceedings of the 2017 CHI Conference on Human Factors in Computing Systems, New York, NY, USA, pp. 6499–6510 (2017)
12. Maurer, B., Nelms, T.C., Swartz, L.: 'When perhaps the real problem is money itself!': the practical materiality of bitcoin. Soc. Semiot. **23**(2), 261–277 (2013)
13. Bohr, J., Bashir, M.: Who uses bitcoin? An exploration of the bitcoin community. In: 2014 Twelfth Annual International Conference on Privacy, Security and Trust, pp. 94–101 (2014)
14. Yelowitz, A., Wilson, M.: Characteristics of bitcoin users: an analysis of Google search data. Appl. Econ. Lett. **22**(13), 1030–1036 (2015)
15. Christopher, C.M.: Why on earth do people use bitcoin? Bus. Bankruptcy Law J. **2**, 1 (2014, 2015)
16. Khairuddin, I.E., Sas, C., Clinch, S., Davies, N.: Exploring motivations for bitcoin technology usage. In: Proceedings of the 2016 CHI Conference Extended Abstracts on Human Factors in Computing Systems, New York, NY, USA, pp. 2872–2878 (2016)
17. Glaser, F., Zimmermann, K., Haferkorn, M., Weber, M. C., Siering, M.: Bitcoin - Asset or Currency? Revealing Users' Hidden Intentions, Social Science Research Network, Rochester, NY, SSRN Scholarly Paper ID 2425247, April 2014
18. Davis, F.D., Bagozzi, R.P., Warshaw, P.R.: User acceptance of computer technology: a comparison of two theoretical models. Manage. Sci. **35**(8), 982–1003 (1989)
19. Siyam, N.: Factors impacting special education teachers' acceptance and actual use of technology. Educ. Inf. Technol. **24**(3), 2035–2057 (2019). https://doi.org/10.1007/s10639-018-09859-y
20. Folkinshteyn, D., Lennon, M.: Braving bitcoin: a technology acceptance model (TAM) analysis. J. Inf. Technol. Case Appl. Res. **18**(4), 220–249 (2016)
21. Yin, R.K.: Applications of Case Study Research. SAGE, Thousand Oaks (2012)
22. Cooper, D.R., Schindler, P.: Business Research Methods. McGraw-Hill Education, New York (2013)
23. Creswell, W.: Educational Research: Planning, Conducting, and Evaluating Quantitative and Qualitative Research, Enhanced Pearson eText with Loose- Leaf Version–Access Card Package, 5th edn. Pearson Education, Inc., New Jersey (2015)
24. Vyas, C.A., Lunagaria, M.: Security concerns and issues for bitcoin. In: IJCA Proceedings on National Conference Cum Workshop on Bioinformatics and Computational Biology, NCWBCB, vol. 2, pp. 10–12, May 2014

Cryptocurrency Usage Impact on Perceived Benefits and Users' Behaviour

Omar Alqaryouti[1](✉) , Nur Siyam[1] , Zainab Alkashri[1] ,
and Khaled Shaalan[1,2]

[1] The British University in Dubai, Dubai, United Arab Emirates
`omar.alqaryouti@gmail.com, nur.siyam@gmail.com,`
`zainabalkashri@gmail.com, khaled.shaalan@buid.ac.ae`
[2] School of Informatics, University of Edinburgh, Edinburgh, UK

Abstract. This paper aims to analyse the impact of Cryptocurrency usage on users' perceived benefits and behaviour. The Technology Acceptance Model has been used as foundation for this research. In this study, three main factors were examined, namely perceived ease of use, perceived benefits, and usage behaviour. To measure the impact of these factors, a quantitative methodology using surveys is adopted. Twenty-Five (n = 25) specialized individuals in the area of cryptocurrency participated in the electronic survey. The results indicate a positive relationship between perceived ease of use and usage behaviour. Surprisingly, no significant relationship between the perceived benefit in cryptocurrency and usage behaviour was found. In addition, there is no significant relationship between the Perceived Benefit in cryptocurrency and Usage Behaviour. These results indicate the need for further investigation of the factors that influence the usage of cryptocurrency.

Keywords: Cryptocurrency · Cryptocurrency usage · Digital currency · Technology Acceptance Model (TAM) · Cryptocurrency benefits · Cryptocurrency behaviour

1 Introduction

The rapid spread of e-commerce using the Internet and smart phone technology has led to the evolvement of many innovative technologies in the field of secure payment systems [1]. As a result of this evolvement, there has been a need to invent digital currencies that often use technological capabilities that secure digital transactions without the involvement of a central register. These technological capabilities facilitate the peer-to-peer transactions without a central clearing intermediate party. This leads to enhancing the financial efficiency while minimizing the transaction time and cost, particularly across borders. These capabilities have strategically the potential to expand financial coverage through providing cost-effective and secure payment options.

With the development of the Blockchain technology, a new payment method in the form of digital currency had emerged. Cryptocurrency represents the transfer of funds from one individual to another without a financial intermediary between them. Cryptocurrency transactions are performed through encrypted network [2].

© Springer Nature Switzerland AG 2020
M. Themistocleous and M. Papadaki (Eds.): EMCIS 2019, LNBIP 381, pp. 123–136, 2020.
https://doi.org/10.1007/978-3-030-44322-1_10

Cryptocurrency can be defined from a technical perspective as an electronic currency that depends on cryptography scheme [3]. It works in a decentralized network in which the nodes are synchronized to keep the transactions verified and controlled. The encrypted currency Cryptocurrency is safe and provides a level of anonymity, and transactions cannot be synchronized inversed or faked. In addition, cryptocurrency does not need high fees for conversion, even when sent to the farthest place in the world.

This makes Cryptocurrency more reliable than the conventional currency, available to all, and cannot be controlled or observed by any one even governments [4–6].

The digital currencies technological revolution will change the form of funds in this world, and will affect the world's largest and most important financial institutions through changing their mode of operation. Despite all these advantages, the digital currencies raised the fear and doubtfulness of some individuals.

Since a few years ago, digital currencies were not known outside the online video game community, but today they are far beyond. Digital currency offers customers a new option for payment and stimulates large investments in payment technology that has the potential to create new options for customers and investors in the future. However, there is a lack of research in regards to the factors that influence the cryptocurrency users' adoption of the technology. Therefore, this research aims to determine the factors that impact cryptocurrency users' adoption as well as the factors that impact their perception.

The cryptocurrency is dependent on three main correlated elements: the users (individuals), the miners and the blockchain [7]. The blockchain technology offers various advantages [8, 9]. In 2009, Bitcoin was first introduced as the first encrypted digital currency. Bitcoin helped in the appearance of the term "Cryptocurrency". Bitcoin is the most famous among other digital currencies so far. The encrypted digital currency is a form of money that has been designed digitally to be secured and unknown to the exchange parties [10].

The objective of this study is to analyse the impact of the usage of Cryptocurrency on perceived benefits and users' behaviour. In this regard, a questionnaire was designed and developed to understand the user's perceptions according to the factors that impact their perception.

The remainder of this paper is structured as follows. Section 2 provides a summary of the related work according to the literature. Sections 3 and 4 provide details on the constructed conceptual framework and research model, the research questions and the formulated hypotheses. The research methodology and the approach followed are discussed in Sect. 5 followed by the questionnaire design in Sect. 6. In Sect. 7, the data analysis and empirical results are presented. The key findings and the results of testing the hypotheses are presented in Sect. 8. Then, a discussion of the research implications and how it relates to the literature. The last section provides a conclusion of this study and future research prospects.

2 Related Work

As bitcoin first appeared in 2009, many researches were done concerning cryptocurrency and blockchain. However, the patterns of cryptocurrency usage and the ways blockchain characteristics impact users' trust is still understudied [11]. The digital currency is the balance of money electronically recorded on a stored value card or other electronic intermediary or stored on electronic networks, allowing the transfer of value over the Internet. Digital currency can be obtained, stored, accessed, and handled electronically. Also, it can be used for various aims, as long as the deal is approved by the parties [3].

The emergence of cryptocurrency was overshadowed by online banking and other virtual currency concepts. The problem of exchanging money between peers, without a third party, and through a secured network was first solved in 2008 when an anonymous programmer or group of anonymous programmers named Satoshi Nakamoto came up with a paper introducing the soon-to-be-popular virtual currency Bitcoin. The Bitcoin remains the flag bearer for cryptocurrencies because it was able to solve the recurrent problems surrounding digital currencies, such as the problem of Trust and Double-spending [12–14]. Also, Bitcoin has become famous because of its four advantages: conversion speed, low cost, privacy and decentralization [6].

Digital currency offers customers a new option for payment and stimulates large investments in payment technology. However, the current limited regulation and control of the digital currency market and transactions in digital currency means that traders and investors who pay or keep a virtual currency are at high risk [7].

Despite the convenience of Bitcoins guaranteeing a higher level of anonymity, its reputation was soiled when it was misused in suspicious and criminal activities such as trading with drugs, money laundering, illegal activities have shaken the credibility of cryptocurrencies [15].

Few studies aimed at exploring the factors that impact the usage of cryptocurrency. For instance, Abramova and Böhme [16] explored the factors that impact the usage of bitcoin. The authors have used Technology Acceptance Model (TAM) and theories from literature as the framework for their experiment. Moreover, an integration between numerous benefits and risks towards Bitcoin usage to formulate the research constructs.

TAM is a most well-known model used to justify the reason why the users adopted a wide range of new technologies. Also, it is the theory of information systems that describes the way users may accept technologies and use it. The model proposes that when new technology is introduced to users, there are a set of elements that impact their opinions about when and how they can use it [16, 17].

3 Theoretical Background

With regard to the behaviour of individuals towards computer technology, there are currently many theoretical models used to study their acceptance of and use of technology, and although many of these models exist, the TAM for (Davis [18]) remains the most commonly used one [19].

The TAM, which was built based on the theory of justified action, was designed to determine the user acceptance of information systems by limiting the determinants of this acceptance, and to interpret the behaviour of users from different societies towards different types of computer applications. The TAM touches the internal psychological and external variables of individuals, in which a large number of these variables affect the acceptance of computer technology by individuals. This model attempts to provide the basis for tracking the effects of these factors in regards of the internal beliefs of individuals about their use of computer technology, trends of individuals towards the use of computer technology, intentions of individuals to use computer technology, and actual uses of computer technology by individuals [18].

TAM refers to two factors closely related to the individual acceptance behaviour of computer technology: the individual perception factor for computer technology, and the individual perception factor for the ease of use of computer technology. The ease-of-use factor is defined as the degree to which an individual is expected to be free to use computer technology. The interest-rate factor is defined as the degree to which an individual anticipates the likelihood that his use of computer technology will improve his performance [20].

The model assumes that these factors determine together the direction of the individual to use computer technology, and that they are both affected by a set of external factors for the individual. The model also assumes that there is an impact of the user-perception factor in the interest-rate factor. The model assumes that the individual's tendency towards computer technology and the factor of interest recognition together determine an individual's intention to use computer technology because the individual is usually intent on carrying out a positive behaviour. The model also assumes that the intention of the individual to use computer technology determines their actual use [18].

4   Research Questions and Hypothesis

This study seeks to answer the following three questions:

- **Research Question 1 (RQ1):** Is there a relationship between the perceived ease of use and users' behaviour in Cryptocurrency transactions?
- **Research Question 2 (RQ2):** Is there a relationship between the perceived ease of use and perceived benefits of Cryptocurrency?
- **Research Question 3 (RQ3):** Is there a relationship between the perceived benefit in cryptocurrency and usage behaviour?

In this research, we are concerned with two specific factors from the TAM; user's perceived ease of use of cryptocurrency, and perceived benefits represented by Transaction processing, security and control, and decentralization. This research studies the impact of these several factors in usage intended behaviour. Figure 1 shows the research conceptual framework which represents the foundation in which the hypotheses were formulated.

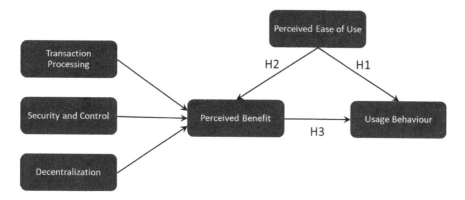

Fig. 1. Research conceptual framework

Through the problem of the study and its questions, the study tries to test the validity of the following hypotheses:

- **Hypothesis 1 (H1):** There is a significant relationship between the perceived ease of use and users' behaviour in Cryptocurrency transactions.
- **Hypothesis 2 (H2):** There is a significant relationship between the perceived ease of use and perceived benefits of Cryptocurrency.
- **Hypothesis 3 (H3):** There is a significant relationship between the perceived benefit in cryptocurrency and usage behaviour.

5   Research Methodology

The main objective of this study is to analyse the impact of use Cryptocurrency on perceived benefits and users' behaviour. To achieve this objective, the current study uses quantitative method through survey. The survey approach is considered most suitable for testing theories when it comes to testing and verifying the quantified description of perceptions for participants [21].

In this research, a purposeful sample was selected. The purposeful sample ensures that particular groups within the target population are sufficiently represented through the sample. The sample of this study was selected from specialized individuals who use Cryptocurrency, where the sample size is ($n = 25$) individuals.

6   Questionnaire Design

Questionnaire responses are summarized and described based on defined variables of the current study, as shown in Tables 2, 3, and 4 for the three main variables of the study: Perceived Benefit, Perceived Ease of Use, and Usage Behaviour, respectively. Each variable represents a questionnaire construct that is measured by a number of items that are measured on a five-point Likert scale.

The questionnaire of this study was adopted from Abramova and Böhme [16] and was re-designed and developed to suite the objective of this study. The questionnaire consists of 19 questions falling under 3 main constructs in addition to the demographic questions. The first construct is the "Perceived Benefit" which consists of 3 sub-constructs, namely; Transactions Processing, Security and Control, and Decentraliza-tion. There are 4 questions under Transaction Processing, 2 questions under Security and Control, and 3 questions under Decentralization. The second construct is "Per-ceived Ease of Use" which consists of 5 questions. Each of these questions in the first two constructs are assigned with a 5-point Likert scale ranging from "Strongly Agree" (5) for full agreement to "Strongly Disagree" (1) for full disagreement for the question or argument. The third construct is Usage Behaviour which consists of 5 questions. Each of these questions are assigned with five-point Likert scale ranging from "Never" (1) for not using cryptocurrency to "All the time" (5). The demographic questions consist of three elements including gender, age, education level, and the number of years the participant has used cryptocurrency. The questionnaire was developed using Google Forms and the participants were asked to answer the questions through the online form link.

Reliability Analysis

Reliability refers to the consistency of the results obtained concerning the extent to which the research instrument produces the same findings when repeated [22]. The most popular approach to measure the internal consistency reliability for a set of items is the Cronbach's alpha coefficient, a. The values of Cronbach's alpha range from 0 to 1. In the social sciences, a with values greater than or equal to 0.7 are considered to be desirable [23].

Reliability analysis of the current study constructs revealed that the constructs have acceptable reliability. Perceived Benefit had a Cronbach's alpha of 0.816 based on nine items set, which is very good. Perceived Ease of Use had Cronbach's alpha of 0.617 based on five items set, while Usage Behaviour had a Cronbach's alpha of 0.858, which are acceptable levels of reliability. Reliability statistics for constructs and sub-constructs are reported in Table 1.

Table 1. Reliability statistics

Construct	No. of items	Cronbach's alpha	Mean	SD
Perceived benefit	9	.816	4.17	.532
Transaction processing	4	.819	4.22	.798
Security and control	2	.055	3.98	.603
Decentralization	3	.617	4.32	.573
Perceived ease of use	5	.634	3.46	.585
Usage behaviour	5	.858	2.10	.878

7 Data Analysis

In this section, data are described and summarized in tables and graphs to best represent the sample characteristics and responses. Sample characteristics are described and summarized using four personal background variables: gender, age, education, and number of years using cryptocurrency. Data obtained from participants responses are described and summarized by frequencies, percentages, means, and standard deviations. Questionnaire responses are summarized and described based on defined variables of the current study, as shown in Sects. 7.2, 7.3 and 7.4 for the three main variables of the study: Perceived Benefit, Perceived Ease of Use, and Usage Behaviour, respectively. Each variable represents a questionnaire construct that is measured by a number of items that are measured on a five-point Likert scale.

7.1 Personal Background

Based on descriptive analysis reported in Table 2, the majority of the sample are males representing 84% of the total number of participants. The majority of participants are under 39 years, representing 68% of the whole sample. Also, 28% of the sample are middle aged, while only one participant is 59 years or older. The sample is well educated, 60% hold bachelor degrees, and 28% hold Master's degrees and two participants hold PhDs. Also, the majority of respondents have been using cryptocurrency for less than one year, representing 64% of the sample, and 32% have been using it for 1 to 2 years. Personal background data are summarized in Table 2, broken down by each variable category.

Table 2. Descriptive statistics of personal background (N = 25)

Personal background		Frequency	Percentage
Gender	Male	21	84.00%
	Female	4	16.00%
Age	18–28	2	8.00%
	29–38	15	60.00%
	39–48	7	28.00%
	59 or more	1	4.00%
Education	High School	1	4.00%
	Bachelor	15	60.00%
	Master	7	28.00%
	PhD	2	8.00%
How long have you been using Cryptocurrency?	Less than 1 year	16	64.00%
	1 to 2 years	8	32.00%
	3 to 4 years	1	4.00%

7.2   Perceived Benefit

Perceived Benefit is the first construct in the questionnaire and is measured by three sub-constructs and nine items, all measured on a five-point Likert scale starting with score "1" for "Strongly Disagree" and ending with score "5" for "Strongly Agree". From the univariate analysis as shown in Table 3, it can be said that, on average, the majority of respondents gave high scores; either 4 or 5, to items measuring Perceived Benefit, represented by 83% of the sample, with a mean score of 4.17 and standard deviation of 0.531. Detailed statistics are reported in Table 3.

Transaction Processing and Decentralization had higher mean scores (M = 4.22 and M = 4.32, respectively) than Security and Control (M = 3.98). However, there is a general trend to score highly on all items measuring these sub-constructs as mean scores ranged between 3.84 and 4.44, indicating that the majority of participants tend to score around "4" for these items, which suggests tendency to "Agree" to these items' statements.

Table 3. Descriptive statistics for perceived benefit (N = 25)

Questionnaire variables	(1) Strongly Disagree	(3) Disagree	(3) Neutral	(4) Agree	(5) Strongly Agree	Mean	SD
Perceived benefit	3	9	26	89	98	4.17	.531
	1.33%	4.00%	11.56%	39.56%	43.56%		
Transaction processing	**3**	**4**	**10**	**34**	**49**	**4.22**	**.798**
	3.00%	**4.00%**	**10.00%**	**34.00%**	**49.00%**		
With Cryptocurrency, I can instantly transfer money	2	1	1	10	11	4.08	1.187
	8.00%	4.00%	4.00%	40.00%	44.00%		
With Cryptocurrency, I can transfer money worldwide	0	1	1	9	14	4.44	.768
	0.00%	4.00%	4.00%	36.00%	56.00%		
Cryptocurrency allows me to transfer money with cheaper transaction fees	1	0	5	3	16	4.32	1.069
	4.00%	0.00%	20.00%	12.00%	64.00%		
Cryptocurrency allows me to easily transact money	0	2	3	12	8	4.04	.889
	0.00%	8.00%	12.00%	48.00%	32.00%		
Security and control	**0**	**3**	**9**	**24**	**14**	**3.98**	**.603**
	0.00%	**6.00%**	**18.00%**	**48.00%**	**28.00%**		
Cryptocurrency allows me to transfer money securely	0	0	5	12	8	4.12	.726
	0.00%	0.00%	20.00%	48.00%	32.00%		
Cryptocurrency enables me to control my money	0	3	4	12	6	3.84	.943
	0.00%	12.00%	16.00%	48.00%	24.00%		
Decentralization	**0**	**2**	**7**	**31**	**35**	**4.32**	**.573**
	0.00%	**2.67%**	**9.33%**	**41.33%**	**46.67%**		
Cryptocurrency decentralization enables me to do transactions faster	0	1	3	10	11	4.24	.831
	0.00%	4.00%	12.00%	40.00%	44.00%		
With Cryptocurrency, I do not have to deal with any authority	0	1	2	11	11	4.28	.792
	0.00%	4.00%	8.00%	44.00%	44.00%		
When using Cryptocurrency, there is no central authority that has custody of my deposits	0	0	2	10	13	4.44	.651
	0.00%	0.00%	8.00%	40.00%	52.00%		

7.3   Perceived Ease of Use

This construct is measured by five items, as shown in Table 4. The fourth item was reversely recoded in order to match the flow of wording of other items. On average, about half of the sample gave high scores; either 4 or 5, to items measuring Perceived Ease of Use, represented by 52% of total participants, with a mean of 3.46 and a standard deviation of 0.585.

Mean scores of items ranged between 3.24 and 3.68, with the lowest value being for the item "I don't feel that it would be hard to gain advanced skills at using Cryptocurrency" and the highest value for the item "Learning how to use the Cryptocurrency is easy for me".

Table 4. Descriptive statistics for perceived ease of use (N = 25)

Questionnaire variables	(1) Strongly Disagree	(3) Disagree	(3) Neutral	(4) Agree	(5) Strongly Agree	Mean	SD
Perceived ease of use	5	19	35	57	9	3.46	.585
	4.00%	15.20%	28.00%	45.60%	7.20%		
Cryptocurrency is easy to use	1	2	5	15	2	3.60	.913
	4.00%	8.00%	20.00%	60.00%	8.00%		
Learning how to use the Cryptocurrency is easy for me	0	4	4	13	4	3.68	.945
	0.00%	16.00%	16.00%	52.00%	16.00%		
I can easily convert fiat money into Cryptocurrencies and vice versa	1	4	8	11	1	3.28	.936
	4.00%	16.00%	32.00%	44.00%	4.00%		
I don't feel that it would be hard to gain advanced skills at using Cryptocurrency	0	6	10	6	3	3.24	.970
	0.00%	24.00%	40.00%	24.00%	12.00%		
It is easy for me to get and learn new tools for Cryptocurrency	0	3	8	12	2	3.52	.823
	0.00%	12.00%	32.00%	48.00%	8.00%		

7.4   Usage Behaviour

Five items measured Usage Behaviour, shown in Table 5. With a mean of 2.10 and standard deviation of 0.878, respondents' usage is around "rarely". That is, 43% of the sample never used any of the cryptocurrency features, while 42% use them between rarely and sometimes, and 15% use them more often.

However, investigating each aspect of this construct, it can be observed that the most frequent aspect is using Cryptocurrency legitimate transactions as 32% of participants stated that they use it either "Often" or "All the time", while the least frequent aspect is using Cryptocurrency to make donations as only 4% of participants stated that they use Cryptocurrency "All the time" to make donations.

Table 5. Descriptive statistics for usage behaviour (N = 25)

Questionnaire variables	(1) Never	(2) Rarely	(3) Sometimes	(4) Often	(5) All the time	Mean	SD
Usage behaviour	54	26	26	16 .	3	2.10	.878
	43.20%	20.80%	20.80%	12.80%	2.40%		
How frequently do you use Cryptocurrency legitimate transactions?	3	5	9	6	2	2.96	1.136
	12.00%	20.00%	36.00%	24.00%	8.00%		
How frequently do you use Cryptocurrency to buy goods?	13	5	4	3	0	1.88	1.092
	52.00%	20.00%	16.00%	12.00%	0.00%		
How frequently do you use Cryptocurrency to buy online web services (software, digital goods, hosting, cloud computing, etc.)?	13	6	4	2	0	1.80	1.000
	52.00%	24.00%	16.00%	8.00%	0.00%		
How frequently do you use Cryptocurrency to make cross-border money transfers	12	3	5	5	0	2.12	1.236
	48.00%	12.00%	20.00%	20.00%	0.00%		
How frequently do you use Cryptocurrency to make donations	13	7	4	0	1	1.76	1.012
	52.00%	28.00%	16.00%	0.00%	4.00%		

7.5   Correlation Analysis

Correlation analysis is performed to measure the existence of significant relationships between each pair of variables in this study. Pearson's r correlation coefficients were calculated and reported in Table 6. The analysis revealed no significant correlation between Perceived Benefit and Perceived Ease of Use and between Perceived Benefit and Usage Behaviour as p-values exceeded 0.05. However, there was a significant correlation between Perceived Ease of Use and Usage Behaviour, r = 0.451 and p-value = 0.024. No significant correlation was found between Perceived Benefit and Usage Behaviour, r = −0.150 and p-value = 0.474.

More significant correlations were observed; namely, the relationships between the sub-constructs of Perceived Benefit Construct (Transaction Processing, Security and Control, and Decentralization) and the construct itself, and among the sub-constructs and each other. That is, there were significant positive strong relationship between each of the sub-constructs and the construct itself. Also, there were significant moderate positive relationships between Transaction Processing and Decentralization, and between Security and Control and Decentralization.

Table 6. Pearson's r correlation coefficients

		Transaction processing	Security and control	Decentralization	Perceived ease of use	Usage behaviour
Perceived benefit	Pearson correlation	.857[a]	.731[a]	.818[a]	.139	−.150
	Sig. (2-tailed)	.000	.000	.000	.507	.474
Transaction processing	Pearson correlation	1	.388	.584[a]	.223	−.168
	Sig. (2-tailed)		.055	.002	.284	.423
Security and control	Pearson correlation		1	.441[b]	−.055	−.098
	Sig. (2-tailed)			.027	.793	.641
Decentralization	Pearson correlation			1	.135	−.080
	Sig. (2-tailed)				.519	.704
Perceived ease of use	Pearson correlation				1	.451*
	Sig. (2-tailed)					.024

[a]Correlation is significant at the 0.01 level (2-tailed).
[b]Correlation is significant at the 0.05 level (2-tailed).

8 Findings

The findings of the research were tackled with regards to the research hypotheses. These hypotheses can be tested by performing the correlation analysis as they are investigating the relationships between pairs of the study variables; results of correlation analysis were previously reported in Table 6.

8.1 H1: There Is a Significant Relationship Between the Perceived Ease of Use and Users' Behaviour in Cryptocurrency Transactions

This hypothesis is supported by the correlation analysis results as, based on the results reported in Table 6, there is a significant relationship (at significance level of a = 0.05) between Perceived Ease of Use and users' behaviour in Cryptocurrency transactions, r = 0.451 with p-value = 0.024.

8.2 H2: There Is a Significant Relationship Between the Perceived Ease of Use and Perceived Benefits of Cryptocurrency

This hypothesis is not supported by results reported Table 5, as correlation of Perceived Ease of Use and Perceived Benefits was not statistically significant (at significance level of a = 0.05), r = 0.139 with p-value = 0.507. That is, there is no significant relationship between the Perceived Ease of Use and Perceived Benefits of Cryptocurrency.

8.3   H3: There Is a Significant Relationship Between the Perceived Benefit in Cryptocurrency and Usage Behaviour

This hypothesis is not supported by results reported in Table 5, as correlation of Perceived Benefits and Usage Behaviour was not statistically significant (at significance level of a = 0.05), r = −0.150 with p-value = 0.474. That is, there is no significant relationship between the Perceived Benefit in cryptocurrency and Usage Behaviour.

9   Discussion

In this research, two particular factors from the TAM were examined; user's perceived ease of use of cryptocurrency, and perceived benefits represented by Transaction processing, security and control, and decentralization. This research studies the impact of these several factors in usage intended behaviour. The figure below (Fig. 2) shows the research conceptual framework along with the hypothesis results assigned. TAM represents the foundation in which the research and the hypotheses were formulated.

The analysis of the questionnaire illustrated that participants have positive attitudes towards the use of cryptocurrency in general. This is evident from the mean scores for each construct being 3.24 and above according to Tables 3 and 4. However, participants usage behaviour was reported as relatively low with an average mean score of 2.1. These results may imply that even though users perceive cryptocurrency as beneficial and easy to use, they are still hesitant to use it as frequently as they intend to.

The hypothesis results reported different findings from Abramova and Böhme [16] in terms of the relationship between the perceived ease of use and perceived benefits as well as the perceived benefits and usage behaviour. This could be due to the limitation of the sample size and the context of the study. The research results did not agree with TAM in terms of ease of use impact on benefits. TAM is considered as an assumption that succeeds in many concepts and areas but did not fit in the cryptocurrency context for this research.

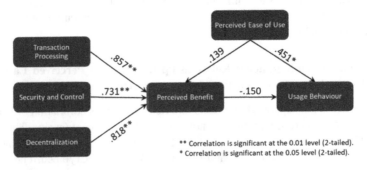

Fig. 2. Research results

10   Conclusion

This study aimed to analyse the impact of the usage of Cryptocurrency on perceived benefits and users' behaviour. TAM was selected as the foundation to formulate the hypotheses and two specific factors from the TAM were considered in cryptocurrency context, namely user's perceived ease of use, and perceived benefits. A total of 25 cryptocurrency users completed an electronic survey containing perceived benefit, perceived ease of use and usage behaviour.

The results indicate a positive relationship between perceived ease of use and usage behaviour. Surprisingly, no significant relationship between the perceived benefit in cryptocurrency and usage behaviour was found. In addition, there is no significant relationship between the perceived benefit in cryptocurrency and usage behaviour. As a conclusion, the participants usage behaviour was reported as relatively low. These results may imply that even though users perceive cryptocurrency as beneficial and easy to use, they are still hesitant to use it as frequently as they intend to. These results indicated the need for further investigation of the factors that influence the usage of cryptocurrency. Furthermore, the sample size might be considered a limitation and may make the results hard to generalize.

References

1. Baur, A.W., Bühler, J., Bick, M., Bonorden, C.S.: Cryptocurrencies as a disruption? Empirical findings on user adoption and future potential of bitcoin and co. In: Janssen, M., et al. (eds.) Open and Big Data Management and Innovation. I3E 2015. LNCS, vol. 9373, pp. 63–80. Springer, Cham (2015). https://doi.org/10.1007/978-3-319-25013-7_6
2. Raymaekers, W.: Cryptocurrency bitcoin: disruption, challenges and opportunities. J. Paym. Strategy Syst. 9(1), 30–46 (2015)
3. Ahamad, S., Nair, M., Varghese, B.: A survey on crypto currencies. Presented at the 4th International Conference on Advances in Computer Science, AETACS, pp. 42–48 (2013)
4. Ametrano, F.M.: Hayek money: the cryptocurrency price stability solution. Social Science Research Network, Rochester, NY, SSRN Scholarly Paper ID 2425270, August 2016
5. Nakamoto, S.: Bitcoin: a peer-to-peer electronic cash system (2008). http://bitcoin.org/bitcoin.pdf
6. Nseke, P.: How crypto-currency can decrypt the global digital divide: bitcoins a means for African emergence. Int. J. Innov. Econ. Dev. 3(6), 61–70 (2018)
7. Turban, E., Outland, J., King, D., Lee, J.K., Liang, T.-P., Turban, D.C.: Electronic commerce payment systems. In: Electronic Commerce 2018. STBE, pp. 457–499. Springer, Cham (2018). https://doi.org/10.1007/978-3-319-58715-8_12
8. Kakavand, H., Kost De Sevres, N., Chilton, B.: The blockchain revolution: an analysis of regulation and technology related to distributed ledger technologies. Social Science Research Network, Rochester, NY, SSRN Scholarly Paper ID 2849251, January 2017
9. Alqaryouti, O., Shaalan, K.: Trade facilitation framework for e-commerce platforms using blockchain. Int. J. Bus. Inf. Syst. (in press)
10. Hileman, G., Rauchs, M.: 2017 global blockchain benchmarking study. Social Science Research Network, Rochester, NY, SSRN Scholarly Paper ID 3040224, September 2017

11. Sas, C., Khairuddin, I.E.: Design for trust: an exploration of the challenges and opportunities of bitcoin users. In: Proceedings of the 2017 CHI Conference on Human Factors in Computing Systems, New York, NY, USA, pp. 6499–6510 (2017)
12. Nair, M., Cachanosky, N.: Bitcoin and entrepreneurship: breaking the network effect. Rev. Austrian Econ. **30**(3), 263–275 (2017). https://doi.org/10.1007/s11138-016-0348-x
13. Fanning, K., Centers, D.P.: Blockchain and its coming impact on financial services. J. Corp. Account. Financ. **27**(5), 53–57 (2016)
14. Fridgen, G., Radszuwill, S., Urbach, N., Utz, L.: Cross-organizational workflow management using blockchain technology - towards applicability, auditability, and automation. In: Hawaii International Conference on System Sciences 2018 (HICSS-51) (2018)
15. Christin, N.: Traveling the silk road: a measurement analysis of a large anonymous online marketplace. In: Proceedings of the 22nd International Conference on World Wide Web, New York, NY, USA, pp. 213–224 (2013)
16. Abramova, S., Böhme, R.: Perceived benefit and risk as multidimensional determinants of bitcoin use: a quantitative exploratory study. In: ICIS 2016 Proceedings (2016)
17. Siyam, N.: Factors impacting special education teachers' acceptance and actual use of technology. Educ. Inf. Technol. **24**(3), 2035–2057 (2019). https://doi.org/10.1007/s10639-018-09859-y
18. Davis, F.D.: Perceived usefulness, perceived ease of use, and user acceptance of information technology. MIS Q. **13**(3), 319–340 (1989)
19. Venkatesh, V.: Determinants of perceived ease of use: integrating control, intrinsic motivation, and emotion into the technology acceptance model. Inf. Syst. Res. **11**(4), 342–365 (2000)
20. Davis, F.D., Bagozzi, R.P., Warshaw, P.R.: User acceptance of computer technology: a comparison of two theoretical models. Manage. Sci. **35**(8), 982–1003 (1989)
21. Merriam, S.B., Tisdell, E.J.: Qualitative Research: A Guide to Design and Implementation. Wiley, Hoboken (2015)
22. Andrew, D.P.S., Pedersen, P.M.: Research Methods and Design in Sport Management. Human Kinetics, Champaign (2011)
23. Julie, P.: SPSS Survival Manual. McGraw-Hill Education, London (2013)

Cloud Computing

Test Recommendation for Service Validation in 5G Networks

Marios Touloupos[1,2], Evgenia Kapassa[1,2(✉)], Dimosthenis Kyriazis[2], and Klitos Christodoulou[1]

[1] Institute for the Future (IFF), School of Business, University of Nicosia, Nicosia, Cyprus
{touloupos.m,kapassa.e,christodoulou.kl}@unic.ac.cy
[2] Department of Digital Systems, University of Piraeus, Piraeus, Greece
{ekapassa,mtouloup,dimos}@unipi.gr

Abstract. System Testing is the testing of a fully integrated software, as well as a series of different tests whose purpose is to exercise the full computer-based system. Software testing though, is an arduous and expensive activity. In the context of manual testing, any effort to reduce the test execution time and to increase defect findings is welcome. One of the biggest challenges in the upcoming 5G era is the validation and verification of VNFs and NSs, so that operators can be sure of their behavior in different execution environments. 5G technologies as well as SDNs are already introducing great challenges in the field service validation, testing and optimization of the underlying network. Considering the above, we propose a recommendation system acting as a Decision Support Mechanism integrated in an SDN environment. Its purpose is the proposition of tests to the software developers towards a stable NS ready to be deployed to the production environment.

Keywords: 5G networks · Recommendations · Software testing · Validation · Decision support · Network services

1 Introduction

Undisputedly, the rapid evolution of mobile communications delivers a remarkable impact on the social and economic development. The design of the fifth generation (5G) mobile wireless standard introduces the reconstruction of the prevalent network infrastructure and the enhancement of the wireless connectivity [1]. It is of no doubt that the advent of 5G will provide the support of a plethora of innovating services with improvements in system capacity and spectrum coverage. With the aim of bridging the gap between the capacity improvement and scalable connectivity of the multiple users, the advent of 5G mobile networks will introduce paramount changes from the perspective of flexible network management [2]. The Telecommunications Service Providers (TSPs) anticipate demanding requirements from the 5G network, such as high throughput, low latency, increased capacity, and unlimited scalability. The principles of Software Defined Networking (SDN) and Network Function Virtualization (NFV) can effectively diminish these challenges with aligned optimization of short-service life

M. Themistocleous and M. Papadaki (Eds.): EMCIS 2019, LNBIP 381, pp. 139–150, 2020.
https://doi.org/10.1007/978-3-030-44322-1_11

cycles, playing a pivotal role with the respect to the commercialization of 5G networks [3]. In the 5G ecosystem, the exploitation of SDN and NFV concepts offers agility enhancement and maintenance automation compared to the legacy technologies, while it provides the necessary tools to simplify the vertical system organization [4, 5].

Through the virtualization of lower level functions, SDN and NFV supplies the necessary tools for the composition of the 5G architecture with network functionalities in software components, namely the Virtual Network Functions (VNFs), through their deployment onto standard devices [6]. The combination of VNFs as Network Services (NSs) can be twinned with respect to the target performance parameters and mapped onto the infrastructure resources. The optimum design and management of the VNFs leverages the peak benefits of NFV landscape of reducing the Capital Expenditure (CAPEX) and Operating Expense (OPEX) in 5G networks, by means of dynamic resource allocation and traffic load balancing [7, 8].

As 5G network services and applications are key in several enterprise domains, VNF/NS developers and consumers are still lacking tools to verify functional and non-functional properties of these services. Such tools should consider properties such as functional correctness, service availability, reliability, performance and security guarantees. The close interaction between high-integrity VNFs and VNFFGs, with their operating environments (SDN/NFV/MEC Infrastructures), places a high priority on understanding and satisfying both functional and nonfunctional requirements of their configuration [37].

However, in this plethora of the NSs and VNFs, a big challenge of choosing the appropriate test for validating and/or verifying the on boarded NSs arises. Due to the many test combinations it seems impossible to test each and every combination both in automatic and manual testing. Also, many times, test developers need to communicate with the service developers in order to discuss the service requirements. If the test developer fails to completely understand the service's needs, then it's mostly sure that the chosen test won't be the correct one. Furthermore, most of the testing projects are trying to translate their manual test cases to automated ones, in order to improve productivity and coverage. One of the key steps to commence automation testing is – selecting the appropriate test cases and determining the Return on Investment (ROI). Automation though, does not overpower or replaces manual testing, but it compliments it. Like manual, automation to, needs a strategy with proper planning, monitoring and control. Automation, when implemented correctly, can become an asset to the team, project and ultimately to the organization.

In this paper, moving towards the automated testing, we present a Decision Support Mechanism (DSM), which is based on a recommendation system, aiming to support the test developers at the selection of the most relevant test cases, for a given NS. The presented mechanism is integrated in a real 5G environment, the SONATA (powered by 5GTANGO) development and validation platform. The DSM, as part of the Validation and Verification Platform (V&V) of 5GTANGO, aims at providing a set of recommendation tests to the end users, when they choose to trigger a test for a specific NS.

The rest of this paper is organized as follows. Section 2 presents the state of the art regarding software defined networks, network service validation and recommendation systems in general. Section 3 describes the general architecture of SONATA (powered by 5GTANGO), but also how the recommendation engine is positioned into the V&V platform. Section 4 presents the internal architecture of the proposed DSM and the algorithms used for the provided recommendations.

2 State of the Art

2.1 Software Defined Networks

Software Defined and 5G Networks - a combination of SDN and NFV- is a significant area that tend to make NSs and applications more flexible. NFV decouples network functions from the underlying hardware and centralizing them at network servers making the network architecture highly flexible from quick and adaptive reconfiguration [9]. The services' complexity and specialized requirements could be easily handled by transforming them to NFV and deploying the underlying applications in a software-defined environment. In addition, it is worth mentioning the fact that many service providers are anticipated to adjust network operations to promote a business model where NSs and network resources are managed and verified properly. SDN brings ease of programmability in changing the characteristics of whole networks. This simplifies the management of the network, since it is decoupled from the data plane. Therefore, network operators can easily and quickly manage, configure and optimize network resources with dynamic, automated and proprietary-free programs [10]. VNFs are at the heart of NFV that manage specific network functions such as firewalls and load balancing. In order to establish a completely virtualized environment, individual VNFs can be chained as building blocks, namely NSs [11]. VNF transfers network functions from dedicated hardware devices into a software layer running on commercial off-the-shelf servers (COTs), offering a huge reduction in network costs. Improved mobility and faster time-to-market for new services is also an advantage [12]. Moving a step forward, there are also many NFV platforms that support the quick deployment of new NSs while they also try to validate and verify them [13–15].

2.2 Network Service Validation

One of biggest challenges facing the 5G environments is the validation and verification of VNFs and NSs against various execution platforms so that network providers can be confident that services perform as anticipated. Such V&V processes not only include functional testing of VNFs and NSs but also non-functional tests, for example performance measurements [16]. One could define validation as the ability to predict the impact of different actions, reason about correctness, and diagnose unexpected network behavior, for a selected VNF or NS [17]. There are many different tools for the verification of NSs. Batfish [18] is an open source network configuration analysis tool which is used for verification in pre-deployment taking advantage of model-based analysis. Moreover, GNS3 [19] and vrnetlab [20] are tools for non-functional testing also in pre-deployment, with which test developers can deploy configurations and check the resulting network behavior through emulation.

2.3   Recommendation Systems

A Recommender System (RS) is a software application or algorithm, which collects and analyzes the preferences (i.e. ratings) given by users aiming to suggest relevant items to the interested users (e.g. books to read, mobile applications to download, VNFs to instantiate or even tests to validate a whole NS) [21]. RSs are moving a step forward since recommendations can be of various types of items, depending on the underlying domain (such as web sites, applications, software, VNFs, NSs or test functions). A recommendation system plays an extremely important role in the emerging SDNs and especially in NS validation and verification platforms, since it helps the platform to promote validation flows to the test developers and finally lead to greater commercial benefits. Currently, collaborative filtering is the most widely used commercial recommendation algorithm.

2.4   Related Work

In parallel with the vast development of the web, the arrival of the rapid expansion of the information available to the users became apparent. Recommender Systems pioneered the web with the goal of integrating contextual data and offering practical feedback to the end-user. While the research field of RSs has expanded in various fields, there is a steady interest in the application of RSs to SDN environments. In this context, a predictive, automated network management recommendation was also introduced with surprising results in [22]. The main driver of these recommendations was the appropriate trading policies to enforce the recommendation module and to propel the actions required to get the best value per VNF. However, the absence of RSs in SDNs is crucial in the tacit use of the multiple quality of service-oriented elements, such as monitoring systems, regulation, VNF/NS storage. RSs approaches and procedures therefore include a range of tools that must be thoroughly examined.

An approach is discussed in [23], where authors proposed a deep neural network model (SDAE-BPR) based on Stack Denoising Auto-Encoder and Bayesian Personalized Ranking for the problem of accurate product recommendation. Their results shown high accuracy of parameters estimation and the efficiency of model training. Moreover, authors in [24] introduced a novel approach for service multi-label recommendation using deep neural networks as well. The difference between this research and the previous one lies on the fact that the approach not only satisfy the demands of service multi-label recommendation, but also provide the importance with an ordered label ranking. Moving forward, Liang et al. presented a graph-based approach [25] to automatically assign tags to unlabeled API services by exploiting both graph structure information and semantic similarity. This work has been a basis to the current research, as NSs can also be represented in form of graphs.

Taking into consideration the background presented in the previous paragraphs, more effective decision support mechanisms are required in order to recommend to test developers the necessary VNF and NS tests that are of importance. The latter would allow NS developers, V&V test developers, and systems integrators, the ability to provide high quality services, since the targeted tests will reply to the specific requirements of network operators.

3   Architecture Overview

SONATA (powered by 5GTANG) is a 5GPPP Phase2 Innovation Action that enables the flexible programmability of 5G networks with (a) an NFV-enabled Service Development Kit (SDK), (b) a Catalogue with advanced validation and verification mechanisms for VNFs/Network Services qualification (including 3rd party contributions) and (c) a modular Service Platform with an innovative orchestrator so it can bridge the gap between business needs and network operational management systems.

3.1   Software Development Kit (SDK)

The SDK aims at providing the developer with a powerful set of tools to develop, examine and evaluate NFV-based Network Services. Thus, it includes tools and mechanisms for the unified development of the NSs, namely from their creation and validation, until their final packaging and advertisement to the NFV Marketplace. Thus, the latter comprises the key storage point of publishing the emerging services directly from the developer to the diverse stakeholders. Consequently, NFV Marketplace conceptualizes the idea of exploiting existed web services and providing inspiration from the hosted developments. Developers can rapidly initiate projects of Network Services on–the–fly, either by fetching already-advertised Network Services from the NFV Marketplace, or by commencing new developments. The ability of optionally enabling easy re-use of existing components comprises a crucial advantage, which can be blended into the overall service under creation [26].

3.2   Validation and Verification Framework

The V&V framework servers the validation and verification of the developed network services [27]. Via the V&V platform, the different stakeholders are able to validate and qualify the reliability of their produced designs prior to release. The advent of the NFV Marketplace constitutes a paramount lever in the V&V ecosystem as it integrates the entire test lifecycle of the VNFs/NS from the execution of the tests to the storage of the results. As it is obvious, the test process demands a plethora of information from low level metrics, logging, system reporting, all of which are included in the NFV Marketplace. The inclusion of the concrete information in the NFV Marketplace provides a holistic insight to the end–user and propels the dynamic nature of the NFV Marketplace for the optimum composition and proposal of innovative test scenarios to the end-user.

3.3   Service Platform (SP)

The SP comprises a set of components that provide a service delivery architecture. In the SP, one of the core components of the 5G ecosystem is the flexible MANagement and Orchestration (MANO) framework [28], responsible for the orchestration features and the management of VNFs/NSs. Along with the MANO, several other key enablers coexist as introduced in the 5G environment, such as the Slice [29, 30], Policy [31] and the SLA management [32]. The components of the SP produce an abounding amount of information for each respective NS. The MANO framework exports relative information with resource allocation of the instantiated VNFs/NS across the infrastructure. The positioning of the NFV Marketplace comprises the centralized storage entity of all the components of the SP from the necessary files for the deployment of VNFs/NS to the corresponding business rules. This type of information is rendered as profitable knowledge and allows the efficient characterization of the VNFs/NS through their enrichment with valuable metadata in the Catalogue.

3.4 Catalogue

The Catalogue is an instrumental component in the SONATA (powered by 5GTANGO) environment present in different parts of it (a common building block with the V&V). Primarily, it hosts the different descriptors of the 5GTANGO packages. Since SONATA (powered by 5GTANGO) aims at a multi-platform environment, it enables the NS developers to orchestrate and deploy their NSs using different Service Platforms. In this context the 5GTANGO Catalogue is being adapted to support the storing and retrieval of new packages, that are "marked" like ONAP [33], OSM [34] or 5GTANGO packages. Moreover, the Catalogue is aligned with the principle of persistent storage by extending the hosted VNFDs and NSDs with valuable fields for successful data integration, accuracy in the format of the document, confirmed time of creation, etc. In this way, it enables the development of enhanced operations for Creating, Retrieving, Updating and Deleting (CRUD) descriptors inside it, while reassures the correct data format of the stored documents. Going beyond a conventional data storage, the presented 5GTANGO Catalogue provides intelligent functionalities in this 5G environment. Since the types of information vary, one of the requirements, satisfied by the Catalogue, is the full-text search capabilities in structure-agnostic documents. Since the schema of the diverse is variable, the Catalogue provides searching capabilities without the necessity of indexes. Thus, it provides seamless retrieval abilities in deep-hierarchical machine-readable document structures. Furthermore, besides the plain NoSQL document store for the diverse descriptors, Catalogue provides a scalable file system for hosting the artifact files, required for the instantiation life cycle of the NSs. Finally, Catalogue provides a set of endpoints where the CRUD methods are supported for the different descriptors of the project.

3.5 Positioning of the DSM in the V&V Framework

The decision support mechanism constitutes a vital component in the V&V platform of a 5G environment, implementing methods for suggesting relevant items to the users (i.e. items being tests to execute). This section provides the architectural description of the DSM with the underlying recommendation engine, its consolidation in the 5G environment, in terms of interacting with other software components.

The emergence of the rapid growth of the available information became clear to its users with the massive advancement of the Internet. RSs has been exploring the internet with the goal of integrating contextual data and offering practical feedback to the end user. While the RSs research field has skyrocketed in a number of domains, there is a steady, but sluggish, interest in applying RSs in 5G environments by defining them in network management applications [35]. Telecom networks generate massive amounts of data monitoring through the advent of the virtualized era, consisting of observations on network failures, configuration, accounting, performance, and safety. E-stream also included a predictive, automated recommendation for network management with surprising results due to the increasing complexity of the networks, associated with specific business level constraints [36]. Through manipulating deep data streams and efficiently applying dimensional reduction techniques, E-stream was focused on recommending behavior with four specific related variables, namely context, audience, existing responses, and validation. The main factor of these recommendations was the appropriate trading policies to enforce the recommendation module and to propel the actions necessary to get the best price per VNF. However, the absence of RSs in 5G telecom systems is crucial in the tacit use of the multiple element QoS/QoE metrics, such as monitoring systems, regulation and SLA modules, etc. RSs approaches and methods therefore form a subset of tools to be thoroughly examined.

In the case of our implementation, a recommendation system which is integrated in the V&V of the SONATA (powered by 5GTANGO) framework, is running at the background "listening" to activities such as choose of a test by a user, upload of a new test package etc. To elaborate more, the most worth mentioned activity is the upload of a new test package. A callback request is arriving at the recommendation engine when a test package is successfully uploaded to the catalogue. Then, the recommendation engine extracts the testing tags from the package descriptor, as well as the owner/user of the package and stores that information in an inside database. At a next step, using the prediction techniques described in Sects. 4.2 and 4.3 the recommendation model is calculated and its ready to provide test recommendations at the next execution of a test case. As it is depicted in Fig. 1, the recommendation engine is integrated in the V&V platform, which is communicating with the SP in order to deploy the service and run the recommended test cases. Among others, the SP to execute the test is chosen based on what the user have chosen. Service package can be either OSM, ONAP or SONATA. Thus, based on the kind of the service package, the corresponding SP is automatically chosen.

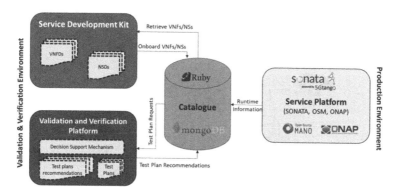

Fig. 1. Positioning of the DSM in the V&V

4 Proposed Decision Support Mechanism

4.1 Overview

The purpose of the recommendation engine is to automate the process of the test selection, providing some recommendation preferences based on the user's previous activity. The recommendation engine uses singular-value decomposition (SVD) methods that are based on collecting and analyzing large amounts of information on users' behaviors, activities or preferences and predict what users will prefer based on their similarity to other users. The main capabilities of the recommendation engine are:

- Retrieve the mechanism's health.
- Retrieve the items' *"testing tags"*, the recommendation engine is trained for.
- Retrieve the users, the recommendation engine is trained for.
- Add a new user-item pair based on the uploaded package to the Catalogue.
- Add a new user-item pair based on what test a user has executed.
- Get the top n recommendations for a user.
- Delete a user along with the associate activity.

Aligned with the escalating development of the NFV landscape, the number of services is increasingly overwhelming in the Catalogue. The publishing of the services from the various stakeholders yields a plethora of VNFs/NSs selections to the end-user in the development phase. Therefore, the infiltration, prioritization and delivery of optimum information about VNF selections is considered necessary. The process of optimum selection of VNFs/NSs by the operators is no exception and there is a clear need to facilitate their decision-making process by providing recommendations that match their preferences and needs. The proposed DSM is based in a Collaborative Filtering techique, which makes recommendations based on how users (i.e. test developers) rated items (i.e. test cases) in the past - not based on the items themselves. Specifically, the implemented collaborative-filtering-based recommendation engine is a recommendation system that has no knowledge of the actual item (i.e. test case) it is recommending. On the contrary, it only knows how other users (i.e. test developers) rated the item, as depicted in Fig. 2.

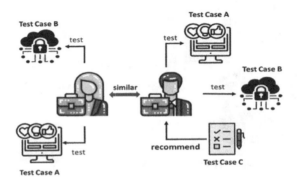

Fig. 2. Collaborative filtering in the proposed DSM

4.2 Collaborative Filtering

Collaborative Filtering methods are based on collecting and analyzing a large amount of information on users' behaviors, activities or preferences and predicting what users will like based on their similarity to other users. A key advantage of the collaborative filtering approach is that it does not rely on machine analyzable content and therefore it is capable of accurately recommending complex items such as tests without requiring an "understanding" of the item itself. Many algorithms have been used in measuring user similarity or item similarity in recommender systems. For example, singular-value decomposition (SVD) approach. Collaborative filtering is based on the assumption that people who agreed in the past will agree in the future, and that they will like similar kinds of items as they liked in the past.

4.3 Singular Value Decomposition

Collaborative Singular-Value Decomposition (SVD) In linear algebra, the singular-value decomposition (SVD) is a factorization of a real or complex matrix. It is the generalization of the eigen decomposition of a positive semidefinite normal matrix (for example, a symmetric matrix with positive eigenvalues) to any $m \times n$ matrix via an extension of the polar decomposition. It has many useful applications in signal processing and statistics.

4.4 Continuous Optimization

Upon now, the conventional test planning of the NSs is utterly based on the developer. The continuous optimization service of the recommendation engine introduces dynamicity and adaptability in the operation of the V&V framework. The continuous optimization service it comes to fulfill the integration of V&V platform in the 5G infrastructure. The DSM in collaboration with the Catalogue, target in the assessment of the test performances while considering the actual performance of the deployed VNFs/NS in the SP. Potential differences observed in the performance of the production and the validation environment comprises a basis for extending the strain of the VNFs/NS through the proposal of new test cases to the V&V framework. By means of proposing new test plans, the developer is equipped with innovative tools of improving the design of the VNFs/NSs. The test suggestions will not include only pre– defined script configurations, but also produce innovative tests to explore potential performance bottlenecks. For these reasons, monitoring information both from the test (i.e. validation and verification) and the production infrastructure are collected, along with previous test configurations parameters, that are stored into the Catalogue. After the execution of the new test configurations and the gathering of the corresponding data, the mechanism will propose (i.e. recommend) new V&V tests to be triggered to the V&V framework and thus causing a feedback loop. The activity of the V&V developer is recorded, in the continuous optimization service. Based on this activity, the recommendation engine of the DSM proposes unprecedented test scenarios, according to the test developer history in terms of NS instantiations, corresponding test selections and results.

5 Conclusions

The current paper presented a Decision Support Mechanism built upon available Network Services, in order to recommend to the test developers, the most relevant tests, aiming to validate and verify the services in the best possible way. The proposed recommendation system uses collaborative filtering taking into consideration the end users' historical preferences on a set of items (i.e. NSs and tests). The f sparsity and scalability issues were tried to be solved using Matrix Factorization, with the Singular Value Decomposition algorithm. It is worth mentioning that collaborative filtering provides significant predictive power for recommender systems, while at the same time requiring the least data. But, in some specific situations, it has some drawbacks, such as the problem with the *"cold start"*. The disadvantages of using collaborative filtering are likely to be solved using a more complete and large set of data. As a future work, we aim to use a more complex dataset, enriched also with a set of metadata, so that we could combine content-based filtering by adding some explicable keyword dimensions, and at the same time be able to consider the trade-offs between model - computational complexity and performance improvement effectiveness.

Acknowledgements. This work has been partially supported by the PARITY project, funded by the European Commission under Grant Agreement Number 864319 through the Horizon 2020. Moreover, this scientific work has been performed in the framework of the 5GTANGO project, funded by the European Commission under Grant number H2020ICT-2016-2761493 through the Horizon 2020 and 5G-PPP programs (http://5gtango.eu).

References

1. You, X., et al.: AI for 5G: research directions and paradigms. Sci. China Inf. Sci. **62**(2), 21301 (2019)
2. Andrews, J.G., et al.: What will 5G be? IEEE J. Sel. Areas Commun. **32**(6), 1065–1082 (2014)
3. Abdelwahab, S., et al.: Network function virtualization in 5G. IEEE Commun. Mag. **54**(4), 84–91 (2016)
4. Agiwal, M., Roy, A., Saxena, N.: Next generation 5G wireless networks: a comprehensive survey. IEEE Commun. Surv. Tutorials **18**(3), 1617–1655 (2016)
5. Gupta, A., Jha, R.K.: A survey of 5G network: architecture and emerging technologies. IEEE Access **3**, 1206–1232 (2015)
6. Sun, S., Yanhong, J., Yamao, Y.: Overlay cognitive radio OFDM system for 4G cellular networks. IEEE Wirel. Commun. **20**(2), 68–73 (2013)
7. Liang, C., Yu, F.R., Zhang, X.: Information-centric network function virtualization over 5G mobile wireless networks. IEEE Network **29**(3), 68–74 (2015)
8. Aissioui, A., et al.: Toward elastic distributed SDN/NFV controller for 5G mobile cloud management systems. IEEE Access **3**, 2055–2064 (2015)
9. Akyildiz, I.F., Lin, S.-C., Wang, P.: Wireless software-defined networks (W- SDNs) and network function virtualization (NFV) for 5G cellular systems: An overview and qualitative evaluation. Comput. Netw. **93**, 66–79 (2015)
10. Kuo, T.-W., et al.: Deploying chains of virtual network functions: on the relation between link and server usage. IEEE/ACM Trans. Network. (TON) **26**(4), 1562–1576 (2018)

11. SDxCentral Staff: What is a Virtual Network Function or VNF? (2014). https://www.sdxcentral.com/networking/nfv/definitions/virtual-network-function/
12. Virtual Network Function (2019). https://www.thefastmode.com/wiki-networking/5499-virtual-network-function-vnf
13. Hoban, A.: OSM Release TWO, A Technical Overview. ETSI OSM Community White Paper (2017)
14. Open Orchestrator Project and Linux Foundation: Open-O (2017). https://www.open-o.org
15. Xilouris, G., et al.: T-NOVA: a marketplace for virtualized network functions. In: 2014 European Conference on Networks and Communications (EuCNC). IEEE (2014)
16. Zhao, M., et al.: Verification and validation framework for 5g network services and apps. In: 2017 IEEE Conference on Network Function Virtualization and Software Defined Networks (NFV-SDN). IEEE (2017)
17. The what, when, and how of network validation (2019). https://www.intentionet.com/blog/the-what-when-and-how-of-network-validation/
18. The software that empowers network professionals. https://www.gns3.com/
19. vrnetlab - VR Network Lab. https://github.com/plajjan/vrnetlab
20. Rocca, B.: Introduction to recommender systems: Overview of some major recommendation algorithms (2019). https://towardsdatascience.com/introduction-to-recommender-systems-6c66cf15ada
21. Zaman, F., et al.: A recommender system architecture for predictive telecom network management. IEEE Commun. Mag. 53(1), 286–293 (2015)
22. Bi, Z., Zhou, S., Yang, X., Zhou, P., Wu, J.: An approach for item recommendation using deep neural network combined with the bayesian personalized ranking. In: Wang, X., Gao, H., Iqbal, M., Min, G. (eds.) CollaborateCom 2019. LNICST, vol. 292, pp. 151–165. Springer, Cham (2019). https://doi.org/10.1007/978-3-030-30146-0_11
23. Gan, Y., Xiang, Y., Zou, G., Miao, H., Zhang, B.: Multi-label recommendation of web services with the combination of deep neural networks. In: Wang, X., Gao, H., Iqbal, M., Min, G. (eds.) CollaborateCom 2019. LNICST, vol. 292, pp. 133–150. Springer, Cham (2019). https://doi.org/10.1007/978-3-030-30146-0_10
24. Liang, T., et al.: Exploiting heterogeneous information for tag recommendation in API management. In: 2016 IEEE International Conference on Web Services (ICWS). IEEE (2016)
25. Soenen, T., et al.: Insights from SONATA: implementing and integrating a microservice-based NFV service platform with a DevOps methodology. In: NOMS 2018-2018 IEEE/IFIP Network Operations and Management Symposium. IEEE (2018)
26. Twamley, P., et al.: 5Gtango: an approach for testing NFV deployments. In: 2018 European Conference on Networks and Communications (EuCNC). IEEE (2018)
27. Mijumbi, R., et al.: Management and orchestration challenges in network functions virtualization. IEEE Commun. Mag. 54(1), 98–105 (2016)
28. Zhang, H., et al.: Network slicing based 5G and future mobile networks: mobility, resource management, and challenges. IEEE Commun. Mag. 55(8), 138–145 (2017)
29. Vaishnavi, I., et al.: Realizing services and slices across multiple operator domains. In: NOMS 2018-2018 IEEE/IFIP Network Operations and Management Symposium. IEEE (2018)
30. Alleg, A., et al.: Delay-aware VNF placement and chaining based on a flexible resource allocation approach. In: 2017 13th International Conference on Network and Service Management (CNSM). IEEE (2017)
31. Khodapanah, B., et al.: Fulfillment of service level agreements via slice-aware radio resource management in 5G networks. In: 2018 IEEE 87th Vehicular Technology Conference (VTC Spring). IEEE (2018)

32. Open Network Automation Platform (2019). https://www.onap.org
33. Open Source MANO (2019). https://osm.etsi.org/
34. Núñez-Valdéz, E.R., et al.: Implicit feedback techniques on recommender systems applied to electronic books.". Comput. Hum. Behav. **28**(4), 1186–1193 (2012)
35. Oku, K., Kotera, R., Sumiya, K.: Geographical recommender system based on interaction between map operation and category selection. In: Proceedings of the 1st International Workshop on Information Heterogeneity and Fusion in Recommender Systems. ACM (2010)
36. Serrano-Guerrero, J., et al.: A Google wave-based fuzzy recommender system to disseminate information in University Digital Libraries 2.0. Inf. Sci. **181**(9), 1503–1516 (2011)
37. Tsvetkov, T., et al.: A configuration management assessment method for SON verification. In: 2014 11th International Symposium on Wireless Communications Systems (ISWCS). IEEE (2014)

Modelling 5G Cloud-Native Applications by Exploiting the Service Mesh Paradigm

Ilias Tsoumas[1]($\boxtimes$), Chrysostomos Symvoulidis[1],
Dimosthenis Kyriazis[1], Panagiotis Gouvas[2],
Anastasios Zafeiropoulos[2], Javier Melian[3], and Janez Sterle[4]

[1] Department of Digital Systems, University of Piraeus, Piraeus, Greece
{itsoum, simvoul, dimos}@unipi.gr
[2] R&D Department, Ubitech Ltd., Athens, Greece
{pgouvas, azafeiropoulos}@ubitech.eu
[3] ATOS, Tenerife, Spain
javier.melian@atos.net
[4] Internet Institute, Ljubljana, Slovenia
janez.sterle@iinstitute.eu

Abstract. The new-coming 5G network is considered to be one of the most significant innovations today. This is due to the opportunities that is going to provide to the vertical industries. 5G infrastructures will introduce a new way for low-delay, reliable deployment of services. In fact, such infrastructures can be used for the placement of application services in the form of application graphs. An application graph consists of several application components (i.e. micro-services) that may be hosted in the same infrastructure or in different ones. Conflicting requirements that arise when deploying in such infrastructures are now handled through network slicing, which regards a way for partitioning conventional network and computing resources into virtual elements. In this paper, we define a universal application metamodel of a 5G compatible application in order to guarantee the annotation of each application descriptor with its proper requirements for their fulfillment at the instantiation time. In terms of application architecture, we consider each application graph as a service mesh topology in order to adopt this novel service architecture as a dominant methodology that is well fitting in the promising 5G capabilities.

Keywords: 5G-ready applications · Application components metamodels · Application graphs · Service mesh · Cloud-native applications

1 Introduction

5G comes in a revolutionary way to change forever both the internet, and the World Wide Web (WWW), whereas their combination will certainly change the existing vertical industry. This will be realized through the provision of an ultra-fast wireless WWW that will lead to the 4th Industrial Revolution. More specifically, the main purpose of 5G is to combine multiple technologies of different layers and areas in order to achieve its goals, aiming mainly at higher capacity, higher data rate, lower end-to-end latency, massive device connectivity, reduced cost, as well as consistent quality of

M. Themistocleous and M. Papadaki (Eds.): EMCIS 2019, LNBIP 381, pp. 151–162, 2020.
https://doi.org/10.1007/978-3-030-44322-1_12

experience provisioning [1]. Network softwarization will play a key role to this, hence methodologies such as Network Slicing (NS) and Cloud Computing methodologies will be used in consolidation.

One of the existing major challenges of 5G is the integration of vertical industries. In more detail, the challenge regards the adoption of 5G capabilities from the applications and the procedures of the vertical industries. Nevertheless, it is necessary to define a proper model of them so as to be harmonized with 5G architectures.

There are innumerable non-monolithic applications that run in a distributed manner. For the proper deployment of these distributed applications in the virtual environments of 5G networks, it is crucial to capture their computing and networking requirements, as well as to monitor their components at runtime and adapt to any environment changes may appear [17] in order to make possible their consistent instantiation inside of 5G. Thus, the applications will be ready to be deployed in 5G environments, following and extending the cloud-native rules of the containerization, the dynamic orchestration, and the micro-services orientation [12].

In order to address these challenges, this paper focuses on the provision of a rich description of 5G-ready applications, as a metamodel. A 5G-ready application consists of several chainable components (i.e. micro-services). The interaction between these components can be depicted by a directed acyclic graph, which is referred as a 5G-ready application graph. The proposed approach exploits the service mesh paradigm, since it achieves (i) security with Transport Layer Security (TLS) and key management, (ii) observability via metrics, monitoring, and distributing tracing, (iii) clear separation between business logic and the network layer 7 (L7) functionalities, (iv) primitive routing capabilities, as well as (v) resiliency for inter-service communications (i.e. circuit-breaking, retries and timeouts, fault handling, load balancing, etc.), through the data plane (via sidecar proxies). Through a control plane, policy and configuration for all the running data planes in the mesh transformed into a distributed system are provided [10].

The overall description addresses two fundamental entities; the chainable component, and the 5G-ready application graph. The key outcome is the metamodel of these two entities, which are then used for the request of a computing and network slice in order to deploy the 5G-ready application, both by the network and the cloud computing provider.

Eventually, the application graph metamodel is going to be used by the slice intent metamodel. The latter refers to a description of the request of the Application provider (Vertical/northbound orchestrator) to the Network Service provider (Telco/southbound orchestrator), regarding the network and the compute slice that are needed. In order to provide the requested resources, the Network Service provider needs information regarding the requirements of each application component and the topology of the given application graph. That information is depicted in the application graph metamodel, since it contains information regarding the links between the application components of the application graph.

The chainable application component metamodel describes and verifies (with the aid of some supporting mechanisms – introduced in Sect. 4) the following: (i) the required information for the proper deployment and execution of the components (e.g. resource requirements), and (ii) the alignment with a set of rules in terms of QoS requirements, cloud-nativeness affected by the 12-factor manifest [2]. The application graph (service mesh) metamodel is the collection of the bindings among the exposed and required interfaces per chainable component. Both at component and at graph level, the denotation of a set of computing, memory, storage and network requirements are being supported in correlation with the corresponding slice intent metamodel [3].

The rest of the paper is organized as follows: Sect. 2 presents the State of the Art in the area of modelling applications and services. Section 3 presents the approach of the authors, including a detailed demonstration of the developed metamodels. Section 4 regards the experimental evaluation of the proposed architecture in a real-life deployment scenario. Finally, Sect. 5 concludes the paper and suggests future work based on the current model.

2 Related Work

There exist various researches in the literature concerning the modelling schemas that have been developed and used for application components and services, as well as application graphs and network services so far. Juju [13] is an open-source modelling framework [14] developed by Canonical that is used for managing, deploying and scaling services in the cloud in the form of application graphs. A Juju charm, (i.e. an application component) contains information that is necessary for a service to be orchestratable and composable. Several charms wired together with virtual links create a Bundle that is in fact the application graph. The descriptors of both charms and bundles are created in YAML containing crucial information for the orchestration of a service.

Another interesting approach regards the descriptors used in ARCADIA framework [15], an EU-funded research project that is created for the design and development, as well as the dynamic setup and management of highly distributed applications over a programmable infrastructure. The ARCADIA framework uses a context model to describe these applications. This context model [16] is used for the proper representation of distributed applications designated as service graphs, including four main models, the component model, the service graph model, the service deployment model, and the service runtime model. The component model is used as the descriptor of the nodes that wired together form a service graph, preserves information for the components, for other components to connect with them properly, and the requirements that have to be fulfilled for the component to run smoothly, etc.

On the other side, the service graph model contains information regarding the whole service graph, like the "Virtual Link Descriptor" that holds the information related to the links between two components. Regarding the service deployment model, this is responsible for the placement of the service graph into the Infrastructure as a Service (IaaS) resources, where the service runtime model is a representation of an instance of a deployed service graph by the orchestrator.

The Open-source MANO (OSM) [18] is an ETSI-hosted project offering an Open Source NFV Management and Orchestration (MANO) software stack, aligned with ETSI NFV. For that purpose, a strong data model is created, and is used to describe the ETSI MANO objects, modeled as YANG objects. It consists of several descriptors such as the Network Service descriptor that is responsible for containing information related to the deployment of a Network Service, the virtual network functions (VNF) descriptor that holds information regarding the attributes of a VNF, and the resource requirements, etc. [19].

Finally, Bruneliere et al. [20] present a generic model-based architecture created in YAML language to allow the automation of the management of any cloud system. The proposed architecture consists of two main metamodels, where the first is used for the description of the structure of any given topology, and the second one for the representation of the relationship between nodes and any constraints that may exist.

3 Proposed Approach

This section describes our approach regarding the way a 5G-enabled application should be modeled in order to exploit the advantages of the new-coming 5G era. At first, we present a way to properly introduce cloud services in the 5G world using the service mesh approach. Then, we showcase our approach regarding the way the application components and the application graphs should be described in our metamodel in order to exploit the advantages of 5G enabled cloud infrastructures.

3.1 The Service Mesh Approach

One of the biggest challenges in the 5G evolution lies in the way we properly introduce services and the Service Oriented Architectures (SOAs) in the 5G environments [4].

An approach to address this challenge is by using Mesh Applications and Service Architecture (MASA). The high-level difference of MASA from SOA is summed up on this "The mesh app and service architecture (MASA) is a multichannel solution architecture that leverages cloud and serverless computing, containers and microservices as well as APIs and events to deliver modular, flexible and dynamic solutions. Solutions ultimately support multiple users in multiple roles using multiple devices and communicating over multiple networks" as presented by Panetta in his work at [5].

Thus, each 5G-ready application can be modelled as a Service Mesh. More specifically the service mesh is presented by Morgan [6] as a "dedicated infrastructure layer for handling service-to-service communication. It is responsible for the reliable delivery of requests through the complex topology of services that comprise a modern, cloud native application. In practice, the service mesh is typically implemented as an array of lightweight network proxies that are deployed alongside application code, without the application needing to be aware". This infrastructure layer comes to tackle a deep issue regarding the real properties of network. Specifically, Peter Deutsch [7] describes a list of "fallacies", as a set of the opposite of rules about distributed computing that people often forget based on the assumptions that they are making for the underlying network. These fallacies include the assumption that (i) the network is reliable, (ii) latency is zero, (iii) bandwidth is infinite, (iv) the network is secure, (v) the topology does not change, (vi) there is one administrator, (vii) transport cost is zero and (viii) the network is homogeneous. The removal of these assumptions requires the addition and the satisfaction of many hard requirements [8], something that is feasible in 5G-enabled environments.

The Service Mesh concept is implemented in similar environments with the use of a sidecar pattern, where the functionality of each of the components in the mesh is extended by a sidecar proxy. In general, a sidecar is a service that is coupled to another service (i.e. an application component) that does not interfere with the functionalities of the main service but extends its properties. A typical example could be a monitoring information saver that stores (or even analyses) monitoring information issued by one or more services. In the proposed approach we take the advantages of the sidecar paradigm, attach a proxy to each of the components, taking over the network functionalities of it, regarding interconnection with other components, abstracting the network view to the component the sidecar is attached to, in order to build a more efficient service mesh.

The L7 proxy implements L7VFs (plug in functions that are dynamically loaded by the intelligent proxy) like load balancing, HTTP filter, HTTP routing, service discovery, etc. that operate at the Application level, abstracting the network to the components that are connected to it, making the communication among them more efficient and easier, as it is depicted in Fig. 1.

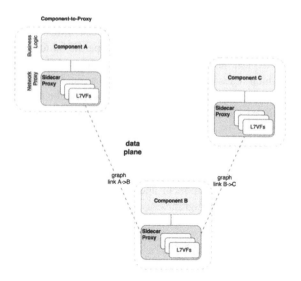

Fig. 1. Proxy-to-Proxy communication example

Moreover, the emergence of cloud computing/programmable infrastructure-as-a-code paradigm along with the dominance of microservice – driven architecture, generated additional requirements. These are related mainly with the: (i) rapid provisioning of compute resources, (ii) basic monitoring, (iii) rapid deployment, (iv) easy to provision storage, (v) easy access to the edge, (vi) authentication/authorization, and (vii) standardized interfaces (e.g. RPC, HTTP).

The requirements of 5G-ready applications coincide with the aforementioned cloud-native requirements. Yet they are much more exhaustive, since provisioning of infrastructure should be "instantaneous", topology is continuously changing, delay tolerance is minimum, etc. The concept of this dedicated infrastructure layer is depicted in Fig. 2.

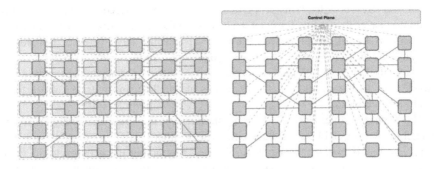

Fig. 2. Service mesh paradigm for cloud-native applications

Based on the above, a 5G-ready application is a distributed application consisting of cloud-native components that rely on a service mesh infrastructure as a mean of network abstraction. The service mesh per se has to operate on top of a programmable 5G environment. To exploit the service mesh added-value, a 5G full-stack architecture has to be used [9], which relies on a solid interplay between various logical layers such as the actual data plane, the service mesh control plane, and the configured virtualized resources that are offered by the telco provider as a proper slice [9].

3.2   Proposed 5G-Ready Application Metamodel

As already described, the 5G-ready application metamodel incorporates two fundamental entities: the chainable component and the 5G-ready application graph, which are presented in the following paragraphs.

Application Component Part

We propose a separation between the business logic part of a component from the layer 4–7 network part of it. We implement a service mesh approach with a dedicated proxy sidecar attached per component. Thus, in this section we present the "core" component. For each component, a proxy sidecar will also be utilized. The sidecar will be exploited by an L7 proxy and communication bus framework, such as Envoy [11]. To this end, the modelling of the proxy is not required.

The component metamodel includes a set of fundamental complex Type elements (except from the 'ComponentIdentifier' element) that uniquely describe each component in the entire Service Mesh. These elements are the following – as depicted also in Fig. 3: (i) The 'Distribution' element, (ii) the 'ExposedInterface' element, (iii) the 'Configuration' element, (iv) the 'Volume' element, (v) the 'MinimumExecutionRequirements' element, (vi) the 'ExposedMetric' element, (vii) the 'RequiredInterface' element, and finally (viii) the 'Capability' element.

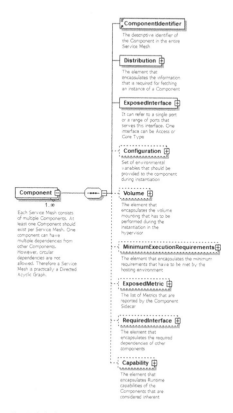

Fig. 3. High-level view of the component metamodel

The first complex type element regards the 'Distribution' element that encapsulates the information that is required for fetching an instance of a Component. It contains information regarding the final image/container of a component and the URI where the component is located in the repository.

The second complex type element, the 'ExposedInterface', is critical since it describes the exposed interfaces. It is a "one-to-many" relation since a component might expose several interfaces. It encapsulates the descriptive identifier of the interface, which is required in order to infer the chainability of dependencies during the Service Mesh deployment. Furthermore, it contains the classification of the exposed interface based on its positioning in the 5G network. It can be ACCESS or CORE. The ACCESS type refers to the UserEquipment-to-component communication, where the CORE refers to the component-to-component communication. Moreover, it contains port declaration and an optional choice for the transport layer protocol. On the other hand, each component requires some inputs. Thus, the required interface section of the component encapsulates via a "one-to-many" relation the information regarding the graph link, which links the current component with another component. Specifically, it encapsulates the identifier of the component that satisfies the current component input needs and the corresponding exposed interface identifier. To this end, it should be mentioned that there is also a descriptive identifier of this logical link ("GraphLink") between two components.

Next stands the "Configuration" element. This aspect represents a set of environmental variables that should be provided to the component during instantiation. In practice, it is a generic collection of key-value pairs to be exploited for deployment and instantiation.

The application component also includes the "Volume" element. This element offers the capability of the Hypervisors to provide storage to a virtual machine (VM) via volumes. To capture the corresponding cases, the model includes three "children" for each volume instance. The definition of the type of the volume since if it has been attached to the guest using one hypervisor type (e.g. Xen), cannot be attached to a guest that is using another hypervisor type (e.g. vSphere, KVM). This happens due to the fact that the different hypervisors use different disk image formats. Additionally, the "Volume" element includes sub-elements for the source and the target of each volume.

Furthermore, a crucial aspect of the component relates to its minimum requirements that have to be met by the hosting environment for the proper execution. This complex 'MinimumExecutionRequirements' element contains the "VCPU" element that refers to the minimum number of vCPUs that should be provided by the hypervisor, the minimum memory (i.e. the "Memory" element) and storage (i.e. the "Storage" element) and an element regarding the type of the hypervisor that is preferred (i.e. "Hypervisor" element) which has the following options; either Esxi, KVM or Xen.

The application component metamodel also includes a section regarding the metrics that will be reported by the proxy sidecar, the "ExposedMetric". It is a key-value structure with the metric identifier as key and the unit of it as value.

Finally, the "Capability" element encapsulates runtime capabilities of the components that are considered inherent. Such a capability is the scaling of the component.

Application Graph/Service Mesh Part

Many chainable components can be combined in order to create a 5G-ready application graph. As already described, an application graph is essentially a directed acyclic graph (DAG) that is implemented as a Service Mesh.

As depicted in the Figs. 4(a) and (b) below, given the adoption of the service mesh paradigm, the form of the application metamodel is simple. It contains a "ServiceMeshIdentifier" for the unique identification of each 5G-ready application, a "Name" that includes the descriptive name of each Service Mesh. As expected, a "one-to-many" relation is used to capture the correlation between the Service Mesh and its components.

While this metamodel may seem simple, it is in fact quite informative. There is no need for declaring graph links and their constraints, since (i) each graph link description is encapsulated in each component as it has been analyzed in the previous subsection of this paper. Specifically, each link is considered as an input required interface of the component which needs it, and (ii) it is a logical link, and each logical link will be

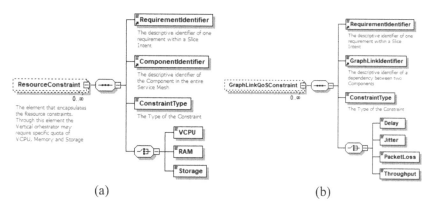

Fig. 4. (a) Slice intent - Resource constraints, (b) Slice intent – Graph link QoS constraints

realized as a network link, with network and compute constraints. These constraints are incorporated in another metamodel that is exploited by the northbound Vertical Orchestrator [9]: The Slice Intent metamodel [3]. The figures below depict the relevant part of the metamodel.

As depicted in Figs. 4(a) and (b) the vertical orchestrator is able to intent more computational quota for the efficient execution of application plus of minimum requirements per component and also it is able to define some serious network QoS constraints per graph link such as delay, jitter, packet loss, throughput.

These capabilities are provided by slice intent metamodel [3] which will elaborate more in a future paper. In conclusion, it's important to underline that there is a direct relation between application graph metamodel and slice intent metamodel which the first seriously affects the second and otherwise.

4   Use Case

The proposed metamodel as described above, was used in a real-life deployment scenario. The orchestration of the testbed was done by a 5G Vertical Application Orchestrator (VAO), fully aligned with the proposed model.

The testbed is located in the TNT-lab at DITEN of University of Genoa. It consists of both radio access and virtualized infrastructure parts. The business scenario regards a 5G-enabled emergency response pilot provided with the iMON product suite [21] for real time intervention monitoring and critical infrastructure protection.

The deployed application was placed in two parallel instances in different data centers. The two datacenters during the whole time were fully synced, to avoid any upcoming issues in case of shutdown. Thus, for the full synchronization of the two instances, between the different locations, the database (DB) component and the binary large objects (BLOB) storage components of the application were communicating continuously.

The deployed application consisted of three application components; a database system that was connected to a PHP service and a BLOB connected to the PHP service.

Regarding the database system the proposed model was fulfilled with information, including the (a) 'ExposedInterface' element that presented the chainable interface to the PHP component, (b) the 'Capability' element that stated that this component is vertically scalable, (c) the 'Distribution' element regarding the image of a MySQL service used, and (d) the 'MinimumExecutionRequirements' element with 2x CPU cores, 2 GB of RAM, and 20 GB of Disk. For the PHP business logic (BL) service in the shape of a tactical dashboard, the described model contained information related to (a) the 'RequiredInterface' element to the DB and BLOB components, (b) the 'ExposedInterface' element that presented the two chainable interfaces to the DB and the BLOB components, (c) the 'Capability' element stating that this component was horizontally scalable, (d) the 'Distribution' element providing information about the Apache web server image used, also hosting the proprietary PHP-based page, and (e) the 'MinimumExecutionRequirements' element with 2x CPU cores, 2 GB of RAM, and 10 GB of Disk. Finally, regarding the BLOB the model contained information related to (a) the 'ExposedInterface' element that offered a chainable interface to the PHP BL component, (b) the 'Capability' element stating that it was vertically scalable, (c) a 'Distribution' element containing information regarding the SAMBA service image used, and (d) the 'MinimumExecutionRequirements' element with 2x CPU cores, 2 GB of RAM, 40 GB of Disk.

More information regarding the slice intent descriptor for the constraints of access links and NFV-based components of the scenario were also described, but are not in the scope of the current paper.

The execution of the application was done without any issues emerging. This happened due to the fact that the model was very informative, and the orchestrator was fully aligned with it. So even in cases where problems could arise (e.g. a stress-tests were executed) there were no problems causing it to shut down or arise deployment issues.

5   Conclusions

In this paper we provided the specification of a 5G-ready application graph as well as the relevant metamodel. The metamodel presented contains valuable information regarding the application graph and the components constituting it, containing the mandatory elements that are used for deployment and instantiation of the components and thus the overall application.

The next step in our work is to create a suite of supporting mechanisms to facilitate in the whole management process. This suite consists of three major supporting mechanisms, (i) the performance estimator, (ii) the graph-level aggregator and (iii) the recommendation engine. The first mechanism, meaning the performance estimator, will be used for the provision of resource estimations regarding the application components in order to facilitate the infrastructure orchestrator on the better deployment and run-time adaptation. The graph-level aggregator will be responsible for collecting all the performance estimates per application component and produce aggregated results for the complete application graph. The last mechanism (i.e. the recommendation engine) will be responsible for proposing components during the composition of an application graph, based on prior usage of the components similar to [22], as well as the performance estimates.

In addition, there will be three validation mechanisms, the chainability evaluator, the configurability checker and the validation optimizer. The first mechanism regards the evaluation of the chainability of a component in an application graph, that will be used to evaluate whether the connected components can be chained or not, based on the interfaces that are exposes by an application component and the required ones from the components with which it is connected. The configurability checker will be responsible for validating whether an application component exposes its configuration parameters and if it's adequate to alter its configuration during runtime if required. Finally, the optimizer mechanism will assist on the more rapid evaluation of each application component with respect to the validation mechanisms as described above. In essence, this mechanism will be in charge of checking if each component on the application graph is already validated or not and if it has there will be no need for re-validation. Note though, that even if an application component has already been evaluated in terms of chainability, it may not be chainable in another application graph, since the topology of the graph plays significant part.

Acknowledgement. The publication of this paper has been partly supported by the University of Piraeus Research Center and by the European Union's Horizon 2020 research and innovation program under grant agreement No. 761898 project Matilda.

References

1. Gupta, A., Jha, R.K.: A survey of 5G network: architecture and emerging technologies. IEEE Access **3**, 1206–1232 (2015)
2. The 12-factor methodology. https://12factor.net/
3. D1.4 – MATILDA Network-aware Application Graph Metamodel (Network Slice Intent and Slice Instance Metamodel). http://www.matilda-5g.eu/index.php/outcomes
4. Katsalis, K., Nikaein, N., Schiller, E., Favraud, R., Braun, T.I.: 5G architectural design patterns. In: 2016 IEEE ICC Workshops 2016, pp. 32–37 (2016)
5. Panetta, K.: Top 10 strategic technology trends for 2017. https://www.gartner.com/smarterwithgartner/gartners-top-10-technology-trends-2017/?lipi=urn%3Ali%3Apage%3Ad_flagship3_pulse_read%3BMN%2B0hmkBTTuRW%2B53QE2hzw%3D%3D
6. Morgan, W.: What's a service mesh? And why do I need one? https://buoyant.io/2017/04/25/whats-a-service-mesh-andwhy-do-i-need-one/
7. Deutsch, P.: Fallacies of distributed computing. White Paper, Wikipedia Google Scholar (1995)
8. Calçado, P.: Pattern: service mesh. http://philcalcado.com/2017/08/03/pattern_service_mesh.html
9. D1.1–MATILDA framework and reference architecture. http://www.matilda-5g.eu/index.php/outcomes
10. Envoy's blog: Service mesh data plane vs. control plane. https://blog.envoyproxy.io/service-mesh-data-plane-vs-control-plane-2774e720f7fc
11. Envoy (an open source edge and service proxy) docs. https://www.envoyproxy.io/docs/envoy/latest/intro/intro
12. Cloud Native Computing Foundation. https://www.cncf.io/

13. Juju Orchestrator. https://jujucharms.com
14. Tsakalozos, K., Johns, C., Monroe, K., VanderGiessen, P., Mcleod, A., Rosales, A.: Open big data infrastructures to everyone. In: 2016 IEEE International Conference on Big Data (Big Data), Washington, DC, pp. 2127–2129 (2016)
15. ARCADIA Framework. http://www.arcadia-framework.eu/
16. Gouvas, P., Fotopoulou, E., Zafeiropoulos, A., Vassilakis, C.: A context model and policies management framework for reconfigurable-by-design distributed applications. Procedia Comput. Sci. **97**, 122–125 (2016)
17. Symvoulidis, C., Tsoumas, I., Kyriazis, D.: Towards the identification of context in 5G infrastructures. In: Arai, K., Bhatia, R., Kapoor, S. (eds.) CompCom 2019. AISC, vol. 998, pp. 406–418. Springer, Cham (2019). https://doi.org/10.1007/978-3-030-22868-2_31
18. Open-source MANO. https://osm.etsi.org
19. OSM Information Model (2016). https://osm.etsi.org/wikipub/images/0/0c/Osm-r1-information-model-descriptors.pdf
20. Bruneliere, H., Al-Shara, Z., Alvares, F., Lejeune, J., Ledoux, T.: A model based architecture for autonomic and heterogeneous cloud systems. In: Proceedings of the 8h International Conference on Cloud Computing and Services Science (CLOSER 2018), Funchal, Portugal, pp. 201–212 (2018)
21. qMon. http://www.qmon.eu/
22. Tsoumas, I., Symvoulidis, C., Kyriazis, D.: Learning a generalized matrix from multi-graphs topologies towards microservices recommendations. In: Proceedings of SAI Intelligent Systems Conference (to appear)

Digital Services and Social Media

Towards an Integrated Theoretical Model for Assessing Mobile Banking Acceptance Among Consumers in Low Income African Economies

Josue Kuika Watat[1]([✉]) and Micheline Madina[2]

[1] AMBERO Consulting GmbH, Yaounde, Cameroon
josuewatat@gmail.com
[2] Catholic University of Central Africa, Yaounde, Cameroon
madinaibrahim250@gmail.com

Abstract. The meteoric rise of mobile banking technologies in Africa is a result of an increasing penetration of smartphones and internet. Although successful studies have covered a set of themes around mobile banking and recognized the great potential existing in Africa, very few of them have examined the motivations related to its adoption and its daily use by consumers in developing countries. To fill this research gap, this study investigates on the adoption of mobile banking by consumers in sub-Saharan Africa. It is based on several theoretical models such as TAM and DeLone and McLean IS success Model to better assess the acceptance of mobile banking on African consumers. The proposed research model was assessed and supported by a data collection from 479 mobile banking users. The last section of the paper focuses on the formulation of practical implications for future work and studies in mobile banking.

Keywords: TAM · DeLone and McLean · Mobile Banking · Sub-Saharan Africa

1 Introduction

Following an exponential penetration of smartphones and internet in Sub-Saharan Africa, Mobile Banking (M-Banking) has emerged as a powerful technology capable of reversing economic, financial and social trends for stakeholders. This technology could transform virtually the entire decision-making financial chain, in particular in the reduction of the costs of financial services, the reduction of the process of purchase/payment of a good or services, or the security of transactions by end-to-end encryption [1, 2].

Although several empirical studies have recognized the value and strategic position of M-Banking for low income consumers, few of them have assessed the real impact in developing countries. As a result, several questions are emerging such as the consumer's attitude and impact of M-Banking in low-income African households as well as the influence on small businesses and informal sector activities, which account for

M. Themistocleous and M. Papadaki (Eds.): EMCIS 2019, LNBIP 381, pp. 165–178, 2020.
https://doi.org/10.1007/978-3-030-44322-1_13

the vast majority of employment in many cities in low-income countries in Africa [3]. The African development Bank revealed that low income countries in Africa have 16.6% of the penetration rate of deposit institution penetration, which is the lowest rate in the world, compared to 63.5% in other countries [4]. The M-Banking is therefore a solution that can stimulate the economy and facilitate access to finance for many low-income households in sub-Saharan Africa. For this reason, this study aims to fill the knowledge gap by modeling an extended approach of the Technology Acceptance model (TAM) that includes the DeLone McLean model along with Social Influence to assess the degree of acceptance and use of mobile banking in low-income African countries.

We rely on successful studies on M-Banking and challenges faced by banks in Africa due to the explosive penetration of technology in the financial system to meet our research objective. After having established the cutting edge of M-Banking in sub-Saharan Africa at the introduction, the first section describes the theoretical development and highlights the results of studies that have been conducted on M-Banking. The following sections of this study are devoted to our research methodology and the presentation of results and various related discussions.

The last part of the paper highlights the implications that emerge from our studies, and limitations that results, following the research perspectives of the study.

2 Background Study

2.1 Mobile Banking in Developing Economies in Africa

Sub-Saharan African Countries are facing several challenges in Technological Infrastructures. In spite of efforts and investments made by governments to harmonize the technological environment, Mobile Banking Services (MFS) are largely unexplored yet promising in the face of growing economic forces. While access to financial services is still a mystery for 2.7 billion people, more than a billion of potential consumers do not have a bank account [4]. Most of Banks in Sub-Saharan Africa are facing the definition of a sometimes-high cost model, which excludes the heavily impacted low-income category. The Consulting firm McKinsey revealed that by 2017, Bank penetration was only 38% of gross domestic product in Africa. This relatively low rate is only the average of the world average for emerging economies [5]. While the proportion of users with a bank account has increased by 4% in Sub-Saharan Africa, the one with a mobile money account has doubled in recent years, up to 21% [6]. Most low-income countries in Africa have the highest mobile money penetration rate in the world, exceeding 10% [6]. In East Africa, where the proportion of mobile money penetration is the highest on the continent with a 34% increase, the penetration of banks and other financial institutions remains constant at 24% [7]. Many Fintech digital ecosystem startups that have access to important investment funds are leaning more and more towards the mobile financial services (MFS) [8] (Fig. 1).

Adults with a mobile money account (%)

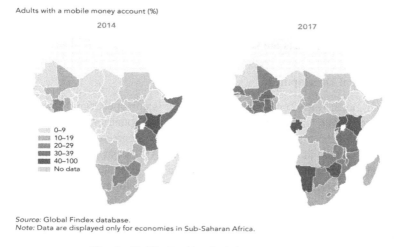

Fig. 1. Mobile Banking in Sub-Saharan Africa

2.2   Related Work

M-Banking in Africa has already proven itself as a reliable, viable and cost-effective system, capable of providing a myriad of inclusive development benefits. Empowering migrant women entrepreneurs in Ghana, its influence in promoting financial inclusion in Kenya [9–11], or in improving and facilitating access to health services by poor people from South Africa and Swaziland [12, 13]. M-Banking has largely contributed to a redistribution of wealth, thus helping to reduce income inequality in several African countries [14]. In sales and marketing, it has facilitated business opportunities and the dematerialization of financial transactions [15] (p. 505).

In Education, [16] used the usual TAM constructs to assess the use of mobile banking services among university students. Further, the work of [17] condensed the TAM and UTAUT models to better examine Generation Y's intention to adopt M-Banking services. In agriculture, M-Banking has confirmed to be a technology that reduces agricultural prodigality while significantly improving household management in Nigeria and Kenya [18, 19]. In Kenya, mobile banking has brought about a revolution in the financial stability of low-income households. The study of [20] revealed that households related to the use of M-PESA were able to significantly increase their income by overcoming problems such as job loss, poor harvests, without reducing their daily consumption. Contrarily, the same study reported that financial difficulties led non-users of the M-PESA banking system to drastically reduce their spending in households by 7%. Mobile Banking Services can therefore be seen as shortcuts to financial inclusion in several low-income countries in Africa [21]. Developed countries, unlike low-income countries, have strong financial institutions that provide widespread financial services. They can rely on this notoriety and ease of access to offer consumers online financial services with upstars like Google Wallet, Stripe, Venmo, Amazon Payment, WePay, Square, Pauline that pushes the envelope.

Following these previous works, it is undeniable not to recognize the strategic position that occupies mobile banking in Sub-Saharan Africa. All sectors of daily life are affected, and the impacts are socially, culturally and financially measurable.

2.3 Theoretical Development

The research model (Fig. 2) proposed in this study is an appendage of the TAM [22, 23] tailored to mobile banking adoption in low income countries in Africa. TAM has been proposed for the first time by Davis to gauge the degree of use or non-use of a technology by an individual. Davis argues that the TAM assists in providing a general answer of the factors contributing to the acceptance of a technology. this answer would therefore be a response to the behavioral analysis of users following the use of a range of computer technologies [22] (p. 985). The TAM has been used and customized in many areas of information systems by several scholars. [24] has extended the TAM with the DeLone and McLean IS success Model to measure the acceptance of M-Banking services in the Jordanian banking system. [25] united the TAM with Innovation and Diffusion Theory to estimate hindrances to M-Banking adoption among young German consumers. [26] linked the TAM with the TPB model in order to understand Emiratis motivations and perceptions in the acceptance of M- Banking. [27] developed and tested several versions of TAM in order to explore the intentions that users can adopt when it comes to M-Banking. [28] schematized a research model hinged on the TAM along with the task-technology fit model (TTF) and perceived risk, all in the expectance-confirmation model (ECM). Furthermore, [29] extended the traditional TAM with social image, trust and perceived risk to evaluate the intention to use mobile banking apps among Spanish customers.

Based on the previous of research, we suggest a set of hypotheses in the context of M- Banking daily usage by consumers in Sub-Saharan Africa:

H1: System Quality (SQ) has a significant positive impact on Perceived Credibility (PC).

H2: System Quality has a significant positive impact on Perceived Ease of Use (PEOU).

H3: Information Quality (IQ) has a significant positive impact on Perceived Usefulness (PU).

H4: Information Quality (IQ) has a significant positive impact on Perceived Ease of Use (PEOU).

H5: Perceived Usefulness (PU) has a significant positive impact on Attitude (ATT).

H6: Perceived Ease of Use (PEOU) has a positive impact on Perceived Usefulness (PU).

H7: Perceived Ease of Use (PEOU) has a positive impact on Attitude (ATT).

Besides, [30] argued that Perceived Credibility (PC) plays a leading role in the context of M-Banking technology in low-income countries.. It is a digest of trust, caution and privacy evoking an individual's perception of believing that another individual has the ability to perform a task reliably [30]. Verily, previous studies have shown the importance of credibility when referring to a technological system, moreover, in relation to its bank account [2, 31, 32].

In addition, social influence (SI) is also considered in several works as being a decisive construct in the adoption of mobile banking. Yu's empirical study on 441 respondents in Taiwan reported that social influence is the most important predictor of acceptance of M-Banking. It mainly contributes to the explanation of the use of an accounting computer system by young entrepreneurs [33]. Many technology enthusiasts among whom the students give a great interest to the new technological inventions because of their curiosity in the use, and their enthusiasm in the handling of the tool. They find themselves being influenced by their peers in the use of mobile banking applications that are usually installed on smartphones [16].

We therefore build on these previous studies and suggest that, with respect to the banking environment in relation to mobile technologies, PC between stakeholders in the M-Banking system will play a key role. This role is not only in mobile banking use, but also in the adoption, continuous use, satisfaction and even for recommendations. Thus, we suggest that:

H8: Perceived Credibility (PC) has a significative positive impact on Attitude (ATT).

H9: Social Influence (SI) has a positive impact on Mobile Banking Adoption (MBA).

H10: Attitude (ATT) has a significant positive impact on Mobile Banking Adoption (MBA).

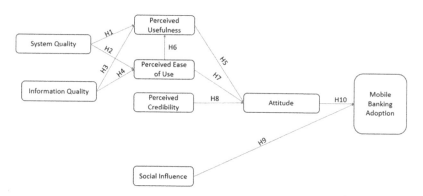

Fig. 2. Research Model

3 Research Approach

3.1 Instrument

To carry out our investigations, a questionnaire of 24 items was set up. It was divided into two components. The first component was the measurement elements of the eight constructs defining the research model (SQ, IQ, PU, PEOU, SI, ATT, MBA). Each construct contains between two and four questions. These questions correspond to items measured following a Likert Scale graduated from 1 - "strongly disagree" to 7 - "strongly agree". The second component contains 05 questions that concern exclusively descriptive statistics data including sex, age, educational level, place of residence, as well as experience in the use of a smartphone (Table 1).

Table 1. Research hypotheses

Hypotheses	Results	Statements
H1	SQ → PU	The quality of the M-Banking system has a significant positive impact on Perceived Usefulness
H2	SQ → PEOU	The quality of the M-Banking system has a significant positive impact on Perceived Ease of Use
H3	IQ → PU	The quality of information from a M-Banking system has a significant positive impact on the Perceived Usefulness
H4	IQ → PEOU	The quality of information from a M-Banking system has a significant positive impact on the Perceived Ease of Use
H5	PU → ATT	Perceived Usefulness of M-Banking has a significant positive impact on the attitude adopted in the use of mobile banking
H6	PEOU → PU	Perceived Ease of Use of M-Banking has a positive impact on perceived Usefulness
H7	PEOU → ATT	Perceived Ease of Use of M-Banking has a positive impact on Attitude towards Mobile Banking
H8	PC → ATT	Perceived credibility has a significative positive impact on Attitude towards mobile banking
H9	SI → MBA	Social influence in the use of M-Banking has a positive impact on Mobile Banking adoption
H10	ATT → MBA	Attitude has a significant positive impact on M-Banking Adoption

A pilot test was run with 50 mobile banking consumers in order to improve the understanding of the items/questions. This pilot test also helped to modify the structure of the questionnaire to eliminate any ambiguities. Subsequently, the survey was inserted on google forms and adapted to match the different ones where it will be open and filled.

3.2 Data Collection

For this study, the data collection was conducted from April to July 2019. The questionnaire was shared according to various web 2.0 platforms such as social media (Facebook, twitter, WhatsApp, Instagram, Telegram), as well as by email. It has also been distributed in banks where there is a high rate of use of mobile banking services. With the purpose of diversifying the type of respondents, the survey was sent to people from various activities, so that we could have a real actual perception and thus better identify the factors contributing to the acceptance of M-Banking.

3.3 Data Assessment Methods

Following the recommendations of [34], we adopted the dual approach for structural equation modeling (SEM). This method has been successfully adopted in several works in the field of Information Systems, where the TAM was used [35–39]. The PLS-SEM method is the most suitable in this study because it takes into account path and factor analysis [40, 41]. SmartPLS v. 3.2.8 was used to conduct the data analysis. According to several aspects of measurements and assessments, PLS-SEM method consider the reliability and the validity of the measuring instruments and the hypotheses of a quantitative study [41]. This method is also used to test the causal model and integrating several latent variables [42]. Its widespread use in quantitative studies is explained by the fact that it jointly estimates the structural coefficients and factors of the measurement elements of the research model [43].

4 Results

4.1 Data

Following the data collection process, we obtained 479 respondents. Since the form was filling out via Google forms, we did not have any missing data in view of the obligation to answer each question. Respondents' descriptive characteristics, including age, gender, education level, and experience with mobile phone use, are recorded in Table 2. We have a high rate of male respondents with a percentage of 57%, compared with 43% of women. In addition, most of our respondents are between 26–35 years old, followed by those between 18 and 25 years old. We also note that many of them went to school and have good experience in the use of smartphones.

4.2 Reliability of the Measurement Model

The reliability of internal consistency can be measured using composite reliability [41, 44]. Furthermore, we observe a composite reliability varying between 0.812 and 0.862, well above the acceptable threshold of 0.7 [45–47]. The same observation is made on the loadings varying between 0.700 and 0.842, being thus higher than the acceptable threshold. In order to better measure the discriminant validity, [48] suggests using the Average Variance Extracted (AVE) following a threshold above 0,5. It's the distributed variance between the measurement elements of a construct [49]. In view of the results recorded in Table 3, the AVEs of all our constructs are between 0.570 and 0.747 (Table 4).

Table 2. Demographic characteristics of respondents

Variable	No.	%
Gender		
Female	208	43%
Male	271	57%
Age		
18–25	161	34%
26–35	233	49%
36–45	50	10%
46–60	19	4%
>60	16	3%
Study level		
Never gone to school	25	5%
Apprenticeship training	38	8%
Undergraduate	90	18%
Postgraduate	290	61%
PhD	36	8%
Experience using smartphone (in years)		
<3	30	6%
4–6	87	18%
7–9	134	28%
>10	228	48%

Table 3. Construct reliability and validity

Variables	Items	Loadings	Composite reliability	AVE
Attitude (ATT)	ATT1	0,748	0.812	0.591
	ATT2	0,709		
	ATT3	0,842		
Mobile Banking Adoption (MBA)	MBA1	0,778	0.841	0.570
	MBA2	0,801		
	MBA3	0,700		
	MBA4	0,737		
Perceived Ease of Use (PEOU)	PEOU1	0,837	0.862	0.676
	PEOU2	0,854		
	PEOU3	0,774		
Perceived Usefulness (PU)	PU1	0,787	0.828	0.617
	PU2	0,832		
	PU3	0,733		
Information Quality (IQ)	QI1	0,771	0.857	0.600
	QI2	0,789		
	QI3	0,749		
	QI4	0,789		
System Quality (SQ)	QS1	0,836	0.825	0.702
	QS2	0,840		
Social Influence (SI)	SI1	0,779	0.818	0.600
	SI2	0,797		
	SI3	0,747		

Table 4. Discriminant validity

	ATT	MBA	PC	PEOU	PU	QI	QS	SI
ATT	**0.711**							
MBA	0.306	**0.757**						
PC	0.419	0.196	**0.821**					
PEOU	0.594	0.201	0.389	**0.822**				
PU	0.662	0.241	0.362	0.621	**0.726**			
IQ	0.541	0.188	0.382	0.501	0.641	**0.775**		
SQ	0.549	0.146	0.366	0.458	0.521	0.602	**0.767**	
SI	0.466	0.225	0.390	0.491	0.424	0.377	0.352	**0.773**

4.3   Hypothesis Testing

Tables 5 and 6 show the results of our structural model. All the assumptions of our research model were supported. The results of the study thus argue that social influence in a neutral economic environment, has a significant positive effect on the M-Banking adoption. In other words, regardless of the economic situation of a developing country, the fact M-Banking is welcomed, used and adopted by a group of individuals influences people who are close to this group to use and adopt mobile banking services.

Table 5. Structural model result

	Beta (Sig.)	T statistics ($|O/STDEV|$)
ATT → MBA	0,306****	6,908
PC → ATT	0,069****	1,737
PEOU → ATT	0,243****	5,167
PEOU → PU	0,277****	6,342
PU → ATT	0,344****	8,770
IQ → PEOU	0,370****	7,699
IQ → PU	0,400****	8,089
SQ → PEOU	0,221****	3,847
SQ → PU	0,178****	4,124
SI → MBA	0,113**	1,382

****$P < 0,001$; *** $P < 0,01$; **$P < 0,05$; *$P < 0,1$

The results also showed the key role of perceived credibility in M-Banking usage. Indeed, for a technology system coupled with finance to be adopted, it must be considered credible. Not only by the people who use it, but also by its ability to secure information, its relationship of trust with user.

Table 6. Hypothesis result

Hypothesis	Results
H1: The quality of the M-Banking system has a significant positive impact on Perceived Usefulness	Supported
H2: The quality of the M-Banking system has a significant positive impact on Perceived Ease of Use	Supported
H3: The quality of information has a significant positive impact on the Perceived Usefulness.	Supported
H4: The quality of information has a significant positive impact on the Perceived Ease of Use	Supported
H5: Perceived Usefulness of M-Banking has a significant positive impact on the attitude adopted in the use of mobile banking	Supported
H6: Perceived Ease of Use of M-Banking has a positive impact on perceived Usefulness	Supported
H7: Perceived Ease of Use of M-Banking has a positive impact on Attitude towards Mobile Banking	Supported
H8: Perceived Risk has a significative positive impact on Attitude towards M-Banking	Supported
H9 Social influence in the use of mobile banking has a positive impact on M-Banking Adoption	Supported
H10: Attitude has a significant positive impact on M-Banking Adoption	Supported

5 Discussion

This study finds a strong endorsement of the Technology Acceptance model coupled with M-Banking in a low-income context. Our results corroborate the assertion that PEOU and PU indirectly influence the adoption of M-Banking through attitude (H1), which is in line with the work of [50–52]. Additionally, our results show that there is a direct positive influence of the SQ and IQ on PEOU and PU. Furthermore, we noticed that all the hypotheses proposed in our study are significant at 0.001 except SI → MBA which is significant at 0.05. Thus, all the suggested hypotheses in this study are supported.

6 Limitations and Future Research Directions

The measurement model developed in this study revealed preliminary analysis of the structural model with respect to the acceptance of M-Banking services by consumers in emerging economies within sub-Saharan Africa. The next step will be to improve the proposed research model and the survey. This improvement will concern the items/questions that will be increased in order to better evaluate the constructs of the research model and therefore the scales of measures of reliability. We also want to investigate potential differences in perceptions that may arise in the use of mobile banking among the groups of respondents. We will therefore distinguish young people from old people, people with strong experience in the use of ICTs and novices in the use of ICT.

Moreover, future studies could extend this research model by incorporating new constructs such as Perceived Risk, or Perceived Privacy in view of the importance of these constructs when it comes to financial transactions [53]. The Task–Technology Fit model (TTF) could also be combined with this research model in future studies to better explain and understand the acceptance of M-Banking not only from an adoption perspective, but also according to adjustments between the features offered by mobile banking applications, and the actual tasks to be performed by users when using mobile banking technologies. Besides, this study will serve as a point of departure in case future longitudinal studies could be conducted to better describe the acceptance of M-Banking within low income countries. Future studies could also focus on the unobserved discrepancy in the use of SEM regarding the acceptance of M-Banking in Sub-Saharan Africa.

7 Conclusion

In this study, we refined a research model regarding the acceptance and use of M-banking by citizens of emerging economies in Africa. Initially, we proceeded to an extension of the original TAM by incorporating new constructs that are prerequisites for a strong acceptance of M-Banking in developing countries: the quality of the banking system, the quality of the information that is diffused as well as other constructs such as the social influence and perceived risk. Subsequently, we've designed a measurement model that was used to complete a survey to better assess the perception of mobile banking users. The survey was sent to 479 consumers of mobile banking system following several channels of communication such as social media, emails. At the end of this data collection, the PLS algorithm on SmartPLS 3.2.8 allowed us to evaluate the reliability and validity of our measurement model. After this step, we obtained the evaluation of the structural model proposed by the Bootstrapping method of Structural Equation modeling. The results of the study show that the adoption of a M-Banking system is subject to a good quality of the system and the good quality of the information that must be disseminated. This means that, for widespread acceptance and efficient use of a mobile banking system in developing countries, banking institutions and even governments should increase their efforts towards a better quality of the proposed system, and better quality of information. In addition, the results also showed that social influence dominates the adoption of mobile banking in Low income economies within Africa. This demonstrates the importance of external pressure when it comes to touting the merits of a technological system to potential users. Financial institutions can use their influencers' strengths to get potential customers to use their products. At the same time, the pressure put on by those close to a potential consumer of mobile banking services also plays a key role in the ambition to make him adopt a mobile banking service. To conclude, the study highlights a number of items to consider when it comes to M-Banking in sub-Saharan African countries.

References

1. Sharma, S.K.: Integrating cognitive antecedents into TAM to explain mobile banking behavioral intention: a SEM-neural network modeling. Inf. Syst. Front. **21**, 815–827 (2019). https://doi.org/10.1007/s10796-017-9775-x
2. Priya, R., Gandhi, A.V., Shaikh, A.: Mobile banking adoption in an emerging economy: an empirical analysis of young Indian consumers. Benchmarking Int. J. **25**, 743–762 (2018)
3. Sparks, D.L., Barnett, S.T.: The informal sector in Sub-Saharan Africa: out of the shadows to foster sustainable employment and equity? Int. Bus. Econ. Res. J. (IBER) **9** (2010)
4. Ondiege, P.: Mobile banking in Africa: taking the bank to the people. Afr. Econ. Brief **1**, 1–16 (2010)
5. Chironga, M., Cunha, L., De Grandis, H.: Roaring to Life: Growth and Innovation in African Retail Banking. McKinsey & Company, New York (2018)
6. Demirguc-Kunt, A., Klapper, L., Singer, D., Ansar, S., Hess, J.: The Global Findex Database 2017: Measuring Financial Inclusion and the Fintech Revolution. The World Bank, Washington, D.C. (2018)
7. Demirguc-Kunt, A., Klapper, L., Singer, D., Van Oudheusden, P.: The Global Findex Database 2014: Measuring Financial Inclusion Around the World. The World Bank, Washington, D.C. (2015)
8. Pasti, F.: State of the Industry Report on Mobile Money: 2018 (2019)
9. Buku, M.W., Meredith, M.W.: Safaricom and M-PESA in Kenya: financial inclusion and financial integrity. Wash. J. Law Technol. Arts **8**, 375 (2012)
10. Donovan, K.: Mobile money for financial inclusion. Inf. Commun. Dev. **61**, 61–73 (2012)
11. Asongu, S., De Moor, L.: Recent advances in finance for inclusive development: a survey (2015)
12. Leon, N., Schneider, H., Daviaud, E.: Applying a framework for assessing the health system challenges to scaling up mHealth in South Africa. BMC Med. Inform. Decis. Mak. **12**, 123 (2012)
13. Kliner, M., Knight, A., Mamvura, C., Wright, J., Walley, J.: Using no-cost mobile phone reminders to improve attendance for HIV test results: a pilot study in rural Swaziland. Infect. Dis. Poverty **2**, 12 (2013)
14. Asongu, S.A., Kodila-Tedika, O.: Is poverty in the African DNA (Gene)? S. Afr. J. Econ. **85**, 533–552 (2017)
15. Mishra, V., Bisht, S.S.: Mobile banking in a developing economy: a customer-centric model for policy formulation. Telecommun. Policy **37**, 503–514 (2013)
16. Govender, I., Sihlali, W.: A study of mobile banking adoption among university students using an extended TAM. Mediterr. Ean J. Soc. Sci. **5**, 451 (2014)
17. Boonsiritomachai, W., Pitchayadejanant, K.: Determinants affecting mobile banking adoption by generation Y based on the Unified Theory of Acceptance and Use of Technology Model modified by the Technology Acceptance Model concept. Kasetsart J. Soc. Sci. (2017). https://doi.org/10.1016/j.kjss.2017.10.005
18. Oluwatayo, I.: Banking the unbanked in rural southwest Nigeria: showcasing mobile phones as mobile banks among farming households. J. Financ. Serv. Mark. **18**, 65–73 (2013)
19. Kimenyi, M., Ndung'u, N.: Brookings Institution. Expanding the Financial Services Frontier: Lessons from Mobile Phone Banking in Kenya. Brookings Institution, Washington, D.C. (2009)
20. Jack, W., Suri, T.: Risk sharing and transactions costs: evidence from Kenya's mobile money revolution. Am. Econ. Rev. **104**, 183–223 (2014)

21. Rosengard, J.K.: A quantum leap over high hurdles to financial inclusion: the mobile banking revolution in Kenya (2016)
22. Davis, F.D., Bagozzi, R.P., Warshaw, P.R.: User acceptance of computer technology: a comparison of two theoretical models. Manag. Sci. **35**, 982–1003 (1989)
23. Venkatesh, V., Davis, F.D.: A theoretical extension of the technology acceptance model: four longitudinal field studies. Manag. Sci. **46**, 186–204 (2000)
24. Alsamydai, M.J.: Adaptation of the technology acceptance model (TAM) to the use of mobile banking services. Int. Rev. Manag. Bus. Res. **3**, 2039 (2014)
25. Koenig-Lewis, N., Palmer, A., Moll, A.: Predicting young consumers' take up of mobile banking services. Int. J. Bank Mark. **28**, 410–432 (2010)
26. Aboelmaged, M., Gebba, T.R.: Mobile banking adoption: an examination of technology acceptance model and theory of planned behavior. Int. J. Bus. Res. Dev. **2** (2013)
27. Gu, J.-C., Lee, S.-C., Suh, Y.-H.: Determinants of behavioral intention to mobile banking. Determ. Behav. Intent. Mob. Bank. **36**, 11605–11616 (2009)
28. Yuan, S., Liu, Y., Yao, R., Liu, J.: An investigation of users' continuance intention towards mobile banking in China. Inf. Dev. **32**, 20–34 (2016)
29. Munoz-Leiva, F., Climent-Climent, S., Liébana-Cabanillas, F.: Determinants of intention to use the mobile banking apps: an extension of the classic TAM model. Span. J. Mark. ESIC **21**, 25–38 (2017)
30. Crabbe, M., Standing, C., Standing, S., Karjaluoto, H.: An adoption model for mobile banking in Ghana. Int. J. Mob. Commun. **7**, 515–543 (2009)
31. Luarn, P., Lin, H.-H.: Toward an understanding of the behavioral intention to use mobile banking. Comput. Hum. Behav. **21**, 873–891 (2005)
32. Amin, H., Hamid, M.R.A., Lada, S., Anis, Z.: The adoption of mobile banking in Malaysia: the case of Bank Islam Malaysia Berhad (BIMB). Int. J. Bus. Soc. **9**, 43 (2008)
33. Yu, C.-S.: Factors affecting individuals to adopt mobile banking: empirical evidence from the UTAUT model. J. Electron. Commer. Res. **13**, 104 (2012)
34. Anderson, J.C., Gerbing, D.W.: Structural equation modeling in practice: a review and recommended two-step approach. Psychol. Bull. **103**, 411 (1988)
35. Rauniar, R., Rawski, G., Jei, Y., Johnson, B.: Technology acceptance model (TAM) and social media usage: an empirical study on Facebook. J. Enterp. Inf. Manag. **27**, 6–30 (2014). https://doi.org/10.1108/JEIM-04-2012-0011
36. Hsu, M.-W.: An analysis of intention to use in innovative product development model through TAM model. Eurasia J. Math. Sci. Technol. Educ. **12**, 487–501 (2016). https://doi.org/10.12973/eurasia.2016.1229a
37. Venkatesh, V., Davis, F.D.: A theoretical extension of the technology acceptance model: four longitudinal field studies. Manag. Sci. **46**, 186–204 (2000). https://doi.org/10.1287/mnsc.46.2.186.11926
38. Schneberger, S., Amoroso, D.L., Durfee, A.: Factors that influence the performance of computer-based assessments: an extension of the technology acceptance model. J. Comput. Inf. Syst. **48**, 74–90 (2008). https://doi.org/10.1080/08874417.2008.11646011
39. Watat, K., Fosso Wamba, S., Kamdjoug, K., Robert, J.: Use and influence of social media on student performance in higher education institutions in Cameroon (2018)
40. Henseler, J., et al.: Common beliefs and reality about PLS: comments on Rönkkö and Evermann (2013). Organ. Res. Methods **17**, 182–209 (2014)
41. Chin, W.W.: The partial least squares approach to structural equation modeling. Mod. Methods Bus. Res. **295**, 295–336 (1998)
42. Chou, C.-P., Bentler, P.M.: Estimates and tests in structural equation modeling (1995)

43. Hair Jr., J.F., Sarstedt, M., Hopkins, L., Kuppelwieser, V.G.: Partial least squares structural equation modeling (PLS-SEM) an emerging tool in business research. Eur. Bus. Rev. **26**, 106–121 (2014)
44. Tenenhaus, M.: L'approche PLS. Revue de statistique appliquée **47**, 5–40 (1999)
45. Fornell, C., Larcker, D.F.: Structural equation models with unobservable variables and measurement error: algebra and statistics. J. Mark. Res. **18**, 382–388 (1981). https://doi.org/10.1177/002224378101800313
46. Nunnally, J.C.: Psychometric Theory. McGraw-Hill, New York (1978)
47. Ab Hamid, M., Sami, W., Sidek, M.M.: Discriminant validity assessment: use of Fornell & Larcker criterion versus HTMT criterion. In: Proceedings of Journal of Physics: Conference Series, p. 012163 (2017)
48. Fornell, C., Larcker, D.F.: Evaluating structural equation models with unobservable variables and measurement error. J. Mark. Res. **18**, 39–50 (1981)
49. Valentini, F., Damásio, B.F.: Average variance extracted and composite reliability: reliability coefficients. Psicologia Teoria e Pesquisa **32** (2016)
50. Karjaluoto, H., Riquelme, H.E., Rios, R.E.: The moderating effect of gender in the adoption of mobile banking. Int. J. Bank Mark. **28**, 328–341 (2010)
51. Püschel, J., Afonso Mazzon, J., Hernandez, J.M.C.: Mobile banking: proposition of an integrated adoption intention framework. Int. J. Bank Mark. **28**, 389–409 (2010)
52. Akturan, U., Tezcan, N.: Mobile banking adoption of the youth market: perceptions and intentions. Mark. Intell. Plan. **30**, 444–459 (2012)
53. Baabdullah, A.M., Alalwan, A.A., Rana, N.P., Kizgin, H., Patil, P.: Consumer use of mobile banking (M-Banking) in Saudi Arabia: towards an integrated model. Int. J. Inf. Manag. **44**, 38–52 (2019)

Smart City Adoption: An Interplay of Constructive and Adverse Factors

Anton Manfreda[(✉)]

School of Economics and Business, University of Ljubljana, Ljubljana, Slovenia
anton.manfreda@ef.uni-lj.si

Abstract. Digital technologies are constantly changing not only the way how business processes are performed at the organizational level but also the way how we live. Digital transformation is affecting many areas. Cities and living in cities is not an exception. Smart cities are developing at an ever-increasing rate. New concepts and technologies such as cloud computing, mobile technology, 5G networks and integration with social media are bringing information solutions closer to end-users and are providing greater flexibility for business solutions as well. The technological aspects of smart cities are already extensively researched; however, the development of smart cities is also presenting significant challenges related to citizens, quality of life, personal preferences, privacy and others. This paper thus focuses on the interplay of different factors that are important for smart city adoption. The impact of this interplay is empirically tested with structural equation modelling using data from 203 millennials.

Keywords: Smart cities · Millennials · Digital transformation · Structural equation modelling

1 Introduction

The concept of digitalization and digital transformation is currently used on a daily basis since it is challenging many areas. Modern technologies affect not only business processes in organizations but also the lifestyle of individuals. Urban areas are not an exception. Since urban populations grow rapidly [29] many cities are facing major changes and challenges. These challenges are arising from global shifts in the environment, rapid urbanization and older infrastructure as well. By the end of 2050, the urban population is expected to reach about 70% of the total population [29]. Thus, the development of information and communication technology may provide future smart urban habitat. Not surprisingly, the concept of smart city is evolving at an increasing speed. Smart cities address the key issues of modern life including transportation, energy, environment, public administration and citizen involvement.

The concept of a smart city is based on the use of information and communication technology, which enables the digitalization of urban living, and covers many areas such as smart mobility, smart living, smart environment, smart citizens, smart government, smart economics, smart architecture and smart technology [23].

The technological aspects of smart cities have already been researched in recent years [17]; however, smart cities are also presenting significant challenges related to the

M. Themistocleous and M. Papadaki (Eds.): EMCIS 2019, LNBIP 381, pp. 179–192, 2020.
https://doi.org/10.1007/978-3-030-44322-1_14

implementation and proper use of technology; and therefore, the focus on aspects such as citizens, quality of life, personal preferences, privacy and sustainability is equally important. New technologies and concepts are particularly relevant to the millennial generation aged from 20 to 35, who are often referred to as confident, open to change, more educated than previous generations, always connected and focused on digital technology and social media [37]. Millennials are therefore an important group to explore adopting the concept of smart cities because they want to embrace technology and new business models.

The purpose of this paper is thus to examine the interplay of different factors important for smart city adoption perceived by millennials. The paper focuses on the impact of modern technology, privacy issues and concerns regarding future consequences in the field of smart cities. The paper is divided into four parts. Firstly, a brief literature review on the relevant concepts is presented, followed by the model conceptualization. In the second part, the research methodology is presented, followed by presenting the results. Lastly, discussion and concluding remarks are outlined.

2 Literature Review

2.1 Digital Transformation

In the last decade, several areas have been exposed to a change, mainly due to the advent and accessibility of various digital technologies. This change is recently labelled as a digital transformation or digitalization. The latter is defined as the use of digital technology to radically improve organizational performance [39] or a specific form of organizational transformation that integrates digital technologies and business processes within an organization [30]. This transformation indicates simultaneous major changes implemented in the short term in the key areas, namely strategy, organizational structures, business models and business processes [41]. Besides, digitalization refers to the use of new digital technologies that are enabling significant business improvements and are affecting many aspects of consumer life or lifestyle [33, 36].

The transformation of existing business processes and business models in organizations is strongly linked with the ubiquitous digitalization. Both, business models and the way of living as well, are exposed to significant changes that deviate from the established habits in the past [31]. Researchers thus address the challenges that different industries are facing while adapting to such changes such as the aerospace industry [43], construction [42], healthcare [20] and others. Cities and living in cities are not excluded.

2.2 Smart Cities

Urban population is rapidly increasing and the growth is expected to continue in the future [29]. Therefore, it is not unexpected that the concept of a smart city is rapidly evolving. Moreover, the development of information and communication technology is expected to make an important contribution to the way of living. Implementing information technology and systems is crucial for improving public services [4], which are particularly important when considering future city habitat. However, for transforming public services it is crucial to understand the priorities and needs of citizens [14]; and therefore, citizen-oriented services are extremely important [1], also for considering the smart city concept.

The smart city is currently quite a popular term. Despite different definition for the smart city concept, they are converging at focusing on information and communication technology as a prerequisite and a driver of smart city, including economic, managerial and social aspects [38]. A smart city is also claimed to be an investment in human and social capital with proper intertwine between the traditional and modern information technology focusing on sustainable economic growth and high quality of life through participatory governance [32]. Smart cities thus address the key issues of contemporary urban life, including transportation, energy, environment, government and citizen involvement [23]. The latter is made possible by extensively using the concept of the Internet of things. The latter is, after all, a key factor in gaining the benefits of delivering advanced services and features as it enables real-time data collection and transmission [3]. The availability of data that can be automatically collected in urban areas, creates new opportunities not only for managing public information services and resources but also for understanding and designing these services. With the popularization of the concept of smart cities, information services are also radically changing, with limited research on the design and impact of these new services. Therefore, understanding the drivers of technology adoption is important for policymakers and technology providers to successfully disseminate the smart city concept [12].

Smart cities are associated with technology that can improve the lives of citizens by providing the core for future services. The concept of smart cities has already been extensively researched from a technological perspective [9, 17]; however, personal considerations and overall impacts including the interplay of different factors interacting with smart infrastructure should also be considered in the future research [23]. This involves examining factors that are associated with both technology adoption as well as personal characteristics [34].

2.3 Research Hypothesis and Model Conceptualization

Since smart cities address the key issues of contemporary urban life, the smart city adoption in this research was thus based on individual preferences regarding the smart economy, smart people, smart governance, smart mobility and smart environment [16]. With the rapid increase of data left behind by individuals and increasing usage of the internet of things, organizations can more precisely observe and forecast our needs. However, the latter is also depended by the preparedness to share the data [2]. The latter is in many cases associated with the preparedness to install different control sensors that are able to constantly measure and transmit the data [15]. Thus, proper privacy management and trust in relevant institutions to properly store all obtained data are crucial as well [6]. Yet, with the proliferating digitalization, cities may become an easier target for cyber-attacks in the future [15], causing additional concerns regarding the future consequences of smart cities.

Considering the literature review and own observations, the following hypotheses were proposed:

- H1: Enthusiasm regarding new technology has a positive impact on preparedness to install different control sensors in cities.
- H2: The perceived trust in proper privacy management has a positive impact on supporting the development of smart cities.
- H3: The perceived trust in proper privacy management has a positive impact on preparedness to share the data.
- H4: The perceived fear regarding future consequences has a negative impact on preparedness to share the data.
- H5: Preparedness to share the data has a positive impact on supporting the development of smart cities.
- H6: Preparedness to install different control sensors has a positive impact on supporting the development of smart cities.

Figure 1 shows the conceptual model of the interplay of the factors supporting the development of smart cities with the proposed hypotheses.

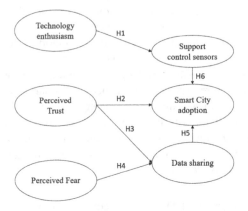

Fig. 1. Conceptual model of Smart City adoption factors

To test the proposed hypotheses, six constructs were formed, namely: (1) Technology enthusiasm; (2) Perceived trust; (3) Perceived fear; (4) Data sharing; (5) Support control sensors; and (6) Smart city adoption. The first three constructs in the model are exogenous latent variables, while the last three are endogenous latent variables.

3   Research Methodology

3.1   Research Instrument

In order to test the research hypotheses, a web-based questionnaire was prepared. The questionnaire was, among other indicators that are not relevant for this research, composed of several items measuring the enthusiasm regarding new technologies, attitude toward smart cities, attitude toward different control sensors, attitude toward sharing the data, perceived concerns regarding future use and trust in proper data management. All latent model variables were measured by items using a 5-point Likert scale ranging from "strongly disagree" (1) to "strongly agree" (5). Items of each construct together with their descriptions are presented in Appendix A.

The construct technology enthusiasm (enthTEC) was measured by three items (tec1 – tec3). The construct Smart city adoption (adpSMART) was measured using six items (sc1 – sc6). Further, four variables (sen1 – sen4) were utilized to measure the construct support control sensors (supSEN). The construct perceived trust (prvTRUST) was measured by three variables (tr1 – tr3), while four variables (data1 – data 4) were used to measure the construct data sharing (shrDATA). Finally, three variables (con1 – con3) were applied to measure the construct perceived fear (prvFEAR).

3.2   Data Collection and Research Methods

The research hypotheses were empirically tested on millennials in Slovenia aged from 20 to 35. An online s questionnaire was randomly disseminated among individuals. Overall, 269 individuals finished the survey; however, 203 individuals were included in the analysis, since they responded with all the data valid for the research. Data collection started in June and was completed in August 2019. The profile of the respondents is presented in Table 1.

As it is evident from the table, the demographic characteristics of the sample are similar to the population characteristics; and therefore the sample resembles the millennials' population in Slovenia.

Table 1. Profile of the respondents.

		Percent (%)	Population (%)
Gender	Male	53.7	51.9
	Female	46.3	48.1
Education	Primary or less	6.3	8.4
	Secondary	59.6	62.3
	Tertiary	34.1	29.3
Type of settlement	Urban settlement	38.9	N/A
	Suburban areas	30.6	
	Small city	24.9	
	Village areas	5.7	
Region (NUTS-2)	West region	43.6	49.1
	East region	56.4	50.9

In order to verify to what extent the hypothesized relations between the latent variables and the relations between the latent variables and their items are consistent with the empirical data, a confirmatory analysis was applied in the research. A co-variance-based structural equation modelling (SEM) and the LISREL 8.80 tool was used to verify the model and the hypotheses.

4   Results

4.1   Descriptive Statistics and Scale Reliability

The measurement model was analyzed regarding reliability. Cronbach's alpha was calculated to determine the internal consistency reliability of the identified factors. Values above 0.7 are generally accepted [25], As it is evident from Table 2, Cronbach's alpha for factors identified in the proposed model is above 0.7, except for the item enthTEC; yet, the latter is close to 0.7. However, in exploratory studies values above 0.50 are also considered to be satisfactory [18]. In the table also mean values together with the standard deviation for all items used in the model are presented.

Table 2. Descriptive statistics and scale reliability

Construct	Item	Mean value	Standard deviation	Cronbach's α
enthTEC	tec1	2.83	0.947	0.670
	tec2	2.93	0.935	
	tec3	3.16	1.035	
adpSMART	sc1	3.48	0.829	0.740
	sc2	3.46	0.915	
	sc3	3.14	0.965	
	sc4	3.43	1.041	
	sc5	3.45	0.919	
	sc6	3.55	0.943	
supSEN	sen1	3.80	1.049	0.702
	sen2	3.90	1.018	
	sen3	2.75	1.087	
	sen4	2.71	1.154	
shrDATA	data1	2.93	1.094	0.819
	data2	2.46	1.048	
	data3	3.45	0.921	
	data4	3.71	0.848	
prvFEAR	con1	3.55	1.065	0.754
	con2	4.21	0.916	
	con3	3.79	1.158	
prvTRUST	tr1	2.78	1.035	0.771
	tr2	2.83	1.028	
	tr3	2.88	0.955	

4.2   Confirmatory Analysis

Figure 2 shows the path diagram of the Smart City adoption model with the completely standardized parameter estimates. Parameters were estimated using a maximum likelihood method as a default estimation method in Lisrel. The purpose of the presented path diagram is to facilitate the presentation of the model.

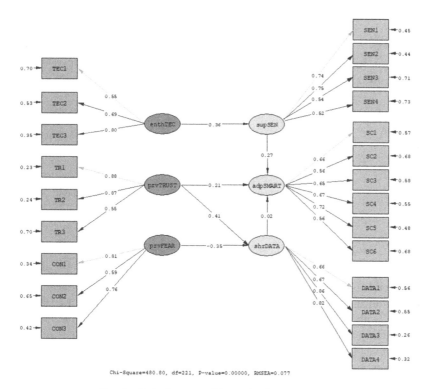

Fig. 2. Path diagram with standardized loadings

An explanation of the parameter estimates between latent variables is presented at the end of the next section. Firstly, the model fit is examined and considered. The latter represents the consistency of a hypothesized model and the data [13]. Testing the model fit refers to the statistical procedure that is comparing the covariance in the observed data and the expected covariance in the hypothesized model.

4.3   Model Assessment and Hypotheses Confirmation

Different fit indices have been developed to assess the model fit; yet, there is no consensus on the overall model fit index [19]. Besides, the model fit indices also depend on the sample size and model complexity [8]. Thus, in Table 3 generally used fit indices with the reference values are presented and discussed.

Five indices are an indication of a good overall fit, while three indices are not indicating a good overall fit, and two are acceptable. Indices that are not indicating a good overall model fit are the p-value for $\chi 2$ statistics, the goodness-of-fit index (GFI) and normed fit index (NFI).

Table 3. Fit indices of the Smart city adoption model

Fit indices	Model value	Reference value	Overall model fit
$\chi 2$	480.799	Not applicable	Not applicable
P value for $\chi 2$	0.000	>0.05	No
$\chi 2$/df	2.176	<5.00 (3.00)	Yes
Standardized RMR	0.097	<0.10 (0.05)	Acceptable
RMSEA	0.077	<0.10 (0.05)	Yes
CAIC	826.931	<CAIC saturated (1736.9) <CAIC independence (3461.5)	Yes
NFI	0.851	>0.90	No
NNFI	0.897	>0.90	Acceptable
CFI	0.910	>0.90	Yes
GFI	0.826	>0.90	No
IFI	0.911	>0.90	Yes

However, it is important to add that in sample sizes larger than 200 the $\chi 2$ statistic is often significant, even though the model has a good fit [18]. Thus, $\chi 2$ statistics in comparison with degrees of freedom is more commonly used to test the model [13] with a reference value of the ratio between the $\chi 2$ statistics and degrees of freedom lower than five [40], or three [26]. In the presented model, this value is 2.2 indicating a good fit even using a more restrictive reference value. In the same way, GFI is questionable in larger samples [35]; and therefore there is no commonly agreed value for accepting GFI, though higher values indicate a better fit [18]. The last index that is not within the reference value is NFI. However, similarly, to GFI there is no commonly agreed value, yet values close to one signify a good fit [24].

The standardized root mean square residual (standardized RMR) index in the proposed model has a value 0.097 indication an acceptable fit. A good model fit requires the value below 0.08 [22], although it is claimed that values below 0.10 also indicate a good model fit [27]. The next index in the table, namely the root mean square error of approximation (RMSEA) is considered as one of the most informative fit indices [13]. Its reference value for a good model varies from around 0.06 [22] or below 0.08 [18], while values exceeding 0.10 indicate a poor fit [7]. In the Smart city adoption model, the value indicates a good fit, as well as other indices like consistent Akaike information criterion (CAIC), non-normed fit index (NNFI), comparative fit index (CFI) and incremental fit index (IFI). Generally, $\chi 2$ per degree of freedom, CFI, and NNFI are used to assess the model fit [28]. Thus, the proposed Smart city adoption model has a good overall fit considering presented indices, their reference values and limitations.

Lastly, it is important to examine the structural model, which refers to assessing the significance of the estimated coefficients in the structural part of the model [18]. Thus, the signs of the parameters measuring the relationship between the latent variables, their statistical significance and the extent of the estimated parameters, together with the squared multiple correlations for the structural equations are examined.

In the proposed Smart City adoption model, all parameters are statistically significant at the 0.01 significance level, except the preparedness to share the data. Besides, the signs of the parameters are consistent with the hypothesized relationships between the latent variables. Thus, only H5 is not supported, as shown in Table 4.

Examining the impact of the estimated standardized parameters it is evident that the preparedness to install different control sensors have the largest impact on Smart City adoption, while perceived trust in proper privacy management has an important influence on preparedness to share the data. Contrary, the perceived fear regarding future consequences has a significant negative impact on preparedness to share the data.

Table 4. Result of the structural model

Hypothesis	Relationship	Std. path coefficient		t-Value	Result
H1	enthTEC → supSEN	+	0.36	3.53	Supported
H2	prvTRUST → adpSMART	+	0.21	2.13	Supported
H3	prvTRUST → shrDATA	+	0.41	5.04	Supported
H4	prvFEAR → shrDATA	–	0.35	−4.25	Supported
H5	shrDATA → adpSMART	+	0.02	0.21	Not supported
H6	supSEN → adpSMART	+	0.27	2.89	Supported

The R^2 for endogenous variables are ranging from 0.13 for supSEN, 0.12 for adpSMART and 0.35 for shrDATA. The latter shows the independent latent variables (prvTRUST and prvFEAR) are able to explain 35% of the variance in the shrDATA latent variable. Based on the criterion, where 0.26 is considered as substantial, 0.13 moderate, and 0.02 weak [11], the relationships are relevant, although according to more restrictive criterion [10] these values represent weak to the moderate predictor.

5   Discussion

The development of smart cities is extensively related to the development of information and communication technology. In the last years, the latter has become available and affordable to different stakeholders. Consequently, many initiatives across the world are moving into the direction of transforming the urban areas into smart cities focusing on future inhabitants as well. However, the smart city concept is not built on the technology itself or merely the technology. Smart cities are also causing important challenges that are related to the proper use of technology. Since the technological aspects of smart cities are already extensively researched, future studies should also focus on aspects covering citizens, personal preferences, privacy and quality of life.

This paper is thus focusing on factors important for smart city adoption as perceived by millennials. The focus on millennials is important since they are presenting future habitats in smart cities. The results indicate that several factors are important when considering smart city adoption. Firstly, the research has shown that preparedness to accept different control sensors both outside and inside buildings as well, is positively related to the smart cities' development support. However, achieving that preparedness should be done by focusing on millennials that are more enthusiastic about new technology. The latter has namely been confirmed as a strong predictor for preparedness to install different control sensors. This finding supports the previous study from healthcare industry claiming that individuals who are more open to technologies will more likely adopt new technologies that are offered to them [21].

On the other side, there are two interplaying factors, namely perceived fear regarding future consequences and perceived trust in proper privacy management, one with the strong positive effect and one with a strong negative effect on preparedness to share the data. The latter was hypothesized to have an important impact on smart city adoption; however, that hypothesis was not confirmed due to insignificant effect. Contrary, the perceived trust in proper privacy management is important factor to consider in the smart city adoption model. Nevertheless, trust is related to security issues, which were already proven to be important in case of smartcard adoption [5].

There are also several limitations related to the research findings. The research findings are constrained by the sample, which is limited to a single country and a single segment of the population, namely millennials. Although the emphasis was on studying millennials, future research should be done on other segments as well, particularly on elder people. The latter are generally not familiar with new technology, yet it can help them in solving daily problems. Further, the study is based on millennials' perception of smart city concepts. The concepts and the technologies are quite new; and therefore, not massively used or used in local initiatives only. Future research should provide an insight into how the perception will change after more intense usage.

Moreover, the research showed that further study of the smart city adoption factors is justified. Since the influence of preparedness to share the data is not significant, future research examining the factor in detail is suggested. Several factors may not have a direct impact on the smart city adoption, yet they may have an important role regarding the perception of the smart city. Lastly, the presented indicators and latent variables did not thoroughly explain the smart city adoption since the exogenous latent variables were able to explain the minor proportion of the variance in the smart city adoption construct. Further studies on the factor indicators and other factors not covered in this research are therefore needed in order to improve understanding the complexity of smart city adoption.

6   Conclusion

The rapid growth of population, particularly in the cities is influencing the quality of living in urban areas. Urban areas are namely facing several challenges due to older existing infrastructure, which is in many cases not being able to cope with this rapid urbanization. Besides, global shifts in the environment and sustainable orientation are presenting additional challenges for the future development of the cities.

In the last years, the development of information and communication technology resulted in the digital transformation of many areas including cities. Several cities are transforming or preparing with different initiatives for the transformation into smart city habitats. However, this transformation will affect many areas including mobility, public governance, environment, architecture and others. Yet, most importantly, it will affect existing and future citizens, namely how they will live and work. The paper; thus, presented a proposed model of the interplay of different factors that are important for smart city adoption including privacy issues, individual fears and perceived benefits. Accordingly, there is a huge challenge to properly implement new technologies, and at the same time to prepare the solutions that will be designed in line with what citizens expect.

Acknowledgements. The research presented in this paper was financially supported in part by the Slovenian Research Agency under research program No. P2-0037 – Future internet technologies: concepts, architectures, services and socio-economic issues.

A Appendix

See Table 5.

Table 5. Item descriptions

Construct	Item	Item description
enthTEC	tec1	Quickly experiment with new technologies
	tec2	Not hesitant in using new technologies
	tec3	Not procrastinating with the new technology
adpSMART	sc1	Prefer smart city because of a smart economy
	sc2	Prefer smart city because of smart people
	sc3	Prefer smart city because of a smart governance
	sc4	Prefer smart city because of a smart mobility
	sc5	Prefer smart city because of smart environment
	sc6	Prefer smart city because of smart life
supSEN	sen1	Support sensors for traffic control
	sen2	Support sensors for air control
	sen3	Support sensors for street control
	sen4	Support sensors' application inside buildings
shrDATA	data1	Not opposing to generating more data
	data2	Willing to share data (without benefits)
	data3	Willing to share data to raise the quality of life
	data4	Willing to share data to reduce costs of living
prvFEAR	con1	Concerned about cyber-attacks
	con2	Concerned about dependence on smart devices
	con3	Concerned about unmanageable artificial intelligence
prvTRUST	tr1	Trust public (state) institutions to keep data secure
	tr2	Trust public (state) institutions not selling the data
	tr3	Public organizations are more trusted than private

References

1. Albino, V., Berardi, U., Dangelico, R.M.: Smart cities: definitions, dimensions, performance, and initiatives. J. Urban Technol. **22**, 3–21 (2015)
2. Allam, Z., Dhunny, Z.A.: On big data, artificial intelligence and smart cities. Cities **89**, 80–91 (2019)
3. Ardolino, M., Rapaccini, M., Saccani, N., Gaiardelli, P., Crespi, G., Ruggeri, C.: The role of digital technologies for the service transformation of industrial companies. Int. J. Prod. Res. **56**, 2116–2132 (2017)
4. Baig, A., Dua, A., Riefberg, V.: Putting Citizens First: How to Improve Citizens' Experience and Satisfaction with Government Services, Washington, D.C. (2014)
5. Belanche-Gracia, D., Casaló-Ariño, L.V., Pérez-Rueda, A.: Determinants of multi-service smartcard success for smart cities development: a study based on citizens' privacy and security perceptions. Gov. Inf. Q. **32**, 154–163 (2015)
6. Braun, T., Fung, B.C.M., Iqbal, F., Shah, B.: Security and privacy challenges in smart cities. Sustain. Cities Soc. **39**, 499–507 (2018)
7. Browne, M.W., Cudeck, R.: Alternative ways of assessing model fit. Sociol. Methods Res. **21**, 136–162 (1992)
8. Byrne, B.M.: Structural Equation Modeling with Lisrel, Prelis, and Simplis: Basic Concepts, Applications, and Programming. Lawrence Erlbaum Associates, Mahwah (1998)
9. Chatterjee, S., Kar, A.K.: Effects of successful adoption of information technology enabled services in proposed smart cities of india: from user experience perspective. J. Sci. Technol. Policy Manag. **9**, 189–209 (2018)
10. Chin, W.W.: The partial least squares approach to structural equation modeling. Mod. Methods Bus. Res. **295**, 295–336 (1998)
11. Cohen, J.: Statistical Power Analysis for the Behavioral Sciences. Lawrence Erlbaum Associates, Hillsdale (1988)
12. Daziano, R.A., Sarrias, M., Leard, B.: Are consumers willing to pay to let cars drive for them? Analyzing response to autonomous vehicles. Transp. Res. Part C Emerg. Technol. **78**, 150–164 (2017)
13. Diamantopoulos, A., Siguaw, J.A.: Introducing Lisrel. SAGE Publications, London (2000)
14. Dudley, E., Lin, D.-Y., Mancini, M., Ng, J.: Implementing a Citizen-Centric Approach to Delivering Government Services. McKinsey & Company, New York (2015)
15. Gharaibeh, A., et al.: Smart cities: a survey on data management, security, and enabling technologies. IEEE Commun. Surv. Tutor. **19**, 2456–2501 (2017)
16. Giffinger, R., Haindlmaier, G., Kramar, H.: The role of rankings in growing city competition. Urban Res. Pract. **3**, 299–312 (2010)
17. Gil-Garcia, J.R., Helbig, N., Ojo, A.: Being smart: emerging technologies and innovation in the public sector. Gov. Inf. Q. **31**, I1–I8 (2014)
18. Hair, J.F., Anderson, R.E., Tatham, R.L., Black, W.C.: Multivariate Data Analysis. Prentice-Hall, New Jersey (1998)
19. Hayduk, L.: Lisrel Issues, Debates, and Strategies. Johns Hopkins University Press, Baltimore (1996)
20. Herrmann, M., Boehme, P., Mondritzki, T., Ehlers, J.P., Kavadias, S., Truebel, H.: Digital transformation and disruption of the health care sector: internet-based observational study. J. Med. Internet Res. **20**, 8 (2018)

21. Hossain, A., Quaresma, R., Rahman, H.: Investigating factors influencing the physicians' adoption of electronic health record (EHR) in healthcare system of bangladesh: an empirical study. Int. J. Inf. Manag. **44**, 76–87 (2019)
22. Hu, L., Bentler, P.M.: Cutoff criteria for fit indexes in covariance structure analysis: conventional criteria versus new alternatives. Struct. Equ. Model. Multidiscip. J. **6**, 1–55 (1999)
23. Ismagilova, E., Hughes, L., Dwivedi, Y.K., Raman, K.R.: Smart cities: advances in research —an information systems perspective. Int. J. Inf. Manag. **47**, 88–100 (2019)
24. Jöreskog, K.G., Sörbom, D.: Lisrel 8: Structural Equation Modeling with the Simplis Command Language. Scientific Software International, Chicago (1993)
25. Kline, P.: The Handbook of Psychological Testing. Routledge, London (1999)
26. Kline, R.B.: Principles and Practice of Structural Equation Modeling. Guilford Press, New York (2011)
27. Kline, T.J.B.: Psychological Testing: A Practical Approach to Design and Evaluation. Sage Publications, Thousand Oaks (2005)
28. Koufteros, X.A.: Testing a model of pull production: a paradigm for manufacturing research using structural equation modeling. J. Oper. Manag. **17**, 467–488 (1999)
29. Lierow, M.: B2City: the next wave of urban logistics. Supply Chain **247**, 41–48 (2014)
30. Liu, D.-Y., Chen, S.-W., Chou, T.-C.: resource fit in digital transformation: lessons learned from the CBC bank global e-banking project. Manag. Decis. **49**, 1728–1742 (2011)
31. Loebbecke, C., Picot, A.: Reflections on societal and business model transformation arising from digitization and big data analytics: a research agenda. J. Strat. Inf. Syst. **24**, 149–157 (2015)
32. Praharaj, S., Han, H.: Cutting through the clutter of smart city definitions: a reading into the smart city perceptions in India. City Cult. Soc. **18**, 100289 (2019)
33. Reis, J., Amorim, M., Melão, N., Matos, P.: Digital transformation: a literature review and guidelines for future research. In: Rocha, Á., Adeli, H., Reis, L.P., Costanzo, S. (eds.) WorldCIST'18 2018. AISC, vol. 745, pp. 411–421. Springer, Cham (2018). https://doi.org/10.1007/978-3-319-77703-0_41
34. Shabanpour, R., Golshani, N., Shamshiripour, A., Mohammadian, A.: Eliciting preferences for adoption of fully automated vehicles using best-worst analysis. Transp. Res. Part C Emerg. Technol. **93**, 463–478 (2018)
35. Sharma, S., Mukherjee, S., Kumar, A., Dillon, W.R.: A simulation study to investigate the use of cutoff values for assessing model fit in covariance structure models. J. Bus. Res. **58**, 935–943 (2005)
36. Stolterman, E., Fors, A.C.: Information technology and the good life. In: Kaplan, B., Truex, D.P., Wastell, D., Wood-Harper, A.T., DeGross, J.I. (eds.) Information Systems Research. IIFIP, vol. 143, pp. 687–692. Springer, Boston, MA (2004). https://doi.org/10.1007/1-4020-8095-6_45
37. Taylor, P., Keeter, S.: Pew Research Center: Millennials: A Portrait of Generation Next: Confident, Connected, Open to Change. Pew Research Center, Washington, D.C. (2010)
38. Van den Bergh, J., Viaene, S.: Unveiling smart city implementation challenges: the case of Ghent. Inf. Polity **21**, 5–19 (2016)
39. Westerman, G., Calméjane, C., Bonnet, D., Ferraris, P., McAfee, A.: Digital transformation: a roadmap for billion-dollar organizations. MIT Cent. Digit. Bus. Capgemini Consult. **1**, 1–68 (2011)
40. Wheaton, B., Muthen, B., Alwin, D.F., Summers, G.F.: Assessing reliability and stability in panel models. Sociol. Methodol. **8**, 84–136 (1977)

41. Wischnevsky, J.D., Damanpour, F.: Organizational transformation and performance: an examination of three perspectives. J. Manag. Issues **18**, 104–128 (2006)
42. Woodhead, R., Stephenson, P., Morrey, D.: Digital construction: from point solutions to iot ecosystem. Autom. Constr. **93**, 35–46 (2018)
43. Zaharia, S.E., Pietreanu, C.V.: Challenges in airport digital transformation. Transp. Res. Procedia **35**, 90–99 (2018)

Supervised Machine Learning Approach for Subjectivity/Objectivity Classification of Social Data

Rim Chiha[1(✉)] and Mounir Ben Ayed[1,2]

[1] REGIM-Lab.: REsearch Groups in Intelligent Machines,
National School of Engineers (ENIS), University of Sfax, BP 1173,
3038 Sfax, Tunisia
{rim.chiha,mounir.benayed}@ieee.org
[2] Faculty of Science of Sfax, University of Sfax, BP 802, 3038 Sfax, Tunisia

Abstract. With the exponential growth of critiques available on social media, the distinction between subjective (i.e., emotional terms) and objective (i.e., factual terms) information is a non-trivial natural language processing task. Therefore, we focus in this paper on the subjectivity/objectivity classification of social data precisely Facebook which is the most popular social network. The proposed approach is based on supervised machine learning techniques. Similar to any supervised application, our approach is composed of three main steps which are features extraction, training and prediction. Our main contribution in this work is to introduce new features such as ontology-based N-grams feature which represent good a indicator for predicting subjective text. Multiple classifiers like Naive Bayes, Support Vector Machine, Random Forest and Multi Layer Perceptron are applied on our data set. The experimental results show that the Random Forest model achieved the highest performance metrics 0.676 of accuracy, 0.697 of precision, 0,677 of recall and 0.683 off-score.

Keywords: Social data · Subjectivity/objectivity · Supervised · Machine learning

1 Introduction

Nowadays, we have witnessed to the exponential growth of social networks such as Facebook, Instagram, Twitter, etc., through which the users can communicate, exchange different types of information and express their opinions and attitudes about on almost all aspects of everyday life.

Indeed, social data aren't including only subjective information, but also objective information. Subjective sentences express emotional state while objective sentences can describe factual information. However, the subjectivity/objectivity classification is not simple task due to the non availability of annotated data and the subjectivity can take different forms. Such task is based on machine learning techniques and can be performed at sentence and/or document level. Various research works such as [8, 9] and [10] focus on the subjectivity prediction of twitter data. But none that focus on Facebook data. Despite, Facebook is considered as the most popular social network and

© Springer Nature Switzerland AG 2020
M. Themistocleous and M. Papadaki (Eds.): EMCIS 2019, LNBIP 381, pp. 193–205, 2020.
https://doi.org/10.1007/978-3-030-44322-1_15

the comments may contain both emotional and factual information. Therefore, we propose in this paper a supervised approach based on a set of features for predicting the subjectivity of Facebook comments associated to Samsung Mobile USA page.

In addition, the majority of works cited in the literature [3–5] and [7] assumed that the existence of adjectives in a sentence represents as good feature for detecting the subjectivity. However, in some case we can find the existence of adjective in objective sentences which can reduce the performance of such approaches.

For this, we introduced in this paper N-grams features combined with their grammatical roles (i.e., POS) in order to improve the subjectivity prediction task. For example, "The screen has good pixels". The combination between "good" adjective and "pixels" noun as a bigram can facilitate the detection of subjective sentence and improve the performances of classification models.

As our approach is oriented domain (e.g., mobile phone domain), we proposed to use the ontology notion for two reasons: (i) handling the extraction of N-grams features using mappings between the nouns of N-grams and the ontology concepts. (ii) filtering out irrelevant reviews in which users express opinions about things that are not related to the domain.

The rest of this paper is organized as follows. In Sect. 2, we reviewed the previous works in subjectivity/objectivity classification. In Sect. 3, we described the proposed approach. In Sect. 4, we presented the experimental setup of the classification application. The evaluation results are discussed in Sect. 5. Section 6 concludes the paper and gives some future directions.

2 Related Works

The first research works that studied the subjectivity/objectivity classification issue affirmed that the existence of adjectives in sentences is a strong predictor of subjectivity. So, Bruce and Wiebe [2] assumed that the probability of a sentence being subjective is 55.8%, if the sentence contains at least one adjective. Hatzivassiloglou and Wiebe [3] are interested in the existence of dynamic adjectives, semantically oriented adjectives and gradable adjectives for the classification of a large collection of new stories and human evaluation documents. They applied the Naive Bayes (NB) algorithm that achieved very high performance upwards of 97% precision and recall. In addition to the use of adjectives, Riloff et al. [4] take into account the nouns.

Kamal [5] proposed new features such as TF-IDF (Term Frequency- Inverse Document Frequency), part of speech, opinion indicator seed word, position, the presence of negation and modifier words. In this work, the author applied different classifiers such as NB, J48, MLP (Multi Layer Perceptron) and Bagging for detecting the subjectivity of each word present in a review sentence then the subjectivity of the whole sentence using an unigram model. Thus, NB has a higher recall (0.916), precision (0.932) and f-score (0.922).

In addition to the classical features such as n-gram feature and sentiment information, Chenlo and Losada [6] studied the importance of new features such as the position and the rhetorical structure of sentence in a discourse for subjectivity detection. Then, they proposed two types of feature representation such as unigrams and unigrams/bigrams models. The experimental results showed that the use of SVM (Support Vector Machine) classifier combines with unigrams/bigrams model perform well compared to the OpinionFinder subjectivity classifier. Palshikar and colleagues [7] focused on the identification of subjective sentences which contain or not explicit sentiment markers. This approach is based on several features such as number of adjectives, number of nouns, word count, number of strongly subjective words, number of named entities, number of comparatives, number of superlatives, tense, number of adverbs, number of date and time. In the experimentation step, they applied different classifiers such as J48, MLP, NB, Random Forest (RF), SVM and Logistic Regression (LR). Then, they investigated the combination of multiple classifiers in order to improve the results of classification. The evaluation is based on OpinionFinder system and TextBlod a python library.

Other works such as [8, 9] and [10] focus on the subjectivity prediction of data generated from Twitter Micro-blogging. Due to the specifications of Twitter data such as Hashtags, user references, existence of URLs, the length restriction (140 characters), the feature extraction becomes quite different compared to the works mentioned above. Addressing this challenge, Sixto et al. [10] studied the effect of contextual information for improving the classification task. Different classifiers such as LR, NB and RF were tested on multiple training models like Meta-Information (MI), Bag of Words (BoW), MI+ BoW and staking MI+ BoW. The result of experimentation showed that the use of regression models combined with staking MI+ BoW produces the best performance results.

Hajj et al. [11] focus on the subjectivity prediction of sports articles extracted from Amazon. They proposed several features that can be divided into two categories semantic and syntactic. For finding the subset of features required for optimal classification, the authors proposed Cortical Algorithm (CA) for features reducing. Then, CA* is used for classifying the texts on subjective and objective. Several classifiers were compared such SVM and LMSVM with CA*. The latter achieved the best value of accuracy 85,6% while reducing 40% of features.

Table 1 summarizes the most relevant approaches cited above are based on such criteria: Data source, features and used algorithms. Through Table 1 we found out that the data sources in all approaches are heterogeneous. None of such works used Facebook data as input. Despite, the domain Facebook message is boundless and may contain both subjective, objective and irrelevant information [1]. In addition, the majority of such approaches are based on the following hypothesis "the existence of adjectives represents a good indicator for finding the subjectivity". However, such a hypothesis is not always valid precisely in the case of the existence of adjectives in objective sentences.

For this, we proposed in this paper new feature the N-grams feature combined with their grammatical roles (i.e., POS) in order to improve the subjectivity prediction task of Facebook data. Moreover, we proposed to use the ontology notion for handling the extraction of such feature and filtering out irrelevant reviews.

Table 1. Summary of reviewed works.

	Data source	Features	Used algorithms
Hatzivassiloglou and Wiebe [3]	New stories, Human evaluation documents	Dynamic adjectives, semantically oriented adjectives, gradable adjectives	NB
Kamal [5]	Amazon	TF-IDF, PoS, opinion words, position, negation, modifier	NB, J48, MLP, Bagging
Chenlo and Losada [6]	NTCIR-7 English Moat	Position, opinion, RST, Length	SVM
Palshikar et al. [7]	Opinosis dataset, biomedical abstracts	Number adjective, noun, opinion words, named entities, superlative, comparative, adverb, tense, date	J48, MLP, NB, RF, SVM, LR
Sixto et al. [10]	Twitter	URL, Exclamation marks, Emoticons and Uppercase words Uppercase Percent, Favorites, Modularity Class, Graph Degrees, Retweet, Ellipsis	LR, RF, NB, GradientBoosting
Hajj et al. [17]	Amzon	Semantic and Syntactic features	SVM, LMSVM, CA*

3 Proposed Approach for Finding Subjective Sentence

Figure 1 shows a flowchart of the proposed approach for the subjectivity/objectivity prediction of social data.

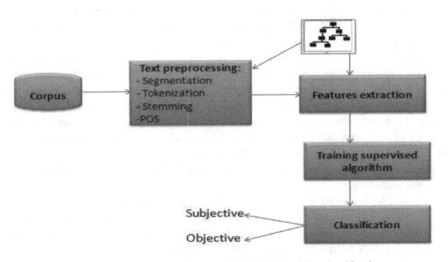

Fig. 1. Proposed approach for subjectivity/objectivity classification

As mentioned above, we are interested to the mobile phone domain. Therefore, we proposed to use the ontology proposed by Kontopoulos et al. [12] at the preprocessing step for filtering the noise reviews and at the features extraction step for handling the extraction of N-grams features.

Firstly, we provided an overview of the ontology proposed by Kontopoulos et al. [12] which represents a description of Smartphone concepts and its relationships. For the design of such ontology, authors start with the central element (i.e., Smartphone concept), then they presented its sub-categories such as Nokia Lumia, Htc One, Apple Iphone and Samsung Galaxy through the sub-concept of relationship. Thereafter, they defined the aspects of each category through the sub-concept-of relationship. To augment the underlying semantics of the ontology, authors proceed to enrich the aspects with their synonyms and hyponyms using the WordNet lexical database. In our work, we focused only on the sub-class which describes Samsung Galaxy Smartphones. Figure 2 shows the ontology using the OntoGen software tool.

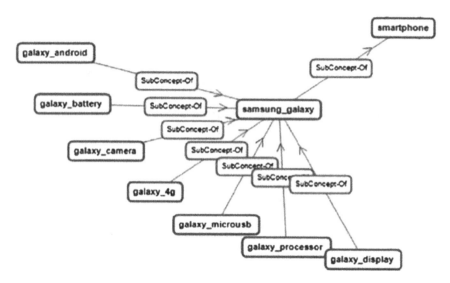

Fig. 2. Ontology visualization through OntoGen tool

3.1   Data Collection

The first step of our approach is the collection of Facebook comments associated with such post. Then, the gathered data are provided to human readers for interpreting and categorizing the text content that are based mainly on the existence of opinion words and the adjectives in sentences.

3.2   Text Preprocessing

In this step, we performed on our corpus preprocessing operations, including the filtering of the comments. Indeed, Facebook comments can be written in various languages. We are interested in the English language. So, we used DetectLanguage API for this purpose. Then, we proposed to clean the comments from the noise such as name identification (i.e., @ user name), hyperlinks, etc. For segmenting the comments, we considered only the dots as separators because the other punctuation marks such as commas or semicolons can be part of emoticons. For the tokenization of sentences into words, we used PTBTokenizer provided by SNLP group. In addition, we used PorterStemmer for reducing the words to their root forms.

Moreover, we propose to filter out the irrelevant comments which contain opinion about things which are not related to the object or its aspects. For example "I am disappointed to customer service of Samsung Galaxy". In this comment, user introduced your opinion about customer service which is not considered as an aspect of Samsung Galaxy Smartphones. For this, we compare the nouns of sentences with the ontology concepts. The matched nouns mean that the comment will be considered for the subjectivity prediction, otherwise it will be eliminated.

3.3 Features Extraction

Feature extraction is the most important stage in the text classification field [5]. This step consists to transform each text in the form of numeric vectors representing the features set. For the classification of text into subjective and objective, we proposed the following features:

Number of Opinion Words (f1). This feature represents the number of words which express sentiment and feeling whether positive or negative. For the detection of opinion words, we used a SentiWordNet tool [13] that assigns a score for each word according to its grammatical role. For instance, the word "much" has a score equal to 0.125 if it is tagged as a noun, 0.875 as an adverb and 0 as adjective.

Number of Negation (f2). Within the user reviews, the negating terms such as not, no, never, etc., are frequently used. Indeed, the presence of negation terms represents a good cue for detecting subjectivity of a sentence.

Number of Enhancing Terms (f3). This feature counts the number of adverbs in a sentence. An adverb, also called, a modifier is defined as a word that modifies a verb, an adjective, another adverb or even the whole sentence. In the English language, we can distinguish five basic types of adverbs namely that of manner, degree, time, place and frequency. In our work, we focus on the two first categories. Indeed, the adverbs that describe the manner and degree are the most appropriate and used in the sentiment analysis and subjectivity detection contexts.

Number of Exclamation & Interrogation (f4). Generally, the use of exclamation and interrogation punctuations is associated with the subjective content [14].

Number of Superlative and Comparative Words (f5). The existence of superlative and comparative cues checks the subjectivity of the sentence. For this, we used the words set proposed in [15].

Number of Emoticons (f6). Facebook is a social network in which users frequently use the emojis. Indeed, the existence of emoticons in a sentence is considered as a strong indicator for indicating that the sentence is subjective. For this, we defined a dictionary that contains the most used emoticons and their short cut codes. Then, we performed mappings between the emojis used in comments and those defined in the dictionary.

N-Grams Features The bigrams and trigrams features are taken as a good indicator for detecting the subjectivity of a sentence. Each word in the bigrams and trigrams features is combined with its grammatical role, such as noun, verb, adverb, adjective, etc. We used the Part Of Speech (POS) Tagger of the Stanford Natural Language Processing (SNLP) for word tagging. The extraction of such features is assisted with the ontology mentioned above.

Bigrams Feature (f7): If a sentence contains a bigrams tagged as JJ (i.e., adjective) followed by NN (i.e., NN) in which the adjective expresses an opinion information and the noun belongs to the concepts of Smartphone ontology, so the sentence is classified as subjective. Examples of bigrams: "Excellent battery". "Good screen".

Trigrams Feature (f8): The majority of subjectivity detection approaches are based on the existence of simple adjectives in a sentence. In our work, we are interested in the compound adjectives. In the English Language, we distinguished ten formats of compound adjectives. In this paper, we focus only on the four formats which are described in the following. Such compound adjectives are the most suitable for subjectivity detection context and they are represented as trigrams tagged as follows:

- JJ (i.e., adjective) + NN (i.e., noun) + NN.
  Example: high quality screen
- JJ + VBG (i.e., Verb + ing) + NN.
  Example: nice looking phone
- RB (i.e., Adverb) + VBG + NN.
  Example: hard working battery
- RB + VBN (i.e., Verb + past participle) + NN.
  Example: highly valued Smartphone

These trigrams are taken as a good indicator if the following conditions are checked:

- The adjectives of the first two cases are opinion terms.
- The adverbs of the two last cases are manner or degree adverbs.
- The mapping between the noun of each trigram and the concepts of Smartphone ontology is checked.

Consequently, a sentence which contains at least one of the trigrams mentioned below is classified as subjective.

Class Attribute. The Facebook social network does not impose conditions on the comment length. In some cases, we can find very long comments. Therefore, we proposed to divide the comment into sentences. Then, we checked the subjectivity of each sentence based on such features. If the comment contains a subjective sentence, then it is considered as subjective. The class value set 'S' if a comment is subjective, otherwise 'O'.

The textual corpus is transformed to a numeric matrix in which each comment is represented as a numeric feature vector. Such matrix is prepared for training and prediction steps. Table 2 shows the feature vectors of the first ten comments of the corpus.

3.4 Training and Prediction

The subjectivity/objectivity prediction is based on supervised machine learning techniques which are divided into two main steps: training and test. The training is fed with the feature matrix which is generated from the previous step and produces the classification models which are used to make the predictions.

Table 2. Sample of training dataset

f1	f2	f3	f4	f5	f6	f7	f8	Class
5	2	1	2	17	1	1	0	S
1	0	0	2	0	1	0	0	O
6	0	1	0	1	1	0	3	S
12	7	6	10	8	1	1	0	S
2	1	0	3	0	1	0	0	O
1	0	0	1	4	1	0	0	O
4	1	0	1	2	1	0	0	S
7	0	2	2	5	3	0	1	S
0	1	0	2	0	2	0	0	O
11	1	4	3	0	1	2	1	S

4 Experimentation

Generally, the extraction of Facebook data is ensured through Graph API Explorer. However, the API has become more restricted which makes data collection complex. Therefore, we used Facepager [16] an application for generic data retrieval through APIs for extracting the Facebook comments. Their number is up to 1250 and their length varied between 36 and 1473 of words.

Then we performed on the extracted data preprocessing operations as described in Sect. 3.2. We defined under Java such functions for feature extraction. Finally, we split the data set into 75% for training and 25% for the test and we tested under WEKA the most cited classifiers in the literature like NB, SVM, RF and MLP for the classification of the comments. Table 3 shows the parameters used in each classifier. In all models, we used batch size = 100 and number place = 4

Table 3. Models'parameters

Table 3. Models'parameters

RF	SVM	MLP	NB
Maxdepth = 8 NumFeatures = 4 NumIterations = 100	PolyKernel numFolds = 5	LearningRate = 0.7 normalizeAttribute = true	useKernelEstimator = true

5 Results and Evaluation

5.1 Results

Different metrics are taken into account to measure the performance of each classifier such as:

- Accuracy: Allows to measure the performance of classifier in terms of correctly and incorrectly classified instances.
- Precision and Recall: They used for checking the success of prediction and calculated based on Eqs. (1) and (2).

$$Precision = \frac{TP}{TP + FP} \tag{1}$$

$$Recall = \frac{TP}{TP + FN} \tag{2}$$

In subjectivity/objectivity classification context, the TP means the number of subjective/objective instances correctly labeled as belonging to the associated class. FP is the number of subjective/objective items incorrectly labeled as belonging to the associated class. FN presents the number of subjective/objective items whose system fails to assign the appropriate label.

- F-score: is the harmonic average of the precision and recall.

$$f_{score} = 2 * \frac{Precision * recall}{Precision + recall} \tag{3}$$

Firstly, we present the performances of such classifiers over training and test steps.

Table 4. Classifiers performances on training dataset

Classifier	Accuracy	Precision	Recall	F-score
NB	0.567	0.624	0.568	0.563
SVM	0.637	0.628	0.638	0.612
RF	**0.780**	**0.787**	**0.780**	**0.782**
MLP	0.707	0.709	0.708	0.708

Table 5. Classifiers performances on test dataset

Classifier	Accuracy	Precision	Recall	F-score
NB	0.506	0.619	0.506	0.503
SVM	0.652	0.627	0.652	0.629
RF	**0.676**	**0.697**	**0.677**	**0.683**
MLP	0.664	0.675	0.665	0.669

Through Tables 4 and 5 we found out that: (i) the performance values on train and test are much closed which show there is no over fitting problem happened to the all models, (ii) RF achieve the high performance measures on both training and predicting steps.

Afterwards, we investigated the feature's importance in the classification task. Random forest classifier is among the most popular supervised machine learning technique, thanks to its simplicity of use, robustness and good accuracy. Two methods for feature selections are provided by such classifier like mean decrease impurity and mean decrease accuracy. The first one can determine how much each feature can reduce the weighted impurity in a tree. It is based on Gini impurity or information gain/entropy for classification and the variance for regression tree. The second can determine the impact of each feature on the accuracy of the model. The main idea of this method is to permute values of each feature, then determine how much these changes reduce the accuracy of the model. Clearly, the permutations of unimportant variables have a little or any impact on model accuracy, while the permutations of important variables decrease it. In this work, random forest contributes with the best accuracy value. For this, we investigated the feature's importance on accuracy of the classifier. Table 6 shows the importance rate of each feature with the random forest classifier.

Table 6. Features importance with RF

Features	Scores
Opinion words	0.3323
Interrogation & exclamation	0.1976
Superlative & comparative	0.1701
Negation	0.1133
Modifier	0.0727
Bigrams	0.0518
Emoticons	0.0462
Trigrams	0.0154

OpinionWords is considered as the most important feature. The permutation of this feature decreases the model performance by 33.23%. The Interrogation & Exclamation, Comparative & Superlative, and Negation features have scores which belong to an interval [10%, 20%]. So, the impacts of these features are ranked as medium.

Modifiers, Bigrams, Emoticons and Trigrams features participate with the less importance value which belonging to the same interval [0%, 10%]. Trigrams feature has the poor importance value (1.5%). This does not mean such feature is not a good cue for subjectivity detection. But, in our data set (i.e., Facebook comments) users rarely express their opinions with compound adjectives. So, when we use the other dataset in which compound adjectives are frequently used, the relative importance of trigrams feature will be increased. Hence, we will focus on future works on the effectiveness of such features.

5.2   Evaluation

As mentioned above the data sources of previous works are heterogeneous and there is no work that focuses on Facebook data. Therefore, we used subjectivity classifier of OpinionFinder (OF) against the same collection of (i.e., our corpus) data for comparison purposes. OF [17] is a system that identifies the subjectivity of sentences based on various aspects of subjectivity such as agents who are sources of opinion, direct subjective expressions and speech events, and sentiment expressions. The evaluation metrics obtained with OF are 0.562 of accuracy, 0.316 of precision, 0.562 of recall and 0.405 of F-score. When we compare the results of OF with the predicted results of RF classifier, we found out that the results of our model outperform OF (Table 7).

Table 7. Performances comparison of our method with OF

	RF	OF
Accuracy	0.676	0.562
Precision	0.697	0.316
Recall	0.677	0.562
F-score	0.683	0.405

6   Conclusion

In this paper, we presented a supervised approach for distinguishing the factual and emotional information from a corpus composed of a set of Facebook comments. Indeed, the success of classification task is strongly related to the good features management. Thus, we selected a set of features based on sentiment information, namely OpinionWords, Bigrams, Trigrams features, sense modification terms like negation and modifier features and visual information such as the emoticons and the exclamation/interrogation punctuations for detecting the subjectivity of comments.

Afterwards, different classification models were tested in our dataset and the obtained performance values are considered reasonable compared to OF classifier. As future work, we focus at short time on the evaluation of the proposed approach on larger datasets which come from other commercial web sites. Then, we intend to extend this work with sentiment analysis process in which we will study the polarity detection.

Acknowledgment. The research leading to these results has received funding from the Ministry of Higher Education and Scientific Research of Tunisia under the grant agreement number LR11ES48.

References

1. Ortigosa, J.M., Carro, R.M.: Sentiment analysis in facebook and its application to e-learning. Comput. Hum. Behav. **31**, 527–541 (2014)
2. Bruce, R.F., Wiebe, J.M.: Recognizing subjectivity: a case study in manual tagging. Nat. Lang. Eng. **5**(2), 187–205 (1999)
3. Hatzivassiloglou, V., Wiebe, J.M.: Effects of adjective orientation and gradability on sentence subjectivity. In: Proceedings of the 18th Conference on Computational Linguistics - Volume 1, Stroudsburg, PA, USA, pp. 299–305 (2000)
4. Riloff, E., Wiebe, J., Wilson, T.: Learning subjective nouns using extraction pattern bootstrapping. In: Proceedings of the Seventh Conference on Natural Language Learning at HLT-NAACL 2003 - Volume 4, Stroudsburg, PA, USA, pp. 25–32 (2003)
5. Kamal, A.: Subjectivity classification using machine learning techniques for mining feature-opinion pairs from web opinion sources. CoRR, abs/1312.6962 (2013)
6. Chenlo, J.M., Losada, D.E.: An empirical study of sentence features for subjectivity and polarity classification. Inf. Sci. **280**, 275–288 (2014)
7. Palshikar, D.G.K., Apte, M., Singh, V.: Learning to identify subjective sentences. In: Proceedings of the 13th International Conference on Natural Language Processing, pp. 239–248 (2016)
8. Barbosa, L., Feng, J.: Robust sentiment detection on Twitter from biased and noisy data. In: Proceedings of the 23rd International Conference on Computational Linguistics: Posters, Stroudsburg, PA, pp. 36–44 (2010)
9. Davidov, D., Tsur, O., Rappoport, A.: Enhanced sentiment learning using Twitter hashtags and smileys. In: Proceedings of the 23rd International Conference on Computational Linguistics, Posters, Stroudsburg, PA, USA, pp. 241–249 (2010)
10. Sixto, J., Almeida, A., López-de-Ipiña, D.: An approach to subjectivity detection on Twitter using the structured information. In: Nguyen, N.-T., Manolopoulos, Y., Iliadis, L., Trawiński, B. (eds.) ICCCI 2016. LNCS (LNAI), vol. 9875, pp. 121–130. Springer, Cham (2016). https://doi.org/10.1007/978-3-319-45243-2_11
11. Hajj, N., Rizk, Y., Awad, M.: A subjectivity classification framework for sports articles using improved cortical algorithms. Neural Comput. Appl. **31**, 8069–8085 (2019). https://doi.org/10.1007/s00521-018-3549-3
12. Kontopoulos, E., Berberidis, C., Dergiades, T., Bassiliades, N.: Ontology-based sentiment analysis of Twitter posts. Expert Syst. Appl. **40**(10), 4065–4074 (2013)
13. Baccianella, S., Esuli, A., Sebastiani, F.: SentiWordNet 3.0: an enhanced lexical resource for sentiment analysis and opinion mining. In: Proceedings of LREC, pp. 2200–2204 (2010)
14. Agarwal, A., Xie, B., Vovsha, I., Rambow, O., Passonneau, R.: Sentiment analysis of Twitter data. In: Proceedings of the Workshop on Languages in Social Media, Stroudsburg, PA, USA, pp. 30–38 (2011)
15. Jindal, N., Liu, B.: Identifying comparative sentences in text documents. In: Proceedings of the 29th Annual International ACM SIGIR Conference on Research and Development in Information Retrieval, New York, NY, USA, pp. 244–251 (2006)

16. Jünger, J., Keyling, T.: Facepager. An application for generic data retrieval through APIs. Source code and releases (2019). https://github.com/strohne/Facepager/
17. Wilson, T., et al.: OpinionFinder: a system for subjectivity analysis. In: Proceedings of HLT/EMNLP on Interactive Demonstrations, Stroudsburg, PA, USA, pp. 34–35 (2005)

e-Government

Smart Cities and Citizen Orientation: The Growing Importance of "Smart People" in Developing Modern Cities

Mariusz Luterek[✉]

Department of Journalism, Information and Book Studies, University of Warsaw,
Warsaw, Poland
m.luterek@uw.edu.pl

Abstract. The smart people dimension of smart cities becomes more important in recent years and is broadly discussed in the literature. The main goal of this paper is to verify if citizen orientation can be proven not only by research papers, but also actual strategic documents enacted by city officials. For this purpose we discuss citizen orientation of smart city strategies from 30 smart cities from IESE Cities in Motion Index, following two main hypothesis: H1: Smart cities do have strategic documents laying their path to "smartness", H2: Smart city strategies contain goals proving their citizen orientation. Most of the cities from the sample include "smart" concept in their strategic planning, either as part of general strategy (e.g. New York) or dedicated smart city strategy (e.g. London). Others define only a set of undertaken actions, without setting measurable goals. Many of the cities from the sample tend to include more human-oriented goals, however technology-oriented approach still seems to be dominant.

Keywords: Smart city · Smart city strategy · Strategic planning · Citizen orientation

1 Introduction

There are many scientific studies trying to collect definitions and approaches to what a smart city is, but the term remains fuzzy [1]. Although it is not a new concept, still, with over 20 years of research and practice, as many authors notice, there is very little agreement over what smart cities actually are [2]. It grows from e-government solutions and experiences [3], however it's about (1) even more technologies and (2) even more informed decisions based on (3) even more information (data) collected, as case of Singapore's "intelligent island" shows [4]. It can be defined as "a city well performing in a forward-looking way in six dimensions: economy, people, governance, mobility, environment, and living, built on the 'smart' combination of endowments and activities of self-decisive independent and aware citizens" [5], or more comprehensively as "a well-defined geographical area, in which high technologies such as ICT, logistic, energy production, and so on, cooperate to create benefits for citizens in terms of well-being, inclusion and participation, environmental quality, intelligent development;

© Springer Nature Switzerland AG 2020
M. Themistocleous and M. Papadaki (Eds.): EMCIS 2019, LNBIP 381, pp. 209–222, 2020.
https://doi.org/10.1007/978-3-030-44322-1_16

governed by a well-defined pool of subjects, able to state the rules and policy for the city government and development" [6].

There are many battling concepts for modern urban development, some overlapping, like: smart cities, digital cities and intelligent cities [7], while others are presented as more distinctive: networked city [8], world city or global city [9], ubiquitous city [10], informational city [11], creative city [12], knowledge city [13], resilient city [14] or sustainable city [15]. In reality even those concepts are quite often discussed together, because the obvious question is if a city can be smart without being sustainable [16]? Some researchers even use the term Smart Sustainable City (SSC) to emphasize inseparability of those concepts [17], some claim that "smart" is the next stage of city's development, after digital city and intelligent city [18], while others define smart city as a city in which issues limiting sustainable urban development are tackled by ICT [19]. Sustainability and resilience also cannot exist without another [20], as smart technologies are being used to create resilient cities [14], which adds to the confusion.

In recent years, the smart people dimension of smart cities becomes more important, as addressing the topic of people and communities as part of smart cities is seen as critical [21]. This paper falls in line with this approach, as its main goal is discuss citizen orientation of smart city strategies from 30 smart cities. For this purpose we follow two main hypothesis: H1: Smart cities have strategic documents laying their path to "smartness" (meaning they are implementing smart solutions in a planned, cohesive way), H2: Smart city strategies contain goals proving their citizen orientation.

The reminder of this paper is organized as follows. First, we define what citizen orientation means through analysis of previous smart city research. Then we will try to identify what a smart city actually is by analyzing composition of indicators used in selected smart city rankings. This is also important from the point of view of sample selection, which will be discussed in Sect. 4. Finally, before presenting results and final remarks, we will describe our methodological approach.

2   Citizens Orientation in the Smart City Research

Smart city domain attracts researchers from many disciplines, which leads to growing publication output, as Web of Science and Scopus indexing proves [22]. Nonetheless, scientific process requires time, and in case of research in the smart city domain time is limited, as evolution of technology changes the landscape constantly. It is especially true when we analyze papers with IT oriented case studies, sometimes already obsolete upon publication. That's why some city officials question the need for scientists' involvement in creating smart solutions. While scientific input to smart city domain grows constantly, it still fails to provide necessary strategic, technological and organizational knowledge, that cities need for successful urban development [19]. It makes also smart city research more problematic, as previous research tends to focus primarily on the technology dimension and the way it affects other dimensions of the city [7].

In recent years the term "smart" is used more and more often with terms like "open" and "participatory" [23], which makes the "people" pillar of this concept even more important, putting much emphasis on skills and human capital. It is also the fundament of the "holistic path", defined in the literature by [2], which refers to bottom-up, decentralized and diffused, oriented towards more collaborative and inclusive solutions city management model, giving more space to involve broad spectrum of stakeholders, like NGOs or public libraries [24], and average citizens by unlocking their knowledge and skills potential [4]. This leads to knowledge-based vision of the smart city, oriented on people's information and knowledge of people, so shifting the organization more from explicit knowledge (knowledge gained from city's information systems) towards tacit knowledge (citizen's knowledge) [25]. As a result, public officials start to understand, that people are an important component of smart cities, they are not only passive recipients/users, but active participants, or even creators [6]. In consequence, the top-down approach in planning must be balanced with bottom-up community participation [26]. It is important to create suitable environment to foster the growth of creative class, as social infrastructure (intellectual and social capital) is essential fundament of any smart city [27].

This can lead to adopting an open innovation system in the city, and, as a consequence, to multilayer innovation ecosystem [26], allowing citizens to engage directly in co-production of public services and policies [28]. There are many ways to involve people of the city e.g. urban labs, living labs, hackatons, citizen dashboards, open datasets, online voting and consultation [31]. All of this comes together under the umbrella of so-called human smart cities [29] and would be impossible without introducing mechanisms for reducing digital divide and promoting smart social inclusiveness [30].

Although the research on citizen orientation of smart city specialization seems to be growing, giving theoretical fundaments for more open and inclusive governance models, some authors claim it doesn't necessarily reflect what is actually being introduces in real life, and people are usually hardly aware of local smart initiatives [30].

3   Smart Cities Rankings

Smart city is a concept which attracts a lot of attention, not only in research word, but also in media. As a result many different rankings were presented in recent years, some of them with global reach [32], while others are limited to specific countries like Italy [33]. Rankings in general can provide an important empirical base and be an effective instrument for enhancing territorial capital and identifying city's development paths [34], as they should include indicators referring to various aspects of city's activities, however, as analysis of their composition shows, they tend to focus on a particular dimension, and in some cases, they can even be biased.

At first glance *Top 50 Smart City Governments* [35] looks like a tailored solution to the sample selection problem of this research. It uses ten factors to determine smart city government ranking: (1) vision (if city has a clear "smart" vision for itself), (2) leadership (dedicated leaders responsible for "smart" projects), (3) budget (adequate financing allocated to those projects), (4) financial incentives and (5) support programs (both to efficiently attract public sector), (6) talent-readiness (in case of smart-skills), (7) people-centricity (as core value of city's future design), (8) innovation ecosystems (engagement of stakeholders to sustain change), (9) smart policies (regarding e.g. open data) and (10) track record (understood as past, successful endeavors related to "smart" initiatives). However, the report has very little data on the scoring process itself, providing only information that every city was ranked on a scale of one to five in each category. In fact, it is even unknown who was responsible for the scoring, which, considering that the process has characteristics of peer-review evaluation, is rather fundamental information.

The *Smart Cities Index* [36] provides a ranking of top 100 cities, selected on the basis of 24 factors, grouped into eight categories: (1) Transport and Mobility (which constitutes for 22.5% of the final score), (2) Sustainability (12.5%), (3) Governance (15%), (4) Innovation Economy (5%), (5) Digitalization (17.5%), (6) Living Standard (10%), (7) Cyber Security (7.5%) and (8) Expert Perception (10%). Assigning almost ¼ of the final score to the category "Transport and Mobility" (which includes indicators like availability of parking apps and their usage penetration, number of parking spaces in the city center, number of car sharing services, levels of congestion and percentage of people satisfied with public transportation services) can be a good example of company bias – as it is created by EasyPark Group - entity providing digital solutions for parking.

Global Cities Report analyzes 130 using 40 metrics divided into two main groups: "current performance" and "future potential" [37]. Current performance uses total of 27 indicators in five dimensions: business activity (30%), human capital (30%), information exchange (15%), cultural experience (15%) and political engagement (10%); while future potential uses 13 metrics to describe four aspects: personal well- being, economics, innovation and government (with each assigned equal value of 25%). However, the report doesn't provide actual list of specific indicators, giving some general labels instead (e.g. human capital equals "education levels").

Sustainable Cities Index is created on the basis of three pillars: people (17 indicators), planet (16 indicators) and profit (15 indicators) [38]. Some of those indicators are grouped under common label, for example "connectivity" label from "profit" pillar refers to four indicators: mobile connectivity, broadband connectivity, importance in the global networks and internet speeds. From methodological point of view it is a well-documented analysis -each label has a clear data source and rationale, however it is a very human-centric ranking, which makes its usability as a sample source for this research limited, as it could generate a list of cities more likely of being citizen oriented, and possibly making our results biased.

IESE Cities in Motion Index (CIMI), developed by the Business School (University of Navarra), includes total of 83 indicators, describing 165 cities from 80 countries [32]. As authors claim, it has been designed as a revolutionary indicator in terms of its scope, allowing measurement of city's performance in the context of future sustainability and quality of life. CIMI introduces nine dimensions: (1) human capital (nine indicators, including: number of universities that are in the top 500 of QS Top Universities Ranking, number of theaters, or expenditure on leisure and recreation per capita), (2) social cohesion (13 indicators, e.g.: crime rate, price of property as percentage of income, or number of terrorist acts of vandalism in the previous three years), (3) economy (8 indicators, e.g.: number of calendar days needed so a business can operate legally, gross domestic product per capita, or number of headquarters of publicly traded companies), (4) governance (11 indicators, e.g.: number of research and technology centers, number of embassies and consulates, or number of government buildings and premises), (5) environment (11 indicators, e.g.: average amount of municipal solid waste (garbage) generated annually per person (kg/yr), total renewable water sources per capita, or PM 2.5 emissions), (6) mobility and transportation (9 indicators, e.g.: number of gas stations, length of the metro system, or number of arrival flights), (7) urban planning (5 indicators, e.g.: number of bike-rental or bike-sharing points, or number of people per household), (8) international outreach (6 indicators, e.g.: number of McDonald's restaurants per city, Number of international conferences and meetings, or number of hotels per capita), (9) technology (11 indicators, which include number of registered users of Twitter, LinkedIn and Facebook, number of Apple Stores, or percentage of households with access to the Internet). Apart from simple indexes, those dimensions also take advantage of many complex domain-specific indexes, published by other bodies, like: Pollution index and Health Index (by Numbeo), Corruption perceptions index (Transparency International), E-Government Development Index (United Nations), Happiness index (World Happiness Index) or Global Slavery Index (Walk Free Foundation). It is the most complex index, referring to the broad list of city activities.

4 Sample Selection

The main problem in case of sample selection was how to select a valid from scientific point of view list of cities, containing a cohesive, and most importantly, comparable group of objects? Both "city" and "smart city", as was discussed in previous sections, are very broad categories: economical, technological, geographical, demographical, political parameters have to be taken under consideration, among others. There are many cities around the world defined by third parties (researchers, consulting companies, authors of smart city rankings) as, or calling themselves "smart".

Researchers take different approaches to this problem. Some use pre-existing lists of smart cities, for example, [27] analyses 80 smart cities identified by Intelligent Community Forum, from Kabul (Afghanistan) to Eindhoven (The Netherlands). Others use more vague approaches, for example [39] defines "Informational World City", which means a city that (1) is referred to as a World City in the literature, and (2) is referred to as digital, smart, knowledge or creative city. It is an interesting concept, as it combines not only characteristics related to "smartness" but also includes demographical, economical and population-related factors through "world city" category.

In case of our research we have to take under consideration that citizen orientation requires certain cultural and political climate, which is necessary to allow e- participation and public cooperation to grow. Thus, it is crucial to identify a sample containing cities with similar characteristics also in this aspect. That's why, based on information presented in Sect. 3 of this paper, we have decided to use IESE Cities in Motion Index, as it uses the broadest range of indexes to compose final ranking. The final list of 30 cities used in this research is presented in Table 1. Almost all of them, except Bern, were included in other smart cities rankings, proving their "smartness".

Table 1. Ranking positions of cities from the sample in selected smart city rankings.

City	IESE Cities in Motion Index (2018)	Top 50 Smart City Governments (2018)	Smart Cities Index (2019)	Global Cities Report (2019)	The Sustainable Cities Index (2018)
New York	1	4	23	1	14
London	2	1	45	2	1
Paris	3	46	36	3	15
Tokyo	4	28	48	4	33
Reykjavik	5	44	27	X	X
Singapore	6	2	10	6	4
Seoul	7	3	60	13	13
Toronto	8	39	22	17	30
Hong Kong	9	18	70	5	9
Amsterdam	10	13	4	20	12
Berlin	11	29	21	14	18
Melbourne	12	8	47	16	56
Copenhagen	13	24	5	X	11
Chicago	14	17	24	8	48
Sydney	15	31	38	11	34
Stockholm	16	15	6	X	2
Los Angeles	17	26	17	7	45
Wellington	18	37	X	X	49
Vienna	19	12	9	24	5
Washington DC	20	21	16	10	39
Boston	21	7	11	21	22
Helsinki	22	5	19	X	X
Oslo	23	X	2	X	8
Zurich	24	X	1	X	6
Madrid	25	X	52	15	21
Barcelona	26	9	71	23	28
San Francisco	27	11	40	22	16
Auckland	28	X	50	X	X
Bern	29	X	X	X	X
Dublin	30	41	58	X	20

From geographical point of view, European cities make of exactly half of the sample, 7 are located in North America, 4 in Asia and 4 in Australia and New Zealand. Most of them are national capitals.

5   Methodological Approach

The verification of hypothesis H1: Smart cities have strategic documents laying their path to "smartness" (meaning they are implementing smart solutions in a planned, cohesive way), was addressed through answering 4 consecutive research questions: Q1: Is there a "smart city strategy" on the city's website?, if not Q2: Is there a general strategy for city development?, if not Q3: Is there subsite/portal on "smart" initiatives of the city?, if not Q4: Are there sectoral strategies for city's development? Answering those questions was basis for grouping cities from the sample in four categories: (1) with smart city strategy, (2) with general strategy, (3) with subsites/portals on their "smartness", and (4) with sectoral strategies.

Data collection was conducted in March 2019. In case of each city the search for strategic documents was began with analysis of the city's official website.

For the purpose of this research as a strategic document we understand a written document containing vision of the city and at least goals, which are defined as a way to achieve that vision. In reality, strategic document should also include specific actions and key performance metrics [40]. Well-structured organization of strategic documents should provide good material for analysis.

The verification of the hypothesis H2: Smart city strategies contain goals proving their citizen orientation was done through document analysis of general strategies and smart city strategies. In case of general strategies we wanted to answer additional research question Q5: Does general strategy for city's development contain goals introducing "smart" approach? If so, Q6: Can it replace a smart city strategy for the purpose of this research?

Finally, we have analyzed smart city strategies to answer the next research question: Q6: What categories of goals (smart city dimensions) are present in smart city strategies. This was done with bottom-up approach, which is often used in information science and allows to identify groups based on common characteristics of given objects (in our case – strategic goals). This allowed us to answer final research question Q7: Do goals defined in smart city strategies prove their citizen orientation?

It is important to underline, that this research is a part of bigger research project on "Smart City Research and Library and Information Science", and as the result our analysis is conducted from the library and information science point of view, with main hypothesis that citizen re-orientation gives more space for public libraries and information specialists to participate actively in "smart" initiatives.

6   Results

The conducted analysis allowed to group cities into four categories: (1) those with general strategies of city's development, addressing broad range of topics (6 cities); (2) cities with various sectoral strategies (San Francisco); (3) those without a published strategic document on how to become "smart", but with a set of smart initiatives presented on their websites and/or dedicated portals (10 cities); and finally, (4) cities with smart city strategies or other documents outlining them in detail, published on their own websites or linking those strategic documents from other portals (13 cities).

Set of initiatives presented on dedicated subsites of local authorities websites were found in case of Reykjavik, Toronto, Melbourne, Oslo, Madrid and Barcelona. The way they are presented doesn't proof existence of written strategic vision in those cities and doesn't give proper material for comparison. It seems that those subsites are more to give the statement "we are smart", supported with information on the "smart" projects within city. Some of them, like Barcelona, are discussed in scientific literature as cities with a "plan" [41], however even those publications don't provide any reference to that "plan". Amsterdam (amsterdamsmartcity.com), Helsinki (helsinkismart.fi), Washington DC (smarter.dc.gov) and Dublin (smartdublin.ie) also fall into this category, although they present information on their initiatives on dedicated portals, also used as platforms to engage third parties.

General strategies were found in case of: New York [42], Chicago [43], Los Angeles [44], Boston [45], Auckland [46] and Bern [47].

Smart cities strategies were identified in case of: London [48], Paris [49], Tokyo [50], Singapore [51], Seoul [52], Hong Kong [53], Berlin [54], Copenhagen [55], Sydney [56], Stockholm [57], Wellington [58], Vienna [59], and Zurich [60].

6.1   General Strategies

General strategies identified in the cities from the sample come with diverse shapes and forms as well as different approaches. Their length spans from 20 (Bern) to 472 (Boston) pages, as some of them present mostly city's vision for the future, while others go into detail on how to achieve declared goals presenting action plans and key performance metrics, proving more business-like approach (e.g. New York, Chicago). In case of general strategies for city's development our goal was to verify if they incorporate "smart city" approach, and if so – to what extent, with no specific strategy on becoming "smart", general strategies fill this void. Goals related to implementing smart solutions were identified in case of 5 cities from this group, however they are very few and mostly limited to ecology, infrastructure, utilities management and transport.

New York is addressing environmental issues by expanding green infrastructure and smart design for stormwater management, as well as adopting smart grid technologies and reduce transmission bottlenecks. Los Angeles is planning to deploy air quality tracking system, launch residential thermostat demand response program, use energy efficiency to limit electricity usage, implement policies to decarbonize new buildings, deploy community air quality monitoring networks and strengthen Green Business Certification Program.

Actions like installing intelligent transportation systems, developing a smarter electric grid and implementing smart grid technology to assess utility system conditions in real time (New York), implementing so-called the Array of Things (Chicago), installing 3 MW of solar panels at city facilities (Los Angeles), setting foundational "smart city" infrastructure (Boston) are also going to be taken.

Boston is the only city from this group introducing goals matching citizen orientation, as described in Sect. 3 of this paper. It plans to make every resident's experience of the city personalized and intuitive, take action to limit digital exclusion and to unlock new ways of citizen's collaboration. Auckland sets very general goal of achieving the vision of the world's most livable city through smart city initiatives, among others.

6.2   Smart City Strategies

Most smart city strategies prove strong citizen orientation in the vision section. Copenhagen is aiming to develop solutions to sustain a well-functioning city, with citizens enjoying a high quality of life [55], while Stockholm is going to be smarter, greener, more inclusive and creative city for all citizens, innovating with the citizens' interest and well-being in mind [57]. Paris wants to combine collective human intelligence with technology to achieve means to create city of tomorrow [49], and Singapore's vision is to make people more empowered by new technologies to live meaningful and fulfilled lives full of exciting opportunities [51]. Wellington puts more meaning into economic dimension, trying to find a way to make the best use of knowledge, investments and technology to create a better city, with a diverse and resilient economic base [58], while Berlin tries to create a place which is suitable for both living and economic activity [54]. Finally, Sydney wants to become 'smarter' and learn from customer feedback in a more systematic way, learning how to deliver better services that are more relevant to the needs of city's communities [56].

Berlin's smart city strategy identifies 6 areas of action: (1) smart administration and urban society, (2) smart housing, (3) smart economy, (4) smart mobility, (5) smart infrastructures, and (6) public safety [54]. However, from strictly editorial point of view, it is a very badly organized document, and the way in which headlines are used makes it impossible to differentiate between goals and activities. Similarly, Sydney's strategy is limited to presentation of 6 very general priorities, which include: (1) champion digital inclusion and lifelong learning, (2) create people-centered digital programs and services, (3) transform how we engage with all our communities, (4) support businesses to build digital skills, knowledge and infrastructure, (5) actively participate in urban renewal, advocating for, and where appropriate providing, smart infrastructure needed to ensure Sydney's global competitiveness, and (6) innovate ethically in the information marketplace [56]. As the result, cities of Berlin and Sydney are excluded from further analysis in this paper. Finally, Tokyo's strategy is in fact a general strategy, divided into 3 sections: (1) safe city, (2) diverse city and (3) smart city. For the purpose of this research third part of said document is treated as a smart city strategy.

The analysis of collected documents allowed to identify 5 smart city dimensions: (1) citizens, (2) ecology and environment, (3) economy, (4) ICT and data, and (5) transport, to which goals from each strategy were classified (Table 2). In case of goals matching more than one dimension, the decision on their allocation was based on the character of activities planned under that goal. In general, in almost every case, except Tokyo, "smart" strategies include goals related to citizen orientation. Their number varies, and is dependent on their length and their level of detail.

Citizen orientation is approached in many different ways in the cities from the sample, and can take shape of user-centered design of services, promoting digital leadership and skills, limiting effects of digital exclusion, stimulating citizen participation and collaboration in projects. Shorter strategies offer more general goals, like

Table 2. Categorization of goals from smart city strategies.

City	Smart dimension				
	Citizens	Ecology	Economy	ICT and data	Transport
London [48]	7	0	1	9	0
Paris [49]	1	4	1	5	0
Tokyo [50]	0	3	2	0	2
Singapore [51]	3	0	2	3	0
Seoul [52]	3	1	3	6	1
Hong Kong [53]	2	6	3	6	3
Copenhagen [55]	3	1	0	3	1
Stockholm [57]	5	6	5	2	0
Wellington [58]	4	4	1	2	1
Vienna [59]	1	3	1	2	1
Zurich [60]	4	1	1	3	1

"building a digitally ready workforce to seize new opportunities" or "ensuring everyone benefits from Smart Nation" (Singapore). Sometimes they target specific groups of citizens, like elderly (Hong Kong) or people with disabilities (Hong Kong, Seoul), making sure they can benefit from smart solutions. Some include goals targeting young people, through "nurturing young talent" (Hong Kong) or "support computing skills and the digital talent pipeline from early years onwards" (London). e-Participation and public collaboration are also important topics, as Seoul wants "smart government that actively interacts with citizens", Paris puts strong emphasis on citizen participation and Stockholm wants to "simplify and enhance citizens influence and participation in the democratic process through digitalization".

London plans to explore new civic platforms to better engage citizens, including Civic Innovation Challenge, which is a form of open innovation in public sector. Similarly, Copenhagen wants to develop co-creation partnerships, using e.g. "Fablab, where residents, students and businesses can work with prototyping and production using laser cutters, 3D printers, opensource hardware as well as more traditional equipment", Wellington wants to foster active communities that support innovation and resilience and Zurich plans to test Living Labs.

7   Conclusions

Discussion on what actually makes a city smart is ongoing, and it doesn't seem that the answer to this question will be found soon. The fast changing technological landscape, which is the fundament of everything "smart", makes this even less likely. In our research we have decided to use smart city strategies for analysis of "smart" policies, as existence of such document proves not only that city sees itself as a smart city, but also takes actions to achieve that state.

Most cities from our sample don't have published strategies dedicated to becoming smart, and some of those which do (Berlin, Sydney), produced very vague documents. It is surprising, as almost all of them are not only discussed in scientific literature as having a "plan" or "strategy" on how to become smart, but they are also included in most popular smart city rankings. As it seems, "smartness" can be achieved without written strategy (mission, vision, goals, actions).

In case of existence of more general strategies for city's development we have found that they do in fact incorporate "smart" solutions, however they address specific issues related to infrastructure, utilities management, transport and ecology, and do not prove existence of cohesive "smart" vision in the city.

Almost every smart city strategy, except Tokyo's (which is actually not a separate smart city strategy but a section in general strategy), includes goals proving citizen orientation of chosen vision for city's development. It is especially visible in cases of London, Stockholm and Wellington. It is safe to say, that although technology oriented approach still seems to be dominant, cities put more effort into e- participation, public collaboration, including co-creation, fighting digital exclusion and broadly understood bottom-up approach. That in turn connects "smart city" solutions more with "creative city" concept.

In the future we plan to increase the number of the cities in the sample and limit them to those having smart city strategies trying to identify citizen orientation models.

References

1. Barth, J., et al.: Informational urbanism. A conceptual framework of smart cities. In: Proceedings of the 50th Hawaii International Conference on System Science (HICSS- 50), Waikoloa Village, Hawaii, USA, pp. 2814–2823 (2017)
2. Mora, L., Deakin, M., Reid, A.: Smart-city development paths: insights from the first two decades of research. In: Bisello, A., Vettorato, D., Laconte, P., Costa, S. (eds.) SSPCR 2017. GET, pp. 403–427. Springer, Cham (2018). https://doi.org/10.1007/978-3-319-75774-2_28
3. Bernardo, M.R.M.: Smart city governance: from e-government to smart governance. In: Carvalho, L.C., (ed.) Handbook of Research on Entrepreneurial Development and Innovation Within Smart Cities, pp. 290–326. Information Science Reference, Hershey (2017)
4. Tan, M.: Plugging into the wired world: perspectives from the Singapore. Inf. Commun. Soc. 1(3), 217–245 (1998)
5. Giffinger, R., Fertner, C., Kramar, H., Kalasek, R., Pichler-Milanović, N., Meijers, E.: Smart cities: ranking of European medium-sized cities, Vienna (2007)
6. Dameri, R.P.: Searching for a smart city definition: a comprehensive proposal. Int. J. Comput. Technol. 11(5), 2544–2551 (2013)
7. Ojo, A., Dzhusupova, Z., Curry, E.: Exploring the nature of the smart cities research landscape. In: Gil-Garcia, J.R., Pardo, T.A., Nam, T. (eds.) Smarter as the New Urban Agenda. PAIT, vol. 11, pp. 23–47. Springer, Cham (2016). https://doi.org/10.1007/978-3-319-17620-8_2
8. Mitchell, W.J.: Me++: The Cyborg Self and the Networked City. MIT Press, Cambridge (2003)
9. Tabuchi, T.: Agglomeration in world cities. Proc. - Soc. Behav. Sci. 77, 299–307 (2013)

10. Gil-Castineira, F., Costa-Montenegro, E., Gonzalez-Castano, F., López-Bravo, C., Ojala, T., Bose, R.: Experiences inside the ubiquitous oulu smart city. Comput. (Long. Beach. Calif) **44**(6), 48–55 (2011)
11. Castells, M.: The Informational City: Economic Restructuring and Urban Development. Blackwell Publishers, Oxford (1989)
12. Martini, L.: Knowledge sharing in a creative city. Proc. Comput. Sci. **99**, 79–90 (2016)
13. Franz, P.: From university town to knowledge city: strategies and regulatory hurdles in Germany. In: Yigitcanlar, T., Velibeyoglu, K., Baum, S. (eds.) Knowledge-Based Urban Development: Planning and Applications in the Information Era, pp. 101–115. IGI Global (2008)
14. Papa, R., Galderisi, A., Vigo Majello, M.C., Saretta, E.: Smart and resilient cities a systemic approach for developing cross-sectoral strategies in the face of climate change. Tema-J. L. Use Mobil. Environ. **8**(1), 19–49 (2015)
15. Cohen, S.: The Sustainable City. Columbia University Press, New York (2018)
16. Yigitcanlar, T., Kamruzzaman, M., Foth, M., Sabatini-Marques, J., da Costa, E., Ioppolo, G.: Can cities become smart without being sustainable? A systematic review of the literature. Sustain. Cities Soc. **45**, 348–365 (2019)
17. Höjer, M., Wangel, J.: Smart sustainable cities: definition and challenges. In: Hilty, L., Aebischer, B. (eds.) ICT Innovations for Sustainability, pp. 333–349. Springer, Cham (2014). https://doi.org/10.1007/978-3-319-09228-7_20
18. Esteven, E., Lopes, N.V., Janowski, T.: Smart sustainable cities: reconnaissance study. United Nations UNU-EGOV (2016). http://collections.unu.edu/eserv/UNU:5825/Smart_Sustainable_Cities_v2final.pdf. Accessed 05 May 2019
19. Mora, L., Daekin, M., Aina, Y., Appio, F.: Smart city development: ICT innovation for urban sustainability. In: Leal Filho, W., Azul, A.M., Brandli, L., Özuyar, P.G., Wall, T. (eds.) Sustainable Cities and Communities. ENUNSDG, pp. 1–17. Springer, Cham (2019). https://doi.org/10.1007/978-3-319-71061-7_27-2
20. Sharma, D., Singh, S.: Instituting environmental sustainability and climate resilience into the governance process: Exploring the potential of new urban development schemes in India. Int. Area Stud. Rev. **19**(1), 90–103 (2016)
21. Chourabi, H., et al.: Understanding smart cities: an integrative framework. In: Proceedings of the 45th Hawaii International Conference on System Sciences (HICSS- 45), pp. 2289–2297. IEEE, Maui (2012)
22. Mora, L., Daekin, M., Reid, A.: Stylized facts on smart specialization research. In: 27th International Scientific Conference on Economic and Social Development: Book of Proceedings, pp. 176–185 (2018)
23. Scholl, H.J., Scholl, M.C.: Smart governance: a roadmap for research and practice. In: Proceedings of the 9th iConference. Illinois Digital Environment for Access to Learning and Scholarship (IDEALS), Berlin, Germany, pp. 163–176 (2014)
24. Johnson, I.M.: Smart Cities, Smart Libraries, and Smart Librarians. In: Shanghai International Library Forum (2012)
25. Negre, E., Rosenthal-Sabroux, C., Gascó, M.: A knowledge-based conceptual vision of the smart city. In: Proceedings of the 48th Hawaii International Conference on System Sciences (HICSS-48), pp. 2317–2325 (2015)
26. Zygiaris, S.: Smart city reference model: assisting planners to conceptualize the building of smart city innovation ecosystem. J. Knowl. Econ. **2**(2), 217–231 (2011)
27. Nam, T., Pardo, T.A.: Conceptualizing smart city with dimensions of technology, people, and institutions. In: 12th Annual International Conference on Digital Government Research (dg.o 2011), pp. 282–291. ACM, College Park (2011)

28. Castelnovo, W., Misuraca, G., Savoldelli, A.: Smart cities governance: the need for a holistic approach to assessing urban participatory policy making. Soc. Sci. Comput. Rev. **34**(6), 724–739 (2016)
29. Oliveira, A., Campolargo, M.: From smart cities to human smart cities. In: Proceedings of the 48th Hawaii International Conference on System Sciences (HICSS- 48), pp. 2336–2344 (2015)
30. Dameri, R.P.: Smart City Implementation. Springer, Cham (2017)
31. Webster, C.W.R., Leleux, C.: Smart governance: opportunities for technologically- mediated citizen co-production. Inf. Polity **23**, 95–110 (2018)
32. Berrone, P., Ricart, J. E.: IESE cities in motion index. IESE Business School, University of Navarra (2018). https://media.iese.edu/research/pdfs/ST-0471-E.pdf. Accessed 05 May 2019
33. D'Acunto, A., Mena, M., Polimanti, F., Quintiliano, C.: Polis 4.0: rapporto smart city index 2018. EY (2018). https://www.ey.com/Publication/vwLUAssets/Smart_City_Index_2018/$FILE/EY_SmartCityIndex_2018.pdf. Accessed 05 May 2019
34. Giffinger, R., Haindlmaier, G.: Smart cities ranking: an effective instrument for the positioning of cities? ACE Archit. City Environ. **IV**(12), 7–25 (2010)
35. Top 50 Smart City Governments. Eden Strategy Institute. ONG&ONG Pte Ltd. (2018). https://static1.squarespace.com/static/5b3c517fec4eb767a04e73ff/t/5b513c57aa4a99f62d168e60/1532050650562/Eden-OXD_Top+50+Smart+City+Governments.pdf. Accessed 05 May 2019
36. Smart Cities Index 2019. EasyPark Group (2019). https://www.easyparkgroup.com/smart-cities-index/. Accessed 05 May 2019
37. Hales, M., Pena, A.M., Peterson, E., Dessibourg-Freer, N.: A Question of talent: how human capital will determine the next global leaders. In: 2019 Global Cities Report, ATKearney (2019)
38. Batten, J.: Citizen centric cities. The Sustainable Cities Index 2018, Arcadis (2018). https://www.arcadis.com/media/1/D/5/%7B1D5AE7E2-A348-4B6E-B1D7-6D94FA7D7567%7DSustainable_Cities_Index_2018_Arcadis.pdf. Accessed 20 June 2019
39. Mainka, A., Hartmann, S., Orszullok, L., Peters, I., Stallman, A., Stock, W.G.: Public libraries in the knowledge society: core services of libraries in informational world cities. Libri **64**(4), 295–319 (2013)
40. Johnson, G., Scholes, K., Whittington, R., Regnér, P., Angwin, D.: Exploring Corporate Strategy: Text & Cases, 11th edn. Pearson, Carmel (2017)
41. Vives, A.: Smart City Barcelona: The Catalan Quest to Improve Future Urban Living. Sussex Academic Press, Brighton (2017)
42. de Brassio, B., Shorris, A.: One New York. The Plan for a Strong and Just City, The City of New York (2015). http://www.nyc.gov/html/onenyc/downloads/pdf/publications/OneNYC.pdf. Accessed 07 Jun 2019
43. Emanuel, R.: Resilient Chicago: A Plan for Inclusive Growth and a Connected City, Chicago (2019)
44. Garcetti, E.: L.A.'s Green New Deal. Sustainable City Plan, Los Angeles (2019)
45. Walsh, M.J.: Imagine Boston 2030. A plan for the Future of Boston, Boston (2017)
46. Brown, L.: Working together to build Resilient Auckland (2016). https://www.aucklandemergencymanagement.org.nz/media/1054/19-pro-0212-_resilient-auckland_-online-doc-update_proof1.pdf. Accessed 05 Mar 2019
47. Tschapat, A.: Strategie Bern 2020 (2009). https://www.google.pl/url?sa=t&rct=j&q=&esrc=s&source=web&cd=1&cad=rja&uact=8&ved=2ahUKEwj7g7P6sOzkAhWFp4sKHa0hBhUQFjAAegQIABAC&url=https%3A%2F%2Fwww.bern.ch%2Fpolitik-und-verwaltung%2Fgemeinderat%2Flegislaturrichtlinien%2Fdownloads%2Fstrategie-bern-2020. Accessed 12 Mar 2019

48. Khan, S.: Smarter London Together. The Mayor's roadmap to transform London into the smartest city in the world. Greater London Authority, City Hall (2018). https://www.london. gov.uk/sites/default/files/smarter_london_together_v1.66_-_published.pdf.   Accessed   08 June 2019

49. Hidalgo, A., Missika, J.-L.: Paris: Smart and Sustainable. Looking ahead to 2020 and beyond, Mairie de Paris (2016). https://api-site-cdn.paris.fr/images/99354. Accessed 09 June 2019

50. Koike, Y.: New Tokyo: New Tomorrow. The Action Plan for 2020. Tokyo Metropolitan Government   (2016).   http://www.metro.tokyo.jp/english/about/plan/documents/pocket_ english.pdf. Accessed 08 June 2019

51. Smart Nation: The Way Forward (2018). https://www.smartnation.sg/docs/default-source/ default-document-library/smart-nation-strategy_nov2018.pdf. Accessed 23 Mar 2019

52. Smart Seoul 2015. Basic Strategic Plan for Informatization of Seoul Metropolitan City. Seoul Metropolitan   Government   (2014).   http://ebook.seoul.go.kr/Viewer/92E7DHQWT49V. Accessed 08 July 2019

53. Hong-Kong Smart City Blueprint. Innovation and Technology Bureau (2017). https://www. smartcity.gov.hk/doc/HongKongSmartCityBlueprint(EN).pdf. Accessed 11 June 2019

54. Smart City Strategy Berlin (2015). https://www.stadtentwicklung.berlin.de/planen/foren_ initiativen/smart-city/download/Strategie_Smart_City_Berlin_en.pdf.   Accessed   14   Mar 2019

55. Smart City Copenhagen (2016). https://www.gate21.dk/wp-content/uploads/2016/06/Smart_ City_Copenhagen_FOLDER_2016.pdf. Accessed 17 Mar 2019

56. Moore, C.: Sydney 2030. Digital Strategy (2017). https://www.cityofsydney.nsw.gov.au/ data/assets/pdf_file/0005/288167/Digital-Strategy.pdf. Accessed 24 Mar 2019

57. Strategi för Stockholm som smart och uppkopplad stad Bilaga 1. Strategi (2016). https:// insynsverige.se/documentHandler.ashx?did=1856826. Accessed 16 Mar 2019

58. Wade-Brown, C.: Wellington Towards 2040: Smart Capital (2011). https://wellington.govt. nz/~/media/your-council/plans-policies-and-bylaws/plans-and-policies/a-to-z/ wellington2040/files/wgtn2040-brochure.pdf. Accessed 19 Mar 2019

59. Häupl, M., Vassilakou, M.: Smart City Wien: Framework Strategy (2014). https://smartcity. wien.gv.at/site/files/2019/07/Smart-City-Wien-Framework-Strategy_2014-resolution.pdf. Accessed 20 Mar 2019

60. Strategie Smart City Zürich (2018). https://www.stadt-zuerich.ch/content/dam/stzh/prd/ Deutsch/Stadtentwicklung/Grafik_und_Foto/SmartCity/STE_Strategie_Dez2018_Mail_ Low_neu.pdf. Accessed 23 Mar 2019

Digital Transformation in the Public Sector: Identifying Critical Success Factors

Gideon Mekonnen Jonathan[(⊠)]

Department of Computer and Systems Sciences, Stockholm University,
Stockholm, Sweden
gideon@dsv.su.se

Abstract. Regardless of size and sector, organisations in today's market are rushing to join the journey of digital transformation. Empirical studies, opinion pieces and publications from practitioner outlets present recorded benefits of digitalisation from well-known traditional businesses that chose to adopt the use of IT to radically change the way they do their businesses. A closer look into the findings of these studies reveal that success from digital transformation endeavour is realised when firms manage to make necessary adjustments to their business and IT strategies, organisational structure as well as their processes. Recently, public organisations found themselves under pressure from political leaders and citizens to digitally transform the provision of their services. However, the majority of digitalisation initiatives fail to produce the anticipated results. Building upon findings of previous studies and data collected from 12 interviews with leaders in public organisations, this study presents a list of factors that could determine the success of digitalisation in the public sector. The findings could be invaluable for public organisations as they attempt to realise the value from their digital transformation initiatives.

Keywords: Critical success factors · Digitalisation · Digital transformation · Digitisation · Public organisations

1 Introduction

The extensive adoption of information technology (IT) in the private and commercial organisations to provide improved services and products has not gone unnoticed by the public organisations. In recent years, the heavy investment in IT across federal, state and local governments as well as other public agencies demonstrates the anticipated benefits that may stem from execution of various IT initiatives [1–5]. To denote this trend of widespread IT adoption, the terms *"Digital Transformation"* and *"Digitalisation"* have become fashionable among researchers and practitioners. Even though the literature does not provide consistent definition, a closer look into past studies suggest that digital transformation came to garner the attention of many because large organisations previously not known to use IT intensively have transformed their businesses with the adoption of IT solutions [6].

Berman [7, p. 17] defines digitalisation (also referred to as '*digital transformation*' in this study) as *"a set of complementary activities–reshaping customer value*

M. Themistocleous and M. Papadaki (Eds.): EMCIS 2019, LNBIP 381, pp. 223–235, 2020.
https://doi.org/10.1007/978-3-030-44322-1_17

propositions and transforming their operations using digital technologies for greater customer interaction and collaboration". In the same vein, Shaughnessy [8] describes digital transformation as an organisation-wide endeavour which involves a variety of technical and cultural changes. According to Horlacher et al. [9], digital transformation refers to firms' use of such technologies as social media, mobile, analytics or embedded devices with the aim of maximising customer experience or enabling the design and adoption of new business models. Another term "digitisation" which refers to the "*technical process of converting streams of analogue information into digital bits of 1 s and 0 s with discrete and discontinuous values*" [10, p. 17] is often used interchangeably with digitalisation or digital transformation. However, scholars in various disciplines agree that digital transformation entails much more than replacing the storage of information in analogue to a digital form [9]. For today's organisations, digital transformation means moving away from traditional forms of communication channels to embrace innovative ways of interacting with customers, suppliers as well as collaborators and partners [4, 11, 12].

In the context of the public sector, digital transformation is considered as the application of IT solutions to improve the accessibility and efficiency of public organisations. The analysis of the findings of empirical and conceptual studies reveals two potential benefits of digital transformation for the public sector [2, 5, 13–16]. To start with, digital transformation improves organisational efficiency by bringing down running costs and increasing productivity. Second, the quality and variety of service provisions are found to improve as public organisations embrace digital transformation. In a nutshell, scholars argue that digital transformation in the public sector is an important endeavour that is instrumental in public administration effectiveness as well as the promotion of democratic values and mechanisms [14]. However, researchers identify several factors that need to be identified and configured appropriately to realise the benefits of digital transformation [12, 17, 18]. To this end, the extant literature provides a long list of models and frameworks designed to identify antecedents and evaluate the success of the digital transformation.

On the other hand, scholars argue that digital transformation is one of the new phenomena which is garnering the attention of researchers [19]. A closer look at extant literature seems to suggest two unexplored areas. First, even though researchers have attempted to explore how organisations approach digital transformation, the focus of most of these studies is found to be on the outcome of the use of information technology, i.e. improved efficiency and productivity, access to new markets, and optimised supply chain [7]. According to Bharadwaj et al. [20], digitalisation has enabled many organisations to come a long way in their effort to fundamentally transform how they formulate their strategies; design their business processes; deliver their products and services; communicate with their customers, and extend their networks. However, how organisations plan and navigate through the digital transformation process and which obstacles they encounter is not addressed sufficiently. Thus, the different organisational factors that can influence the digital transformation process need to be identified. Second, findings of previous studies suggest that there is a lack of knowledge on the different organisational challenges that make the digital transformation journey difficult in the public organisations' context. Consistent with previous studies (for instance, [21–23]), public organisations have not been represented in digital transformation research. Aichholzer and Schmutzer [24] also argue that leaders in the public sector have not acknowledged the organisational changes required to realise the value from digital transformation. To address this gap in literature, this study aims to explore the critical success factors that influence digital transformation in the public sector. To meet the aim of the study, the following research question is formulated: *How can a public organisation be managed to drive digital transformation, and what are the critical success factors?*

The rest of the paper is structured as follows. First, a brief review of the extant literature on digital transformation in the public sector and related areas is presented. Second, the research strategy, as well as the data collection and analysis methods, are described. The subsequent section discusses the results and analysis of the study.

Finally, the last section presents the concluding remarks, along with the limitations of the study and future research directions.

2   Literature Review

2.1   Managing Digital Transformation

Even though the rapid changes in the adoption of IT is acknowledged to affect the whole organisation, those with IT leadership responsibilities are expected to deal with the different challenges of digital transformation than what their predecessors had to do in the past [25]. What is new with the current wave of digital transformation is that the strategic significance of IT is heightened to a new level. In addition to automating various processes and functions in organisations, digital transformation is viewed as a means that provides proactive and innovative solutions. According to Kane et al. [18], organisations that successfully manage their digital transformation process are characterised by their approaches of IT management. The authors argue that organisations with mature digital transformation orientation are likely to have the support and leadership of top management. In the same vein, the significance of top leaders' involvement in formulating digital transformation strategy is acknowledged by researchers [12, 21, 26]. Such organisations see IT as a strategic enabler that shape organisational goals and scope. The strategic view of IT, according to Bharadwaj et al. [20], enables organisations to adopt practices that foster the alignment between IT and overall organisational objectives.

A review of previous studies indicates that researchers identify three aspects of digital transformation that need to be recognised by leaders [11, 14, 16, 18, 27, 28]. To start with, the outcome of digital transformation in terms of added value needs to be established. For instance, one of the important conditions for organisations to gain value from their digital transformation attempt is to achieve organisational agility [16]. Organisational agility, particularly in the public sector is necessary to meet the needs of citizens or sudden changes in the political environment that might have implications for the provision of services. Second, organisations have to systematically identify the various activities and processes as well as required organisational changes that help them to meet the goal of digital transformation. Third, the underlying IT solutions that can drive the digital transformation must also be identified.

To put it in a nutshell, it is in organisations' best interest to distinguish between the various issues that enable or inhibit the digital transformation process. Unfortunately, the evidence seems to suggest that digital transformation has become one of the biggest challenges for organisations. Hess et al. [12] argue that digital transformation is a complex issue that has an implication on different aspects of an organisation. As such, the management of digital transformation calls for exploration of all resources and making continuous adjustments to the configuration of these resources. Yet, empirical evidence suggests that the focus of many digital transformation initiatives have been on technological issues while overlooking other organisational factors. The extant literature also reveals that there is a lack of research recognising holistic approaches of firm-wide digital transformation process [18].

Looking back into the findings of the previous studies, the various factors that are found to influence the digital transformation process in the public sector could be categorised and related to one of the three challenges—organisational and managerial challenges, information technology challenges, and environment challenges [11, 14].

2.2 Organisational and Managerial Factors

As one of the new research areas in the IS research domain, various organisational and managerial issues that might influence the success of digital transformation have been identified in the literature. For instance, Vogelsang et al. [29] argue that organisational culture, change management practices, employee and leaderships' engagement, knowledge management, and business-IT alignment have attracted the attention of scholars and practitioners. Henriette et al. [30], on the other hand, present these organisational factors as managerial challenges falling under the category of strategic, structural and cultural, as well as implementation related.

Strategic issues in the context of digital transformation are reflected in how well an organisation recognises IT as a driver of the overall business strategy [31]. The recognition of the strategic role of IT, and the continuous effort to align the IT strategy with the overall organisational goal, also referred to as 'Business-IT alignment' is found to improve the value derived from IT investment [32, 33]. The success of the digital transformation is also found to be influenced by the organisational- culture and structure in place. For instance, organisational culture determines the mindsets of employees and leadership towards embracing digitalisation as a necessary endeavour for value creation and transforming the way public organisations deliver services to citizens [14, 34]. Besides, organisational culture is found to influence the extent to which employees and leaders are open to change, willingness to learn, accept failures, and adopt exploratory character [25, 35]. On the other hand, the organisational structure's role in the successful implementation of IT solutions is established in previous studies (e.g., [22, 32]). In the context of digital transformation in the public sector, scholars argue that appropriate organisational structure is paramount to facilitate communication which fosters the engagement of internal and external stakeholders [11, 25, 29]; knowledge management [35]; business model innovation and process automation [19, 25]; and organisational agility [34, 35].

Managing digital transformation is a challenging endeavour with various elements that need to be configured appropriately to fit the context of organisations.

Organisations initiate the plan and set-up their journey of digital transformation by identifying transformation activities tailored to their needs [36]. In the implementation phase, leaders are expected to manage the identified activities to realise the value of their digital transformation. The literature provides a list of factors that are related to the implementation of digital transformation—business process re-engineering, the involvement of leaders, change management, capability and skills development, aligning business and IT strategies [25, 29, 35].

2.3   Information Technology Factors

Organisations' move towards a digitalised business demands a considerable sociotechnical change that has an implication on the overall organisational- structure and strategy [14, 25]. However, Dremel [37] argue that there seems to be a consensus among researchers and practitioners that digital transformation is mainly the adoption of IT to improve processes and achieve overall organisational success. Thus, the literature provides a list of IT-related factors influencing digital transformation. For instance, Legner et al. [25] identify various key areas that determine the success of digitalisation endeavours. These include data-driven agility (the appropriate use of data to improve analytics capability); digital platform management (assessment of the need for new digital platforms); IT architecture transformation (anticipating changes and making sure the IT architecture is ready to meet the challenge); security and compliance (making sure the cyber-threats are recognised, and countermeasures are put in place).

In addition to the IT capabilities and resources within an organisation, researchers argue that IT infrastructure of a country, as well as the existence of IT standards, is found to affect the success of digital transformation [35]. For instance, Altameem et al. [11] argue that the level of quality of national information infrastructure of a country—landlines and telecommunication systems—is one of the important determinants of success in eGovernment initiatives. Citizens are expected to benefit when different agencies and government bodies collaborate and improve the quality of the services delivered. However, the problem of interoperability and lack of standards is restricting the collaboration between public organisations [11, 25].

2.4   Environmental Factors

Previous studies recognise the significant role of external environmental factors on digital transformation. Particularly in the case of public organisations, scholars argue that the success of public organisations attempt to digitalise their services is dependent on the restrictiveness of legal and regulatory frameworks as well as industry-related factors such as intergovernmental relationships [11, 14]. According to Holotiuk and Beimborn [34], the collaboration between organisations embarking in digitalisation need to extend to other stakeholders (even service providers as well as suppliers) who might possess the expertise of innovation enabling digital transformation. Citizens" participation in digital transformation by adopting the use of, for instance, eGovernment services is required to gain the value from IT investment [38].

Public organisations are expected to operate under more restrictive laws and regulations than organisations in the private sector. For instance, digitalisation projects in the public sector have to be negotiated and approved by those who hold political and administrative powers [14]. Besides, the political environment might also change abruptly prompting a shift in priority which might mean redirection of funds away from IT projects. Altameem et al. [11] cite lack of funding as one of the main reasons for the failure of eGovernment initiatives in many countries. Other environmental factors such as the cost and quality of IT infrastructure, the availability of skilled human capital, as well as the dynamism and the openness of the economy, are also found to determine how public organisations manage the digital transformation [39].

3   Research Methodology

This study is conducted applying the case study research strategy, which is known to be suited to investigate a phenomenon that involves several actors, processes and goals in detail without altering the characteristics of *"real-life events"* [40]. The complex organisational structure, decision-making arrangement, and the relationships between leaders and other staff in the public organisations call for a case study research strategy that could help to provide an in-depth insight in a specific setting [41]. The research strategy choice is also justified as the study aims to explore the various factors that influence digital transformation. The investigation requires the identification of factors relevant to the planning and execution of activities related to digitalisation.

Case study as a research strategy provides a researcher with different data collection methods that might be invaluable to improve the credibility of findings [40]. For this study, interviews, as well as internal organisational documents, were used to collect data. According to Denscombe [41] and Yin [40], interviews are invaluable when researchers are interested in gaining people's insights, opinions and experiences. The use of different data collection method also referred to as multiple sources of evidence, is intended to improve the validity and reliability of the various construction of realities, a phenomenon which Yin [40] referred to as triangulation. Semi-structured interviews with 12 administrative and IT leaders lasting between 60 to 80 were conducted in one city administration (anonymously labelled in this report as CA). An interview guide was used to ensure comparability of the results. Both IT and administrative leaders with varying degree of authority are represented. The interviews were recorded and transcribed to facilitate data extraction. The transcripts were sent to the respondents for comments and/or correction. Thematic data analysis which is a widely used qualitative analysis method, is chosen for the study. The choice of the analysis method is justified due to the flexibility it provides while it is not restricted to a particular theory and epistemology [42]. The 6-phase guide thematic analysis (familiarising with the data; generating initial codes; searching for themes; reviewing potential themes; defining and naming themes, and producing report) by Braun and Clarke [43] was followed to identify the final list of success factors.

4   Results and Discussions

4.1   The Case Organisation

The case organisation investigated for this study, CA, is one of the city administrations in Ethiopia with around six hundred thousand population. CA is among one of the public organisations mandated by the regional government to improve the accessibility and quality of services for its residents. The elected political leaders serving for a term limit of five years are responsible for overseeing the implementation of the countrywide digital transformation strategy at the level of the city administration.

The administrative head is responsible for leading CA while the Head of Digitalisation (DH) and is in charge of modernising the city administrations services adopting IT solutions. The DH reports to the CIO who works under the supervision of the administrative head. The IT department serves the whole city administration with its nine departments (i.e. culture and tourism; education; finance; health and environment; information and public relation; justice and security; real state; tax administration; trade, industry and transport) as well as two government bodies located in the city. Even though the departments have the autonomy to run their core services, the central administration service is responsible for HR, IT, legal services, budget and finance, registry, security and readiness, public relations, and procurement.

The DH is responsible for executing the five-year digital transformation initiative (running between 2016 and 2021) in consultation with a committee of six deputy heads from selected departments. So far, the documents obtained indicate that the city administration has managed to accomplish 42% of the digitalisation project in three years. The respondents also claim that most of the services offered to private customers at the tax administration, real state, as well as the trade, industry and transport departments are mostly digitalised.

4.2   Organisational and Managerial Factors

Even though the focus of past studies on digitalisation was on the technological aspects, the critical role of other organisational factors is established in recent empirical studies [29]. The finding of the study has also confirmed how organisational culture, employees and leaderships' engagement played into the digitalisation work at the case company. The DH (IT1) recalls how the digitalisation project was initiated in early 2016…*"we had several meetings with employees in all departments and tried to let them know about the vision…less cost, better service, more efficiency…you can't get a better deal than that, right? We did not know what was coming"*. His story was shared by the remaining participants from the IT department (IT2, IT3, IT4). According to their responses, there were several obstacles for the digitalisation initiatives from the very beginning. As Mithas et al. [31] pointed out, the introduction of IT in a workplace might attract resistance from employees who are not willing to change their work behaviour. The committee working in the digitalisation did not meet resistance only from employees but also from some of the department heads and top management at CA.

A closer look at the findings seems to indicate two reasons for the resistance for the digitalisation. To start with, the leadership at the CA might not be convinced of the strategic role of IT [32, 33]. On the other hand, as in most public organisations, the organisational culture and structure in place might not be suited to embrace digitalisation as a necessary endeavour for value creation and transforming the delivery of services [14, 34]. As respondents from three of the departments contend (A2, A3, A8), CA is a centralised and highly bureaucratic organisation providing employees with little room for flexibility and exploration of new ways of doing their work, which in turn was found to be problematic for digitalisation.

Looking back after three years of the start of the digitalisation journey, IT1 and IT2 agree that the realised success so far was the result of a thorough dialogue with the top leaders at CA who came to recognise the strategic role of IT. The fact that the federal government *"sees digitalisation the only way forward to improving the lives of citizens"* (IT2) has also helped us to gain the sponsorship of the CA's leadership. The CIO now sits at the central leadership's meetings. The department heads (A1, A3, A4) also acknowledge that IT is now seen as a strategic partner to meet the overall objective. This phenomenon referred to as business-IT alignment is invaluable to achieve successful digital transformation [32, 33]. Other organisational and managerial issues were also found to have influenced digitalisation at the case company. For instance, IT2, IT3 and respondents from the administration departments (A2, A3, A5, A6) mention the lack of capability and skills development programmes to lift up the digital literacy among employees. As indicated in the literature [29, 35], human resource management programmes fostering the necessary technical and related competencies is paramount for success in digital transformation.

4.3   Information Technology Factors

Respondents from both sides—IT and administration—agree that most of the digitalisation work, starting from the initiation of many of the deliverables, are almost left for the IT personnel. Consistent with the findings in the literature, digitalisation is assumed to be a change in technology and how its adoption is to be managed [37]. What was interesting from the analysis of the results is that four of the administrative directors (A3, A2, A5, and A7) did not acknowledge the difficulty of organisational issues that need to be addressed to facilitate the digital transformation in the city administration. However, they were quick to point out the factors that are related to IT. For instance, according to A3, *"the residents of the city could have seen an improved and fast delivery of services if the IT solutions are in par with the current technology and needs of the citizens. For instance, many young adults in our school system are conversant with social media and mobile phones, but the city has a long way to provide mobile solutions"*. On the other hand, A7 criticises the IT department's lack of data analytics capabilities. In his opinion, *"...the city administration collects a huge amount of data from residents which could have been used to make better predictions and plans"*.

The respondents raised the different technology factors identified by Legner et al. [25]. For instance, the CIO (IT2) and one of the IT managers (IT4) agree that the current IT architecture is not in good standing to facilitate the kind of transformation planned. Unfortunately, access to funding, red tape and availability of skilled IT personnel is making the needed changes difficult. According to the head of digitalisation (IT1), the digitalisation process is not going as fast to meet the expectation from the residents and the city administration. Even though the lack of sufficient resources and capabilities in the city administration is acknowledged, the interviewees have also blamed the lack of good IT infrastructure in the region. IT 4, who is responsible for procurement of IT services, argue that the IT department and those working in the digital transformation are assumed to be at fault *"when actually the telecom service provider and outside contractors could not meet their responsibilities"*. As Altameem et al. [11] point out, the quality of telecommunication services is one of the reasons for the failure of eGovernment services in many countries.

Another IT-related issue brought up during the interview was data security and compliance. As it appears in the city administration, some departments are refraining from openly accepting the introduction of digital services because they could not be certain that the security and integrity of their residents are warranted. For instance, the respondents from the education (A2) and health services (A8) argue that the IT department should take steps to make satisfactory progress in securing data and work with the legal department to put compliance assurance measures before they fully digitalise their services. The literature is clear about the significance of data protection practices and laws for the successful digital transformation [11, 14].

Even though the results of the study suggest the consensus among participants on the importance of collaboration with other agencies in the city, the lack of common IT standards is cited to be a barrier. For instance, the respondents from two of the departments—justice and security, and trade, industry, and transport—confirm that they have a close working relationship with two government bodies located within the boundary of the city administration. However, the interoperability between their systems is making communication impossible. As Legner et al. [25] found out, interoperability issues and lack of standards is defeating the very essence of collaboration between public organisations.

4.4   Environmental Factors

The implication of political instability on digital transformation is already established in the literature (e.g., [14, 19, 39]). Upon analysing the interview data, it became apparent that the influence of environmental factors on digitalisation is noted. Many of the respondents describe the turbulent political situation in city administration as well as the country as problematic. The DH recalls *"it was not even after four months since the beginning of the project that the whole administration of the municipality resigned. I was not sure if I was also about to be replaced or our work will not be a priority. There were many resistances to digitalisation at the beginning"*. Another committee member also pointed out another problem related to the political environment. In his own words, *"...the political stability not only in the region but also in the country was affecting our work. The Internet service is being cut off for security purposes.... we don't know for how long the interruptions were going to last"* (A5). According to Dewan and Kraemer [39], the quality and reliability of telecommunication services is one of the determinant factors for digital transformation. In contrast, one respondent seems to be grateful for the current political climate *"I can proudly say that we have accomplished a lot thanks to the bold move by the government. We have had a very good situation for almost two years now"* (A6).

On the other hand, respondents blamed the restrictive regulations and frameworks as it prevented them from doing what they need to do to succeed in the digital transformation. In one of the director's own words *"the biggest issue we had is that we do not have the budget to hire the best IT experts. Even very young and new enterprises could attract very young and energetic IT nerds"* (A2). This is consistent with the findings of previous studies acknowledging the lack of adequate funding for digital transformation in the public sector [11].

Other environmental factors influencing digitalisation were also brought up during the interview. For instance, the lack of collaboration with other organisations is found to be an issue. One respondent from the IT department says *"...we could do a lot to transform how we serve our residents only if we were able to integrate our services with the offerings from other private and public organisations. We don't even have a network to access data from the regional state where we closely work...our systems are simply not compatible"* (IT3). On the other hand, one of the concerns for the respondents is the lack of engagement from citizens, *"in my opinion, what we lack is the adoption of our IT services by the residents...it is a pity that the services we rolled out are not being used. I suspect most people who come to us are not digitally literate."* The literature is clear about the significance of stakeholders' participation for the success of digitalisation initiatives in the public sector [11, 14, 38].

5   Conclusion

This case study attempted to identify various factors that determine the effective implementation of digital transformation in the context of public organisations. Figure 1 shows the different factors identified to have influenced the digitalisation journey at the case company.

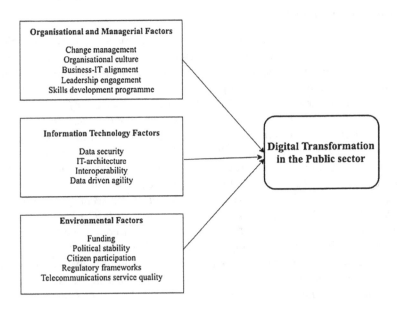

Fig. 1. Success factors for digital transformation in the public sector

The findings of the study confirm some of the results of previous studies. For instance, the benefits of digital transformation initiatives are highly dependent on how well the organisational variables are configured rather than the sophistication of the IT solutions. In this regard, the issue of IT alignment—the extent to which the IT strategies are in congruence with the overall objectives as well as the formal and informal organisational structures—has been raised by most of the respondents.

A closer look at the findings also suggests that the various challenges of digital transformation in the public sector stem from the fact that public organisations are expected to meet the interests of multiple stakeholders while navigating through complex decision- making processes. As noted from the responses of the IT and administrative leaders, IT investment decisions in the public sector are almost always influenced by the politically charged debates. For instance, unlike the private and commercial firms, public organisations could not make IT investment decisions based on cost-effectiveness or selected target groups. Organisational structure changes necessary to enable seamless digital transformation or provision of digital services are strictly regulated by political guidelines and legislation rather than informed managerial decisions.

Consistent with the findings of past studies, this study has also found that digital transformation brings numerous benefits for public organisations. However, it is also worth noting that leaders in public organisations need to address the numerous challenges. To this end, the findings of the study are invaluable for Public organisations as they attempt to gain the best out of their digital transformation journey. Researchers may also find the identified critical factors as a starting point for further investigation. Similar studies may apply quantitative research method to see if the findings are replicated in other public organisations.

The limitations of this study relate to the chosen research strategy and the data collection method. Even though case studies are known to be appropriate for eliciting in-depth insights, the generalisability of the findings is limited [40]. However, it is the author's conviction that the strategy has revealed a unique insight from a Swedish public organisation that might not be present in other settings. Future studies employing similar research methodology might be carried out in similar contexts to validate the findings of this study. In addition to comparative studies in different settings, quantitative research methods could be applied to test the generalisability of the results of this study.

References

1. Angelopoulos, S., Kitsios, F., Papadopoulos, T.: New service development in e-government: Identifying critical success factors. Transform. Gov. People Process Policy 4(1), 95–118 (2010)
2. Napitupulu, D., Sensuse, D.I.: The critical success factors study for eGovernment implementation. Int. J. Comput. Appl. 89(16), 23–32 (2014)
3. Nograšek, J., Vintar, M.: E-government and organisational transformation of government: black box revisited? Gov. Inf. Q. 31(1), 108–118 (2014)

4. Matt, C., Hess, T., Benlian, A.: Digital transformation strategies. Bus. Inf. Syst. Eng. **57**(5), 339–343 (2015)
5. Cordella, A., Tempini, N.: E-government and organizational change: reappraising the role of ICT and bureaucracy in public service delivery. Gov. Inf. Q. **32**(3), 279–286 (2015)
6. Haffke, I., Kalgovas, B.J., Benlian, A.: The role of the CIO and the CDO in an organization's digital transformation. In: Proceedings of the International Conference on Information Systems (ICIS). Association for Information Systems, AIS Electronic Library (AISeL) (2016)
7. Berman, S.J.: Digital transformation: opportunities to create new business models. Strategy Leadersh. **40**(2), 16–24 (2012)
8. Shaughnessy, H.: Creating digital transformation: strategies and steps. Strategy Leadersh. **46**(2), 19–25 (2018)
9. Horlacher, A., Klarner, P., Hess, T.: Crossing boundaries: organization design parameters surrounding cdos and their digital transformation activities. In: Proceedings of the Americas Conference on Information Systems (AMCIS). Association for Information Systems, AIS Electronic Library (AISeL) (2016)
10. Brennen, J.S., Kreiss, D.: Digitalization. The International Encyclopaedia of Communication Theory and Philosophy, pp. 1–11 (2016)
11. Altameem, T., Zairi, M., Alshawi, S.: Critical success factors of egovernment: a proposed model for e-government implementation. In: 2006 Innovations in Information Technology, pp. 1–5. IEEE (2006)
12. Hess, T., Matt, C., Benlian, A., Wiesböck, F.: Options for formulating a digital transformation strategy. MIS Q. Exec. **15**(2), 6 (2016)
13. Anthopoulos, L., Reddick, C.G., Giannakidou, I., Mavridis, N.: Why eGovernment projects fail? An analysis of the healthcare. gov website. Gov. Inf. Q. **33**(1), 161–173 (2016)
14. Gil-García, J.R., Pardo, T.A.: E-government success factors: Mapping practical tools to theoretical foundations. Government Information Quarterly 22(2), 187–216 (2005)
15. Rosacker, K.M., Rosacker, R.E.: Information technology project management within public sector organizations. J. Enterp. Inf. Manag. **23**(5), 587–594 (2010)
16. Janowski, T.: Digital government evolution: from transformation to contextualization. Gov. Inf. Q. **32**(3), 221–236 (2015)
17. Caudle, S.L., Gorr, W.L., Newcomer, K.E.: Key information systems management issues for the public sector. MIS Q. **15**(2), 171–188 (1991)
18. Kane, G.C., Palmer, D., Phillips, A.N., Kiron, D., Buckley, N., et al.: Strategy, not technology, drives digital transformation. MIT Sloan Manag. Rev. Deloitte Univ. Press **14**, 1–25 (2015)
19. Tarutė, A., Duobienė, J., Klovienė, L., Vitkauskaitė, E., Varaniūtė, V.: Identifying factors affecting digital transformation of SMEs (2018)
20. Bharadwaj, A., El Sawy, O.A., Pavlou, P.A., Venkatraman, N.: Digital business strategy: toward a next generation of insights. MIS Q. **17**(2), 471–482 (2013)
21. Jonathan, G.M., Abdul-Salaam, A., Oluwasanmi, O., Rusu, L.: Business-IT alignment barriers in a public organisation: the case of federal inland revenue service of Nigeria. Int. J. Innov. Digit. Econ. (IJIDE) **9**(1), 1–13 (2018)
22. Rusu, L., Jonathan, G.M.: IT alignment in public organizations: a systematic literature review. In: Rusu, L., Viscusi, G. (eds.) Information Technology Governance in Public Organizations. ISIS, vol. 38, pp. 27–57. Springer, Cham (2017). https://doi.org/10.1007/978-3-319-58978-7_2
23. Jonathan, G.M., Rusu, L.: IT governance in public organizations: a systematic literature review. Int. J. IT/Bus. Alignment Gov. (IJITBAG) **9**(2), 30–52 (2018)

24. Aichholzer, G., Schmutzer, R.: Organizational challenges to the development of electronic government. In: Proceedings 11th International Workshop on Database and Expert Systems Applications, pp. 379–383. IEEE (2000)
25. Legner, C., et al.: Digitalization: opportunity and challenge for the business and information systems engineering community. Bus. Inf. Syst. Eng. **59**(4), 301–308 (2017)
26. Ylinen, M., Pekkola, S.: A process model for public sector IT management to answer the needs of digital transformation. In: Proceedings of the 52nd Hawaii International Conference on System Sciences (2019)
27. Brown, T.L., Potoski, M., Van Slyke, D.M.: Managing public service contracts: aligning values, institutions, and markets. Public Adm. Rev. **66**(3), 323–331 (2006)
28. Osman, I.H., et al.: Cobra framework to evaluate e-government services: a citizen-centric perspective. Gov. Inf. Q. **31**(2), 243–256 (2014)
29. Vogelsang, K., Liere-Netheler, K., Packmohr, S., Hoppe, U.: A taxonomy of barriers to digital transformation. In: Proceedings of the 14th International Conference on Wirtschaftsinformatik, pp. 736–750. Association for Information Systems. AIS Electronic Library (AISeL) (2019)
30. Henriette, E., Feki, M., Boughzala, I.: The shape of digital transformation: a systematic literature review. In: Proceedings of the Mediterranean Conference on Information Systems (MCIS). Association for Information Systems. AIS Electronic Library (AISeL) (2015)
31. Mithas, S., Tafti, A., Mitchell, W.: How a firm's competitive environment and digital strategic posture influence digital business strategy. MIS Q. **17**(2), 511–536 (2013)
32. Jonathan, G.M.: Influence of organizational structure on business-IT alignment: what we do (not) know. In: Proceedings of the 17th International Conference Perspectives in Business Informatics Research (BIR 2018), Stockholm, Sweden. pp. 375–386. CEUR-WS.org (2018)
33. Prahalad, C.K., Krishnan, M.S.: The dynamic synchronization of strategy and information technology. MIT Sloan Manag. Rev. **43**(4), 24 (2002)
34. Holotiuk, F., Beimborn, D.: Critical success factors of digital business strategy. In: Proceedings der 13. Internationalen Tagung Wirtschaftsinformatik (WI2017), pp. 991–1005. Association for Information Systems. AIS Electronic Library (AISeL) (2017)
35. Osmundsen, K., Iden, J., Bygstad, B.: Digital transformation: drivers, success factors and implications. In: Proceedings of the Mediterranean Conference on Information Systems (MCIS). Association for Information Systems. AIS Electronic Library (AISeL) (2018)
36. Berghaus, S., Back, A.: Stages in digital business transformation: results of an empirical maturity study. In: Proceedings of the Mediterranean Conference on Information Systems (MCIS), p. 22. Association for Information Systems. AIS Electronic Library (AISeL) (2016)
37. Dremel, C., Herterich, M., Wulf, J., Waizmann, J.C., Brenner, W.: How Audi AG established big data analytics in its digital transformation. MIS Q. Exec. **16**(2), 81–100 (2017)
38. Jonathan, G.M., Rusu, L.: eGovernment adoption determinants from citizens' perspective: a systematic literature review. Int. J. Innov. Digit. Econ. (IJIDE) **10**(1), 18–30 (2019)
39. Dewan, S., Kraemer, K.L.: Information technology and productivity: evidence from country-level data. Manag. Sci. **46**(4), 548–562 (2000)
40. Yin, R.K.: Case Study Research and Applications: Design and Methods. SAGE Publications, Thousand Oaks (2017)
41. Denscombe, M.: The Good Research Guide: For Small-Scale Social Research Projects. McGraw-Hill Education, UK (2014)
42. Boyatzis, R.E.: Transforming Qualitative Information: Thematic Analysis and Code Development. SAGE Publications, Thousand Oaks (1998)
43. Braun, V., Clarke, V.: Using thematic analysis in psychology. Qual. Res. Psychol. **3**(2), 77–101 (2006)

Employing the Once-Only Principle in the Domain of the Electronic Public Procurement

Maria Siapera, Konstantinos Douloudis, Gerasimos Dimitriou, and Andriana Prentza

Department of Digital Systems, University of Piraeus, Piraeus, Greece
{mariaspr, kdoul, jerouris, aprentza}@unipi.gr

Abstract. This paper presents a case study for the application of the "Once Only Principle" (OOP) for cross-border public services where citizens and businesses provide data only once in contact with public administrations. In order to support the European Union (EU)'s vision of a Single Digital Market, a generic federated OOP architecture has been developed, within the context of the European Union funded "The Once-Only Principle Project" (TOOP). The federated architecture is showcased in a real-life use case scenario that demonstrates in practical ways how OOP can be implemented to aid the elimination of administrative burdens in the domain of electronic public procurement. More specifically, the scenario focuses on the case of the Greek "European Single Procurement Document" (ESPD) public service, acting as a system that requests and receives data from the TOOP infrastructure. Finally, the paper presents the results of testing connectivity scenarios between the Greek and other Member State systems.

Keywords: Once-Only Principle · Interoperability · eProcurement · Data reuse · Interconnection · Cross-border public digital services

1 Introduction

There is no doubt, that Information and Communication Technology (ICT) systems are nowadays the core of government processes, and enterprise business as well. In addition, one of the core strategies of the European Commission is that of a Digital Single Market [1], meaning an internal European Union (EU) market that people are able to move freely and conduct their business outside of their home country, in any Member State. Thus, there is a significant need for citizens, enterprises and organizations to carry out their business seamlessly and easily in any Member State of the EU.

There are many practical difficulties though, for businesses engaging in cross-border activities. Things like, for example, complying with different national regulations or with different administrative requirements of foreign public agencies, form serious impediments. On the other hand, public agencies also face many difficulties when it comes to collecting, but also verifying the validity of foreign official information on companies and their legal representatives due to multiple data sources and

M. Themistocleous and M. Papadaki (Eds.): EMCIS 2019, LNBIP 381, pp. 236–246, 2020.
https://doi.org/10.1007/978-3-030-44322-1_18

the cost of manual back-office procedures. In this context, the interaction with public services and the governments within the EU needs to be also reformed and digitally "transformed" to keep up with the new digital economic pace and reality. There are several steps to be taken though, in order to ensure the improvement of the delivery of services. These steps are made not only by providing tools, utilizing eGovernment practices and rethinking internal processes [2], but also by making them a significant priority through political commitment at the EU level. This kind of political commitment is showcased by the signing of the Tallinn Declaration on eGovernment at the ministerial meeting during Estonian Presidency of the Council of the EU on 6 October 2017 [3]. As part of this digital reform, the European Commission is taking concrete actions for the development of Cross-Border Digital Public Services [4], such as the creation of European interoperable platforms that implement the "Once-Only Principle" [5] (OOP) and the provision of guidelines for the better use of ICT systems of public authorities. Something that aims at aiding the plans of the EU regarding the Digital Single Market, by reducing the administrative burden in the Member States.

According to the "Once Only Principle", sharing information and data across the public administration systems is cheaper than collecting them more than once from citizens and businesses. Thus, the OOP is based on the simplification of administrative processes and the notion that information is collected only once and then can become available and shared across the different systems that request for this information, respecting constraints that are imposed by regulations. This kind of digital information availability, not only increases the efficiency of the public administrations but also reduces the time and cost of the administrative processes, improving the quality of public services, both at national levels and cross-border [6].

To address the OOP related challenges and ease the implementation of OOP in cross-border settings, the Once-Only Principle Project (TOOP) [7] was selected and funded under the scope of the "EU Horizon 2020 Research and Innovation Funding Programme" [8]. TOOP aims to facilitate the cross-border application of OOP by demonstrating it in practice through multiple real wide-scale pilots [9] using a federated architecture that is designed on a pan-European collaboration, enabling the connection of different registries and architectures in different countries and domains for better exchange of information across the public administrations [10]. TOOP's main goal is to demonstrate the feasibility of its proposed federated architecture in real-world pilots. This means that the aforementioned pilots are systems that are either already in production, conducting real transactions connected to TOOP or are starting technical development and will reach production level within the lifetime of TOOP [11].

In order to explore the viability of TOOP's proposed federated architecture, there are three pilot areas selected that serve as proof of feasibility across Europe. These pilot areas are the following:

1. Cross-border eServices for Business Mobility
2. Updating Connected Company Data
3. Online Ship and Crew Certificates

Each pilot area consists of different pilot use cases and usage scenarios that are of interest to the participating Member States. Such a particular use case scenario, of interest, is the Greek ESPD (European Single Procurement Document) system [12] which demonstrates the use of OOP in the eProcurement domain within the first pilot area and it is further examined in this paper.

2 Background and Motivation for the Study

2.1 Digital Single Market Strategy and Once Only Principle

In October 2015, the "Single Market Strategy" was introduced by the European Commission (EC) [13]. According to the EC, this strategy is "*at the heart of the European project*" [13], foreseeing that people, services, and goods are freely moving within the EU. The vision of the Single Market Strategy is backed by Initiatives and Action Plans, ensuring that citizens/businesses can fairly access goods and services, irrespective of their nationality and place of residence. One of the strategy's backing Action Plans is the "eGovernment Action Plan 2016–2020" [14].

The eGovernment Action Plan 2016–2020 focuses "on the wide-scale implementation of eGovernment", making sure that the citizens and businesses in the EU can experience the tangible benefits of technological enablers being used in public services. According to that, there are three policy priorities identified:

- *Public administration modernization using digital enablers such as Connecting Europe Facility (CEF)'s [15] building blocks (i.e. eID, eSignature, eDelivery, and eInvoicing);*
- *High-quality public services that ease the digital interaction between administrations and citizens/businesses;*
- *The facilitation of mobility of citizens/businesses by cross-border interoperability [14].*

To enhance cross-border activities within the EU, the introduction of the "Once Only Principle" (OOP) was made by the European Commission. According to the eGovernment Action Plan 2016–2020, the EC defines the Once Only Principle as follows:

"public administrations should ensure that citizens and businesses supply the same information only once to a public administration. Public administration offices take action if permitted to internally re-use this data, in due respect of data protection rules, so that no additional burden falls on citizens and businesses" [14].

In October 2017, the Tallinn Declaration on eGovernment was signed by the ministers of 32 Member States of the EU. The declaration focuses on the benefits and potential savings to be achieved, through political commitment to "*take steps to identify redundant administrative burden in public services and introduce once-only options for citizens and businesses in digital public services*" [3]. Meaning that both the Tallinn Declaration and the eGovernment Action Plan 2016–2020 establish the "Once Only Principle" and data re-use, as political priority and commits to reduce administrative burdens in public services.

2.2 Once Only Initiatives and Implementations

As part of the eGovernment Action Plan 2016–2020, two projects were funded under the "EU Horizon 2020" research and innovation program in order to address the OOP challenges: "The Once-Only Principle Project" (TOOP) and the "Stakeholder Community Once-Only Principle for Citizens" (SCOOP4C) [16]. TOOP, which was launched in January 2017 and is being coordinated by the Tallinn University of Technology in Estonia, focuses on reducing the administrative burden for businesses by employing the OOP. TOOP's proposed solution is based on already existing working systems and building blocks in the Member States implementing *"multiple sustainable pilots by using a federated IT architecture on cross-border, pan-European scale."* [17]. The SCOOP4C project, launched in November 2016 and coordinated by the University of Koblenz-Landau in Germany, aims to *"investigate, discuss, and disseminate how co-creation and co-production in public service provisioning for citizens can be achieved by implementing the once-only principle"* [16].

Another case of an initiative employing the OOP is the Business Registers Interconnection System (BRIS) [18] providing cooperation across European business registers. It provides to the citizens and the businesses an interface for accessing information about companies and their branches across all Europe.

There are also many examples of using OOP in national implementations. For example, in the Netherlands, the Dutch Tax office provides pre-filled tax reports. Citizens don't have to manually fill in tax forms, but only check and change things in case of an error [19].

2.3 eProcurement and the European Single Procurement Document (ESPD)

eProcurement refers to the exchange of supplies, services, goods and work through the Internet or any other electronic channels [20] and is the focus of the 2014/24/EU Directive [22]. According to the EC [21], *"public procurement is undergoing a digital transformation. The EU supports the process of rethinking of public procurement processes with digital technologies in mind"*. eProcurement is considered at the heart of EU Directives (2014/24/EU [22] on public procurement, 2014/23/EU [23] on the award of concession contracts). The purposes of these directives are enhancing the free movement of goods and services during procurement processes by making them simpler and easier for the Small Medium-sized Enterprises (SMEs) to gain access to procurement processes and bid for public contracts. Taking into consideration the lessening of administrative burdens and the continuation of the public procurement reform across the EU, the EC established the standard form for the ESPD [24] issuing an implementing regulation at January 5, 2016.

An ESPD *"is a self-declaration of the business's financial status, abilities, and suitability for a public procurement procedure [25]. The access and participation in cross-border tendering opportunities is simplified since the tenderers no longer need to provide full documentary evidence and different forms previously used in the EU procurement. In addition, the service is available in all EU languages and can be used as preliminary evidence of condition fulfillment required in public procurement procedures across the EU" [26].* With the introduction of the ESPD, companies can participate in procurement processes without having to submit various documents as evidences satisfying certain criteria in order to participate. Only the winner of a procurement process needs to provide the actual documents and evidences. Almost all EU countries provide national ESPD services, since the use of the ESPD is obligatory. Also, since all Contracting Authorities are legally obliged to accept the standard layout of the ESPD, the Economic Operators can easily and safely qualify for any public tender in Europe increasing the competitiveness.

3   Methodology

3.1   The Generic Federated OOP Architecture

The aim of TOOP's generic federated OOP architecture is to support the interconnection and interoperability between national registries at the EU level. The architecture consists of loosely coupled service components which utilize already existing available building blocks, such as the CEF [15] eID and eDelivery infrastructures and standards. The main benefit of re-using such components is the fact that they have already been used by the Member States and proven successful, avoiding the imposition of any technological specific solutions on citizens, businesses and public administrations. Figure 1 shows a component architecture overview. A legal entity that can be either a natural or legal person is the user of a Public eService provided by a Member State. The Member State Authority providing the public service that requests and receives data from a registry in another Member State, acts in the role of Data Consumer (DC), whereas the Member State Authority providing the data acts in the role of Data Provider (DP). The TOOP infrastructure fetches information from the Member State Authority who acts as a DP making it available to the foreign Public Authority who acts as a DC. The end-user only needs to provide minimum information in order to be identified, authenticated and authorized allowing the TOOP infrastructure to discover what information is available for the needs of the DC Service. The cross-border interoperability is guaranteed via retrieving information in machine-readable format, packaged in a specific TOOP message format that uses the TOOP semantic building block in order to preserve meaning. In addition, an eDelivery Gateway is used providing secure transport between the DC and the DP and trust establishment between the participants.

As shown in Fig. 1, green components are deployed centrally either at TOOP or CEF infrastructure. Components in purple consist the TOOP connector, which is provided by TOOP as a facilitation, but Member States are free to replicate its functionalities using their own development. Components in blue are the responsibility of the Member State systems. It is worth to mention that since TOOP's architecture is a reference architecture, there is no fixed way of how to deploy TOOP services. TOOP is providing components and guidelines as a facilitation but does not impose their usage.

The central components include the following:

- TOOP Directory: provides global search functionality over all participants,
- CEF BDMSL (Business Document Metadata Service Location): facilitates the retrieval of participant identifiers.
- Semantic Mapping Service: maintains mappings between national data models and the TOOP Common Semantic Model.

The services that need to be deployed at a Member State (MS) level are the following:

- Service Metadata Publisher (SMP) Service: decentralized registry that links identifiers to endpoint URLs and certificates for document exchange.
- eIDAS Node: Optional component that oversees identification and authentication of the user.
- TOOP Connector: Optional component that encapsulates several functions that support the data exchange from one participant to another. Some of its main functions are the transformation of data input into a proper TOOP message, routing metadata discovery and endpoint discovery. It is provided by TOOP as facilitation, but its usage is not imposed to the Member States.
- AS4 (Applicability Statement 4 standard for the secure and payload-agnostic exchange of business-to-business documents) Gateway: eDelivery Gateway that provides secure transport between the participants.

The DC User Interface, DC Business Processing and DP Business Processing components can vary and be specific to each Member State's eService.

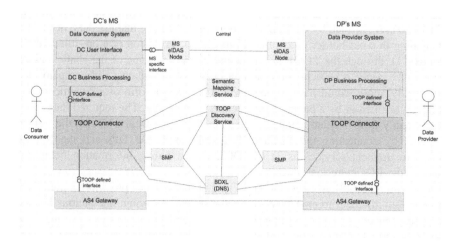

Fig. 1. Component architecture (Color figure online)

3.2   ESPD Service as TOOP Data Consumer

3.2.1   Use Case Description

A typical usage scenario of the ESPD service with the TOOP integration is the following: Firstly, a Contracting Authority (CA) has published a call for tender containing among others the ESPD template for a specific call. The legal representative of an Economic Operator (EO) that wishes to take part in the tender process, gets the ESPD request from the public call for tender and is being authenticated to the ESPD service, providing information for the identification of the company for which creates an ESPD response and the country of origin. The ESPD service requests via the TOOP Infrastructure the requested information (i.e. company details) by the designated DP of the country of origin. The TOOP DP receives the request, processes it and sends a response back to the ESPD service. Upon a successful TOOP response reception from a DP, the ESPD service validates the response, extracts the available data from the response and after getting the user's consent, automatically fills the part of the ESPD form that is relevant with the requested information. Afterwards, the ESPD system asks of any additional information and generates the requested ESPD. The legal representative previews the generated ESPD response, completes and submits it and finally, proceeds with the tender process.

The EOs can easily and safely qualify for any public tender of a CA in Europe since all CAs are legally obliged to accept the standard layout of the ESPD. This fact makes the use case a perfect instance of demonstrating the elimination of redundant provision of data, by the legal representatives of the business's during the fulfillment process of an ESPD, through the TOOP infrastructure.

3.2.2   Advantages Integrating TOOP with an ESPD Service

The provision of company details, as well as the provision of evidences to selection and exclusion criteria defined by the CAs is cumbersome for EOs, making them hesitant on participating in cross-border procurement procedures. Provision of a pre-filled version of the ESPD, through the TOOP infrastructure, alleviates some of the challenges that the EOs face, since it reduces the time and hassle of providing valid company data. Traditionally, these would have to be provided either in a form of a document (i.e. a certificate) or filled in by a business representative manually. The required data can be pulled directly from verified sources, such as the Business Registries that the EOs are registered, by connecting the Business Registries as TOOP DPs and the National ESPD/eProcurement services as TOOP DCs, thus avoiding information being submitted by the EOs more than once.

Furthermore, the eIDAS Regulation [27] is put into practice providing a predictable regulatory environment to enable secure and seamless electronic interactions between businesses, citizens and public authorities. People and businesses can use their own national electronic identification schemes (eIDs) to access public services in other Member States since companies that have their information in Business Registries that act as TOOP DPs, can access those data by using their eIDAS credentials. The ESPD service that acts as a TOOP DC asks its users for their eIDAS credentials and consent for requesting any data required, respecting and taking into consideration regulations about the protection of personal data like the General Data Protection Regulation (GDPR) [28].

Data exchange is implemented in a way that reduces human interaction during the provision and consumption of the exchanged information, aiming as much as possible to machine-processable information sharing. In addition, the services are open to all Member States, avoiding bilateral agreements that do not scale EU-wide and thus, eliminating discriminations.

The ESPD service that acts a TOOP DC can connect and fetch data from every TOOP DP that is available in the TOOP eDelivery Network. There is no need for specific point-to-point connections due to TOOP's federated architecture. The TOOP DC requests for data and then the TOOP Infrastructure is responsible for the discovery and retrieval of the data.

Finally, the messages sent and received across the TOOP infrastructure are packaged, signed and encrypted in a certain way before transmission, ensuring their integrity, establishing trust between the TOOP DC and the TOOP DP.

3.2.3   The Greek ESPD Service as TOOP Data Consumer

Greece is participating in the TOOP infrastructure as a DC with the Greek ESPD service called *"Promitheus"*. Each of TOOP's pilots deploy the required subset of TOOP service components necessary for the specific application scenario. Likewise, only the TOOP components necessary for the ESPD service scenario are deployed.

The implementation architecture, as shown in Fig. 2, follows the TOOP architecture as described previously. The existing ESPD application is used without modification to its core components. A component called *"TOOP Interface"* acts as a bridge between the ESPD application and the rest of the TOOP infrastructure. The ESPD application can request data in its own format while the "DC Interface" (instance of TOOP Interface) converts that to a "TOOP Data Request" which is the proper request that can be made through the TOOP network. The "TOOP Response" that comes back can also then be converted to data that the ESPD application can work with.

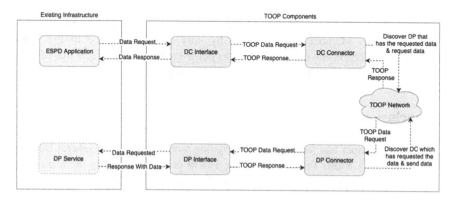

Fig. 2. TOOP architecture of the Greek Data Consumer

4   Results

TOOP has defined a multi-step process to conduct tests that check the readiness and maturity of the pilot MS implementations. The last step of these series of tests is called a "Connectathon" which consists of thorough connectivity tests between a MS DC and a MS DP following the pilot scenario. When enough MSs are ready, a "Connectathon" can take place. In each "Connectathon", every MS uses their implementation and attempt to exchange data with other MSs through a set of specified test scenarios. These include example sets of data and some test cases for the DP and DC software. The results of these exchanges are logged and discussed in order to address any issues that may come up. This method of testing was selected because it simulates a real-life scenario of exchanging data within the TOOP premises and aids in discovering issues with the TOOP components and the MS' implementations.

Table 1. Successful connections made with the Greek ESPD service acting as TOOP DC

#	DC	DP	Date
1	Greece	Sweden	23.05
2	Greece	Slovakia	23.05
3	Greece	Italy	07.06
4	Greece	Romania	04.07
5	Greece	Austria	16.09
6	Greece	Poland	16.09
7	Greece	Norway	26.09
8	Greece	Slovenia	26.09

Currently, the Greek ESPD Service acting as a TOOP DC has been successfully integrated and exchanged information with the Swedish, Slovakian, Slovenian, Italian, Romanian, Austrian, Polish and Norwegian systems acting as TOOP DPs, as it is shown in Table 1. The Greek ESPD service managed to exchange information with eight (8) different Member State systems by only connecting once to the TOOP infrastructure. There is no need for point-to-point connection between the Member States due to the way the TOOP federated architecture is designed.

5   Conclusions and Future Work

To sum up, this paper has focused on the ongoing work done in the General Business Mobility pilot area within the context of the TOOP project, especially the use case of the Greek ESPD Service, acting as a TOOP DC in the eProcurement domain. It is anticipated that more Member States will join, acting as TOOP DPs and demonstrate more cross-border exchanges. Finally, regarding the Greek ESPD service, there is ongoing work with the purpose of using the TOOP infrastructure to discover and retrieve Evidences and Documents, needed for the fulfillment of a CA's criteria requirements at the time of awarding or when is needed and not only fetching e.g. company data, thus eliminating the need for the businesses to upload documents from their local IT infrastructure.

Acknowledgments. This work is supported financially by the TOOP (The Once-Only Principle) Project, which is partially funded by the European Union's Horizon 2020 research and innovation program under G.A. No. 737460. We acknowledge the work and contributions of the TOOP project partners.

References

1. Digital Single Market. https://ec.europa.eu/commission/priorities/digital-single-market_en. Accessed 25 Sept 2019
2. EU eGovernment Action Plan 2016–2020 communication. https://ec.europa.eu/digital-single-market/en/news/communication-eu-egovernment-action-plan-2016-2020-accelerating-digital-transformation. Accessed 25 Sept 2019
3. Tallinn Declaration: https://ec.europa.eu/digital-single-market/en/news/ministerial-declaration-egovernment-tallinn-declaration. Accessed 25 Sept 2019
4. eGovernment and Digital Services. https://ec.europa.eu/digital-single-market/en/public-services-egovernment. Accessed 25 Sept 2019
5. Once Only Principle. https://ec.europa.eu/cefdigital/wiki/display/CEFDIGITAL/Once+Only+Principle. Accessed 25 Sept 2019
6. Gallo, G., Giove, M., Millard, J., Thaarup, R.: Study on eGovernment and the Reduction of Administrative Burden (2014). http://ec.europa.eu/newsroom/dae/document.cfm?doc_id=5155. Accessed 25 Sept 2019
7. The Once Only Principle Project (TOOP). http://www.toop.eu/. Accessed 26 Sept 2019
8. Horizon 2020. https://ec.europa.eu/programmes/horizon2020/en/what-horizon-2020. Accessed 25 Sept 2019
9. TOOP pilots. http://www.toop.eu/pilot-area1. Accessed 26 Sept 2019
10. Krimmer, R., Kalvet, T., Toots, M., Cepilovs, A.: The Once-Only Principle Project: position paper on definition of OOP and situation in Europe (2017)
11. Krimmer, R., Kalvet, T., Toots, M., Cepilovs, A., Tambouris, E.: Exploring and demonstrating the once-only principle: a European perspective. ACM (2017)
12. Greek ESPD System. https://espdint.eprocurement.gov.gr/. Accessed 26 Sept 2019
13. Single Market Strategy. https://ec.europa.eu/growth/single-market/strategy_en. Accessed 25 Sept 2019
14. eGovernment Action Plan 2016–2020. https://ec.europa.eu/digital-single-market/en/european-egovernment-action-plan-2016-2020. Accessed 25 Sept 2019
15. CEF – Connecting Europe Facility. https://ec.europa.eu/inea/en/connecting-europe-facility. Accessed 26 Sept 2019
16. SCOOP4C project site. https://www.scoop4c.eu/project. Accessed 25 Sept 2019
17. The Once Only Principle Project (TOOP) info page. http://www.toop.eu/info. Accessed 26 Sept 2019
18. BRIS, Business Registers Interconnection System. https://ec.europa.eu/cefdigital/wiki/display/CEFDIGITAL/2017/09/19/Business+Register+Interconnection+System. Accessed 25 Sept 2019

19. Dutch Tax Office website. https://www.belastingdienst.nl/wps/wcm/connect/bldcontentnl/belastingdienst/prive/werk_en_inkomen/jongeren/teruggaaf_jongeren/aangifte_invullen/aangifte_invullen. Accessed 25 Sept 2019

20. Davila, A., et al.: Moving procurement systems to the internet: the adoption and use of e-procurement technology models (2003). https://www.sciencedirect.com/science/article/abs/pii/S026323730200155X. Accessed 25 Sept 2019

21. Digital Procurement. https://ec.europa.eu/growth/single-market/public-procurement/digital_en. Accessed 25 Sept 2019

22. Directive 2014/24/EU of the European Parliament and of the Council of 26 February 2014 on public procurement and repealing Directive 2004/18/EC, OJ L 94, pp. 65–242, 28 March 2014

23. Directive 2014/23/EU of the European Parliament and of the Council of 26 February 2014 on the award of concession contracts, OJ L 94, pp. 1–64, 28 March 2014

24. Commission Implementing Regulation (EU) 2016/7 of 5 January 2016 establishing the standard form for the European Single Procurement Document, OJ L 3, pp. 16–34, 6 January 2016. Accessed 27 Sept 2019

25. European Single Procurement Document. https://ec.europa.eu/growth/single-market/publicprocurement/digital/espd_en. Accessed 27 Sept 2019

26. Public procurement guidance for practitioners. https://ec.europa.eu/regional_policy/sources/docgener/guides/public_procurement/2018/guidance_public_procurement_2018_en.pdf. Accessed 27 Sept 2019

27. Regulation (EU) No 910/2014 of the European Parliament and of the Council of 23 July 2014 on electronic identification and trust services for electronic transactions in the internal market and repealing Directive 1999/93/EC, OJ L 257, pp. 73–114, 28 August 2014

28. Regulation (EU) 2016/679 of the European Parliament and of the Council of 27 April 2016 on the protection of natural persons with regard to the processing of personal data and on the free movement of such data, and repealing Directive 95/46/EC (General Data Protection Regulation), OJ L 119, 4 May 2016

Embracing Modern Technologies and Urban Development Trends: Initial Evaluation of a Smart City Enterprise Architecture Frameworks

Hong Guo[1,2]([⊠]), Sobah Abbas Petersen[1], Shang Gao[3], Jingyue Li[1], and Anthony Junior Bokolo[1]

[1] Norwegian University of Science and Technology, Trondheim, Norway
{hong.guo,sobah.a.petersen,jingyue.li,
Anthony.j.bokolo}@ntnu.no
[2] Anhui University, Hefei, People's Republic of China
homekuo@gmail.com
[3] Örebro University, Örebro, Sweden
shang.gao@oru.se

Abstract. The development of smart cities becomes increasingly reliant on leveraging modern technologies such as Internet of Things (IoT), big data, cloud computing, and Artificial Intelligence (AI). While the importance of applying such technologies has been widely recognized, they might not have been effectively discussed in the early design phase. As a widely applied planning and architecting tool, traditional Enterprise Architecture Frameworks (EAF) are not always able to meet requirements of urban development in an expected way. This might be alleviated by applying a smart city-oriented EAF which supports discussion of modern techniques in the early design phase. In the EU smart city project +CityxChange, an EAF was proposed to address such issues. In this article, we focus on an initial evaluation of the EAF proposed in the +CityxChange project according to the Design Science Research (DSR) method. We discuss how the EAF has enhanced the widely used EAF (i.e., The Open Group Architecture Framework, TOGAF for short) by extending its layer-based Enterprise Architecture (EA). We also present a sample scenario demonstrating how the EAF can be used.

Keywords: Enterprise Architecture Framework · Smart cities · TOGAF · Service management · Data management · Physical infrastructure · Urban development

1 Introduction

More than half of the world's population lives in cities [1]. Smart cities construction becomes a global focus as it utilizes Information and Communications Technology (ICT) resources to alleviate unprecedented city challenges such as producing more wealth, encouraging wide innovation, and keeping sustainability. To solve the

M. Themistocleous and M. Papadaki (Eds.): EMCIS 2019, LNBIP 381, pp. 247–257, 2020.
https://doi.org/10.1007/978-3-030-44322-1_19

complexity issues that we often encountered when managing the ICT systems in smart cities, Enterprise Architecture (EA) has been commonly utilized [2, 3].

However, when EA was applied in governments, public sectors, and cities, various challenges have been met which hindered its successful application. The challenges include unique business driven approach, lack of an agreement on a vision and the extent of the EA initiative, and unclear organizational strategies [4].

This might partly be because existing EA Frameworks (EAFs), such as the most widely used The Open Group Architecture Framework (TOGAF) [5], have been designed many years ago. Therefore, they do not highlight important roles of new technologies such as cloud computing and Internet of Things (IoT), and therefore have caused the invisibility of relevant concepts in the early stage of design. As a result, effective design of them is hindered.

In addition, existing EAFs were initially designed for enterprises rather than for cities. Previous research [6] indicated that more attention had been paid to general EAFs than governmental EAFs [7], despite that the existence of several important government EAFs such as the Federal Enterprise Architecture Framework (FEAF) has confirmed the importance of government EAFs. Important concepts like city infrastructure and data services/elements/sources that are specific to city scenarios are missing in general EAFs. On the other hand, the required analysis on specific government domains was usually conducted on a local and adhoc basis, which makes the results hard to be reused in a general scenario [8].

As indicated in [9], EA in governments has been driven to a large extent by fashion. EA is not a clear-cut cure that would produce similar results to all organizations. It is important that, many different stakeholders, such as senior managers and domain experts, should build a common and holistic view of the organization's strategy, processes, information, and technology assets that must not be underestimated in EA programs. Similarly, according to the study on 21 interviews with stakeholders like government officials and IT companies in Finland [10], "shared understandings" and "implementation ability" were thought as two of the most pivotal challenges of EA when applied in governments.

In the EU smart city project +CityxChange [11, 12], an EAF was proposed [13] to better consider urban specific technologies and requirements based on earlier research results [14]. As "shared understanding" is critical to implement EAF, in this article, we clarify how the EAF proposed in [13] enhanced the traditional EAF TOGAF by extending its layer-based enterprise architecture. We also explain the possible application of the proposed EAF with a sample scenario. We refer to the +CityxChange EAF proposed in [13] as "*the EAF*" in the rest of this article unless otherwise specified.

The rest of this paper is organized as below. Section 2 introduces our research methods. Section 3 introduces some background information. Especially, three groups of modern technologies and urban development trends that might bring significant impacts to smart city EAs are presented. Then, we brief introduce the EAF and discuss how it enhances the layered enterprise architecture of TOGAF in Sect. 4. In Sect. 5, we further demonstrate the usage the EAF through a sample scenario. In Sect. 6, we talk about related studies in the smart city domain. At last, we conclude this paper and direct some future studies in Sect. 7.

2 Research Methods

The methodology we used follows the DSR paradigm described in [15]. The DSR has been widely applied in information systems research [16]. It describes a problem-solving paradigm in which organization capability boundaries are extended through building and applying design artifacts. The EAF proposed in the +CityxChange project is such a design artifact as it might help architects and other stakeholders to perform architecture design of smart cities in a consistent and visualized way.

According to [15], the evaluation of one design science artifact may cover two parts, namely the *Rigorous* to the knowledge base and the *Relevance* to the environment as shown in Fig. 1. While rigorous is achieved by appropriately applying existing foundations and methodologies, relevance is assured by framing research activities to address business needs.

In this article, we evaluate the rigorous of the EAF by reviewing relevant literature (in Sects. 3 and 6) and especially, comparing it with one existing EAF that is notable and have been used widely in various domains, namely TOGAF (in Sect. 4). We use the method of *Informed Argument* for this part which means to use information from existing studies to build an argument for the artifact's utility. We then evaluate the relevance of the EAF by presenting a scenario to demonstrate how to use the EAF and what benefits could be expected through using it (in Sect. 5). We use the method of *Scenarios* for this part which means constructing a detailed scenario around the artifact to demonstrate its utility.

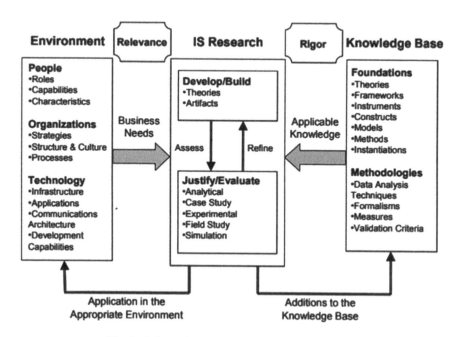

Fig. 1. Information system research framework [15]

Both Informed Argument and Scenarios are *Descriptive* evaluation methods [15]. Because +CityxChange is at present in its early development phase, other forms of evaluation might not be feasible yet. Further evaluation of other forms such as *Case Study* and *Structural Testing* might be planned along with the further development/ enhancement of the EA.

3 Background

Smart city development has relied more and more on effective usage of modern *techniques* such as big data and IoT. In [3], four enabling technologies that have been used in state-of-the-art smart city platforms was summarized, i.e., big data, cloud computing, IoT, and cyber physical systems. Furthermore, around ten functional/non-functional *requirements* as well as ten *challenges* that have been addressed in most existing smart city platforms were enumerated based an intensive review [3]. There are tight connections among such techniques, requirements, and the challenges that smart city platforms are facing.

The leverage of such modern *techniques* as well as the pursue of urban development *trends* (requirements to achieve and challenges to overcome) might bring significant impact to the business architecture of smart cities. In this section, we introduce three groups of technologies and corresponding requirements or challenges for smart city development. Relevant studies where specific EAs were constructed to better leveraging technologies and address requirements/challenges for smart cities will be presented in Sect. 6.

3.1 SOA, Service Management, Interoperability, and Provision of Services

There are different paradigms to create EA. The most important one is to encapsulate the functions of ICT resources into services. For example, Service Oriented Architecture (*SOA*) has been a widely used technique in various smart city architectures. In addition, *service management* was explicitly achieved as a functional requirement in many smart city platforms [3]. Partly decided by services management, *interoperability* is thought as the most important non-functional requirements of smart city platforms as summarized in [3]. On the other hand, the *provision of services* is regarded as one of the most challenging part of future cities by EU [17]. Here services are referred to public and commercial services that are provided in a city to its residents and the population in its hinterland. Such city services should be modular and reusable [17], and therefore might indicate a service-oriented implementation.

3.2 Big Data, Cloud/Edge/Fog Computing, and Data Management

During the last decade, technologies related to data management have emerged and gradually become the most commonly used technologies. Such technologies include *cloud computing, edge computing, fog computing, big data* techniques, and techniques which combine some of them [3, 18–20]. As a result of utilizing them in smart cities, it is unsurprising that *data management* (including external data access and data processing) are highlighted as important requirements in most existing smart city platforms as reviewed in [3].

3.3   IoT, City Sensing, and Context Awareness

IoT has been used more and more commonly in smart city construction. By embracing it as a direct result of utilizing it, *city sensing* has been mentioned by many platforms and were perceived as the mostly applied domain of smart city platforms. Not surprisingly, *context awareness*, which means smart cities applications/service can provide better results using context information such as user location and city traffic condition, was fulfilled in many platforms as one of the most important non- functional requirements [3].

4   Comparing the +CityxChange EAF and TOGAF

In the +CityxChange project, an EAF has been proposed which consists of three parts, namely, the stakeholder perspectives part, the data perspectives part, and the central part [13]. In the central part of the EAF, a layered approach is presented where lower layers support higher layers. Seven layers are defined (as shown in the right part of Fig. 2). Among them, three layers can be thought as approximately correspondent to the three layers that are defined in TOGAF (as shown in the left part of Fig. 2). A new context layer was defined to provide general information such as strategy and motivations which sits at the top. Three extra new layers (as marked by stars at layers in the right part of Fig. 2) are highlighted in the EAF. In these extra layers, three groups of artefacts, namely city services, data, and physical infrastructures that are often used in the high-level design of smart cities development (as described in Sect. 3) are captured. By doing so, new technologies could be better embraced and critical requirements in smart city scenarios satisfied. While in the traditional EAF TOGAF, they are not explicitly highlighted.

- *Business (Virtual Enterprise) Layer*: focuses on capturing business collaborations among two or many business actors.
- *Application and Data Processing Layer*: contains applications and relevant APIs for businesses to use. It is also described about how data is processed from the (+CityxChange) Data Space layer.
- *Technologies Layer*: enumerates network and communication technologies in order to capture data and transfer data to the Data Space Layer.
- *Context Layer*: is defined where components including but more than those in the Strategy & Motivation Stage of TOGAF are captured, from the city perspective.

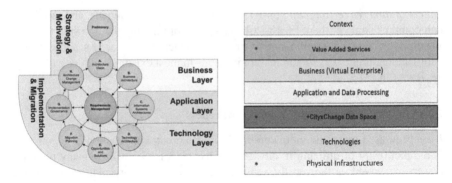

Fig. 2. The +CityxChange EAF [13] as an extension of TOGAF [5]

- *Value Added Services Layer*: is designed service is defined as specific value- added city services that are offered to users such as "zero emission" and "lower usage of power". For traditional enterprises, businesses are the primary goal. While in smart city scenario, services are often used to characterize the primary requirements for urban development. Smart cities are constructed to fulfill specific city services for citizens, government, or other stakeholders. By highlighting services in the top-level smart city architectures, stakeholders could start discussion based on diverse services that are expected to be provided by the smart city implementation.

- *+CityxChange Data Space Layer*: Data is used to describe the data that are available which might physically come from either cloud sides, local databases, or edge (IoT). Data is the main driver of the smart city implementation which decides whether and how diverse services could be satisfied. By highlighting this part, stakeholders could get better understanding of the data flow among different sub- systems and ensure the feasibility of target smart city systems. By using the business layer and this layer, concepts like data markets and data as a commodity can be supported. One thing needs to mention is, although this layer was named with the project name [11], the idea of this layer can be generalized to other smart city projects.

- *Physical Infrastructures Layer*: physical devices (data sources) was used to indicate real objects that are used to provide important user/city information in smart cities such as city cameras, mobile phones, and vehicles which are equipped with sensors. Infrastructure is the base of smart city. In addition, infrastructure construction is costly and takes time. By highlighting this part, not only IoT technologies could be better employed in smart city construction, but also the construction of infrastructure could be planned in an early stage of a project.

5   A Sample Scenario

In this section, we use Scenario [15] to demonstrate the utility of the +CityxChange EAF. The sample scenario was sketched for eMobility and eMaaS (eMobility-as-a-Service) which was inspired by the +CityxChange project. We use the EAF to perform enterprise architecture design in two stages to identify major architectural component concepts, and model implementations. The design results are presented in the Archi-Mate modelling language with the Archi modelling toolkit as shown in Fig. 3. ArchiMate is hosted by The Open Group and is fully aligned with TOGAF. Archi is an open source and cross-platform toolkit which supports modelling in the ArchiMate modelling language [21]. In Archi, different colors and icons can be used to visualize the differences for artefacts in different layers. For instance, artefacts in the business layer are usually painted as yellow rectangles, while artefacts in the technology layer are usually presented as green rectangles.

5.1 Case Description

The scenario is described from the perspective of a citizen who wants to use a car sharing service, and the car is possibly an Electric Vehicle (EV). The citizen uses a service looking for transportation options between two locations, and selects the best options based on personal preferences. He/she receives guidance on how to access the vehicle and then starts the journey accordingly. If the EV needs charge on the way, the driver looks for a charging station, stops the vehicle, charges, and makes a micro payment using a specific transaction infrastructure. When the citizen arrives at the destination, he/she makes another micro payment.

5.2 Identifying Concepts

In this stage, we identify all relevant concepts that are involved in different layers of the EAF. For instance, in the *Services Layer*, we identified two services: The Traffic Management Service and the EMaaS Service. In the *Business Layer*, several companies were identified such as a Car Renting Software Provider, a Payment Company, a Car Renting Company, and a Transportation Sector in charge of public transportation administration. In addition, a Car Renting Platform was also identified. In the *Application and Data Processing Layer*, existing APIs and libraries were enumerated. Similarly, existing or expected data bases, open data, social data were identified in the *Data Space Layer* and technologies which can be used were identified in the *Technologies Layer*. At last, physical infrastructures such as scooters, city bikes, city buses, airport shuttle busses, EVs, EV Charging stations involved were presented in the *Data Sources Layer*.

5.3 Modeling Implementations

In the second stage, we model the implementations by specifying relationship among all artefacts that we have identified in previous stage. The relationship includes col-laboration among businesses, data flow among data sources within one layer. In addition, relationships between different layers, especially close layers, are also pre-sented to describe how technology intensive components in lower layers can support to implement business-oriented goals in high layers. A tentative overall view drawn using ArchiMate tool is presented in Fig. 3.

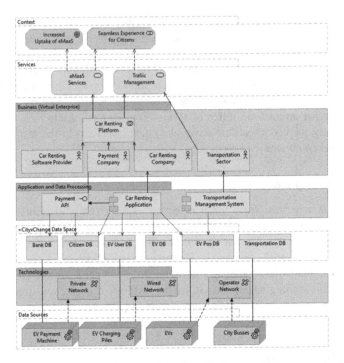

Fig. 3. An Enterprise Architecture view for eMaaS example based on the EAF

Through this scenario, we demonstrate that the EAF could help enterprise architects highlight important artefacts as well relationships among them. In addition, we believe that it might facilitate the communication among stakeholders in a visualized way.

6 Related Work

There are some relevant researches in which frameworks or models were proposed for smart city architectures.

Many researchers and practitioners utilized the name of service in designed architectures of smart cities. However, it is often referred to different meanings. For instance, in [22], a six layered architecture was proposed according to how data is processed, namely acquisition, transmission, storage, preprocessing, service, and application layers. In this architecture, service is defined as "modules of software that provide the data requested by the user in a transparent manner." In [18], the logic (IoT application) was encapsulated as external services formalized as microservices and exposed by the proposed smart city platform. Similarly in [23], a three tier architecture was proposed consisting of a service layer, a digital layer, and an urban infrastructure layer where service is referred to smart city services as "electric vehicle charging and parking services to tourism applications." While [24] tried to define the relationship between various SOAs from each domain to be integrated, [20] discussed how a service-oriented middleware can be used to develop and operate city services using Cloud of Things (CoT) and Fog Computing.

The importance and complexity of data management has been realized and illustrated in many smart city architectures. For instance, in the middle of the proposed architecture stack in [25], an industrial data space was positioned which connects lower-level communication and basic data service architectures with higher- level smart data service architectures. In [26], a data federation component was proposed to answer users' queries over federated data streams.

In [27], a scalable data storage component was designed to provide data Application Programming Interfaces (API) by managing metadata, historical data and real time data based on lower layer sensor/actuator nodes. Similarly, a data management component sits in the middle of overall platform which supports the application through technologies such as ZigBee, WiMax, Ethernet and 4G/5G to get data from diverse sources in [28]. While in [6], an architectural component which details all phases and components in the big and open linked data lifecycle was illustrated, including data archiving, data processing and analysis, data visualization, and data publication.

In [29], perception layer was proposed in the architecture which is the closest level to actual environment, known as the sensor layer to collect and convert physical information into digital signals. Similarly, the smart city infrastructure layer which includes wireless sensor and actuators networks, utilities HW and municipality HW was highlighted to provide information to smart city kernel platform in [30]. While in [31], a sensing & actuation layer is proposed to enable physical sensors to collect real-time observations and support the networking and communication layer.

To summarize, despite that the concepts of services, data management, and physical infrastructure have been mentioned and highlighted in many smart city architectures, especially during recent years while corresponding techniques are getting more popular and intensively used in urban platforms, few studies has emphasized all these three architectural components at the same time. In addition, to our knowledge, few studies have presented intensive theoretical base and practical adoption/validation of EAFs in real smart city project. On the one hand, some studies have detailed the theoretical base, and proposed enriched frameworks as well as more detailed components [18], but have not shown actual adoption/validation in practical project. On the other hand, most practical projects did not detail their theoretical base or concreted extension/adaption, which makes the EAF difficult to be generally applied elsewhere [32].

7   Conclusions

Modern techniques have brought significant influences on the architecture of smart city platforms as they are often tightly connected to crucial requirements/challenges of urban development. There is a need to highlight relevant concepts and clarify relationship among them during earlier architecture design stage. An EAF was proposed in the EU smart city project +CityxChange which addressed such issues to some extent. In this article, we present an initial evaluation on the EAF through a discussion of how it has enhanced TOGAF layered enterprise architecture and a sample scenario to demonstrate how to use it and what benefits can be expected by using it. The result shows that the EAF may help enterprise architects better capture important concepts as well as the relationship among them. Communication among stakeholders could be improved correspondingly.

There are some limitations of current research. As it is only an early phase of the project, the development and validation of the EA is not completed. Based on this basic structure, the framework could be further refined. We thereby point out possible future works. *Firstly*, smart city relevant architectures, frameworks, and models could be systematically examined so that more intensive knowledge regarding important architectural components can be obtained. *Secondly*, along with the further development of the EAF, continuous observation and evaluation will be necessary based on deeper and more rigorous forms of evaluation methods such as case studies and structural testing. Other possible future works might include enhancing the architecture tool to better differentiate artefacts in different layers as well as formalizing the approach and process of using the EAFs.

Acknowledgements. +CityxChange is a smart city project funded by the European Union's Horizon 2020 Research and Innovation programme under Grant Agreement No. 824260. The authors would like to thank the project partners from Trondheim Municipality, Limerick City Council and all the participants in the project team.

This research is financially supported by The European Research Consortium for Informatics and Mathematics. (ERCIM).

References

1. United Nations. World Urbanization Prospects (2018). https://population.un.org/wup/
2. Toh, K., Nagel, P., Oakden, R.: A business and ICT architecture for a logistics city. Int. J. Prod. Econ. **122**(1), 216–228 (2009)
3. Santana, E.F.Z., Chaves, A.P., Gerosa, M.A., et al.: Software platforms for smart cities: concepts, requirements, challenges, and a unified reference architecture. ACM Comput. Surv. (CSUR) **50**(6), 78 (2018)
4. Guo, H., Li, J., Gao, S.: Practical Insights of Applying Enterprise Architecture in Public Sectors: A Survey IEEE EDOC 2019, Paris, France (2019)
5. The Open Group. The Open Group Architecture Framework TOGAF Version 9.1 (2011)
6. Lnenicka, M., Komarkova, J.: Developing a government enterprise architecture framework to support the requirements of big and open linked data with the use of cloud computing. Int. J. Inf. Manag. **46**, 124–141 (2019)
7. Goudos, S.K., Loutas, N., Peristeras, V., et al.: Public administration domain ontology for a semantic web services egovernment framework. In: IEEE International Conference on Services Computing, pp. 270–277. IEEE (2007)
8. Peristeras, V., Tarabanis, K.: Governance enterprise architecture (GEA): domain models for e-governance. In: Proceedings of the 6th International Conference on Electronic Commerce, pp. 471–479. ACM (2004)
9. Hjort-Madsen, K., Pries-Heje, J.: Enterprise architecture in government: fad or future? In: 2009 42nd Hawaii International Conference on System Sciences, pp. 1–10. IEEE (2009)
10. Isomäki, H., Liimatainen, K.: Challenges of government enterprise architecture work – stakeholders' views. In: Wimmer, Maria A., Scholl, Hans J., Ferro, E. (eds.) EGOV 2008. LNCS, vol. 5184, pp. 364–374. Springer, Heidelberg (2008). https://doi.org/10.1007/978-3-540-85204-9_31

11. European Union. +CityxChange. https://cityxchange.eu/
12. Ahlers, D., Wienhofen, Leendert W.M., Petersen, S.A., Anvaari, M.: A smart city ecosystem enabling open innovation. In: Lüke, K.-H., Eichler, G., Erfurth, C., Fahrnberger, G. (eds.) I4CS 2019. CCIS, vol. 1041, pp. 109–122. Springer, Cham (2019). https://doi.org/10.1007/978-3-030-22482-0_9
13. Petersen, S.A., Pourzolfaghar, Z., Alloush, I., Ahlers, D., Krogstie, J., Helfert, M.: Value-added services, virtual enterprises and data spaces inspired enterprise architecture for smart cities. In: Camarinha-Matos, Luis M., Afsarmanesh, H., Antonelli, D. (eds.) PRO-VE 2019. IAICT, vol. 568, pp. 393–402. Springer, Cham (2019). https://doi.org/10.1007/978-3-030-28464-0_34
14. Pourzolfaghar, Z., Bastidas, V., Helfert, M.: Standardisation of enterprise architecture development for smart cities. J. Knowl. Econ. 1–22 (2019)
15. Von Alan, R.H., March, S.T., Park, J., et al.: Design science in information systems research. MIS Q. **28**(1), 75–105 (2004)
16. Peffers, K., Tuunanen, T., Rothenberger, M.A., et al.: A design science research methodology for information systems research. J. Manag. Inf. Syst. **24**(3), 45–77 (2007)
17. Union, E.: The Future Of Cities (2019)
18. Badii, C., Bellini, P., Difino, A., et al.: Sii-mobility: an IoT/IoE architecture to enhance smart city mobility and transportation services. Sensors **19**(1), 1 (2019)
19. Gaur, A., Scotney, B., Parr, G., et al.: Smart city architecture and its applications based on IoT. Procedia Comput. Sci. **52**, 1089–1094 (2015)
20. Mohamed, N., Al-Jaroodi, J., Jawhar, I., et al.: Smartcityware: a service-oriented middleware for cloud and fog enabled smart city services. IEEE Access **5**, 17576–17588 (2017)
21. Beauvoir, P.: Archi – Open Source ArchiMate Modelling (2019)
22. Massana i Raurich, J., Pous i Sabadí, C., Burgas Nadal, L., et al.: Identifying services for short-term load forecasting using data driven models in a smart city platform. Sustain. Cities Soc. **28**, 108–117 (2017)
23. Sivrikaya, F., Ben-Sassi, N., Dang, X.-T., et al.: Internet of smart city objects: a distributed framework for service discovery and composition. IEEE Access **7**, 14434–14454 (2019)
24. Clement, S., McKee, D.W., Xu, J.: Service-oriented reference architecture for smart cities. In: 2017 IEEE Symposium on Service-Oriented System Engineering (SOSE), pp. 81–85. IEEE (2017)
25. Otto, B., Lohmann, S., Steinbuß, S., et al.: IDS Reference Architecture Model, Industrial Data Space, Version 2.0. International Data Spaces Association & Fraunhofer (2018)
26. Puiu, D., Barnaghi, P., Tonjes, R., et al.: CityPulse: large scale data analytics framework for smart cities. IEEE Access **4**, 1086–1108 (2016)
27. Vilajosana, I., Llosa, J., Martinez, B., et al.: Bootstrapping smart cities through a self-sustainable model based on big data flows. IEEE Commun. Mag. **51**(6), 128–134 (2013)
28. Rani, S., Chauhdary, S.H.: A novel framework and enhanced QoS big data protocol for smart city applications. Sensors **18**(11), 16 (2018)
29. Park, J.-H., Salim, M.M., Jo, J.H., et al.: CIoT-net: a scalable cognitive IoT based smart city network architecture. Hum.-Centric Comput. Inf. Sci. **9**(1), 29 (2019)
30. Sanchez, L., Elicegui, I., Cuesta, J., et al.: Integration of utilities infrastructures in a future internet enabled smart city framework. Sensors **13**(11), 14438–14465 (2013)
31. Simmhan, Y., Ravindra, P., Chaturvedi, S., et al.: Towards a data-driven IoT software architecture for smart city utilities. Soft. Pract. Exp. **48**(7), 1390–1416 (2018)
32. Janssen, M., Hjort-Madsen, K.: Analyzing enterprise architecture in national governments: the cases of denmark and the Netherlands. In: 2007 40th Annual Hawaii International Conference on System Sciences (HICSS'07), p. 218a. IEEE (2007)

Enterprise Systems

Process Chunks Selection in the Context of Loose Inter-Organizations Cooperation in Cloud Computing

Yosra Lassoued[1,2(✉)], Selmin Nurcan[1], and Faiez Gargouri[2]

[1] Université Paris1 Panthéon-Sorbonne, CRI Laboratory, Paris, France
{Yosra.Lassoued,nurcan}@univ-paris1.fr
[2] ISIMS, MIRACL Laboratory, University of Sfax, Sfax, Tunisia
faiez.gargouri@isims.usf.tn

Abstract. Cloud Computing has been attracting the interest of the Information and Communication Technology Community. It has emerged as a compelling paradigm that assures reliable on-demand computing services over Internet. However, the potential that this new model offers for organizations is still not fully explored. In fact, this technology has not been explored yet to manage Loose Inter-Organizations Cooperation (LIOC). Loose Inter-Organizations Cooperation corresponds to occasional cooperation without structural constraints in which the partners involved and their numbers are not predefined. In order to handle LIOC in Cloud Computing we have proposed the notion of Cloud Workflow Services (CWS). CWS is an Inter-Organizations business process having loosely coupled fragments of process that we called Process Chunks (PCs) whose description and execution are accessible through the Cloud. In our previous work, we have used the Model-Driven Engineering approach to deal with modeling and specifying Contextualized Flexible Cloud Workflow Services. In this work, we focus on the selection of PCs. We propose an ontology based approach permitting a PC_Consumer to select the appropriate PC satisfying its requirements. This selection is done according to two different strategies "MIC-selection" and "MAC-selection". In MIC-Selection, every PC will be selected using the assembling strategy, that's mean we have the possibility to assemble multiple PCs. In MAC-Selection, for each PC we will select only the best PC with the highest score of similarity. This work has been validated through the "Drug Development process" with the help of experts from the pharmaceutical field.

Keywords: Cloud Computing · Context · Workflow service · Versioning · Process Chunks · Selection · Description · Ontology

1 Introduction

The blooming of Cloud Computing is rapidly changing the landscape of information technology in both academic and industry communities. It is defined by the National Institute of Standards and Technology (NIST) as a model for enabling convenient, on-demand network access to a shared pool of configurable computing resources (e.g., networks, servers, storage, applications, and services) that can be rapidly provisioned

© Springer Nature Switzerland AG 2020
M. Themistocleous and M. Papadaki (Eds.): EMCIS 2019, LNBIP 381, pp. 261–278, 2020.
https://doi.org/10.1007/978-3-030-44322-1_20

and released with minimal management effort or service provider interaction [1]. The adoption of Cloud Computing is growing rapidly, hence more and more organizations are using Cloud services for their applications, software or infrastructure.

Although the increasing number of researches dedicated to propose methods, processes and tools focused on Cloud-related technology, the innovative opportunities offered by this new paradigm are not fully explored. Indeed, this new paradigm has not been explored yet in the context of Loose Inter-Organizations Cooperation (LIOC) [2]. LIOC corresponds to occasional cooperation without structural constraints in which the partners involved and their numbers are not predefined. Using Cloud Computing in Loose Inter-Organizations Cooperation presents a shift away that guarantees: (i) the heterogeneity and the distribution of the involved organizations: each organization publishes its services in any Cloud Computing platform; (ii) the autonomy of each organization insofar as it can only publish its public activities without going into details; (iii) the evolution of the composition of Cloud services through time; (iv) the scalability of cooperation (no a priori limitation to the number of potential partners); (v) better Quality of Service such as scalability, reliability, availability and performance than intra-organizational solutions; (vi) enabling inter-organizations services sharing from different service providers; (vii) reducing developing costs for business services (viii) combining Cloud services from various organizations.

In order to describe LIOC in Cloud Computing, we have defined a new concept, which is the Cloud Workflow Service (CWS). The key element of a CWS is its Process Chunks. A Process Chunk (PC) is a fragment of process of an organization that can be described, published, discovered and selected through the Cloud. It is structured around three views. The local view of a PC represents its private (i.e., internal) parts, while the global view of a PC represents its public (i.e. external) activities along with their corresponding interaction. The outsourced view has private and public parts that are outsourced to the Cloud. To deal with CWS modeling in a conceptual framework we have used the Model-Driven Engineering approach. The basic principle of MDE is the separation of business concerns from their technical achievement. Following this practice, we have proposed in our previous work a CWS description model [3]. A CWS is a loosely coupled inter-organizations business process having dynamically (on the fly) discovered PCs of the involved organizations. A CWS is defined on the consumer side of PCs (PC-Consumer). Hence a PC-Consumer has to specify a CWS having missing PCs to be integrated. On the providers' side (PC-provider), they have to configure their respective PCs to be published. PC-provider must provide a PC that can be used by multiple organizations at the same time, independent of in-house processes or legacy applications. We have therefore used a reengineering approach for in-house processes using microservices technology [4]. This reengineering approach is used to create microservices from in-house applications. A microservice represents the smallest functional unit not decomposable that can be automatically executed. Microservices could be implemented in different technologies or languages. Microservices could be deployed locally, in Docker or in the Cloud. Hence each PC-Provider has a registry of microservices to configure its PCs. So behind each selected PC resides a dynamic orchestration of microservices to be executed (Fig. 1).

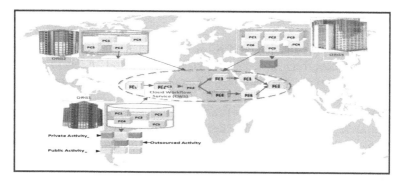

Fig. 1. Loose Inter-Organization Cooperation in Cloud Computing environment

A CWS description model has a set of functional and non-functional requirements relative to the definition of a CWS. The functional requirements are related to the expression of three main complementary perspectives of a CWS, usually described by three different but dependent models, well known in process modeling literature: organizational, informational and behavioral models [5, 6]. The behavioral model defines the PCs of a CWS and their interaction. The organizational model structures the involved partners and the used resources in the realization of these PCs. The informational model defines the structure of documents and data that are produced, required or exchanged. A CWS has also a set of non-functional requirements. First of all, potential users of Cloud workflow solutions might be hesitant because of the vulnerabilities related to the Cloud Computing. Hence, security requirements should be taken into account such as privacy, access control, non-repudiation and integrity. In addition to that, a CWS will be executed alternatively in a Cloud environment as well as in-house in the cooperating organizations. So, when specifying a CWS, one should also consider its deployment parameters. Besides to the requirements mentioned above, in order to face the dynamic, open and competitive environment, LIOC requires flexible CWS as the involved organizations are distributed, autonomous and heterogeneous. The flexibility requirement of a CWS is consequent to the changes in the involved organizations, and their PCs (as components of a CWS) and their interaction schema e. g any modification (update, add, delete) in organizations' PCs. The last requirement calls for the definition of a CWS context and capacity and subsequently the definition of the involved (in its configuration) PCs contexts and capacities. A PC context defines the conditions of use of a PC while a PC capacity defines the intention of use of a PC. The problem addressed in this paper is how we could select PCs in order to run a CWS? The remainder of this paper is organized as follows. Section 2 presents related works relevant to our research problem. Section 3 presents our Drug Development case study in order to better understand the Loose Inter-Organizations Cooperation application. Section 4 presents our proposed PC selection approach. Section 5 concludes the paper and gives our research perspectives.

2 Background and Related Work

Through our deep investigation of IOC works through our Systematic Literature Review [7], we have been able to distinguish several eras of Inter-Organizations Cooperation. The first era was marked by Centralized Tight Cooperation. This type of cooperation answers the following question: *How a set of well identified organizations, each organization has its own intra-organizational process, will cooperate to realize a common project?* This project is specified through a well-defined inter-organizations process. Among the most known approaches proposed for Tight Centralized Cooperation are EDI and ESB [8, 9]. This type of cooperation is well suited for long-term and well-structured cooperation projects involving well-known organizations. Hence, Tight Centralized Cooperation doesn't cover dynamicity or flexibility of cooperation. The second era of cooperation is the one who has experienced an explosion in terms of proposed approaches to ensure a Tight Decentralized Cooperation that responds mainly to the following question: *How to dynamically discover organizations as part of a well-structured Inter-Organizations process?* Tight Decentralized Cooperation remedies the inflexible nature of Tight Centralized Cooperation. Indeed, in this type of cooperation the organizations are not known in advance. One of the most known approaches in Tight Decentralized Cooperation is the eSourcing [10, 11]. Several variants of this Framework have been proposed [12, 13]. eSourcing in Tight Decentralized Cooperation consists in four main tasks, the definition of the consumer process, to project the consumer process through process views [14] hence only public activities are visible, to match the consumer process with a provider process, to negotiate and create a contract. Following the eSourcing framework [15], the consumer subprocess will be matched with a provider subprocess. In this type of cooperation, an organization has the sufficient knowledge to model the exact structure of the subprocess. The negotiation and contracting can result on a modification of the subprocess structure. The main limits of Tight Decentralized Cooperation can be summed up in the following points:

- In Tight Decentralized Cooperation the matching between a consumer subprocess and the provider subprocess does not handle the problem of composition of sub processes from different providers. Here we suppose that we could find perfectly the exact structure of the subprocess from the provider's side.
- Once a subprocess has been selected we cannot modify its structure or replace it dynamically. In fact, in the execution step, all the selected subprocesses are tightly coupled with other private activities from in-house processes.
- In Tight Decentralized Cooperation a well defined consumer subprocess will be matched with a provider subprocess. In reality the following problems emerge:
  - If the consumer has not the sufficient knowledge of the exact structure of the subprocess to be integrated.
  - If the consumer founds a provider that just satisfies a part of the process.
  - How an organization could be sure that the integrated subprocess is the best compared to other providers' process?
  - How to compose multiple subprocesses from different providers each one satisfies a part of the process?

- The specification of the subprocesses in the provider's side as well as in the consumer's side is mainly based on the notion of process views [14] which tries to remedy the fact that we are dealing with processes tightly coupled with other elements of in-house processes or legacy applications. A process view defines level of visibilities of the activities. This notion has not resolved the problem of tightly coupled activities but it has assured the security of some activities not being exposed.
- Tight Decentralized Cooperation has data-flow and control flow problems. In fact the subprocess to be integrated is tightly coupled with other elements of in-house applications and/or legacy systems. This poses a problem at the execution level of non termination of processes or deadlocks.
- Tight Decentralized Cooperation is not scalable in terms of composing multiple subprocesses from different Organizations during execution.
- Tight Decentralized Cooperation is not flexible in terms of replacing a subprocess by another during execution.

All these limitations have made us think that a third era must define Loose Inter-Organizations Cooperation (LIOC) responding to the following questions:

- *Question 1: From a consumer side: How an organization could define an Inter-Organizations process when it doesn't know exactly the structure of the processes to be integrated or their number? How to select the best fragment of process satisfying its requirements? How to compose different fragments of processes from different providers?*
- *Question 2: From a provider side: How to propose a loosely coupled fragment of process that has not a dependency with other in-house processes or legacy applications? How to assure that this fragment of process could be automatically executed once selected, no configuration is needed? How to assure that this fragment of process could be easily composed with other providers fragments?*

To answer those questions, we have proposed the notion of a CWS. A CWS is an Inter-Organizations business process having loosely coupled fragments of process that we called Process Chunks (PCs) that could be selected and composed through the Cloud. In this paper, we are dealing with the dynamic selection of PCs.

3 Case Study: Drug Development Process

Throughout this paper we will use the Drug Development Process (DDP) to illustrate and to validate our contributions. This case study has been used in our previous work [3]. We have conducted several interviews with pharmacologists from the research laboratory of the "Faculty of Pharmacy of Monastir" in Tunisia.

The process starts when pharmacology's laboratory detects the need of treatment for a specific disease or the possibility of improvement of the current ones. First, the Laboratory will search for new ideas to create the new molecule. About 10000 molecules will be sent to Laboratories of biochemistry where it will undergo 'chemical tests'. The selected molecules will undergo 'screening tests'. Based on this test, only 20 molecules will be selected. Therefore, the laboratory will seek the help of industries to create samples for further researches. These samples will undergo four types of tests to validate the effects of this drug on animals such as Toxicology Test in a Toxicology Laboratory, Teratology Test in Embryology Laboratory, Mutagenicity Test in Histology Laboratory and Pharmacology Test in Pharmacology Laboratory. Following these tests, several hospitals will be asked for help to perform the rest of the process on human beings. Finally, the tests reports will be sent to bio statistical centers for statistical studies. It is important to note that a CWS has not a definite and final way to be modeled. That's mean an organization can have different versions for a CWS. From a PC-Consumer side, an organization model PCs to be discovered as unknown elements. It can be content to only specify their capacities and contexts. Figure 2 represents an extract of the first version of the Drug Development Process. To improve the performance of this process, in the second version represented in Fig. 3 some activities will be outsourced to the Cloud mainly those whose execution is long or consume or produce a large size of data. The outsourced activities are represented by green rectangles. In this version, the activities which execution is estimated to be too long, "Chemical tests" and "Create samples", will be executed by different organizations offering the same activity. Hence we add two new outsourced activities "Select Biochemistry Laboratories" and "Select Medical Industries". Process Chunks are modeled with red rectangles. A PC having an unknown structure is represented with a red circle. Elementary Activities of each PC are either private represented by blue rectangles or public represented by yellow rectangles or outsourced represented by green rectangle.

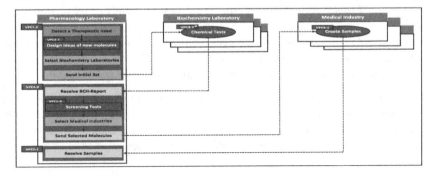

Fig. 2. First version of the Drug Development Process (Color figure online)

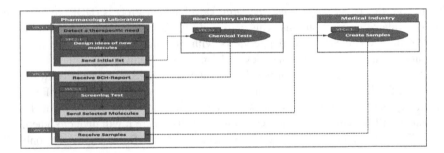

Fig. 3. Second version of the Drug Development Process (Color figure online)

For the first version VCWS1-1 it has seven Process Chunks VPC1-1, VPC2-1, VPC3-1, VPC4-1, VPC5-1, VPC6-1 and VPC7-1. "VPC3-1: Chemical Tests" and "VPC6-1: Create Samples" are two Process Chunks to be discovered and selected.

For the second version VCWS1-2 it has ten Process Chunks VPC1-2, VPC2-1, VPC3-2, VPC4-2, VPC5-2, VPC6-1 and VPC7-1. "VPC3-2: Chemical Tests" correspond to a new version to be discovered. In order to describe a PC we have developed a graphic editor called PC-Editor. Our PC-Editor offers two types of PC definition: PC-offer and/or PC-request. This editor has been implemented using ADOxx tool [16]. The pharmacology laboratory doesn't know the exact structure of the chemical test Process Chunk to be discovered; only the capacities and contexts are specified. Figure 4 present the first version of the chemical tests Process Chunk (VPC3-1) modeled from a

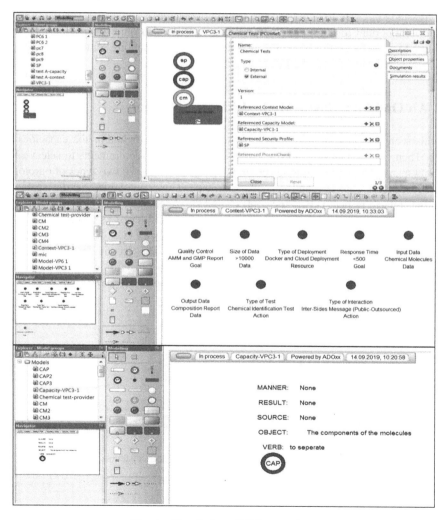

Fig. 4. Chemical test PC first version

consumer side perspective. The context model is based on nine context attributes "Quality Control", "Size of Data", "Type of Deployment", "Response Time", "Input Data", "Output Data", "Type of Test", "Type of Interaction" and "Security Control" having the respective values for VPC3-1 "AMM and GMP report", ">10000", "Docker and Cloud Deployment", "<500", "Chemical Molecules", "Composition Report", "Chemical identification test", "Inter-Sides Message (public-outsourced)" and "None". In the second version of the chemical tests Process Chunk (VPC3-2), the values of these parameters are respectively "AMM and GMP report", ">100000", "Cloud Deployment", "<300", "Chemical Molecules", "Toxicology analysis report", "Toxicology analysis", "Inter-Sides Message (Private-outsourced)" and "Authentification". The capacity model of VPC3-1 is:

To separate $_{verb}$ (the components of the molecules) $_{object}$

The capacity model of VPC3-2 is:

To study $_{verb}$ (the toxicology aspect of the molecules) $_{object}$

It is important to note that our PC Editor handles also other interesting elements relative to a CWS description. In this paper, we are just presenting some parts related to the behavioral dimension of a PC.

4   An Ontology-Based Method for PC Selection

In this section, we show first how we compare the contexts and/or the capacities of PCs. Then, we explain how a PC-Consumer expresses its requirements to select a PC among many. To facilitate this selection, we propose the use of two types of ontology, namely context ontology and capacity ontology. These ontologies handle semantic conflicts related respectively to the contexts and the capacities of PCs. The specification of contexts and capacities is done through two abstraction levels as depicted in Fig. 5. The first level represents the invariant structure shared by all PCs. This level is defined by the context ontology and the capacity ontology. The second level defines the specification of contexts and capacities. Hence, each specification of context (respectively capacity) is generated as an instance and described with OWL (Ontology Web Language) [17].

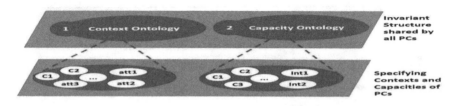

Fig. 5. Specification of PCs contexts and capacities

4.1   Context Ontology

The context of a PC is defined by its context attributes and their respective values. Figure 6 presents the Context Ontology (CO) for specifying contexts. This ontology is used to describe the attributes and values of a given context. We distinguish two types of links: between concepts or between concepts and attributes. Links between concepts are semantic links, namely equivalence, subsumption and part_of. The links between context attributes and concepts express the meaning of context attributes as well as the meaning of their values. Figure 7 represents an extract of context ontology for the PC "chemical tests" of the DDP.

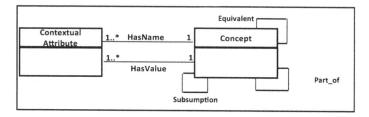

Fig. 6. UML class diagram that represents the context ontology

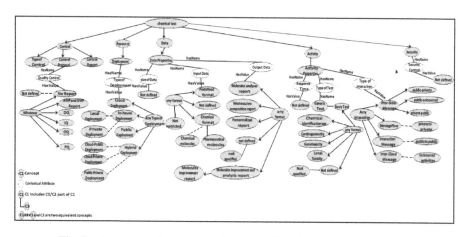

Fig. 7. An extract of context ontology regarding the PC "Chemical tests"

4.2   Capacity Ontology

The capacity of a PC is defined by an intention, with a verb, a domain and parameters, namely manner, target (object or result) and source. Figure 8 presents the capacity ontology. Figure 9 represents an extract of capacity ontology for the PC "chemical tests".

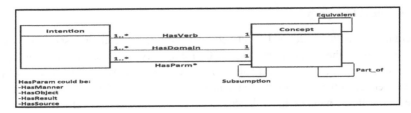

Fig. 8. UML class diagram that represents the capacity ontology

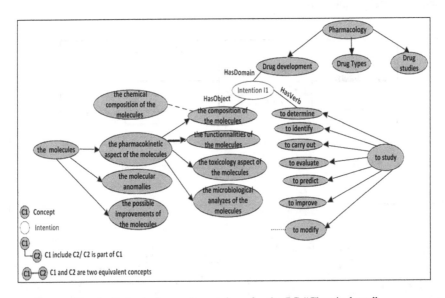

Fig. 9. Extract of capacity ontology for the PC "Chemical test"

4.3 Principles of Contexts/Capacities Matching

We propose a contexts/capacities matching method for PCs based on two main principles: (i) the method considers two matching types (context matching and capacity matching); (ii) it provides three matching modes, namely Exact mode ((PC consumer context (capacity) = PC provider context (capacity); Plugin mode ((PC consumer context (capacity) < PC provider context (capacity)) and the Subsume mode ((PC consumer context (capacity) > PC provider context (capacity)).

In the following we present some of PC comparison algorithms regarding contexts (it's the same for capacity).

The function "Englobe" returns a Boolean, true if E1 encompasses E2, otherwise false. We verify that E1 is a concept that encompasses the concept E2 in the ontology represented by a tree "A".

For that reason, we assume the existence of the following high-level functions:

- Father (E): returns the father of an element E in the tree A.
- Root (A): Returns the root of the tree A.

4.4   Selection of PCs

The consumer of a PC expresses its context using the concepts of context ontology and its capacity using the concepts of capacity ontology. Matching contexts (respectively capacities) means selecting the most appropriate PC among others.

Selecting a PC is essentially based on the calculation of the degree of similarity between the preferences specified in the request of the PC-consumer and the specified elements in the contexts/capacities of PCs. The main selection algorithm accepts two data parameters: the request sent by the PC-Consumer and the repository of PCs. The selected PCs are those whose degrees of similarity are higher than a predetermined threshold. The algorithm provides as an output all PCs that match the request, ranked in descending order (the PC having a low degree of similarity is presented at the bottom of list and vice versa) according to their degree of similarity. If the threshold is 0.5, the algorithm hides all PCs whose degree of similarity is less than 50% with respect to the customer request. The threshold can be determined by experimentation. It is also possible to consider it as a parameter of the matching algorithm. The main function of the generic algorithm "PC-Match" calculates the degree of similarity between a query or a request and the PC attributes. The degree of similarity is calculated using the following formulas:

$$SimCON\ (PC,\ Request) = \frac{sim(CON, ReqCON)^* wcon}{wcon + wcap}$$

$$SimCAP\ (PC,\ Request) = \frac{sim(CAP, ReqCAP)^* wcap}{wcon + wcap}$$

$$Sim(PC,\ Request) = (SimCAP + SimCON)/2$$

The degree of similarity is composed of similarity degree of CONTEXT and CAPACITY. We defined weights, represented by CON and CAP to balance these degrees of similarity in order to have the possibility to give more importance to the context in the comparison or vice versa. The value "0" for a weight indicates that the corresponding element is not taken into account.

4.4.1   MAC-Selection

In our work, we provide PC-Consumer two strategies of PC selection the first strategy is MAC-Selection. In this type of selection, PC-Consumer will select the PC with the highest score of similarity. Tables 1 and 2 resume the obtained results respectively of "VPC3-1: chemical tests" and "VPC3-2: chemical tests" selection with MAC-Selection strategy. It is important to note that we have created a registry of PCs from ten providers. Each provider is a biochemistry laboratory offering chemical test PCs. The obtained results have been validated by experts from the laboratory of pharmacology.

Table 1. VPC3-1: chemical tests selection according to MAC-Selection strategy

	Score
PC1	0,55
PC2	0,45
PC3	0,45
PC4	0,1
PC5	0,1
PC6	0,05
PC7	0,05
PC8	0,05
Execution time	0,8 s

Table 2. VPC3-2: chemical tests selection according to MAC-Selection strategy

	Score
PC8	0,6
PC7	0,6
PC6	0,6
PC5	0,25
PC4	0,25
PC3	0,1
PC1	0,1
PC2	0,05
Execution time	0,8 s

4.4.2 MIC-Selection

The second strategy of selection is MIC-Selection. In this type of selection every PC will be selected using the assembling strategy, that's mean we have the possibility to assemble multiple PCs to ameliorate the score of similarity. Before presenting our assembling strategy, we will discuss in which cases we can apply this strategy:

PC1 PC2	PC1 and PC2 have different contexts and capacities. In this case we can apply the assembling strategy.
PC1 PC2	PC1 and PC2 have the same capacity. PC1 and PC2 have overlapping contexts i.e. they have some different values of contexts. The PC-Consumer has not the right to modify the structure of a provider PC (to add, modify or delete an activity). In this case the assembling strategy is not applicable. PC-Consumer must choose between the two PCs according to their score of similarity.
PC1 PC2	PC2 includes PC1: the capacity of PC2 includes the capacity of PC1. The assembling strategy is not applicable, PC-Consumer must choose between the two PCs according to their score of similarity.

Hence before assembling PCs a comparison must be made between the capacities and contexts of the PCs candidate by the algorithms presented above (Sect. 3). Only different PCs would be maintained. After this step, we will calculate the score of similarity for each PC. At the end of this step, only different PCs must be maintained (if we have two PCs having the same capacity or one of them includes other's capacity, only the PC with the highest score of similarity is maintained). Then we generate binary assemblies. We determine the execution order of the two PCs by comparing the

Input and Output Data of the different activities (only the initial and final activities are examinated for each PC as we can't modify the structure of the PCs). If we found an activity that consumes the output data of another we will create a new message between the two. Elsewhere we create a new activity to preserve the output data being produced. For each pair of PCs we will calculate its new score of similarity. If none of the binary combinations has exceeded a threshold determined by the PC-Consumer, we will continue with tertiary assemblies and so on. In fact, one of the advantages of LIOC in CC using loosely coupled automatically executable PCs is the scalability of cooperation. Hence no limitation of the number of PCs to be assembled. However a PC-consumer could introduce score and time thresholds. Finally, a list of assembled PCs will be returned to PC-Consumer with their respective score (Fig. 10).

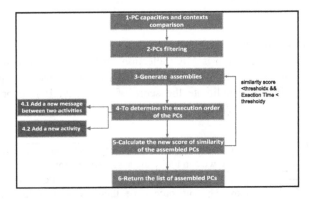

Fig. 10. PC-assembling strategy

Tables 3 and 4 resume the results obtained respectively of "VPC3-1: chemical tests" and "VPC3-2: chemical tests" selection with MIC-Selection strategy.

Table 3. VPC3-1: chemical tests selection according to MIC-Selection strategy

PC assemblies	Score
PC1-PC9-PC0	0,95
PC1-PC9-PC11	0,95
PC1-PC9	0,82
PC1-PC10	0,82
PC1-PC11	0,82
PC1-PC12	0,7
PC1-PC13	0,7
PC1-PC14	0,7
PC1-PC12-PC13	0,7
Execution time	1,65

Table 4. VPC3-2: chemical tests selection according to MIC-Selection strategy

PC assemblies	Score
PC8-PC9-PC10	0,9
PC8-PC9-PC11	0,9
PC8-PC9	0,77
PC8-PC9-PC12	0,77
PC8-PC9-PC13	0,77
PC8-PC9-PC14	0,77
PC8-PC10	0,72
PC8-PC11	0,72
PC8-PC12	0,65
PC8-PC13	0,65
Execution time	1,69 ms

As we can see using MIC-Selection has ameliorated significatively the score of similarity but the execution time has also increased. Figures 11 and 12 resume the comparison between using MIC-Selection and MAC-Selection for PC-selection in the DDP. We can conclude that MIC-selection is more effective when we have a limited number of PCs to discover. In fact the execution time of PC selection in MIC-selection is high compared to MAC-Selection. Hence, if a CWS has not a significant number of PCs to discover, we can assemble multiple PCs to ameliorate the score of similarity for each discovered PC. MAC-Selection is more effective when we have a big number of PCs to select. In this case it's better to select the PC having the highest score of similarity without proceeding to the PC assembling (Fig. 13).

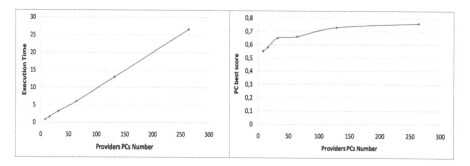

Fig. 11. PC selection for DDP using MAC-Selection

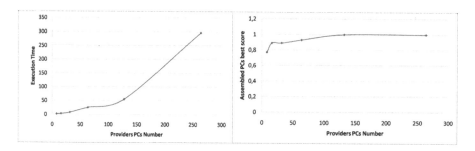

Fig. 12. PC selection for DDP using MIC-Selection

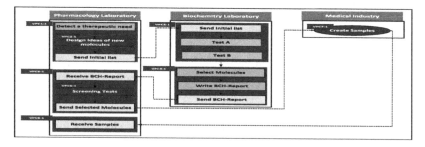

Fig. 13. First version of the DDP after "VPC3-1: chemical tests" using MIC-selection strategy

5 Conclusion

In this paper, we have tackled the process chunk (fragment) selection issue in the context of Loose Inter-Organizations Cooperation in Cloud Computing for the configuration of a business process, from the consumer perspective, by exporting some missing capacities to the cloud. LIOC in Cloud Computing corresponds to occasional cooperation without structural constraints in which the partners involved and their numbers are not predefined. In fact, our goal is to propose an approach that allows Decentralized, distributed, open and scalable cooperation. Cloud Computing ensure the deployment of fragment of processes in multiple providers, no limitation of the number of organizations, or technologies used in each fragment. In order to ensure the interoperability between the different process fragments, we have proposed an approach to reengineer in-house processes tightly coupled to produce decoupled functional units using the microservices technology. Hence a PC is a configuration of microservices deployed in Cloud Computing to be discovered, selected and composed. LIOC in Cloud Computing offers to organizations the possibility to select PCs specified only by their capabilities and contexts. In order to specify LIOC we have proposed in our previous work the notion of CWS which is a loosely coupled Inter-Organizational process containing fragments of processes deployed in the Cloud called Process Chunks. In this paper, we have approached the dynamic selection of these Process Chunks. This selection is made through an ontology based approach that permits to calculate the score of similarity between the context and capacity of a PC-Consumer request with the list of PC-Providers contexts and capacities. The proposed approach permits also to handle as a first class citizen the capacity and the context of a PC. A PC-Consumer can also wish to give more importance to some elements of the context and/or the capacity. The PC-Consumer has the possibility to selection the best PC with the highest score through the MAC-strategy or to assemble several PCs through the MIC-selection. A comparison between these two strategies was made that favored MAC-strategy in case the number of PCs in the CWS is important. This selection strategy favors the total execution time of the CWS. MIC-selection is more efficient in terms of the qualities of returned PCs. This strategy is recommended in case we have a limited number of PCs to discover. So, we can assemble several PCs from different PC-providers in order to improve the score of similarity. Finally, to implement the different contributions, we have developed a PC-Editor (to define a PC) and PC-Matchmaker (to support the selection of PCs). These contributions have been applied to the Drug Development Process which is known as a complex Inter-Organization process which execution requires the participation of different organizations. The data processed and exchanged are also known to be large. Through our work with domain experts from the pharmacology of Monastir, we have modeled the CWS structure as well as its different PCs. We believe that our work constitute the first attempt to create an open distributed free of structural constraints open space of cooperation between unlimited number of organizations. This cooperation cuts with structural dependency with hidden in-house applications, as the fragments of processes being discovered and selected are decoupled and automatically executable. This cooperation is scalable so the PCs can be dynamically assembled at the time of the execution. As future direction, we are working on reference architecture for Loose IO in Cloud Computing.

References

1. NIST Cloud Computing Reference Architecture. NIST, September 2011. http://www.nist. gov/customcf/getpdf.cfm?pubid=909505
2. Bouzguenda, L.: How to design a loose inter-organizational workflow? An illustrative case study. In: Andersen, K.V., Debenham, J., Wagner, R. (eds.) DEXA 2005. LNCS, vol. 3588, pp. 1–13. Springer, Heidelberg (2005). https://doi.org/10.1007/11546924_1
3. Lassoued, Y., Nurcan, S.: Modeling contextualized flexible cloud workflow services: an MDE based approach. In: 11th International Conference on Research Challenges in Information Science RCIS, pp. 44–55 (2017)
4. Hassan, S., Ali, N., Bahsoon, R.: Microservice ambients: an architectural meta-modelling approach for microservice granularity. In: IEEE International Conference on Software Architecture (ICSA), pp. 1–10 (2017)
5. Van der Aalst, W.M.P., Weske, M.H., Wirtz, G.: Advanced topics in workflow management: issues, requirements and solutions. Int. J. Integr. Des. Process Sci. **7**(3), 47–77 (2003)
6. Daoudi, F., Nurcan, S.: A benchmarking framework for methods to design flexible business processes. Softw. Process Improv. Pract. **12**(1), 51–63 (2007). Journal on Business Process Management, Development and Support
7. Lassoued, Y., Nurcan, S.: Inter-Organizational Cooperation: A Systematic Review. A paper under revision
8. Krathu, W., Engel, R., Pichler, C., Zapletal, M., Werthner, H.: Identifying inter-organizational key performance indicators from EDIFACT messages. In: 15th IEEE International Conference on Business Informatics (CBI 2013), Vienna, Austria, pp. 15–18, July 2013
9. Eckartz, S.M., Katsma, C., Wieringa, R.: Using value models to improve the cost/benefit analysis of inter-organizational system implementations. In: Camarinha-Matos, L.M., Xu, L., Afsarmanesh, H. (eds.) PRO-VE 2012. IAICT, vol. 380, pp. 529–538. Springer, Heidelberg (2012). https://doi.org/10.1007/978-3-642-32775-9_53
10. Norta, A., Grefen, P.: Discovering patterns for inter-enterpriseal business collaboration. Int. J. Coop. Inf. Syst. (IJCIS) **16**, 507–544 (2007)
11. Norta, A.: eSourcing: electronic Sourcing for business to business (2006). http://www.cs. helsinki.fi/u/anorta/research/eSourcing/
12. Norta, A.: Establishing distributed governance infrastructures for enacting cross-organization collaborations. In: Norta, A., Gaaloul, W., Gangadharan, G.R., Dam, H.K. (eds.) ICSOC 2015. LNCS, vol. 9586, pp. 24–35. Springer, Heidelberg (2016). https://doi.org/10.1007/ 978-3-662-50539-7_3
13. Norta, A.: Designing a smart-contract application layer for transacting decentralized autonomous organizations. In: Singh, M., Gupta, P.K., Tyagi, V., Sharma, A., Ören, T., Grosky, W. (eds.) ICACDS 2016. CCIS, vol. 721, pp. 595–604. Springer, Singapore (2017). https://doi.org/10.1007/978-981-10-5427-3_61

14. Eshuis, R., Norta, A., Roulaux, R.: Evolving process views. Inf. Softw. Technol. **80**, 20–35 (2016)
15. Norta, A., Grefen, P., Narendra, N.C.: A reference architecture for managing dynamic inter-organizational business processes. Data Knowl. Eng. **91**, 52–89 (2014)
16. https://www.adoxx.org/live/adoxx-development-tools
17. Bechhofer, S., et al.: OWL Web Ontology Language Reference (2004). http://www.w3.org/TR/owl-ref/

Agile Software Engineering Practices in ERP Implementation

Adnan Kraljić$^{(\boxtimes)}$ and Tarik Kraljić

Ghent University, Ghent, Belgium
{adnan.kraljic, tarik.kraljic}@ugent.be

Abstract. The Enterprise Resource Planning (ERP) implementation is a complex and active process, one that involves a mixture of technological and organizational interactions. Often it is the largest IT project that an organization has ever launched and requires a mutual fit of system and organization. Concept of an ERP implementation supporting business processes across different departments in organization is not a generic, rigid and uniform process - it is a vivid one and depends on number of different factors. As a result, the issues addressing the ERP implementation process have been one of the major concerns in industry. Therefore, ERP implementation process receives profound attention from practitioners and scholars in academic or industry papers. However, research on ERP systems so far has been mainly focused on diffusion, use and impact issues. Less attention has been given to the methods/methodologies used during the configuration and the implementation of ERP systems; even though they are commonly used in practice, they still remain largely undocumented in Information Systems research domain. This paper aims to provide insight from practice (SAP ERP implementation team up with 20 SAP consultants including authors of this paper) regarding the agile engineering practices in ERP implementation process. One of stubbornly persists belief was that ERP systems cannot be part of agile development due to their complexity and nature. However, it is becoming obvious that agile engineering practices will not be anymore exclusively linked to software development as SAP (biggest world ERP vendor) recently introduced its first agile ERP implementation methodology named SAP Activate Methodology.

Keywords: ERP · ERP implementation · Agile implementation methodology · Sprints · Phases

1 Introduction

Implementing an ERP system is a major project demanding a significant level of resources, commitment and adjustments throughout the organization.

Problem Description. Often the ERP implementation project is the single biggest project that an organization has ever launched. As a result, the issues surrounding the implementation process have been one of the major concerns in industry. And it further worsens because of numerous failed cases including a few "fatal" disasters which lead to the demise of some companies. In previous studies can be found that almost 70% of ERP implementations fail to achieve their estimated benefits [1]. Although ERP can

© Springer Nature Switzerland AG 2020
M. Themistocleous and M. Papadaki (Eds.): EMCIS 2019, LNBIP 381, pp. 279–290, 2020.
https://doi.org/10.1007/978-3-030-44322-1_21

provide many benefits for organization, goals are often changed to getting the system operational instead of realizing the goals. Reflecting such a level of importance, the largest number of articles in literature belongs to this theme. It comprises more than 40% of the entire articles. Less attention has been given to the methods/methodologies used during the configuration and the implementation of ERP systems; even though they are commonly used in practice, they still remain largely unexplored and undocumented in Information Systems research domain. However, practically relevant research that addresses industry sectors that have to apply more than just agile (e.g., due to the development of safety critical systems or legal regulations) is rare. Back in 2003, Boehm and Turner [2] described a first approach how to combine agile and traditional software development for defining a balanced software development strategy, and Diebold and Zehler described how agile can be integrated into rich processes. Yet, as also argued in, systematic construction procedures are missing as most available research documents ad-hoc and user specific approaches to construct organization- and project-specific development approaches.

Objective. The overall goal of the research presented in this paper is to provide an insight from industry regarding the ERP implementation methodologies trend (focusing on world's biggest ERP provider SAP). The research presented aims to show the key components of SAP ERP implementation methodologies focusing on differences between agile and waterfall elements in each of them (and their evolution).

Contribution. In this paper, we present the ongoing research on agile software engineering practices applied on ERP implementation methodologies in practice.

2 ERP Implementation Methodologies in Literature

Several models of ERP implementation methodologies are provided in literature and they vary according to e.g. the number of phases. The phases in ERP implementation frameworks are often counted as between three and six, according to Somers and Nelson. However, the model of includes 11 phases and it gives practical checklist- type guidance for an ERP implementation. On the other hand, the models of Markus and Tanis or Parr and Shanks are very general, and are merely used for analyzing ERP implementation projects [3]. The models are useful in studying, analyzing and planning ERP implementation. The selection of ERP implementation method mentioned in paper is based on the degree of "institutionalization" in the scientific community. Livari and Hirschheim described six criteria to determine institutionalization: including (1) the existence of scientific journals, (2) scientific conferences, (3) textbooks, (4) professional associations, (5) informational and formal communication networks, and (6) citations. There are number of different ERP implementation methodologies mentioned and described in literature. However, there is an issue with methodology scope, context and its ambiguity. For example, some methodologies treat the phases before the acquisition of an ERP system (and are focused on it), while some methodologies put stress on phases after the ERP system has started to be used (production phase) [4]. Next table summarize list of proposed implementation methodologies followed by the degree of institutionalization in scientific community [5] (Table 1).

Table 1. ERP implementation models

Author(s)	ERP implementation model
Bancroft et al. (1998)	(1) Focus, (2) Creating As – Is picture, (3) Creating of the To-Be design, (4) Construction and testing and (5) Actual Implementation
Kuruppuarachchi et al. (2000)	(1) Initiation, (2) Requirement definition, (3) Acquisition/development, (4) Implementation, and (5) Termination
Markus and Tanis (2000)	(1) Project chartering, (2) The project, (3) Shakedown, and (4) Onward and upward
Makipaa (2003)	(1) Initiative, (2) Evaluation, (3) Selection, (4) Modification, Business process Reengineering, and Conversion of Data, (5) Training, (6) Go – Live, (7) Termination, and (8) Exploitation and Development
Parr and Shanks (2000a)	(1) Planning, (2) Project: a. setup, b. reengineer, c. design, d. configuration and testing, e. installation (3) Enhancement
Ross (1999)	(1) Design, (2) Implementation, (3) Stabilization, (4) Continues improvement and (5) Transformation
Shields (2001)	Rapid implementation model of three phases and 12 major activates
Umble et al. (2003)	(1) Review the pre-implementation process to date, (2) Install and test any new hardware, (3) Install the software and perform the computer room pilot, (4) Attend system training, (5) Train on the conference room pilot, (6) Established security and necessary permissions, (7) Ensure that all data bridges are sufficiently robust and the data are sufficiently accurate, (8) Document policies and procedures, (9) Bring the entire organization on – line, either in a total cutover or in a phased approach, (10) Celebrate, and (11) Improve continually
Verviell and Halingten	(1) Planning, (2) Information search, (3) Selection, (4) Evaluations, and (5) Negotiation

It is evident that there is no ground based ERP implementation methodology - widely accepted and tested. Even though they are commonly used in practice (ERP implementation methodologies) they still remain largely unexplored and undocumented in Information Systems research domain. Additionally, academic literature does not provide any relevant material regarding the influence of agile software engineering practices on ERP implementation methodology. In next paragraph we will describe newly introduced SAP ERP implementation methodology (SAP Activate Methodology).

3 SAP Activate Methodology (Agile Based Methodology)

In business informatics, software project methodologies define implementation and development guidelines for "out-of-box" software implementation as SAP. Historically, SAP had its own project methodology called ASAP, which stands for Accelerated SAP (and was completely based on waterfall project management principles). Few years ago, SAP introduced SAP Launch project methodology for its Cloud product portfolio which was also based on waterfall principles. Launch methodology has been transformed into SAP Activate Implementation methodology (currently in use for SAP ERP products) and presents the first agile based ERP implementation methodology introduced by SAP. The SAP Activate methodology comprises of six phases as highlighted in Fig. 1, which is a disciplined approach to managing complex projects, organizational change management, solution management, & industry specific implementations [6]. In next paragraph, we will briefly describe SAP Activate ERP implementation phases.

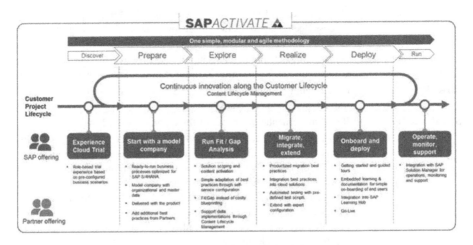

Fig. 1. SAP activate methodology

Prepare - This phase encompasses the entire project preparation and planning activities with infrastructure, hardware/network sizing requirements completed. It involves setting up the infrastructure, team, project goals, charter, and agree upon schedule, budget, risk baseline, proof- of-concept planning if applicable with implementation sequence. The project manager on the ground will discuss with the customer project manager to identify risks early on with a mitigation plan. The PM will be responsible for drafting a high-level project plan with all milestones with a detailed task level plan chalked out with critical dependencies. Each phase deliverable should be agreed between both parties. Finally, a project organization, steering committee is organized with assigned resources [7].

Explore - This is the most crucial phase of the project for a project manager as he just about to steer the ship, like a captain. The objective of this phase is to be on a common platform on how the company plans to run SAP for their business operations. Thus, a PM is responsible for analyzing the project goals and objectives and revise the overall project schedule if required. In simple terms, it is the critical requirements gathering phase, A PM might use appropriate tools to collect requirements with required traceability. The result is the Business Blueprint, which is a detailed flow of business process AS-IS, how they run the business operations with a TO-BE mapped in SAP, on how these business operations will run in SAP. Depending on the implementation complexities, number of business process, Blueprint workshops might span for a few days or weeks or even months, in a complex environment. The output of this phase is the baseline configuration in SAP with detailed custom code requirements analysis done [8].

Realize - In simple terms, realization is the actual development phase of the project, where you'd configure, develop custom code and conduct required testing. It involves coding-unit testing- integration testing-User acceptance testing (UAT). As per the business blueprint and mapping the SAP system as agreed with business, all the business process requirements will be implemented. In reality, there are two major work packages: (a) Baseline (major scope); and (b) Final configuration (remaining scope). The success of any implementation project relies on how closely you're able to develop custom code, test and release it to the UAT phase, in order to support adequate testing by the users. Also, the challenge is to adopt changes as indicated during the UAT. This phase is resource intensive and the team is at peak team size to ensure all deliverables are met and sign-off. Often times Integration fail due to lack of test data, and testing in a "PRD" like environment to be able to test all critical business scenarios. A good practice is to copy a "PRD"-like environment and start testing if the system already exists. If it is GreenField environment, ensure adequate test data is available to test it rigorously [9].

Deploy - Final preparations before cutover to production ensure that that the system, users, and data are ready for transition to productive use. The transition to operations includes setting up and launching support, then handing off operations to the organization managing the environment.

In next few paragraphs we will provide industry report from major medical institution in Bosnia and Herzegovina.

4   Report from the Industry

This industry report provides insight into an implementation of SAP ERP solution in a major medical institution in Bosnia and Herzegovina, with several thousands of employees. The project was initiated by management of the hospital with purpose to eliminate the ineffectiveness of the current information system. Analysis of the current financial system and the list of new system requirements have been prepared by external consulting company. This was prerequisite for announcing a public tender for selection of ERP software solution integrator. After several months of tender procedure and assessment of the best vendor (price was eliminatory criteria, in accordance with the law), software integrator was selected. At the end, SAP All-in One solution was preferred one. In next few paragraphs are briefly provided some quick facts regarding the project. As recommended by external consultants the main tasks of the project were:

To centralize the information system;
To increase data integrity and consistency;
To focus on accounting and financial department processes;

To improve drug warehouse management and billing system;
To provide comprehensive and accurate reports for top management;

The project incorporated five SAP modules: FI (Finance), CO (Controlling), MM (Material management), SD (Sales and Distribution) and HR (Human resources). SAP integrator offered a team of 20 SAP solution consultants, including one SAP system administrator. Additionally, two consultants (ABAP programmers) were teamed up for specific ABAP developments. The implemented system was standard SAP ERP All-in-One. Since it was not specialized health care solution, additional industry-specific functionalities needed to be developed to fulfill basic needs. They were mostly related to the processes of Materials Management and Sales and Distribution.

Remarks from Participations

Agile SAP implementation methodology named SAP Activate was presented to team members at the kick off meeting. Some of the remarks presented in next paragraphs are also mentioned in industry whitepaper named Whitepaper "Scrum and ERP – do they go together" from Mr. Boris Dloger. Some of the most repeated remarks from participants were:

> "What is the intention for using agile practices for standard ERP implementations? Typically ERP implementation does not involve any kind of development, just customizing of software to the customer's needs."

> "Agile terminology is ambiguous for us – it is terminology of software development process, not ERP implementation process!"

> "Team structure is ambiguous and not possible in ERP implementation process – lack of the rigid hierarchy will create chaos"

> "In order to customize ERP and adjust the diverse and complex ERP components we need dedicated experts. Work in cross functional teams is complex!"

We will describe those remarks in detail in next chapters providing the experience of team members.

Agile Terminology in SAP ERP Implementation

Getting the terminology right is often a complex task. In order to have a better insight in this topic author used industry experience and knowledge of Mr. Anton Karnaukhov, SAP expert, available on his blog. Agile project management brings a number of new terms that are critical to understand in order to be able to comprehend how agile can help you implement SAP solutions in a better way. Projects, especially large and complex, typically should have both waterfall and agile characteristics and elements to them. A combination of elements from both approaches usually works best for any given project, regardless of context, complexity, size or any other factor. The key roles that should be integrated in an organization that mixes traditional waterfall and agile practices in are simplified in Table 2 [10].

Table 2. Agile and waterfall terminology

Waterfall role	Meet half way	Agile role
Sponsor	Same	Sponsor
Product manager	Product manager would typically be accountable for the whole product or product line, and oversee potentially many product owners, or act as a product owner herself	Product owner
Project manager	Solution architect would be elevated to oversee programs and dependencies of projects, leaving teams to manage more autonomously	Solution Architect
Project methodology "champion"	Same idea here, if either practices are applied, care should be taken to apply with true understanding of why they are applied to not dilute the intent and effect	Scrum master (Scrum being by far the most widely adopted agile framework, hence this role used here)
End users	Active involvement from the beginning to the end. Traditional stage gates with wider presentation, key roles from core stakeholder groups involved continually	End users
Other stakeholders	Address and respect the product owner	Other stakeholders

Furthermore, those are "items" of terminology used regarding agile implementation process, shown in Table 3 [11].

Table 3. Agile process terminology

Agile terminology	Description (analogy to SAP ERP implementation terminology)
Release	Each release is associated with some type of go-live where a number of features are moved to production. For example, a "big bang" SAP implementation project could have just a single large release. A more phased approach could lead to many releases within a single SAP implementation project - SAP ERP Finance and Human Resources in one release and Logistics modules taking place in a separate release shortly after
Feature	These are sometimes called Epic Stories or Epics. Features represent large sets of functionality, for example - sales order processing, warehouse management picking, month-end close, etc. We often try to build our feature around SAP's list of best practice scenarios

(*continued*)

Table 3. (*continued*)

Agile terminology	Description (analogy to SAP ERP implementation terminology)
User Story	Each user story describes a particular business requirement and is assigned to a single feature. In many ways a user story is the next level down in terms of detail after a feature. We try to generally follow the traditional user story format of "As a a WHO I need WHAT so that I can WHY" replacing the WHO, WHAT and WHY accordingly. For example, "As a Sales Administrator I need to capture the authorization code when I am creating a sales order so that I can ensure that we are authorized to send an invoice". User stories are business- centric, not technology-centric. They do not capture HOW something will be accomplished technically (that comes later)
Task	We generally try to avoid tracking detailed tasks, but sometimes we need to breakdown a single user story into multiple tasks and assign those to different people. For example this can by handy for tracking ABAP development tasks. Each task belongs to one and only one user story. Generally speaking, it is the lowest level entity that we track
Sprint	A sprint is typically a pre-determined period of time (2 weeks, 4 weeks, 6 weeks, etc.) within which a set of identified user stories needs to complete - have found sprints to be too rigid for SAP implementation projects and prefer to use the Kanban variation of agile project management methodology, which doesn't make use of sprints
Kanban Board	A visual board where columns represent a state that a user story can be in, for example - planned, blueprinting, realization, testing, done. Stories are arranged on the Kanban board and moved from one column to another as progress is being made. Many teams build physical Kanban boards by using tape and post-it notes
Retrospective	A retrospective is a focused session where your team looks back at how the current agile approach is working and which areas can be improved. Many agile teams conduct retrospectives at set intervals of time (every 8 weeks or at the end of every sprint)

Team Structure of Project

In the past, different variations of project team composition was suggested as standardized, but the fact is that there is no canned project team setup that will work on every project [10].

At the very beginning of any SAP implementation project there is a process of defining a baseline of features that make up the general scope of a particular product. A release is typically associated with a go-live - for example going live with Material Management (MM) and Finance (FI) modules of SAP ERP, or a particular business unit going live with an SAP Extended Warehouse Management (EWM) system. One important thing to note is that the initial list of features in a release is not "frozen for changes". Most of the time, if not all of the time, new features will be added to the list as the project progresses and some of the old features will be either moved to a later release or even removed entirely from the project. This is perfectly normal and even encouraged. In fact, part of embracing change is constantly re-evaluating the prioritization of project features and user stories and focusing on the ones that bring the most business value.

A good starting point for building a list of features for an SAP implementation project is SAP's Best Practices library. Once a baseline or industry-specific package is chosen customer is able to see its requirements presented with a list of SAP best practice scenarios, each designated by a unique number. For example, under the baseline package you will be able to find scenario 112 called "Sales Quotation". The end result is a list of features that outlines the first pass at defining the overall scope of what we think we are going to accomplish in a particular project [12].

Once the initial feature list is put together we can start building our project team structure. Here are some general guidelines that we try to follow.

Leadership

In the context of an agile SAP implementations these roles are much less about management and are much more about leadership, which is often a source of tension in many organizations that are trying to do agile for the first time [10]. What is meant by this is that many traditional managers are used to working in an environment where they create layers of superfluous entities (status reports, WBS structures, functional and technical specification documents, detailed tracking of estimated vs actual time) all typically under the banner of "proper management" and for purposes of historical reference, and then depend on "data" from those entities to reveal red flags in order to take some "corrective action". With agile the use of such activities is greatly discouraged and many managers who are not successful leaders often struggle to find their niche within an agile project.

Self-directed Teams

In general, each team is responsible for managing all of the work (features, user stories, tasks, etc.) from start to finish. They are responsible for gathering user stories and tasks (blueprinting), prioritize the stories; performing the configuration and development work (realization), testing, providing documentation, and even of training end-users. All teams are expected to create their own user stories (and tasks) and keep their Kanban boards up-to-date. Teams are expected to engage in continuous dialog with business users and prioritize their own workload [10]. One of the most crucial techniques for promoting self-directed teams is the use of daily stand-ups. These are short and focused meetings, typically at the beginning of each day, where each team member answers the following 3 questions

- What have I accomplished yesterday?
- What am I planning to accomplish today?
- Is there anything in my way that is preventing me from making progress?

Product Owner

Four product owners where assigned to project team structure. They are important part in providing help with prioritization of user stories, but given the volume of stories in an average SAP implementation (from 1000 to 5000), their involvement in prioritization at the individual story level is limited [13]. We can summarize product owner's primary objectives as:

Identification and prioritization of features (in tandem with project manager aka Scrum Master)
Review and acceptance of delivered solutions through a live demo (usually a batch of 15–30 user stories)

Solution Architect

One solution architects was assigned to project team structure whose role was to ensure that the overall SAP implementation across sub-teams is synchronized. Solution architect is professional with extensive technical experience across many SAP systems and modules. And even though cross-functional sub-teams often rely on solution architects to get direction in complex integration scenarios, the teams themselves still retain the responsibility of aiming all of their user stories and tasks forward [14]. Solution architects are typically responsible for:

Cohesiveness and robustness of the overall delivered solution for the entire project Integration design and testing across teams, systems and modules.

Cross – functional teams

This is often a source of confusion in SAP project as the term cross-functional has historically referred to cross-module (for example SD, FI, MM, etc.) in the SAP world. However, in the context of an agile team structure for an SAP project cross- functional refers to the various functions performed by the project team - requirement gathering, configuration, development, documentation, training, etc. [13]. Typically a number of such cross-functional sub-teams is build, each focused on a small number of SAP systems/modules. For example:

Sales and Distribution team - 4 BPOs, 3 analysts, 1 developer, 1 trainer/instructional designer
Materials Management team - 5 BPOs, 2 analyst, 1 developer, 1 trainer/instructional designer

Impact on Project Managers

In Agile engineering practices, a traditional project manager role may not be required to manage an implementation, as the agile teams are self-sufficient (common Project Management roles in an agile project are product owners, scrum masters and scrum team)

Scrum master coaches the development team to use scrum principles.
A product owner will generally come from the customer side and will own the requirements and will be part of the scrum team.

Product owner will be responsible for documentation of requirements which are normally written as user stories. He will also be in charge of the prioritization of the requirements [11].

Impact on Project Stakeholders and Sponsors
SAP Activate Methodology ensures consistent involvement of project stakeholders and sponsors. Project stakeholders are involved in project planning and retrospective meetings every 2–4 weeks. In a traditional/Waterfall project management scenarios, the client gets involved at a much later stage which results in a mismatch of expectations and project delivery [13].

5 Conclusion

It is evident that agile practices will not be exclusively linked to software development anymore. Some of the remarks that arise from team members were stated in previous chapter. We will restate them again, but this time, providing an insight as a result of "hands on" experience in agile SAP ERP implementation project.

> *"Why should agile methods be used for standard ERP implementations? This does not normally involve any kind of development, just adapting software to the existing processes."*

ERP implementations intervene in the way many employees work, whether standard or in-house development: changes give rise to uncertainty. In agile engineering practices, great scope is given to communication with the user by means of regular interviews. The users test the product increments and give feedback as to what works well and what does not.

> *"We don't understand agile terminology – it is terminology of software development process, not ERP implementation process!"*

Getting the terminology right is very important part adopting agile engineering practices truly [15]. Agile project management brings with it a number of new terms that are critical to understand in order to be able to comprehend any of the detailed discussions on how agile can help you implement SAP solutions in a better way. Listed in this paper, in the form of table, we showed that it is possible to map agile and waterfall terminology "one – to – one"

> *"Team structure is ambiguous and not possible in ERP implementation process – lack of the rigid hierarchy will create chaos"*

In general, each team is charged with owning and managing all of their logical units of work (features, user stories, tasks, etc.) from start to finish. That means they are responsible for gathering user stories and tasks (blueprinting), working with the business to prioritize those stories, performing the configuration and development work (realization), testing, documentation, demoing solutions and even training end- users [7].

> *"To be able to configure and adapt the diverse and complex ERP components we need specialized experts. That makes work in cross-functional teams more difficult."*

It has also proved effective in ERP projects to unite different skills in one team: ERP consultants work with ERP developers, CRM experts with MM experts, while business analysts or system architects also enhance such teams. In this way the requirements are viewed from different perspectives and the exchange of ideas within the team brings aspects to light that the individual alone would not have detected –this again ensures that the "right" product is delivered [13].

In upcoming years we will see more and more research papers and case studies about the influence of agile practices on ERP implementation process. It is expected that all major ERP providers present theirs unique agile driven ERP implementation methodologies [15]. In upcoming papers (and as a part of PhD project) we will focus on providing hybrid Agile Waterfall ERP implementation methodology designed on design science postulates.

References

1. Abrahamsson, P., Salo, O., Ronkainen, J., Warsta, J.: Agile Software Development (2002)
2. Methods: Review and Analysis, Research Report (478) (2002). http://www.vtt.fi/inf/pdf/publications/2002/P478.pdf
3. Aiken, L.S., West, S.G.: Multiple Regression: Testing and Interpreting Interactions. Sage, Newbury Park (1992)
4. Akgün, A.E., Byrne, J., Keskin, H.: Knowledge networks in new product development projects: a transactive memory perspective. Inf. Manag. 42(8), 1105–1120 (2005)
5. Akgün, A.E., Keskin, H., Byrne, J., Imamoglu, S.Z.: Antecedents and consequences of team potency in software development projects. Inf. Manag. 44(7), 646–656 (2007)
6. Al-Fatish, F., Roemer, M., Fassunge, M., Reinstorf, T., Staader, J.: ASE: Immer busser mit starken Teams! Agile Software Engineering bei der SAP. Object Spectr. 1, 1–3 (2011)
7. Anderson, D.J.: Agile Management for Software Engineering: Applying the Theory of Constraints for Business Results. The Coad Series. Prentice Hall, Upper Saddle River (2004)
8. Denecken, S., Musli, J.: SAP S/4HANA cloud: implementation with SAP activate. SAP Press 1, 42–43 (2017)
9. Argote, L.: Input uncertainty and organizational coordination in hospital emergency units. Adm. Sci. Q. 27(3), 420–434 (1982)
10. http://www.xpertminds.net/blog/111
11. Baccarini, D.: The concept of project complexity: a review. Int. J. Project Manage. 14(4), 201–204 (1996)
12. Balijepally, V.G., Mahapatra, R.K., Nerur, S., Price, K.H.: Are two heads better than one for software development? The productivity paradox of pair programming. Manag. Inf. Syst. Q. 33(1), 91–118 (2009)
13. https://go.forrester.com/consulting/
14. Jalali, S., Wohlin, C.: Global software engineering and agile practices: a systematic review. J. Softw. Evol. Proc. 24(6), 643–659 (2012)
15. Glogler, B.: Scrum and ERP: do they go together? Industry whitepaper (2014). https://borisgloger.com/wpcontent/uploads/2014/07/Whitepaper_Scrum_and_ERP_en.pdf

Exploring Machine Learning Models to Predict Harmonized System Code

Fatma Altaheri$^{(\boxtimes)}$ and Khaled Shaalan

British University of Dubai, Dubai, UAE
20181351@student.buid.ac.ae,
khaled.shaalan@buid.ac.ae

Abstract. The Harmonized System (HS) Code is widely used across all customs administrations because of the several benefits including a more convenient and easier approach for calculating duties as well as preventing the potential loss of revenue. This paper aims to explore various machine learning models to predict the HS Code based on the customers' input commodity descriptions. This prediction model helps in reducing the complexity, gaps and many other challenges in using HS Code in any Customs administration. This study follows the Cross-Industry Process for Data Mining methodology which comprises six phases, namely business understanding, data understanding, data preparation, building prediction model, performance evaluation and model deployment. The results of the study indicate that machine learning models are effective tools in predicting HS Code based on user's inputs. The linear support vector machine model was able to achieve the highest accuracy of 76.3%.

Keywords: Harmonized System Code (HS Code) · Customs, revenue protection · Machine learning · Predictive models · Trade

1 Introduction

The emergence of globalization has paved way to opening a number of opportunities towards achieving economic growth and prosperity. However, there are still certain challenges that pose as barriers to the effective implementation of processes within local governments. Customs is one of the most important government agencies, in the global perspective, that governs international trade and services process such as the declaration of goods and services, particularly in the aspect of trade and commerce. Generally, the verifying commodity descriptions ensures that goods and/or services are in compliance with government regulations to prevent improper or unlawful entry to the country of destination (Che et al. 2018). In this sense, Customs has the responsibility of ensuring that declared goods and/or services to be imported or exported are classified accordingly based on commodity descriptions.

Goods classification is one of the most important obligation of importer and exporter compliance. As such, it has become vital to customs departments worldwide to ensure that there is a delicate balance of reducing classification uncertainties and promoting effective classification systems. In response to this, several customs departments across the globe has integrated the use of modern technology by adopting

M. Themistocleous and M. Papadaki (Eds.): EMCIS 2019, LNBIP 381, pp. 291–303, 2020.
https://doi.org/10.1007/978-3-030-44322-1_22

the Harmonized System (HS) Code. According to Ding, Fan and Cheng (2015), the HS Code, also known as the Harmonized Commodity Description and Coding System, was developed by Brussels-based World Customs Organization (WCO) in order to cope with the rapidly increasing international trade worldwide. In line with this, Weerth (2008) explained that goods in a customs tariff must be described fully within the customs declaration so they can be classified accordingly. For example, a wooden chair can be classified according to material condition or its function as furniture (Weerth 2008). This means that the use of HS Code has become important for customs departments because it promotes easier ways of calculating duties, fees and taxes, determining appropriate permits, licenses and certificates required and collecting trade statistics (Ding et al. 2015).

Traditionally, declared goods are analyzed and inspected by inspectors using inspection images wherein results are used as grounds for decision making (Che et al. 2018). Using this approach, a number of weaknesses and concerns can be identified such as difficulty in identifying hazards in substances and ineffective classification of declared goods due to possible inefficiencies in the designation of harmonized system codes (Che et al. 2018; United Nations 2013). Aside from these weaknesses, there are also some challenges in the application of HS Code in relation to achieving satisfactory accuracy. These challenges include HS complexity, gaps in terminology and the evolving nature of the HS Code among others (Ding et al. 2015).

This study aims to contribute to reducing HS complexity and gaps by exploring various machine learning-based prediction models. In order to provide a better outlook as to the impact of the adoption of the machine learning-based HS Code Prediction model, the case of Dubai Customs is used. This means that this study employs a case study approach focusing on the Customs Department in Dubai, UAE. It is expected that the integration of technological advancement to the HS Code classification can contribute to addressing HS Code complexity and to enhancing its accuracy.

The paper is divided into 5 sections. Section 1 provides introductions about the HS Code and the importance of this study. Section 2 explores the related work that have been done to address the HS code research gaps. Section 3 illustrates the research methodology in details and the various machine learning models that have been implemented. Section 4 discusses the main findings. The last section provides the conclusion of this work and the future prospects.

2 Related Work

Machine learning methods are currently being integrated in various programs and systems in order to help organizations make better decisions particularly with regards to predictive analysis and pattern recognition. For example, machine learning methods are majorly being integrated in the security field such as to enhance facial recognition from using large amount of data from various sources which is difficult for humans to do manually (Mohammed et al. 2017). In addition, machine learning is also being integrated to various systems to promote automation and improve efficiency and accuracy. For example, machine learning techniques are being integrated in HS codes to foster accuracy, intelligence and automation (Zang et al. 2008). This suggests that multiple machine learning strategies integrated in various programs and systems can contribute to enhancing system performance, continuous learning and promoting more informed decision making.

In the perspective of customs organizations/departments, the integration of machine learning has become vital in order for them to stay competitive in the international trade facilitation (Ding et al. 2015). As explained by Ding and colleagues, different machine learning techniques are already being applied in capturing and learning long term and stable criteria for text categorization. For example, the use of keywords is one of the most common approaches of machine learning through the adoption of the vector space model (VSM) (Ding et al. 2015). In addition, machine learning approaches are also being integrated in HS in pursuit of addressing HS code prediction problems (Luppes 2019).

Furthermore, machine learning strategies are also being integrated in HS in order to enhance automation process. According to KPMG International (2018), machine learning can be used to develop a knowledge base towards learning and developing a set of algorithms from large amount of data in order to make informed predictions. KPMG International (2018, p. 37) explained that "A combination of natural language processing and machine learning makes it possible to automate the capture, array and analysis of unstructured data and transform it into structured data that may be used in a tax application". This suggests that the integration of machine learning in HS can contribute to process efficiency by means of improving quality, consistency and accuracy of code classification due to reduced likelihood of human errors. There are several machine learning tools and techniques that have been developed. Yet, machine learning can be viewed as the one that provides the technical basis for data mining (Witten et al. 2011).

In order to promote effective application and integration of machine learning to HS, it is important to understand how it works. In the general perspective, machine learning can be viewed as the new technology for mining knowledge from data in order to learn and generate accurate predictive outcomes (Witten et al. 2011). As such, machine learning can be viewed as being directly correlated with data mining. In line with this, machine learning techniques integrated with HS can also foster smart matching and classification through building data driven smart customs (Youyi 2017). As explained by Youyi (2017), a data driven smart customs can promote intelligent law enforcement, intelligent risk control and intelligent revenue collection wherein data collections can lead to intelligent applications (see Fig. 1).

Therefore, data mining is an important part of creating a machine learning framework that can contribute to promoting accurate and efficient classification and detection of tariff code as integrated in HS code systems. Collecting large amount of data set and generating useful information from collected data will not become a challenge due to the integration of machine learning in HS. Using machine learning based approaches and models can help enhance predictive analysis on streaming data and detect changes and inconsistencies in data to address HS code classification and description and business intelligence problems.

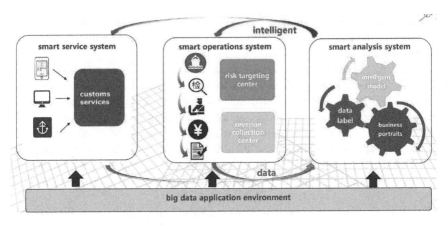

Fig. 1. Architecture of data driven smart customs (Youyi 2017)

3   Research Methodology and Experiments

This study aims to investigate the possibility of implementing machine learning model to predict the HS code for the commodities based on the provided descriptions by the users. To perform this text mining task, we adopted the Cross-Industry Process for Data Mining methodology (CRISP-DM) (Shearer 2000). As illustrated in Fig. 2, this methodology consists of the following processes, namely business understanding, data understanding, data preparation, data modelling, performance evaluation and deployment. Business understanding refers mainly to the importance of the problem that is being address which is reducing the loss revenue by building machine learning model to correctly predict the HS Code. Data Understanding refers to the process of analyzing the available input information in order to produce an efficient machine learning model. Data preparation represents the preprocessing steps which are typically performed in order to remove any factor which may degrade the performance of the machine learning model. The machine learning modelling, evaluation and deployment involves the selection the appropriate machine learning techniques in order to investigate and evaluate these models and figure out the best machine learning model that produces the highest performance for deployment.

This section starts by describing the source of the HS Codes dataset that is used to conduct the machine learning experiments. Furthermore, a detailed analysis on how the obtained dataset can be used to answer the driving research question. And this is followed by the data preparation tasks that includes data cleansing, sample processing and tokenization that will be used to build the inputs features to the machine learning models. This section also explains in details the machine learning models that are adopted and implemented throughout the HS Code prediction models.

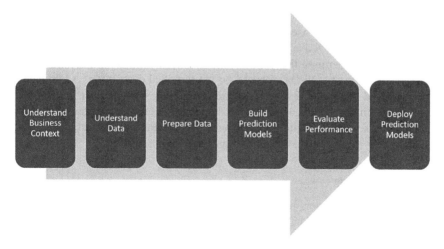

Fig. 2. Research methodology

3.1 Business Understanding

The importance of this work scope is to reduce the loss revenue caused by misclassifying the goods. This misclassification results in loss of duties. Such misclassification normally occurs to either the ability to the user not to correctly determine the required HS Code or in another situation the manipulation by the users to reduce the amount of duty that he/she is required to pay. In this work, the focus is on the first issue since the second issue requires other authentication techniques to determine whether the user is intentionally misclassifying the goods.

3.2 Data Understanding

The data used in this work are provided by Dubai Customs through the Artificial Intelligence (AI) hackathon competition that was conducted on October 2019. This data consists of 22,346,194 records where each record has two attributes; the Harmonized System Code (HS Code) and the user inputs description. In this section, we will describe the processing techniques that we adopted in order to review, analyse and prepare the input data.

3.3 Data Analysis

During the analysis of the provided data, we have noticed several major factors which must be taken into consideration during the development of the machine learning based model. These factors are mainly related to the quality of the user's description and the number of expected classes (labels).

About the user's description, several issues have been noted. For instance, some of the descriptions do not contain any valuable keywords from the English dictionary. In another words, the spelling mistakes in these descriptions are too severe to the point that they could not be understood by the human mind. Also, we have noticed that the same description has been used several times to describe totally different items.

Regarding the expected number of classes, the provided data has almost 8,000 labels. And this underlines the problem associated with establishing any machine learning model to predict the label based on the provided description. Additionally, it has been noticed that they are severe variations in terms of the number of records that are associated with each class. For instance, some of the classes have around 10 records while other classes may have up to 700 records. This factor must be addressed in order to avoid having any bias behavior in the machine learning model.

3.4 Data Cleansing

The above-mentioned factors have been taken into consideration during the cleaning of the data. And in this section, we will present the procedural steps that have been performed during the cleaning of the data. These steps can be summarized as follows:

(1) remove duplications (2) remove punctuation and remove stop words (3) remove non-English words (4) remove numbers and (5) lemmatization.

Remove Duplications: Duplicated records might have negative impact on the overall performance of the machine learning models. Therefore, we have removed all duplicated records based on the users' description as a pre-processing step.

Remove Punctuation and Stop Words: Eventually, the punctuation and stop words have no impact in the training behavior of any machine learning model since they are common words that do not add any distinct features to the description. Therefore, the punctuation and stop words have been removed in order to speed up the training process.

Remove Non-English Words: Normally, the descriptions are provided by users who have basic understanding of the English language. And this may result in writing words with spelling mistakes which may confuse the behavior of the training because at the training stage, these non-English words will be interpreted with different words that have different meaning. Therefore, these non-English words were removed during the cleansing step.

Remove Numbers: In this domain, it has been noticed that numbers do not provide any valuable features to the goods. Thus, the number have been removed as well in order to speed up the training for the machine learning model.

Lemmatization: This process is used to return the word to its origin. Thus, applying lemmatization is expected to reduce the vocabulary size and improve the performance since words that have the same origin must be treated equally.

In addition to the above-mentioned cleansing steps, all text has been converted to lower case in order to reduce the vocabulary size since any machine learning model is case sensitive.

3.5 Sample Processing

Having classes with very big variation in terms of records is expected to create a significant impact on the training behavior. For instance, if we assume using the

K- nearest neighbor to predict a binary class label where the first class has 100 records and the second class has only 10 records. In this case, the model may mis-classify the data towards labeling the reading by the 100-records label class. Accordingly, this sampling issue must be addressed to ensure consistency in terms of the classification behavior. To address this problem, we have reported the minimum and maximum records for the 8,000 classes that are provided in the dataset. During this step, it has been noticed the gap between the minimum and the maximum reaches to 750 records. Thus, we have performed down sampling to achieve 100 records as a gap between the minimum and maximum class size.

In this work, due to computational limitation of the used machine, we have selected only 500,000 at random as the input data. Additionally, once all pre-processing steps are performed, 217,700 records are kept as the final data set input.

3.6   Tokenization

In NLP, tokenization is an important step in order to determine weight (importance) of each word in the text. In general, two major techniques have been widely used to perform tokenization. These techniques are: (1) bag of words and (2) Term Frequency - Invert Document Frequency (TF-IDF). The bag of words is simply a counting method where each word is given a value that represents the frequency in which the word appears in the text. Accordingly, the use of this technique depends whether the number of appearances of each word in the text is considered as distinct features in each model (Alqaryouti et al. 2019).

However, the TF-IDF is considered as a more advanced technique since it uses the frequency of the word in order to determine the uniqueness of each word in the text. The TF-IDF starts by calculating the frequency of each word in the text $(Fr(w))$. This is calculated by dividing the number of times word (w) appears in the text over the total number of words. This denotes the term frequency in the calculation (TF). The inverse document frequency (IDF) is calculated as follows:

$$IDF(w) = \log(\frac{N}{Nw})$$

Where N denotes to the total number of records (the users' HS Code descriptions), and Nw denotes the number of records that has the word w. This inverse is normally calculated to associate a weight value with each word where words with less appearance have more weight. Eventually, the TF-IDF score for a word w can be represented as follows:

$$TF - IDF(w) = TF(w) \times IDF(w)$$

The equation shows that the TF-IDF aims to magnifies the weight of the words that appears in a smaller number of records (Alqaryouti et al. 2018).

3.7   Experiments

In this section, we present and discuss the machine learning models that are used in this work and the corresponding performance of each model. These experiments were performed using Python 3.5 with scikit learn library for model specifications. To evaluate the performance for each model, we have adopted the following evaluation metrics: precision, recall, F1-measure and accuracy. The machine learning prediction approach is illustrated in Fig. 3.

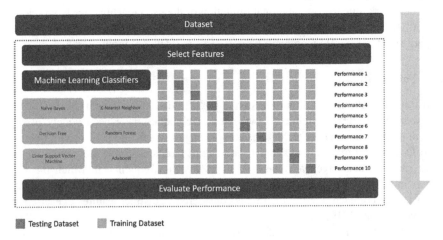

Fig. 3. Machine learning prediction and evaluation approach

3.7.1   Performance Measures

For each HS Code label, precision refers to the number of correctly classified description that belongs to this label. For instance, the precision for HS Code (00000000) refers to the percentage of correctly classified goods that belong to this label where the equation of calculating the precision is show below:

$$P = \frac{TP}{TP + FP}$$

Where, number of goods that are classified as (00000000) label is referred as True-Positive (TP). The False-Positive (FP) denotes the number of goods (descriptions) that have been misclassified as (00000000) label.

Recall (R) denotes the correctly classified labels. For instance, the recall for the class (00000000) in the above example refers to the correctly classified goods that belong to this label and is calculated as per the below equation:

$$R = \frac{TP}{TP + FN}$$

Where, false-negative (FN) denotes the number of goods (records) that belong the class (00000000) and are misclassified as other classes.

The F1-score is used a measure to determine the quality of the classification, where a higher F1-measure score highlights better classification quality. The F1-measure score is calculated according to the following equation:

$$F1 = 2 \times \frac{R \times P}{R + P}$$

The accuracy refers to the number correctly classified goods by the machine learning model and it is calculated as follows:

$$Accuracy = \frac{TP + TN}{(TP + TN + FP + FN)}$$

3.7.2   HS Code Prediction Models

In the experiments that are presented in this work, we have performed 10-fold cross validation technique. This technique which is also denoted as rotation estimation is typically used to assess the performance of the machine learning model by generating different independent equal sets (k = 10). In general, any machine learning model works by using the training set to learn the behavior of the data. Whereas, the test set is the unseen data that is used to measure the accuracy of the learning behavior of the machine learning model. In cross validation, the experiment is performed k times where in each round the data is divided into training and testing sets. In each round the selected testing set must be different where the performance is monitored over the k runs in order to better analyze the model performance.

The main ingredients of this work are to use the following machine learning models in order to evaluate and answer the proposed research question. These machine learning models are: Naïve Bayes, K-Nearest Neighbor, Decision Tree, Random Forest, Linier Support Vector Machine and Adaboost. In these machine learning models, we will perform the prediction model on two experiment settings. The first setting, we will test whether the machine learning model is able to predict the entire HS Code Correctly. Whereas, in the second setting, we will test the ability of only predicting the header of the HS Code. The header denotes the first four digits of the HS Code which represent the chapter (2 digits) and section (2 digits). The chapter and section represent the commodity type (e.g. coffee, skin products).

The input data for the machine learning models are expressed as a tuple that consists of the following features: <HS Code, Description Text> where, once the tokenization is performed, the description text is converted to several features that represent the weights of the words in each description. HS Code represents the label that will be predicted.

In its core, the Naiive Bayes classifier uses the Bayes theorem to predict the probability of membership. The main idea in this classifier is to use conditional probability in which the probability is calculated between each input feature and the corresponding classes. In other words, if we assume that we have 5 features and 2

classes, the mechanism of this classifier works by determining the conditional probability of each feature and the 2 classes. This classifier is very efficient in text- based
modelling where the input is expected to have distinct words that highlight the
advantages of using the conditional probability concept. To test the performance of the
Naïve Bayes classifier in predicting the HS Code, we ran the experiment where Table 1
shows the performance metrics. From the table, we can see that the accuracy of this
classifier is relatively low (52.43%) and this highlights the fact that the input
description consists of relatively common words that do not distinguish between the
input record efficiently.

Table 1. Performance evaluation adopted machine learning models

Machine learning model	Experiment settings	Precision	Recall	F1-Measure	Accuracy
Naïve Bayes	HS Code header	73.66%	55.66%	63.40%	66.21%
	Entire HS Code	59.67%	29.45%	39.44%	52.43%
K-Nearest Neighbor	HS Code header	72.83%	57.75%	64.42%	71.72%
	Entire HS Code	55.30%	26.66%	35.97%	57.94%
Decision Tree	HS Code header	70.21%	46.92%	56.25%	61.62%
	Entire HS Code	51.00%	20.72%	29.47%	47.84%
Random Forest	HS Code header	96.35%	64.39%	77.19%	79.99%
	Entire HS Code	94.00%	38.19%	54.31%	66.21%
Linear Support Vector Machine	HS Code header	**96.35%**	**70.55%**	**81.46%**	**84.58%**
	Entire HS Code	**95.06%**	**51.41%**	**66.73%**	**75.40%**
Adaboost	HS Code header	73.66%	67.44%	70.41%	75.40%
	Entire HS Code	51.00%	25.10%	33.65%	57.02%

Table 1 shows the performance measure of this classifier where the label of each
class only represents the header. Recall that the header represents the first 4 digits of the
HS Code. And this header classifies an abstract level the goods type. From this table,
we can see that the by considering the header of the label, the performance of the
classifier has improved significantly, where the classifier achieves 66.21% accuracy.
This is related to the fact that by aggregating the records and only perform the classification on the HS Code header, we reduce the pressure on the classifier since the
number of labels have been reduced significantly.

K-Nearest Neighbor is a discriminated classifier in which the prediction works by
taking into consideration the observation around the location of the new data to be
predicted. To clarify this concept, assume that we are planning to predict the class label
of an input record using 5-Nearest Neighbor. In this example, once the new record is
represented in the solution space, the 5-Nearest Neighbor works by determining the
class label of the 5 nearest point to the new record. Then, a voting mechanism is
applied and the new record is assigned to the label with the major points. The key
performance factor of this classifier is the number of neighbors that are considered
during the search (k). in this work, we have noticed that the performance of this

classifier stabilizes once the k reaches to 15 (k = 15). Thus, in the experiment shows below, we have sat k to 15.

Table 1 illustrates the performance measures for this classifier. From the table, we can see that the K-Nearest Neighbor classifier performs slightly better than the Naïve Bayes model. This improvement (around 5%) in performance is related to the cleansing procedures that are applied in this work since it contributes towards eliminating unnecessary features and therefore reduce the dimensionality of the solution space. In addition, Table 1 shows the performance for only the header of the HS Code. From this table, it is clear that the accuracy of this classifier has been improved (71.72% accuracy) due to the above-mentioned factors similar to Naïve Bayes. Decision Tree classifier uses the input data to build a tree. This tree is eventually a conditional statement (if-else statement). In this mechanism, the node of the trees is selected based on the corresponding label. In other words, by starting from the root, the selection of the node will be based on the features and their impact on the class label. In each level, the features with the most impact on the class label will be selected as this particular level nodes. The behavior and performance of this classifier depends on the length of the tree and the number of labels. In our experiment it is not expected that this classifier to obtain significant classification behaviors due to the high number of labels. This is confirmed by the results which is shown in Table 1, where this classifier achieves 47.84% accuracy for the entire HS-code matching experiment. Random Forest is an ensemble learning technique in which the classification is performed based on the outcome of several learning models. In this work, the sub- learning model represents decision trees. By combining several decision trees into a random forest, the boundary of prediction is expected to be more accurate. And this is was clearly illustrated by the achieved results (66.21%) where the accuracy has improved significantly compared to the previously discussed Decision Tree classifier as shown in Table 1. Linear Support Vector Machine is an efficient well-known method that has been widely adopted to address several machine learning problems. Typically, a machine learning model tries to determine a hyperplane which divides the solution space according to the classes. For instance, assume that we have a binary problem, a hyperplane in this case is expected to divide the space such that one of the classes will be located to the right of the hyperplane and the other is located to the left of the hyperplane. In Linier Support Vector Machine, the optimization objective is to determine the location of this hyperplane such that the distance between the nearest point in each class and the hyperplane is maximized. This distance is typically referred to as a margin and therefore, the problem addressed in this situation can be denoted as maximizing the total margin. The results shown in Table 1 indicates that the linear Support Vector Machine achieves significant results than other classifiers in all of the cases (75.4%), where in the header only case, the improvement is much significant compared to the entire HS Code experiment (84.58%). This is related to the fact that in the header only case, the number of classes will be significantly lower and this reduces the complexity of locating an efficient hyperplane to separate the classes. In other situation where the experiment is performed to predict the entire HS Code, the complexity of the solution space increases the pressure on the classifier to obtain an efficient hyperplane locality.

Adaboost is an ensemble learning technique where the main idea of this classifier is to determine the weight of each sub-classifier based on its behavior in the overall evaluation. For instance, assume that Adaboost consists of three round optimizations. In each round, the weight of the classification factors depends on the outcome of the previous round of evaluations. Thus, this classifier aims to optimize the classification factors weights in iterative manner based on the behavior of the previous round. Unexpectedly, this classifier performance was relatively low compared to other machine learning classifiers as shown in Table 1. This is related to the fact that in our problem the number of features (after tokenization) is high. Therefore, Adaboost, failed to obtain an efficient classification behavior during the experiments which is bounded by 24 h running time.

4 Discussion

This study aims to investigate the problem of predicting the HS Code for the goods based on the users' input description. This prediction aims to reduce the revenue loss caused by using wrong HS Codes in order to reduce amount of duty that the trader is expected to pay to the customs administration. From the results, it is clear that the machine learning models can be used to help in predicting the HS Code for the user goods descriptions. The relatively low classification performance can be contributed by different factors such that the quality of the description and in some situations the planning of providing falsified descriptions. Since any machine learning model will be able to predict the description quality is bad due to poor English skills or due to the intention of the user to provide such low-quality description. The work that has been carried out to answer the research question which deals with the ability of using machine learning techniques to build HS Code Prediction Model establishes the ability to perform such tasks using machine learning techniques. To address the main objective question of this research, the dataset that is provided by Dubai Customs was used to predict the HS Code of the provided users' description using six machine learning models. The adopted machine learning models have achieved promising results specially the linier Support Vector Machine which achieved the highest accuracy of 76.3%.

5 Conclusion

This study underpins the challenges that confront Customs relating to the use of Harmonized System (HS) Code in their operations. Through the use of the case study approach and the development of a machine learning-based HS Code Prediction Model. Considering the benefits of using the HS code, there is subsequently a need to also address the issues it entails. The significance of this study is rooted on the interest of the research to contribute to empirical knowledge, especially in filling in gaps about the use of machine learning approaches in improving HS Code at Dubai Customs. As the results of the study reveal, the machine learning models are useful in predicting HS Code for the user goods descriptions. In addition, it is also noted that one of the six machine learning models used, the Linear Support Vector Machine, reveals a high accuracy of 76.3% in relevance with predicting HS Code using the dataset provided by the Dubai Customs.

However, this study is also not without limitations. Since a case study approach was adopted, the research is only limited to Dubai Customs as the machine learning models were only used on the dataset obtained from said government agency for predicting HS Code. On the other hand, information presented in the study can be used for future research, specifically on how gaps and other challenges in HS Code can be addressed among government agencies that use the modern technology. It can also be used to explore and identify strategies that will positively affect the efficiency of using HS Code in the public sector. The adoption of machine learning models as predictive frameworks and their respective effectiveness and/or efficiency can additionally be examined in future.

Due to the complexity of the problem, as a future step, we will explore the applicability of developing a divide-and-concur approach to address this problem. Whereas, hieratical prediction can be build starting from the HS Code header until identifying all of the HS Code subsections. Additionally, we are planning to explore the benefits of employing deep learning-based approaches to address this problem.

References

Alqaryouti, O., Khwileh, H., Farouk, T., Nabhan, A., Shaalan, K.: Graph-based keyword extraction. In: Shaalan, K., Hassanien, A.E., Tolba, F. (eds.) Intelligent Natural Language Processing: Trends and Applications. SCI, vol. 740, pp. 159–172. Springer, Cham (2018). https://doi.org/10.1007/978-3-319-67056-0_9

Alqaryouti, O., Siyam, N., Monem, A.A., Shaalan, K.: Aspect-based sentiment analysis using smart government review data. Appl. Comput. Inform. (2019, Accepted Manuscript)

Che, J., Xing, Y., Zhang, L.: A comprehensive solution for deep-learning based cargo inspection to discriminate goods in containers. IEEE Xplore (2018)

Ding, L., Fan, Z., Chen, D.: Auto-categorization of HS Code using background net approach. Procedia Comput. Sci. 60, 1462–1471 (2015)

KPMG International: Transforming the tax function through technology (2018). https://home.kpmg/content/dam/kpmg/au/pdf/2018/transforming-the-taxfunction-au.pdf

Luppes, J.: Classifying short text for the harmonized system with convolutional neural networks. Master Thesis, Radboud University (2019)

Mohammed, M., Khan, M.B., Bashier, E.B.M.: Machine Learning-Algorithms and Applications. CRC Press, Boca Raton (2017)

United Nations: Globally Harmonized System of Classification and Labelling of Chemicals (GHS), 5th Revised edn. United Nations, Geneva (2013)

Shearer, C.: The CRISP-DM model: the new blueprint for data mining. J. Data Warehous. 5(4), 13–22 (2000)

Weerth, C.: Basic Principles of Customs Classifications under the Harmonized System. Global Trade Customs J. 3(2), 61–67 (2008)

Witten, I.H., Frank, E., Hall, M.A.: Data Mining: Practical Machine Learning Tools and Techniques, 3rd edn. Elsevier, Burlington (2011)

Youyi, W.: Exploration of Data-Driven Intelligent Customs (2017). https://www.eiseverywhere.com/file_uploads/c7e054aa02ad13907d6ad513ea57b8d_session3-YouyiWu.pdf

Zang, B., Li, Y., Xie, W., Chen, Z., Tsai, C., Laing, C.: An ontological engineering approach for automating inspection and quarantine at airports. J. Comput. Syst. Sci. 74, 196–210 (2008)

Adopting Industry 4.0 Technologies in Citizens' Electronic-Engagement Considering Sustainability Development

Aliano Abbasi[1(✉)] and Muhammad Mustafa Kamal[1,2]

[1] Brunel Business School, Brunel University London, Uxbridge, UK
aliano.abbasi@brunel.ac.uk,
muhammad.kamal@coventry.ac.uk
[2] School of Strategy and Leadership, Coventry University, Coventry, UK

Abstract. In today's modern world, societies are utterly attached to internet and technologies to access more information, switching the traditional modes of communication to virtual – all at large scale simultaneously. Governments are using advanced innovative technologies to provide end-to-end integrated public services e.g. in the form of electronic government (e-Government); nevertheless, how effective and efficient their communication with public society are and where citizens engagement has been considered to deliver the services – these still remain unexplored. This developing paper is considering Industry 4.0 (I4.0), Society 5.0 (S5.0), sustainability and circular economy in order to review the impact of I4.0 on manufacturing, what various governments planned to adopt I4.0 technologies within public services and direct communication with citizens. Eventually introducing some of the opportunities, challenges and gaps within citizen's electronic engagement (e-Engagement) which is a term of digital communication between citizens and public decision makers.

Keywords: Industry 4.0 · Society 5.0 electronic citizen engagement · Sustainable development · Circular economy

1 Introduction

A digital transformation road map needed to identify the business opportunities within every cooperation. In the beginning, the organisation needs to draw a clear business objectives, then the organisation should choose effective and potential technologies to be adopted. Such development required a great level of understanding in relevant digital innovations, testing the technologies and analysing the data collection from the simulation process. Eventually the organisation have to priorities their capabilities and understand the benefits the initiatives brings to business such as environmental, social and financial prospective (Savastano et al. 2019). Industry 4.0 strategies and researches have been mainly focused on communication systems within industry digital transformation to develop production line, creating a new business models, collaboration strategies and so on. When it comes to adopting I4.0 within human society, I4.0 benefits the quality of life, human resource development, addressing long term economic stagnation, and creating an opportunity to engage citizens in governments' decision making.

© Springer Nature Switzerland AG 2020
M. Themistocleous and M. Papadaki (Eds.): EMCIS 2019, LNBIP 381, pp. 304–313, 2020.
https://doi.org/10.1007/978-3-030-44322-1_23

The 4th industrial revolution, refers to industrial internet of things (IoT) and cyber physical system (CPS). The value creation would resolve current industries challenges, and establish highly dynamic environment, smart and decentralised automation network, flexibility and customisation, quality standards, proactivity and so on. In the meanwhile, public society and policy makers also expect manufacturers consider triple bottom line sustainability, which are ecological, economic and social dimensions (Birkel et al. 2019), when they adopt technologies in their production process. Therefore the public initiatives and development road map would be studied from every crucial prospective when they observe, learn and apply the innovation within public services.

2   Industrial Revolution

In the mid 18th century, England invented steam engine to replace manual labor work with mechanical production factories to run the production engines. In the second half of 19th century, mass production became the main concept of industries in Europe and America, powered by chemical energies and electricity. Assembly line and automated operation were the technologies of that period of time. These two first industrial revolution development, relied heavily on increasing number of employees and urbanisation. Manufacturing production advanced in late 1960s, owing to the advanced computing, improving optimisation and automation, benefited from programmable virtual control system. Eventually the production line was more efficient and quality improved (Ślusarczyk 2018). Industry 4.0 concept was primarily created In Germany (Beier et al. 2017), adopting Cyber-Physical System (CPS) innovation and smart plant (Lin et al. 2017) in order to maintain the country's leadership within manufacturing and industrial transformation and move toward smart automation by integrating labor and machine within production line. On the other hand, Japan was the first country to adopt I4.0 to actively utilise its robotic technology, speed up the socio-economy and increasing the competitiveness within manufacturing industries.

3   Key Industrial 4.0 Technologies

The main scope of I4.0 technologies are IoT or internet of everything (IoE), including objects and people, Big Data, Robotics, Cloud Computing, Artificial Intelligent, BlockChain, Virtual Reality (3D) and Cyber Security. IoT and CPS systems are the main players in forth industrial revolution (Lin et al. 2017). In I4.0, by benefiting from robots and their connections to computer systems, computers and automation come together to minimise the human input operation. Smart factory is the main concept within I4.0 where CPS integrated with IoT, monitors the physical production line to decentralise decision making in the factory which communicates with the human through the wireless system and web. Following we briefly explain I4.0 concept and the main technologies.

Mohamed (2018) describes the I4.0 main components such as:

- Identification (RFID) and Location which is referred to real time location system (RTLS).
- CPS which is describing the combination of digital with physical workflows.
- IoT which is part of CPS to collect the data in real time, enabling communication capability within several CPSs, also between CPS and users.

On the other hand, the main principles related to I4.0 are:

- Interoperability which describes the connectivity between human, companies and CPS through IoT.
- Service orientation in order to provide software services to the other components.
- Real time capability to respond.
- Security and privacy of data.
- Decentralisation and virtualisation.

3.1 Cyber-Physical System

In general speaking, the definition of Cyber-Physical Systems is the connection and communication between applications or software and digital hardware, via cabled or wireless data infrastructure such as internet or wireless, to monitor and manage production line (Waibel et al. 2017).

3.2 Internet of Things

Internet of Things is a network of computerised devices with unique identification, connected to a computer systems. The interconnection between IoT and CPS is achieved through combination of sensors, software, processor and communication technologies (Kamble et al. 2018).

3.3 Big Data

Big Data analytic and related technologies are aiming to manage the data collected from various sources, analyse and help real time decision making which lead to enhance and improve flexibility, energy efficiency, and quality of product and maintenance prediction (Kamble et al. 2018). Production line will also be able to meet the demand, identifying the potentials to enhance self-optimisation through analysing the big data (Rauch et al. 2017).

3.4 Robots

Robots in human society, assists human to prepare working environment more flexible and ergonomic (Waibel et al. 2017). Robots are built to interact with each other, learning from human to make smart decision and operate in human's unsafe environment (Kamble et al. 2018).

3.5 Additive Manufacturing

Additive Manufacturing (AM) also known as 3D printing, is a digital process adding raw material into 3D printing-data-modeling machine which produce the product through tiny droplet of layer upon layer to shape the product. AM machine will reduce the cost, time, and increase the product's quality. It also has an impact on "supply chain including purchasing, operations, distribution and integration" (Murmura and Bravi 2018).

3.6 Cloud Computing

Cloud computing not only filling the storage gap but also provides vast computing capacity in order to process accumulated data within self-contained environment (Stock et al. 2018). Cloud Computing is one of the main technologies within I4.0 to share data across the organisation boundaries, improving performance through flexibility features and reducing the cost by keeping the system online (Kamble et al. 2018).

3.7 Augmented Reality

Augmented Reality (AR) displays real time data. The real time data helps system, for instance, to track digital objects' accurate location within physical world, as soon as the agent or operator requires such information (Masood and Egger 2019).

4 I4.0 and Sustainability

Industry 4.0 delivers sustainable environment by offering new business models and using smart data to support the operation systems and infrastructure. In order to promote sustainability, refurbishing and recycling patterns are the main elements within life-cycle product management (Gu et al. 2019). Sustainable Development (SD) is one of the most players within Forth Industrial Revolution (Garbie 2017). Linking sustainability development within firms operation and I4.0 will benefit customer's demand in timely manner. Therefore it is crucial to bring innovation within operation management (Shim et al. 2017).

Kamble et al. (2018) introduced I4.0 sustainability's framework, which includes 3 categories:

- Technologies related are Big Data, IoT, Simulation and Prototype, Cloud Competing, 3D Printing, Robotic Systems and Augmented Reality.
- Integration operation includes human-machine collaboration.
- Sustainable result which describe economic, automation operation and safety and environmental protection.

The industry 4.0 implantation will have Technical, Economic, Social and Environmental' impact. Manufacturing firms must adopt technologies network to connect their production with end users and respond quicker on changes but also reduce waste and overproduction in the same time (Waibel et al. 2017). Three of those dimensions mentioned such as environmental, social and economic (excluding technical), can have conflict whilst they are interacting with each other too. I4.0 seems to be a new business model to support business development within organisations and society to appreciate the sustainable development's Concept (Luthra and Mangla 2018).

5   I4.0 and Circular Economy Impact

The circular economy (CE) concept is referred to boosting industrial ecology from open loop to closed loop resources cycle, including promoting renewable energy and direct the production to less wasteful, resulting resource efficiency operation. In order to achieve the CE potential, new business models needed to power up and integrate sustainable development within economic, technological and environmental. Lifetime extension either through service or maintenance, reduction, reuse, remanufacturing and recycling are the main CE principals which are linked to waste management by European commission (Jensen and Remmen 2017). CE principal in practice help increasing Gross Domestic Product (GDP) within European Union countries to 11%, which comes with net benefit of 1.8 trillion by 2030 and resource saving by 1 trillion USD (Bressanelli et al. 2018). Implementing CE is designed in 3 different level within their scale of analysis: micro, meso and macro. CE in micro level is dealing with single company. In meso level several companies collaborate to create eco-industrial parks. The macro scale is establishing an expanded view contains CE implementation within cities, regions and countries (Bressanelli et al. 2018).

For instance, CE concept is going to be expanded within leasing product is benefiting environment directly alongside with reduce waste and consuming raw materials. This type of business model called Servitized Business Model (SBM) aiming to strengthening consumer relation, improving market competition and create new revenue stream for businesses (Bressanelli et al. 2018). Combining I4.0 innovations such as IoT, 3D printing, Big Data, Data Analytics, Virtual and augmented reality and etc., would massively benefit advanced management toward circular economy, and with such processed information, outcome would be sustainability-oriented decision making procedure. However, it is not fully cleared yet, how technologies would impact circular economy within economic, business and social prospective (Rajput and Singh 2019). Although, I4.0 is major player to build a route toward sustainability, but how industries need to act technologically toward sustainable operations and gain circular economy (Rajput and Singh 2019).

6   I4.0 Issues and Challenges

Industry 4.0 delivers prediction to the business operation in order to take an appropriate action before facing the challenges. This will give manufacturers a road map what to do next (Waibel et al. 2017). However, there is still uncertainty about the consequences when it comes to the operation level, although the author claims that late adopters within I4.0 will be forced out of the market. Big Data is the other main challenges as the data collection would be from abundance of sources in relation to the operation in a smart production system (Waibel et al. 2017). I4.0 needs intelligence structure such as worldwide data sharing protocols and standards to collect and process the data which needs preconditions protocols to respect data owners (Rajput and Singh 2019). Also data security must be maintained within I4.0 technologies networks and throughout the value chain to avoid security vulnerability and system attacking.

Luthra and Mangla (2018) describes other risks within I4.0 implementing are:

- Lack of appropriate definition and understanding of every I4.0 elements by both researchers and practitioners.
- Applying digitalisation requires digital culture for business environment to adopt I4.0.
- Economic benefit uncertainty within digital investment.
- Global standards and protocol needed for data transaction.
- Poor internet based network infrastructure.
- Lack of ability to adopt new business models.
- Lack of high quality data.
- Lack of technology integration.
- Lack of government policies and support.

7   I4.0 and Government Impact

All countries all pushing innovation to adopt technologies faster, in order to respond to the new business model which involves different society management and human role. Telecommunication industry is particularly the main ICT industry on the supply side with its high potential linkage (Min et al. 2019). Big open data policy innovation along with its related technologies and application have been increasingly adopted both at local and central government in all levels. Public sector bodies responsible to collect, generate, monitor and publish the data online. However, limited attention has been given on how these new innovative ideas can gain prominence on government plan within public sector (Khurshid et al. 2019). Big Open Data (BOD) has various advantages to improve economic growth such as commercialising product and services, increasing employment opportunity, government taxing revenue, productivity and smooth operation. Adopting BOD's would benefit public ability to have e-Engagement with government, but also improving the quality of citizens' life.

The data quality and transparency of citizens and users increases more, whenever human interference decrease within data collection process. Therefore, I4.0 will help to feed national data base with reliable information (Bonilla et al. 2018). However some of BOD challenges within public administration are related to data management and fostering public trust and interest to share or use and control the quality of data. Also governments traditionally reluctance in publishing data in large scale whilst there is lack of effective communication between citizens and most governments, within public decision making's set of policies. For instance, citizens in the UK make millions of calls every year panicking whether their application had submitted successfully or the payment has been received by the government. The UK is trying to reducing such contact to its contact center. The government claims "We want to transform the way citizens communicate with government" (UK Digital Strategy 2017). But the question here is whether the government fully understood what society needs are to be more proactive by delivering a fundamental digital and political services which meet public demands?

8 Society 5.0

Japanese government cabinet office published a document in 2017 to prepare society for I4.0, its elaboration and the issues that might face through this transformation (Riminucci 2018). It is included explaining several challenges such as long term economy stagnation. "Society 5.0" paradigm is not only integrated industries but also considering society within industry 4.0 innovation and human resource improvement. The highlights are included creating standards and policies for human resource development in order to increase individual working skills such as standardise IT skills' revision, cooperation and collaboration among governments, academia, private sector industries, aiming working skills development, workers IT skill's expansion, the formation of IT specialists for the industry leadership and IT education in primary school specifically programming.

The concept is also enhancing the working style for improvement in innovation and productivity. The plan creates an ambitious working environment by adding new amendments to the current policies such as discovering diversity and flexibility at work, limiting long hours, accepting and promoting side jobs, increasing wages, supporting young workers in their carrier and promote employment of disable workers. However, employing foreign workers, robots implementation and information exchange between public administration and citizens, have been expected to investigate more in the future (Riminucci 2018).

Japanese government "Society 5.0" is aimed to create first super smart cyber-physical society which means more human centered than what currently most societies are (Gladden 2019). This human centered society is surrounded by rapidly innovative technologies such as social robots, Internet of Things, Augmented and Virtual Reality, advanced computer-human interface, artificial agent, and other artificial operations which as intelligent enough to learn, make decision and behave accordingly by themselves instead of being passive and getting controlled by human operator all the time. This type of smart society paradigm links physical world with cyber space by maximised capacity of information communication technologies (Government of Japan 2016).

9 I4.0 and Citizens' Impact

Industry 4.0 development is promising an interaction between virtual world and physical space which in other word, it is virtual space, technology (networking) and human (Gladden 2019). Such interaction is not only meet citizens' livelihood and care they needed to survive, but it is also a "guarantee citizens' richness in minds and high-quality way of life" (Gladden 2019). The Society 5.0 demonstrate a vision of a high-tech society network in the future where new innovative technologies such as robots,

Artificial Intelligence and virtual entities (3D) will create human e-engagement in society through a rich and beneficial way. One of barriers adopting technologies implementation is the negative impact the innovation has on users, and their distrust on using the technology. The level of success within the technology's implementation could be measured by users, based on witnessing the technology's potential in its service delivery and its willingness to adopt the ongoing enhancement and development. End users will be pursue further involvement with the technology if they convinced by the firm's efforts to overcome the barriers in every prospective (Masood and Egger 2019). Piccarozzi et al. (2018) claimed the organisations and companies by adopting correct and appropriate approaches "as the result of purposely formulated strategy" could improve the welfare and quality of human life in society along with helping to establish enhanced sustainability.

10 Research Gap

53% of EU citizens believe that their voice and wishes are not heard (Bruno 2015). Despite on the percentage improvement in 2013, only half of EU citizens believe their vote in European Election is impacting political decision making in comparison with the result of 70% of same outcome within their countries' local and national level. However EU citizens still looking to find a way directly impacting decision making at EU level through participation on online/offline petition and also expressing their idea and concerns on social media and internet. EU recommends citizens online involvement by highlights the importance of digital technologies and creating an easy-to-use platform to engage as many citizens as possible in design policies, connect the platform with social media and also deliver offline activities to engage citizens who have lack of IT skills (Bruno 2015). The question remains, how the I4.0 innovation would impact the channel of communication between citizens and public administration and how this bridge would impact citizens e-engagement within public administration decision making.

In other hand, despite on opportunities and promising that I4.0 innovations bring to deliver a sustainable environment, there are still challenges and barriers which have not been fully addressed, such as uncertainty in "to what extent, with which delay, and at which stage of deployment the digitisation of industrial production will promote or hinder transformations that will affect environmental sustainability" (Bonilla et al. 2018).

11 Conclusions

This paper has studied industry 4.0, society 5.0, sustainability and circular economy, identifying the necessity of adopting I4.0 technologies in citizens' e-engagement, in order to help creating an ideology which adopting I4.0 technology to reduce complexity through public service delivery, increase transparency in decision making process and address public demands in more effective way. The concept needs to consider environmental, social and economic sustainability within the policy making.

This will fill a necessary public engagement paradigm within public administration's service delivery. In order to prove the ideology, previous investigations was studied to learn the concept's keywords, main players and where those elements make a link. The research was also reviewed industry 4.0 adoption within manufacturing to learn the possibilities and opportunities of such innovation within public service engagement. Limited number of academic and governments publication plan, to adopt I4.0 technologies within citizens' engagement in policy making and public service delivery, is the paper's main barrier.

References

Bányai, T., Tamás, P., Illés, B., Stankevičiūtė, Ž., Bányai, Á.: Optimization of municipal waste collection routing: impact of industry 4.0 technologies on environmental awareness and sustainability. Int. J. Environ. Res. Public Health 16(4), 634 (2019)

Bednar, P.M., Welch, C.: Socio-technical perspectives on smart working: creating meaningful and sustainable systems. Inf. Syst. Front., 1–18 (2019). https://doi.org/10.1007/s10796-019-09921-1

Beier, G., Niehoff, S., Ziems, T., Xue, B.: Sustainability aspects of a digitalized industry–a comparative study from China and Germany. Int. J. Precis. Eng. Manuf. Green Technol. 4(2), 227–234 (2017)

Birkel, H.S., Veile, J.W., Müller, J.M., Hartmann, E., Voigt, K.I.: Development of a risk framework for Industry 4.0 in the context of sustainability for established manufacturers. Sustainability 11(2), 384 (2019)

Bonilla, S., Silva, H., da Silva, M.T., Franco Gonçalves, R., Sacomano, J.: Industry 4.0 and sustainability implications: a scenario-based analysis of the impacts and challenges. Sustainability 10(10), 3740 (2018)

Bressanelli, G., Adrodegari, F., Perona, M., Saccani, N.: Exploring how usage-focused business models enable circular economy through digital technologies. Sustainability 10(3), 639 (2018)

Bruno, E.: Co-deciding with citizens: towards digital democracy at EU level. ECAS Brussels (2015)

Ding, B.: Pharma industry 4.0: literature review and research opportunities in sustainable pharmaceutical supply chains. Process Saf. Environ. Prot. 119, 115–130 (2018)

Garbie, I.H.: Incorporating sustainability/sustainable development concepts in teaching industrial systems design courses. Procedia Manuf. 8, 417–423 (2017)

Gladden, M.E.: Who will be the members of Society 5.0? Towards an anthropology of technologically posthumanized future societies. Soc. Sci. 8(5), 148 (2019)

Government of Japan: The 5th Science and Technology Basic Plan, Provisional translation (2016). https://www8.cao.go.jp/cstp/english/basic/5thbasicplan.pdf. Accessed 15 Aug 2019

Gu, F., Guo, J., Hall, P., Gu, X.: An integrated architecture for implementing extended producer responsibility in the context of Industry 4.0. Int. J. Prod. Res. 57(5), 1458–1477 (2019)

Kamble, S.S., Gunasekaran, A., Gawankar, S.A.: Sustainable Industry 4.0 framework: a systematic literature review identifying the current trends and future perspectives. Process Saf. Environ. Prot. 117, 408–425 (2018)

Khurshid, M.M., Zakaria, N.H., Rashid, A., Kazmi, R., Shafique, M.N., Ahmad, M.N.: Analyzing diffusion patterns of big open data as policy innovation in public sector. Comput. Electr. Eng. 78, 148–161 (2019)

Jensen, J.P., Remmen, A.: Enabling circular economy through product stewardship. Procedia Manuf. **8**, 377–384 (2017)

Li, B., Zhao, Z., Guan, Y., Ai, N., Dong, X., Wu, B.: Task placement across multiple public clouds with deadline constraints for smart factory. IEEE Access **6**, 1560–1564 (2017)

Lin, K., Shyu, J., Ding, K.: A cross-strait comparison of innovation policy under Industry 4.0 and sustainability development transition. Sustainability **9**(5), 786 (2017)

Luthra, S., Mangla, S.K.: Evaluating challenges to Industry 4.0 initiatives for supply chain sustainability in emerging economies. Process Saf. Environ. Prot. **117**, 168–179 (2018)

Masood, T., Egger, J.: Augmented reality in support of Industry 4.0—implementation challenges and success factors. Rob. Comput. Integr. Manuf. **58**, 181–195 (2019)

Min, Y.K., Lee, S.G., Aoshima, Y.: A comparative study on industrial spillover effects among Korea, China, the USA, Germany and Japan. Ind. Manag. Data Syst. **119**(3), 454–472 (2019)

Mohamed, M.: Challenges and benefits of Industry 4.0: an overview. Int. J. Supply Oper. Manag. **5**(3), 256–265 (2018)

Murmura, F., Bravi, L.: Additive manufacturing in the wood-furniture sector: sustainability of the technology, benefits and limitations of adoption. J. Manuf. Technol. Manag. **29**(2), 350–371 (2018)

Piccarozzi, M., Aquilani, B., Gatti, C.: Industry 4.0 in management studies: a systematic literature review. Sustainability **10**(10), 3821 (2018)

Rajput, S., Singh, S.P.: Industry 4.0 − challenges to implement circular economy. Benchmarking Int. J. (2019)

Rauch, E., Dallasega, P., Matt, D.T.: Distributed manufacturing network models of smart and agile mini-factories. Int. J. Agile Syst. Manag. **10**(3–4), 185–205 (2017)

Savastano, M., Amendola, C., Bellini, F., D'Ascenzo, F.: Contextual impacts on industrial processes brought by the digital transformation of manufacturing: a systematic review. Sustainability **11**(3), 891 (2019)

Shim, S.O., Park, K., Choi, S.: Innovative production scheduling with customer satisfaction based measurement for the sustainability of manufacturing firms. Sustainability **9**(12), 2249 (2017)

Ślusarczyk, B.: Industry 4.0: are we ready? Pol. J. Manag. Stud. **17**(1), 232–248 (2018)

Stock, T., Obenaus, M., Kunz, S., Kohl, H.: Industry 4.0 as enabler for a sustainable development: a qualitative assessment of its ecological and social potential. Process Saf. Environ. Prot. **118**, 254–267 (2018)

Tsai, W.H., Lu, Y.H.: A framework of production planning and control with carbon tax under Industry 4.0. Sustainability **10**(9), 3221 (2018)

UK Digital Strategy: Digital government - maintaining the UK government as a world leader in serving its citizens online, Department for Digital, Culture, Media and Sport (2017). https://www.gov.uk/government/publications/uk-digital-strategy/6-digital-government-maintaining-the-uk-government-as-a-world-leader-in-serving-its-citizens-online. Accessed 21 Aug 2019

Waibel, M.W., Steenkamp, L.P., Moloko, N., Oosthuizen, G.A.: Investigating the effects of smart production systems on sustainability elements. Procedia Manuf. **8**, 731–737 (2017)

HealthCare Information Systems

The Case for mHealth Standardization for Electronic Health Records in the German Healthcare System

Max-Marcel Theilig[1]([⊠]), Johannes Werner[1], Florian Schoffke[2],
and Rüdiger Zarnekow[1]

[1] Chair of Information and Communication Management,
Technische Universität Berlin, Berlin, Germany
{m.theilig, johannes.werner,
ruediger.zarnekow}@tu-berlin.de
[2] Technische Universität Berlin, Berlin, Germany

Abstract. New impulses for the development of an electronic health record in Germany were given with passing the *Terminservice- und Verordnungsgesetz*. Looking into adjacent legislative work, we find that the existent international standard for Fast Healthcare Interoperability Resources (FHIR) is not sufficient and consequently, German FHIR objects (gFR) are mandatory. Therefore, we investigate the necessity and capability of this German format and evaluate the interaction with current health interfaces. Hence, an app prototype was developed to assess the ability for mobile use and integration with *Apple HealthKit*. We find, the use of gFRs and electronic health records prevents media discontinuity and has the potential to improve patient care and empowerment. We recommend that developing gFRs according to FHIR should be done in the following order: Medication, Clinical, Diagnostics, Workflow, Finance. Proceeding with clinical and diagnostic gFRs according to population prevalence, has best chances for quick, yet sustainable, success.

Keywords: Electronic health records · Mobile Health · Standardization · FHIR · Design science

1 Introduction

The German healthcare system is one of the strongest growing sectors in Germany. In 2016, spending of about 356.5 billion Euro was tracked, making up for a share of 11.3% of GDP. Projections for 2018 are 370 billion and more than 12% of the GDP respectively [1]. However, the number of hospitals as well as available working hours for physicians is shrinking [1, 2], leading to issues in the clinical and out-patient sectors.

But especially when patients are provided with their own health data, chances of recovery or to maintain a positive state of health are improved. E.g. using electronic health record (EHR) for the case of diabetes was shown to lead to significantly improved healthcare service [3]. Therefore, enabling technologies carry certain advantages for patients and the healthcare sector in general. Since a variety of

M. Themistocleous and M. Papadaki (Eds.): EMCIS 2019, LNBIP 381, pp. 317–330, 2020.
https://doi.org/10.1007/978-3-030-44322-1_24

applications are supposed to interact with an EHR and electronic devices being used in all countries around the world, an international standard is in demand. This standard would be able to increase interoperability, homogeneity, and availability of data in the healthcare system.

As early as 1987 an American organization named *Health Level Seven* (HL7) started to work on communications standards in medicine [4]. The most recent version 4 of the HL7 Fast Healthcare Interoperability Resources (FHIR) offers various opportunities for potential application in the German healthcare system [5]. With the use of FHIR it is possible to provide an EHR allocating comprehensive data and information on medical, financial, and administrative matters for all stakeholders within the healthcare system. This provision and standardization is supposed to save costs and improve integration across domain healthcare [6]. Therefore, enabling the patients to carry their health relevant data conveniently, e.g. via smartphone, has the potential to be beneficial for the mobile Health (mHealth) sector in specific.

Due to the *Terminservice- und Versorgungsgesetz* that was put into effect in May 2019 [7], the German health insurance funds are obligated to provide insurees with an EHR that is officially approved by the *Society of Telematik* (*gematik*) by 2021. To allow for modular expandability following § 291a Abs. 5c SGB V [8], a broadly compatible EHR is in need of a uniform format. Therefore, this format has to comply with German legislation, consider international standards and will become mandatory once this EHR is available [7]. Supposedly derived from HL7 FHIR, to have a most common ground, it represents a composition of German FHIR objects (gFRs).

Towards this end, this work depicts the data exchange between patient and physician with such an EHR to investigate the appropriateness of gFRs that are currently under development. Implied advantages and obstacles of the implementation will be discussed. Furthermore, by the interaction with a health API we derive perspectives for users and potential developers. Since the German market is largely dominated by the Apple and Google smartphone ecosystems [9], we follow a mobile first approach. Accordingly, our work will be visualized by an app prototype. The developed functions resemble the create, read, update, and delete (CRUD) operations and interaction will be simulated with the *Apple HealthKit*. To test validation against a specified EHR standard of a FHIR server, we chose the use cases of vaccination and blood sugar.

2   Methodology

To explore an effective contribution, theoretical background and related work are systematically assessed and a possible approach is developed. This venture does not only call for an inquiry on scientific literature, but also for relevant legislative work. After developing a basic understanding of the German healthcare system, the required gFRs are then used to show that our prototype is able to reduce media discontinuities and improve patient care when implemented in a mobile EHR.

In order to achieve this goal, we utilize Hevner's three cycle view of design science research [10, 11]. To guide the creation, evaluation, and presentation of the prototype, the approach proposes to learn about the problem first. Then, design a draft, which is concurrently and conclusively evaluated. In accordance with design science research methodology (see Fig. 1) [12], a viable artifact in the form of a system architecture design, a mobile application, a graphical web frontend, and recommendations on how to proceed is developed. Feasibility checks made against recent public media discussion are used for assessing outcomes and assuring relevance. For a rigor outcome, we aim at giving further recommendations or insights that might build the foundation for future research or provide a practical roadmap. Finally, this work communicates the steps of the process, guidelines for moving forward, insights and outlooks.

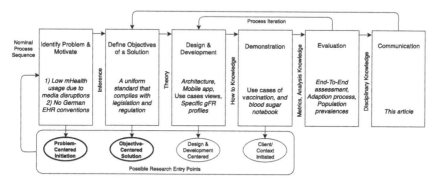

Fig. 1. The design science approach adopted from Peffers et al. [12] and adjusted to context

3   Background and Related Work

As the first country worldwide, Germany introduced a national health insurance policy in 1883. Already back then, health insurance funds were organized in self-governing. The lawmakers declared legislative constraints and regulations, while the health insurance funds were free to define premiums and health benefits [13]. These principles still exist and were even expanded by various executive organs. In addition, we find a strict inter-sectoral divide of the in- and out-patients that sustains until now.

The federal ministry and its associated institutes (e.g. *Bundeszentrale für gesundheitliche Aufklärung*, or *Robert Koch Institut*) carry the duty of supervision and assure homogenization on a national level. The health insurance funds cooperate on an executive level to carry out treatment and administrative tasks. These collaborations include (1) the *Spitzenverband der Krankenkassen*, (2) the *Kassen[zahn]ärztliche Bundesvereinigung* (K[Z]BV), and (3) the *Deutsche Krankenhausgesellschaft* [13]. The public bodies each send members into the largest organ of self-government, the *Gemeinsamer Bundesausschuss* (GBA). The *GBA* develops guidance on areas of coverage, the reimbursement catalogue, evaluation of health technologies, and regulates the disease management programs for improved evidence based health care [13]. Various sub-organs on a regional level exist, like one *Kassenärztliche Vereinigung* (KV) for any given state authority. This fragmentation is only one reason for media discontinuities, since there was neither a common integration approach, nor a wide attempt to connect information systems.

As early as in the 1960's IBM developed one of the first information technology (IT) systems for hospitals, while systems for the out-patients followed a few years later [14]. Since then, health IT systems have come a long way. The electronic settlement for health services became mandatory in Germany in 2009, and the term eHealth was coined, describing the application of information and communication technologies in health related activities [15]. Hence, the fields of application multiplied over the years, expanding to e.g. telemedicine, telemonitoring, mobile Health (mHealth), decision support systems, and many more. Nowadays, patients are at the center of eHealth applications, due to smartphones being able to gather and process health relevant data. The Commonwealth Fund is a private foundation putting EHR implementation into an international perspective [16]. Interestingly, none of the 19 compared nations has a national uniform EHR that is sued by health insurance funds, healthcare providers, and patients. Denmark seems to have the state of the art, were all data standards are described, with the slight notion that systems to write health data are only on a regional level. The best practice seems to be homogenizing health care provider systems first, while enabling patient access is the last step. The primary goal is to cut costs and improve provided health care. Adverse examples could be China or Canada, where almost every health insurance fund developed its own solution. No standards exist, and hence, cooperation is scarce. When any form of gFRs are specified and legislation is implemented as intended, Germany could rank in a top spot, according to that list [16].

3.1 Technical Environment

The EHR in general contains data and documents that are generated within the healthcare system and are, therefore, mostly disease related. In contrast to that, the electronic health card carries core data about the patient himself, e.g. age, insurance coverage. But it will possibly be extended with patients' context data like nutrition.

The FHIR standard employs the REST paradigm for data exchange, which describes the client server connections [17, 18]. Here, the server offers a REST API to which the client can send CRUD requests via HTTP protocol using a path-like structure. This gives the advantage of full server-client decoupling so that the development can be independent. Furthermore, REST is stateless, resulting in saved resources, and increased performance as well as scalability. REST is a widely adopted paradigm in industry and research [18].

With more than 80 million inhabitants in Germany and a non-optional health insurance, no single point of contact would be able to account for the amount of data. Thus, a standard for medical data interoperability is necessary. Three categories of interoperability are separated [14]: (1) Transport Interoperability, referring to exchanging data similarly in regards to the medium (e.g. Fax, Email, HTTP), (2) Structured Interoperability, defining how the data is setup or segmented, and (3) Semantic Interoperability, as a high-level view of interoperability, which does not only define the structure of data, but also its meaning. FHIR has inherited transport and structure interoperability from REST, while semantics originate from standardized data models and terminologies. Within FHIR so called FHIR resources are exchanged and at the time of this work about 140 different resources were defined and grouped into the categories: foundation, base, clinical, financial, and specialized. While FHIR offers XML, JSON, and Turtle (RDF) as concrete formats, yet a FHIR server, depending on its implementation, might be limited. Since HL7 is engaged for years within the healthcare sector, older versions, named differently, are used by various software products. But products are believed to use only about 10 of 300 version two objects [19], while acceptance of FHIR seems to be more popular. At least in the U.S., where about 82% of clinical software system and 64% of out-patients physicians support FHIR [20].

3.2 Related Work

While there are indicators that the smartphone market saturation is soaring, its introduction simplified many aspects of daily life and data access. Due to the possibility to get data from the internet when on the go, it is also possible to access, view, and analyze health data. EHRs in Germany, and therefore medical health data integration, are still on hold as described but adjacent relevant research exists internationally or on related subjects. For instance, telemonitoring, the mean of delivering remote diagnosis and therapy, was investigated in a literature review with over 1400 studies [21], and showed immense potential for patients.

EHR and mHealth. Marceglia et al. [22] discuss a standardized approach integrating EHRs with mHealth apps, using not FHIR but the XML CDA2 format. Clinical Document Architecture (CDA) is a data standard that can visualize medical documents similar to HTML. The *Apple HealthKit* in specific has proven to be suitable [23], while especially older age groups could benefit from such mHealth services [24]. Furthermore, studies have investigated the interplay of EHRs and mHealth, depicted a scenario based on the processing of blood sugar measurements and forwarding them to the *Apple HealthKit* [25]. The physician was able to view the data on short notice and that lead to more and improved therapy adjustments. Gay and Leijdekkers [26] describe how an mHealth app might be used to aggregate health data to reach interoperability. They developed an Android app that was able to accumulate data from different sensors and generate a holistic health impression.

FHIR. Proof of concept has been made for specific use cases of FHIR applications for smartphones, e.g. by [27]. In that study, patients were instructed to use an EHR app to get an overview of their vaccinations, while the use data was utilized to optimize clinical processes. Re-using an existing EHR for the integration with *Substitutable Medical Apps and Reusable Technologies* (SMART) seems convenient [28]. SMART apps are based on FHIR and were designed as modules to enable fast replacements of health records. As a result, EHRs were able to utilize various other applications to process and visualize patient data, and the potential for using SMART was shown [26]. Our work consequently is an inter-technological approach with all the introduced technologies and concepts (e.g. *Apple HealthKit*, FHIR, and mHealth) to investigate, and eventually demonstrate the fit of gFRs for the German EHR interoperability.

3.3 Exploratory Work for German FHIR Resources

HL7 employs an 80/20 principle in its FHIR standard. That means FHIR is supposed to cover about 80% of use cases, while 20% of specifications might be extended to local or application specific needs. gFRs, as we define them, follow similar design principles as FHIR profiles. Multiple FHIR resources may be bundled in such.

Due to growing attention, there already is a German branch of HL7 (www.hl7.de), that promotes the FHIR standard and lobbies on behalf of German interests on an international level. We identified the need for specific adjustments as follows. In accordance with § 22 IfSG [29], a vaccination entry explicitly has to contain the following information: (1) date of appliance, (2) vaccination term, (3) identity and local of implementing physician, (4) signature of implementation physician. Furthermore, the patient has to be informed about side-effects, rights, and responsibilities (compare §§ 60 to 64 IfSG [34]). The vaccination record should provide a text field for proposed future vaccination refreshments. Fields in the according international FHIR profile are all optional and in arbitrary order. Hence, for the German derivative a cardinality had to be introduced, and a disclaimer to account for medical clarification was added.

4   Prototype Implementation

The aforementioned prototype was developed for iOS using *Apple HealthKit* to simulate the data exchanged in FHIR format with constraints given by the proposed gFRs. A website, which served as a graphical user interface, is the pendant to a clinical information system (CIS) here but shall not be described in more detail.

4.1   Application System Architecture

The app was developed following the idea of the model view controller pattern, and therefore every view depicts the corresponding function that is possible for that data. While that is not particularly user friendly, it segments necessary functions and helps investigating them. The developed architecture components and their interactions for the used scenarios are shown in Fig. 2. They explain the functions and possibilities for our solution and for potential gFRs to interact with the *Apple HealthKit*.

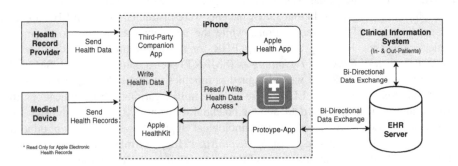

Fig. 2. Scenario architecture

Apple iOS contains an app to record and analyze medical data per default, the *Health App*. For instance, a patient is able to gather his blood sugar level in this app. Devices with Bluetooth are able, without user action, to write data via a companion app. Since the *Apple HealthKit* works as a uniform interface it is very suitable for developers of additional services.

The functionality for health records is integrated in the *Health App* as a module, that was introduced by Apple in 2018. At the moment they are only available in the U.S. and about 300 American health providers are able to send patient health results via these health records. That includes for instance laboratory results of a blood analysis, which the user is able to view in the familiar graphics of its iOS device. Hence, these Health Records are the Apple variant of an EHR. Interestingly, Apple provides the user with the original FHIR entry so that it is possible to have a look at what health insurance funds put in what field. However, in general these health records are read-only, and for Germany, Apple even only provides sample records via the Xcode simulator in macOS. For access to the medical data, the user first has to authorize the *HealthKit Store*.

The user then is shown a view provided by Apple to specifically grant access to the data he wants the respective app to use. When this process is done, reading and writing data is possible via queries. Deleting or changing data is only possible from the same app, i.e. one app cannot delete or change the data generated by another app. Therefore, the *HealthKit* is a solid and secure way of writing data with a 3rd party device, through a custom app, or by the user itself via the *Apple Health* app.

The prototype app was developed intended as a client for a FHIR server, which also acts as an EHR validation tool. Therefore, no data was saved on the device itself, but requested from the Server, written into *HealthKit*, and visualized. For a convenient user experience and reasons of efficiency, data might be saved on the device. This requires only new or modified data to synchronize and is beneficial when the amount of data is increasing. These remote data sources are visualized by *Bi-Directional Data Exchange* in Fig. 2. As last item, the CIS represents a various number of possible participants from the healthcare sector: clinics, doctors' offices, pharmacies.

4.2   Vaccination and Blood Sugar Scenarios

The scenarios chosen for our app are vaccination and blood sugar since as of today, communication between patient and doctor happen predominately via paper. Delay of time between vaccination may be significant so that the patient is not able to find the immunization card anymore. While on the other hand that data has to be available on short notice, even when it comes to minor incisions that carry the possibility for tetanus. For blood sugar related diseases, it is the other extreme in the sense that patients have to keep track of many protocolary measurements since glucose levels may change significantly within short windows of time. Therefore, patients keep track of glucose levels in a notebook, which is used by the physician for monitoring and adjusting medication (i.e. insulin).

While many scenarios are in focus of recent public discussions, we investigated the creation, exchange, and processing of vaccination entries with the use of preliminary specified gFRs, derived from the FHIR standard. The app was able to read and write data from the *Health Store* of the *Apple HealthKit*. Synchronization with the FHIR server was possible in every direction. Hence, the data was available to patients and physicians on a consistent basis. We find that the implementation of the FHIR server will be key, since it is able to do a validation of given data against a proposed schema. Since a standard implementation of the FHIR server was used, validation failed due to adjusted FHIR entries that did not fit the international standard anymore.

The case of blood sugar tracking was primarily used to investigate the necessity for new on-device entry generation, in the home or an individual environment. After generating the new measurement records according to the given FHIR template, the record is sent to the FHIR server via a standard post-request. After validation on the FHIR server, the CIS is able to pull the entry from the FHIR server and provide access to this, and possible historic entries, to the physician. Since JSON is a very common format, processing and visualization was very easy, and might be implemented for different technologies (i.e. Android) in a similar fashion. Simply that mean of generating valid data poses a significant benefit for the system.

Generating new entries might be particularly interesting for data acquisition tasks that take place in the private or home environment, like for the use case of tracking blood sugar levels in a notebook. Unfortunately, that notebook has to be maintained very regularly, carried to the doctor's office, and transcribing values to another system is very prone to errors. Electronic transmission reduces errors and saves time. Additionally, ahead of a scheduled appointment the physician is able to look into the data and do an ad-hoc evaluation. If the purpose was related to medication tuning, which then shows to be unnecessary, he may give the patient a positive feedback and cancel or postpone the appointment. This reduces stress and burden for patients and doctors alike.

4.3 Application Views

Authentication and authorization are an essential factor for security, especially for sensible data. Hence, the app carries a login screen that could function as a selector for different EHR providers, i.e. health insurance funds in a later iteration. After login the app is granted access to all necessary data from the chosen end point. Available functions (i.e. gFRs) of the EHR have been realized with a tab bar. For the vaccination case the most interesting views for the prototype are depicted in Fig. 3.

The *personal gFRs* view displays all available distinct gFRs for the patient, and part of the EHR. Here, that is vaccinations and blood sugar measurements (top left screen in Fig. 3). A more detailed view for one specific diagnosis, e.g. for the *Vaccination View*, is available on the next tab. This view gives an overview of related FHIR records, here for instance, an entry for Measles from the 30th of November, or an entry for Vericella from the 12th of April. On the next level there is a visualization of the concrete FHIR details with according fields, and it is also possible to add an entry on its own with the *New Entry View*. In this scenario, this option becomes relevant for the case of Influenza immunizations, which are also given at the place of work in Germany. To differentiate, a source of origin was implemented, here *primarySource*, or *reportOrigin*. More cascading sub views, depending on the use case, are easily implementable.

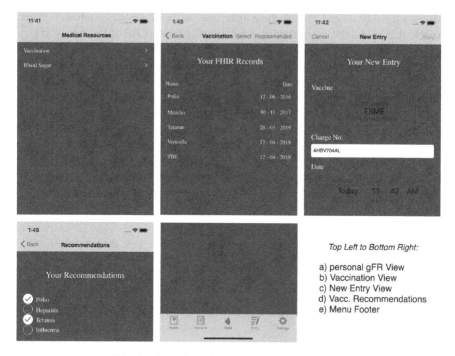

Fig. 3. App views for the gFR vaccination case

As a best practice for a meta-function, the *Vaccination Recommendations* were implemented. The patient can see what immunizations he might lack according to national or environmental requirements (e.g. by the RKI). Analog, cascading views for supplementary information are possible. The potential user is able to maneuver the EHR app, adjust settings, or log out via an appropriate footer.

5 Evaluation

For the chosen use cases we were able to proof the concept for a mobile EHR on iOS with integration into the *Apple HealthKit*. Especially the FHIR data structure with JSON was very convenient, as multiple third party libraries provide parsing and generation of such JSON structures, here smart-on-fhir [30]. FHIR supports all kinds of data, even media data, to be sent to mobile devices. That holds the potential for even further information, visualization, and explanation for the users. Hence, we find potential for an increased user engagement which is believed to support a better recovery and improved therapy outcome [31].

5.1 Population Prevalence and Implementation Proposal

Due to the given time schedule we assume that the assigned public organs have already started developing a certification process for gFRs. Nonetheless, questions remain what obstacles might be ahead and if there is a way of prioritizing, or another general approach, that is optimal for achieving a functionally broad EHR at the date of release. HL7 already suggests some kind of roadmap for the implementation [32]. That roadmap has 5 levels: Foundation, Supporting Implementation, Administration, Record-Keeping, and Clinical Reasoning.

Following § 291a Abs 5c SGB V [8], the *gematik* was assigned with deploying the necessary infrastructure and technical feasibility for the EHR. Hence, level 1 to 3 are a concern for the so called *Telematik Infrastruktur*. Since level 5 resources are not necessary for daily operations, but have more of an add-on character, health insurance funds should focus on the sequence of deploying gFRs to their EHR. Questions remain if for these gFRs a roadmap matching German specifications is ideal. Therefore, an implementation sequence based on the level 4 modules of FHIR, displayed in Fig. 4, is proposed.

Fig. 4. Recommended gFR implementation sequence for level 4: Record-Keeping

Starting with the module of *Medication* seems mandatory, due to the draft for a new legislation regarding more safety in medication provision, that requires that the *gematik* is to introduce means that enable the transmission of medical e-prescriptions by June 30th 2020 [33]. Otherwise, another round of changes to integrate that e- prescription for the EHR, due by Jan 1st 2021, would be required. For a practical EHR the succeeding *Clinical* and *Diagnostics* gFRs are required. The *Clinical* module carries supplementary information about a patient like allergies, pre-conditions, or family plans, and the *Diagnostics* carries previous and recent anamneses. It has to be stressed, that these (2 & 3) are the main modules for the daily operations of the healthcare system in any given scenario. Therefore, they should be released in a short window of time, ideally parallel. Their interdependences have to be taken into account.

After these fundamental modules, the *Workflow* should be deployed, thereby enabling a more connected case management with appointments, nurse tasks, referrals to specialists, and alike. Most of these processes are already supported today, so that primarily integrative work is expected. Finally, the *Finance* module should be addressed. It allows for creation, exchange, and clearance of claims within the healthcare system.

The *Clinical* and *Diagnostics* modules are related to the population prevalence and gFRs addressing most prevalent diseases could cover the demand to process according data efficiently. Table 1 shows the biggest disease groups in Germany [34], and gives ICD and distribution examples for the insurance fund area of Nordrhein [35], which we look at as a recent surrogate (Q1 2019) for the epidemiology. Hence, this data allows for conclusions on what gFRs potentially will be used to the biggest extend.

Table 1. Top 5 disease groups by patients with ICD examples and according group shares of the KV Nordrhein region. Disease groups from 2015 [34], and ICD from Q1 2019 [35].

Rank	(Mio. PT)	Disease group	Exemplary ICD	ICD share
1	(36.7)	Musculoskeletal system	M54	17.3%
2	(35.1)	Respiratory system	J06	12.7%
3	(29.5)	Metabolic disorder	E78	23.3%
4	(28.5)	Cardiovascular system	I10	34.4%
5	(25.6)	Behavioral disorder	F32	10.6%

Those diseases are in need for a broad list of data collection activities, that can in the future be carried out by patients with a mobile device as well as transferred to the physician with electronic means. Such data includes information about pre-existing conditions, stress at work, or bad sleep but also parameters that are specific to the diagnosis. For cardiovascular problems, vital parameter like blood pressure and heart rate have to be investigated ahead of treatment, similar to the blood sugar use case. Metabolic disorders are also largely examined by consecutive blood work and require circadian notes. And at least nowadays, diagnosing back pain (e.g. *ICD* M54) or a depressive disorder (e.g. *ICD* F32) requires a lot of descriptive interaction with a physician. It is noteworthy that most of these diseases are treated with medication, for which entrainment is required.

6 Conclusion

We developed a proof of concept EHR and showed that integration with modern standards like REST and FHIR leads to convenient handling of medical data. Therefore, synchronization and management, including CRUD operations, of an EHR via smartphone was implemented. As shown with a prototype app, an interaction of patients, care providers, and insurances is possible without further ado, because of the universal standardization. The communicated requirements of the *gematik* are essential to that, since regulation and legislation requires data format adjustments for gFRs. While Google Fit also offers similar functionality and allows for individual format definitions, iOS has a superior level of maturity and is a suitable platform for EHR related data. As to our knowledge, both platforms will continue to extend their portfolio and could be considered moving forward. Since the majority of data is generated within the out-patient part, a minimal EHR implementation, would enable smartphone users to use their device immediately, which would likely result in an accelerated acceptance. Since our work is only proof of concept and was used in a constrained environment, one has to take into account that we did not take appropriate security measures, which is known to increase breaches [36]. While it could require a significant additional effort to integrate security concepts, it does not affect the prototype in any way. Implementing the different requirements of HL7 and the legislation led to minor issues. While the charge number is optional in international standards, it is obligatory in German regulations, requiring further extensions to add according data fields. Additionally, validation of gFRs was not possible without a custom FHIR server to verify against the German standard. Providing an adjusted FHIR server poses a challenge due to the immense daily stream of healthcare data. Some aspects of a comprehensive EHR, e.g. medical images, are not supported by the prototype as of today.

Moving forward, an API would allow to expand on the context by building connections to other resources, e.g. the *Weisse Liste* [37]. Furthermore, a dedicated industry cooperation could be considered to benefit from the experience made with already existing international EHR pendants. One example is the *Argonaut Project* and its guidelines [38]. A collaboration on developing EHRs within a shared scope of such a project might be beneficial for both sides, possible lock-in effects aside. It could reduce time to market for apps of the according ecosystem, while the public institution is able to concentrate on essential resources of the FHIR catalogue. Authentication and authorization are equally important and a recent point of discussion. Building on that, solutions have to be found for situations in which the patient is not able to provide consent, e.g. after an accident. Popular use cases would provide access to known allergies, preexisting conditions, advance directives or even organ donation declarations, when it comes to emergency care. Related to all those measures, the economic aspects like costs of development, implementation, and roll out lack sufficient research. When the benefits for physician and patient are quantified, biases for all stakeholders could reduce and general acceptance might be improved.

Many public and private companies put a lot of time and effort into healthcare digitalization, not only to increase revenue, but to improve patient care. With our contribution, we enable the introduction of an EHR that is conform with current regulation and legislation in Germany. When gFRs, and therefore common data exchange standards, are specified comprehensively, they represent a catalyst to multifarious applications and convenient service in the German healthcare system. In consequence, disruptions in communication, waiting times, and costs will reduce while patient care will be improved in quantity and quality.

References

1. Bundesministerium für Gesundheit: Bedeutung der Gesundheitswirtschaft. https://www.bundesgesundheitsministerium.de/themen/gesundheitswesen/gesundheitswirtschaft/bedeutung-der-gesundheitswirtschaft.html. Accessed 30 July 2019
2. Statistisches Bundesamt (Destatis): Einrichtungen, Betten und Patientenbewegung. www.destatis.de/DE/Themen/Gesellschaft-Umwelt/Gesundheit/Krankenhaeuser/Tabellen/gd-krankenhaeuser-jahre.html. Accessed 30 July 2019
3. Weber, V., Bloom, F., Pierdon, S., Wood, C.: Employing the electronic health record to improve diabetes care: a multifaceted intervention in an integrated delivery system. J. Gen. Intern. Med. **23**, 379–382 (2008). https://doi.org/10.1007/s11606-007-0439-2
4. Benson, T., Grieve, G.: Principles of Health Interoperability: SNOMED CT, HL7 and FHIR. Springer, New York (2016). https://doi.org/10.1007/978-3-319-30370-3
5. Health Level Seven International (HL7): HL7 FHIR, https://www.hl7.org/fhir/. Accessed 23 July 2019

6. Haas, P.: Einrichtungsübergreifende elektronische patientenakten. In: Fischer, F., Krämer, A. (eds.) eHealth in Deutschland, pp. 183–201. Springer, Heidelberg (2016). https://doi.org/10. 1007/978-3-662-49504-9_9

7. Bundesministerium für Gesundheit: TSVG - Terminservice- und Versorgungsgesetz. In: Bundesgesetzblatt, pp. 646–691 (2019)

8. Bundesministerium der Justiz und für Verbraucherschutz: § 291a SGB V - Elektronische Gesundheitskarte und Telematikinfrastruktur, www.gesetze-im-internet.de/sgb_5/291a.html. Accessed 01 Aug 2019

9. Statista: Marktanteile von Android und iOS am Absatz in Deutschland. www.statista.com/ statistik/daten/studie/256790/umfrage/marktanteile-von-android-und-ios-am-smartphone-absatz-in-deutschland/. Accessed 01 Aug 2019

10. Hevner, A.R.: A three cycle view of design science research. Scand. J. Inf. Syst. **19**, 4 (2007)

11. Hevner, A.R., March, S.T., Park, J., Ram, S.: Design science in information systems research. MIS Q. **28**, 75–105 (2004)

12. Peffers, K., Tuunanen, T., Rothenberger, M.A., Chatterjee, S.: A design science research methodology for information systems research. J. Manag. Inf. Syst. **24**, 45–77 (2007). https://doi.org/10.2753/MIS0742-1222240302

13. Busse, R., Blümel, M., Spranger, A.: Das deutsche Gesundheitssystem: Akteure, Daten. Analysen. Medizin. Wissenschaftliche Verlagsgesellschaft, Berlin (2017)

14. Braunstein, M.L.: Health Informatics on FHIR: How HL7's New API is Transforming Healthcare. Springer, Heidelberg (2018). https://doi.org/10.1007/978-3-319-93414-3

15. Fischer, F., Aust, V., Krämer, A.: eHealth: hintergrund und begriffsbestimmung. In: Fischer, F., Krämer, A. (eds.) eHealth in Deutschland, pp. 3–23. Springer, Heidelberg (2016). https:// doi.org/10.1007/978-3-662-49504-9_1

16. The Commonwealth Fund: Electronic Health Records: International Health Care System Profiles. https://international.commonwealthfund.org/features/ehrs/. Accessed 01 Aug 2019

17. Fielding, R.T.: REST: architectural styles and the design of network-based software architectures (2000)

18. Fielding, R.T., et al.: Reflections on the REST architectural style and principled design of the modern web architecture. In: Proceedings of the 2017 11th Joint Meeting on Foundations of Software Engineering, pp. 4–14. ACM (2017)

19. Shaver, D.: How Widely Adopted Is HL7?. http://healthstandards.com/blog/2007/08/30/ how-widely-adopted-is-hl7/. Accessed 02 Agu 2019

20. Posnack, S., Barker, W.: Heat Wave: The U.S. is Poised to Catch FHIR in 2019 | Health IT Buzz. www.healthit.gov/buzz-blog/interoperability/heat-wave-the-u-s-is-poised-to-catch-fhir-in-2019. Accessed 02 Aug 2019

21. Totten, A.M., et al.: Telehealth: mapping the evidence for patient outcomes from systematic reviews. Agency for Healthcare Research and Quality (US), Rockville (MD) (2016)

22. Marceglia, S., Fontelo, P., Rossi, E., Ackerman, M.J.: A standards-based architecture proposal for integrating patient mHealth apps to electronic health record systems. Appl. Clin. Inform. **06**, 488–505 (2015). https://doi.org/10.4338/ACI-2014-12-RA-0115

23. North, F., Chaudhry, R.: Apple HealthKit and health app: patient uptake and barriers in primary care. Telemedicine e-Health **22**, 608–613 (2016). https://doi.org/10.1089/tmj.2015. 0106

24. Parker, S.J., Jessel, S., Richardson, J.E., Reid, M.C.: Older adults are mobile too! Identifying the barriers and facilitators to older adults' use of mHealth for pain management. BMC Geriatr. **13**, 43 (2013). https://doi.org/10.1186/1471-2318-13-43

25. Kumar, R.B., Goren, N.D., Stark, D.E., Wall, D.P., Longhurst, C.A.: Automated integration of continuous glucose monitor data in the electronic health record using consumer technology. J. Am. Med. Inf. Assoc. **23**, 532–537 (2016). https://doi.org/10.1093/jamia/ocv206

26. Gay, V., Leijdekkers, P.: Bringing health and fitness data together for connected health care: mobile apps as enablers of interoperability. J. Med. Internet Res. **17**, e260 (2015). https://doi.org/10.2196/jmir.5094

27. Coons, J.C., Patel, R., Coley, K.C., Empey, P.E.: Design and testing of Medivate, a mobile app to achieve medication list portability via Fast Healthcare Interoperability Resources. J. Am. Pharm. Assoc. **59**, 78–85 (2019). https://doi.org/10.1016/j.japh.2019.01.001

28. Bloomfield, R.A., Polo-Wood, F., Mandel, J.C., Mandl, K.D.: Opening the Duke electronic health record to apps: implementing SMART on FHIR. Int. J. Med. Inform. **99**, 1–10 (2017). https://doi.org/10.1016/j.ijmedinf.2016.12.005

29. Bundesministerium der Justiz und für Verbraucherschutz: IfSG - Gesetz zur Verhütung und Bekämpfung von Infektionskrankheiten beim Menschen. www.gesetze-im-internet.de/ifsg/. Accessed 02 Aug 2019

30. GitHub Repository: FHIR Swift Classes. https://github.com/smart-on-fhir/Swift-FHIR. Accessed 06 Aug 2019

31. Hibbard, J.H., Greene, J.: What the evidence shows about patient activation: better health outcomes and care experiences. Fewer Data Costs. Health Affairs. **32**, 207–214 (2013). https://doi.org/10.1377/hlthaff.2012.1061

32. Health Level Seven International (HL7): Level 1 to 5 Implementation Roadmap. www.hl7.org/fhir/index.html. Accessed 02 Aug 2019

33. Bundesministerium für Gesundheit: Entwurf eines Gesetzes für mehr Sicherheit in der Arzneimittelversorg. www.bundesgesundheitsministerium.de/fileadmin/Da-teien/3_Downloads/Gesetze_und_Verordnungen/GuV/G/GSAV_Bundestag.pdf. Accessed 02 Aug 2019

34. Kassenärztliche Bundesereinigung: Die häufigsten Krankenheiten in deutschen Arztpraxen. https://www.presseportal.de/pm/34021/3446781. Accessed 12 Aug 2019

35. Kassenärztliche Vereinigung Nordrhein: Die 100 häufigsten ICD-10-Schlüssel und Kurztexte (2019). https://www.kvno.de/downloads/verordnungen/100icd_19–1.pdf

36. Kim, S.H., Kwon, J.: How Do EHRs and a meaningful use initiative affect breaches of patient information? Inf. Syst. Res. (2019). https://doi.org/10.1287/isre.2019.0858

37. Thranberend, T.: Weisse Liste - For patients, for quality. https://www.bertelsmann-stiftung.de/en/our-projects/weisse-liste/weisse-liste-project-description/. Accessed 15 Nov 2019

38. Health Level Seven International (HL7): HL7 Argonaut Project Wiki. https://argonautwiki.hl7.org, www.fhir.org/guides/argonaut/. Accessed 31 July 2019

Assessing Digital Support for Smoking Cessation

Alessio De Santo[✉] and Adrian Holzer

University of Neuchâtel, Neuchâtel, Switzerland
{alessio.desanto,adrian.holzer}@unine.ch

Abstract. Tobacco still kills more than 7 million people each year. Research points to several evidence-based interventions to support smoking cessation which, if applied widely, could considerably reduce premature deaths. There is a huge range of mobile apps targeting this concern, which could potentially be powerful catalysts to provide this support. Yet it is unclear how much of their design is evidence-based and how effective they are. To address this issue, this paper provides an analysis of 99 popular smoking cessation apps. The results show that only two apps come from a credible source, provide support for user engagement through advanced motivational affordances and have been evaluated for efficacy.

Keywords: Smoking cessation · Smartphone apps · Digital support · mHealth · User engagement · Content analysis

1 Introduction

Do you think smoking is a public health concern of the past? Think again. According to the World Health Organization (WHO) tobacco use is still the single biggest preventable cause of death in the world today [30]. Tobacco kills 7 million people a year, which could potentially increase to more than 8 million by 2030 if left unchecked [30]. Most smokers, aware of the dangers of tobacco, would like to quit but they need help [30]. Simple behavioral change interventions can considerably reduce premature deaths of tobacco users [29].

Digital resources are increasingly available to support individuals in adopting healthier behaviors [13, 18]. An ever-increasing global adoption of mobile devices, such as smartphones and connected devices, has spurred rapid growth in the field of electronic health. New technologies are giving individuals the potential to engage more fully in their healthcare decision-making, opening possibilities to improve health outcomes [8, 17].

Face-to-face counseling is the most universally effective means of helping people quit [8] but, currently, participation rates in these programs are low [15] and they are not affordable globally [28]. Digital solutions to support smoking cessation can provide some advantages over traditional face-to-face methods, for example in terms of scalability and user proximity. Participation rates could be improved by leveraging features such as real-time data collection, feedback and low-cost dissemination [16].

Supported by the Swiss Learning Health System project.

M. Themistocleous and M. Papadaki (Eds.): EMCIS 2019, LNBIP 381, pp. 331–343, 2020.
https://doi.org/10.1007/978-3-030-44322-1_25

Current literature establishes mobile phones as potentially useful in helping smokers quit [8]; however, among the thousands of mobile applications (apps) it is unclear how much of their design is evidence-based and how effective their use is. To address this issue, this paper provides a critical analysis of the most popular smoking cessation apps and identifies open research gaps and future promising research avenues.

2 Smoking Cessation – What Works

Government organizations, medical societies, research networks and research centers establish guidelines to provide a comprehensive review of the scientific evidence for treating tobacco use and dependence [9]. A review of 26 current guidelines allowed us to identify globally recommended smoking cessation interventions, with four of them providing strong evidence of efficacy: *brief advice, behavioral support, pharmacotherapy* and *abstinence evaluation* [27].

- *Brief advice.* Brief advice is 5 to 10 min of advice to encourage smokers to improve their health by quitting their smoking habit, primarily by triggering a cessation attempt. Some frameworks, such as the 5A's and the ABC framework, provide a structure for providing brief advice. The 5A's stands for *Ask, Assess, Advise, Assist* and *Arrange* a follow-up. The ABC stands for: (A) *Ask* all people about their smoking status, (B) provide *Brief advice* to stop smoking to all people who smoke, (C) make an offer of evidence-based *Cessation treatment.*
- *Behavioral support.* Often when smokers try to quit, they need behavioral support to avoid relapses. There are three main methods of providing behavioral support: (1) self-help material, (2) peer group meetings, (3) health professional counseling. The first method, self-help information, can support patients without outside help. When self-help is personalized it is even more effective [19]. In the second method, peers meet regularly and provide each other with support and encouragement. Compared to self-help, peer group support is more effective in helping smokers quit [19, 20]. In the third method, health professionals provide individual counseling through face-to-face appointments. This patient-centered approach is the most effective. Providing multiple and longer sessions also increases the effectiveness [19].
- *Pharmacotherapy.* Guidelines suggest the use of pharmacotherapy such as nicotine replacement therapy, bupropion and varenicline to assist patients with nicotine withdrawal [27]. In situations such as abruptly quitting smoking, a combination of behavioral support and pharmacotherapy is recommended [19].
- *Abstinence evaluation.* Guidelines suggest that abstinence evaluation confirmed by objective measurements is providing strong evidence in smoking cessation programs [27]. Measurement forms include various techniques such as tracking systems, biochemical markers and clinical tests. Even though tracking systems can in principle be bypassed, research suggests that increasing smoking awareness and providing tools such as goal setting [11] and tailored feedback [6] helps smokers to quit. These tools are important, since smokers are generally unaware of their daily smoking patterns [7].

3 Smoking Cessation Apps – What Research Says

Early attempts to assess mobile support for smoking cessation have primarily rated apps according to their adherence to smoking cessation treatment guidelines [1–3, 5, 10]. Overall, apps identified by Abroms et al. [1, 2] presented low adherence to established US guidelines for smoking cessation. The recommendation of Abroms et al. [1, 2], for future development, was to greatly adhere to such guidelines and other evidence-based practices. Bennett et al. [3] provided conclusions consistent with those of Abroms et al. [1, 2]. These US findings were echoed around the world, as smoking cessation apps also have low levels of adherence to Chinese [5] and Australian smoking cessation treatment guidelines [25]. Research suggests that the more a smoking cessation app is opened and accessed, the more likely the user is to quit smoking [4]. Thus, factors that might influence routine use are particularly important to consider for mobile app interventions, as 26% of apps are discontinued after first use, and 74% are used no more than 10 times [12]. *User engagement* and *source credibility* are two dimensions that appear to be important aspects of mHealth routine use [12, 14, 23].

In this paper, we build on these findings and critically assess existing digital smoking support solutions not only on their adherence to guidelines, but also on how their design encourages user engagement, and on their source credibility. The source credibility of an app relates to the emitting authority and significantly influences mHealth routine use [14]. *Competence* and *trustworthiness* are the main subdimensions of source credibility [24]. Competence refers to expertise, while trustworthiness is a function of the perceived character and integrity of the source. An app's emitting authority is not always mentioned, making the evaluation of its competence and trustworthiness difficult. Note, however, that source credibility refers to a user's perception of the credibility of an emitting authority, reflecting nothing about the app itself.

User engagement can be measured through the activity of a user of the app (number of visits, time spent, actions performed, etc.). It can be enhanced through motivational affordances, i.e. design features that trigger psychological levers such as intrinsic motivation, sociometric status and reciprocity [23]. Suh et al. [23] identified four types of motivational affordance, leading people to be better engaged in an activity:

- *Rewards.* By obtaining points as a pay-off for completing pre-designed tasks, users reach levels or milestones rewarded by virtual badges and trophies demonstrating their accomplishments.
- *Competition.* Users have the opportunity to compare with, and compete against, other people through components such as leaderboards, permitting them to visualize their standing against other users or friends.
- *Self-expression.* Personal identities can be created by users, through avatars and emoticons, enabling them to express their emotions.
- *Altruism.* Points and virtual goods can be exchanged between users.

Figure 1 provides an overview of the three-dimensional perspective for building an evidence-based app that will potentially encourage user engagement and routine use.

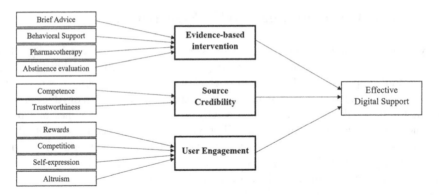

Fig. 1. Research three-dimensional perspective.

4   App Landscape – What Currently Exists

To identify current practices, we collected a subset of the most popular apps and reviewed them on: *evidence-based* practice adherence, *source credibility* and motivational affordance that encourages *user engagement*. We also investigated whether apps were *validated* through evaluation studies. The app collection was conducted through the Explorer research tool provided by 42Matters (https://42matters.com/), on 19 November 2018. The following search terms were used to perform the queries on the title and description of the apps: *quit smoking*, *smoking cessation* and *stop smoking*. For each search term, the 40 most popular apps were retrieved on the number of downloads and on a rating basis, resulting in 120 Android apps and 120 iOS apps. Duplicate apps were removed, resulting in 92 iOS apps, 78 Android apps and 18 apps available on both platforms. Inclusion and exclusion criteria, as presented in Table 1, were applied to exclusively select smoking cessation apps. Figure 2 depicts the results of the process. The remaining 99 apps were then manually coded by parsing the app description, screenshots and website (where available).

Table 1. Inclusion and exclusion criteria.

Inclusion criteria
Apple iOS and Google Android app
Only apps available in the English language
Only apps published in the Apple App Store or the Google Play Store
Only apps containing in their description or title "quit smoking", "smoking cessation" or "stop smoking"
Exclusion criteria
Unrelated app
General health and wellbeing app
Exact duplicates between different app stores

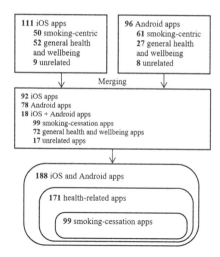

Fig. 2. Procedure for our smoking cessation app sample selection.

4.1   Adherence to Evidence-Based Practices

As a first dimension of our review, apps were coded in respect of adherence to evidence-based practices: *brief advice, behavioral support, pharmacotherapy* and *abstinence evaluation*. The coding process was inspired by grounded theories and open coding techniques [21, 22], making the categories emerge by their proximity. For the *brief advice* subdimension, we coded whenever apps provided smoking cessation *tips*, *pieces of advice* or *recommendations*. Apps' descriptions and screenshots were parsed, looking for this specific content addressed to smokers and representing brief advice interventions. Brief advice in a smoking cessation app can, for instance, be "Rejecting is easier if you do it with someone who has the same problem and understands you completely. [...]" (Ex Smoker, Sopharma AD), or when a smoker is reporting a craving, tips such as "drink something (water, juice)", "eat some fruit" or "brush your teeth" (Stop-tobacco, Université de Genéve).

Concerning the *behavioral support* subdimension, we identified three different levels of support: (1) apps providing *self-help* support with cessation facts, (2) apps having a *social* dimension and (3) apps providing a guided smoking cessation *program*. Self-help cessation facts, are usually related to monitoring information and provide smokers with statistics about their behavior. For instance, apps can inform about the time elapsed since their last cigarette, the number of cigarettes smoked daily, or empowering facts triggered after quitting, such as "You have no more physical dependence on nicotine" (Qwit, Team Geny) or "Taste and smell senses regained" (Smoke – quit, NikNormSoft). Apps providing peer group support offer features such as community chat, permitting sharing and the discovery of peer experience, but also features allowing smokers to share their progress and achievements about smoking cessation on social networks such as Facebook and Twitter. Apps can also rely on specific programs, conducting smokers through the use of the app. Programs can have different formats, such as animated video clips, audio sessions including interactive exercises and mindfulness sessions. Finally, indications of *validation* studies were sought on the app description and website.

The *pharmacotherapy* subdimension was coded on whether apps provided information about existing pharmacotherapies. For instance, apps can provide tablet intake instructions or support.

The *abstinence evaluation* subdimension was coded by categorizing the various self-monitoring possibilities offered by the apps. Most of the apps provided monitoring features such as an *unsmoked cigarettes* counter, *unsmoked days* representing the number of days since the smoker quitted, the number of *cigarettes smoked* since the installation of the app, the *interval* of time between two smoked cigarettes or the report of *cravings and urges*.

4.2 Source Credibility as Routine Use Influencer

As a second dimension of our review, the source credibility of each app was coded. Apps could be developed and published by everyone, enabling developers of any kind to come with their batch of smoking cessation interventions. Metadata found in an app's description, screenshots and website allowed the identification of the emitting authority of the app. Competence and trustworthiness are the two consistently emerging dimensions of source credibility [24]. Trustworthiness is a function of the perceived character and integrity of the source and can therefore not be universally categorized. Competence refers to expertise of the source. Coding was simply categorized as follows:

- *Unspecified.* No information about the people involved in the development process of the app is found.
- *Peer.* A smoker or an ex-smoker developed or participated in the development of the app.
- *Specialists.* The creation of the app involved medical professionals, researchers or universities.
- *Governmental.* A governmental institution, such as the public health department, mandated or participated in the development of the app.

4.3 User Engaging Motivational Affordance

As a third dimension of our review, user engagement was evaluated. According to Suh et al. [23]: *rewards, competition, self-expression* and *altruism* provide motivational affordance, being meaningful antecedents of needs satisfaction, stimulating intrinsic motivation (enjoyment) and causing users to engage more deeply in target activities within a gamified app. User engagement was coded by noting the presence of the following motivational affordances in the apps:

- *Rewards.* Through using the app, points are obtained as a pay-off for completing pre-designed tasks, such as staying smoke-free. By obtaining points, users can also reach levels or milestones rewarded by virtual badges and trophies demonstrating their accomplishments. Associated design elements are: points, levels and badges/trophies.

- *Competition.* Users engage in competition with each other through components such as leaderboards, enabling them to compare points, levels or badges. Associated design elements are: points, levels, badges and leaderboards.
- *Self-expression.* Personal identities can be defined through dynamics, allowing users to, for instance, create an avatar, upload a personal profile photo or communicating with emoticons expressing their emotions. Associated design elements are: points, levels, badges, leaderboards, avatars and emoticons.
- *Altruism.* Points and virtual goods can be exchanged between the users. For instance, a user can make a present by offering a virtual gift to another user. Associated design elements are: points and virtual gifts.

5 Results

The content of 99 apps was reviewed and coded, following the three previously presented dimensions: *evidence-based* practices adherence and *validation* studies, *user engagement* and *source credibility*. Table 3 presents the results of the analysis, with the supported subdimension and scores. Scores allow us to compare evaluated apps on the evidence-based, user engagement and source credibility dimensions. Scores range goes

Table 2. Attribution of the dimensions' scores.

Score	Evidence-Based	User Engagement	Source Credibility
0	No use of any evidence-based practices	No use of motivational affordance	Unknown emitting authority
1	Use of at least one evidence-based practice	Use of at least one motivational affordance design element	Peer (e.g. ex-smoker) emitting authority
2	Use of at least one evidence-based practice and the app is backed up by scientific validation	Use of two or more motivational affordances	Specialists or governmental emitting authority

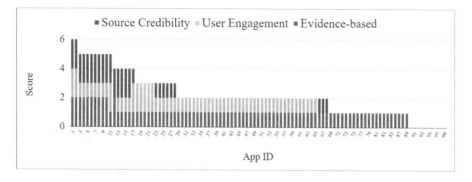

Fig. 3. Overview of the reviewed apps' scores.

Table 3. Overview of the reviewed apps sorted y score.

id	App name (Editor)	OS		Evidence-based										User Engagem.				Source Cred.			Scores			
					Behav. Supp.				Abstinence Evaluation															
		Android	iOS	Validation	Brief Advice	Self-help	Peer-support Program	Pharmacotherapy	Unsmoked cig.	Unsmoked days	Smoked cigarettes	Cigarettes Interval	Urges/Cravings	Rewards	Competition	Self-expression	Altruism	Peer	Specialists	Governmental	Evidence-based	User Engagement	Source Credibility	Total
1	Stop-tobacco (Université de Genève)		√						√											√	2	2	2	6
2	Quit Genius - Best way to quit smoking for good (Digital Therapeutics)	√	√	√	√	√	√				√			√	√			√	√		2	1	2	5
3	Stoptober (Public Health England)	√	√	√	√	√	√				√			√						√	2	1	2	5
4	Craving To Quit! (Claritas MindSciences/Goblue International LLC)																							
5	Quit Smoking - Stop Tobacco Mobile Trainer (Iteration Mobile S.L)	√	√	√			√			√				√							2	1	2	5
6	Quit smoking - Smokerstop (Dr. med. Titus Brinker)	√		√	√	√				√		√		√							2	1	2	5
7	Smoke Free - Stop Smoking Now (David Crane)	√	√	√			√					√		√						√	2	1	2	5
8	2MorrowQuit (was SmartQuit) (2Morrow, Inc.)																				2	1	2	5
9	Smoke Free, quit smoking now and stop for good (The Quit Smoking Specialists)	√	√	√			√			√				√							2	1	2	5
10	Stay Quit Coach (US Department of Veterans Affairs (VA))	√	√	√			√			√				√					√		2	1	2	5
11	Quit Now: My QuitBuddy (ANPHA)	√	√	√		√	√			√				√	√			√	√		1	2	2	5
12	Stop Tobacco Mobile Trainer. Quit Smoking App Free (Iteration Mobile & Vialsoft Apps)				√			√		√		√							√		2	0	2	4
13	Smokefree (Public Health England)	√	√		√	√	√			√					√					√	1	1	2	4
14	Tabac info service, l'appli (l'Assurance Maladie)	√	√																		1	1	2	4
15	Ex Smoker (Sopharma AD)				√																1	1	2	4
16	Sacabo (Amarutek S.L.)	√			√			√	√					√							1	1	2	4
17	QuitNow! (Fewlaps, S.C)	√								√				√	√	√		√			1	2	1	4
18	Quit It - stop smoking today (digitalsirup)	√			√	√			√					√							1	2	0	3
19	Quit It Lite (digitalsirup)				√	√			√					√							1	2	0	3
20	Quitbit - Quit Smoking Cigarettes And Gently Stop (Quitbit, Inc)	√			√	√				√				√	√						1	2	0	3
21	Stop Smoking - EasyQuit free (Mario Hanna)	√			√					√				√							1	2	0	3
22	Stop tabac - Quit smoking and cigarette cessation (Cedric Martin)	√							√					√	√						1	2	0	3
23	Quit Smoking Now: Quit Buddy! (HQmedia)				√				√					√				√			1	1	1	3
24	My Quit Smoking Coach (Andreas Jopp)	√			√	√	√		√					√				√			1	1	1	3
25	Quit Smoking Pro (EpicLapps)				√					√				√				√			1	1	1	3
26	Quit Smoking: Cessation Nation (Ron Horner)									√								√			1	1	1	3
27	Stop Smoking — quit smoking, be smoke free (The Quit Smoking Professionals)	√			√	√			√					√				√			1	1	1	3
28	LIVESTRONG MyQuit Coach (LIVESTRONG.COM)	√			√				√					√				√			1	1	1	3
29	SmokeFree — quit smoking slowly (MotiveBite)	√			√				√	√											1	1	0	2
30	Quit Pro (Etago)	√			√	√			√	√				√							1	1	0	2
31	quitSTART - Quit Smoking (ICF International)	√			√					√		√									1	1	0	2
32	101 days to quit smoking for good Free (GreenTomatoMedia)	√		√	√				√					√							1	1	0	2
33	Quit Smoking - Quit now (Dhurandhar apps)													√							1	1	0	2
34	Quit-Smoking Coach (Brainlag Studios)	√			√	√								√							1	1	0	2
35	Quit-Smoking Coach Free (Brainlag Studios)				√				√												1	1	0	2
36	QuitGuide - Quit Smoking (ICF International)	√			√							√	√								1	1	0	2
37	Smoke — quit (NikNormSoft)	√																			1	1	0	2
38	Quit Smoking Now: Stop Forever (TreePie)	√			√				√					√							1	1	0	2
39	Stop Smoking 3D (World Cloud Ventures)	√					√		√					√							1	1	0	2
40	Drop It! Quit Smoking (Nikola Mladenovic)				√				√					√							1	1	0	2
41	Kwit — quit smoking for good - smoking cessation (Kwit SAS)	√	√		√	√			√	√				√							1	1	0	2
42	Smoke FREE Finally Non Smoking (sg-pages - Marcus Steller)	√			√	√			√					√							1	1	0	2
43	Smoke Revoke - Gradually Quit Smoking (Alek Branch)	√					√			√				√							1	1	0	2
44	Cigarette Analytics (Alvakos)									√											1	1	0	2
45	Get Rich or Die Smoking (Tobias Gruber)				√				√					√							1	1	0	2
46	I Give Up Smoking (Stand Dev)	√																			1	1	0	2
47	myQuitTime (Arete World Enterprises)				√				√	√											1	1	0	2
48	myQuitTime Free (Arete World Enterprises)	√			√				√												1	1	0	2
49	Quit Smoking - Goodbye Tobacco (Your Health)	√			√				√	√				√							1	1	0	2
50	Quit Smoking - My Last Cigarette (Mastersoft)																				1	1	0	2
51	Quit Smoking !!! (Dennis Ebbinghaus)		√		√				√	√				√							1	1	0	2

(Continued)

Table 3. (*Continued*)

id	App name (Editor)	Android	iOS	Validation	Brief Advice	Self-help	Peer-support	Program	Pharmacotherapy	Unsmoked cig.	Unsmoked days	Smoked cigarettes	Cigarettes Interval	Urges/Cravings	Rewards	Competition	Self-expression	Altruism	Peer	Specialists	Governmental	Evidence-based	User Engagement	Source Credibility	Total
		OS			Evidence-based	Behav. Supp.				Abstinence Evaluation					User Engagem				Source Cred.			Scores			
52	Quit Smoking (Luis Salcedo)																					1	1	0	2
53	Quit Smoking (Morisson Software)	✓				✓					✓				✓							1	1	0	2
54	Quit Tracker: Stop Smoking (despDev)	✓				✓						✓	✓		✓							1	1	0	2
55	Qwit (Quit Smoking) (Team Geny)																					1	1	0	2
56	Smoke FREE - Non Smoking (sg-pages)									✓	✓											1	1	0	2
57	Stop & Quit Smoking – Smoke & vaping Cessation Now (Ibrahim Khalil)	✓				✓						✓			✓							1	1	0	2
58	Stop smoking helper (Roxoft)					✓						✓	✓		✓							1	1	0	2
59	Time To Quit Smoke (VantusMantus)	✓				✓									✓							1	1	0	2
60	Non Smoking Timer (LinQ)	✓									✓	✓	✓	✓	✓							1	1	0	2
61	Quit Smoking - Butt Out (Ellisapps Inc.)	✓		✓							✓	✓		✓	✓							1	1	0	2
62	Quit Smoking - Butt Out Pro (Ellisapps Inc.)	✓									✓		✓		✓							1	1	0	2
63	Smoking reduction free (hashisoft)	✓																✓					1	1	0	2
64	Smoking reduction Trial (hashisoft)	✓										✓											1	1	0	2
65	Tabex – quit smoking (Sopharma Ukraine Limited Liability Company)	✓							✓						✓							1	1	0	2
66	Stop Smoking In 2 Hours (Juice Master)	✓						✓												✓			1	0	1	2
67	Quit Smoking Audio Help Tips Stop Now and Forever (Pitashi! Mobile Imagination.)	✓	✓		✓	✓															✓		1	0	1	2
68	Stop Smoking Personal Stories of Success Quit Now (Pitashi! Mobile Imagination.)	✓	✓		✓	✓						✓									✓		1	0	1	2
69	Quit Smoking with Willpower (Pocket Pixels)																						1	0	0	1
70	Smoktivation : Ma motivation pour arreter de fumer (JCD Software)	✓	✓		✓	✓	✓			✓	✓												1	0	0	1
71	Can I Smoke? (Steven Dakh)	✓				✓							✓	✓									1	0	0	1
72	Ecig-Coach (E-CIG GROUP)																						1	0	0	1
73	No smoking (antonfil84)					✓	✓				✓	✓											1	0	0	1
74	Quit Smoking Hypnosis (Mindifi)	✓		✓																			1	0	0	1
75	Quit Smoking NOW - Max Kirsten (Life Change Media Ltd)	✓				✓		✓															1	0	0	1
76	iQuit - Stop Smoking Counter (Vidal de Wit)					✓					✓	✓											1	0	0	1
77	Nextlater (App2Bizz)	✓										✓											1	0	0	1
78	NoSmokingLife (bamboo)	✓																					1	0	0	1
79	Quit Smoking (Azati)	✓	✓			✓						✓											1	0	0	1
80	Quit Smoking (HC)										✓	✓											1	0	0	1
81	Smokenote - Quit Smoking (NXCARE)					✓																	1	0	0	1
82	Smoking Log - Stop Smoking (Cory Charlton)	✓										✓											1	0	0	1
83	Quit Smoking with Andrew Johnson (Michael Schneider)	✓				✓	✓																1	0	0	1
84	iCan Stop Smoking: learn self hypnosis and quit smoking (iCan Hypnosis)	✓				✓																	1	0	0	1
85	Quit and Stop Smoking Hypnosis (Mindifi)																						1	0	0	1
86	Quit Smoking Hypnosis Program (Mindifi)																						1	0	0	1
87	Quit Smoking in 28 Days Audio Program (Pitashi! Mobile Imagination.)	✓				✓																	1	0	0	1
88	Smoking Cessation Hypnosis (Hyptalk)																						1	0	0	1
89	Stop Smoking! (On Beat Limited)	✓				✓																	1	0	0	1
90	Cigarette Smoke Simulator Free (Gravy Baby Media)	✓																					0	0	0	0
91	Help You to Quit 100% (Nightingale WebApp)																						0	0	0	0
92	Roll and Smoke 3D FREE (Sakis25)																						0	0	0	0
93	Simulator Cigarette Vape Joke (StarApps7)	✓																					0	0	0	0
94	Smoke a virtual cigarette (MaxZieli)																						0	0	0	0
95	Smoke Cigarette Simulator (Yami Apps)	✓																					0	0	0	0
96	Smokerface (Dr. med. Titus Brinker)	✓																					0	0	0	0
97	Smoking virtual cigarettes (ScreenPranks)	✓																					0	0	0	0
98	Virtual cigarette (SmileTools)																						0	0	0	0
99	Virtual Hookah/Shisha (Iris Studios and Services)	✓																					0	0	0	0
		61.6%	49.5%	11%	31.3%	61.6%	24.2%	25.3%	3.0%	43.4%	29.3%	19.2%	3.0%	6.1%	64.6%	2.0%	7.1%	0.0%	13.1%	12.1%	4.0%				
																			Average			1.01	0.74	0.42	2.17

from 0 to 2, 0 representing a lowest level of adherence, 2 corresponding to the highest level of adherence. The addition of evidence-based, user engagement and source credibility scores provides the total score. Detailed attribution of scores is further detailed in Table 2.

Figure 3 provides an overview of the cumulative scores. The maximum achievable total score is 6. The best score of our sample is 6 and was obtained by only two apps (2%) while the average total score was 2.17. The average score for evidence-based adherence is 1.01. The average score for user engagement is 0.74. The average score for source credibility is 0.42. Of the reviewed apps, 10.1% do not support any evidence-based practice or any motivational affordance stimulating user engagement. Of the sample, 24.2% support some form of evidence-based practices without implementing any motivational affordances to increase user engagement. Finally, 72.7% of the reviewed apps do not provide enough information to clearly identify the emitting authority and therefore the source credibility. Note that only 11% of the apps indicated that their efficacy was validated through a scientific study.

6 Discussion

This research has shown that even though the subject is well-known, and smoking cessation apps are plentiful, research that provides information for system designers, users and medical professionals is not yet mature. One main issue is the lack of evaluation of smoking cessation apps. Of the 99 applications reviewed, only 11 (11%) were validated by scientific research, seven other apps (7.1%) claimed to be scientifically based, but no proof of this claim was found on the developer website. The lack of large empirical studies on effectiveness of smoking cessation apps provides an open avenue for future research. Furthermore, at this stage, most of the research papers referenced by the reviewed apps deal with the effectiveness of cognitive and behavioral theories [13, 26], but none deal with the app itself.

Current popular smoking cessation apps still have much room for improvement. Adherence to evidence-based guidelines and best practices continues to be low, as mentioned by previous research. It is often difficult to evaluate the source credibility, as most of the time the source is unknown or no guarantee of legitimacy is available. Regarding user engagement, the great majority of apps automatically reward smokers without requiring their intervention or being based on their actual behavior. In terms of motivational affordances, providing rewards is the most used mechanism. Although rewards are recognized as motivational affordances that encourage user engagement, they only weakly contribute to it when they are not coupled with other mechanisms (such as competition or self-expression) [23]. To maximize user engagement, future apps should consider such combinations.

The findings of this study should be interpreted in the context of certain limitations, the main limitation being that the apps were reviewed on the sole basis of the information provided by their developer (description, screenshots and website), which could be incomplete, erroneous or outdated. For a more comprehensive assessment, each app should be installed and used just as a smoker would.

While actual apps are potentially useful, they vastly underutilize the potential of mobile technologies. Mobile technology provides an unprecedented environment for reaching and interacting with smokers. Arguably the greatest strength of mobile technology is its ability to infer user activity, potentially providing a better idea of the smoker's actual behavior and in turn delivering personalized content in an appropriate context, in terms of space and time. Such technology also enables ubiquitous connectivity, enabling communication with peers and experts. Currently, popular apps only poorly implement such possibilities; for instance, only 2% permit smokers to engage in competition with peers and only one app (Quit Now: My QuitBuddy, ANPHA) provides access to experts through a quitline.

Future research should further exploit the opportunity of the device being in the smoker's pocket anytime and anywhere, thus providing an inconspicuous, accurate and efficient monitoring of smoking activity. Of the reviewed apps, only one (Quitbit, Quitbit Inc) uses a connected device (lighter) to monitor smoked cigarettes. There is a lack of research into the evaluation of such tracking devices and their efficiency. These devices would definitely introduce an important feedback loop for the smoker's actual behavior with potentially high effectiveness [6, 19]. In addition, the sensors (e.g. GPS) already built into most smartphones make it possible for apps to provide sophisticated just-in-time and in-the-moment intervention for smoking cessation. Evaluation of previous smoking activity monitoring and digital support tailorization should be further investigated. A major challenge with such features is the privacy concern that they raise. It is therefore crucial to understand how to best find trade-offs to enable privacy-by-design while enabling personalization through data analytics.

Future work could also investigate social media interactions, which have been found to be poorly implemented. Designing interactions with peers (behavioral support functionalities) would not only reinforce the evidence-based practices, but would also facilitate the design, evaluation and understanding of what additional motivational affordances (competition, self-expression, altruism) are most effective besides rewards.

Finally, a majority of reviewed apps were emitted by an unspecified authority, leading to concerns of source credibility. Emitting sources of mHealth apps could be certified to help smokers in their choice. As interest in using apps for smoking cessation grows, it may become more difficult for consumers to find an app that is likely to be helpful. Further research should investigate how the emitting source could be legitimated and how sensitive content such as pharmacotherapy could be integrated.

7   Conclusion

This study provides an updated review of the most popular smoking cessation apps and suggests directions for further research to improve the efficacy of future digital support for smoking cessation. As interest in using apps for smoking cessation grows, it may be difficult for consumers to find an app that is likely to be helpful. Helping individuals quit smoking is a challenging task that requires an interdisciplinary approach. The volume of available apps makes the process of selecting a smoking cessation app difficult. The information systems community can provide support for this challenge by investigating how to best design digital support systems to help smokers quit.

Even though there are a significant number of apps to help smokers quit, most of them are not aligned with evidence-based guidelines, nor are they encouraging user-engagement and source credibility, and there is also a lack of research for evaluating their effectiveness.

References

1. Abroms, L.C., Lee Westmaas, J., Bontemps-Jones, J., Ramani, R., Mellerson, J.: A content analysis of popular smartphone apps for smoking cessation. Am. J. Prev. Med. **45**(6), 732–736 (2013)
2. Abroms, L.C., Padmanabhan, N., Thaweethai, L., Phillips, T.: iPhone apps for smoking cessation: a content analysis. Am. J. Prev. Med. **40**(3), 279–285 (2011)
3. Bennett, M.E., Toffey, K., Dickerson, F., Himelhoch, S., Katsafanas, E., Savage, C.L.: A Review of Android Apps for Smoking Cessation (2014)
4. Bricker, J.B., et al.: Randomized, controlled pilot trial of a smartphone app for smoking cessation using acceptance and commitment therapy. Drug Alcohol Depend. **143**(1), 87–94 (2014)
5. Cheng, F., Xu, J., Su, C., Fu, X., Bricker, J.: Content analysis of smartphone apps for smoking cessation in china: empirical study. JMIR mHealth uHealth **5**(7), e93 (2017)
6. Dijkstra, A., De Vries, H., Roijackers, J.: Long-term effectiveness of computer- generated tailored feedback in smoking cessation. Health Educ. Res. **13**(2), 207–214 (1998)
7. El Ali, A., Matviienko, A., Feld, Y., Heuten, W., Boll, S.: VapeTracker: tracking vapor consumption to help e-cigarette users quit. In: Proceedings of the 2016 CHI Conference Extended Abstracts on Human Factors in Computing Systems (2016)
8. Hartmann-Boyce, J., Stead, L.F., Cahill, K., Lancaster, T.: Efficacy of interventions to combat tobacco addiction: Cochrane update of 2013 reviews. Addiction **109**(9), 1414–1425 (2014)
9. Clinical Practice Guideline Treating Tobacco Use and Dependence 2008 Update Panel, Liaisons, Staff: A clinical practice guideline for treating tobacco use and dependence: 2008 update. A U.S. Public Health Service Report. Am. J. Prev. Med. **35**(2), 158–176 (2008)
10. Hoeppner, B.B., et al.: How smart are smartphone apps for smoking cessation? a content analysis. Nicotine Tob. Res. **18**(5), 1025–1031 (2015)
11. Huang, S.C., Jin, L., Zhang, Y.: Step by step: Sub-goals as a source of motivation. Organ. Behav. Hum. Decis. Process. **141**, 1–15 (2017)
12. Information Consumer Health Corporation: Motivating Patients to Use Smart-phone Health Apps. Technical report (2011)
13. Lin, Y., Tudor-Sfetea, C., Siddiqui, S., Sherwani, Y., Ahmed, M., Eisingerich, A.B.: Effective behavioral changes through a digital mHealth app: exploring the impact of hedonic well-being, psychological empowerment and inspiration. J. Med. Int. Res. **20**(6) (2018)
14. Meng, F., Guo, X., Peng, Z., Zhang, X., Vogel, D.: The routine use of mobile health services in the presence of health consciousness. Electron. Commer. Res. Appl. **35**, 100847 (2019)
15. Paay, J., et al.: Quitty: using technology to persuade smokers to quit. In: Proceedings of the 8th Nordic Conference on Human-Computer Interaction Fun, Fast, Foundational – NordiCHI 2014 (2014)
16. Pernencar, C., et al.: Planning a health promotion program: mobile app gamification as a tool to engage adolescents. Procedia Comput. Sci. **138**, 113–118 (2018)
17. Sama, P.R., Eapen, Z.J., Weinfurt, K.P., Shah, B.R., Schulman, K.A.: An evaluation of mobile health application tools. JMIR mHealth uHealth **2**(2), e19 (2014)

18. Sardi, L., Idri, A., Fernández-Alemán, J.L.: A systematic review of gamification in e-Health. J. Biomed. Inform. **71**, 31–48 (2017)
19. Smith, S., Roberts, N., Kerr, S., Smith, S.: Behavioral interventions associated with smoking cessation in the treatment of tobacco use. Health Serv. Insights **6**, 79–85 (2013)
20. Stead, L., Carroll, A., Lancaster, T.: Group behaviour therapy programmes for smoking cessation (review). Cochrane Database of Syst. Revi. Group **3**(3), CD001007 (2017)
21. Strauss, A., Corbin, J.: Basics of Qualitative Research. Sage Publications, London (1990)
22. Strauss, A.L.: Qualitative Analysis for Social Scientists. Cambridge University Press, Cambridge (1987)
23. Suh, A., Wagner, C., Liu, L.: Enhancing user engagement through gamification. J. Comput. Inf. Syst. **58**(3), 204–213 (2018)
24. Sussman, S.W., Siegal, W.S.: Informational influence in organizations: An integrated approach to knowledge adoption. Inf. Syst. Res. **14**(1), 47–65 (2003)
25. Thornton, L., et al.: Free smoking cessation mobile apps available in Australia: a quality review and content analysis. Aust. N. Z. J. Public Health **41**(6), 625–630 (2017)
26. Tudor-Sfetea, C., et al.: Evaluation of two mobile health apps in the context of smoking cessation: qualitative study of cognitive behavioral therapy (CBT) versus Non-CBT-based digital solutions. J. Med. Internet Res. **20**(4) (2018)
27. Verbiest, M., et al.: National guidelines for smoking cessation in primary care: a literature review and evidence analysis. NPJ Prim. Care Respir. Med. **27**(1), 0–1 (2017)
28. West, R., et al.: Health-care interventions to promote and assist tobacco cessation: a review of efficacy, effectiveness and affordability for use in national guideline development. Addiction **110**(9), 1388–1403 (2015)
29. WHO: Global action plan for the prevention and control of noncommunicable diseases 2013–2020, p. 102. World Health Organization (2013)
30. WHO: Tobacco (2019). http://www.who.int/news-room/factsheets/detail/tobacco

The Role of Gender in Supporting Active and Healthy Ageing by ICT Solutions: Learning from Latvian, Polish and Swedish Older Adults

Ewa Soja[1]([⊠]), Piotr Soja[2], Ella Kolkowska[3], and Marite Kirikova[4]

[1] Department of Statistics, Cracow University of Economics, Kraków, Poland
Ewa.Soja@uek.krakow.pl
[2] Department of Informatics,
Cracow University of Economics, Kraków, Poland
Piotr.Soja@uek.krakow.pl
[3] Center for Empirical Research in Information Systems (CERIS),
Örebro University School of Business, Örebro, Sweden
Ella.Kolkowska@oru.se
[4] Department of Artificial Intelligence and Systems Engineering,
Institute of Applied Computer Systems, Riga Technical University, Riga, Latvia
Marite.Kirikova@cs.rtu.lv

Abstract. Facing the challenges related to ageing population with the help of ICT solutions may depend on various socioeconomic factors and differences in attitudes between women and men. This quantitative study investigates the role of gender in the possibility of using ICT for an active and healthy ageing in Latvia, Poland, and Sweden focusing on (1) needs which are considered important for independent and satisfying ageing and (2) technological solutions that should be developed to support independent and healthy ageing. In our approach to statistical data analysis we adopted the ordered logistic model. The findings implicate that gender differences in adoption of ICT for active and healthy ageing may vary between countries. In particular, with respect to the needs, the gender differences appear the greatest in Sweden, while as regards technological solutions, the gender gap is visible only in Poland. The results also show a need to develop some technologies regardless of socioeconomic considerations, such as technologies supporting independent living of elderly women and communication technologies allowing older women to participate in cultural activities.

Keywords: Gender · ICT · Active and healthy ageing · Older adults · Latvia · Poland · Sweden

1 Introduction

Nowadays, population ageing is a typical phenomenon in developed countries, which will deepen in time [9]. To counteract the negative effects of an ageing population and use the potential of older people, various strategies are suggested and developed, such

© Springer Nature Switzerland AG 2020
M. Themistocleous and M. Papadaki (Eds.): EMCIS 2019, LNBIP 381, pp. 344–357, 2020.
https://doi.org/10.1007/978-3-030-44322-1_26

as the policy of active and healthy ageing [31] or productive ageing [28]. Various forms of activity within these strategies can be seen as essential elements for maintaining health of an ageing society. In particular, social participation such as volunteering or informal care are considered as necessary elements in a new holistic approach to care, which, thanks to the use of ICT, should have integrated care support for citizens' health through linked social and health care [21]. However, the use of the ICT-enabled opportunities is not the same for all countries, societies or individuals. This is due to different levels of countries' digital development or digital inclusion of society [13, 26]. Countries may also differ with respect to the social and healthcare systems, which can be manifested in the level of implementation of the strategies for ageing society (e.g. possibilities to access health services, active and independent living, financial security, social participation, and digital inclusion of the elderly) [15, 33].

Previous research suggests that the use of ICT in transition economies, i.e. countries that are transitioning or recently transitioned from centrally planned economy to a free market system, is characterized by different considerations than those experienced by the most developed countries [22]. The level of digital development of transition economies, together with the degree of implemented active ageing strategies, is lower than that of developed countries [26].

Research into the possibility of using ICT for active and healthy ageing at the individual level usually refers to the explanations of socioeconomic and digital considerations, especially if they relate to comparative analyzes [e.g. 4, 15, 24]. Prior studies, mainly qualitative, also reveal that certain individual characteristics such as beliefs, social networks, health, and IT skills can be factors that differentiate the use of ICT for healthy ageing [20, 32]. However, the role of gender, which seems to be an important issue, is rarely considered in research [20] and, in this regard, the results achieved in the field of ICT adoption and use by older adults are ambiguous [30].

Studying the role of gender in the context of ICT and active ageing is justified for several reasons. First, women live longer than men; therefore more older women than men can be left without a partner [7, 23]. On the one hand, this may result in the need for care from third parties; on the other hand, it may motivate women to seek out-of-home activities, in which ICT solutions can be helpful. Another premise for research into the role of gender is the fact that older women are more often involved in spousal and partner care than men [3, 29] and can expect support from modern ICT solutions. However, the availability of such solutions for women may be more limited than for men because of the high costs and the fact that the gender gap in poverty is higher among older age groups and reflects inequalities rooted in the labor market. Women have fewer chances to achieve an adequate pension due to lower employment rates, more frequent part-time employment than men, and lower wages [5, 18].

The aim of this paper is to investigate the role of gender in the possibility of using ICT for an active and healthy ageing in the context of diverse socioeconomic considerations on the example of three countries: Latvia, Poland and Sweden. These three countries appear diverse with respect to the level of digital development [26]. However, Poland and Latvia appear similar to each other as regards the level of the implementation of strategy for active and healthy ageing [25]. They also reveal the considerations of transition economies [26, 27]. This study seeks to answer the following research questions: *(1) Do women and men in Latvia, Poland and Sweden differ in the perception of factors that are important to have an independent and satisfying life as people age? (2) Do women and men in Latvia, Poland and Sweden differ in the perception of technological solutions that should be developed to support independent and healthy ageing?*

The remainder of the paper is organized as follows. In the next section, we describe the background for this study. Next, we present our research method followed by the presentation of the results. We then discuss our findings and explain implications for practice. The study ends with concluding remarks.

2 Background

Prior research among older adults in Latvia, Poland and Sweden showed that regarding factors important for satisfying and independent ageing, older adults in Sweden have higher requirements than respondents in Poland and Latvia. Regarding technological solutions that should be developed to support independent and healthy ageing, Polish respondents identified that a broad spectrum of such technologies should be developed; Latvians were more moderate in their opinions, while Swedish respondents emphasized only a few areas where the technological solutions to support independent and healthy ageing should be developed [26].

Investigating the role of gender in the possibility of using ICT for an active and healthy ageing in the context of diverse socioeconomic considerations (Latvia, Poland and Sweden) is interesting for at least three reasons: (1) demographic differences, (2) differences in IT-skills and adoption of ICT solutions, and (3) different level of involvement in spousal and partner care.

Regarding demographic considerations, life expectancy and the level of health measured by the length of healthy years differs in the three studied countries (see Table 1). Comparing Latvia, Poland and Sweden, we notice that the Swedes live the longest, while the Latvians live the shortest. The similar regularity applies to healthy life years. In each of the three countries, women live longer. However, the biggest differences in life expectancy in favor of women are in Latvia and Poland, but gender gap is rather insignificant in the case of healthy life years. This means that, compared to men, older women in Poland and Latvia may need care for a longer period of time than Swedish women.

The ability to use ICT for active ageing will also depend on the ICT skills and experience of older people and, as suggested by extant research, lack of such skills is a strong barrier [24, 32]. In Europe, the digital skills of older people as well as the level of digital development at the macro level are the highest in the Scandinavian countries and in the UK, in contrast to transition economies, and these characteristics are strongly correlated with the implementation of active and healthy ageing policies, measured using Active Ageing Index (AAI) (see Table 1, [26]). However, the broadly understood acceptance of ICT by older people depending on gender is not well researched and the results are ambiguous [20, 30].

Table 1. Country comparison

	Latvia			Sweden			Poland		
Life expectancy – 2016*									
Female	79.6			83.7			81.9		
Male	69.8			80.1			73.9		
Healthy life years (65+) – 2016*									
Female	4.5			16.6			8.9		
Male	4.4			15.1			8.2		
Individuals using the Internet during last 12 months (%) - aged 55–74**									
Year	2016	2017	2018	2016	2017	2018	2016	2017	2018
Female	53.9	56.4	65.2	92.0	91.1	93.0	41.4	45.2	48.8
Male	55.8	58.1	59.1	93.1	91.3	62.2	44.7	47.6	48.6
Total active ageing index domains and gender gap – 2014***									
Employment	32 (+2.4 Male)			43.4 (+7.1 Male)			22.4 (+12.5 Male)		
Social participation	13.8 (+6.3 Female)			22.9 (+0.8 Female)			12.1 (+2.3 Female)		
Independent Living	58.7 (+3.8 Male)			78.6 (+1.9 Male)			64.9 (+3.2 Male)		
Capacity for Active Ageing	48.2 (+1.2 Male)			69.2 (+0.7 Male)			47.9 (+2.0 Female)		

Notes: *based on Eurostat database, **based on OECD.org, ***based on [33], gender gap shown in parentheses

In the review of studies dealing with ICT and the elderly, Wagner [30] indicated only two studies which have examined the impact of gender on attitudes toward computers, but results have been inconclusive, with one study showing that males have more positive attitudes and the other finding no relationship. In the similar vein, Peek et al. [20] in the literature review regarding acceptance of technology for ageing in place indicated that gender was not present in the reviewed qualitative studies, but was researched in one of three reviewed quantitative studies. This study showed that gender negatively influenced the acceptance of a motion monitoring system, but not the acceptance of a vitals signs monitoring system. Unfortunately, the authors did not specify whether the motion monitoring system was more accepted by males or females [17]. Similar inconclusive pattern is found in the most recent studies [1, 14]. In particular, Hunsaker and Hargittai [14] showed that gender differences are not clear regarding older adults' use of Internet. The gender gap appears for the oldest group of older adults but is not visible among the younger groups of older adults. While Abolhassani et al. [1] indicate that gender matters regarding acceptance of health ICTs, their study showed that the acceptance rate decreased across age categories for women and that women were less likely to accept data accessibility to non-physicians. Abolhassani et al.'s study contradicts prior studies on adoption of health related ICT, which demonstrated no effect of gender [12]. In addition, OECD statistics on individuals using the Internet for older people (see Table 1) show some unexpected trends in relation to men, whose growing participation in the use of the Internet is gradually slowing down in recent years, and in the case of Swedes even dropped significantly. For women in Poland and Latvia, there is a growing tendency, and in all three countries in 2018, more older women than men were Internet users.

Another aspect that may be important for the possibility of using ICT for an active and healthy ageing is women's and men's different way of involvement in spousal and partner care. Prior research shows that both men and women are involved in spousal and partner care, but the level of involvement and the way of caregiving differ [3]. Most caregiving women take care of their spouses and partners on their own while men more often share caregiving with other informal helpers such as family members, friends or neighbors. This fact could be explained by men's higher engagement in the labor market. When it comes to cash for care payments, women are generally more willing to engage in such arrangements than men and low-paid women more often than high-paid women [8]. This fact increases the risk for women poverty in advanced age, but better helps families to integrate family care and paid work. Prior research shows that the gender inequality is highest in countries with a high level of intergenerational care, a low provision of professional care services, and high family obligation norms [3, 8, 11].

3 Method

In our study, we focused on the investigation of the opinions of the older adults concerning the needs related to independent living and the attitudes towards using ICT. Data for Sweden (Örebro County) came from a larger study conducted by the municipality of Örebro, which, among other things, had a goal of assessing the needs related to the ageing of the population. On the basis of a research instrument used by the municipality of Örebro, a survey for Poland (Krakow and its surroundings) and Latvia (Riga and its surroundings) has been constructed. In order to achieve the comparability of country samples, from the Swedish database we randomly drew 10% of respondents taking into account the proportions in the age and gender structure of the analyzed population. Our preliminary survey was directed to older adults aged 50 to 89 years.

The questionnaire included two categories of questions. The first category concerned the needs which the respondents may consider important for an independent and satisfying life as people age. We presented the following 9 factors to the respondents and asked for their evaluation: (1) ability to choose where they will live (e.g. independently at home, at home with family, nursing home, at home with help coming); this factor was named "type of residence", (2) ability to choose what they will eat ("kind of food"), (3) ability to choose when they will eat ("time of meals"), (4) ability to be outside when and as much as they want ("time in outdoors"), (5) ability to participate in cultural activities (e.g. theater, cinema, concerts – "cultural activity"), (6) ability to perform physical activity ("physical activity"), (7) ability to decide what kind of help they will receive (e.g. personal care, cleaning, shopping – "kind of aid"), (8) ability to choose the time of assistance ("time of aid"), and (9) ability to choose the assisting person ("assisting person").

The second category related to the types of ICT solutions that should be developed to support independent and healthy ageing. We presented the following 7 examples of digital solutions for the evaluation by the respondents: (1) robots assisting independent eating (this device was named as "eating"), (2) technologies facilitating communication (e.g. with family, health care, care personnel – "communication"), (3) memory-supporting technology ("memory"), (4) health monitoring technologies (e.g. remote transmission of blood pressure measurement, sugar level – "health monitoring"),

(5) technology that help with personal hygiene ("hygiene"), (6) cleaning robots ("cleaning"), and (7) monitoring and alarming technologies (e.g. fall detection – "alarming"). In each case, a three-point Likert-type scale was employed for factor evaluation: 1 – not important, 2 – important, and 3 – very important. The Swedish sample consisted of 409 people (female/male median age = 67/69), the Polish sample counted 470 people (female/male median age = 67/67), and the Latvian sample consisted of 315 respondents (female/male median age = 69/68).

When examining the role of gender in perceiving the importance of the needs related to active and healthy ageing and attitudes towards the development of technology, a two-stage approach was applied. In the first exploratory step, the simplest method for analyzing categorical (nominal) data was used to assess the attitudes of women and separately the attitudes of men. This approach allowed us to observe the potential impact of varied socioeconomic considerations of the studied countries on women's and men's attitudes.

In the next step, individual countries were analyzed separately for each indicated type of need. It was examined whether women have a lower or higher propensity than men to a higher assessment of the importance of the indicated needs. For this purpose, using the STATISTICA package, the ordered logistic model (OLM) belonging to the generalized linear models (GLM) was employed [6, 19]. In OLM models, the dependent variable defines the consecutive levels of importance as regards the given need: not important, important, and very important. The first independent variable is gender with the category "male" as a reference category. The second independent variable is age, defined as a qualitative variable with four categories (50–59, 60–69, 70–79, 80–89). Age is treated as a control variable with "60–69" as a reference category.

4   Results

Results achieved in the first step, calculated separately for women and men, revealed that women in Sweden have higher requirements regarding needs important for satisfying and independent ageing than women in Poland and Latvia. However, women in Poland are most interested in the development of technology supporting independent ageing, while women in Sweden point more selectively to only certain technological solutions (alarming, communication and memory). Similar results were observed in the subpopulation of men, however, in the case of technology supporting independent ageing, Swedish male respondents were mostly interested in the development of alarming solutions and those facilitating communication.

In Tables 2 and 3 we present the results of ordered logit models for factors for independent life as people age and for supported technologies. In the case of the variable "gender", positive values denote that women reveal a greater propensity than men to evaluate more highly the needs associated with independent and healthy ageing, or to assess more favorably the need for development of given technological solutions. In the case of negative values, the interpretation is the opposite – women reveal a smaller propensity than men to evaluate more highly relevant needs. Similarly, we interpret the control variable age, referring to the reference group 60–69 years. For all statistically significant variables, the results are interpreted based on a *ceteris paribus* assumption.

Table 2. Results of ordered logit models for factors for independent life as people age

Variable	Type of residence	Kind of food	Time of meals	Time in outdoors	Cultural activity	Physical activity	Kind of aid	Time of aid	Assisting person
Latvia									
Cons1	−2.51**	−1.88**	−1.38**	−1.28**	−0.21**	−1.02*	−1.40**	−1.09**	−0.84**
Cons2	−1.08**	0.11	0.53**	0.22	1.25*	0.53*	0.37	0.51*	0.69*
Gender	−0.03	0.09	0.14	0.09	0.22*	−0.21*	0.20*	0.01	0.21*
50–59	0.45*	0.30	0.29†	−0.15	0.02	0.25	0.04	0.14	0.12
70–79	0.06	−0.04	0.10	−0.28*	−0.00	0.06	0.17	0.12	−0.02
80–89	0.10	−0.29†	−0.13	−0.40*	−0.29†	−0.18	0.19	0.18	−0.11
Dev#	0.86	0.98	1.06	0.95	1.08	1.09	1.07	1.10	1.09
Poland									
Cons1	−3.71**	−3.04**	−1.69**	−3.61**	−2.17**	−2.89**	−2.08**	−2.13**	−2.67**
Cons2	−1.06*	0.18	0.73**	−0.64*	0.58**	−0.08	0.25	0.50*	−0.37
Gender	0.15	0.24*	0.09	0.36**	0.42**	0.21*	0.34**	0.14	0.21*
50–59	0.07	−0.07	−0.10	−0.16	−0.47**	−0.28*	−0.02	−0.09	0.25
70–79	−0.12	−0.13	−0.21*	0.03	−0.03	−0.14	−0.05	−0.24*	−0.00
80–89	−0.06	0.03	0.18	−0.10	0.06	−0.03	0.14	0.24	0.20
Dev#	0.85	1.11	0.99	0.92	0.87	0.91	0.95	0.94	0.91
Sweden									
Cons1	−5.16**	−3.85**	−2.93**	−3.83**	−1.82**	−2.59**	−4.19**	−4.11**	2.34**
Cons2	−1.29**	−0.97**	−0.40	−1.06**	0.39	0.03	−1.28**	−1.21**	−0.41
Gender	0.76**	0.39**	0.39**	0.38**	0.24*	0.28**	0.35**	0.43**	0.48**
50–59	−0.19	−0.10	−0.17	−0.21	0.08	0.15	0.06	0.09	−0.07
70–79	−0.17	−0.21	−0.09	−0.42*	−0.13	−0.09	−0.01	−0.00	−0.16
80–89	−0.20	−0.32	−0.01	−0.46*	−0.44*	−0.51**	−0.30	−0.20	−0.19
Dev#	1.18	1.07	0.83	0.62	0.93	0.86	1.29	1.48	0.78

Notes: ref. category: gender – male; age categories: (50–59, 70–79, 80–89) – 60–69;
significance †p < 0.1; *p < 0.05; **p < 0.01; #Goodness of fit: Criterion deviance (Stat/df)

Our results indicate that gender affects the perception of factors that are important for active and healthy ageing. However, the differences vary in the studied countries.

Gender gap is particularly visible for Sweden and Poland. Women in these countries more often have higher requirements than men (they assess the importance of individual needs higher), while in Latvia gender differences are less clear-cut. Namely, the needs for cultural activity, the kind of aid received and the ability to decide on the choice of a helper were more important for women, while the need for physical activity turned out to be more important for men (the only case where men were more demanding).

Age-related differences are selective and different in all countries. Only in the case of the need to be outdoors in Sweden and Latvia older generations proved to be less demanding than younger ones, it also seems that the oldest generations pay less attention to the importance of the need of cultural activity.

Table 3. Results of ordered logit models for technologies for independent life as people age

Variable	Eating	Communication	Memory	Health monitoring	Hygiene	Cleaning	Alarming
Latvia							
Cons1	0.23	−1.89**	−1.35**	−1.91**	−0.49*	−0.79**	−1.86**
Cons2	1.71**	−0.23	0.33	−0.15	1.08**	0.72**	−0.03
Gender	−0.01*	0.13	0.28**	0.08	0.25*	0.05	0.17
50–59	0.27	0.26	0.11	−0.06	0.01	0.10	0.31†
70–79	−0.02	0.17	−0.02	−0.00	−0.01	0.25*	0.22†
80–89	0.34*	0.08	0.28†	0.17	0.04	0.17	0.26
Dev#	0.89	1.02	1.07	0.98	1.08	1.09	1.05
Poland							
Cons1	−0.27	−3.91**	−2.43**	−3.06**	−2.11**	−1.69**	−2.84**
Cons2	1.62**	−1.23**	−0.12	−0.45	0.13	0.72*	−0.59*
Gender	0.36**	0.23*	0.40**	0.21*	0.37**	0.34**	0.39**
50–59	−0.13	0.23	−0.00	0.10	−0.05	−0.20	0.03
70–79	−0.06	0.07	0.15	0.14	−0.04	−0.13	−0.00
80–89	−0.42*	0.01	−0.18	−0.09	−0.09	0.14	−0.04
Dev#	1.06	0.85	0.84	0.90	0.90	0.97	0.75
Sweden							
Cons1	1.89**	−2.24**	−2.02**	−1.35**	−0.03	0.89**	−3.08**
Cons2	3.68**	−0.32	0.66**	0.95**	2.37**	3.22**	−0.34
Gender	0.11	−0.02	0.25*	−0.04	−0.15	0.07	0.02
50–59	−0.02	0.09	0.29*	0.20	−0.02	0.17	−0.14
70–79	0.04	0.20	0.11	0.13	−0.00	0.03	−0.16
80–89	0.04	−0.08	−0.33†	−0.14	−0.29	−0.44*	−0.18
Dev#	0.48	0.93	0.94	1.03	0.96	0.79	0.76

Notes: ref. category: gender – male; age categories: (50–59, 70–79, 80–89) – 60–69; significance †p < 0.1; *p < 0.05; **p < 0.01; #Goodness of fit: Criterion deviance (Stat/df)

Regarding the perception of technological solutions that should be developed to support independent and healthy ageing, gender gap has appeared mainly in Poland. Women perceived the importance of developing such technological solutions stronger than men. In Latvia, this pattern occurred only in the case of solutions supporting memory and personal hygiene, while in Sweden only the development of solutions supporting memory turned out to be more important for women. Regarding other solutions, we did not find any significant differences due to gender.

There was also a slight impact of age on the perception of the importance of technology supporting independent and healthy ageing. It appeared mainly in Latvia and Sweden. The oldest generations to a lesser extent pointed to the need to develop technology that facilitates cleaning and supporting memory in Sweden, while in Poland this relationship concerned only the development of devices supporting independent eating. The opposite situation was found in Latvia, where the oldest also expressed a greater need for the development of devices assisting independent eating and memory-supporting technologies. In addition, generations 70–79 more strongly pointed to the need to develop devices that help in cleaning and alarming technologies. Also, in Sweden the youngest generation expressed a stronger need to develop memory-supporting technologies, while in Latvia the youngest mentioned alarming technologies.

Therefore, summing up, if age-related differences were present (i.e. were statistically significant), these indicated that older generations may be less interested in the development of technologies supporting active and healthy ageing in Sweden and Poland, while the development of technologies was more important for older Latvians. However, for the youngest generations, the differences indicated their stronger perception of the importance of technology development.

5 Discussion

The study addresses two research questions, which we discuss in the following subsections individually.

5.1 RQ1: Do Women and Men in Latvia, Poland and Sweden Differ in the Perception of Factors that Are Important to Have an Independent and Satisfying Life as People Age?

Our results show that gender differentiates older adults' perception of factors that are important for an independent and satisfying ageing in all studied countries. The gender gap is the biggest in Sweden, clearly visible in Poland, but less obvious in Latvia, which was a surprising result. We expected the biggest gender gap in Poland and Latvia, since in these two countries women live considerably longer than men. We assumed that because of the considerable differences in life expectancy, more older women in Poland and Latvia need to live without a partner as they age and that fact could influence their need for care from third parties (e.g. kind of aid, time of aid). Living alone could also motivate women to seek out-of-home activities (such as physical or cultural activities). We expected small or none gender gap in Sweden, since in this country life expectancy and number of healthy life years is almost similar for men and woman (see Table 1). While results from Poland confirmed our expectations, results from Sweden and Latvia surprised us. Further research is needed to explain why the gender gap is the biggest in Sweden and Poland and less visible in Latvia.

One could expect that results from Poland and Latvia should be similar because of comparable demographic and socioeconomic considerations but different from Sweden.

However, by considering the complexity of the considerations in more detail (e.g. interrelationships between various factors), one can try to partially explain the results obtained. The AAI indexes indicate that women are more involved in volunteering activities and caring for the older relatives and children (see "Social participation" domain of Active Ageing Index in Table 1). For this reason women may emphasize the importance of the needs related to caregiving (e.g. assisting person or kind of aid) stronger that men. However, at the same time, the Independent Living indexes show a gender gap related to secure living (see Table 1) [33]. In particular, women are more likely to experience financial problems than men, they more often live alone and feel less safe. These aspects may also influence women's higher evaluation of the importance of the needs related to independent living.

It is worth noticing that the models for elderly care, as well as the level of available funds allocated by the state for elderly care, differ in the studied countries [16]. Sweden is one of the countries with the best-developed elderly care organization and the highest financing of care by the government, while Poland belongs to the group of countries with the least-developed care organization and the lowest level of funds allocated for elderly care. The situation in Latvia is slightly better than in Poland. It is possible that high expectations related to the government's support (as in Sweden) related to caregiving may encourage Swedish women to express higher demands for the quality of care (e.g. type of residence, time of aid or time of meals), while less developed organization of care and low availability of funds offered by the government may result in lower expectations (requirements) in this respect.

Previous research shows that poor health can reduce women's and men's time in active leisure. However, disability status in particular has pervasive negative influence on participation and time in discretionary activities like leisure, as well as time in paid work, care work, and volunteering, but research has not yet examined how disability and time use patterns differ between women and men [23]. This could explain the differences in perceptions of the needs for time in outdoors and physical activity in Latvia compared to Poland and Sweden in the context of differences in healthy life expectancy.

As many different factors may be involved, further research is needed to explain why older woman generally have greater requirements than older men regarding factors important for satisfying and independent ageing and why there are clear differences in gender gap between Latvia, Poland and Sweden.

5.2 RQ2: Do Women and Men in Latvia, Poland and Sweden Differ in the Perception of Technological Solutions that Should Be Developed to Support Independent and Healthy Ageing?

Our results show that the difference in the perception of technological solutions that should be developed to support independent and healthy ageing between women and men is clearly visible in Poland, but not so obvious in Sweden and Latvia. In these two countries gender differences appeared only for single types of ICT. As discussed earlier, prior research is not conclusive regarding the role of gender in adoption of ICTs [e.g. 1, 14, 30]. Our results implicate that gender differences in adoption of ICT may vary between different countries.

The interesting question is why the gender gap in the perception of technological solutions that should be developed to support independent and healthy ageing is more visible in Poland than in Latvia and Sweden. Looking at the patterns in using Internet by older adults (see Table 1), Poland does not differ significantly from Sweden and Latvia. In all countries older women use Internet to a similar extent as older men do; only for 2018 the difference between female and male Internet users in Sweden was bigger than in Poland and Latvia.

ICT solutions for independent and healthy ageing may help older adults to be able to cope with everyday life at home but can also support older adults as caregivers for their partners and spouses. Previous research showed that there is a clear gender gap regarding level of involvement in spousal and partner care in European countries and that the gap is higher in countries with a high level of intergenerational care, a low provision of professional care services, and high family obligation norms [3, 8, 11]. Examples of such countries are Poland and Latvia, however, in Poland the obligations and norms regarding care of the older family members are more obvious and higher than in Latvia. Also, as indicated earlier, Poland has a less developed organization of long-time assistance for the elderly, as well as significantly fewer resources are dedicated for elderly care [10, 16]. This could partly explain the differences in the gender gap between Poland and Latvia. However, more research is needed to better understand the reasons behind the differences in the perception of technological solutions that should be developed to support independent and healthy ageing between men and women and to understand the differences in gender gap between Latvia, Poland and Sweden.

5.3   Implications

Three implications seem to emerge from our study on the role of gender in the possibility of using ICT for an active and healthy ageing in the context of diverse socioeconomic considerations on the example of three countries: Latvia, Poland and Sweden. First, women and men in Latvia, Poland and Sweden differ in the perception of factors that are important for an independent and satisfying ageing. Women have generally higher requirements regarding factors important for independent and satisfying ageing than man. This indicates that gender is an important factor to consider in developing of the so-called silver economy, which should support the implementation of strategies for ageing society.

Second, the differences in the perception of technological solutions that should be developed to support independent and healthy ageing between women and men are clearly visible in Poland, but not so obvious in Sweden and Latvia. Our results may indicate that in countries with more traditional ways of caring for the elderly the recipients of technology may more often be women. As women in such countries may often have limited financial possibilities, there is a need to develop solutions for "home use" (i.e. lighter, cheaper) and also to develop financial solutions that would make the solution more available for poor users (i.e. leasing). Regardless of institutional solutions, the development of alarming and memory supporting technology is desirable. These solutions can increase the level of safe habitation for women that live alone at a more advanced age.

Third, given the stronger need of women related to cultural activity and their restricted financial and communication capabilities (i.e. women more likely than men limit their driving in situations like bad weather or at night, and their health limitations strongly reduce the desire to drive [2]), it appears worth developing various forms of communication technology such as video transmission and social platforms, allowing for greater participation in broadly understood cultural events.

6 Conclusions

The current study investigated the role of gender gap in the context of ICT and active and healthy ageing. We examined older adults in three countries with different socio-economic considerations, i.e. Latvia, Poland and Sweden. Employing the ordered logistic models we achieved the results that implicate that gender differences in adoption of ICT of active and healthy ageing may vary between countries. In the case of factors that are important for an independent and satisfying ageing, the gender gap was the biggest in Sweden, clearly visible in Poland, but less obvious in Latvia. In turn, differences in the perception of technological solutions that should be developed to support independent and healthy ageing between women and men were clearly visible in Poland, but not so manifested in Sweden and Latvia.

Important implications suggested by our research include: (1) The need to take into consideration gender issues in the development of the so-called silver economy and to incorporate different gender-related needs to support the implementation of strategies for ageing society; (2) Development of technological solutions supporting elderly care that are more affordable and better aligned for home, whose users are first and fore-most women from countries with a low provision of professional care services, and high family obligation norms regarding care of the older family members; (3) The need to develop some technologies regardless of socioeconomic considerations, such as technologies supporting independent living of the elderly women (e.g. alarming, technology supporting memory) and communication technologies allowing older women to participate in cultural activities, due to greater mobility barriers experienced by older women.

Our study had an exploratory nature and the problems related to the explanation of the results indicate both some limitations and the possibilities for future research. The reasons of problems might be associated with the focus on the elderly living in large cities and the fact that some characteristics of individuals were not considered in the study. In future research it is worth considering such characteristics as health status, providing or receiving help, or type of residence (including countryside, not just cities). Inclusion of these factors might diversify the examined population to a greater extent. This is an interesting issue to be considered in further research.

Acknowledgments. This research has been financed in part by The Swedish Institute, Sweden, and by the subsidy granted to Cracow University of Economics, Poland.

References

1. Abolhassani, N., Santos-Eggimann, B., Chiolero, A., Santschi, V., Henchoz, Y.: Readiness to accept health information and communication technologies: a population-based survey of community-dwelling older adults. Int. J. Med. Inform. **130**, 103950 (2019)
2. Barrett, A., Gumber, C., Douglas, R.: Explaining gender differences in self-regulated driving: what roles do health limitations and driving alternatives play? Ageing Soc. **38**(10), 2122–2145 (2018)
3. Bertogg, A., Strauss, S.: Spousal care-giving arrangements in Europe. The role of gender, socio-economic status and the welfare state. Ageing Soc., 1–24. https://doi.org/10.1017/s0144686x18001320
4. Carretero, S., Stewart, J., Centeno, C.: Information and communication technologies for informal carers and paid assistants: benefits from micro-, meso-, and macro-levels. Eur. J. Ageing **12**(2), 163–173 (2015)
5. Chan, L., Chou, K.: Poverty in old age: evidence from Hong Kong. Ageing Soc. **38**(1), 37–55 (2018)
6. Dobson, A.J.: An Introduction to Generalized Linear Models, 2nd edn. Chapman & Hall, London (2002)
7. de Jong Gierveld, J., Dykstra, P.A., Schenk, N.: Living arrangements, intergenerational support types and older adult loneliness in Eastern and Western Europe. Demogr. Res. Spec. Collect. **27**(7), 167–200 (2012)
8. Dykstra, P.A.: Cross-national differences in intergenerational family relations: the influence of public policy arrangements. Innov. Aging **2**(1), 1–8 (2018)
9. European Commission: The 2018 Ageing Report. Underlying Assumptions and Projection Methodologies. European Economy Institutional Paper 065 (2017)
10. Golinowska, S.: The Present and Future of Long-Term Care in Ageing Poland. The World Bank (2015)
11. Haberkern, K., Schmid, T., Szydlik, M.: Gender differences in intergenerational care in European welfare states. Ageing Soc. **35**(2), 298–320 (2015)
12. Heart, T., Kalderon, E.: Older adults: are they ready to adopt health-related ICT? Int. J. Med. Inform. **82**(11), e209–e231 (2013)
13. Hill, R., Beynon-Davies, P., Williams, M.D.: Older people and internet engagement: acknowledging social moderators of internet adoption, access and use. Inf. Technol. People **21**(3), 244–266 (2008)
14. Hunsaker, A., Hargittai, E.: A review of Internet use among older adults. New Media Soc. **20**(10), 3937–3954 (2018)
15. Kolkowska, E., Soja, E., Soja, P.: Implementation of ICT for active and healthy ageing: comparing value-based objectives between Polish and Swedish seniors. In: Wrycza, S., Maślankowski, J. (eds.) SIGSAND/PLAIS 2018. LNBIP, vol. 333, pp. 161–173. Springer, Cham (2018). https://doi.org/10.1007/978-3-030-00060-8_12
16. Kraus, M., Riedel, M., Mot, E., Willemé, P., Röhrling, G., Czypionka, T.: A typology of long-term care systems in Europe. ANCIEN Project, ENEPRI Research Report No. 91. CEPS, Brussels (2010)
17. Lai, C.K., Chung, J.C., Leung, N.K., Wong, J.C., Mak, D.P.: A survey of older Hong Kong people's perceptions of telecommunication technologies and telecare devices. J. Telemed. Telecare **16**, 441–446 (2010)
18. Malgesini, G., Cesarini-Sforza, L., Babović, M., Leemkuil, S., Sverrisdóttir, M., Mareková, S.: Gender and Poverty in Europe. The European Anti-Poverty Network (2017)

19. McCullagh, P., Nelder, J.A.: Generalized Linear Models, 2nd edn. Chapman & Hall, London (1989)
20. Peek, S.T.M., Wouters, E.J.M., van Hoof, J., Luijkx, K.G., Boeije, H.R., Vrijhoef, H.J.M.: Factors influencing acceptance of technology for aging in place: a systematic review. Int. J. Med. Informatics **83**(4), 235–248 (2014)
21. Rigby, M., Koch, S., Keeling, D., Hill, P., Alonso, A., Maeckelberghe, E.: Developing a New Understanding of Enabling Health and Wellbeing in Europe: Harmonising Health and Social Care Delivery and Informatics Support to Ensure Holistic Care. European Science Foundation, Strasbourg (2013)
22. Roztocki, N., Weistroffer, H.R.: Information and communication technology in transition economies: an assessment of research trends. Inf. Technol. Dev. **21**(3), 330–364 (2015)
23. Sayer, L.C., Freedman, V.A., Bianchi, S.M.: Gender, time use, and aging. In: George, L.K., Ferraro, K.F. (eds.) Handbook of Aging and the Social Sciences (Eighth Edition), pp. 163–180. Academic Press, San Diego (2016)
24. Soja, E.: Information and communication technology in active and healthy ageing: exploring risks from multi-generation perspective. Inf. Syst. Manag. **34**(4), 320–332 (2017)
25. Soja, E.: Supporting active ageing: challenges and opportunities for information and communication technology. Zarządzanie i Finanse J. Manag. Finan. **15**(1/2017), 109–125 (2017)
26. Soja, E., Soja, P., Kolkowska, E., Kirikova, M.: Supporting active and healthy ageing by ICT solutions: preliminary lessons learned from Polish, Swedish and Latvian older adults. In: Wrycza, S., Maślankowski, J. (eds.) SIGSAND/PLAIS 2019. LNBIP, vol. 359, pp. 48–61. Springer, Cham (2019). https://doi.org/10.1007/978-3-030-29608-7_5
27. Soja, P., Cunha, P.R.: ICT in transition economies: narrowing the research gap to developed countries. Inf. Technol. Dev. **21**(3), 323–329 (2015)
28. Strauss, S., Trommer, K.: Productive ageing regimes in Europe: welfare state typologies explaining elderly Europeans' participation in paid and unpaid work. J. Popul. Ageing **11**(4), 311–328 (2018)
29. Schmid, T., Brandt, M., Haberkern, K.: Gendered support to older parents: do welfare states matter? Eur. J. Ageing **9**, 39–50 (2012)
30. Wagner, N., Hassanein, K., Head, M.: Computer use by older adults: a multi-disciplinary review. Comput. Hum. Behav. **26**(5), 870–882 (2010)
31. Walker, A., Maltby, T.: Active ageing: a strategic policy solution to demographic ageing in the European Union. Int. J. Soc. Welf. **21**(1), 117–130 (2012)
32. Yusif, S., Soar, J., Hafeez-Baig, A.: Older people, assistive technologies, and the barriers to adoption: a systematic review. Int. J. Med. Informatics **94**, 112–116 (2016)
33. Zaidi, A., Stanton, D.: Active Ageing Index 2014: Analytical Report. UNECE, European Commission (2015)

Information Systems Security and Information Privacy Protection

Trust Management Model Based on Mutual Evaluation Method for the Social Internet of Things

Rim Magdich[1]([⊠]), Hanen Jemal[1], and Mounir Ben Ayed[1,2]

[1] REGIM-Laboratory REsearch Groups in Intelligent Machines,
University of Sfax, National Engineering School of Sfax (ENIS),
BP 1173, 3038 Sfax, Tunisia
{rim.magdich,hanen.jemal,Mounir.benayed}@ieee.org
[2] Faculty of Sciences of Sfax, University of Sfax, Sfax, Tunisia

Abstract. The combination of Social Networks with the Internet of Things, has led to the appearance of a new standard dubbed Social Internet of Things (SIoT), where devices are able to make social links between each other. However, ensuring secure and trustworthy interactions between all the agents in the network is still an ongoing challenge. Trust is a notion which assesses the reliability of a communication between two agents namely: the trustor and the trustee. Therefore, there is a need for a Trust Management (TM) model to deal with dishonest nodes and ensure a users' safe communications. In this research, we propose a new TM for SIoT systems called TM-SIoT, for the sake to assess the trustworthiness of SIoT nodes based on mutual evaluation method. The proposed method provides reliable security mechanisms for both the trustor and the trustee, by considering both of quality of service and social metrics that can affect trust in SIoT Systems. In addition, we propose a novel trust metric which is the time aware to deal with nodes' behaviors changing over the time and to limit the influence of reputations given in the past for the trust assessment. The experimentations results performed based on ns-3 simulator show that the proposed model produces a reliable trust level for protecting both the trustor and the trustee toward dynamic nodes' behaviors even for a system with 50% of malicious nodes.

Keywords: Internet of Things · Social Internet of Things · Trust Management · Social networks · Time-aware · Security

1 Introduction

Internet of Things (IoT) is described as the implementation of several smart devices with wireless communication technologies to provide intelligent services and improve the human's quality of life [1]. Scalability and heterogeneity are among the famous challenges that block the large-scale realization of IoT services in our lives [2]. To overcome these challenges, a new standard integrating smart devices of IoT and social

R. Magdich, H. Jemal, B.M. Ayed—IEEE Member.

M. Themistocleous and M. Papadaki (Eds.): EMCIS 2019, LNBIP 381, pp. 361–375, 2020.
https://doi.org/10.1007/978-3-030-44322-1_27

networks systems, dubbed Social Internet of Things (SIoT), has evolved recently. The idea is to make devices not only smart, but also socially cooperative via social networks such as Twitter, Facebook, Instagram, etc. In this paradigm, each node has the ability to make autonomously social links with other nodes in the network [3]. However, the large scale connectivity of SIoT nodes can be managed by dishonest attackers that bring risks and vulnerabilities to devices [4, 5]. In order to ensure users' satisfaction and increase SIoT system consumption and security, it is necessary for SIoT node to assess all the involved agents' trustworthiness [6, 7].

Trust is defined as a crucial feature for ensuring reliable interactions between trusted nodes. Several TM models have been defined [8–14] to deal with misbehaving nodes and ensure user's safe communications. Each one of them has its own constraints and features to assess the trust such as quality of service, nodes' behaviors, social relationships, etc. However, all of them propose a unilateralevaluation method to assess the trustee's trustworthiness before any transaction and to protect the trustor's resources. This method can bring risks to the trustee and damage the SIoT systems security. In addition, all the already mentioned research works have neglected the consideration of the time factor as a trust metric to address the impact of past trans-actions and nodes' behaviors changing in the trust evaluation.The objectives of this contribution are as follows:

- We propose a generic TM model for SIoT systems called "TM-SIoT" based on mutual evaluation method. This model allows us to protect both the trustor and the trustee against malicious nodes and ensure a trustworthy interaction;
- Since the efficiency of the trust evaluation method counts on the required trust metrics, we consider in the TM-SIoT model both qualities of service (QoS) and social metrics to deal with the inherent constraints that can affect trust in SIoT systems;
- In order to deal with the changing behaviors of nodes over the time, we consider in this research work the time-aware factor as a trust metric to consider the impact of past and recent trust data (reputation).

The rest of this paper is structured as follows: Sect. 2 defines the general concept of the trust and discusses related works in TM model for both IoT and SIoT systems. In Sect. 3, we express in detail how each SIoT node in the TM-SIoT model compute the trust level of other nodes based on mutual evaluation. In Sect. 4, the effectiveness of the TM-SIoT model is presented through a wide set of simulation. Finally, Sect. 5 concludes the paper and discusses future works.

2   Background and Related Work

2.1   Trust in the SIoT Systems

The concept of trust is studied in various fields [15] which makes hard to give it a clear and a standard definition. In SIoT, trust is explained as a dynamic process of the trustor, predicated on the assessment and the assumption of the trustee's capacity and confidence, decision to delegate tasks to the trustee, and the utilization of the trustees' resulted action to achieve the goal [6]. By integrating social structures into the IoT devices, the trust level could be assessed based on their social links. Socialization over devices is defined throw five basic inter-social object relationships (I-SoR) [16]:

1. Parental object Relationships (PoR): defined among similar objects that are constructed by the same producer in the same period;
2. Co-location object Relationships (C-LoR): defined among objects (such as actuators, sensors, RFID tag, etc.) used continuously in similar environments;
3. Co-Work Object Relationships (C-WoR): defined whatever objects cooperate to produce a common service;
4. Ownership object Relationships (OoR): defined between varied objects derived from the same owner;
5. Social objects Relationships (SoR): defined when objects communicate with each other, periodically or continuously, predicated on their owners' social relationships.

2.2 Literature Review

To understand the current literature related to this research question, we address researches in two main fields which are IoT and SIoT networks. We are interested in this work to analyze the proposed TM models based on two criteria: (1) the considered trust metrics to assess the trustworthiness and (2) the trust evaluation method between the trustor and the trustee.

Since the efficiency of a TM model counts on the required trust metrics selected for the trust evaluation, we started our study with a comparison between these metrics proposed in the literature. Researches define different metrics to assess the trust level for nodes in both IoT and SIoT networks [17]. Each one of them has its own believes and goals. For example, authors in [8] proposed a subjective model for trustworthiness evaluation in which the trustor assess the trustee based on honesty, centrality, computation capabilities and social relationship factors. In this work, social metrics have been employed for the first time to evaluate the trust level between nodes where does the appearance of the SIoT network. Researches of the work [9] recognize the worthiness of the context in assessing the trustworthiness of dynamic behaviors of IoT nodes. Therefore, a generic context-aware TM protocol for IoT systems has been suggested which provides dynamic trust values to cooperate nodes based on the changing contexts. It considers only the quality of services (QoS) metrics such as services which demonstrate they capability to assess trust. The paper [10] presents an adaptive TM framework for SIoT systems. To measure SIoT nodes' trustworthiness, they consider three social trust properties, i.e., honesty, cooperativeness and CoI. In [11], a schema of access service recommendation is presented for SIoT based on trust level between nodes. Three trust metrics are considered in this work: reputation of the trustee in the SIoT system, social relationship factors and QoS. Authors in [12] consider three types of object relationships for the evaluation of nodes' interaction such as: ownership relationships, domestic relationships and social relationships. In this model, trustees' trustworthiness is assessed based on requestors' satisfaction feedback and reputation. As for researches in [13], they assumed that trustworthiness in SIoT systems can be assessed through three based metrics: reputation, experience with the trustee and knowledge. However, authors in [14] define a distributed TM model for IoT using direct and indirect information. The node's trustworthiness is assessed by the service quality and recommendation from neighbors. IoT nodes locally assess the trustworthiness of their neighbors, without a centralized entity.

These works helped us to improve one's comprehension of the challenges of the proposed TM model. Given that there is no a standard and a clear definition of the trust, trust is assessed in the literature based on various and different trust metrics. Some researchers think that trust can be assessed based only on QoS or only on social trust metrics. Others assume that trust should be assessed based on both QoS and social trust metrics. We believe in the second hypothesis in which both of specifics SIoT devices requirements and social interactions between nodes should be considered for the evaluation of the trustworthiness. However, these works neglected to consider the temporal factor of nodes' transaction in the trust evaluation process. In fact, social metrics such as reputation, rely on the evaluation of nodes' transactions which defines their behaviors that are not always constant but often change with the time. So, it can be efficient to consider recent transactions more than the historical interactions. The second point of comparison concerns the lack of security of the trustee. In fact, all the TM model proposed to carry out a unilateral evaluation of trustworthiness in which only the Trustor evaluates the trustee. This evaluation method brings risks to the trustee who needs also to be sure that the trustor will not damage its resources.

3   Proposed Trust Management for SIoT

In our model, we consider the SIoT environment defined by [18]. Each device in the network maintains its profile (manufacturer, type, capacity, location), owners' profile (friendship, CoI, Co-work), trust values and history of transactions between nodes. When two nodes contact each other, they exchange their profiles and trust data. The mutual evaluation of trustworthiness depends on two phases: the direct-evaluation and the post-evaluation.

3.1   Direct Evaluation

Before the delegation of a task π, both the trustor X and the trustee Y evaluate each other asdescribed in Fig. 1. This phase is achieved based on three steps:

1. Trust composition: the required trust metrics for the evaluation of the trustworthiness will be selected. In our model, trustworthiness is assessed based on three main trust metrics namely: reputation, recommendation and knowledge (see Fig. 2).

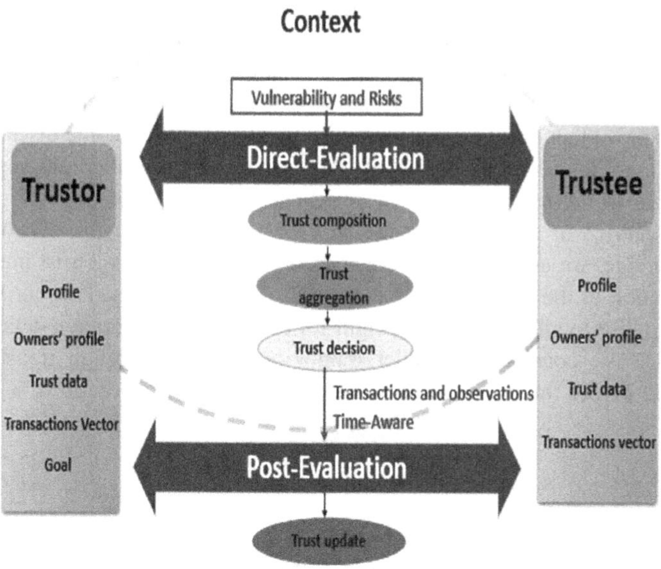

Context

Fig. 1. Illustration of the mutual evaluation of trustworthiness

Recommendation Rec(t): represents opinions produced by trustors' friends to help the trustor X judge the trustworthiness of the trustee Y. A node is considered honest if its recommendations reflect its actual evaluation, which means that it does not try to give false trust value to improve or reduce the importance of other nodes. To evaluate the honesty trust metric, the trustor compares trustees' vector of recommendations R_{YS} of the node S with the vector V_S representing the average trust values of others nodes to the same node S by considering the coefficient similarity of Jaccard (Eq. 1).

$$Rec(t) = sim_f(R_{YS}, V_S) = J(R_{YS}, V_S) = \frac{|(R_{YS} \cap V_S)|}{|(R_{YS} \cup V_S)|} \qquad (1)$$

Reputation Rrep (t): is a notion defines the global reputation of a device D produced by opinions of other nodes than friends n_i in the SIoT system. It is assessed based on the quotient between the number of success transactions and the total number of transactions (Eq. 2).

$$Rrep(t) = \frac{\sum_1^i V_T(n_i, D)}{N_T(n_i, D)} \qquad (2)$$

Where: V_T represents the successful transactions between device D and other node than friends n_i and N_T represents the total number of transactions.

Time-aware: trust is a dynamic concept which varies over time based on nodes' behaviors changing. This variation can be captured through the change of transactions between nodes with the time. In fact, every transaction in the SIoT network is achieved in a particular context and at a given time. Researches in [19] believe that old reputation between two users may become discarded after a period. In this context, we think that we should consider old reputation in addition to the recent reputation to deal with malicious nodes who try to give good service in order to enhance their past reputation in the network. To our knowledge, we are the first to consider the time- aware as a trust metric for the evaluation of the trustworthiness in the SIoT systems. Based on our hypothesis, we propose to affect different weight for each type of reputation data (older and recent). We consider that older reputation is given through transaction performed before the period Δtlfixed according to the Eq. 3.

$$\Delta t_l = \frac{\sum_{i=1}^{n} PT(x,i)}{N} \tag{3}$$

Where P_T represents the elapsed period of the first transaction and the actual date between the trustor X and the trustee i. For the consideration of the time metric in the assessment of trustworthiness, we update the Eq. 2 as follow:

$$Rrep(t) = \alpha_1 \frac{\sum_1^i V_T(n_i, D, \Delta t_1)}{N_T(n_i, D, \Delta t_1)} + \alpha_2 \frac{\sum_1^i V_T(n_i, D, \Delta t_2)}{N_T(n_i, D, \Delta t_2)} \tag{4}$$

Where Δt_2 represent the elapsed period between the first transaction and Δt_1.
Knowledge: represents valuable information describing the trustee's (trustor's) profile. It is assessed based on two trust attributes: Social Similarity and I-SoR.

$$Knowledge(t) = k_1 \text{ Social Similarity}(t) + k_2 \text{ I-SoR} \tag{5}$$

Social Similarity: is considered as a crucial metric for the evaluation of the trustworthiness predicated on the following hypothesis "in social networks, if two agents have an elevated level of similarity, they will be considered more trustworthy [13]. This metric is based on two trust attributes namely CoI and cooperativeness where S_1, S_2 c$[0,1]$.

$$\text{Social Similarity}(t) = S_1 \text{ cooperativeness}(t) + S_2 \text{CoI} \tag{6}$$

Cooperativeness: the trustor X evaluates the cooperativeness' degree of the trustee Y with their similar friends that are considered honest, based on a comparison of the similarity between two friends' vectors F_X and F_Y (Eq. 7).

$$\text{sim}_f(X,Y) = J(X,Y) \frac{|F_X \cap F_Y|}{|F_X \cup F_Y|} \tag{7}$$

CoI: in our SIoT system model, when two devices interact with each other, they exchange the lists of their owners' communities of interest V_X and V_Y (Eq. 8):

$$\text{sim}_{\text{Col}}(X,Y) = J(X,Y)\frac{|V_X \cap V_Y|}{|V_X \cup V_Y|} \qquad (8)$$

I-SoR: The initial trustworthiness values for each node are defined in [0.1] based of the type of the relationship that links two objects in the SIoT network. Table 1 describes the trust value for each relationship type defined and proved in [10, 20]. These values are the inputs of TM-SIoT model. For the consideration of QoS trust metrics, we defined in another form of SoR intitules "Intelligence Object Relationships" (IoR). IoR is defined among objects that have similar functionalities and performances. In fact, a smart device with higher computation capabilities seems to be able to achieve different and complex tasks. In this case, we define two types of devices for IoR: type 1 is assigned to nodes with higher competences and communication capabilities and type 2 for nodes with only sensing competences.

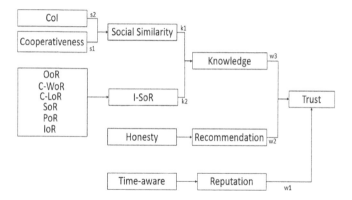

Fig. 2. Trust metrics Overview

Table 1. Inter-Social Object Relationships parameters.

I-SoR		Trust values input
OoR		1
C-LoR		0.6
C-WoR		0.8
SoR		0.4
PoR		0.2
IoR	Smartphone,Tablet, etc.	0.7
	Sensor, RFID	0.3

2 Trust aggregation: as each value may have diverse impacts on the trust assessment, we use the weighted mean technique to aggregate trust metrics values (Eq. 9).

$$T^{\pi}_{pre(X,Y)}(t) = w_1 Rrep + w_2 Rec + w_3 Knowledge \qquad (9)$$

We note that $T^{\pi}_{pre(X,Y)}(t)$ represents the trust assessment of the trustor X toward the trustee Y at time t over task π where w_1, w_2 and $w_3 \in [0.1]$ represent respectively weights parameters for trust metrics. The weights values are defined according to author's choices and experiences yet they are destined to be adapted dynamically to the changing context in our next work.

3 Trust decision: a SIoT device is considered trustworthy if its trust value is higher or equals than a threshold fixed by the trustor X. In this stage, the trustor delegates the task to the trustee Y with the first higher trustworthiness value. The trustee Y performs the same pre evaluation described above to decide whether or not the trustor will give the task with risk. In the case that the trustee Y refuses to produce the task π to thetrustor X, then the trustor X will select another trustee with the second best trust value.

3.2   Post-evaluation

After the completion of the task π, both the trustor X and the trustee Y perform a post-evaluation, to update their trust assessment value toward each other, based on their direct observations (Eqs. 10 and 11).

$$T^{\pi}_{post(X,Y)}(t) = (1 - \alpha)T^{\pi}_{pre(X,Y)}(t - \Delta t) + \alpha Ret^{\pi}_{(X,Y)}(t) \qquad (10)$$

Δt represents the period time between the last trust assessment and the end of the task π execution. $Ret^{\pi}_{(X,Y)}(t)$ defines the rating attributes by the trustor X toward the trustee Y based on a comparison between the resulting action and the expected trustworthiness. If the expected trustworthiness is aligned with the resulting action, then the available SoR factor should be adapted accordingly by trustor.

$$T^{\pi}_{post(Y,X)}(t) = (1 - \alpha)T^{\pi}_{pre(Y,X)}(t - \Delta t) + \alpha Ret^{\pi}_{(Y,X)}(t) \qquad (11)$$

In the other hand, the rating attributes by the trustee $Ret^{\pi}_{(X,Y)}(t)$ describes its level of satisfaction of how the trustor managed her resource for the task π.

4 Experimental Simulation

In this section, we assess the efficiency and the performance of the TM-SIoT model toward malicious nodes based on simulation results. In the field of SIoT research, establishing a network of SIoT in the real scene is very difficult; a test takes up a lot of time and costs. Thanks to simulation tools, we can easily get the analysis, monitor the process and assess the effectiveness of a TM model. As a simulator, we choose the ns_3 [21] because it represents an open simulation platform for networking research.

4.1 Environment Setup

In this simulation, we consider a SIoT environment with 1000 SIoT devices that belong to 200 owners. We started the simulation with a number of nodes equal to 100. This number was partially increased to 1000 in order to evaluate the performance of the model with a large number of nodes. Owners are socially related to each other via social networks and are randomly distributed to 40 CoI. By applying a social relationship matrix [22] a social cooperativeness among SIoT nodes is defined. In this experiment, we study a hostile environment in which the percentage of dishonest nodes is randomly chosen among all SIoT nodes. At the beginning of the simulation, a dishonest node is benign initially and after an interval of time turns malicious. The trust value of all the nodes is fixed with a trust level of 0.8. The candidate node will be selected as the provider of this transaction if its trustworthiness value is higher or equals than a threshold $\sigma = 0$. To set the suitable threshold, we performed several tests by varying this value predicated on the performance measurement "sensitivity" as described in Fig. 3 (Eq. 12) (Table 2).

$$\text{Sensitivity} = \frac{\text{Number of Dishonest Nodes Found}}{\text{Total Number of Nodes Found}} \tag{12}$$

Table 2. List of parameters and values used.

Parameters	Designation	Value
N	SIoT devices	1000
O	Owners	200
N_C	CoI	40
T	Transactions	12000
S_1	Social links between nodes	527

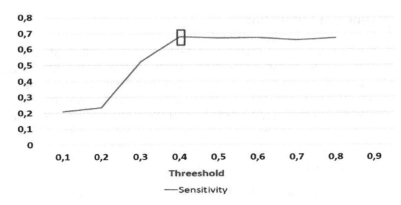

Fig. 3. Variation of sensitivity according to the threshold Experimental results

4.2 Experimental Results

1. Time-aware trust metric performance: we investigate the effect of the time-aware trust metric in the trustworthiness evaluation for an increasing number of dishonest nodes. We compare the results obtained by: (i) our model with time-aware influence, (ii) our model without the consideration of the time-aware metric, (iii) and the ground truth.

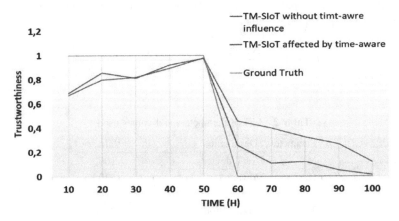

Fig. 4. Evaluation of the Time-Aware trust metric performance

Figure 4 shows a clear difference between the results obtained in the two situations. The time-aware factor that we propose to consider in the trust assessment give better performance compared to the second situation (without time-aware factor consideration). With considering the change of the trust data (past and recent reputation) over the time, results show how the curve of trustworthiness converges in parallel with the ground truth. However, the predicted trustworthiness value assessed in the second situation become aligned to the ground truth as the time increases. This difference due to the consideration of past reputation data that become discarded at a given moment.

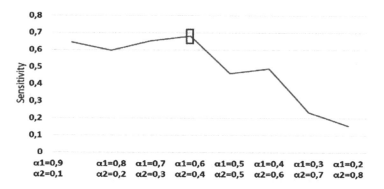

Fig. 5. Variation of sensitivity according to $\alpha 1$ and $\alpha 2$

Results prove that we should pay attention to the time as a crucial factor that influence the trustworthiness between two agents in the network. To set the best weights values for past and recent reputation data, we have compared the performance of our model in terms of sensitivity with different weights values as shown in Fig. 5. Based on the results obtained in Fig. 5 we set the weights 0.6 for recent reputation values and 0.4 for past reputation values. These values are consistent with our hypothesis defined in Sect. 3.1 and confirms the efficiency of the time in nodes' transactions to provide a reliable and accurate trust value.

2. Mutual trust evaluation performance: to demonstrate the performance of the proposed mutual evaluation solution towards malicious trustors, we compare the efficiency of our proposed model with a situation where the trustee accepts all the tasks and the threshold $\sigma = 0$, based on the abuse rate measure. This measure defines the average of abusive uses in relation to the total number of uses of the trustee's devices to achieve the task π. Each trustor is affected with a trust value between [0.1] which is assessed by the trustee based on the Eq. 9. Figure 6 shows the trustee's reactions towards a dishonest trustor who aims to manage trustees' resources abusively. There is a clear difference between the curves of the abuse rate in the two situations: unilateral and mutual evaluation. With unilateral evaluation, we observe a rapid increase in the abuse rate curve in parallel with the decrease of the trustors' trust value. This show that the trustee continues to accept tasks from malicious trustors. Based on our proposed solution, we note that with the decrease of the rate value, the number of abusive uses of the trustees' recourses remains low, constant and does not increase. This experiment has demonstrated the lack security of the trustees' resources in the situation with unilateral evaluation. However, the performance of the proposed mutual evaluation method is reflected in decreased abuse rates of task delegations with the decrease of the trustors' trustworthiness. This proves the resiliency of the proposed solution towards malicious trustors who aims to damage the trustees' resources.

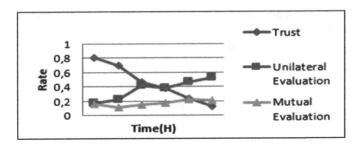

Fig. 6. Comparison of abuse rate with different trustworthiness of the trustor in the reverse evaluation

3. TM-SIoT model performance: for an effective evaluation of the designed TM-SIoT model, we compare our trust evaluation method and metrics with others that were proposed in previous works based on the evaluation measures namely: sensitivity, recall, and F-measure (see Table 3).

Table 3. Summary of the proposed parameters

Work	Metrics	Method
Saied et al., 2013 [7]	Direct information Recommendation	Unilateral evaluation
Chen et al., 2016 [8]	Honesty Cooperativeness CoI	Unilateral evaluation
Truong et al., 2017 [11]	Reputation Experiences	Unilateral evaluation
TM-SIoT	**Knowledge: Social Similarity and I-SoR Recommendation: Honesty Reputation: Time-Aware**	**Mutual evaluation**

$$\text{Recall} = \frac{\text{number of malicious nodes detected}}{\text{total number of malicious nodes}} \tag{13}$$

And

$$\text{F} - \text{mesure} = \frac{2 * \text{Sensitivity} * \text{Recall}}{\text{Sensitivity} + \text{Recall}} \tag{14}$$

As shown in Fig. 7, we note that best values of sensitivity, recall and F-measure are obtained with the proposed TM-SIoT model. The experiment demonstrates well that the proposed features and method of trust evaluation proves display a commanding capability in coping with dishonest nodes whose behaviors change dynamically.

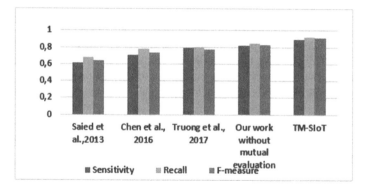

Fig. 7. Comparison of TM-SIoT model with proposed models

This mean how the temporal trust metric of nodes' transaction and the proposed mutual evaluation have an important influence to provide an efficiency TM model and ensure nodes' safe communications.

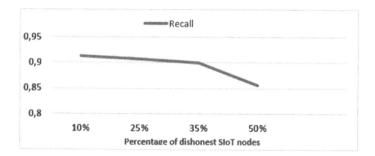

Fig. 8. Comparison of Recall with different number of dishonest SIoT nodes

On the other hand, we compare the performance of our proposed model with a percentage of malicious nodes that ranges from 10% to 50%. Figure 8 demonstrates how the TM-SIoT model provides good results even for a system with 50% of malicious nodes.

5 Conclusion

In this work, we proposed a generic TM model called TM-SIoT that can be deployed in different SIoT systems. Compared to other works, the trust evaluation method is mutual, where both the trustor and the trustee evaluate each other in order to deal with the lack protection of the trustee. For the consideration of the specifics' constraints and assumptions of SIoT nodes, the trust value in TM-SIoT model is assessed based on both QoS and social trust metrics. As the trustworthiness data (reputation) represents the evaluation of nodes' transactions that changes over the time, we define in this work an additional trust metric which is the time-aware. The results showed that the TM-SIoT model can attain better performance in detecting malicious nodes how's behaviors change dynamically over the time. Based on the proposed mutual evaluation, the efficiency of the TM-SIoT model to detect almost of the dishonest nodes is enhanced. In addition, we note that the time factor of nodes' transactions has a remarkable influence on the trust assessment. In the future research, we aim to test and validate the proposed model toward a lot of dynamically environment situations in which a SIoT system can adjust autonomously trust metrics settings based on the available context. Another trend is to add other resources restriction (e.g. energy awareness) that can affect the trustworthiness of SIoT nodes.

Acknowledgement. The research leading to these results has received funding from the Ministry of Higher Education and Scientific Research of Tunisia under the grant agreement number LR11ES48.

References

1. Ray, P.P.: A survey on internet of things architectures. J. King Saud Univ. Comput. Inf. Sci. **30**(3), 291–319 (2018)
2. Lin, J., Yu, W., Zhang, N., Yang, X., Zhang, H., Zhao, W.: A survey on internet of things: architecture, enabling technologies, security and privacy, and applications. IEEE Internet Things J. **4**(5), 1125–1142 (2017)
3. Atzori, L., Iera, A., Morabito, G.: From "smart objects" to "social objects": the next evolutionary step of the internet of things. IEEE Commun. Mag. **52**(1), 97–105 (2014)
4. Atzori, L., Iera, A., Morabito, G.: Siot: giving a social structure to the internet of things. IEEE Commun. Lett. **15**(11), 1193–1195 (2011)
5. Atzori, L., Lera, A., Morabito, G., Nitti, M.: The social internet of things (siot)-when social networks meet the internet of things: Concept, architecture and network characterization. Comput. Netw. **56**(16), 3594–3608 (2012)
6. Lin, Z., Dong, L.: Clarifying trust in social internet of things (2017). arXiv preprint arXiv: 1704.03554
7. Abdelghani, W., Zayani, C.A., Amous, I., Sèdes, F.: Trust management in social internet of things: a survey. In: Dwivedi, Y.K., et al. (eds.) I3E 2016. LNCS, vol. 9844, pp. 430–441. Springer, Cham (2016). https://doi.org/10.1007/978-3-319-45234-0_39
8. Nitti, M., Girau, R., Atzori, L., Iera, A., Morabito, G.: A subjective model for trustworthiness evaluation in the social internet of things. In: 2012 IEEE 23rd international symposium on personal, indoor and mobile radio communications-(PIMRC), pp. 18–23. IEEE (2012)
9. Saied, Y.B., Olivereau, A., Zeghlache, D., Laurent, M.: Trust management system design for the internet of things: a context-aware and multi-service approach. Comput. Secur. **39**, 351–365 (2013)
10. Chen, R., Guo, J., Bao, F.: Trust management for SOA-based IoT and its application to service composition. IEEE Trans. Serv. Comput. **9**(3), 482–495 (2016)
11. Chen, Z., Ling, R., Huang, C.-M., Zhu, X.: A scheme of access service recommendation for the social Internet of Things. Int. J. Commun Syst **29**(4), 694–706 (2016)

12. Jayasinghe, U., Truong, N.B., Lee, G.M., Um, T.W.: RPR: a trust computation model for social Internet of Things. In: 2016 International IEEE Conferences on Ubiquitous Intelligence & Computing, Advanced and Trusted Computing, Scalable Computing and Communications, Cloud and Big Data Computing, Internet of People and Smart World Congress (UIC/ATC/ScalCom/CBDCom/IoP/SmartWorld), pp. 930–937 (2016)
13. Truong, N.B., Lee, H., Askwith, B., Lee, G.M.: Toward a trust evaluation mechanism in the social Internet of Things. Sensors 17(6), 1346 (2017)
14. Mendoza, C.V.L., Kleinschmidt, J.H.: A distributed trust management mechanism for the internet of things using a multi-service approach. Wireless Pers. Commun. 103(3), 2501–2531 (2018)
15. Nam, C., Li, H., Li, S., Lewis, M., Sycara, K.: Trust of humans in supervisory control of swarm robots with varied levels of autonomy. In: 2018 IEEE International Conference on Systems, Man, and Cybernetics (SMC), pp. 825–830. IEEE (2018)
16. Chen, D., Chang, G., Sun, D., Li, J., Jia, J., Wang, X.: TRM-IoT: a trust management model based on fuzzy reputation for Internet of Things. Comput. Sci. Inf. Syst. 8(4), 1207–1228 (2011)
17. Guo, J., Chen, R., Tsai, J.J.: A survey of trust computation models for service management in Internet of Things systems. Comput. Commun. 97, 1–14 (2017)
18. Nitti, M., Girau, R., Atzori, L.: Trust worthiness management in the social Internet of Things. IEEE Trans. Knowl. Data Eng. 26(5), 1253–1266 (2014)
19. Josang, A., Ismail, R.: The beta reputation system. In: Proceedings of the 15th Bled Electronic Commerce Conference, vol. 5, pp. 2502– 2511 (2002)
20. Abderrahim, O.B., Elhedhili, M.H., Saidane, L.: CTMS-SIoT: a context-based trust management system for the social internet of things. In: 2017 13th International Wireless Communications and Mobile Computing Conference (IWCMC), pp. 1903–1908. IEEE (2017)
21. Toor, A.S., Jain, A.: A survey on wireless network simulators. Bull. Electr. Eng. Inform. 6(1), 62–69 (2017)
22. Sobin, C., Raychoudhury, V., Marfia, G., Singla, A.: A survey of routing and data dissemination in delay tolerant networks. J. Netw. Comput. Appl. 67, 128–146 (2016)

A Model for Describing and Maximising Security Knowledge Sharing to Enhance Security Awareness

Saad Alahmari[1]([⊠]), Karen Renaud[2,3], and Inah Omoronyia[1]

[1] School of Computing Science, University of Glasgow, Glasgow, UK
S.alahmari.1@research.gla.ac.uk,
Inah.Omoronyia@glasgow.ac.uk
[2] School of Design and Informatics, Abertay University, Dundee, UK
k.renaud@abertay.ac.uk
[3] Rhodes University, Grahamstown, South Africa

Abstract. Employees play a crucial role in enhancing information security in the workplace, and this requires everyone having the requisite security knowledge and know-how. To maximise knowledge levels, organisations should encourage and facilitate Security Knowledge Sharing (SKS) between employees. To maximise sharing, we need first to understand the mechanisms whereby such sharing takes place and then to encourage and engender such sharing. A study was carried out to test the applicability of *Transactive Memory Systems Theory* in describing knowledge sharing in this context, which confirmed its applicability in this domain. To encourage security knowledge sharing, the harnessing of *Self-Determination Theory* was proposed— satisfying employee autonomy, relatedness and competence needs to maximise sharing. Such sharing is required to improve and enhance employee security awareness across organisations. We propose a model to describe the *mechanisms* for such sharing as well as the means by which it can be *encouraged*.

Keywords: Security Knowledge Sharing · Security awareness · Transactive Memory System · Self-Determination Theory

1 Introduction

Employees play a crucial role in enhancing information security [1]. An essential prerequisite is for employees to know what it is they have to do, and how to do it; in other words, that they possess the required knowledge and skills (know-how). Knowledge sharing, of all types, improves the organisation as a whole and engenders trust between employees [11]. Of particular interest in this paper is information security knowledge sharing (SKS). Knowledge sharing, which improves information security awareness, is important when it comes to preventing security breaches [14]. The knowledge held by an organisation's employees is its most important asset [51]. Moreover, information security can help employees see the importance of information SKS in enhancing security awareness [41]. While awareness drives and training are undeniably valuable and essential, a neglected way of ensuring that all employees gain the requisite knowledge and know-how is to encourage and facilitate SKS across the organisation [37].

© Springer Nature Switzerland AG 2020
M. Themistocleous and M. Papadaki (Eds.): EMCIS 2019, LNBIP 381, pp. 376–390, 2020.
https://doi.org/10.1007/978-3-030-44322-1_28

The biggest challenge of SKS is gathering and sharing information and exploring the key factors which affect it [38]. However, many other factors need more investigation [29]. Previous studies used only a handful of different theories designed to mitigate those challenges [2]. Moreover, there have been other approaches to improving security awareness. They have generally been based on individualistic models (considering an individual in isolation) [7, 44, 45].

A lack of provision of an environment that facilitates and motivates the process of information exchange within organisations was also found, which is a powerful barrier to knowledge sharing. Most of the existing studies did not propose effective solutions to mitigate such barriers [2].

In order to facilitate access to this knowledge, many companies are introducing knowledge repositories. This makes it easier to store and distribute knowledge, and has also facilitated the movement of knowledge to those outside of the organisation. While companies routinely protect their information using firewalls and filtering systems, it is crucial that they do not overlook the importance of security knowledge held within the minds of their employees as well [15]. Organisations should therefore facilitate and engender organisational SKS. The aim should be to make the knowledge accessible to those who need it and ultimately to improve information security across the organisation.

To investigate this, we ask what the challenges are of Security Knowledge Sharing in terms of improving security awareness? After identifying these challenges, we will consider how information security knowledge can be facilitated. Thirdly, we explore how people can be motivated to share security knowledge. The aim is to maximise such sharing to improve and enhance organisational security awareness?

Section 2 reviews related information security and SKS research. Section 3 presents the research methodology, data collection, and data analysis we carried out to model security knowledge sharing. Section 4 proposes a model to *describe* SKS within organizations using *Transactive Memory System* (TMS) Theory. We also incorporate the satisfaction of *Self Determination Theory* (SDT) constructs in order to *encourage* SKS within organizations. Finally, Sect. 5.1 discusses the potential for future work. Section 6 concludes.

2   Literature Review

Knowledge and Information Security: Knowledge, which can be either tacit or explicit [12], is gained when meaning is added to information. People can gain knowledge from their environment [16] or from personal experience [16]. The former refers to skills that cannot easily be recorded or expressed, which makes it difficult to share and retain [17]. It is important for employees to transfer tacit security-related knowledge to other employees – to externalise it [18]. Explicit knowledge can be expressed in numbers and words [20] and can be recorded. In the information security context, people can indeed gain knowledge from training drives, or from recorded explicit sources, but are more likely to gain the knowledge they need from other employees in the workplace [23].

Information Security Knowledge Sharing: Many challenges deter SKS between organisations, such as the reputation of the organisation in the eyes of customers [49]. Vakilinia et al. [49] confirmed a strong relationship between anonymity and sharing of cyberattack information [49]. The researchers proved that the more anonymity there is, the more cyberattack information is shared. Employees are concerned about sharing personal details in the security incident record in case there are consequences that may ensue. Also, He and Johnson's study confirms the importance of sharing security incidents between employees to mitigate the risk in the workplace [23].

Kim and Kim [28] show that social pressure influences compliance intention, and that compliant behaviour is influenced by knowledge. SKS is crucial in the information security arena [28]. Safa and Von Solms [45] explored the process of information SKS in organisations and discovered that "earning a reputation and gaining promotion" and "external motivations" had a positive influence on SKS [45]. Mermoud et al. [37] report that people would share knowledge if they expected to get something valuable in return; reciprocity was deemed to be important. They suggest that organisations incentivise rather than mandate sharing [37]. Safa et al. [45] aimed to deliver an insight into the phenomenon of information SKS. They combined Motivation Theory and the Theory of Planned Behaviour to deliver a SKS module [45]. Dang-Pham et al. [12] aimed to find out why people provided information security advice to others. They discovered that the primary barriers to sharing security of knowledge were behaviour and trust [12]. Rocha Flores et al. [43] examined the impact of cultural factors on SKS. The results show that national and cultural factors are worth considering when it comes to the nature of sharing. They concluded that the most critical barrier to sharing security knowledge was cultural [18]. Feledi et al. [16] examined the efficiency of cooperation between participants during the process of SKS and found a lack of motivation to be the primary barrier to sharing [16].

Summary of the Related Work: Previous research in social network and technical systems has indicated that various reward system indicators can have a significant positive effect on SKS [19, 52]. Conversely, other studies have revealed the negative impacts of reward systems [9]. Such tactics focus on short-term motivation, yet SKS ought to be seen as a long-term solution to low levels of security awareness.

Our literature review revealed that information security investigations generally use a specific limited number of theories, such as the Theory of Planned Behaviour and Theory of Reasoned Action [32]. Also, there have been other approaches to improving security awareness. They have generally been based on individualistic models (considering an individual in isolation) but our proposal is to use a collaborative model to improve security awareness [7, 44, 45].

Yet individual-focused models have more to do with predicting factors leading to security-related behaviours than with factors that lead to security-related knowledge sharing within organisations. We thus consider using the lens offered by TMS in order to understand and encourage SKS. TMS has been used in other contexts to model knowledge sharing between employees [50]. Moreover, researchers in information retrieval have adopted the individual experience directory of TMS to gain access to the data usage of IT-based expertise information [53]. Thus, this study considered using TMS to model the dissemination of security knowledge in organizations. Choi et al. argue that knowledge sharing activities have features that support specific communication and collaboration practices to facilitate team-related TMS [10]. Yet TMS only describes existing knowledge sharing within organizations; our interest is also in encouraging such sharing. We thus propose incorporating the core tenets of Self Determination Theory (SDT) into our model as well, in order to enhance SKS. Furthermore, Tsohouet al. (2015) have confirmed limited studies examining Security awareness in both levels (organisational and individual level) to have effective information security awareness programmes [48].

3 Research Methodology

3.1 Study 1 (Semi-structured Interview)

We conducted semi-structured interviews with participants from a Saudi and a British university to elicit information regarding employees' knowledge and beliefs related to SKS [8]. By so doing we were investigating SKS-related challenges [6]. We engaged in two stages in order to extend previous research which relied purely on either surveys and/or literature reviews. Surveys, on their own, do not deliver in-depth analyses of human behaviours. Only one study was found to have used interviews or focus groups to explore SKS challenges and barriers [2]. This is surprising since observation and interviews are the most powerful techniques for delivering comprehensive insights that lead to enhanced understanding of SKS in natural environments [21, 25].

Data Collection: Our study used interviews [31] in order to facilitate an indepth look into, and exploration of, perceptions and perspectives [8]. In 2018, interviews were conducted with participants from a Saudi university and a British university. The interviews took from 15 to 20 min and explored how participants would respond to a security incident in the workplace. Participants were also asked some general questions about trust, privacy, experience, and the effect of the relationship in terms of sharing security advice in the security knowledge system. Participants were employees between the ages of 20 and 60 years of age. 28 people participated (7 female, 21 male). 8 had a high school certificate, 13 had a Bachelor's degree and 7 had a Masters degree.

Data Analysis: All of the audio recordings (n = 28) were professionally transcribed. All transcripts were read through by the researchers while listening to the audio recordings to confirm the accuracy of the transcripts. Transcripts were de-identified and imported into NVivo 12.0 (QSR, Doncaster, Victoria). A thematic analysis approach was used to analyse the transcripts [47].

Codes were derived and categorised, with researchers using detailed and rich descriptions to represent the findings [5]. The consistency of the coding was verified by matching of the transcripts with their recording, as well as by the researchers' repeated reading and reflecting on the transcripts after coding to ensure that the definition or meaning of the codes remained the same throughout the process. Lastly, a senior colleague unrelated to the research was asked to assess the study, looking at areas such as the relationship between the data and the research questions, the interpretation, and the level of analysis [5].

3.2 Study 2 (Quantitative Approach Survey)

The aim of this study was to examine scale reliability, correlations, and relationships between the TMS scale and other constructs in the security context in order to understand SKS in organizations.

Measurement of Constructs: A questionnaire was used to collect empirical data to support the research model and hypotheses developed from the prior literature review, as presented in Fig. 1. For each of the hypotheses, metrics were derived from the prior research and the probes were rephrased as necessary as the majority of the existing studies did not focus specifically on Security context. In order to measure the constructs of the research model, five-point Likert scales were created with options ranging from 1 (strongly disagree) to 5 (strongly agree).

Pre-test and Refinement of Measurement Items: A pilot test was carried out among a small group of computing science PhD students. The feedback received from the students was used to make improvements to the design of the instrument. Four independent researchers were then asked to carry out a final validation before the questions were distributed.

Data Collection Procedure: A link to the questionnaire was sent to a Saudi and a British university to collect information from a sample of employees. The university's information technology department was asked to send an email containing the questionnaire link and the study objectives to employees across all departments in order to obtain a diverse sample population. Participants were asked to provide basic demographic information, but not their name or email address. 204 people responded to the email request, eight of which were disregarded due to incompleteness. 196 were retained for analysis.

3.3 Findings

Results of Study 1: We now answer the research question: "Which factors impact SKS in organizations?" (Table 1).

Infrastructure: This refers to the software and hardware that enable to facilitate and disseminate the knowledge in the organizations. The participants agreed on the importance of the infrastructure which facilitates communication between people during the working day and after they leave the workplace such as offer an electronic knowledge repository to record information security incidents which offer a high-quality knowledge: *"there is a need for a knowledge management process and database due to the ongoing risk of losing information and knowledge as people transition from one role to another and/or leave the University"* (A21). It is important to note that we found little evidence that the Universities fostered an environment that facilitates SKS.

Table 1. Concepts and categories that emerged from the analysis

1st order concepts	Themes
Offer effective system to facilitate communication among those in the workplace	Infrastructure
Offer an electronic knowledge repository to record information security incidents which offer high-quality knowledge	
Experience, Qualifications and Relationships with colleagues	Knowledge
Experience is more important than qualifications in an information security incident	
Sensitive documents refused to anyone working outside the IT dept	Trust
Trust based on the situation such as critical problems and need for a quick solution. Lack of experience and knowledge in the security field prevents helping others	
Security knowledge sharing, not violation of privacy. Those reporting would rather be anonymous. Recording a bad experience with an employee's skills by the incident reporting which show the employee's name in the knowledge repository. Lack of knowledge of policies, to provide a set of strategies and explain user responsibilities	Personal Factors
Annual evaluation. Financial incentives and moral incentives. Reward system based on their contribution to recording the incident such as attending training and conferences	Motivation
Improving decision making, Reducing information security incidents	IT Advantage
Mitigates the risk through learning from previous incidents	
Gain knowledge by practice and learn lessons from previous incidents.	Employees'
Lessons learnt when knowledge sharing. Reduce the loss of know-how	Advantages

Trust Building: Factors involved building enough trust to request help, which focuses on the motivations, include encouraging employees to trust their colleagues enough to accept their solutions or advice which are already available in the knowledge repository. When the participants were asked about it, the majority commented that experience is one of the most important factors involved in building trust in others, and the majority of respondents revealed that experience is more important than qualifications in an information security incident: *"It is based on the relationship, and I can judge if I can trust him or not. On the other hand, the experience together with an appropriate qualification is essential in building the trust before asking anyone"* (A1).

Factors involved in building enough trust to request help include encouraging employees to trust their colleagues enough to accept their solutions or advice which are already available in the knowledge repository. When the participants were asked about it, the majority considered experience one of the most important factors involved in building trust in others, and the majority of respondents revealed this to be more important than qualifications.

Trust: The third theme is trust, which prevents employees from trusting others in the workplace, such as sensitive documents leading to the refusal of any advice from anyone who works outside the IT department: *"I have sensitive documents which*

prevent me from asking anyone who works outside the IT department" (A1). Moreover, trust based on the situation such as critical problems and need for a quick solution.

Personal Factors: What is surprising is that a lack of anonymity prevents employees from sharing their incidents. Many feel that SKS can violate privacy if they add an incident, which includes personal details, such as their names. Many employees would prefer be anonymous when reporting incidents: *"They don't have to know the personal information about me"* (A13), *"it will appear as a bad experience about me"* (A3).

Motivation: The current study found that a reward system affected the employees' likelihood of sharing knowledge. The most effective reward system is annual evaluation, encouraging employees by financial incentives and moral incentives a reward system based on their contribution to recording incidents.

The Advantage of SKS for Employees and IT Dept.: *Enhancing the IT Dept.'s response to cyber-attacks:* An important finding was that SKS – improving decision making based on recording in the knowledge repository and reducing information security incidents.

Enhancing employees' information security to prevent cyber-attacks: The most interesting finding was that employees can gain knowledge by practising and learning lessons from previous incidents and security advice. This reduces the loss of knowhow and leads to increased security awareness.

4   Security Knowledge Sharing Model

To depict the factors impacting SKS, we propose the model shown in Fig. 1, building on Transactive Memory System (TMS) Theory.

Transactive Memory System (TMS)
TMS has been described as *"a set of individual memory systems in combination with the communication that takes place between individuals"* (p. 186), [51]. A TMS determines the specific division of cognitive labour within a group of people, as a means to facilitate encoding, storage, and retrieval of knowledge pertaining to various domains. When a TMS is being utilised, each group member is aware of *"who knows what, and who knows what"* (p. 260), [10]. Simply put, the characteristics of a TMS mean that three crucial qualities, common to other types of socially shared cognition, are absent; i.e. differentiated knowledge, processes of transactive encoding, storage and retrieval, and the dynamic nature of TMS functions [34]. Thus, an alternative and more suitable approach might involve a shift of focus away from repositories towards processes [27].
    Liang, Moreland, and Argote (1995) described three aspects of TMS:
    Specialisation: this is the term used to describe the degree of differentiation of the knowledge held by team members [35]. Hence the first hypothesis is: **H1:** Specialisation (Employees knowledge) is positively related to SKS transfer within the organization.
    Coordination: this describes the efficiency of the team in terms of knowledge processing while working together. The second hypothesis is: **H2:** Coordination (Infrastructure) is positively related to SKS transfer within the organization.

Credibility: this is the way in which individual team members perceive the reliability of the knowledge held by the other members of the team. The third hypothesis is: **H3:** Credibility (Trust) of shared knowledge is positively related to SKS transfer within the organization. These three dimensions are considered variables that can be used to measure the degree to which a TMS has developed among the members of a group, and they have frequently been used for this purpose in empirical studies [30, 35].

As Lewis [33, 50] (Lewis, 2003, p. 590) asserts, these three variables *"reflect transactive memory itself [33], as well as the cooperative processes illustrative of transactive memory use"* as shown in Fig. 1.

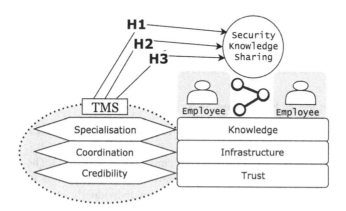

Fig. 1. Using Transactive Memory System (TMS) to Model Organizational Security Knowledge Sharing (SKS)

Davison *et al.* [13] argue that TMS facilitates knowledge sharing, leading to improved team creative performance via team creative efficacy [13]. Our premise is that organisations should facilitate and engender SKS by removing the challenges which prevent SKS i.e. "Specialization, Credibility and Coordination" [30]. The aim is to make security knowledge accessible to all of those who need it and ultimately to improve security awareness across the organisation. Our first qualitative study delivered insights about which factors impact SKS, and we are able to align these factors to the core tenets of TMS theory.

Results of Study 2: The research model and hypotheses were tested using a component-based partial least squares (PLS) regression approach to structural equation modelling (SEM). This kind of approach is the most appropriate for the current study as it has a focus on theory development and the prediction of data [29]. SmartPLS (v.3.0) was used to test the model as it is a powerful, user-friendly instrument for graphical path modelling with latent variables. Our results of a real TMS Model strong support to two hypotheses which are Coordination (t = 3.840, p < 0.001), and Specialisation (t = 2.241, p < 0.001).

Table 2. Path coefficient of the research hypotheses

Hypo	Relationship	Std. Beta	Std. Error	T-value	P-value	Decision
H1	SPE → SKS	0.189	0.075	2.521	0.012	Supported
H2	COO → SKS	0.359	0.090	4.001	0.000	Supported
H3	CRE → SKS	0.132	0.091	1.448	0.148	Unsupported

Path Coefficient of the Research Hypotheses was used to determine whether SPE, COO and CRE variables predict the participants' intentions to SKS transfer within the organization. Dependent variable: Facilities SKS; Independent variables: SPE, COO and CRE as shown in (Table 2). Other results are omitted due to space limitations. H1 and H2 are supported, but H3 is unsupported. We will, however, retain all three tenets of TMS in our model, due to the smallness of our sample, and the fact that we are not at liberty to pick apart TMS. Having modeled SKS within organizations, we now turn to considering how to facilitate and encourage SKS.

4.1   Encouraging & Facilitating SKS

We now proceed to the second question: *"How can security knowledge sharing be facilitated and encouraged?"*

SDT requires the satisfaction of three core human needs. (1) The need for **autonomy**, which refers to an individual's desire for self-organisation of their actions. (2) The need for a sense of **competence**, i.e. an individual's sense of self-efficacy. (3) The need for **relatedness**, which refers to the desire to feel a connection with, and be supported by, people who are important to them [42]. Research has suggested that people are more likely to persist and have better qualitative performance on activities that satisfy these needs [42].

According to recently published policy compliance research, satisfying SDT has been successful in encouraging such compliance in organisations [4]. Moreover, Alkaldi *et al.* confirmed the critical effect of applying SDT to security tool adoption decisions in the security context [3]. That being so, we can *encourage* SKS by satisfying the self-determination needs of employees to enhance the TMS of the organization.

In terms of facilitation, Wang *et al.* [50] suggest that IT systems be used to enhance TMS.

4.2   Modeling SKS Description, Facilitation and Encouragement Model

We propose a model that *describes* SKS based on TMS constructs, *encouraging* SKS by using SDT constructs (Fig. 2). TMS relies considerably on information technology for support. The model complements prior SKS models including Gagne's [19] model of organisational knowledge use. The differences between the models, however, are in the conceptualisation of facilitation by TMS, which is multidimensional in the SKS model and also in the inclusion of psychological factors that can impact on the quality of motivation by SDT. Our model gives a detailed explanation of how and why certain HRM practices impact on engagement with SKS behaviour, thus providing solid advice for employees [19].

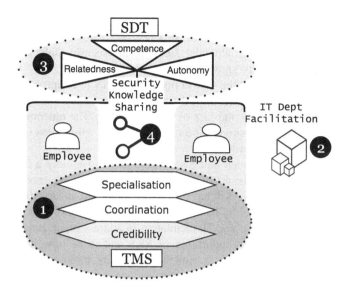

Fig. 2. A Model for Describing (1), Facilitating (2) and Encouraging (3) Security Knowledge Sharing, thereby Enhancing Sharing (4)

There is a crucial need to investigate whether information technology has an influence on the development of TMS within a team, and if so, how this happens [10].

A number of existing studies identify communication as a key determinant of TMS development. Communication is crucial for understanding the knowledge held by others, for the encoding of new knowledge into the TMS of the group, and for the retrieval of information from the TMS [24]. With this in mind, it becomes clear that the processes of communication are crucial in developing and utilising a group TMS [24, 33]. It has also been posited that the frequency of interaction between team members – that is, the quantity of communication – that is important in the development of a TMS; indeed, the usefulness of the shared information in terms of its quality is also an influencing factor [30, 36]. Moreover, the TMS's function is most effectual when there is a reliance between team members on each other to work towards achieving a shared goal [50, 54].

5   General Discussion

Discussion of Study 1. Study 1 showed that the biggest challenges to SKS are (1) facilitating infrastructures, (2) trust, (3) knowledge, and increasing motivation. Our results confirmed that SKS could enhance security awareness, leading to many benefits for both employees and IT department (confirming [18, 39]).

Previous research has indicated the positive effects of trust, which increases interaction among employees in terms of SKS [19, 52]. Prior studies that have noted the importance of trust as an influential factor in the security field as barriers can prevent the sharing of security knowledge advice [2, 46].

The current study is one of the first to investigate SKS in nonprofit organisations. We showed that SKS mitigates risk [40] through learning from previous incidents and security advice [23]. It reduces the loss of knowhow [18], The outcome of the study reveal that SKS can have a positive impact on employees' willingness to comply with information security guidelines [45].

Our literature review revealed that SKS investigations use only a handful of different theories, such as the Theory of Planned Behaviour [2]. We model SKS using TMS [30, 50] (the first time this will have been used in the cyber security context). We augment this descriptive model by incorporating the tenets of SDT in order to address individual sharing motivations, and IT facilitation to address organizational factors.

We wanted to confirm the importance of SKS and show how its influence on employees in the workplace leads to enhanced Security awareness [2]. Our study highlighted the advantages of SKS in an organisational setting, especially in terms of individual security awareness [2]. Hawryszkiewycz and Binsawad [22] describe the impact of barriers deterring SKS. Our study indicated that trust [2, 14, 22], affording anonymity [49], facilitating infrastructure [26] and engendering motivation [19, 52] are factors affecting SKS. In particular, we found a lack of provision of an environment that specifically facilitates SKS. Such an environment could improve incident reporting and inspire employees to participate more fully in recording incidents and sharing their advice.

Discussion of Study 2. The path coefficient of the research hypotheses was utilised to establish whether SPE, COO, and CRE positively affect the transfer of SKS within an organisation. In terms of employees' intention to share knowledge with others, SPE and COO were the strongest predictors here. On the other hand, CRE was not supported as employees need to know who they can trust to take information from and pass knowledge on to. Trust was found to be one of the biggest challenges in the context of security knowledge sharing, mainly due to information security and sensitive issues among employees in the organisation. These challenges can be mitigated through coordination of the TMS, as this can play a key role in increasing credibility among employees and achieving classification of the specialisation. Moreover, Wang et al. suggest that technical system feed into the creation of TMSs. For instance, with the help of IT-empowered collaboration platforms, colleagues may assemble a knowledge index and mutual trust in expertise to maximise effectiveness. Moreover, the researchers referred to the benefits of collective knowledge based on TMS as a useful knowledge network for employees in organisations [50]. We will investigate the impact of SKS model adoption as an effective system for implementation as future work.

5.1   Future Work

Having confirmed the relationship between challenges in TMS and SKS, we plan to implement a SKS facilitating App, which satisfies SDT needs and mitigates SKS challenges. **Firstly,** an electronic knowledge repository of security knowledge and solutions.

Secondly, the app encourages SKS, by motivating employees to share knowledge using the App, with SDT enhancing features.

We will deploy the App in an organization and then determine whether SKS is enhanced, and security awareness accordingly improved, over a period of time.

6   Conclusion

We conducted two studies to confirm factors impacting SKS in organisations; thereby, making key contributions to the study regarding the use of SKS to improve security awareness among employees. We proposed a model that describes, facilitates and encourages security knowledge sharing in organisations; we also relied on TMS Theory (which is a new finding in the security context) and Self Determination Theory. The study investigated significant challenges associated with SKS, required to improve security awareness in organisations. Our aim was to uncover ways to maximise knowledge sharing, both by facilitating and encouraging it. As future work, we plan to build a facilitating App, and to test it in an organisation, to ascertain whether it accentuates knowledge sharing and, as as consequence, improves organisational security awareness.

References

1. Ahmed, G., Ragsdell, G., Olphert, W.: Knowledge sharing and information security: a paradox? In: 15th European Conference on Knowledge Management (ECKM 2014), pp. 1083–1090. Polytechnic Institute of Santarém Portugal, 4–5 September 2014
2. Al Ahmari, S., Renaud, K., Omoronyia, I.: A systematic review of information security knowledge-sharing research. In: Proceedings of the Twelfth International Symposium on Human Aspects of Information Security & Assurance (HAISA 2018), p. 101 (2018)
3. Alkaldi, N., Renaud, K.: Encouraging password manager adoption by meeting adopter self-determination needs. In: Proceedings of the 52nd Hawaii International Conference on System Sciences, Maui, January (2019)
4. Alzahrani, A., Johnson, C., Altamimi, S.: Information security policy compliance: investigating the role of intrinsic motivation towards policy compliance in the organisation. In: 2018 4th International Conference on Information Management (ICIM), pp. 125–132. IEEE (2018)
5. Braun, V., Clarke, V.: Using thematic analysis in psychology. Qual. Res. Psychol. **3**(2), 77–101 (2006)
6. Bryman, A.: Quantitative and qualitative research: further reflections on their integration. In: Brannen, J. (ed.) Mixing Methods: Qualitative and Quantitative Research, pp. 57–78. Routledge, New York (2017)

7. Bulgurcu, B., Cavusoglu, H., Benbasat, I.: Information security policy compliance: an empirical study of rationality-based beliefs and information security awareness. MIS Q. **34** (3), 523–548 (2010)
8. Burnard, P.: A method of analysing interview transcripts in qualitative research. Nurse Educ. Today **11**(6), 461–466 (1991)
9. Cabrera, E.F., Cabrera, A.: Fostering knowledge sharing through people management practices. Int. J. Hum. Res. Manage. **16**(5), 720–735 (2005)
10. Choi, S.Y., Lee, H., Yoo, Y.: The impact of information technology and transactive memory systems on knowledge sharing application and team performance: a field study. MIS Q. **34**, 855–870 (2010)
11. Dang, D., Nkhoma, M.: Effects of team collaboration on sharing information security advice: insights from network analysis. Inf. Res. Manage. J. (IRMJ) **30**(3), 1–15 (2017)
12. Dang-Pham, D., Pittayachawan, S., Bruno, V.: Why employees share information security advice? Exploring the contributing factors and structural patterns of security advice sharing in the workplace. Comput. Hum. Behav. **67**, 196–206 (2017)
13. Davison, R.M., Ou, C.X., Martinsons, M.G.: Information technology to support informal knowledge sharing. Inf. Syst. J. **23**(1), 89–109 (2013)
14. Dixon, N.M.: Common Knowledge: How Companies Thrive by Sharing what They Know. Harvard Business School Press, Brighton (2000)
15. Durcikova, A., Jennex, M.E.: Introduction to confidentiality, integrity, and availability of knowledge, innovation, and entrepreneurial systems minitrack. In: 49th Hawaii International Conference on System Sciences (HICSS), pp. 39:1–39:18. IEEE (2016)
16. Feledi, D., Fenz, S., Lechner, L.: Toward web-based information security knowledge sharing. Inf. Secur. Tech. Rep. **17**(4), 199–209 (2013)
17. Fenz, S., Ekelhart, A.: Formalizing information security knowledge. In: Proceedings of the 4th International Symposium on Information, Computer, and Communications Security, pp. 183–194. ACM (2009)
18. Flores, W.R., Antonsen, E., Ekstedt, M.: Information security knowledge sharing in organizations: investigating the effect of behavioral information security governance and national culture. Comput. Secur. **43**, 90–110 (2014)
19. Gagné, M.: A model of knowledge-sharing motivation. Hum. Res. Manage. **48**(4), 571–589 (2009). Published in Cooperation with the School of Business Administration, The University of Michigan and in alliance with the Society of Human Resources Management
20. Gal-Or, E., Ghose, A.: The economic incentives for sharing security information. Inf. Syst. Res. **16**(2), 186–208 (2005)
21. Gill, P., Stewart, K., Treasure, E., Chadwick, B.: Methods of data collection in qualitative research: interviews and focus groups. Br. Dent. J. **204**(6), 291–295 (2008)
22. Hawryszkiewycz, I., Binsawad, M.H.: Classifying knowledge-sharing barriers by organisational structure in order to find ways to remove these barriers. In: 2016 Eighth International Conference on Knowledge and Systems Engineering (KSE), pp. 73–78. IEEE (2016)
23. He, Y., Johnson, C.: Challenges of information security incident learning: an industrial case study in a Chinese healthcare organization. Inf. Health Soc. Care **42**(4), 393–408 (2017)
24. Hollingshead, A.B., Brandon, D.P.: Potential benefits of communication in transactive memory systems. Hum. Commun. Res. **29**(4), 607–615 (2003)
25. Brinkmann, S., Kvale, S.: Interviews: Learning the Craft of Qualitative Research Interviewing, vol. 3. Sage, Thousand Oaks (2015)
26. Islam, M.Z., Jasimuddin, S.M., Hasan, I.: Organizational culture, structure, technology infrastructure and knowledge sharing: empirical evidence from MNCs based in Malaysia. Vine **45**(1), 67–88 (2015)

27. Jackson, P., Klobas, J.: The organization as a transactive memory system. In: Klobas, J.E. (ed.) Becoming Virtual, pp. 111–133. Springer, Heidelberg (2008). https://doi.org/10.1007/978-3-7908-1958-8

28. Kim, S.S., Kim, Y.J.: The effect of compliance knowledge and compliance support systems on information security compliance behavior. J. Knowl. Manage. **21**(4), 986–1010 (2017)

29. Kim, S., Lee, H.: The impact of organizational context and information technology on employee knowledge-sharing capabilities. Public Adm. Rev. **66**(3), 370–385 (2006)

30. Kotlarsky, J., van den Hooff, B., Houtman, L.: Are we on the same page? Knowledge boundaries and transactive memory system development in cross-functional teams. Commun. Res. **42**(3), 319–344 (2015)

31. Kvale, S.: Interviews: An Introduction to Qualitative Research Interviewing. Sage Publications, Inc, Thousand Oaks (1994)

32. Lebek, B., Uffen, J., Neumann, M., Hohler, B., Breitner, M.H.: Information security awareness and behavior: a theory-based literature review. Manage. Res. Rev. **37**(12), 1049–1092 (2014)

33. Lewis, K.: Measuring transactive memory systems in the field: scale development and validation. J. Appl. Psychol. **88**(4), 587–604 (2003)

34. Lewis, K., Herndon, B.: Transactive memory systems: current issues and future research directions. Organ. Sci. **22**(5), 1254–1265 (2011)

35. Liang, D.W., Moreland, R., Argote, L.: Group versus individual training and group performance: the mediating role of transactive memory. Pers. Soc. Psychol. Bull. **21**(4), 384–393 (1995)

36. Liao, J., Jimmieson, N.L., O'Brien, A.T., Restubog, S.L.: Developing transactive memory systems: theoretical contributions from a social identity perspective. Group Organ. Manage. **37**(2), 204–240 (2012)

37. Mermoud, A., Keupp, M., Huguenin, K., Palmié, M., David, D.P.: Incentives for human agents to share security information: a model and an empirical test. In: 17th Workshop on the Economics of Information Security (WEIS), pp. 1–22 (2018)

38. Ortiz, J., Chang, S.H., Chih, W.H., Wang, C.H.: The contradiction between self-protection and self-presentation on knowledge sharing behavior. Comput. Hum. Behav. **76**, 406–416 (2017)

39. Parsons, K., McCormac, A., Butavicius, M., Ferguson, L.: Human factors and information security: individual, culture and security environment. Technical report, Defence Science and Technology Organization Edinburgh (Australia) Command (2010). https://apps.dtic.mil/docs/citations/ADA535944. Accessed 12 Nov 2019

40. Persadha, P.D., Waskita, A., Fadhila, M., Kamal, A., Yazid, S.: How interorganizational knowledge sharing drives national cyber security awareness?: A case study in Indonesia. In: 2016 18th International Conference on Advanced Communication Technology (ICACT), pp. 550–555. IEEE (2016)

41. Rahim, N.H.A., Hamid, S., Matiah, M.L., Shamshirband, S., Furnell, S.: A systematic review of approaches to assessing cybersecurity awareness. Kybernetes **44**(4), 606–622 (2015)

42. Roca, J.C., Gagné, M.: Understanding e-learning continuance intention in the workplace: a self-determination theory perspective. Comput. Hum. Behav. **24**(4), 1585–1604 (2008)

43. Rocha Flores, W., Holm, H., Svensson, G., Ericsson, G.: Using phishing experiments and scenario-based surveys to understand security behaviours in practice. Inf. Manage. Comput. Secur. **22**(4), 393–406 (2014)

44. Safa, N.S., Maple, C., Watson, T., Von Solms, R.: Motivation and opportunity based model to reduce information security insider threats in organisations. J. Inf. Secur. Appl. **40**, 247–257 (2018)

45. Safa, N.S., Von Solms, R.: An information security knowledge sharing model in organizations. Comput. Hum. Behav. **57**, 442–451 (2016)
46. Tamjidyamcholo, A., Baba, M.S.B., Tamjid, H., Gholipour, R.: Information security–professional perceptions of knowledge-sharing intention under self-efficacy, trust, reciprocity, and shared-language. Comput. Educ. **68**, 223–232 (2013)
47. Thomas, J., Harden, A.: Methods for the thematic synthesis of qualitative research in systematic reviews. BMC Med. Res. Methodol. **8**(1), 45 (2008)
48. Tsohou, A., Karyda, M., Kokolakis, S., Kiountouzis, E.: Managing the introduction of information security awareness programmes in organisations. Eur. J. Inf. Syst. **24**(1), 38–58 (2015)
49. Vakilinia, I., Tosh, D.K., Sengupta, S.: Privacy-preserving cybersecurity information exchange mechanism. In: 2017 International Symposium on Performance Evaluation of Computer and Telecommunication Systems (SPECTS), pp. 1–7. IEEE (2017)
50. Wang, Y., Huang, Q., Davison, R.M., Yang, F.: Effect of transactive memory systems on team performance mediated by knowledge transfer. Int. J. Inf. Manage. **41**, 65–79 (2018)
51. Wegner, D.M.: Transactive memory: a contemporary analysis of the group mind. In: Mullen, B., Goethals, G.R. (eds.) Theories of group behavior, pp. 185–208. Springer, New York (1987). https://doi.org/10.1007/978-1-4612-4634-3_9
52. Wickramasinghe, V., Widyaratne, R.: Effects of interpersonal trust, team leader support, rewards, and knowledge sharing mechanisms on knowledge sharing in project teams. Vine **42**(2), 214–236 (2012)
53. Yuan, Y.C., Fulk, J., Monge, P.R.: Access to information in connective and communal transactive memory systems. Commun. Res. **34**(2), 131–155 (2007)
54. Zhang, Z.X., Hempel, P.S., Han, Y.L., Tjosvold, D.: Transactive memory system links work team characteristics and performance. J. Appl. Psychol. **92**(6), 1722 (2007)

A Formal Environment for Credibility and Accuracy Assessment of Safety Messages Exchanged in VANETs

Ons Chikhaoui[✉], Aida Ben Chehida Douss, Ryma Abassi,
and Sihem Guemara El Fatmi

Digital Security Research Lab, Higher School
of Communication of Tunis (Sup'Com), University of Carthage, Tunis, Tunisia
{ons.chikhaoui, aida.benchehida, ryma.abassi,
sihem.guemara}@supcom.tn

Abstract. One necessary requirement for the well operation of Vehicular Ad hoc NETworks (VANETs) is assessing the credibility and the accuracy of the received safety related messages. Recently, we proposed a scheme [1] dealing with this demand. After defining [1], it has appeared to us necessary to formally validate it to avoid any conflict or lack situations. This is our concern in this paper where we propose in a first step a formal specification using an inference system. In a second step, we propose a formal validation using this inference system in order to prove the soundness and the completeness of propositions in the said scheme.

Keywords: Credibility · Accuracy · Inference system · Formal validation · Soundness · Completeness

1 Introduction

Vehicular Ad hoc NETworks (VANETs) are an instantiation of Mobile Ad hoc NETworks (MANETs) and mainly consist of two types of nodes: vehicles as mobile nodes and infrastructure, deployed alongside the roads, called Road Side Units (RSUs) as fixed nodes.

In VANETs, vehicles mainly exchange safety related messages, comprising information regarding their status (e.g., position, speed, etc.) [2] or roads conditions (e.g., congestion, icing, accidents or other transport incidents) [3], with the aim of bringing safety and expediency to roads traffic. Because critical decisions are based on these information, vehicles' consumption of bogus or imprecise ones could put people's life at jeopardy. Hence, it is of great significance to enable vehicles to evaluate the credibility and the accuracy of these information contained in the received safety related messages.

In our work [1], we proposed a scheme coping with this requirement. [1] is based on three modules: (1) a reputation module to measure the reputations of sending vehicles, (2) a time and location closeness estimation module to evaluate the time closeness and the location closeness towards a received traffic information and (3) a

M. Themistocleous and M. Papadaki (Eds.): EMCIS 2019, LNBIP 381, pp. 391–402, 2020.
https://doi.org/10.1007/978-3-030-44322-1_29

majority module to assess the trueness of a received traffic information. A vehicle can use these modules in a separated or joint way according to the circumstances faced in VANETs. An in-depth security analysis was conducted to demonstrate the security efficiency of the proposal. Case studies illustrating the different modules were presented as well. Figure 1 depicts the three modules and their combination.

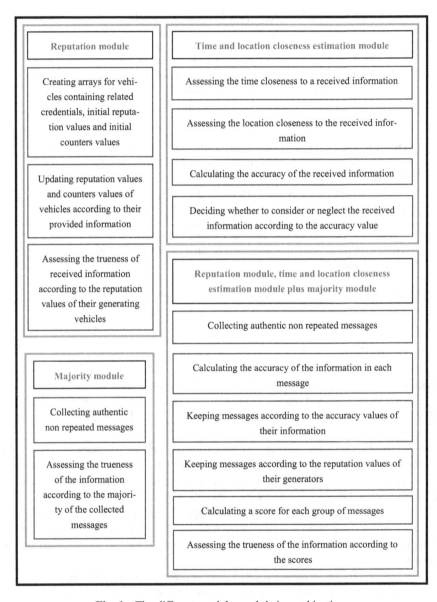

Fig. 1. The different modules and their combination.

Yet, deploying such scheme is error prone and we have found necessary to validate it. According to [4], validation of a model can be done by showing that this model is mathematically sound and that its specification is complete with respect to its input space. More precisely, two main properties have to be considered as proposed in [5]: (1) soundness stating that the proposed model reacts correctly and (2) completeness stating that the model is complete i.e., no other situation can be found. However, the first step towards the validation of a given model is its specification in an automated and generic method [6, 7]. Hence, we first specify the three modules of [1] as well as their combination using a formal and automated method called inference system. In the next, we validate them using the proposed inference system.

The rest of this paper is organized as follows. Section 2 introduces the proposed inference system handling the reputation module, the time and location closeness estimation module, the majority module and the combination of these three modules and elaborates the proposed validation procedure proving the soundness and completeness properties. Section 3 concludes the paper.

2 Formal Specification and Validation

In this section, the various modules of [1] as well as their combination are first specified formally using an inference system. This latter is based on rules called inference rules (i.e., a function that takes premises, analyses their applicability and returns a conclusion [7]). Second, the soundness and completeness properties of the proposed inference system are proved. Soundness is proved by showing that the information trueness assessment using reputation values, the reputation values measuring, the information consideration decision, the information trueness assessment using the majority of messages and the information trueness assessment using the scores of the groups of reporting messages are all logical. Completeness for its part is proved by showing that all the potential situations are handled by the proposed inference system.

2.1 Formal Specification

In this subsection, the proposed inference system describing the three modules and their combination is shown in Fig. 2. Used notations in the proposed inference system are defined in Table 1.

Such as depicted in Fig. 2, the inference rules composing the proposed inference system apply to tuples ($V, E, RP, RT, IR, IC, IN, IM, INM, IT, IF, AC, SC$) whose first component V is a set of couples ($VSEN, vrec$), where $VSEN$ denotes a set of sending vehicles and $vrec$ the vehicle receiving messages from $VSEN$.

The second component E represents the set of events detected by receiving vehicles. In fact, three types of events can be detected by receiving vehicles:

- A positive event *epos*: the receiving vehicle judges that the sending vehicle has provided it with an honest information.
- A negative event *eneg*: the receiving vehicle judges that the sending vehicle has provided it with a bogus information.

Table 1. Inference system's notations

Notation	Meaning
V	A set of couples (*VSEN*, *vrec*) where: • *VSEN*: a set of sending vehicles • *vrec*: the vehicle receiving messages from *VSEN*
E	A set of events detected by receiving vehicles. Three types of events can be detected: • A positive event *epos* • A negative event *eneg* • A neutral event *eneut*
RP	A set of couples (*y(vsen)*, *rp(vsen)*) where: • *vsen* ∈ *VSEN* • *y(vsen)*: the counter of *vsen* used by *vrec* • *rp(vsen)*: the reputation value of *vsen* according to *vrec*
RT	The set of reported vehicles to the TA by receiving vehicles
IR	The set of received information by receiving vehicles
IC	The set of considered information by receiving vehicles
IN	The set of neglected information by receiving vehicles
IM	The set of information that have been approved by the majority of collected received reporting messages by receiving vehicles
INM	The set of information that have not been approved by the majority of collected received reporting messages by receiving vehicles
IT	The set of information believed to be true by receiving vehicles
IF	The set of information believed to be false by receiving vehicles
AC	The set of accuracy values, of received information, calculated by receiving vehicles
SC	The set of scores, of groups of received messages reporting the same information, calculated by receiving vehicles
φ, β	Dynamic weights chosen by the receiving vehicle
S	A fixed step chosen by the receiving vehicle
thrp, thac	A reputation value threshold and an accuracy value threshold, respectively, both are chosen by the receiving vehicle
HighestScore(i)	The status of the score of the group of received messages reporting the information *i*. It is true if that score is the highest in comparison with the scores of the other groups of received messages reporting conflicting information with *i*, otherwise false

- A neutral event *eneut*: the receiving vehicle has no enough evidences for judging the honesty or the dishonesty of the received information.

The third component *RP* is a set of couples (*y(vsen)*, *rp(vsen)*) where:

- *vsen* ∈ *VSEN*,
- *y(vsen)* is the counter of *vsen* used by *vrec* to count the number of times *vsen* has sent to it a bogus information,
- *rp(vsen)* is the reputation value of *vsen* according to *vrec*.

The fourth component *RT* represents the set of reported vehicles to the TA, by receiving vehicles, for sending bogus information. Initially, *RT* is empty.

The fifth component *IR* is the set of received information by receiving vehicles.

The sixth component *IC* represents the set of considered information by receiving vehicles. Initially, *IC* is empty.

The seventh component *IN* is the set of neglected information by receiving vehicles. Initially, *IN* is empty.

The eighth component *IM* represents the set of information that have been approved by the majority of collected received reporting messages by receiving vehicles.

The ninth component *INM* is the set of information that have not been approved by the majority of collected received reporting messages by receiving vehicles.

The tenth component *IT* represents the set of information believed to be true by receiving vehicles. Initially, *IT* is empty.

The eleventh component *IF* is the set of information believed to be false by receiving vehicles. Initially, *IF* is empty.

The twelfth component *AC* represents the set of accuracy values of received information calculated by receiving vehicles.

The thirteenth component *SC* is the set of scores, of groups of received messages reporting the same information, calculated by receiving vehicles.

The inference system stops when all the couples of communicating vehicles, the detected events, the received information, the information that have been approved by the majority of collected received reporting messages, the information that have not been approved by the majority of collected received reporting messages, the accuracy values of received information and the scores of groups of received messages are handled. In the following, the main proposed inference rules are elaborated.

True – info – rep inference rule: This inference rule is concerned with a received information *i*: ($\{i\} \cup IR$) by a receiving vehicle *vrec* from a sending vehicle *vsen*: (($\{vsen\}, \{vrec\}) \cup V$) where the reputation value of *vsen* is greater than or equal to a certain threshold *thrp* chosen by *vrec*: (($\{y(\{vsen\})\}, \{rp(\{vsen\})\} \geq thrp) \cup RP$). In this case, *vrec* considers the information to be true: ($IT \cup \{i\}$).

False – info – rep inference rule: This inference rule is concerned with a received information *i*: ($\{i\} \cup IR$) by a receiving vehicle *vrec* from a sending vehicle *vsen*: (($\{vsen\}, \{vrec\}) \cup V$) where the reputation value of *vsen* is less than a certain threshold *thrp* chosen by *vrec*: (($\{y(\{vsen\})\}, \{rp(\{vsen\})\} < thrp) \cup RP$). In this case, *vrec* considers the information to be false: ($IF \cup \{i\}$).

Epos inference rule: This rule deals with a positive event detected by a receiving vehicle *vrec* concerning a sending vehicle *vsen*: (($\{vsen\}, \{vrec\}) \cup V$) and ($\{epos\} \cup E$). In this case, *vrec* increments the reputation value of *vsen* by $+ \frac{\varphi}{\{y(\{vsen\})\}+1} * S$ as follows: (($\{y(\{vsen\})\}, \{rp(\{vsen\})\} + \frac{\varphi}{\{y(\{vsen\})\}+1} * S) \cup RP$).

Eneg inference rule: This rule is concerned with a negative event detected by a receiving vehicle *vrec* regarding a sending vehicle *vsen*: (($\{vsen\}, \{vrec\}) \cup V$) and ($\{eneg\} \cup E$). In this case, *vrec* increments the counter value of *vsen* by +1:

$(\{y(\{vsen\})\}+1)$ and decrements the reputation value of $vsen$ by $-\beta * (\{y(\{vsen\})\}$ $+1) * S$ as follows: $((\{y(\{vsen\})\}+1, \{rp(\{vsen\})\}) - \beta * (\{y(\{vsen\})\}+1) * S)$ $\cup RP)$. $vrec$ also reports $vsen$ to the TA: $(RT \cup \{vsen\})$.

Eneut inference rule: This rule deals with a neutral event detected by a receiving vehicle $vrec$ concerning a sending vehicle $vsen$: $((\{vsen\}, \{vrec\}) \cup V)$ and $(\{eneut\} \cup E)$. In this case, $vrec$ keeps the current counter value and the current reputation value of $vsen$ the same. Hence, no updating occurs to RP.

Consideration – info inference rule: This rule addresses the case where a receiving vehicle $vrec$ finds that the obtained accuracy value concerning a received information i: $(\{i\} \cup IR)$ from a sending vehicle $vsen$: $((\{vsen\}, \{vrec\}) \cup V)$ is greater than or equal to a certain threshold *thac* chosen by $vrec$: $((\{ac(\{i\})\} \geq thac) \cup AC)$. In such case, the information is considered by $vrec$: $(IC \cup \{i\})$.

Neglect – info inference rule: This rule addresses the case where a receiving vehicle $vrec$ finds that the obtained accuracy value concerning a received information i: $(\{i\} \cup IR)$ from a sending vehicle $vsen$: $((\{vsen\}, \{vrec\}) \cup V)$ is less than a certain threshold *thac* chosen by $vrec$: $((\{ac(\{i\})\} < thac) \cup AC)$. In such case, the information is neglected by $vrec$: $(IN \cup \{i\})$.

True – info – majo inference rule: This rule is concerned with the case where a vehicle $vrec$, receiving conflicting information from a set of sending vehicles $VSEN$: $((VSEN, \{vrec\}) \cup V)$, finds that a received information i: $(\{i\} \cup IR)$ is approved by the majority of the collected received reporting messages: $(\{i\} \cup IM)$. In such case, the information is considered to be true by $vrec$: $(IT \cup \{i\})$.

False – info – majo inference rule: This rule is concerned with the case where a vehicle $vrec$, receiving conflicting information from a set of sending vehicles $VSEN$: $((VSEN, \{vrec\}) \cup V)$, finds that a received information i: $(\{i\} \cup IR)$ is not approved by the majority of the collected received reporting messages: $(\{i\} \cup INM)$. In such case, the information is considered to be false by $vrec$: $(IF \cup \{i\})$.

True – info – combine inference rule: This rule addresses the case where a vehicle $vrec$, receiving conflicting information from a set of sending vehicles $VSEN$: $((VSEN, \{vrec\}) \cup V)$, finds that the score of the group of received messages reporting a received information i: $(\{i\} \cup IR)$ is the highest in comparison with the scores of the other groups of received messages reporting conflicting information with it: $(\{sc(\{i\})\} \cup SC)$ and $(HighestScore(\{i\}) \equiv True)$. In such case, $vrec$ considers the information to be true: $(IT \cup \{i\})$.

False – info – combine inference rule: This rule addresses the case where a vehicle $vrec$, receiving conflicting information from a set of sending vehicles $VSEN$: $((VSEN, \{vrec\}) \cup V)$, finds that the score of the group of received messages reporting a received information i: $(\{i\} \cup IR)$ is not the highest in comparison with the scores of the other groups of received messages reporting conflicting information with it: $(\{sc(\{i\})\} \cup SC)$. In such case, $vrec$ considers the information to be false: $(IF \cup \{i\})$.

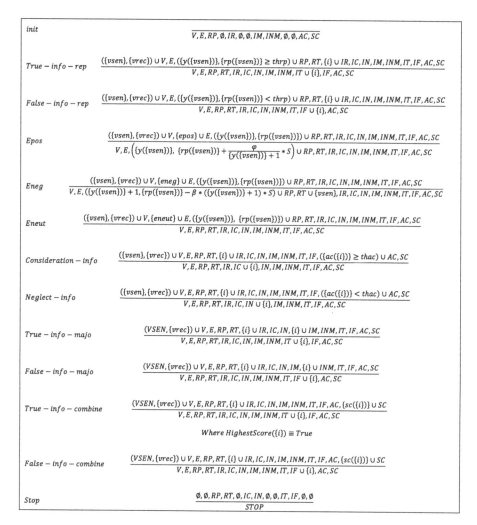

Fig. 2. The proposed inference system.

2.2 Soundness and Completeness Validation

In this subsection, the validation of the soundness and the completeness of the proposed inference system is achieved.

Soundness Validation. The goal is to check whether the proposed inference system is sound by considering the following formal properties: (1) logical assessment of information trueness using reputation values, (2) logical reputation values, (3) logical decision of information consideration, (4) logical assessment of information trueness using the majority of messages, and (5) logical assessment of information trueness using the scores of the groups of reporting messages.

In what follows, we define each one of these properties and we propose adequate theorems proving their preservation.

Property 1 (Logical assessment of information trueness using reputation values):
The assessment of the trueness of a received information through the reputation value of the sending vehicle is logical iff the information believed to be true is sent by a vehicle with a reputation value greater than or equal to a certain threshold chosen by the receiving vehicle.

Theorem 1: Assuming that initially, the assessment of the trueness of received information using reputation values is logical. If $(V, E, RP, \emptyset, IR, \emptyset, \emptyset, IM, INM, \emptyset, \emptyset, AC, SC)|-^*STOP$ then the property of logical assessment of information trueness using reputation values is preserved.

Proof: If $(V, E, RP, \emptyset, IR, \emptyset, \emptyset, IM, INM, \emptyset, \emptyset, AC, SC)|-^*STOP$ then only one inference rule among *True − info − rep, False − info − rep, Epos, Eneg, Eneut, Consideration − info, Neglect − info, True − info − majo, False − info − majo, True − info − combine* and *False − info − combine* applies for each received information. Hence, we have to verify whether the application of each inference rule locally keeps this property.

- When a received information is sent by a vehicle having a reputation value greater than or equal to a certain threshold chosen by the receiving vehicle, only the inference rule *True − info − rep* is applied by considering the information to be true. Then, the property is preserved.
- When a received information is sent by a vehicle having a reputation value less than a certain threshold chosen by the receiving vehicle, only the inference rule *False − info − rep* is applied by considering the information to be false. Then, the property is preserved.

Therefore, the property of logical assessment of information trueness using reputation values is preserved.

Property 2 (Logical reputation values): A reputation value is logical iff the detection of a positive event engenders the increase of the reputation value of the sending vehicle. The detection of a negative event engenders the decrease of the reputation value of the sending vehicle and the detection of a neutral event engenders the keeping of the current reputation value of the sending vehicle the same.

Theorem 2: Assuming that initially, reputation values are logical. All sending vehicles have the neutral reputation value and the neutral counter value that are equal to 0. If $(V, E, RP, \emptyset, IR, \emptyset, \emptyset, IM, INM, \emptyset, \emptyset, AC, SC)|-^*STOP$ then the property of logical reputation values is preserved.

Proof: If $(V, E, RP, \emptyset, IR, \emptyset, \emptyset, IM, INM, \emptyset, \emptyset, AC, SC)|-^*STOP$ then only one inference rule among *True − info − rep, False − info − rep, Epos, Eneg, Eneut, Consideration − info, Neglect − info, True − info − majo, False − info − majo, True − info − combine* and *False − info − combine* applies for each sending vehicle *vsen*. Hence, we have to verify whether the application of each inference rule locally keeps this property.

- When a positive event is detected by a receiving vehicle $vrec$, only the inference rule $Epos$ is applied by incrementing the reputation value of the sending vehicle $vsen$ by $+ \frac{\varphi}{\{y(\{vsen\})\} + 1} * S$. Then, the property is preserved.
- When a negative event is detected by $vrec$, only the inference rule $Eneg$ is applied by incrementing the counter value of $vsen$ by $+1$: $(\{y(\{vsen\})\} + 1)$ and decrementing the reputation value of $vsen$ by $-\beta * (\{y(\{vsen\})\} + 1) * S$. Then, the property is preserved.
- When a neutral event is detected by $vrec$, only the inference rule $Eneut$ is applied by keeping the current counter value and the current reputation value of $vsen$ the same. Then, the property is preserved.

Therefore, the property of logical reputation values is preserved.

Property 3 (Logical decision of information consideration): The decision of considering a received information is logical iff the information has an accuracy value greater than or equal to a certain threshold chosen by the receiving vehicle.

Theorem 3: Assuming that initially, the decision of information consideration is logical. If $(V, E, RP, \emptyset, IR, \emptyset, \emptyset, IM, INM, \emptyset, \emptyset, AC, SC)|-^*STOP$ then the property of logical decision of information consideration is preserved.

Proof: If $(V, E, RP, \emptyset, IR, \emptyset, \emptyset, IM, INM, \emptyset, \emptyset, AC, SC)|-^*STOP$ then only one inference rule among $True - info - rep$, $False - info - rep$, $Epos$, $Eneg$, $Eneut$, $Consideration - info$, $Neglect - info$, $True - info - majo$, $False - info - majo$, $True - info - combine$ and $False - info - combine$ applies for each received information. Hence, we have to verify whether the application of each inference rule locally keeps this property.

- When a received information has an accuracy value greater than or equal to a certain threshold chosen by the receiving vehicle $vrec$, only the inference rule $Consideration - info$ is applied by taking the information into consideration. Then, the property is preserved.
- When a received information has an accuracy value less than a certain threshold chosen by the receiving vehicle $vrec$, only the inference rule $Neglect - info$ is applied by neglecting the information. Then, the property is preserved.

Therefore, the property of logical decision of information consideration is preserved.

Property 4 (Logical assessment of information trueness using the majority of messages): The assessment of the trueness of a received information using the majority of messages is logical iff the information believed to be true is approved by the majority of the received reporting messages.

Theorem 4: Assuming that initially, the assessment of the trueness of received information using the majority of messages is logical. If $(V, E, RP, \emptyset, IR, \emptyset, \emptyset, IM, INM, \emptyset, \emptyset, AC, SC)|-^*STOP$ then the property of logical assessment of information trueness using the majority of messages is preserved.

Proof: If $(V, E, RP, \emptyset, IR, \emptyset, \emptyset, IM, INM, \emptyset, \emptyset, AC, SC)|-^*STOP$ then only one inference rule among *True – info – rep, False – info – rep, Epos, Eneg, Eneut, Consideration – info, Neglect – info, True – info – majo, False – info – majo, True – info – combine* and *False – info – combine* applies for each received information. Hence, we have to verify whether the application of each inference rule locally keeps this property.

- When a received information is approved by the majority of the received reporting messages, only the inference rule *True – info – majo* is applied by considering the information to be true. Then, the property is preserved.
- When a received information is not approved by the majority of the received reporting messages, only the inference rule *False – info – majo* is applied by considering the information to be false. Then, the property is preserved.

Therefore, the property of logical assessment of information trueness using the majority of messages is preserved.

Property 5 (Logical assessment of information trueness using the scores of the groups of reporting messages): The assessment of the trueness of a received information is logical iff the group of received messages reporting the information believed to be true has the highest score in comparison with the scores of the groups of received messages reporting conflicting information with it.

Theorem 5: Assuming that initially, the assessment of the trueness of received information using the scores of the groups of reporting messages is logical. If $(V, E, RP, \emptyset, IR, \emptyset, \emptyset, IM, INM, \emptyset, \emptyset, AC, SC)|-^*STOP$ then the property of logical assessment of information trueness using the scores of the groups of reporting messages is preserved.

Proof: If $(V, E, RP, \emptyset, IR, \emptyset, \emptyset, IM, INM, \emptyset, \emptyset, AC, SC)|-^*STOP$ then only one inference rule among *True – info – rep, False – info – rep, Epos, Eneg, Eneut, Consideration – info, Neglect – info, True – info – majo, False – info – majo, True – info – combine* and *False – info – combine* applies for each received information. Hence, we have to verify whether the application of each inference rule locally keeps this property.

- When the group of received messages reporting a received information has the highest score in comparison with the scores of the groups of received messages reporting conflicting information with it, only the inference rule *True – info – combine* is applied by considering the information to be true. Then, the property is preserved.
- When the group of received messages reporting a received information does not have the highest score in comparison with the scores of the groups of received messages reporting conflicting information with it, only the inference rule *False – info – combine* is applied by considering the information to be false. Then, the property is preserved.

Therefore, the property of logical assessment of information trueness using the scores of the groups of reporting messages is preserved.

Corollary (Soundness): Since all the above-mentioned properties are preserved, we can conclude that the soundness property of the proposed inference system is satisfied.

Completeness Validation. Having that the soundness of the proposed inference system is proved, we proceed to the validation of its completeness. This is fulfilled by showing that all the potential situations are handled by the inference system. First, for the reputation module, the two cases of the reputation value of the sending vehicle being greater than or equal to a certain threshold chosen by the receiving vehicle or less than that threshold are handled. If the reputation value is greater than or equal to the set threshold, the *True – info – rep* inference rule is triggered. However, if the reputation value is less than the set threshold, then the *False – info – rep* inference rule is triggered. In addition, all the possible cases of detected events are handled. In fact, if the reception of an honest information is detected, then the *Epos* inference rule is triggered. If the reception of a bogus information is detected, then the *Eneg* inference rule is triggered. And if a lack of enough evidences is detected, then the *Eneut* inference rule is triggered. Second, for the time and location closeness estimation module, the two cases of the obtained accuracy value being greater than or equal to a chosen threshold or less than that threshold are handled. In fact, if the accuracy value of a received information is greater than or equal to the set threshold, then the *Consideration – info* inference rule is triggered. Else, the *Neglect – info* inference rule is triggered. Third, for the majority module, the two cases of a received information being endorsed by the majority of the received reporting messages or not are handled. In fact, if the information is endorsed by the majority of the messages, then the *True – info – majo* inference rule is triggered. Otherwise, the *False – info – majo* inference rule is triggered. Finally, for the combination of the three above-mentioned modules, the two cases of the group of messages reporting the same information having the highest score, in comparison with the scores of the groups of messages that report conflicting information, or not are handled. In fact, if the score of a group of messages is the highest, then the *True – info – combine* inference rule is triggered. Otherwise, the *False – info – combine* inference rule is triggered.

It follows that in all the situations, there is always an applicable rule in the proposed inference system. Therefore, we can conclude that the completeness property of the proposed inference system is satisfied.

3 Conclusion

In VANETs, vehicles exchange safety related messages in order to increase the safety of roads traffic. These messages are with a critical nature. If they are not secured properly, attackers may take advantages of this loophole to launch dangerous attacks. Recently, we proposed a scheme assessing the credibility and the accuracy of received safety related messages. The scheme in question is based on three modules: a reputation module mainly evaluating the reputation of sending vehicles. A time and location closeness estimation module judging the accuracy of a received information and a majority module assessing the trueness of a received information. These modules can be used in a separated or combined manner according to the circumstances faced in VANETs. In this paper, we formally validated the three modules as well as their combination by first proposing a formal and automated expression of them using an inference system and next building a validation process that uses the proposed inference system and proves soundness and completeness. Soundness was proved by showing that a set of defined properties are preserved. Completeness was proved by showing that all the potential situations are handled by the proposed inference system.

References

1. Chikhaoui, O., Ben Chehida Douss, A., Abassi, R., Guemara El Fatmi, S.: Towards a privacy preserving and flexible scheme for assessing the credibility and the accuracy of safety messages exchanged in VANETs. In: 13th International Conference on Availability, Reliability and Security, Hambourg, p. 55. ACM (2018)
2. Whitefield, J., Chen, L., Giannetsos, T., Schneider, S., Treharne, H.: Privacy-enhanced capabilities for VANETs using direct anonymous attestation. In: 2017 IEEE Vehicular Networking Conference, Torino, pp. 123–130. IEEE Press (2017)
3. Gong, C., Xu, C., Zhou, Z., Zhang, T., Yang, S.: A reputation management scheme for identifying malicious nodes in VANET. In: 2019 IEEE 20th International Conference on High Performance Switching and Routing, Xi'an, pp. 1–6. IEEE Press (2019)
4. Lindsay, P.A.: Specification and validation of a network security policy model. Technical report, 97-05, Software Verification Research Centre, the University of Queensland, April 1997
5. IEEE Guide to Software Requirements Specification. ANSI/IEEE Std 830 (1998)
6. Abassi, R., Guemara El Fatmi, S.: A novel validation method for firewall security policy. J. Inf. Assur. Secur. 4, 329–337 (2009)
7. Ben Chehida Douss, A., Abassi, R., Ben Youssef, N., Guemara El Fatmi, S.: A formal environment for MANET organization and security. In: Reiter, M., Naccache, D. (eds.) CANS 2015. LNCS, vol. 9476, pp. 144–159. Springer, Cham (2015). https://doi.org/10.1007/978-3-319-26823-1_11

A Security Mechanism Against the RSU Compromise Attack in a Ticket-Based Authentication Scheme for VANETs

Ons Chikhaoui$^{(\boxtimes)}$, Ryma Abassi, Aida Ben Chehida Douss, and Sihem Guemara El Fatmi

Digital Security Research Lab, Higher School of Communication of Tunis (Sup'Com), University of Carthage, Tunis, Tunisia
{ons.chikhaoui, ryma.abassi, aida.benchehida, sihem.guemara}@supcom.tn

Abstract. In Vehicular Ad hoc NETworks (VANETs), a major necessity is to enable the receiving vehicles to authenticate the received safety related messages while conditionally preserving the privacy of the real identities of the sending vehicles. In order to achieve the aforementioned objectives, we proposed a Ticket-based Authentication Scheme for VANETs Preserving Privacy (TASVPP) [1] and the Optimization of a Ticket-based Authentication Scheme for VANETs (OTASV) [2]. Unfortunately, the problem of the RSU compromise attack has not been considered in both TASVPP and OTASV. Our objective in this paper is then to mitigate this problem by providing two main mechanisms: a RSU compromise prevention mechanism which focuses on resisting side-channel attacks and a RSU compromise detection and reaction mechanism which focuses on detecting, revoking, recovering and isolating compromised RSUs. An in-depth security analysis is also performed to demonstrate that our scheme can meet the targeted security requirements.

Keywords: RSU compromise attack · Prevention · Detection · Reaction

1 Introduction

In order to deal with the requirement of authenticating the received safety related messages while conditionally maintaining the privacy of the real identities of the sending vehicles in the Vehicular Ad hoc NETworks (VANETs), we proposed in a previous work a Ticket-based Authentication Scheme for VANETs Preserving Privacy (TASVPP) [1] in which vehicles use temporary tickets to communicate with each other while conditionally preserving their privacy. The Optimization of a Ticket-based Authentication Scheme for VANETs (OTASV) [2] was proposed to improve the computation and communication efficiency of [1].

Unfortunately, in both [1] and [2], the problem of RSU compromise has not been considered. In fact, an adversary can conduct a physical attack on RSUs and retrieve secret information and stored data from them particularly in an unwatched location [3]. Even with putting RSUs' inner information in Tamper Proof Devices (TPDs), the assumption of ideal TPDs (devices from which no attacker can ever extract any stored

M. Themistocleous and M. Papadaki (Eds.): EMCIS 2019, LNBIP 381, pp. 403–416, 2020.
https://doi.org/10.1007/978-3-030-44322-1_30

data) is too strong to be practical. In practice, manufactured TPDs can be expected to resist known attacks, but not all future attacks. Even if an attacker cannot probe the inside of a TPD, he might collect substantial information through side-channel attacks [4].

The main contribution of this paper is then, the definition of a security mechanism extending our earlier works [1] and [2], and used for mitigating the RSU compromise problem. This proposition is two-folds: a RSU compromise prevention mechanism and a RSU compromise detection and reaction mechanism. The RSU compromise prevention mechanism focuses on resisting side-channel attacks by introducing an RSU's identity/corresponding private key pair updating strategy, so that the secret cryptographic information stored in the TPD of the RSU can be updated before an attacker manages to collect enough side-channel information to extract them. The RSU compromise detection and reaction mechanism focuses on detecting, revoking, recovering and excluding compromised RSUs. To enable the TA to detect compromised RSUs, the traceability phase of [1] is developed. Here, when the TA receives reports to trace misbehaving vehicles, it detects compromised RSUs by verifying that they have signed revoked credentials. In fact, it checks the revocation status of the credentials included in the reports. If a credential is validly signed while it is revoked, the TA deducts that its signing RSU is compromised. For revoking and recovering the detected compromised RSUs, an RSU revocation and recovering phase is proposed. In this phase, the TA revokes a detected compromised RSU by including its identity(s) into the current RSUs identities' revocation list and immediately sending the updated revocation list to the non-revoked RSUs which in their turn broadcast it within their coverage areas. The revocation of an RSU's identity automatically revokes all the messages generated under that identity. The TA then recovers the detected compromised RSU by repairing it from physical attacks, if any exist, and then loading its TPD directly with the required security materials. In order to exclude the revoked RSUs from the network, both the authentication phase and the signature generation and verification phase of [1] are developed. In fact, here, during the authentication phase, when a vehicle intends to request from its current RSU to sign its credential, it is enabled to, before that, verify the validity period of the RSU's identity and then the RSU's revocation status by checking its identity against the latest RSUs identities' revocation list. If the identity is found to be revoked, then the vehicle aborts its communication with the RSU. The signature generation and verification phase is developed to become a second line of defense to exclude revoked RSUs. In fact, when a vehicle receives a message from a sending vehicle, it is here enabled to verify the validity period of the identity of the RSU that signed that sending vehicle's credential (i.e., the validity period of the RSU's identity included in the received ticket) and then to verify the revocation status of that RSU by checking its identity against the latest RSUs identities' revocation list. If the identity is found to be revoked, then the vehicle drops the received message.

The remaining part of this paper is structured as follows. Section 2 reviews some related works dealing with the RSU compromise attack. In Sect. 3, TASVPP and OTASV are recalled. Section 4 describes the RSU compromise attack's impact. In Sect. 5, a background of our proposed scheme is provided. Section 6 focuses on the proposed scheme. In Sect. 7, a security analysis of this scheme is performed. Finally, Sect. 8 concludes this paper.

2   Related Work

In this section, we recall some works that were conducted to deal with the RSU compromise attack.

In [5], authors dealt with this attack by not granting the RSUs a full access to the vehicles' information. However, no method for preventing and/or detecting the attack is provided. In [6], an elliptic curve ElGamal threshold-based key management scheme is used to tolerate partial compromising of RSUs; and in [4], authors proposed to periodically update the private/public key pairs of the RSUs to prevent side-channel attacks. However, in both these schemes, no method to detect compromised RSUs is provided. Moreover, the updating procedure suggested in [4] is not detailed. In [7], compromised RSUs are detected through the fake link tags they generate; and in [8], the TA revokes a compromised RSU by broadcasting the information of the domain to which it belongs and its identity. However, in both these schemes, no method to prevent the RSU compromise attack is provided.

To the best of our knowledge, this is the first scheme that provides a complete strategy to deal with the RSU compromise attack. This strategy starts from preventing this attack to detecting, revoking, recovering and isolating compromised RSUs.

3   TASVPP and OTASV

In this section, we recall our works TASVPP [1] and OTASV [2].

In TASVPP [1], we proposed a scheme that enables the receiving vehicles to authenticate the received safety-related messages while conditionally preserving the privacy of the real identities of the sending vehicles. [1] is built upon five phases: (1) The network initialization phase in which the TA initializes the network. (2) The authentication phase in which a mutual authentication between a vehicle and its present RSU takes place whenever the vehicle joins a new domain and/or the validity period of the vehicle's current ticket expires. The authenticated vehicle also gets its credential signed by the authenticated RSU. The vehicle then uses its signed credential to form its ticket. (3) The signature generation and verification phase in which vehicles sign their outgoing safety-related messages and authenticate received ones. (4) The traceability phase in which the TA traces the real identity of a misbehaving vehicle. And (5) the revocation phase in which misbehaving vehicles are abrogated from the network. In fact, the TA includes the credentials of misbehaving vehicles into revocation lists and sends these latter to the RSUs. The RSUs do not sign the credentials included in the received revocation lists disabling then misbehaving vehicles from forming valid tickets and consequently evicting them from the network. OTASV [2] was proposed to improve the computation and communication efficiency of [1]. The computation efficiency's improvement is achieved by introducing the Identity Based Online/Offline Signature (IBOOS) technique and Shamir's trick as well as enabling receiving vehicles to store already verified tickets for reference later. The communication efficiency's improvement is achieved by reducing the signature size.

4 RSU Compromise Attack's Impact

In this section, we present the RSU compromise attack's impact.

Let us recall that in [1] and [2], RSUs are responsible for verifying the revocation status of vehicles' credentials and signing non-revoked ones. Hence, if an RSU gets compromised, it may launch the following attacks: The compromised RSU may totally neglect the revocation list of the current time slot and sign all the received credentials of that time slot regardless of being included in the revocation list or not. Also, the compromised RSU may partially neglect the revocation list of the current time slot and sign certain received credentials of that time slot in spite of being included in the revocation list. Besides, the compromised RSU may only sign received credentials that are included in the revocation list of the current time slot while neglecting non-revoked ones. In addition, the compromised RSU may collude with a misbehaving vehicle and then sign its credential in spite of being included in the current revocation list; the compromised RSU may too sign credentials, of the colluding vehicle, that are related to future time slots.

Following the launch of the aforementioned attacks, a legitimate vehicle that requests, a compromised RSU, for signing its credential may waste its resources without getting its credential signed when the compromised RSU intentionally neglects its request. Also, the requirement of isolating revoked vehicles from the network becomes unattainable and hence during the signature generation and verification phase, a receiving vehicle may unknowingly accept a ticket that includes a revoked credential. Besides, the requirement of resisting the GPS spoofing attack becomes unattainable when a compromised RSU colludes with a misbehaving vehicle and then signs future credentials of its accomplice; in fact, using the valid tickets formed from its reserve of these signed credentials, the misbehaving vehicle may pretend, without being detected by receiving vehicles, during the signature generation and verification phase, to be in the vicinity of the signing compromised RSU while in reality, it is out of that zone.

However, it is worth recalling that in [1] and [2], vehicles use credentials to authenticate themselves to RSUs. Hence, even if all the RSUs are compromised, the identity privacy preservation and the long-term unlinkability requirements are still maintained.

Let us consider the scenario depicted by Fig. 1 in which we assume that the RSU $RSU_{3,1}$, belonging to the domain D_1, is compromised. $RSU_{3,1}$ neglects the request of the legitimate vehicle V_1 despite that its credential, related to the current time slot TS_x, is not revoked ($Cred_{V_1,TS_x}$ is not included in the current credentials' revocation list RL_{TS_x}), whereas it accepts the request of the revoked vehicle V_4 and signs its revoked credential ($Cred_{V_4,TS_x}$ is included in the current credentials' revocation list RL_{TS_x}).

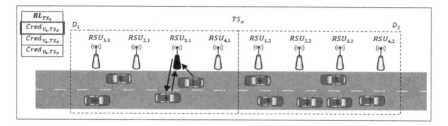

Fig. 1. The attack of neglecting the revocation lists.

5 Background

In this section, we introduce the security requirements and the assumptions of our proposed scheme.

5.1 Security Requirements

The main goal of designing our scheme is to achieve the following security requirements. These requirements are critical for the end-result.

- **The prevention of the RSU compromise attack:** the attack of compromising RSUs can be prevented to the maximum possible extent.
- **The detection of the RSU compromise attack:** the TA is able to detect compromised RSUs.
- **The revocation and recovering of the detected compromised RSUs:** the TA is able to revoke and then recover the detected compromised RSUs.
- **The eviction of the revoked RSUs:** the revoked RSUs can be evicted from the network.

5.2 Scheme Assumptions

Our scheme is based on the following assumptions:

- During the network initialization phase, the TA generates its own updatable (i.e., with a certain validity period VP) initial identity $ID_{TA,VP}$ and extracts the corresponding private key $s_{TA,VP}$ by performing the Key Extraction algorithm of the B-IBOOS scheme [9]. The TA will use $s_{TA,VP}$ to sign its outgoing messages during VP. Then, the TA publishes $ID_{TA,VP}$ and $R_{TA,VP}$ with the network's public parameters mentioned in [1], (*Remark:* see [9] for the definition of $R_{TA,VP}$).
- In this scheme, we will consider the scenario in which a fraction of RSUs in the network could be compromised.
- The TA assigns and preloads into each registered RSU:
  - An updatable initial identity $ID_{RSU,VP}$ and the corresponding private key $s_{RSU,VP}$ where VP is the validity period of the pair $ID_{RSU,VP}/s_{RSU,VP}$. The RSU will use $s_{RSU,VP}$ to sign its outgoing messages during VP, (*Remark:* the validity period of the identity of the TA is different from the validity period of the identity of an RSU).

- A secure symmetric key cryptographic algorithm with key *Key*. In our scheme, the encryption is non-deterministic.
- An updatable initial symmetric key Key_{TA-RSU}^{VP}. This key will be used by both the TA and the RSU for the secure updating of the $ID_{RSU,VP}/s_{RSU,VP}$ pair.

- Each RSU is equipped with a Tamper Proof Device (TPD) to store and physically protect the RSU's security materials as well as performing the cryptographic operations. Any failed attempt to extract any information from the TPD through physical attacks will cause it to self-delete all its inner information. Besides, once the validity period of a stored security material expires, the TPD deletes it.
- The TA periodically checks the RSUs in the network physically and loads their TPDs with the required security materials directly.

6 The Proposed Scheme

In this section, we first present the RSU's identity/corresponding private key pair updating strategy. In the next, we provide the new version of each of the authentication phase, the signature generation and verification phase and the traceability phase in relation to [1]. Finally, we describe the RSU revocation phase.

6.1 RSU's Identity/Corresponding Private Key Pair Updating Strategy

In [1] and [2], the TA sets the identity of each RSU as its geographical coordinates concatenated with the sequence number of the domain to which it belongs. The identity of $RSU_{a,b}$ is: $ID_{RSU_{a,b}} = <GC_{RSU_{a,b}}, D_b>$.

In this scheme, we append an auxiliary information to the identity of an RSU in relation to this latter's identity in [1] and [2]. This information is the validity period *VP* of the identity and consequently the corresponding private key, and it should be a short time period. Hence, the identity of $RSU_{a,b}$ during the validity period VP_h is: $ID_{RSU_{a,b},VP_h} = <GC_{RSU_{a,b}}, D_b, VP_h>$.

One *VP* contains ρ time slots where $\rho \in \mathbb{N}^*$. *VP* has the following structure, i.e., the start and end time of *VP* coincide with the start and end time of a certain number ρ of consecutive time slots, to save the vehicle from performing the authentication phase whenever the *VP* of the identity of the RSU that signed the current credential of the vehicle expires, in addition to the cases already mentioned in [1].

Let us assume that $ID_{RSU_{a,b},VP_h}/s_{RSU_{a,b},VP_h}$ is the current identity/corresponding private key pair of $RSU_{a,b}$. Before the expiration of VP_h, the TA prepares and delivers to $RSU_{a,b}$ an Identity/corresponding Private Key pair Updating Message $IPKUM_{RSU_{a,b},VP_{h+1}}$ as follows:

(1) The TA sets the new identity $ID_{RSU_{a,b},VP_{h+1}}$ of $RSU_{a,b}$ as: $ID_{RSU_{a,b},VP_{h+1}} = <GC_{RSU_{a,b}}, D_b, VP_{h+1}>$.
(2) The TA extracts the private key $s_{RSU_{a,b},VP_{h+1}}$ that corresponds to $ID_{RSU_{a,b},VP_{h+1}}$ by performing the Key Extraction algorithm of the B-IBOOS scheme.
(3) The TA generates a symmetric key $Key_{TA-RSU_{a,b}}^{VP_{h+1}}$.

(4) The TA sets $\gamma = <ID_{RSU_{a,b},VP_{h+1}}, R_{RSU_{a,b},VP_{h+1}}, s_{RSU_{a,b},VP_{h+1}}, Key_{TA-RSU_{a,b}}^{VP_{h+1}}>$.

(5) The TA encrypts γ using $Key_{TA-RSU_{a,b}}^{VP_h}$ to get the ciphertext C_{update}.

(6) The TA selects a timestamp t used for freshness.

(7) The TA generates $\sigma_{TA,VP}(ID_{RSU_{a,b},VP_h}, t, C_{update})$ by performing the Signature Generation algorithm of the B-IBOOS scheme.

(8) The TA sends $IPKUM_{RSU_{a,b},VP_{h+1}} = <ID_{RSU_{a,b},VP_h}, ID_{TA,VP}, t, C_{update}, \sigma_{TA,VP}$ $(ID_{RSU_{a,b},VP_h}, t, C_{update})>$ to $RSU_{a,b}$.

Once $RSU_{a,b}$ receives $IPKUM_{RSU_{a,b},VP_{h+1}}$, it performs the following steps:

(1) $RSU_{a,b}$ checks whether $ID_{RSU_{a,b},VP_h}$ included in $IPKUM_{RSU_{a,b},VP_{h+1}}$ matches its current identity to make sure that it is the intended recipient of the TA.

(2) If there is a match then $RSU_{a,b}$ checks t.

(3) If t is fresh then $RSU_{a,b}$ checks whether $ID_{TA,VP}$ included in $IPKUM_{RSU_{a,b},VP_{h+1}}$ matches the current identity of the TA.

(4) If there is a match then $RSU_{a,b}$ verifies the validity of $\sigma_{TA,VP}(ID_{RSU_{a,b},VP_h},$ $t, C_{update})$ by performing the Signature Verification algorithm of the B-IBOOS scheme.

(5) If $\sigma_{TA,VP}(ID_{RSU_{a,b},VP_h}, t, C_{update})$ is valid then $RSU_{a,b}$ decrypts C_{update} using $Key_{TA-RSU_{a,b}}^{VP_h}$ to get the plaintext γ.

Should any of these verification steps fail, $RSU_{a,b}$ drops the message and exits.

$RSU_{a,b}$ has to confirm the well reception of $IPKUM_{RSU_{a,b},VP_{h+1}}$ by sending a signed acknowledgement ACK to the TA. If a predefined timeout expires without receiving the ACK from $RSU_{a,b}$, the TA re-encrypts γ using $Key_{TA-RSU_{a,b}}^{VP_h}$ to get a different C_{update} (since we use non-deterministic encryption), selects a new timestamp t, and finally generates and sends the new $IPKUM_{RSU_{a,b},VP_{h+1}}$ to $RSU_{a,b}$. If the predefined timeout expires also for the second $IPKUM_{RSU_{a,b},VP_{h+1}}$ without receiving a related ACK from $RSU_{a,b}$, the TA checks $RSU_{a,b}$ physically, repairs it if needed and loads its TPD with the required security materials directly.

6.2   Authentication Phase

As in [1] and [2], the mutual authentication between vehicles and RSUs should occur in these two cases. **Case 1:** whenever a vehicle enters into a new domain, so the vehicle should update its current ticket. **Case 2:** whenever the current ticket of a vehicle expires (i.e., the ticket's corresponding time slot ends), so the vehicle should change its current ticket.

The Mutual Authentication in Case 1

Each RSU must periodically announce itself to the vehicles as follows:

(1) $RSU_{a,b}$ with the current identity $ID_{RSU_{a,b},VP_h}$, selects a timestamp t used for freshness and generates $\sigma_{RSU_{a,b},VP_h}(t)$ by performing the Signature Generation algorithm of the B-IBOOS scheme.

(2) $RSU_{a,b}$ broadcasts $<ID_{RSU_{a,b},VP_h}, t, \sigma_{RSU_{a,b},VP_h}(t)>$ within its coverage area.

Once a vehicle V_i receives $<ID_{RSU_{a,b},VP_h}, t, \sigma_{RSU_{a,b},VP_h}(t)>$, it performs the following steps:

(1) V_i checks t.
(2) If t is fresh then V_i verifies $GC_{RSU_{a,b}}$ in $ID_{RSU_{a,b},VP_h}$ by using the GPS.
(3) If $GC_{RSU_{a,b}}$ are correct then V_i verifies D_b in $ID_{RSU_{a,b},VP_h}$.
(4) If D_b is a new domain for V_i then V_i verifies the validity period of $ID_{RSU_{a,b},VP_h}$ by checking whether VP_h includes the current time slot TS_{x+k}, i.e., V_i checks whether $TS_{x+k} \subset VP_h$, (*Remark:* see [1] for the definition of k).
(5) If $TS_{x+k} \subset VP_h$ then V_i checks $ID_{RSU_{a,b},VP_h}$ against the most recent RSUs identities' revocation list RL_{RSU} to verify the revocation status of $RSU_{a,b}$.
(6) If $ID_{RSU_{a,b},VP_h}$ is not in RL_{RSU} then V_i verifies the validity of $\sigma_{RSU_{a,b},VP_h}(t)$ by performing the Signature Verification algorithm of the B-IBOOS scheme.
(7) If $\sigma_{RSU_{a,b},VP_h}(t)$ is valid then V_i uses its triple $\{Cred_{V_i,TS_{x+k}}, R_{V_i,TS_{x+k}}, S_{V_i,TS_{x+k}}\}$ corresponding to the current time slot TS_{x+k} in order to authenticate itself to $RSU_{a,b}$: V_i selects a timestamp t used for freshness, generates $\sigma_{V_i,TS_{x+k}}(ID_{RSU_{a,b},VP_h}, t)$ by performing the Signature Generation algorithm of the B-IBOOS scheme and then sends $<ID_{RSU_{a,b},VP_h}, Cred_{V_i,TS_{x+k}}, t, \sigma_{V_i,TS_{x+k}}(ID_{RSU_{a,b},VP_h}, t)>$ to $RSU_{a,b}$.

Should any of these verification steps fail, V_i drops the message and exits.

Once $RSU_{a,b}$ receives $<ID_{RSU_{a,b},VP_h}, Cred_{V_i,TS_{x+k}}, t, \sigma_{V_i,TS_{x+k}}(ID_{RSU_{a,b},VP_h}, t)>$, it performs the following steps:

(1) $RSU_{a,b}$ checks whether $ID_{RSU_{a,b},VP_h}$ included in the received message matches its current identity to make sure that it is the intended recipient of V_i.
(2) If there is a match then $RSU_{a,b}$ checks t.
(3) If t is fresh then $RSU_{a,b}$ checks whether the validity period indicated in $Cred_{V_i,TS_{x+k}}$ corresponds to the current time slot (i.e., TS_{x+k}).
(4) If the indicated validity period corresponds to the current time slot then $RSU_{a,b}$ checks $Cred_{V_i,TS_{x+k}}$ against the current credentials' revocation list $RL_{TS_{x+k}}$.
(5) If $Cred_{V_i,TS_{x+k}}$ is not in $RL_{TS_{x+k}}$ then $RSU_{a,b}$ verifies the validity of $\sigma_{V_i,TS_{x+k}}(ID_{RSU_{a,b},VP_h}, t)$ by performing the Signature Verification algorithm of the B-IBOOS scheme.
(6) If $\sigma_{V_i,TS_{x+k}}(ID_{RSU_{a,b},VP_h}, t)$ is valid then $RSU_{a,b}$ generates $\sigma_{RSU_{a,b},VP_h}(Cred_{V_i,TS_{x+k}})$ by performing the Signature Generation algorithm of the B-IBOOS scheme and sends $<Cred_{V_i,TS_{x+k}}, ID_{RSU_{a,b},VP_h}, \sigma_{RSU_{a,b},VP_h}(Cred_{V_i,TS_{x+k}})>$ to V_i.

Should any of these verification steps fail, $RSU_{a,b}$ drops the message and exits.

Once V_i receives $<Cred_{V_i,TS_{x+k}}, ID_{RSU_{a,b},VP_h}, \sigma_{RSU_{a,b},VP_h}(Cred_{V_i,TS_{x+k}})>$, it performs the following steps:

(1) V_i checks whether $Cred_{V_i,TS_{x+k}}$ included in the received message matches its current credential to make sure that it is the intended recipient of $RSU_{a,b}$.

(2) If there is a match then V_i verifies the validity of $\sigma_{RSU_{a,b},VP_h}(Cred_{V_i,TS_{x+k}})$ by performing the Signature Verification algorithm of the B-IBOOS scheme.

(3) If $\sigma_{RSU_{a,b},VP_h}(Cred_{V_i,TS_{x+k}})$ is valid then V_i sets its ticket $TK_{V_i,TS_{x+k}}$ as the concatenation of $ID_{RSU_{a,b},VP_h}$, $Cred_{V_i,TS_{x+k}}$ and $\sigma_{RSU_{a,b},VP_h}(Cred_{V_i,TS_{x+k}})$.

Should any of these verification steps fail, V_i drops the message and exits.

The Mutual Authentication in Case 2

In this case, the same steps are performed as in case 1 except that V_i omits the verification of D_b in $ID_{RSU_{a,b},VP_h}$ and it directly moves from verifying $GC_{RSU_{a,b}}$ in $ID_{RSU_{a,b},VP_h}$ to verifying the validity period of $ID_{RSU_{a,b},VP_h}$.

6.3   Signature Generation and Verification Phase

After forming $TK_{V_i,TS_{x+k}}$, V_i uses $\{Cred_{V_i,TS_{x+k}}, R_{V_i,TS_{x+k}}, S_{V_i,TS_{x+k}}\}$ to sign its safety-related messages, in TS_{x+k}, by performing the following steps:

(1) V_i selects a timestamp t used for freshness, sets $M_{V_i,TS_{x+k}} = <m, t>$, where m is the safety message's content, and generates $\sigma_{V_i,TS_{x+k}}(ID_{RSU_{a,b},VP_h}, M_{V_i,TS_{x+k}})$ by performing the Signature Generation algorithm of the B-IBOOS scheme, (*Remark:* $ID_{RSU_{a,b},VP_h}$ is the identity of $RSU_{a,b}$ included in $TK_{V_i,TS_{x+k}}$).

(2) V_i sends $<TK_{V_i,TS_{x+k}}, M_{V_i,TS_{x+k}}, \sigma_{V_i,TS_{x+k}}(ID_{RSU_{a,b},VP_h}, M_{V_i,TS_{x+k}})>$.

Once a receiving vehicle V_j receives $<TK_{V_i,TS_{x+k}}, M_{V_i,TS_{x+k}}, \sigma_{V_i,TS_{x+k}}(ID_{RSU_{a,b},VP_h}, M_{V_i,TS_{x+k}})>$, it should perform the following steps in order to authenticate $M_{V_i,TS_{x+k}}$:

(1) V_j checks t.

(2) If t is fresh then V_j checks whether TS_{x+k} indicated in $TK_{V_i,TS_{x+k}}$ (more precisely in $Cred_{V_i,TS_{x+k}}$) corresponds to the current time slot.

(3) If TS_{x+k} corresponds to the current time slot then V_j checks whether VP_h indicated in $TK_{V_i,TS_{x+k}}$ (more precisely in $ID_{RSU_{a,b},VP_h}$) includes TS_{x+k}, i.e., whether $TS_{x+k} \subset VP_h$.

(4) If $TS_{x+k} \subset VP_h$ then V_j checks $ID_{RSU_{a,b},VP_h}$ indicated in $TK_{V_i,TS_{x+k}}$ against the most recent RL_{RSU} to verify the revocation status of $RSU_{a,b}$.

(5) If $ID_{RSU_{a,b},VP_h}$ is not in RL_{RSU} then V_j verifies the validity of $\sigma_{RSU_{a,b},VP_h}(Cred_{V_i,TS_{x+k}})$ by performing the Signature Verification algorithm of the B-IBOOS scheme.

(6) If $\sigma_{RSU_{a,b},VP_h}(Cred_{V_i,TS_{x+k}})$ is valid then V_j verifies the validity of $\sigma_{V_i,TS_{x+k}}(ID_{RSU_{a,b},VP_h}, M_{V_i,TS_{x+k}})$ by performing the Signature Verification algorithm of the B-IBOOS scheme.

(7) If $\sigma_{V_i,TS_{x+k}}(ID_{RSU_{a,b},VP_h}, M_{V_i,TS_{x+k}})$ is valid then V_j accepts the message.

Should any of these verification steps fail, V_j drops the message and exits.

Let us mention that if V_j stores already verified tickets in a table as in [2], then it will perform the same aforementioned steps until reaching the fifth step. After that, if $ID_{RSU_{a,b},VP_h}$ is not in RL_{RSU} then V_j verifies whether the hash value of $TK_{V_i,TS_{x+k}}$ exists in its storing table. If it exists then V_j omits the verification of $\sigma_{RSU_{a,b},VP_h}\left(Cred_{V_i,TS_{x+k}}\right)$ and directly moves to the verification of $\sigma_{V_i,TS_{x+k}}\left(ID_{RSU_{a,b},VP_h}, M_{V_i,TS_{x+k}}\right)$. However, if it does not exist, no omission occurs.

6.4 Traceability Phase

This phase is developed to permit the TA to trace compromised RSUs.

Assuming that a vehicle V_j using a ticket $TK_{V_j,TS_{z+u}} = <ID_{RSU_{v,l},VP_e}, Cred_{V_j,TS_{z+u}},$ $\sigma_{RSU_{v,l},VP_e}\left(Cred_{V_j,TS_{z+u}}\right) >$ intends to accuse a vehicle V_i for sending a bogus message $M_{V_i,TS_{x+k}}$ and the corresponding signature $\sigma_{V_i,TS_{x+k}}\left(ID_{RSU_{a,b},VP_h}, M_{V_i,TS_{x+k}}\right)$ under the ticket $TK_{V_i,TS_{x+k}} = <ID_{RSU_{a,b},VP_h}, Cred_{V_i,TS_{x+k}}, \sigma_{RSU_{a,b},VP_h}\left(Cred_{V_i,TS_{x+k}}\right) >$. V_j prepares and sends, to the TA, a signed report $Report_{V_j}(V_i)$ against V_i that includes its own ticket $TK_{V_j,TS_{z+u}}$ and the ticket $TK_{V_i,TS_{x+k}}$ of the accused vehicle V_i.

When the TA receives $Report_{V_j}(V_i)$, and in order to detect compromised RSUs, it checks whether VP_e indicated in $ID_{RSU_{v,l},VP_e}$ includes TS_{z+u} indicated in $Cred_{V_j,TS_{z+u}}$, i.e., whether $TS_{z+u} \subset VP_e$. Next, it verifies the validity of $\sigma_{RSU_{v,l},VP_e}\left(Cred_{V_j,TS_{z+u}}\right)$ by performing the Signature Verification algorithm of the B-IBOOS scheme. Should any of these verification steps fail, the TA drops the message and exits. Otherwise, the TA proceeds to verifying the revocation status of $Cred_{V_j,TS_{z+u}}$ by checking it against $RL_{TS_{z+u}}$. If $Cred_{V_j,TS_{z+u}}$ is in $RL_{TS_{z+u}}$, then the TA deducts that $RSU_{v,l}$ is compromised and thus it triggers the RSU revocation phase to deal with it.

After that, the TA repeats the same procedure on the fields of $TK_{V_i,TS_{x+k}}$ to verify whether $RSU_{a,b}$ is compromised or not.

6.5 RSU Revocation and Recovering Phase

The TA maintains a table, for all the registered RSUs in the network, that includes the following information (Table 1):

Where: Status of the next identity of RSU $\in$ {sent, not yet sent} and $VPRM_{RSU}$ denotes

Table 1. RSUs' table

RSU	Current identity of RSU	Status of the next identity of RSU	$VPRM_{RSU}$
...	...	...	...

the Validity Period of: the last Revoked identity of RSU or the last identity of the RSU after which this latter has had its physical Maintenance.

Let us assume that the TA detects that $RSU_{a,b}$ is compromised. The TA deals with $RSU_{a,b}$ by performing the following steps:

(1) The TA checks whether the validity period VP_h included in $ID_{RSU_{a,b},VP_h}$ (i.e., the identity under which the revoked credential $Cred_{V_i,TS_{x+k}}$ has been signed) comes before or corresponds to $VPRM_{RSU_{a,b}}$.

(2) If VP_h comes before or corresponds to $VPRM_{RSU_{a,b}}$, which means that $RSU_{a,b}$ has already been detected and revoked for being compromised or it has already been repaired through physical maintenance from any potential compromise attack, then the TA aborts the process and exits. Else, the TA verifies if the next identity of $RSU_{a,b}$ is already sent to it or not yet.

(3) If the next identity of $RSU_{a,b}$ is not yet sent then the TA adds the current identity of $RSU_{a,b}$ to the current RL_{RSU}. Else, the TA adds the current and the next identities of $RSU_{a,b}$ to the current RL_{RSU}.

(4) The TA broadcasts the updated RL_{RSU} to all the non-revoked RSUs which in their turn broadcast it in their coverage areas. In the case of consecutive compromised RSUs, the vehicle to vehicle (V2V) communication is used to disseminate the updated RL_{RSU} in that gap.

(5) The TA repairs $RSU_{a,b}$ from physical attacks, if any exist, and loads its TPD with the required security materials directly, (*Remark:* the start time of the new loaded identity of $RSU_{a,b}$ and consequently the related security materials comes after the end time of its last revoked identity).

7 Security Analysis

7.1 The Prevention of the RSU Compromise Attack

In the schemes [1] and [2], an RSU $RSU_{a,b}$ could be compromised as follows:

- An attacker could launch physical attacks on $RSU_{a,b}$ to extract its inner information.
- An attacker could launch side-channel attacks on $RSU_{a,b}$ to learn the secrets stored in it.

To deal with the physical attacks, we assumed that each RSU is equipped with a TPD that erases all the information stored in it with any failed attempt of any information extraction through this type of attacks.

As for the side-channel attacks, we proceeded as follows: In a first step, we added a validity period VP to the identity/corresponding private key pair ID_{RSU}/s_{RSU} in [1] and [2] to limit its use time. This made us have the following two secrets stored in the TPD of an RSU $RSU_{a,b}$ during a validity period VP_h: the private key $s_{RSU_{a,b},VP_h}$ and the symmetric key $Key^{VP_h}_{TA-RSU_{a,b}}$. The key $s_{RSU_{a,b},VP_h}$ is frequently used by $RSU_{a,b}$ to sign its outgoing messages during VP_h. If VP_h is a long time period, an attacker may have enough time to gather sufficient side-channel information to extract $s_{RSU_{a,b},VP_h}$. Once this latter is extracted, the attacker can start impersonating $RSU_{a,b}$ by generating valid signatures on behalf of it. However, as we mentioned earlier in this paper, VP_h is a short time period so that before an attacker succeeds to collect enough side-channel information to recover $s_{RSU_{a,b},VP_h}$, the pair $ID_{RSU_{a,b},VP_h}/s_{RSU_{a,b},VP_h}$ is already updated. In the worst case, even if the attacker manages to recover $s_{RSU_{a,b},VP_h}$, the key compromise attack can only last for a short period of time as $s_{RSU_{a,b},VP_h}$ will be self-revoked with the expiration of its validity period. The second secret $Key_{TA-RSU_{a,b}}^{VP_h}$ is used to decrypt the confidential part C_{update} of $IPKUM_{RSU_{a,b},VP_{h+1}}$. If a side-channel attacker manages to learn $Key_{TA-RSU_{a,b}}^{VP_h}$, it can decrypt C_{update} of $IPKUM_{RSU_{a,b},VP_{h+1}}$, and thus get $s_{RSU_{a,b},VP_{h+1}}$ and $Key_{TA-RSU_{a,b}}^{VP_{h+1}}$. By obtaining $Key_{TA-RSU_{a,b}}^{VP_{h+1}}$, the attacker can decrypt C_{update} of $IPKUM_{RSU_{a,b},VP_{h+2}}$, and thus get $s_{RSU_{a,b},VP_{h+2}}$ and $Key_{TA-RSU_{a,b}}^{VP_{h+2}}$ ... However, in our scheme, $Key_{TA-RSU_{a,b}}^{VP_h}$ is used at most two times because: (1) The TA sends at most a $IPKUM_{RSU_{a,b},VP_{h+1}}$ for a second time if it does not receive a valid ACK from $RSU_{a,b}$ during the first round. (2) When $RSU_{a,b}$ receives $IPKUM_{RSU_{a,b},VP_{h+1}}$, it first checks whether $ID_{RSU_{a,b},VP_h}$ included in $IPKUM_{RSU_{a,b},VP_{h+1}}$ matches its current identity to make sure that it is the intended recipient of the TA. Next, $RSU_{a,b}$ checks the timestamp t to verify its freshness and hence preventing the replay attack. Then, $RSU_{a,b}$ checks whether $ID_{TA,VP}$ included in $IPKUM_{RSU_{a,b},VP_{h+1}}$ matches the current identity of the TA to prevent accepting messages from an attacker that impersonates the TA. After that, $RSU_{a,b}$ verifies the validity of $\sigma_{TA,VP}(ID_{RSU_{a,b},VP_h}, t, C_{update})$ to make sure that the message is sent by the TA under its current identity $ID_{TA,VP}$ and that it has not been modified during its transit. Finally, $RSU_{a,b}$ uses $Key_{TA-RSU_{a,b}}^{VP_h}$ to decrypt C_{update} in order to get the plaintext γ. To recapitulate, $RSU_{a,b}$ only uses $Key_{TA-RSU_{a,b}}^{VP_h}$ after validating that it is the intended recipient of the TA, that the message is not replayed, and that it is indeed sent by the TA under its current identity and has not been altered, in order to protect $RSU_{a,b}$ from using $Key_{TA-RSU_{a,b}}^{VP_h}$ to decrypt dummy messages and hence giving attackers the opportunity to launch successful side-channel attacks to learn $Key_{TA-RSU_{a,b}}^{VP_h}$. In the worst case, even if the attacker manages to learn $Key_{TA-RSU_{a,b}}^{VP_h}$, we dealt with this problem by assuming that the TA performs a periodic physical maintenance to the RSUs in the network during which it loads their TPDs with the required security materials directly to break the aforementioned chain of keys compromises.

Hence, our scheme can prevent the RSU compromise attack to the maximum possible extent.

7.2   The Detection of the RSU Compromise Attack

To detect compromised RSUs, the TA proceeds as follows: when it receives a report, among the steps it performs, it checks the validity of the signature of the RSU on the credential of the vehicle that generated the report to make sure that the RSU is the one that signed the credential under the indicated identity included in the ticket of the vehicle, and that the message has not been modified. If the signature is valid, then the TA verifies the revocation status of the credential by checking it against the adequate credentials' revocation list. If the credential is found to be revoked, the RSU is considered to be compromised. After that, the TA repeats the same method to verify the status of the RSU that signed the credential of the reported vehicle.

To support the aforementioned procedure, we assumed that the TA performs a periodic physical maintenance to the RSUs in the network to detect the RSUs that are compromised through physical attacks.

Thus, the detection of the RSU compromise attack is achieved.

7.3   The Revocation and Recovering of the Detected Compromised RSUs

The TA revokes a detected compromised RSU by adding its current identity (and the next identity if this latter has already been sent to the RSU) into the current RSUs identities' revocation list. Then, the TA immediately publishes the updated revocation list by broadcasting it to all the non-revoked RSUs which in their turn broadcast it in their coverage areas. After that, the TA repairs the compromised RSU from any found physical attack and loads its TPD directly with the required security materials. The RSU resumes its work with the beginning of the validity period of these loaded security materials.

So, the revocation and recovering of the detected compromised RSUs are fulfilled.

7.4   The Eviction of the Revoked RSUs

To exclude revoked RSUs from the network, we developed both the authentication phase and the signature generation and verification phase of [1]. Here, during the authentication phase, among the steps of authenticating an RSU we have the check of the validity period of its identity and then the check of the identity against the latest RSUs identities' revocation list. If the identity is found to be revoked, the vehicle drops the received message. The signature generation and verification phase is developed to become a second layer of defense to prevent communicating with revoked RSUs. In fact, when a vehicle receives a safety-related message from another vehicle, it is here enabled to check the validity period of the identity of the RSU that is included in the received ticket, and after that to check this identity against the newest RSUs identities' revocation list. If the identity is included in the revocation list, then the vehicle drops the received message; it is worthy to mention that this measure will also discourage malicious vehicles from interacting with the revoked RSUs since their messages will be filtered out during this phase.

Therefore, the revoked RSUs are evicted from the network.

8   Conclusion

In our schemes [1] and [2], the RSU compromise attack is not dealt with. In this work, we proposed a scheme to strengthen [1] and [2] against this attack. Our proposal treats the RSU compromise attack on two levels complementary to each other. On the first level, we proposed a RSU compromise prevention mechanism by mainly introducing an identity/corresponding private key pair updating strategy; while on the second level, we proposed a RSU compromise detection and reaction mechanism in which compromised RSUs are detected, revoked, recovered and isolated. The detailed security analysis proved that our scheme can attain the desired security requirements.

References

1. Chikhaoui, O., Ben Chehida, A., Abassi, R., Guemara El Fatmi, S.: A ticket-based authentication scheme for VANETs preserving privacy. In: Puliafito, A., Bruneo, D., Distefano, S., Longo, F. (eds.) ADHOC-NOW 2017. LNCS, vol. 10517, pp. 77–91. Springer, Cham (2017). https://doi.org/10.1007/978-3-319-67910-5_7
2. Chikhaoui, O., Ben Chehida Douss, A., Abassi, R., Guemara El Fatmi, S.: Towards the optimization of a ticket-based authentication scheme for VANETs. In: Seventh International Conference on Communications and Networking, pp. 1–4. IEEE Press, Hammamet (2018)
3. Li, C., Zhang, X., Wang, H., Li, D.: An enhanced secure identity-based certificateless public key authentication scheme for vehicular sensor networks. J. Sens. **18**(1), 194 (2018)
4. Zhang, L., Wu, Q., Domingo-Ferrer, J., Qin, B., Hu, C.: Distributed aggregate privacy-preserving authentication in VANETs. J. IEEE Trans. Intell. Transp. Syst. **18**(3), 516–526 (2016)
5. Tan, H., Gui, Z., Chung, I.: A secure and efficient certificateless authentication scheme with unsupervised anomaly detection in VANETs. J. IEEE Access **6**, 74260–74276 (2018)
6. Ruan, N., Nishide, T., Hori, Y.: Elliptic curve ElGamal threshold-based key management scheme against compromise of distributed RSUs for VANETs. J. Inf. Process **20**(4), 846–853 (2012)
7. Balamahalakshmi, D., Vimal Shankar, K.N.: Sybil attack detection with reduced bandwidth overhead in urban vehicular networks. IJCSMC **3**(1), 578–584 (2014)
8. Zhu, X., Jiang, S., Wang, L., Li, H.: Efficient privacy-preserving authentication for vehicular ad hoc networks. J. IEEE Trans. Veh. Technol. **63**(2), 907–919 (2014)
9. Yasmin, R., Ritter, E., Wang, G.: An authentication framework for wireless sensor networks using identity-based signatures: implementation and evaluation. J. IEICE Trans. Inf. Syst. **E95-D**(1), 126–133 (2012)

Innovative Research Projects

Monitoring the Gait Process During the Rehabilitation of Patients Using Computer Vision Techniques and UWB Technology

Damian Grzechca[1]([⊠]), Adam Ziebinski[1], Dariusz Komorowski[2],
Krzysztof Hanzel[1], Sebastian Pokucinski[1], Kamil Klonowski[1],
and Slawomir Siwek[2]

[1] Department of Electronics, Electrical Engineering and Microelectronics,
Silesian University of Technology, Ul. Akademicka 16, 44-100 Gliwice, Poland
{Damian.Grzechca, Adam.Ziebinski,
Krzysztof.Hanzel}@polsl.pl, {SebaPok553,
KamiKlo610}@student.polsl.pl
[2] Faculty of Biomedical Engineering, Department of Biosensors and Processing
of Biomedical Signals, Silesian University of Technology,
Ul. Roosevelt 40, 41-800 Zabrze, Poland
Dariusz.Komorowski@polsl.pl,
SlawSiw908@student.polsl.pl

Abstract. The document presents the process of creating a tool for the rehabilitation of people with lower-limb dysfunctions. The monitored metrics, hardware, communication, and software layer of the entire solution were presented in a cross-sectional way. In addition, the work analyzed the possibility of using UWB technology (tags) and vision (using markers in the form of diodes) to monitor the position of hip, knee, and ankle. The tests showed that the system has an accuracy of 1.3 cm for monitoring movement in two dimensions and 5.8 cm for a three-dimensional reflection of the position of the said joints. Low cost, combined with low invasiveness in patient movements, easy application and high accuracy of received data as well as cooperation with companies interested in proposed research allows for further investigation on the proposed system.

Keywords: Gait · Rehabilitation · UWB · Vision · Point tracking · Multilateration

1 Introduction

Rehabilitation is the adaptation to normal life in society of people who have lost physical or mental fitness or have birth defects [1]. The task of the physiotherapist is to choose appropriate exercises and to monitor the patient's condition during his recovery [2–4]. The assessment of the patient is usually made in a general and subjective way, which makes it difficult and not very accurate. However, it is possible to attempt to parameterize human gait, and thus - to take measurements before and after the rehabilitation process [5, 6]. Even without statistical tests and reference to the general population, it becomes possible to analyze the progress of the examined person for

© Springer Nature Switzerland AG 2020
M. Themistocleous and M. Papadaki (Eds.): EMCIS 2019, LNBIP 381, pp. 419–437, 2020.
https://doi.org/10.1007/978-3-030-44322-1_31

himself [7]. To collect such data and then be able to analyze the progress of rehabilitation, it is necessary to use all available technical tools, from simple electronic sensors (used more and more often in the wider society as wearable devices) [8–10] to advanced vision systems and location in space. In the rehabilitation process, mechanical devices encapsulating the patient's limb and allowing movements only within a certain range and in a predefined manner are increasingly used [11, 12], however, due to their level of complexity, size, required staff and price, they are not yet widely used. The publication first presents commonly used metrics that have been used in this system. Section 2 describes the hardware implementation as well as the algorithms used together with the data workflow from the acquisition devices to the - also described - operator interface. Section 3 describes what the process of validation of the accuracy of sensors used was, while in the last chapter the authors concluded their work.

2   Method

Various metrics are used to assess the progress of rehabilitation. This section presents a set of metrics that were taken into account as a reference when constructing the discussed system. For the lower limb, mainly functionality is assessed, i.e. walking [5, 6].

2.1   Angular Ranges

The angular ranges of individual joints are determined for specific planes and human anatomical axes [13–16]. There are three axes and three planes.

The human body axes

- **sagittal axis** – runs from front to back (from abdominal to dorsal),
- **longitudinal axis** – (also known as vertical) defines the upper and lower directions relative to the torso. It runs from the top of the head to the residual tail. The vertical axis is the longest of all axes,
- **frontal axis** – (also known as transverse) runs from one side of the body to the other (e.g. from right to left).

Human body planes
They are set at right angles to each other. Their arrangement allows for a very detailed determination of the location of organs, nerves or blood vessels.

- **sagittal plane** – divides the body into two parts: right and left. It is determined by the sagittal axis and the vertical axis. Parallel to the sagittal plane, further sagittal planes can also be routed.
- **frontal plane** – divides the body into two parts: front and back. It is determined by a number of parallel planes can be guided relative to the frontal plane.
- **transverse plane** – divides the body into two parts: upper and lower. It is determined by the transverse and sagittal axes. A number of parallel planes can be carried out relative to the horizontal plane.

To better illustrate the occurrence of the above in the human body, they are shown in the diagram (Fig. 1).

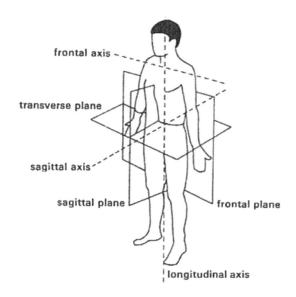

Fig. 1. Axis and planes in human body [16].

2.2   Movement Ranges in the Hip Joint

Movement in the hip joint occurs in all three planes.

In the sagittal plane, there are bending and straightening movements. Bending is the forward movement and straightening in the rear. When the person is in the neutral position, the flexion angle in the hip joint is 0°. The hyperextension can reach values up to 45° and the bend up to 140°. In total, the maximum range of motion is 185° (see Fig. 2).

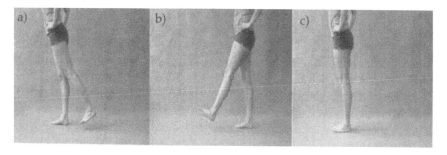

Fig. 2. Straightening and bending movements in the hip joint: (a) hyperextension, (b) flexion, (c) neutral position [15].

There are adduction and abduction movements in the frontal plane. The maximum angle in the adduction movement with the straight leg in the hip joint is 40° and in the abduction movement 50°. The range may increase when bending in the hip joint. When the thigh is bent at an angle of 60°, the traffic of visits increases to 90°, and the addresses 55°. In detail in Fig. 3 (Table 1).

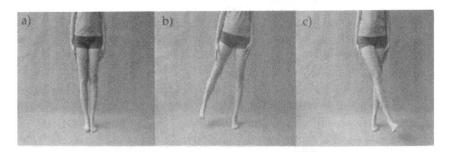

Fig. 3. Adduction and abduction movements in the hip joint: (a) neutral position, (b) visiting, (c) adduction [15].

In the transverse plane, there are rotation motions. The maximum value of the angle of internal rotation is 60°, and the external one 50° (as shown in Fig. 4).

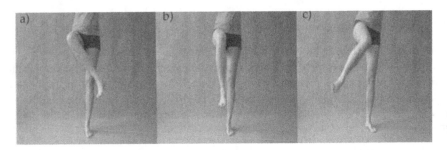

Fig. 4. Rotation movements in the hip joint: (a) inward rotation, (b) neutral position, (c) outward rotation [15].

Table 1. Angular ranges of motion in the hip joint

Plane	Sagittal		Front		Transverse	
Move	Bending	Straightening	Visiting	Adduction	Inward rotation	Outward rotation
Maximum angle	140°	45°	50°	40°	60°	50°
Total angle	185°		90°		110°	

3 Hardware and Software Description

For the needs of the project, it was decided to make and program a specified marking module, which in its construction will contain both components necessary for positioning based on UWB technology (DecaWave DWM1000 module) [17], the necessary connection output for the video-tracked diode, as well as additional components such as the inertial sensor module, barometer and connection interfaces to facilitate programming of the proposed prototype.

3.1 Marking Module

A printed circuit design was drawn up, paying special attention to the layering and impedance of the paths in the high-frequency section. Laying layers recommended by the manufacturer of the DW1000 system was non-standard and constituted a significant cost of the device. However, this was a necessary element in maintaining the proper impedance of the connections with their required dimensions. The layers were divided due to their purpose: signal upper and lower layers, power supply and ground layer, which is a reference for high-frequency signal paths on the upper layer that determines their impedance. Much attention was paid to the appropriate design of the radio section of the circuit. Incorrect routing could lead to incorrect operation or even damage to the system. The high-frequency paths had to be properly shielded with mass planes and a connection with the least impedance and possibly constant geometrical parameters should be ensured to prevent signal attenuation and reflection [18].

The most important functional blocks of the module are numbered in Fig. 5.

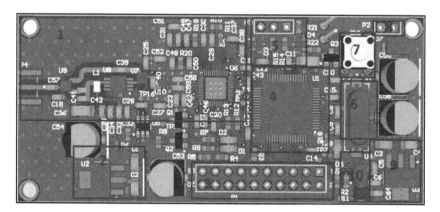

Fig. 5. Three-dimensional visualization of the marking module.

1. Radio section with the DW1000 system
2. 5 V stabilizer for a power amplifier system
3. JTAG/SWD programming interface
4. STM32F1 microcontroller
5. UART serial interface
6. Quartz resonator clocking for the microcontroller

7. Button resetting the microcontroller (Reset)
8. Power connector
9. 3.3 V stabilizer for the digital part of the system
10. Barometer and IMU

3.2 Multilateration Algorithm

In the entire work, we use the multilateration from all four reference points. In the document, for simplification, an outline of the algorithm is presented on the example of three (minimum number for 3D positioning) reference points.

The principle of the operation flows from fundamental geometry and the main idea is depicted in Fig. 6 [19]. There were three reference points (anchors), which were selected from all of those that were available, for example, $A1$, $A2$ and $A3$. The positions of the anchors were well known in three dimensions $A1 \rightarrow (x_1, y_1, z_1)$, $A2 \rightarrow (x_2, y_2, z_2)$, $A3 \rightarrow (x_3, y_3, z_3)$ as was the distance from a tag to a specific anchor d_{A1}, d_{A2} and d_{A3}.

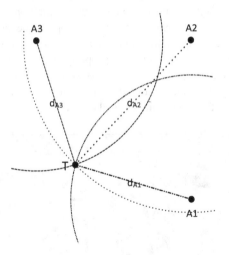

Fig. 6. Trilateration – an example of the operation given for the point – tag T and for the three distances d_{A1}, d_{A2} and d_{A3} from the three reference points (anchors) $A1$, $A2$ and $A3$.

Determining the coordinates of the location point (tag) $T \rightarrow (x, y, z)$ is equivalent to determining the coordinates of a system of quadratic Eq. (1).

$$\begin{cases} (x - x_1)^2 + (y - y_1)^2 + (z - z_1)^2 = d_{A1}^2 \\ (x - x_2)^2 + (y - y_2)^2 + (z - z_2)^2 = d_{A2}^2 \\ (x - x_3)^2 + (y - y_3)^2 + (z - z_3)^2 = d_{A3}^2 \end{cases} \quad (1)$$

Equation (1) can be arranged in a matrix representation (2)

$$
\begin{bmatrix}
1 & -2x_1 & -2y_1 & -2z_1 \\
1 & -2x_2 & -2y_2 & -2z_2 \\
1 & -2x_3 & -2y_3 & -2z_3
\end{bmatrix}
\begin{bmatrix}
x^2+y^2+z^2 \\
x \\
y \\
z
\end{bmatrix}
=
\begin{bmatrix}
d_{A1}^2 & -x_1^2 & -y_1^2 & -z_1^2 \\
d_{A2}^2 & -x_2^2 & -y_2^2 & -z_2^2 \\
d_{A3}^2 & -x_3^2 & -y_3^2 & -z_3^2
\end{bmatrix}
\tag{2}
$$

Then, using the matrix properties we get the Eq. (3),

$$
\boldsymbol{x} = \boldsymbol{x}_p + t \cdot \boldsymbol{x}_h \tag{3}
$$

where t is the actual parameter, x_p is a specific solution of (3) and x_h is the solution of a homogeneous system of (4) – a Basis of Kernel (A_0).

$$
\boldsymbol{A_0} \cdot \boldsymbol{x} = 0 \tag{4}
$$

The x_p and x_h vectors can be determined using the Gaussian elimination method. The specific solution x_p can also be excluded by the pseudo-inverse of the matrix A_0.

To determine the parameter t, use Eq. (5).

$$
\begin{aligned}
\boldsymbol{x_p} &= \left(x_{p0}, x_{p1}, x_{p2}, x_{p3}\right)^T \\
\boldsymbol{x_h} &= \left(x_{h0}, x_{h1}, x_{h2}, x_{h3}\right)^T \\
\boldsymbol{x} &= \left(x_0, x_1, x_2, x_3\right)
\end{aligned}
\tag{5}
$$

After inserting Eqs. (5) through (3), (6) is obtained.

$$
\begin{cases}
x_0 = x_{p0} + t \cdot x_{h0} \\
x_1 = x_{p1} + t \cdot x_{h1} \\
x_2 = x_{p2} + t \cdot x_{h2} \\
x_3 = x_{p3} + t \cdot x_{h3}
\end{cases}
\tag{6}
$$

Where after further transformations described in detail in [20] can be obtained (7).

$$
\begin{aligned}
\boldsymbol{x_1} &= \boldsymbol{x}_p + t_1 \cdot \boldsymbol{x}_h \\
\boldsymbol{x_2} &= \boldsymbol{x}_p + t_2 \cdot \boldsymbol{x}_h
\end{aligned}
\tag{7}
$$

In the case of a positioning using three anchors, the position of $T \rightarrow (x, y, z)$ can be represented as $x_1 \rightarrow (x, y, z)$ or $x_2 \rightarrow (x, y, z)$ depending on the expected range of the positions in the X, Y, and Z axes. The multilateration algorithm that is used does not require any additional range selection because an additional reference point is used that enables us to indicate the point in three-dimensional space.

3.3   Vision System

In the vision system, the most important device was the camera. The used device had to be able to record at high framerate and with high resolution. The possibility of software steering of the device was also taken into account. It was decided to use a camera easy to use and get – GoPro Hero 7 in the black edition. Such camera allowed settings adjustments, software steering and had specification good enough to record at 60 frames per second with a resolution of 2704 × 1520 pixels. After the camera, it was crucial to select a diode. Two types of diodes were discussed: infrared and classic red. The results of the red diode were as good as the infrared. The red diode was much easier to use and selected for the whole project. In the end, it was necessary to define threshold levels used in the analysis algorithm. They were defined with the use of the HSV palette. Selected levels are presented in Table 2.

Table 2. Selected thresholding levels

	H	S	V
Lower threshold level	0	0	200
Upper threshold level	255	255	255

3.3.1   Algorithm of Video Processing

The whole process of recording analysis has multiple steps. At the very beginning interaction with the operator is required. After the first frame of the record is loaded and displayed - the operator is asked to mark subareas of interest. In these subareas of the first frame, it is searched for the LED diodes. Such implementation allows to significantly reduce the number of mathematical operations done for each frame and increase the quality of analyzing results. Instead of the whole frame, only the subareas are taken into account. Next, the operator can check if in given subareas the algorithm can correctly find the diodes. If not, it is possible to restart marking. If the operator is satisfied with the test result – the main loop of analysis is started. The main loop repeats as long as there exist not analyzed frames in the recording. Steps done in each loop are shown in the diagram in Fig. 7.

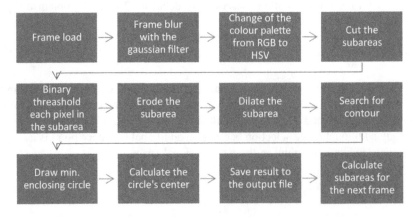

Fig. 7. Diagram showing the individual steps of video processing.

Each frame's analysis starts with the frame loading. Not every frame of the recording is correctly saved to the camera and read errors may occur. If the loading end successfully the next step is gaussian blurring. The blur allows softening the sharp objects. After blurring the color palette is changed from RGB to HSV [21]. In the HSV palette, it is much easier to properly define the thresholding color levels [22, 23]. After the preparations of the whole frame, the subareas of interest are cut and thresholding is done [24]. On the threshold results, there are two computer vision technics applied – firstly erosion and then dilation. They are introduced to reduce the noise of small, incorrectly thresholded pixels. In such a prepared subarea, the contours are searched for. If the dilation and erosion iterations amount are properly selected – there is only one contour of the object found. This object is the observed diode. Just contour is rather not enough to determine the LED's center, so the minimum enclosing circle of the contour is drawn. In such a circle the circle's center is calculated and saved to the output file as the found LED's localization. The last step of each frame analysis is the preparation of subareas of interest for the very next frame. Each time the subareas are calculated based on the last known diode's position. If all frames are analyzed the algorithm ends.

3.4   System Integration

Communication between system components was mainly realized with the use of the Robot Operating System (ROS), which allows taking advantage of C++ and Python libraries as well as connection to the MATLAB environment. ROS serves to deliver measurements from modules, where the data is collected to PC, where the data is analyzed. The schematic diagram is shown in Fig. 8.

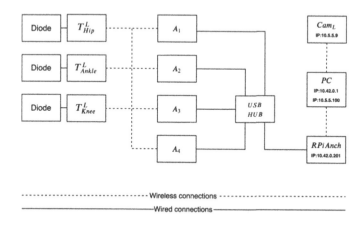

Fig. 8. Proposed system architecture with the division into wired and wireless communication.

Positioning modules form between each other an independent system with their own way of wireless communication. UWB system consists of anchors ($A1$, $A2$, $A3$, $A4$), which are placed in known positions around the treadmill and tags (T_{Hip}, T_{Knee}, T_{Ankle})

situated in characteristic points of the patient's leg. Tags' coordinates can be calculated with the use of reference points, measured distances and trilateration algorithm.

Measured distances are initially sent from anchors to Raspberry Pi (RPiAnch) by wired connection and then via Wi-Fi to PC, similarly, video from camera is sent to PC via Wi-Fi. Measurements received on the computer are analyzed in a MATLAB software. Filtrated and interpolated data are converted to medical metrics and visualized in the user interface.

3.5   Application for Data Visualization and Analysis

The part of the presented system for monitoring and analysis the gait process during the rehabilitation of patients is the MATLAB based software. The application is used to visualize the data collected from sensors and calculate the metrics that are used to assess gait correctness. The metrics, that were implemented, are presented as values as a function of time $y_i = f(x_i)$, where y_i is the appropriate metric, and x_i is a data obtained from the sensors.

The metrics that have been implemented are:

- angular ranges:
  - hip joint: $\varphi_{hip}^{L/R}$
  - knee joint: $\varphi_{knee}^{L/R}$,
  - ankle joint: $\varphi_{ankle}^{L/R}$
- gait determinants:
  - pelvic rotation (around the vertical axis), $\varphi_{pelvis}^{rotation}$,
  - pelvic tilt, $\varphi_{pelvis}^{inclination}$,
  - pelvic lateral movements, $\varphi_{pelvis}^{lateral}$,
- space-time parameters:
  - step frequency, f_{step},
  - stride length, L_{step},
  - movement speed V_{step}.

3.5.1   User Interface

As part of the user interface, charts for real-time analysis (for the needs of the rehabilitation process), as well as charts presenting statistical data and the progress of the patient's work, were prepared. In addition, the interface also allows full system management (configuration, the ability to edit preferences) as well as patient database management (registration, selection, preview, and data analysis). The main window of the conducted medical examination interface is a preview of the patient's current status (can be seen on Fig. 9) with the system components listed (for the purposes of the article, the issue of analyzing data from the strain gauge insert that is also included in the system has been omitted).

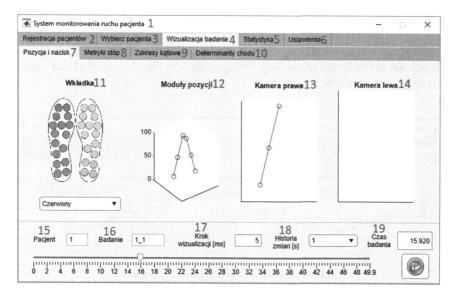

Fig. 9. User interface tab "Test visualization", subsection "Position and pressure".

The most important view from the point of view of rehabilitation is the screen showing movement ranges in the hip joint. As part of the view, the rehabilitator has a constant view of the patient's movement parameters, all irregularities are signaled from times by crossing the statistics line on the fields marked in red on the chart, as can be seen in Fig. 10.

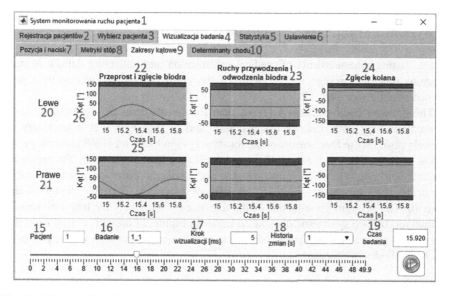

Fig. 10. The user interface, tab "Test visualization", subsection "Angular ranges". (Color figure online)

An additional element of the interface for analyzing historical information is the tab presenting the movements of the joints - hips, knees, and ankles in the sagittal plane for the vertical and horizontal axis. In addition, the characteristics of the movement are also analyzed due to the length of the step - the graphic – in Fig. 11 – is marked in green, blue and red, respectively.

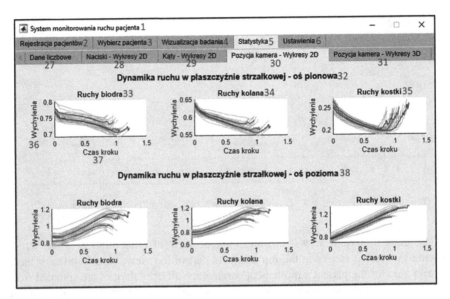

Fig. 11. User interface, "Statistics" tab, subsection "Camera position - 2D charts". (Color figure online)

4   System Parameters Validation

Before starting measurements of medical examination and collecting data, it is necessary to properly arrange the elements of the entire system, according to a pre-planned scheme (see Fig. 12).

The drawing itself presents a layout plan for the elements of the entire system, represented along with distance dimensioning and in "top view". It is necessary to precisely position the four sensors of the location system based on UWB technology, as well as to place them in the area of the treadmill they have designated. To ensure an adequate working field of the camera image and a specific precision of camera measurements, they should be located at a distance of 60 cm from the center of the treadmill. The diagram presents one of the directions – ultimately the treadmill should be observed by two symmetrically spaced cameras. Figure 13 presents a view from the GUI showing a preview of a person during tests of the apparatus with visible points in which the diodes are located.

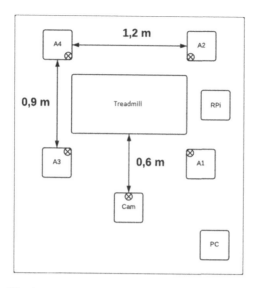

Fig. 12. Arrangement plan of the elements of the test stand.

Fig. 13. Screenshot from the GUI presenting the moment of validation of the position of LEDs informing about the position of the sensors.

No.	English Translation
1	Patient movement monitoring system
2	Patient registration
3	Select a patient
4	Visualization of the examination
5	Statistics
6	Settings
7	Position and pressure
8	Foot metrics
9	Angular ranges
10	Gait determinants
11	Insert
12	Position modules
13	Right camera
14	Left camera
15	Patient
16	Examination
17	Visualization step
18	History
19	Time of examination
20	Left
21	Right
22	Hyperextension and flexion of hip
23	Adduction and abduction movements of the hips
24	Knee flexion
25	Time
26	Angle
27	Numerical data
28	Pressure - 2D graph
29	Angles - 2D graph
30	Camera position - 2D graph
31	Camera position - 3D graph
32	Movement dynamics in the sagittal plane - vertical axis
33	Hip movements
34	Knee movements
35	Ankle movements
36	Inclination
37	Step time
38	Dynamics of movement in the sagittal plane - horizontal axis
39	Press "c" to check detection!

4.1   Evaluation of the Measuring Range of the Monitoring System

During the preparation of the project, the accuracy of individual components was also validated. Below is a description of the research on the accuracy of the determined distance between individual points of the system.

4.1.1   Measurement Results Based on the UWB

For positioning modules based on UWB technology, the key element determining the accuracy of the position was the appropriate measurement of the distance between the reference point and the tag. The manufacturer himself declares the accuracy of his commercial version of the product based on the same chip at a level of up to 10 cm [25], however, due to the nature of the use case, we particularly wanted repeatability with the possible correction proposed below. First, static measurements were made for points in the range from 0.1 m to 1 m. The average results obtained with errors are presented in Table 3.

Table 3. Distance values obtained for the UWB system without constant error correction.

Real distance [m]	Measured distance [m]	Relative error [m]
0.1	0.240	0.140
0.3	0.604	0.304
0.5	0.841	0.341
0.7	1.067	0.367
0.9	1.413	0.513
1	1.404	0.404

The conducted analysis shows a high relative error value expressed as a percentage. This is due to the occurrence of a permanent error - especially visible at low distance values, which is visible in columns on the chart in Fig. 14.

Then, for the distances obtained it was decided to design a curve approximation based on 2nd-degree polynomials (see 8). The difference between the expected curve and the curve was supposed to be the basis for correction for data obtained from the system.

$$f(x) = p1 * x^2 + p2 * x + p3 \tag{8}$$

Obtained coefficients (with 95% confidence bounds) was:

- p1 = −0.37 (−1.44, 0.7)
- p2 = 1.725 (0.501, 2.95)
- p3 = 0.08428 (−0.2022, 0.3708)

Based on the received function, data correction was performed. Each of the values obtained from the system was shifted by the value of the difference between the function at the point of occurrence of the value and the expected value. The results in the form of a graph for raw, filtered data, target values, and relative error percentage bars are shown in Fig. 14.

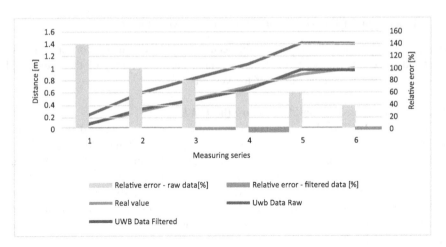

Fig. 14. A graph showing the comparison of values and percentage error for readings from the UWB system before and after making an adjustment based on approximation of the 2nd-degree polynomial function.

4.1.2   Measurement Results Based on a Vision System

The vision system based its measurements on the difference in diodes localization between consecutive frames of captured recording. To provide enough data and research material – taken recordings were 45 s long, repeated 5 times and for two different patients. The changing parameter was speed. Walks at the speed of 1.0, 1.5 and 2.0 mph were recorded. There were 30 recordings taken in total. The camera was set to capture at 60 frames per second and with a resolution of 2704 × 1520 pixels. Summarizing, each recording had about 2695 frames, which gives about 40.000 frames per patient and 80.000 frames in the whole research. The results are presented in the table (Table 4).

Table 4. Statistically obtained results for both patients - raw data.

Patient	Diode 1				Diode 2			Diode 3		
	Speed	Mean	Max	Std. Dev.	Mean	Max.	Std. Dev.	Mean	Max.	Std. Dev.
1	1.0	2	11	2	9	40	11	14	60	16
	1.5	3	15	4	13	54	15	18	64	19
	2.0	4	16	4	15	57	18	21	67	21
2	1.0	3	13	3	8	37	10	12	58	15
	1.5	3	29	4	10	42	12	15	55	16
	2.0	4	20	4	12	45	14	19	88	20

Presented values are in pixels. Movement calculated between frames was rounded to the whole pixel. Diode 1 was placed on the patient's hip, Diode 2 on the knee and Diode 3 on the ankle. As it was expected to base on the natural walk – the hip's movement in the smallest next is the knee and then is the ankle. Movement of the ankle is the biggest and the most dynamic. For both patients the movement of the corresponding diodes was similar. Differences are not bigger than several pixels. With the increase of the walk's speed, the movements of diodes also increase. So are the maximum value and standard deviation of the results.

Known positions and sizes of the whole system's elements allowed to convert the movement from pixels to millimeters. The taken multiplier was 0.7 mm per pixel. Recalculated statistics of recorded movements are presented in the table (Table 5).

Table 5. Statistically obtained results for both patients - recalculated values in mm

Patient	Diode 1				Diode 2			Diode 3		
	Speed	Mean	Max	Std. Dev.	Mean	Max.	Std. Dev.	Mean	Max.	Std. Dev.
1	1.0	1.4	7.7	1.4	6.3	28.0	7.7	9.8	42.0	11.2
	1.5	2.1	10.5	2.8	9.1	37.8	10.5	12.6	44.8	13.3
	2.0	2.8	11.2	2.8	10.5	39.9	12.6	14.7	46.9	14.7
2	1.0	2.1	9.1	2.1	5.6	25.9	7.0	8.4	40.6	10.5
	1.5	2.1	20.3	2.8	7.0	29.4	8.4	10.5	38.5	11.2
	2.0	2.8	14.0	2.8	8.4	31.5	9.8	13.3	61.6	14.0

5   Conclusion

As part of the proposed gait process analysis method during the rehabilitation of patients, UWB technology and vision were used. Prepared research environment and applied technologies allowed for an analysis of lower limb movement during rehabilitation. The proposed solution provides cheaper tracking options for the patient's movements than full exoskeletons. Although it does not give the ability to block specific movements of the proposed joints, it allows the rehabilitator to monitor - in real-time the patient's movements and all possible deviations from accepted norms. In addition, due to the very individual nature of the process of rehabilitation, the proposed system also allows you to keep a record of previous rehabilitation sessions, which makes it possible to analyze archived data and the patient's progress in returning to previous fitness. As proven in preliminary non-clinical tests, the system prototype allows for two-dimensional analysis based on a vision system with high declarative precision of movements for the worst-case scenario at the level of 6.2 cm and analysis of movements in three-dimensional space with mean accuracy to 5.8 cm. In the next stage of work, the accuracy of measurements will be increased and an initial medical assessment based on non-clinical tests will be carried out.

Acknowledgments. This work was supported by the Ministry of Science and Higher Education of Poland funding for statutory activities.

References

1. Sjölund, B.H.: Rehabilitation. In: Gellman, M.D., Turner, J.R. (eds.) Encyclopedia of Behavioral Medicine, pp. 1634–1638. Springer, New York (2013). https://doi.org/10.1007/978-1-4419-1005-9_924

2. Embry, K.R., Villarreal, D.J., Gregg, R.D.: A unified parameterization of human gait across ambulation modes. In: 2016 38th Annual International Conference of the IEEE Engineering in Medicine and Biology Society (EMBC), pp. 2179–2183 (2016). https://doi.org/10.1109/EMBC.2016.7591161

3. Goswami, A.: A new gait parameterization technique by means of cyclogram moments: application to human slope walking. Gait Posture. **8**, 15–36 (1998). https://doi.org/10.1016/S0966-6362(98)00014-9

4. Villarreal, D.J., Poonawala, H.A., Gregg, R.D.: A robust parameterization of human gait patterns across phase-shifting perturbations. IEEE Trans. Neural Syst. Rehabil. Eng. **25**, 265–278 (2017). https://doi.org/10.1109/TNSRE.2016.2569019

5. Baker, R.: Gait analysis methods in rehabilitation. J Neuroeng Rehabil. **3**, 4 (2006). https://doi.org/10.1186/1743-0003-3-4

6. DeLisa, J.A.: Gait Analysis in the Science of Rehabilitation. DIANE Publishing (1998)

7. Sharif Shourijeh, M., McPhee, J.: Forward dynamic optimization of human gait simulations: a global parameterization approach. J. Comput. Nonlinear Dyn. **9** (2014). https://doi.org/10.1115/1.4026266

8. Tao, W., Liu, T., Zheng, R., Feng, H.: Gait analysis using wearable sensors. sensors. **12**, 2255–2283 (2012). https://doi.org/10.3390/s120202255

9. Kong, K., Tomizuka, M.: A gait monitoring system based on air pressure sensors embedded in a shoe. IEEE/ASME Trans. Mechatron. **14**, 358–370 (2009). https://doi.org/10.1109/TMECH.2008.2008803

10. Niazmand, K., et al.: Freezing of gait detection in parkinson's disease using accelerometer based smart clothes. In: 2011 IEEE Biomedical Circuits and Systems Conference (BioCAS), pp. 201–204 (2011). https://doi.org/10.1109/BioCAS.2011.6107762

11. Michener, L.A.: Patient- and clinician-rated outcome measures for clinical decision making in rehabilitation. J. Sport Rehabil. **20**, 37–45 (2011). https://doi.org/10.1123/jsr.20.1.37

12. Duschau-Wicke, A., von Zitzewitz, J., Caprez, A., Lunenburger, L., Riener, R.: Path control: a method for patient-cooperative robot-aided gait rehabilitation. IEEE Trans. Neural Syst. Rehabil. Eng. **18**, 38–48 (2010). https://doi.org/10.1109/TNSRE.2009.2033061

13. Gedliczka, A., Pochopień, P.: Atlas miar człowieka: dane do projektowania i oceny ergonomicznej: antropometria, biomechanika, przestrzeń pracy, wymiary bezpieczeństwa. Centralny Instytut Ochrony Pracy, Warszawa (2001)

14. Bober, T., Zawadzki, J.: Biomechanika układu chu człowieka. Wydawnictwo BK, Wrocław (2006)

15. Tejszerska, D., Świtoński, E., Gzik, M., Głowacka, A.: Biomechanika narządu ruchu człowieka: praca zbiorowa. Katedra Mechaniki Stosowanej, Wydział Mechaniczno-Technologiczny, Politechnika Śląska , Wydawnictwo Naukowe Instytutu Technologii Eksploatacji - PIB, Gliwice; Radom (2011)

16. Goniometer Crosstalk Compensation for Knee Joint Applications. https://www.researchgate.net/publication/51872929_Goniometer_Crosstalk_Compensation_for_Knee_Joint_Applications. Accessed 16 Sept 2019

17. Alarifi, A., et al.: Ultra wideband indoor positioning technologies: analysis and recent advances. Sensors (Basel) **16**, 707 (2016)

18. DW1000   Application   Note.   https://www.decawave.com/wp-content/uploads/2018/08/aps009_dw1000_under_laes_v1.4.pdf
19. An Algebraic Solution to the Multilateration Problem (PDF Download Available). https://www.researchgate.net/publication/275027725_An_Algebraic_Solution_to_the_Multilateration_Problem. Accessed 02 Feb 2018. http://dx.doi.org/10.13140/RG.2.1.1681.3602
20. Grzechca, D., Hanzel, K.: The positioning accuracy based on the UWB technology for an object on circular trajectory. Int. J. Electron. Telecommun. **64**, 487–494 (2018)
21. Thompson, D.: How to Use Color Spaces to Talk About Color| First Source Worldwide, LLC. http://www.fsw.cc/color-spaces/. Accessed 30 Sept 2019
22. Howse, J.: OpenCV Computer Vision with Python. Packt Publishing, Birmingham (2013)
23. Wesolkowski, S., Jernigan, M.E., Dony, R.D.: Comparison of color image edge detectors in multiple color spaces. In: Proceedings 2000 International Conference on Image Processing (Cat. No.00CH37101), vol. 2, pp. 796–799. IEEE, Vancouver (2000). https://doi.org/10.1109/ICIP.2000.899829
24. Liao, P.-S., Chen, T.-S., Chung, P.-C.: A fast algorithm for multilevel thresholding. J. Inf. Sci. Eng. **17**, 713–727 (2001)
25. ScenSor Module DWM1000 - WSN | DecaWave. https://www.decawave.com/products/dwm1000-module. Accessed 19 Oct 2017

Innovation and Competitiveness of Universities – An Empirical Research

Zornitsa Yordanova$^{(\boxtimes)}$ (iD), Vasil Bozev, Borislava Stoimenova,
and Petia Biolcheva

University of National and World Economy, Sofia, Bulgaria
{zornitsayordanova, vbozev,
b.stoimenova, p.biolcheva}@unwe.bg

Abstract. The paper aims at investigating through an empirical research what is the interconnection between innovativeness on country level (based on The Global Innovation Index) and university competitiveness (based on the world university ranking U-Multirank). As a result of statistical analyses, we present the main indicators, part of university competitiveness, which are significant for the Global Innovation Index of a country. The results are based on data from 44 countries and 1394 universities. In addition, the end-result of the study presents a full picture of the interaction between educational innovations for achieving and improving main challenges in universities and universities main functions all together with the relevant indicators, bringing innovation performance on country level.

Keywords: Innovation management · Global Innovation Index · University competitiveness · Higher education

1 Introduction

Innovation plays a crucial role in defining contemporary economic growth patterns and is one of the major factors influencing industry development. For many organizations, improving and increasing innovativeness and the ability to develop innovations is the most substantial factor for growth [1, 2]. The fast-paced globalization of global competition, countries and businesses that are innovating their range of products and services take the lead. Therefore, it is becoming increasingly important for innovation management, innovation to be measured [3]. It is equally important for industries, humanity, civilization. For education, it is a must since higher education encompasses the core values of each country in the latest years. Each university and policy making institution is eagerly looking forward as to what will happen in the future so that it can decide how to prepare its education process. The universities of future will be characterized by educational methods that we are searching for constantly, predominantly with the means of technology [4]. The internationalization of higher education, widely growing number and diversity of educational services providers, increasing demand for transparency and information on academic quality have increased the competitive pressure on universities worldwide to improve their performance [5].

© Springer Nature Switzerland AG 2020
M. Themistocleous and M. Papadaki (Eds.): EMCIS 2019, LNBIP 381, pp. 438–447, 2020.
https://doi.org/10.1007/978-3-030-44322-1_32

University rankings may influence the perceptions and priorities of different user groups. Governmental authorities, funding agencies and the media use university rankings as a source of information and as a tool for assessment of the competitiveness of universities. Governments also use universities' ranks to set their national higher education agendas and as a signal for the competitiveness of their economies. Students and their parents use university rankings as a selection instrument when choosing where to study. Employees address rankings when looking at career opportunities. Researchers may rely on rankings to find new collaborative partners. The institutions from the private sector use rankings to identify mutually beneficial partnerships with universities. Rankings are used by universities to benchmark themselves against global competitors. University policy-makers use rankings to learn more about the strengths and weaknesses of their institutions and to identify potential areas for improvement. In such cases, rankings serve as marketing and management tools to define universities' strategic development towards the ideal "world-class university" and for attracting better students, employees and partners. In the contemporary world, strengthening the connection between science, education and business is vital for building world-class universities and competitive economies. According to Tee [6], the concept of a "world-class" university refers to universities that: (1) perform well in the international university ranking systems; (2) produce excellent outputs including cutting-edge research through licenses, patents and publications in high-quality top ranked journals; (3) produce skilled and professional graduates; (4) attract the best academics and students; (5) possess abundant and diversified funding sources; (6) offer a rich learning and research environment; (7) provide favourable and autonomous governance; (8) encourage strategic vision and innovation; (8) respond effectively to the demands of a fast changing global market.

The current empirical study explores the link between innovation on country level and university competitiveness. Innovation has been analysed by employing The Innovation Global Index for 44 countries and university competitiveness has been analysed by some common parameters, elicited from U-Multirank. In addition, 19 educational innovation types were also introduced as part of relevant and non-relevant university indicators in order to give to readers the whole picture for innovation performance of a country, competitiveness of universities, education innovations applied and university functions. This whole interconnectivity may be used for further exploration.

2   Theoretical Background

The theoretical background in this research is focused on the three main objectives of the study: educational innovations, Global Innovation Index and competitiveness of higher educational institutions.

2.1   Educational Innovations

Innovations are equally important for the private and governmental sectors, important for the humanity in general. Since it has been clarified in many researches that innovations are the most reliable tool for transforming the past and present up to a superior level [7], the issue how more effectively and successfully innovations should be managed is still valid [8]. The issue is critical when it comes to education as this is the other recognized growth engine for humanity. Educational innovations are defined by Taylor et al. [9] as any novel teaching technique, strategy, tool, or learning resource that could be used by an instructor to lead to effective (or promising) instructional techniques that benefit student learning and engagement. According to Fullan [10], educational innovation must contain three elements: use of new revised materials (curriculum materials or technologies); use of new teaching approaches (teaching strategies or activities); alteration of beliefs (pedagogical assumptions).

Much research has been done on problems that education is facing. Utilizing the idea of problem driven innovation [11], the current research aims at extracting some commonly identified problems and challenges because of the understanding that these would be the directions for education innovation in the future. According to OECD [12] the main issue in education and the starting point for innovation in the sector are productivity and efficiency. In education, efficiency means the balance between resources invested and the outcomes in terms of students' performance and equity. According to Kozma [13], educational innovation means supporting a shift from traditional paradigms towards emerging pedagogical approaches based on information and Communication technologies (ICT) solutions such as fostering learner-centred and constructivist processes, and the acquisition of lifelong learning skills. Hannon [14] refers innovation to a complete shift in the educational paradigm, driven by the four principles of social innovation, i.e. openness, collaboration, freedom, and direct participation of those involved. Innovation has become an essential ingredient in creating and sustaining a culture of performance in higher education and keeps transforming higher education [15].

Staley and Trinkle [16] formulated ten trends in managing higher education and respectively included the educational innovations. These are: Increasing Differentiation of Higher Education; Transformation of the General Education Curriculum; Changing Faces of Faculty; Surge in Global Faculty and Student Mobility; The New "Invisible College"; The Changing "Traditional" Student; The Mounting Pressure to Demonstrate Value; The Revolution of "Middle-Skill" Jobs; College as a Private vs. Public Good; Lifelong Partnerships with Students. Ebersole [17] has defined the following challenges which higher education leaders face: a trend toward competency based education, tougher accreditation standards, an emphasis on assessment, voids in leadership, and the growing diversity of students as challenges that will plague higher education in the coming years. Wai [15] detected globalization and collaboration as big challenges, which the educational innovation should be, addresses as cross-disciplinary collaboration received increasing attention. Sustainability has also been identified as a crucial factor for encompassing the different effects of human resources for sustainable development [18]. According to Budzinskaya [19] one of the key criteria for assessing the competitiveness of universities is the commercialization of developments and the possibility of the same to export educational services. Tsvetkova and Lomer [20] summarized that academic excellence is the competitiveness enhancement in higher education. The recently increased number of research in the field of higher education, rankings and educational innovation put even more pressure to universities' management [21].

2.2 Innovation Global Index

The Global Innovation Index came into operation in 2013. What is specific to this type of ranking is the comparative factor in calculating the index and the considerations of innovation performance of all other countries participating in the assessment. It consists of a ratio of innovation efficiency, which in turn contains a sub-index for introducing innovations and a sub-index of innovation realization. The overall result is the simple average of the input and output sub-indices. The Innovation Sub-Index evaluates the infrastructure for innovation (institutions, human capital and research, infrastructure, market complexity, business status), insofar as the Innovation Sub-index evaluates specific innovative results [22]. Countries find themselves at different stages of economic development and innovation performance and so their relative levels of innovation inputs and outputs are likely to be different [23].

2.3 Competitiveness of Universities

As per Hazelkorn [24], the literature on rankings can be roughly divided into two categories: methodological concerns and theoretical understanding. In most papers the focus has been mainly placed on methodological concerns, questioning and challenging the basis by which the indicators have been chosen, the weightings assigned to them, and the statistical method and accuracy or appropriateness of the calculations. This paper makes an attempt to emphasize the theoretical ground of ranking systems used to measure university competitiveness [24]. The ranking systems used to assess the quality of education and the competitiveness of universities are two types – national and global. National ranking systems are typically resource distribution systems based on "input-output" performance indicators [25–27]. They include a more comprehensive and a larger number of indicators because of their access to information and in-depth knowledge about local institutions. The national rankings' indicators primarily focus on educational and institutional parameters, whereas global ranking systems tend to have fewer indicators and are generally mainly focused on research performance [28].

Global ranking systems use information from different sources to develop league tables. The most widely used information sources are internationally accessible bibliometric databases (mainly Thomson Reuters's Web of Science or Elsevier's Scopus data bases); reputation surveys (student, peer, employer or other stakeholder surveys); independent third parties, such as government databases; institutional data. The absence of internationally meaningful available data continues to present a considerable problem for any reliable comparisons [29]. Still, according to the International Association of Universities [30], there are over 16 000 higher education universities, but global rankings focus on the characteristics and performance of only the top 100. This was the reason why this research has been performed and put main focus on global indices and rankings.

3 Methodology

The analysis was performed on 1394 universities from 44 countries. These are: Australia; Austria; Bangladesh; Belarus; Belgium; Bulgaria; Canada; China; Croatia; Cyprus; Czech Republic; Denmark; Estonia; France; Georgia; Germany; Greece; Hungary; India; Iran; Ireland; Israel; Italy; Japan; Kazakhstan; Latvia; Lithuania; Luxembourg; Netherlands; Norway; Portugal; Romania; Russian Federation; Saudi Arabia; Slovakia; Slovenia; Spain; Sweden; Switzerland; Turkey; Ukraine; United Kingdom; United States of America; Vietnam. The number of countries is determined depending on which countries in the U-Multirank base have an Innovative Index. U-Multirank is a multidimensional, user-driven approach to international ranking of higher education institutions. It compares the performances of higher education institutions – in short: universities – in the five dimensions of university activity: (1) teaching and learning, (2) research, (3) knowledge transfer, (4) international orientation and (5) regional engagement [31].

After identifying the specific countries that will participate in the study, they are divided into two groups - High Innovation Index Countries and Low Innovation Index Countries. To distribute each country in one of the two groups, a median between the lowest innovation index and the highest is found. All countries with a smaller index than the average are defined as having a low innovative index and those above the average with a high innovative index. The calculated country-specific limit is 45.75. Among all, 20 countries were rated as low innovation indexed countries and 25 as high innovation indexed countries.

After the countries are divided into two groups, it is checked whether there is a statistically significant difference between the two groups in the specific indicators:

- Citation rate Group
- Co-publications with industrial partners Group
- External research income Group
- Graduating on time (bachelors) Group
- Graduating on time (masters) Group
- Income from continuous professional development Group
- Income from private sources Group
- Income from regional sources Group

If a statistical difference is found, it can be said that the innovative index influences the studied variable and distinguishes two groups that differ significantly from each other. In order to verify that there is a statistically significant difference, it must be determined whether a parametric or non-parametric method of verification is used. For this purpose, the distributions of the variables are checked. If it appears that the distribution of any of the variables is not normally distributed, a non-parametric method is used to test the hypothesis for the difference between two averages of two samples.

4 Results and Discussion

The main results from the empirical research show a statistically significant difference between both analyzed groups with countries when it comes to the main metrics for university competitiveness: Citation rate; Co-publications with industrial partners; External research income; Graduating on time (bachelors); Graduating on time (masters); Income from continuous professional development; Income from private sources Group; Income from regional sources. Table 1 shows the list with 44 countries within the scope of the research, their Innovation Index and the number of universities, part of the U-Multirank index.

Table 1. Global Innovation Index of countries and the number of universities part of the study

Country	Global Innovation Index	Number of universities
Bangladesh	23,1	2
Belarus	29,4	6
Kazakhstan	31,4	2
Iran	33,4	21
Saudi Arabia	34,3	5
Georgia	35	6
India	35,2	19
Turkey	37,4	37
Romania	37,6	44
Vietnam	37,9	3
Russian Federation	37,9	36
Ukraine	38,5	28
Greece	38,9	20
Croatia	40,7	4
Lithuania	41,2	18
Bulgaria	42,6	12
Slovakia	42,9	9
Latvia	43,2	15
Hungary	44,9	14
Portugal	45,7	29
Italy	46,3	48
Slovenia	46,9	4
Cyprus	47,8	8
Spain	48,7	75
Czech Republic	48,7	18
Estonia	50,5	3
Belgium	50,5	11
Austria	51,3	21

(*continued*)

Table 1. (*continued*)

Country	Global Innovation Index	Number of universities
Australia	52	29
Norway	52,6	13
Canada	53	38
China	53,1	96
France	54,4	60
Luxembourg	54,5	1
Japan	55	42
Israel	56,8	8
Ireland	57,2	18
Germany	58	98
Denmark	58,4	8
United States of America	59,8	231
United Kingdom	60,1	156
Sweden	63,1	12
Netherlands	63,3	53
Switzerland	68,4	13
44		**1394**

The average border of Innovation Index, dividing both groups of countries is set to 45,75. Table 2 presents a summary of the statistical tests revealing which of the analyzed indicators are relevant to the Global Innovation Index.

Table 2. Indicators, which are statistically significant for countries with low Global Innovation Index and High Global Innovation Index

Indicators	Statistically significant difference between groups
Citation rate group	Yes
Co-publications with industrial partners group	Yes
External research income group	Yes
Graduating on time (bachelors) group	No
Graduating on time (masters) group	No
Income from continuous professional development group	No
Income from private sources group	Yes
Income from regional sources group	No

In Fig. 1, as an end result of the study, we employed a combinative approach for presenting the linkage between all objectives of the study: educational innovation as they are defined in 19 types by Yordanova [32], for achieving the main university functions as they are identified in a Researchgate discussion involving 26 researchers from all around the world and raised by Gülin Ülker from Sakarya University [33]. The figure presents purposefully how to develop educational innovations in order they to directly contribute to increasing the Innovation Index of the country (based on data from 44 countries and 1394 universities).

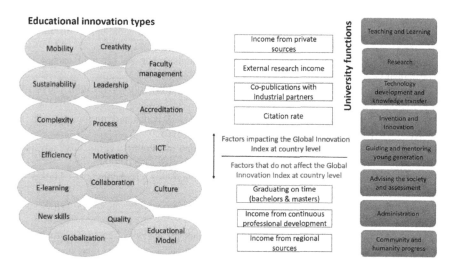

Fig. 1. Linkage between educational innovation, higher education functions and factors, impacting the Global Innovation Index

5   Conclusion

The presented study may be of interest of wide range of audiences, but mainly the target are scholars and higher education management as well as policy makers who are in position to stimulate the purposefulness of educational innovations for achieving concrete targets. In this research, we targeted educational innovations for performing concrete university functions, achieving university competitiveness and also impacting the overall innovation performance of a country. We also would like to reach audience interested in employing educational innovations and gamification for different cases and purposes [34].

Acknowledgements. The paper and the study are supported by BG NSF Grant No DM 15/1-2017 (M 15/4); KP-06 OPR01/3-2018 and NID NI 14/2018.

References

1. Lopesa, A.: Innovation management: a systematic literature analysis of the innovation management evolution. Braz. J. Oper. Prod. Manag. **13**(1), 16–30 (2016). https://doi.org/10.14488/BJOPM.2016.v13.n1.a2
2. Damanpour, F.: Organizational innovation – Ameta – analysis of effects of determinants and moderators. Acad. Manag. J. **34**, 555–590 (1991). https://doi.org/10.1093/icc/dtw004
3. Hamidi, S., Berrado, A.: Segmentation of innovation determinants: case of the Global Innovation Index. In: Proceedings of the 12th International Conference on Intelligent Systems: Theories and Applications, SITA 2018, Article no. 48 (2018)
4. Richardson, S., Tan, Y.: Forecasting future demands: what we can and cannot know, Australian Government, NCVER (2007)
5. Jongbloed, B., Enders, J., Salerno, C.: High. Educ. **56**, 303 (2008). https://doi.org/10.1007/s10734-008-9128-2
6. Tee, K.F.: Suitability of performance indicators and benchmarking practices in UK universities. Benchmarking: Int. J. **23**(3), 584–600 (2016)
7. Distanont, A., Khongmalai, O.: The role of innovation in creating a competitive advantage. Kasetsart J. Soc. Sci. (2018). https://doi.org/10.1016/j.kjss.2018.07.009
8. Tidd, J., Bessant, J.: Managing Innovation: Integrating Technological, Market and Organizational Change (2018)
9. Taylor, C., et al.: Propagating the adoption of CS educational innovations. In: ITiCSE 2018, Larnaca, Cyprus, June 2018
10. Fullan, M.: The New Meaning of Educational Change, 5th edn. Teachers College Press, New York (2007)
11. Coccia, M.: Theorem of not independence of any technological innovation. J. Econ. Bibliogr. **5**(1), 29–35 (2018). https://doi.org/10.1453/jeb.v5i1.1578. SSRN https://ssrn.com/abstract=3163703
12. OECD: Innovating Education and Educating for Innovation: The Power of Digital Technologies and Skills. OECD Publishing, Paris (2016)
13. Kozma, R.B.: Technology, Innovation, and Educational Change. A Global Perspective: A report of the Second Information Technology in Education Study Module 2. ISTE Publisher (2003)
14. Hannon, V.: 'Only Connect!': A New Paradigm for Learning Innovation in the 21st Century, Centre for Strategic Innovation (2009)
15. Wai, C.: Innovation and social impact in higher education: some lessons from Tohoku university and the open university of Hong Kong. Open J. Soc. Sci. **5**, 139–153 (2007). https://doi.org/10.4236/jss.2017.59011
16. Staley, D.J., Trinkle, D.A.: The changing landscape of higher education. Educause Rev. **46**, 15–31 (2011)
17. Ebersole, J.: Top Issues Facing Higher Education in 2014. Forbes, 13 January 2014
18. Yordanova, Z.: Educational innovation: bringing back fads to fundamentals. In: ISPIM Innovation Conference – Celebrating Innovation: 500 Years Since daVinci, Florence, Italy (2019)
19. Budzinskaya, O.: Competitiveness of Russian Education in the World Educational Environment, Astra Salvensis - revista de istorie si cultura, issue year VI/2018, issue no 11, pp. 565–576 (2018)
20. Tsvetkova, E., Lomer, S.: Academic excellence as "competitiveness enhancement" in Russian higher education. Int. J. Comp. Educ. Dev. **21**(2), 127–144 (2019). https://doi.org/10.1108/IJCED-08-2018-0029

21. Erkkilä, T., Piironen, O.: Rankings and Global Knowledge Governance: Higher Education, Innovation and Competitiveness. PSGHE. Springer, Cham (2018). https://doi.org/10.1007/978-3-319-68941-8. ISBN 331968941X, 9783319689418
22. WIPO: The Global Innovation Index (GII) 2019: Creating Healthy Lives—The Future of Medical Innovation (2019). https://www.globalinnovationindex.org/Home
23. Menna, A., Walsh, P., Ekhtari, H.: Identifying enablers of innovation in developed economies: a national innovation systems approach. J. Innov. Manag. 7(1), 108–128 (2019)
24. Hazelkorn, E.: Rankings and the Reshaping of Higher Education: The Battle for World-Class Excellence. Palgrave Macmillian, London (2015)
25. Lindblad, S.: Navigating in the field of university positioning: on international ranking lists, quality indicators and higher education governing. Eur. Educ. Res. J. 7(4), 438–450 (2008)
26. Liu, N.C., Liu, L.: University rankings in China. High. Educ. Eur. 30(2), 217–227 (2005)
27. Tochkov, K., Nenovsky, N., Tochkov, K.: University efficiency and public funding for higher education in Bulgaria. Post-Commun. Econ. 24(4), 517–534 (2012)
28. Çakır, M.P., Acartürk, C., Alaşehir, O., Çilingir, C.: A comparative analysis of global and national university ranking systems. Scientometrics 103(3), 813–848 (2015)
29. Hazelkorn, E.: World-class universities or world-class systems? Rankings and higher education policy choices. In: Rankings and Accountability in Higher Education: Uses and Misuses. Unesco Publishing (2013)
30. International Association of Universities: International Handbook of Universities, Basingstoke, UK, Palgrave Macmillan (2014)
31. U-Multirank. https://www.umultirank.org/
32. Yordanova, Z.: A model for evaluation of Innovative universities. In: Educational Innovations and Applications, pp. 459–462 (2019)
33. Ülker, G.: What are the common functions of universities?, discussion (2017). https://www.researchgate.net/post/What_are_the_common_functions_of_universities
34. Yordanova, Z.: Educational innovations and gamification for fostering training and testing in software implementation projects. In: Hyrynsalmi, S., Suoranta, M., Nguyen-Duc, A., Tyrväinen, P., Abrahamsson, P. (eds.) ICSOB 2019. LNBIP, vol. 370, pp. 293–305. Springer, Cham (2019). https://doi.org/10.1007/978-3-030-33742-1_23

Application of Automated Trust Verification and Delegation Mechanisms in PEPPOL eProcurement Network

Konstantinos Douloudis[(⊠)], Maria Siapera, Gerasimos Dimitriou,
and Andriana Prentza

Department of Digital Systems, University of Piraeus, Piraeus, Greece
{kdoul,mariaspr,jerouris,aprentza}@unipi.gr

Abstract. In the domain of public procurement, more and more of the transactions that are taking place are becoming electronic. For the European Union (EU), PEPPOL is the "standard" for eProcurement with most of the required transactions being done through its eDelivery network. Those transactions need to be trustworthy, and by using the components provided by the EU funded LIGHTest project, trust information can be easily published in its infrastructure, using the global Domain Name System (DNS) network and queried when needed. Two scenarios have been identified in PEPPOL as potential pilots for testing trust establishment schemes and are presented in this paper. The first one focuses on the use of automated trust verification within the eDelivery network and the second one on trust delegation in eProcurement tender transactions.

Keywords: eProcurement · PEPPOL · Trust verification · Trust delegation · DNS · eDelivery · Electronic transaction · OpenPEPPOL

1 Introduction

In the modern world, more and more of the traditional processes are being transformed with the use of technology. In particular, business processes that were done by using paper are being or have been replaced by automated electronic ones. This has many benefits including reduced costs and increased speed and overall efficiency.

In addition to replacing paper transactions with electronic equivalents, it is also needed to replace other aspects of those traditional processes as well. Such an aspect is trust verification. Traditionally, trust was done by using signatures and other related methods to certify that a physical document and its contents were valid. Many electronic equivalents exist today, such as electronic signatures, which may have legal backing in some countries. However, there is no standardized way to verify electronic identities which makes the process complicated on a global scale.

As a solution to this problem, the EU-funded LIGHTest project (http://lightest.eu/) strives to not only create the necessary infrastructure but also automate the process of trust verification [1]. LIGHTest stands for Lightweight Infrastructure for Global Heterogeneous Trust Management in support of an open Ecosystem of Stakeholders and Trust schemes. One of the key aspects of LIGHTest is the use of the readily available

© Springer Nature Switzerland AG 2020
M. Themistocleous and M. Papadaki (Eds.): EMCIS 2019, LNBIP 381, pp. 448–457, 2020.
https://doi.org/10.1007/978-3-030-44322-1_33

Internet Domain Name System (DNS) infrastructure with its organization, governance and security standards [2]. The main benefit that comes from the usage of DNS is the fact that anyone can publish their trust information. By using the open-source infrastructure of LIGHTest, anyone (i.e. companies, citizens and administrations) can query the trust information that they may need with ease [3].

Another key aspect of electronic processes is for everyone involved to be able to understand the way they are accomplished. Ideally, all participants would work in the same, standard, way to accomplish that task. Pan-European Public Procurement On-Line (or PEPPOL for short) was a project funded partly by the European Union aiming at providing the technical standards to enable businesses to participate electronically in the procurement of all European government institutions in a uniform way. The project ran from 2008 to 2012. Today, PEPPOL is in use in more than fifteen European countries, some of which made its use mandatory. The project is now overseen by OpenPEPPOL AISBL, a not-for-profit organization based in Belgium. It has more than 250 members from across Europe, both governmental agencies as well as vendors and service providers [4].

PEPPOL does not constitute an eProcurement platform of its own but rather provides the technical and legal means to allow interoperation between existing platforms. Specifically, it provides three components:

- the PEPPOL eDelivery Network, a network for securely and reliably exchanging messages between participating entities,
- PEPPOL Business Interoperability Specifications (BIS), specifications of standardized document formats for procurement processes, and
- PEPPOL Transport Infrastructure Agreements (TIA), providing the legal framework for communication between the many connected parties.

2   Related Work

In the domain of trust establishment, LIGHTest has expanded upon the work of the now completed EU-funded project called FutureID [5, 6]. FutureID aimed to create an identity management infrastructure for Europe by replacing the classic password credentials with the use of trusted and secure identities. Those identities would be provided by identity intermediation services and the users would be able to choose from several such services through a marketplace. The intermediation is by design completely decentralized and allows intermediation services to join the infrastructure without the need for central registration or approval. The trust backbone of FutureID is based on DNS which has the benefit of using a decentralized, global and pre-existing infrastructure [7]. LIGHTest builds upon the same decentralized trust infrastructure [1] and instead of verifying the trust in user identities, it goes one step further and attempts to verify the trust in any kind of transaction. Just like FutureID, anyone can join the LIGHTest trust infrastructure without approval and use it for their needs.

3   Methodology

PEPPOL uses the eDelivery Network [8] to connect different eProcurement systems by establishing a set of common business processes and technical standards. This provides an interoperable and secure network connecting all Access Points (APs) using the same electronic messaging protocols and formats and applying digital signature technologies to secure message content.

Once connected to the PEPPOL eDelivery Network, public agencies and private enterprises can quickly and easily reach any other trading partner, also using PEPPOL.

3.1   The OpenPEPPOL Network

This network operates on an open four-corner model, shown in Fig. 1. In this model, each organization participating in PEPPOL chooses an AP that acts on their behalf for sending and receiving messages via the delivery network. Communication between an organization and its AP is not regulated by PEPPOL and can happen in whatever form they agree on to accommodate existing systems or procedures. The AP then uses the PEPPOL eDelivery network to communicate with the AP chosen by the receiving organization to deliver the document.

Two directories facilitate this delivery. First, each organization publishes their receiving capabilities, contact information, and other information through a Service Metadata Publisher (SMP). This publisher is typically operated by the AP directly. To find the SMP responsible for a given organization, a centralized directory, the Service Metadata Locator (SML) is employed.

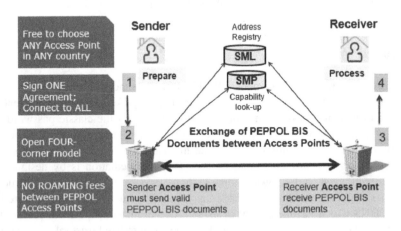

Fig. 1. PEPPOL four-corner model [8]

To ensure that the transactions done through the PEPPOL eDelivery network are secured, a Public Key Infrastructure (PKI) is used [9]. A PEPPOL Digital Certificate is given to the AP providers who sign the PEPPOL TIA. All the information that is needed for validating communications is contained in that certificate. The validity of the certificate is tethered to the TIA; if it is found that a service provider is in breach it will be revoked. This way only trusted providers can operate within the eDelivery Network. These certificates are used in the eDelivery Network of PEPPOL, where trust is established by the use of digital signatures in the messages exchanged between the APs, using secure and reliable protocols like OASIS (Organization for the Advancement of Structured Information Standards) AS2 (Applicability Statement 2) and AS4 (Applicability Statement 4).

3.2   The LIGHTest Tools

The LIGHTest reference architecture, as shown in Fig. 2, incorporates all of the necessary software tools which a verifier can use to validate an electronic transaction. Its major benefit is the use of a pre-existing single trust root, the DNS infrastructure. By using existing DNS servers (with security extension), any organization can publish their trust information [10]. The trust information that can be published and used in LIGHTest includes trust schemes, trust lists, trust translation, and delegation data.

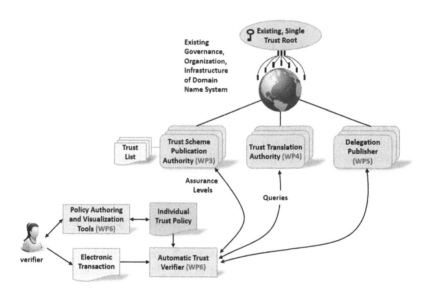

Fig. 2. The LIGHTest architecture

Trust scheme data can be published by using a Trust Scheme Publication Authority (TSPA) [7]. To publish a trust scheme, a trust list (Trust Service Status List, standardized by European Telecommunications Standards Institute or ETSI [11]) is required. This trust list includes information about the authorities which are deemed trusted under the published trust scheme.

Trust translation data can be published by using a Trust Translation Authority (TTA). To ease the use of different trust schemes under different jurisdictions, a TTA can provide the necessary translation data that can map conceptually equivalent information.

Delegation data can be published by using a Delegation Publisher (DP). The DP can provide information about the contents of the delegation as well as information about its validity, including its revocation status [12].

A verifier can validate an electronic transaction by using the Automated Trust Verifier (ATV). For the ATV to validate any transaction, it needs a trust policy. The trust policy contains all the necessary information for the trust verification including the conditions that need to be met for the provided transaction to be valid. Policy Authoring and Visualization Tools can be used to aid non-technical users in understanding and creating trust policies. The ATV performs the validation of the transaction by parsing the verifier's trust policy and by querying the LIGHTest trust infrastructure. The result is a yes/no answer with some information explaining the verification process.

3.3   LIGHTest Within PEPPOL

Out of all the possible scenarios, it was concluded that the best two to demonstrate the LIGHTest technology with the PEPPOL eDelivery network are a trust scheme migration scenario, which focuses on trust list publication and automated verification features, and an eProcurement scenario which utilizes the delegation publishing capabilities [13].

The first scenario is about trust scheme migration and shows the value of the LIGHTest trust list publication infrastructure. PEPPOL acts as its certificate authority and certifies APs to the PEPPOL network. Upon completing the certification process, an AP submits a certificate signing request (CSR) to the OpenPEPPOL authority which creates a certificate signed within the PEPPOL trust chain. Every PEPPOL message must be signed using such a PEPPOL signed certificate. Every message received by an OpenPEPPOL AP must be authenticated by verifying that it is properly signed using the embedded certificate and that the signing certificate is itself signed by within the OpenPEPPOL trust chain. The OpenPEPPOL root and intermediate certificates were originally signed using the SHA-1 (Secure Hash Algorithm 1) signing algorithm. At some point in time, the SHA-1 algorithm was demonstrated to be breakable and it became imperative that everyone (including OpenPEPPOL) migrate to using SHA-2 (Secure Hash Algorithm 2) algorithms. Unfortunately, there are hundreds of APs, upon which thousands of trading partners depend, which have the current SHA-1 trust chain installed.

A migration plan would have to comprise of four phases as demonstrated in Fig. 3. The first step would be for all the APs to move to SHA-2, re-sign every certificate with the new trust chain, and distribute all the newly signed certificates. In the second phase, all the APs need to load the new certificates alongside the old certificates so that they sign using SHA1 but can verify either SHA1 or SHA2. This may require programming changes to some of the APs, so they need to be given time to modify and test their systems. Once all the APs confirm that they have both sets of trust chains loaded and can sign and verify using either, then phase three begins where all the APs are told to start using the SHA2 certificates to sign messages. The fact that all APs can handle either trust chain means that the APs do not need to synchronize their changes during this phase. Finally, after some time, the APs can be told to disable support for SHA1 and delete the old certificates.

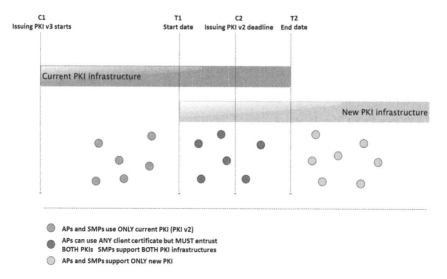

Fig. 3. PKI migration phases [7]

The second scenario is about a cross-border eProcurement procedure. For this scenario, it is assumed that a Medical Device Manufacturer in Germany needs to send a tender to a hospital in France. Since those two countries have PEPPOL access points, the Medical Device Manufacturer can send a signed and encrypted tender for 200 insulin pumps over the PEPPOL network, using the PEPPOL specifications. Since the preparation and signing of the tender, according to the PEPPOL specifications is a complex task, the German Medical Device Manufacturer delegates the ASiC-E (Associated Signature Containers Extended) packaging and signing (Delegation Publishing) of the tender to be submitted to his pre-award PEPPOL Service Provider (Fig. 4).

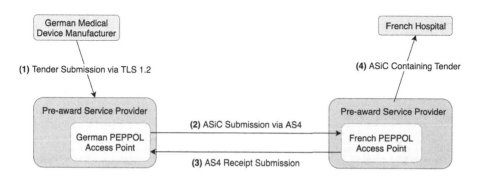

Fig. 4. Conceptual flow of the eProcurement scenario

Upon packaging and signature, the pre-award PEPPOL Service Provider sends the tender, using the PEPPOL eDelivery network.

4 Results

When applying the LIGHTest technologies, significant improvements can be seen in the processes that occur in the proposed scenarios. The benefits are explored in more detail for each one of those scenarios in the following sections.

4.1 Access Point Verification

By using the tools provided by LIGHTest, the migration can be easily performed. No AP would have the trust chain loaded, so there is no need to redistribute the updated Certification Authority certificates and wait for every AP to load them, nor do APs have to modify their code to support multiple trust chains. Verification is handled by ATV [6]. By integrating the ATV into the APs, it is possible to use the certificate of the receiving message and a trust policy that checks if the certificate exists in the trust list which is published under the PEPPOL AP trust scheme. Then, the ATV can inform the AP if the certificate (and thus the message) is trustworthy, possibly with an explanation of its reasoning (in particular if not trustworthy). The ATV automatically knows which trust chain to apply and where to go to get it, so support for multiple trust chains is already there. All that needs to be done is for OpenPEPPOL to re-sign the AP certificates and distribute them. APs do not need to synchronize, and they can swap out the old certificates at a time that is convenient for them.

4.2 Trust Establishment in a PEPPOL Tender

In the case of tender submission, the LIGHTest tools can be used to verify the trustworthiness of the transaction. The German Medical Device Manufacturer can use LIGHTest to create and publish the delegation, for the signing and packaging of the tender, to the Delegation Publisher. In addition to its use in the APs, the ATV can also verify the signature of the ASiC and the validity of the delegation.

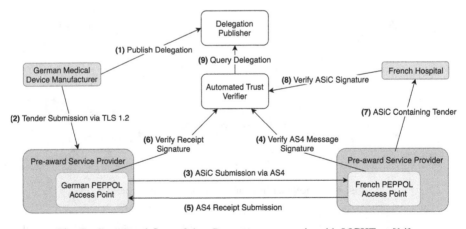

Fig. 5. Conceptual flow of the eProcurement scenario with LIGHTest [14]

The process, as shown in Fig. 5, comprises the following steps:

1. Initially, the German Medical Device Manufacturer creates a bilateral delegation between it and its pre-award service provider and publishes it to the Delegation Provider using the Delegation Tools provided by LIGHTest.
2. The German Medical Device Manufacturer creates and submits the tender details to its pre-award Service Provider for packaging, signing, and submission to the French hospital.
3. The pre-award Service Provider packages and signs the tender details into an ASiC-E and submits the tender using the PEPPOL AP. The submitting PEPPOL AP creates, signs and submits an AS4 message to the receiving PEPPOL AP.
4. The receiving AP receives the AS4 message, verifies the message signature and validates the certificate used for signing using the ATV.
5. If the validation succeeds, it then creates a signed AS4 receipt and sends it back to the submitting AP of the German Medical Device Manufacturer.
6. The submitting AP verifies the receipt signature and validates the certificate used for signing using the ATV.
7. The Receiving AP pushes the tender ASiC-E Container to the French Hospital.
8. The French hospital verifies the signature of the ASiC-E using the ATV, including the delegation verification.
9. The ATV performs a Query to the Delegation Provider [13], to validate the delegation of signature and returns the result to the French Hospital.

All trust configuration for the steps is done with the Policy Authoring and Visualization Tools.

5 Discussion and Conclusions

Without the use of LIGHTest, the migration of the PKI in PEPPOL becomes more cumbersome and time-consuming. All the APs that are part of the PEPPOL eDelivery network will have to synchronize and update their trust chains before the migration is complete. If they do not support having multiple trust chains loaded, as required by the second and third part of the migration process, they will need to update their AP implementations and ensure that they are working properly through rigorous testing. It is estimated that that process would take six months. By using LIGHTest, this six-month process with much higher risk is replaced by a one-week process with low risk. The same applies to a potential case where a root certificate needs to be replaced either because of a routine certificate replacement or because the private key of the current certificate is compromised. Particularly, in the latter case, a six-month process is hardly acceptable and quick exchange is of the essence.

In the case of the tender submission, the use of LIGHTest adds three layers of trust verification between the sender and the receiver:

- The first layer ensures that the message exchange between the APs is trustworthy. This means that the APs can always verify that the messages they receive come from a trusted source.

- The second layer ensures that the data exchanged between the Service Providers is intact and trustworthy. This means that the Service Providers can always verify that the data they receive come from a trusted source and that their integrity is intact.
- The third layer ensures that the data exchange between the sender and the receiver of the tender submission is trustworthy. This means that the receiver can verify that the contents of the container that carries the tender are intact, that it comes from a trusted source, and that the signing and packaging of the tender were authorized by the receiver.

If OpenPEPPOL wants to adopt LIGHTest, they would have to follow several steps to incorporate it into their ecosystem:

1. The first step would be to set up the LIGHTest components in the OpenPEPPOL premises. This means setting up an PEPPOL TSPA and DP but also configuring the PEPPOL DNS to support DNSSEC (DNS with SECurity extensions).
2. After having the basic infrastructure set up, it is possible to move on to the creation of the trust artifacts and the configuration which will be used by the LIGHTest tools. These include the PEPPOL trust lists, trust policies, and trust schemes.
3. The last step after having all the infrastructure and artifacts ready is to integrate the ATV with the PEPPOL components that require trust verification, like the Access Point and Service Provider software.

When the above steps are completed, all the APs and SPs that are part of PEPPOL would have to update their implementations with the new versions that include LIGHTest's advanced trust verification technologies. Eventually, after all the members have migrated and several tests are done to verify that everything is working as intended, LIGHTest becomes the standard method of trust verification within PEPPOL.

To sum up, establishing trust is crucial when performing electronic transactions. The EU funded LIGHTest project can make trust verification effortless with a global trust infrastructure based on DNS, where anyone is free to publish their trust information. In this paper, we present a description of scenarios that are based on the PEPPOL eDelivery network and eProcurement specifications and can greatly benefit from the use of LIGHTest technologies.

Acknowledgments. This research is supported financially by the LIGHTest (Lightweight Infrastructure for Global Heterogeneous Trust Management in support of an open Ecosystem of Stakeholders and Trust schemes) project, which is partially funded by the European Union's Horizon 2020 research and innovation program under G.A. No. 700321. We acknowledge the work and contributions of the LIGHTest project partners.

References

1. Bruegger, B.P., Lipp, P.: Lightest - a lightweight infrastructure for global heterogeneous trust management. In: Hühnlein, D., Roßnagel, H., Schunck, C.H., Talamo, M. (Hrsg.) Bonn: Gesellschaft für Informatik e.V.. (S. 15–26) (2016)
2. The LIGHTest Project, LIGHTest Deliverable D2.10 - Legal, Ethical and Societal Requirements and Constraints, August 2017

3. The LIGHTest Project, LIGHTest Deliverable D2.3 - Requirements and Use Cases, April 2017. https://www.lightest.eu//static/deliverables/D2.3.pdf. Accessed 28 Sept 2019
4. OpenPEPPOL AISBL, About OpenPEPPOL. https://peppol.eu/about-openpeppol/. Accessed 24 Sept 2019
5. Bruegger, B.P., Roßnagel, H.: Towards a decentralized identity management ecosystem for Europe and beyond. In: Hühnlein, D., Roßnagel, H., Schunck, C.H., Talamo, M. (Hrsg.) Bonn: Gesellschaft für Informatik e.V.. (S. 55–66) (2016)
6. Bruegger, B.P.: The Globally Scalable FutureID Trust Infrastructure. In: World e-ID and Cybersecurity. Marseille (2015)
7. Wagner, G., Wagner, S., More, S., Hoffmann, M.: DNS-based trust scheme publication and discovery. In: Roßnagel, H., Wagner, S., Hühnlein, D. (eds.) Open Identity Summit 2019, pp. 49–58. Bonn, Gesellschaft für Informatik (2019)
8. OpenPEPPOL AISBL, PEPPOL eDelivery Network - An Overview. https://peppol.eu/what-is-peppol/peppol-transport-infrastructure/. Accessed 20 Sept 2019
9. PEPPOL PKI explained. In: PEPPOL practical - PEPPOL PKI explained. https://peppol.helger.com/public/locale-en_US/menuitem-docs-peppol-pki. Accessed 22 Sept 2019
10. Bruegger, B.P., Özmü, E.: A DNSSEC-based trust infrastructure. In: Hühnlein, D., Roßnagel, H. (eds.) Open Identity Summit 2014, pp. 133–139. Gesellschaft für Informatik e.V., Bonn (2014)
11. ETSI TS 119 612, Technical Specification: Electronic Signature and Infrastructure; Trusted Lists. https://www.etsi.org/deliver/etsi_ts/119600_119699/119612/01.01.01_60/ts_119612v010101p.pdf. Accessed 22 Sept 2019
12. Wagner, G., Omolola, O., More, S.: Harmonizing delegation data formats. In: Fritsch, L., Roßnagel, H., Hühnlein, D. (eds.) Open Identity Summit 2017, pp. 25–34. Bonn, Gesellschaft für Informatik (2017)
13. The LIGHTest Project, LIGHTest Deliverable D9.5 - eProcurement Requirements, scenarios, and demo data (2018). https://www.lightest.eu//static/deliverables/D9.5.pdf. Accessed 24 Sept 2019
14. The LIGHTest Project, LIGHTest Deliverable D9.6 eProcurement: Design of LIGHTest Integration (2019)

A Smart Distributed Marketplace

Evgenia Kapassa[1,2(✉)], Marios Touloupos[1,2], Dimosthenis Kyriazis[2],
and Marinos Themistocleous[1]

[1] Institute for the Future (IFF), University of Nicosia, Nicosia, Cyprus
{kapassa.e, touloupos.m, themistocleous.m}@unic.ac.cy
[2] Department of Digital Systems, University of Piraeus, Piraeus, Greece
{ekapassa, mtouloup, dimos}@unipi.gr

Abstract. Online marketplaces are incredibly popular with customers around the globe selling products, also providing everyone as an online seller with a platform to reach a large, ready-to-buy products. Nonetheless, the issue is that it can be difficult to determine which one to trust as a seller. Especially in the world of 5G, where a marketplace is a mandatory component where developers can upload and verify their developed Network Services (NSs) or chained Virtual Network Functions (VNFs). Since those NSs are provisioned for a production environment, their consumers would need to trust the developer or the owner of that NS. To this end, in this paper we propose a smart distributed NFV Marketplace, in which we try to resolve security weaknesses related to the verification of the integrity of the developed VNFs and NSs.

Keywords: Blockchain · Distribution · Licensing · Smart contracts · Marketplace · NFV · 5G networks

1 Introduction

Undisputedly, the rapid evolution of mobile communications delivers a remarkable impact on the social and economic development. Network Function Virtualization (NFV) is expected to be the key enabler for agile network management in the upcoming 5G networks, as it will allow optimized service management through softwarization and virtualization of network components [1]. It is of no doubt that the advent of 5G will provide the support of a plethora of innovating services with improvements in system capacity and spectrum coverage. A challenge that arises, is the efficient composition of those Network Services (NSs) from heterogeneous Virtual Network Functions (VNFs). The paramount requirement of a unified framework is deemed indispensable for the exposure and the regulation of the services. Within this scope of the future Internet, an open marketplace comprises a key element in the advertisement and publication of the developed services from different vendors, introducing diversity in the context of network services [2]. The plethora of packages and diverse developers though, introduces an even more critical challenge regarding the incorporation of trust between end-users [3].

Distributed Ledger Technology (DLT) could redefine trust [4] due to the fact that spreads the idea that any type of transaction should be processed without a mediator.

M. Themistocleous and M. Papadaki (Eds.): EMCIS 2019, LNBIP 381, pp. 458–468, 2020.
https://doi.org/10.1007/978-3-030-44322-1_34

DLT gained notoriety by being used for the trading of cryptocurrencies, such as Bitcoins, which are issued and validated by the underlying Blockchain users rather than by a central authority. Recent Blockchain developments focused on the provisioning of trust, including also smart contracts. In the NFV context, these characteristics can be used to resolve security weaknesses related to the verification of the integrity of the developed VNFs and NSs.

The notion of such a decentralized marketplace of storing, retrieving, advertising, purchasing and comparing services is in absence in the 5G concept. To this effect, service providers and developers will be provisioned with a plethora of developed services from the various stakeholders, with seamless and expeditious deployments [5]. Consequently, the ultimate aim of the decentralized marketplace is to introduce the notion of an economic plane in the exchanges of VNFs/NS via the several stakeholders by promoting trust, anonymity and transparency.

To this end, in this paper we are proposing a design of a smart distributed NFV marketplace as a multi–faceted repository, supporting the storage, publication and proposal of the developed VNFs/NSs in a 5G infrastructure. Such component will not only provide a solution for exchanging and trading VNFs/NSs on the-fly, but also rely on the use of publicly auditable smart contracts, deployed in a blockchain that increase the transparency and trust, with respect to the provenance tracking and accountability of the provided NSs. As such, the proposed smart distributed NFV marketplace will act as a mean to commercialize new virtualized products and network-aware applications, by providing also licensing models, verified with smart contracts.

The remaining of the paper is organized as follows. Section 2 presents the related work and motivation of this study while in Sect. 3 we introduce the overall architecture of the proposed "Smart NFV Marketplace" and its internal components. Finally, in Sect. 4, we conclude our work with some thoughts and ideas for future research.

2 Literature Review

In the context of a 5G infrastructure, a smart distributed marketplace can facilitate the high-availability storage of VNFs/NS, as well as a database containing the necessary meta-data of enriching the information of these entities. The ChoiceNet architecture [5] proposed a meeting ground for providing NFV advertisements and user requirements through common minimal semantics. In the ChoiceNet framework, the deployment of several open marketplaces provided their hierarchical arrangements of offering service bundling and auction services. This proposed approach was structured with the aim of the utmost importance of economic perspective of the services yet ignoring the integration with the production environment of a 5G infrastructure. On top of this marketplace template, NetEx [6] constitutes a network marketplace extending to the physical layer for a cloud datacenter. That approach provided the ground for the telecommunication service providers to deploy their services in the infrastructure and publish the relevant set prices, requirements and policies. NetEx had the aim of motivating providers to expose necessary information for offering and, correspondingly, receiving accountable services. However, it was designed without the vision of integrating it in a production environment of the 5G infrastructure. The T-NOVA project [7] introduced the realization of an NFV marketplace, targeting to the user selection of the services and the virtual appliances already published. Additionally, to this point, the T-NOVA marketplace involved multiple metrics from trading and billing policies in order to optimize the VNF combinations and selections. The diverse stakeholders interact with the several instances of the marketplace in different ways depending on the role of each stakeholder in the system. Every relationship between stakeholders involved a commercial transaction with consequent billing information and agreements.

Although there is large research and development of centralized marketplaces for VNF packages, there is a lack in distributed ledger technologies adoption, in order to promote privacy and openness. Till now, the available solutions require that the users trust completely the database integrity of the provider [8]. An initial work that tries to solve this challenge is presented by Scheid in [9], where he proposes a blockchain-based, trusted VNF package repository for securing the underlying 5G environment. Blockchain design must provide high data integrity, protection, consistency and privacy to guarantee the confidentiality of a Blockchain system [10]. Usually, information is distributed and processed throughout the participants in a blockchain. Updating this information requires the approval of most participants who validate that requested update is legitimate and permissible in compliance with the blockchain's programmed rules. The participants serve as both users and data controllers within each blockchain implementation, which effectively eliminates the data [11].

Therefore, the combination of these properties contributes towards research on the use of Distributed Ledger Technologies (DLT) in the sense of NFV. A suggested solution is also discussed in [12] where authors presented a blockchain-based NFV Management and Orchestration (MANO), named SINFONIA. SINFONIA (Secure Virtual Network Function Orchestra for Non-Repudiation, Integrity, and Auditability) is intended for network infrastructure where multiple Network Services (i.e. chained VNFs) are deployed from different customers.

Although there is an escalating interest in the delivery of a decentralized repositories in 5G environments, a major lack exists in the consolidation of an open marketplace as a secure and trustful component, which return the VNFs, NSs and their metadata control, back to the users. Thus, a challenge exists in the orientation of this component beyond the plain storage functionalities. With the evolving plethora of 5G network requirements and the DLT, the verification of VNF package's integrity without relying on a Trusted Third Party (TTP) is deemed of paramount importance.

3   Preliminaries

3.1   Blockchain

A blockchain involves many machines working together in a decentralized network, thus, it is a shared computer system infrastructure. This infrastructure is consisted of distributed computers which are documented in a manner that prevents their subsequent modification. Blockchain technology helps to increase security, accelerates information exchange in a manner that is more cost-effective and transparent, and also is a key technology for validation and verification of any kind of applications and services [17]. Thus, a blockchain is essentially a virtual contract allowing an individual party to conduct any kind of transaction (i.e. storing and/or retrieving a VNF) directly (peer-to-peer) with another party.

Main Characteristics. The key characteristics that could describe the blockchain technology include the (a) Distributed Ledger Technologies (DLTs), (b) Consensus Algorithms and (c) Smart Contracts. An overview of these concepts is described below.

- *Distributed Ledger Technologies (DLTs):* One form of a distributed ledger is blockchain. Distributed ledgers use independent computers (called nodes) to register, exchange and synchronize transactions in their respective electronic ledgers (instead of keeping data centralized like in a traditional ledger) [24].
- *DApps:* Distributed Applications (dApps) are open-source applications that represent a contract between a network and its users and operate on a ledger, such as the Bitcoin or Ethereum blockchains. The user interface of a dApp does not look any different than any website or mobile app today. The smart contract represents the core logic of a decentralized application [25].
- *Smart Contracts:* A smart contract is an arrangement for self-enforcement implemented in a blockchain-managed computer code. The code includes a set of rules under which the smart contract parties agree to communicate. If the predefined rules are met, the agreement will be followed automatically [26].
- *Consensus Algorithms:* One of the big advantages of blockchain is the verification of the data. The purpose of the verification process is to reach consensus about the distributed ledger content. Consensus-based verification is a decentralized and distributed process, implemented on the blockchain itself. Consensus algorithm is a crucial element of every blockchain network, as it is responsible for maintaining the integrity and security of these distributed systems. The first consensus algorithm to be created was the Proof of Work (PoW), which was designed by Satoshi Nakamoto and implemented on Bitcoin as a way to overcome the Byzantine faults [27].

3.2   5G Networks

5G is a new innovative kind of network that improves today's mobile broadband infrastructure and extend mobile networks to serve a wide range of devices and services and connect new industries with better performance, reliability and cost.

Main Characteristics. The NFV Repository is considered to be a multi-sided catalogue, addressing different stakeholder needs in the entire lifecycle of the NSs.

- *Network Function Virtualization (NFV):* NFV is the decoupling of network functions from proprietary hardware appliances and running them as software in virtual machines or containers. Virtual network functions (VNFs) are called the different functions — such as firewalls, traffic control, and virtual routing. Network Services (NSS) are chained VNFs, leading to more complex functionalities [30].

- *Software Defined Networking (SDN):* SDN can make possible to run the network using software rather than hardware. It also proposes a split between control and data planes, adding speed and versatility into 5G networks [29]
- *Network Slicing*: In 5G, a network slice is defined as an instantiation of the physical infrastructure or the network services and capabilities that underlie it. 5G network slicing allows an operator to use the same infrastructure to serve a large variety of user services and applications [28].

4 Proposed Architecture

The proposed smart distributed NFV Marketplace constitutes a vital component in the 5G environment. This section provides the architectural description of the NFV Marketplace, in terms of interacting software components and entities. Taking into consideration the inter-connection between a distributed set of users, developers and service providers, the implementation of the Marketplace aims to take advantage of a blockchain-based approach to support VNFs, NSs, packages and license transactions integrity, accountability and provenance tracking, in order to ensure trust and transparency in the 5G ecosystem. The proposed architecture is consisted of three main blocks: (a) the dPortal, (b) the NFV Marketplace and (c) the blockchain-enabled Validation System, as depicted in Fig. 1. The description of the aforementioned components is discussed in the following sub-sections. It should be pointed out, that the NFV MANO and NFV Infrastructure are not discussed in the current study, as we assume that third-party solutions are included. Although, the proposed architecture can be integrated into existing NFV solutions, such as orchestration platforms that are able to manage deployed VNFs, such as SONATA (powered by 5GTANGO) platform [13].

4.1 dPortal

In this sub-section, the proposed distributed portal (aka "dPortal") which is a dApp (i.e. decentralized application). It is worth mentioning that dApps are considered to be the fourth stage for the evolution of applications, as they are distributed, resilient and transparent [14]. The "dPortal" is a Graphical User Interface (GUI) in order to be accessible to the end-users. The "dPortal" is responsible for user interaction and presenting information, such as available and acquired VNFs and NSs, as well as licenses and prices. The proposed "dPortal" is divided into sections that include Packages, VNFs and NSs management, Licensing management, as well as an Operation section for NS instantiation management. The entities that are expected to take part in the distributed process and are identified by the "dPortal" are (a) the service developers, (b) the SP providers and (c) the end-users. The main role of the "dPortal" is to help the developers to register their NS packages in a trustworthy NFV Marketplace, support the provider for the formulation of smart licenses for each package and finally benefit the end-users by providing an end-to-end verification system based on blockchain that verifies the integrity of the deployed NSs.

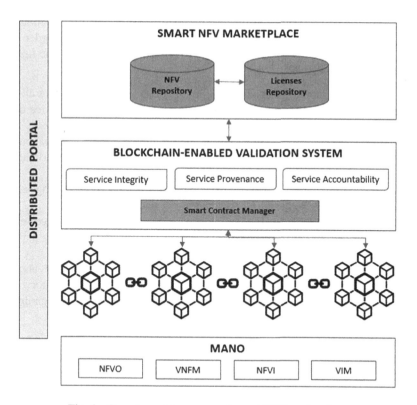

Fig. 1. Overview of the proposed smart NFV marketplace

4.2   Smart NFV Marketplace

The below sub-section describes the key component of the proposed architecture, which is consisted by two components namely (a) NFV Repository and (b) Licenses Repository.

NFV Repository. The NFV Repository is considered to be a multi-sided catalogue, addressing different stakeholder needs in the entire lifecycle of the NSs. The inclusion of the correlated information refers to the NS enables the annotation of VNFs/NSs with metadata. The attached information contributes to the enhancement of the key functions and interfaces of the NFV Repository for storing, searching and retrieving VNFs/NS based on these metadata, as well as providing added value services.

Our approach incorporates the selection of one of the most famous databases from the family of the Documents Stores, MongoDB [15]. The aim of selecting MongoDB for our approach is the convenient management of complex data document and the developer-friendly environment for interpretable JSON/JSON–like data types. Furthermore, MongoDB introduces considerably enhanced performance in the time complexity of the available CRUD operations, along with advanced query engine and index structures [16]. The deployment of a NoSQL MongoDB addresses the management and storage necessities of the template files of NSDs, VNFDs and packages.

The stored descriptors are required for the selection, development and instantiation of the NS by the NFV Orchestrator (NFVO) as well as for data analysis in order for the added value functionalities of NFV Repository to operate properly. Thus, the following object categories are defined:

- Network Service Stored Objects: Feasibility of storage information about all the on boarded NSs, aiding the creation and management of the network service deployment templates.
- Virtual Network Function Stored Objects: Feasibility of storage information about VNFs, referring to the description template, reference to the software images (or even the software image itself) and manifest files.
- Package Stored Objects: Feasibility of storage information about packages, acting as an index to describe the files contained in the package.
- Acquired Licenses Objects: Feasibility of storage information about correlations between the end-user the corresponding licenses and the corresponding payments, resulting from the successful instantiations.
- Verification Information Objects: Feasibility of storage information about the integrity of the VNFs, NSs, packages that are stored into the repository. Additionally, this kind of objects are storing verification information regarding the anonymity of the user's wo sign smart contracts related to the licenses.

As depicted in Fig. 2, prior to the attachment of the metadata to the stored objects, the inspection of the validity and integrity of the document structure is a critical step. Thus, a Validation System based on blockchain technology is introduced. Since the documents are specified in machine-readable formats, the review of the integrity contributes to data security into the NFV Repository.

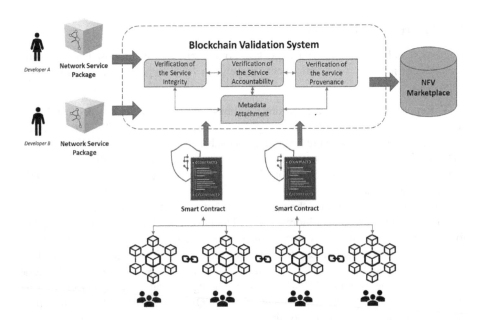

Fig. 2. Blockchain enabled validation

Licenses Repository. The Licensing Repository is responsible for handling customers requests to acquire VNFs and NSs. The License Management process that takes place in the presented work covers the license acquisition by the end-user, leaving the legal agreements to the "Smart Contract Manager" as we will describe in the Subsect. 4.3 below. Each license object stored into the Licenses Repository adopts a service-based licensing model, which links a license to a specific end-user and an instantiated NS, by specifying also the number of allowed NS instances. The licenses are being verified by creating smart contracts through the blockchain verification system of the proposed solution. The Licensing Repository stores the following licensing types:

- Public License: The Public License refers to an open source NS, which the descriptor (i.e. source code) is available to the end-users for instantiation free of charge. As previously mentioned, the Public License comes with no instantiation restrictions.
- Trial License: The Trial License refers to the NSs which end-users can try before they buy. Once the end-user in registered and selects to instantiate a NS with a Trial license he or she activates the license "silently", and can use it for the time period specified in the smart contract. Apart from the constrained period, the Trial License has a limited amount of free NS instances that the end-user can have it activated at the same time.
- Private License: In the proposed architecture, the Private License means that the customer needs to buy a license before instantiating a service. Additionally, this type of license specifies the number of allowed simultaneous instances per customer.

4.3   Blockchain Validation System

In this sub-section we are going to describe the proposed blockchain-enabled verification system which is the component that promotes trust and transparency among all the services and licenses transactions, toward the "Smart NFV Marketplace".

Blockchain Infrastructure. A blockchain involves many machines working together in a decentralized network, thus, it is a shared computer system infrastructure. This infrastructure is consisted of distributed computers which are documented in a manner that prevents their subsequent modification. Blockchain technology helps to increase security, accelerates information exchange in a manner that is more cost-effective and transparent, and also is a key technology for validation and verification of any kind of applications and services [17]. In this section we are going to describe our approach related on how we can ensure the security and provenance of the VNFs and NSs that are going to be stored into the NFV Marketplace. Additionally, the proposed approach promotes the trust and transparency of the licenses' payment transactions, between the service provider and the end-user (e.g. service customer). The verification process is based on the security policy language used by smart contracts, as introduced by the Model-based Security Toolkit (SecKit) [18].

Smart Contracts Manager. In this sub-section we are going to describe the proposed Smart Contract Manager which is responsible for handling end users' requests to store and/or retrieve VNF and NS packages, in a trustful way. The proposed Smart Contract Manger helps to extend the underlying Blockchain Infrastructure by including pieces of code that are the "smart contracts". These small programs are stored in the blockchain and programmed to autonomously behave in a given manner when some conditions are met [19]. We could define the smart contracts as digital contracts which "allow terms contingent on decentralized consensus that are tamper-proof and typically self-enforcing through automated execution" [20]. The aim of smart contracts is to evaluate the conformity that is defined as the fact that a service, method, license or even an individual (e.g. developer) meets stated requirements and can boost business interests, transparency and trust between all the stakeholders, with respect to the verification process.

The proposed Verification System is a framework for building privacy preserving smart contracts in order to (a) verify the network services' integrity, (b) verify the network services' accountability, (c) verify the network services' origin and d) provide trust to licenses payment transactions between the service provider and the customer. The creation and execution of the smart contracts are facilitated by a specific entity, namely "Smart Contract Manager". The "Smart Contract Manager" can see the developer's inputs to the system (i.e. VNFs, NSs, packages) and is trusted not to disclose developer's private data. At this point we should mention that the manager needs also to be a trusted entity, and that's why it is distributed and at the same time verified among each blockchain user. For instance, if multiple contract instances are running concurrently, each smart contract may specify an individual manager, distributed among the infrastructure [21].

Moving forward, when a service developer enters the system and requests the storage or retrieval of a NS package, automatically subscribes to a specific Smart Contract Manager. The manager then is responsible to create a policy-based data usage contract specifying constraints on the usage and redistribution of any service obtained explicitly or implicitly by the system. The manager in this approach functions as a data provenance monitor, policy validation entity and event logger, allowing the system to easily verify all network service transfers and license transactions, ensuring that only transactions in compliance with the smart contract policy are allowed and recorded in the blockchain [22, 23]. Once the Smart Contract Manager verify and validate the integrity, accountability and provenance of all the actions related to the services and licenses, the information is forwarded into the NFV Marketplace for further usage.

5 Conclusions

Security and trust in the 5G environment are still a central concern for users and enterprises, which are increasingly relying on NFV infrastructures to support their business models and deliver their services. In this paper, we introduced a novel prototyping distributed NFV marketplace that goes beyond the plain NFV data repository. The proposed architecture is based in a blockchain infrastructure, taking advantage of the advantages of smart contracts in order to validate all the marketplace-oriented transactions of the VNFs, NSs, packages and license integrity, accountability and provenance tracking, towards trust and transparency in the 5G ecosystem.

It is doubtless that there is a lot of work ahead of us, till this work is ready to be adopted in a production environment. Therefore, we are planning to use business blockchain approaches, such as Hyperledger, as the implementation solution toward this direction. Moreover, we are planning to enhance the capabilities of the proposed smart contract manager, to automatically generate contracts from specified policies.

Acknowledgements. This work has been partially supported by the PARITY project, funded by the European Commission under Grant Agreement Number 864319 through the Horizon 2020. Moreover, this scientific work has been performed in the framework of the 5GTANGO project, funded by the European Commission under Grant number H2020ICT-2016-2761493 through the Horizon 2020 and 5G-PPP programs (http://5gtango.eu).

References

1. Karl, H., et al.: DevOps for network function virtualisation: an architectural approach. Trans. Emerg. Telecommun. Technol. **27**(9), 1206–1215 (2016)
2. Kim, J.B., Segev, A.: A web services-enabled marketplace architecture for negotiation process management. Decis. Support Syst. **40**(1), 71–87 (2005)
3. Network Functions Virtualisation (NFV) ETSI Industry Specification Group (ISG): ETSI GS NFV-MAN 001 - V1.1.1 - Network Functions Virtualisation (NFV); Management and Orchestration (2014). http://tiny.cc/NFVMANO. Accessed 1 Apr 2019
4. The Difference Between Blockchain & Distributed Ledger Technology. https://tradeix.com/distributed-ledger-technology/. Accessed 2019
5. Wolf, T., et al.: ChoiceNet: toward an economy plane for the Internet. ACM SIGCOMM Comput. Commun. Rev. **44**(3), 58–65 (2014)
6. Yu, D., et al.: Towards a network marketplace in a cloud. In: 8th {USENIX} Workshop on Hot Topics in Cloud Computing (HotCloud 2016) (2016)
7. Xilouris, G., et al.: T-NOVA: a marketplace for virtualized network functions. In: 2014 European Conference on Networks and Communications (EuCNC). IEEE (2014)
8. Bozic, N., Guy, P., Stefano, S.: Securing virtual machine orchestration with blockchains. In: 2017 1st Cyber Security in Networking Conference (CSNet). IEEE (2017)
9. Scheid, E.J., Keller, M., Franco, M.F., Stiller, B.: BUNKER: A Blockchain-based trUsted VNF pacKagE Repository. In: Djemame, K., Altmann, J., Bañares, J.Á., Agmon Ben-Yehuda, O., Naldi, M. (eds.) GECON 2019. LNCS, vol. 11819, pp. 188–196. Springer, Cham (2019). https://doi.org/10.1007/978-3-030-36027-6_16
10. Porru, S., et al.: Blockchain-oriented software engineering: challenges and new directions. In: 2017 IEEE/ACM 39th International Conference on Software Engineering Companion (ICSE-C). IEEE (2017)
11. Blockchain Solves For Trust, Not Data Management. https://www.forbes.com/sites/forbestechcouncil/2018/11/02/blockchain-solves-for-trust-not-data-management/#88c4e55132a1. Accessed 2019
12. Rebello, G.A.F., Alvarenga, I.D., de Teleinformática, G.: SINFONIA: Gerenciamento Seguro de Funções Virtualizadas de Rede através de Corrente de Blocos. In: Anais do I Workshop em Blockchain: Teoria, Tecnologias e Aplicações (WBlockchain-SBRC 2018), vol. 1, no. 1/2018. SBC (2018)
13. 5 GTANGO Project Consortium, "5GTANGO: 5G Development and Validation Platform for global Industry-specific Network Services and Apps". https://5gtango.eu. Accessed 2019

14. What Are Dapps? The New Decentralized Future. https://blockgeeks.com/guides/dapps/. Accessed 2019
15. Zhang, Y., et al.: Big data storage technology suitable for the operation and maintenance of new generation power grid dispatching control system operation. In: IOP Conference Series: Earth and Environmental Science, vol. 300, no. 4. IOP Publishing (2019)
16. Ali, W., et al.: Comparison between SQL and NoSQL databases and their relationship with big data analytics. Asian J. Res. Comput. Sci., 1–10 (2019)
17. Themistocleous, M., Morabito, V., da Cunha, P.R.: Introduction to the Minitrack on Blockchain and Fintech (2018)
18. Neisse, R., Steri, G., Nai Fovino, I., Baldini, G.: SecKit: a model-based security toolkit for the internet of things. Comput. Secur. **54**(2015), 60–76 (2015)
19. Gatteschi, V., et al.: Blockchain and smart contracts for insurance: is the technology mature enough? Fut. Internet **10**(2), 20 (2018)
20. Cong, L.W., He, Z.: Blockchain disruption and smart contracts. Rev. Finan. Stud. **32**(5), 1754–1797 (2019)
21. Kosba, A., Miller, A., Shi, E., Wen, Z., Papamanthou, C.: Hawk: the blockchain model of cryptography and privacy-preserving smart contracts. In: 2016 IEEE Symposium on Security and Privacy (SP), San Jose, CA, pp. 839–858 (2016)
22. Neisse, R., Steri, G., Nai-Fovino, I.: A blockchain-based approach for data accountability and provenance tracking. In: Proceedings of the 12th International Conference on Availability, Reliability and Security, vol. 1, pp. 1–10 (2017)
23. Tosh, D., et al.: Data provenance in the cloud: a blockchain-based approach. IEEE Consum. Electron. Mag. **8**(4), 38–44 (2019)
24. Rouse, M.: Distributed Ledger Technology (DLT). https://searchcio.techtarget.com/definition/distributed-ledger
25. Decentralized Applications – dApps. https://blockchainhub.net/decentralized-applications-dapps/
26. Smart Contracts. https://blockchainhub.net/smart-contracts/
27. Nakamoto, S., Bitcoin, A.: A peer-to-peer electronic cash system. Bitcoin. https://bitcoin.org/bitcoin.pdf (2008)
28. Foukas, X., Patounas, G., Elmokashfi, A., Marina, M.K.: Network slicing in 5G: survey and challenges. IEEE Commun. Mag. **55**(5), 94–100 (2017)
29. Gupta, A., Jha, R.K.: A survey of 5G network: architecture and emerging technologies. IEEE Access **3**, 1206–1232 (2015)
30. SDxCentral, "What is NFV (Network Functions Virtualization)? Definition". https://www.sdxcentral.com/networking/nfv/definitions/whats-network-functions-virtualization-nfv/

IT Governance

Organisational Structure's Influence on IT Alignment: The Case of a Public Organisation

Gideon Mekonnen Jonathan[(⊠)], Lazar Rusu, and Erik Perjons

Department of Computer and Systems Sciences, Stockholm University,
Stockholm, Sweden
{gideon,lrusu,perjons}@dsv.su.se

Abstract. IT alignment, even though extensively researched in the last decades, remains to be challenging. Previous studies are criticised for two reasons. First, the majority of the studies focus on the conceptual debate, while practical issues that have implications on IT alignment are overlooked. One of these issues is the influence of organisational structure on IT alignment. Second, studies in few organisational settings, namely private and commercial organisations, have resulted in findings that are not applicable for organisations in other sectors–public organisations. To address the gap in the literature, this study aims to explore the influence of formal and informal organisational structures on IT alignment in a public organisation. As public organisations are joining the trend of digital transformation, identifying appropriate organisational structure that foster IT alignment is an important and timely issue. The result of the case study, conducted in one Swedish municipality, revealed the influence of centralised organisational structure as well as three types of informal organisational structure—interpersonal relationships, professional networks, and cross-departmental relationships—on IT alignment. The findings could be used by leaders in public organisations to design an effective organisational structure that can improve IT alignment and its maturity.

Keywords: Business-IT alignment · IT alignment · Formal organisational structure · Informal organisational structure · Organisational structure · Public organisations

1 Introduction

Business-IT alignment (referred to as 'IT alignment' in this study) is defined as "*the application of Information Technology (IT) in an appropriate and timely way, in harmony with business strategies, goals and needs*" [1, p. 3]. Scholars argue that the continued interest in IT alignment for the past few decades emanates from the empirical evidence confirming its relationship with the improved organisational performance [6]. Despite the widespread attention among researchers and practitioners, the publications in academic and practitioner outlets continue to demonstrate the challenges of aligning business and IT strategies [2–4]. It is, therefore, no surprise that IT alignment has been ranked to be one of the top concerns for IT executives as shown in the yearly surveys carried out across industries around the globe for more than three decades in a row [5]. Even though IT alignment has attracted the attention of many researchers, literature

© Springer Nature Switzerland AG 2020
M. Themistocleous and M. Papadaki (Eds.): EMCIS 2019, LNBIP 381, pp. 471–485, 2020.
https://doi.org/10.1007/978-3-030-44322-1_35

reviews [3, 6–8] indicate that the focus of previous studies was mainly at addressing IT alignment issues at the conceptual levels while practical challenges in different organisational contexts are rarely pursued. The other criticism on the extant literature is the disproportional attention provided to a few contextual settings. For instance, the majority of IT alignment studies were conducted in the commercial and private organisations (banking, insurance, manufacturing as well as the healthcare sectors) while only a few empirical studies targeted public organisations [8]. However, as noted by Caudle et al. [9, p. 172], there are *"pronounced differences between the public and private sectors"*. Studies have identified several factors that are significant to warranty empirical IT alignment investigation in the public sector. To mention a few, the long list of stakeholders with competing or opposing interests; the wide range of services provided to citizens; and the complex decision-making structures with political and administrative powers can make IT alignment more challenging in public organisations [10].

On the other hand, there are calls for more empirical studies to further our understanding of the different organisational factors that influence IT alignment. The influence of both formal and informal organisational structure on alignment is one of the research agendas acknowledged to be relevant and timely but less explored [2, 11]. This study is, therefore, set out to investigate the role of formal and informal organisational structure on IT alignment in public organisational settings. Thus, the following research question is formulated: *"How can the formal and informal organisational structures influence IT alignment and its maturity in a public organisation?"*

The paper is structured as follows. First, a brief review of the extant IT alignment as well as organisational structure literature is presented together with a theoretical framework underpinning the study. Second, the research strategy and the methods used to collect and analyse the data are described. The subsequent section presents the results and analysis of the study, starting with the description of the organisation where the study was conducted. Finally, the last section presents the conclusion and puts forward future research directions.

2   Literature Review

2.1   IT Alignment

The early research by Henderson and Venkatraman [12] is credited to have provided the platform for the subsequent studies that came to contribute to further the different conceptualisations, definitions and numerous IT alignment models. According to Luftman et al. [4], IT alignment is now viewed as an optimised position where an organisation has successfully managed to maximise the business value of IT. Even though there are different definitions in the literature, scholars agree that the purpose of IT alignment is to enable organisations to plan appropriate use of resources which aligns IT strategies with the overall organisational strategy [3]. To this end, researchers have attempted to develop different models, frameworks and identify different dimensions that point firms toward an aligned position. Reich and Benbasat [13] argue that IT alignment need to be viewed from a two-dimensional perspective (i.e., social, and intellectual). The social dimension describes the extent to which the business and the IT leaders within an organisation understand each other. The social dimension also shows how well the leaders are committed to realising the mission, objectives and plans of each other's units. On the other hand, the intellectual dimension is expressed as the extent to which the IT and business units have managed to match each other plans. In addition to these dimensions, researchers have also recognised the significance of looking into IT alignment at different levels within an. Gutierrez and Lycett [14] argue that assessing different levels of IT alignment within an organisation (i.e., at strategic, tactical and operational levels) might reveal appropriate approaches for achieving and maintaining alignment.

The literature provides a long list of models and frameworks identifying different factors that play significant roles in whether organisations succeed in aligning their IT strategies with the overall organisational strategies. One of these models, Strategic Alignment Maturity Model (SAMM) [1, 4] is used to assess IT alignment and its maturity in this study.

As indicated in Fig. 1, the six different areas considered to be vital for IT alignment, referred to as dimensions in the model are: Communications; Value Analytics (how metrics can be used to measure the contribution of IT in a language that would be understood by the business and IT organisation); IT Governance (how organisations allocate the decision-making authority in relation to IT); Partnering; Dynamic IT Scope (the adaptability or flexibility in terms of emerging technologies and provision of tailored solutions); and Business and IT Skills Development. SAMM and the IT alignment dimensions [1, 4] are adopted for this study. Analysis of the six dimensions results in the IT alignment maturity level of an organisation in a scale of 1 to 5. Firms at level 4 are considered to have reached an IT aligned position while level 5 indicates sustained IT alignment [1, 4]. The model is validated by a survey of organisations across 16 different industries thus making its application valid across various industries, business functions or organisations.

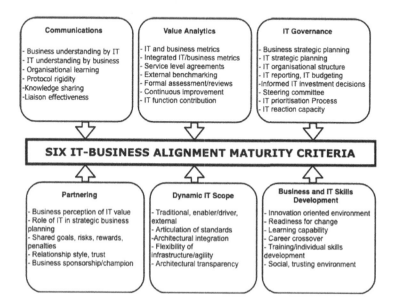

Fig. 1. Strategic Alignment Maturity Model [1, p. 12], [4]

2.2   Organisational Structure

Organisational structure, in organisational theory, and management literature, is defined as a conscious, rational and deliberate arrangement which is sanctioned by leaders to facilitate the smooth running of a business [15]. According to Dalton et al. [16] the level of hierarchy, administrative intensity, specialisation, formalisation or centralisation can be used to determine organisational structure. However, centralisation, i.e. the extent to which the decision making is concentrated at the head office is commonly discussed in the literature. As depicted in organisational charts of many management textbooks [17], the image most of us have about organisational structure resembles what Weber [18] describes as a bureaucratic organisation. This structure which is also commonly referred to as *"formal organisational structure"* is intended to make sure the division of labour is put in such a way that functional divisions are not overlapped to guarantee favourable coordination and control. Three types of formal organisational structure (centralised, decentralised and federated) are widely referred in the literature [17, 19, 20]. Centralised organisations are characterised by interdependence between units resulting from close vertical control, formal authority, standardisation as well as centralised planning. Decentralised organisations allow structural autonomy through lateral coordination and local decision making. Federal organisation structure is aimed at combining some of the characteristics of centralised and decentralised organisational structure.

On the other hand, a different form of organisational structure, referred to as *"informal organisational structure"* has been identified to exist alongside the formally recognized structure within an organisation. The simultaneous existence of both forms of organisational structure is recognised by researchers [2, 20–22]. According to Simon [19, p. 148] *"it would probably be fair to say that no formal organisational structure will operate effectively without an accompanying informal organisational structure"*. In many organisations, informal organisational structure manifests itself in many forms. A closer look into the literature shows that there is a lack of consistency in describing what constitutes as informal organisations [2, 20, 21, 23, 24]. Chan [2], Tshuman and Nadler [24] characterise informal organisational structure as connections and procedures used by employees to get their work done. Informal organisations may take the form of *"interpersonal relationships"*, *"social networks"*, *"professional networks"*, *"cross-departmental relationships"*, *"informal working arrangements"*, and *"flexible division of labour"* [2, 21, 23–26].

Scott [27, p. 82] describe formal organisational structure as *"the normative system designed by management or the blueprint for behaviour"* while informal organisational structure is considered to reflect the actual behaviour of those who work within an organisation. Selznick [28] argues that informal organisations come to existence because formal structures reflecting the rational rules emerging from the formal administration fail to accommodate the "non-rational" dimensions of organisational behaviour. Zenger et al. [20] argue that leaders who are well informed about the relationship between the two organisational structures can make assessments on whether the informal organisational structure supports, complements, substitutes or undermines the contributions of formal organisational structure. Research in organisational theory [29] as well as IT alignment studies in IS [2, 3] show that informal organisational structure plays a significant role for many organisations as they define how the employees perform their work and discharge their responsibilities.

2.3 Organisational Structure and IT Alignment

Even though the role of organisational structure in IT alignment is explored in IS studies [30], researchers are criticised for ignoring the simultaneous existence and interplay between the formal and informal organisational structures. While studies on informal structure and social networks behind the chart overlook the role of formalised structure and processes, the remaining studies seem to have minimised the significance of informal organisational structure. However, findings of empirical studies, for instance, [2] reveal that the influence of informal organisational structure is pronounced than acknowledged in the literature. Thus, both informal and formal organisational structures need to be studied together in terms of their mutual interplay not only because this provides a comprehensive view to warranty how organisations function, but also because the two forms of structures and their interrelationship has an influence on IT alignment [2, 31, 32]. The message from these studies suggests that appropriate organisational structure makes it possible for firms to be more apt to implement strategies that foster IT alignment.

2.4 Research Conceptual Framework

The conceptual framework depicted in Fig. 1 is applied to address the research question. The various types of organisational structure in the literature are studied along with SAMM's six dimensions of IT alignment [1, 4]. The conceptual framework is also used to analyse and present the findings.

As shown in Fig. 2, the influence of formal organisational structure (the solid box in the left) on IT alignment is analysed by looking into the six dimensions of IT alignment (the solid box in the right). Scholars agree that both formal and informal organisations exist simultaneously [2, 21, 22, 31, 32]. However, informal organisations come to existence in response to the shortcomings of the formal rules [28]. Informal organisational structure is known to complement or undermine the formal structure. The different types of routines as well as unofficial processes influence how employees behave and how work is done [33]. Thus, the influence of informal organisational structure (shown in the lower middle box) on each of the IT dimensions is also analysed.

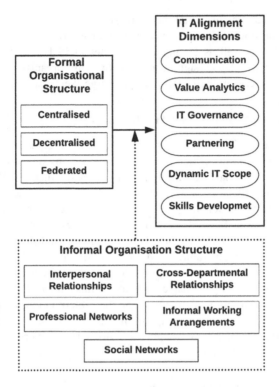

Fig. 2. Research Conceptual framework

3   Research Methodology

As the study aims addressing a "how" question about a phenomenon within a public organisation with a complex natural setting, a case study research strategy is selected [34]. Case study is the most widely employed research strategy among IS researchers [35, 36]. Review of the extant literature has also revealed that case study is the most adopted strategy in IT alignment studies in the public sector [8]. The critical appraisal guidelines for single case study research [37] was followed to determine the appropriateness of a single case study. A single case study rather than multiple case studies was deemed appropriate as the study attempts to establish a theoretical relationship, i.e. between different forms of organisational structure and dimensions of IT alignment. Single case studies are invaluable to describe a phenomenon opulently [38] providing a deeper understanding and rich description of a phenomenon [39]. Single case studies were also used in previous IT alignment studies (for instance, [10, 14, 40]).

One of the strengths of a case study as a research strategy is that it provides a researcher with various data collection methods improving the credibility of the findings [34, 41]. Interviews, observations (three meetings), as well as internal organisational documents were used to collect data. The documents obtained include: governance model of the municipality, organisational chart of the municipality and departments, IT department's strategic plan and process description. The municipality's webpage was also consulted to complement the data collected.

According to Denscombe [41] and Yin [34], interviews are appropriate to gain detailed and in-depth accounts as well as insights into people's opinions and experiences. Interviews were mainly used to gain an explanation on how employees interpret and operationalise the formally sanctioned structure as well as describe how the informal organisational structure looks like [41]. Table 1 shows the list of respondents, length of the interviews, as well as their roles and the departments they represent.

Table 1. List of respondents with their roles and departments

Role	Level	Department	Duration
Administrative Manager	Strategic	Central Administration	50 min
CEO	Strategic	Municipality Owned Enterprise	79 min
CIO	Strategic	IT	68 min
Director	Strategic	Elderly Care	65 min
Business Developer	Tactical	Central Administration	56 min
Business Developer	Tactical	Culture, Sport and Leisure	63 min
Business Developer	Tactical	Labour and Welfare	59 min
IT Architect	Tactical	IT	86 min
Development Manager	Operational	Education	75 min
IT Service Manager	Operational	IT	75 min
Total interview		**duration**	**751 min**

The merit of multiple sources of evidence is found to result in relatively more valid, reliable and diverse construction of realities, a phenomenon which is referred to as triangulation [34]. Ten semi-structured interviews lasting between 60 to 85 min with administrative and IT personnel were conducted in one Swedish Municipality (anonymously labelled in this report as SM). Nonprobability sampling strategy was adopted to select respondents based on the potential of unique insights they are expected to possess [41]. The recorded interviews were transcribed to facilitate data extraction.

The transcript as well as the data collected from the internal organisational documents were coded and analysed thematically. Thematic analysis is widely used qualitative data analysis method which is not tied to a particular theory and epistemology [42]. The 6-phase guide thematic analysis by Braun and Clarke [42] was followed to identify and analyse themes revealing the formal and informal organisational structure types as well as their influence on the six dimensions of IT alignment. First, the interviews were transcribed and reviewed to be familiarised with the data. In the second phase, initial codes were generated. The conceptual research framework in Fig. 1 was used to guide the initial coding. The codes were sorted into potential themes in the third phase. The extant literature was also consulted to review the identified themes. Before the final report was produced in step 6, the themes were defined and named in step 5.

Analysis was also made to determine the IT alignment maturity according to the SAMM instrument [4, p. 40]. The assessment reflects how the respondents rate the different attributes related to IT alignment dimensions shown in Fig. 1. For instance, for communications, the interviewers from the IT side were asked the extent to which they understand the municipality's customers, processes, and partners. On the other hand, those from the other departments were asked the extent to which they understand the IT environment, its capabilities, etc. In total, the instrument contained 39 questions. The IT alignment maturity level is then calculated as the average of the sum of the scores of the dimensions which were assessed using a 1 to 5 Likert scale.

4   Results and Discussions

The results of the study based on the empirical data and the conceptual research framework suggest the simultaneous presence of centralised formal organisational structure as well as various forms of informal organisational structure. This section starts with the description of the case organisation. Subsequently, the various forms of organisational structure, and their influence on the dimensions of IT alignment is discussed.

4.1   The Case Organisation

The case organisation investigated for this study, SM, is one of the mid-size municipalities in Sweden with around one hundred thousand population. SM considers itself to be among the most ambitious public organisations allocating a considerable amount of resources to improve the accessibility and quality of services for its residents. Even though the elected political leaders are responsible for the overarching strategic vision and direction, the focus of this study is on how the civil servants, i.e. the IT and administrative personnel work towards achieving the overall goals of the municipality. The administrative head (equivalent to a CEO position in private firms) is responsible for leading SM while the CIO is in charge of delivering IT solutions to meet the need of all of SM's departments as well as the enterprises owned by the municipality. The seven departments at SM led by department directors (frvaltningschef) are organised based on the services they provide to citizens, i.e. education; elderly care; culture, sport and leisure; agriculture and cadastral; labour and welfare; technical administration; and health and environmental protection. While the departments are responsible for running their core service provisions, the municipality's 'Management and Administration Department' is responsible for providing basic and common services, support and expertise to all departments. These include HR, IT, research and development, legal services, budget and finance, registry, security and readiness, procurement, and sustainability. The CIO and the directors of each department reports to the administrative head.

4.2   IT Alignment Maturity

To analyse the influence of different organisational structures on IT alignment, assessment of current IT alignment maturity level was deemed necessary. The assessment was done using SAMM [1, 4]. The analysis shows that SM has reached level 3 IT alignment maturity. A closer look at the result indicates that the municipality scores lower on dynamic IT scope (2.8), business and IT skills development (2.5), as well as value analytics (2.5). On the other hand, the IT alignment maturity scores are higher for communication (4.25), IT governance (3.8) and partnership (2.7). The following sections discuss the identified organisational structures and their influence on the six IT alignment dimensions.

4.3   Formal Organisational Structure

Even though the characteristics do not exactly fit with the description of an ideal centralised organisation, according to the literature [17], the internal documents obtained indicate that SM has a centralised organisational structure. Particularly looking at the IT, Finance and the legal services, SM seems to be centrally run. The interview with directors from the different departments, reveals that the responsibility and decision-making authority on IT matters is placed at the IT department, which is located within the central Management and Administration Department. Strategic IT decisions are taken at the central steering committee level. The steering committee which is led by the administrative head consists of the CIO, the directors of the seven departments, as well as the CEOs of the municipality held enterprises. The internal documents obtained also indicate a formal hierarchy outlining a clear division of responsibility between the different departments and the Central Administration Management. SM's governance model stipulates regular meetings at three different levels – strategic meetings (1–4 times a year), tactical meetings (4–12 times a year), and operational meetings (1–4 times a month). During the interview, it was revealed that the municipality follows the RACI governance model which requires employees to be responsible, accountable, consulted and informed (CIO, and Director).

As indicated in the literature, the formal organisational structure is considered to be the central nervous system for firms [15, 23]. In the IS context, scholars argue that appropriate formal organisational structures are necessary to adequately support capability, reduce redundancy as well as resolve anticipated issues that might arise in the course of IT implementation and use [25]. The CIO is adamant that the central organisational structure is the key to keep things in order. The respondents seem to agree that centralisation has enabled SM to make sure the IT system is aligned with the main objective of the municipality (delivery of service) while transparency and accountability are maintained. This is consistent with the characteristics of the formal organisational structure in the literature [15, 18]. Formal organisation arrangements, according to Tushman and Nadler [24] provide organisations clarity and direction with formally sanctioned systems and procedures. Most of the respondents underscored the need for order and structure in a public organisation citing the accountability and responsibilities they have for the residents of the municipalities. However, their responses reveal contrasting views on the implications of the centralised organisational structure on IT alignment. At the top level, for instance, the CIO and one of the department directors seem to agree on the benefit of the centralised structure in fostering effective IT governance and clarity of strategy. Even though the CEO of one of the enterprises and another director agree on the shared understanding of strategy as well as good value for investment, they admit the formal structure has created a rigid protocol which has affected how people work. The inflexible division of labour, and the lack of environment which encourages staff to find alternative ways of solving problems are thought to be the result of the centralised organisational structure. The implication of centralisation on communication seems to be mixed. According to the CIO, the municipality has a system to facilitate current and relevant information flow, which is confirmed by one director and CEO. The interview has also revealed different formal forms of arrangements in place to make sure the communication between IT and other departments is maintained. For instance, the steering committee at the top; and the regular meetings at the strategic, tactical and operational levels are brought up in the interview. The CIO, one of the administrative directors and the CEO argued that the formally assembled steering committee had helped them to make the IT and administration strategies of the municipality clear. Since all directors of departments and CEOs of the enterprises are represented in the committee, the IT investment decisions have been fruitful (CIO).

The responses from those at the strategic level seems to suggest that the formal organisational structure in place have improved the shared strategic understanding. However, participants from the tactical and operational levels report the opposite effect. One business developer characterises the formal channels to be *"not the best"'*. In her own words *"there are intranets and email bulletins, but no one relies on them. Either there is too much irrelevant information, or it is too old news. The planned committee meetings do not help us when we have urgent matters"*. Unit managers at the departments and one IT manager also agree that the information flow and time for decision may be long most of the time.

Another issue raised regarding the formal structure is its effect on value analytics and skills development. The respondents mention, in particular, the IT metrics, which are only understood by the IT. According to the CEO of the SM owned enterprise, the IT metrics are not good enough to make reasonable assessments since these are formulated by central administration which is out of touch with the individual departments and enterprises. One of the business developers also says *"I am not aware of how the cost-effectiveness of our systems is calculated. The fact that we are working in the public sector might have resulted in some confusion about what to measure, but the instruction comes from the central administration. We have to give them some figures."* Even though the those in the IT department (for instance, the IT manager and the IT architect) are convinced that the KPIs already stated in the process description are invaluable to assess the IT value, none of the respondents from the other units seem to the effectiveness of these measures. Another area that was related to IT metrics was the use of service level agreements which was found to be sporadic. Only those from the IT department acknowledged the comprehensiveness of the SLAs reflecting the IT needs of all departments at the municipality. Even though the business developers and the administration manager know about the SLAs, none of them recall the time when these were consulted.

In sum, the analysis of the data suggests that the centralised organisational structure at SM has influenced the four dimensions of IT alignment—communication, value analytics, IT governance, and business and IT skills development. While IT governance is high, the results indicate that the business and IT skills development, as well as the value analytics, are unfavourably influenced by the formal organisational structure at SM.

4.4   Informal Organisational Structure

The literature present informal organisational structures in various ways [2, 21, 23–26]. Even though scholars acknowledge the simultaneous existence of formal and informal organisational structures, identifying the informal organisational structures might be difficult. The themes identified reveal three informal organisational strategies at SM–interpersonal relationships, professional networks, and inter- departmental relationships. However, it is worth noting that the majority of respondents did not acknowledge the presence of informal structures out right and attribute what they see as a success to the centralised organisational structure. This is noted particularly from the interviews with respondents in senior positions. For instance, one of the administrative directors says "…*we are managing a very big and complex organisation, it is very important that we have established rules and routines for everyone to follow. I am sure it is the same in other departments as well…*". This conviction is shared by the CIO and one of the CEOs of the municipality held enterprises. Both of them reiterate the importance of consistency and accountability as the reason. Some of the business developers at departments also agree that standardised processes and routines help the municipality save a lot of man hours every year.

Previous studies [22, 23, 26, 43] have reported respondents' lack of awareness on informal organisational structures which is also the case in this study. When asked to reflect about the way work is done at SM or how communication goes between IT and other departments, the respondents seem to acknowledge different practices deviating from the formal routines brought up in the interviews or shown in the organisational chart. For instance, many of the respondents mention to have used the **interpersonal relationships** they have with colleagues in other departments to get work done promptly. As one business developer puts it, "…*I have worked here for more than 10 years…so, most people in IT are my friends than colleagues. I can get things done pretty quick*". Similar stories were told from the IT side as well. On the other side, one of the respondents who is new in SM agrees that those who have connections find it easier to navigate through the system. What is common in these stories is that inter-personal relationships have been found to speed up communication, and improve knowledge sharing. The response from IT service manager and another business developer confirms the role of interpersonal relationships in business and IT development skills, particularly by creating social and trusting environment. Zolper et al. [26] found interpersonal relationships between IT and other departments at the top level to be the most critical aspect of IT alignment which seems to be reckoned by the CIO, the IT architect and one director. According to one of the respondents, "…*good personal relationship and chemistry is vital for a success of a collaboration work… I want to be able to call someone to ask for a favour without thinking about it twice. I have* *some people placed somewhere in the municipality. I can rely on them, so yes, it is very important. It may be some small things as information on upcoming projects, or get some experts come to us to help us without having to wait..."* (Director).

The findings also suggest that employees in different departments but with close proximity in terms of physical location and function seem to have developed what Farris [21] and Zolper et al. [26] called a **cross-departmental relationship**. Even though respondents, mostly at the tactical and operational level acknowledge the significance of the interpersonal relationship, they recognise some collaborative works require a relationship between different departments. According to one administration manager and a business developer, the frequent contact between the IT and their department has led them to forge a partnering relationship which is also reflected in knowledge sharing. According to the respondents, some problems are too big to be dealt with unless many in a department can be mobilised to help. For instance, IT manager recalls that the partnering relationships they build in one of the departments enabled them to provide flexible IT solutions matching their needs.

Consistent with the literature [21], people with related profession and background are found to belong to a **professional network**. For instance, two of the respondents mention the ease of communication with people holding similar position in other departments. The IT manager, who has long experience from the private sector, also acknowledge to interact better with colleagues coming from the private sector. Analysis of the data seems to suggest the positive influence of professional networks on IT governance, communication and partnering.

Even though informal working arrangements were brought up during the interviews, the respondents did not reveal the existence of any form of flexible working arrangements. However, the benefit of informal working arrangements for business and IT skills development seem to be recognised by the respondents.

5 Conclusion

This case study was set out to explore the influences of different organisational structures on IT alignment in a public organisation. Centralised organisational structure as well as three different forms of informal organisational structures were identified at the case organisation. Even though the representativeness of the case organisation was not established, the analysis provides insights on how the identified structures enable or hinder IT alignment. IS researchers have raised the role of organisational structure on IT alignment with contradictory findings [2, 14, 30–32, 44]. However, this study contributes to the body of knowledge by establishing the relationship between specific forms of organisational structures and the various dimensions of IT alignment. Centralised organisational structure is found to influence four of the six IT alignment dimensions (communication, value analytics, IT governance, and business and IT skills development). Consistent with the findings of organisational studies [16, 20], the analysis provides a clear association between centralised organisational structure and shared strategic understanding. The shared understanding has in turn helped the municipality in formulation of IT governance arrangements which is well accepted by the departments. On the other hand, the formal structure with rigid working arrangements has negatively influenced value analytics as well as skills development among employees.

It is reasonable to assume that the shortcomings of the centralised organisational structure have encouraged employees to look for other arrangements to get their work done. The literature supports this assumption [2, 19, 27, 28]. The analysis of the result shows that all the six dimensions of IT alignment, but value analytics, are favourably influenced by informal organisational structures. For instance, the findings indicate that employees use their interpersonal relationships and professional networks when the formal organisational structure makes communication slow. Cross departmental relationships were found to be effective in forging a partnership relationship as well as improving IT agility.

The limitations of this study arise from the research strategy and methods used to collect and analyse data. Case studies provide the benefit of in-depth observations while suffering from the limited generalisability [34]. However, each case study is also an opportunity to reveal a unique insight that might not be found in other settings. Future studies might explore the influence of organisational structure on IT alignment maturity in other municipalities in Sweden to validate the findings of this study. On the other hand, the data collection method applied might not have revealed all the informal organisational structures at the municipality. Formal organisational structures could be identified from interviews and the documents showing workflow, procedures and organisation chart. However, informal organisations might not be revealed readily. Organisational as well as IS studies, for instance, [21, 23, 26, 43] argue that respondents might not have the awareness of the informal organisations. Alternative data collection methods such as observations could be employed to mitigate this limitation in future studies.

References

1. Luftman, J.: Assessing business-IT alignment maturity. Commun. Assoc. Inf. Syst. **4**(1), 1–51 (2000)
2. Chan, Y.E.: Why haven't we mastered alignment? The importance of the informal organization structure. MIS Q. Exec. **22**(4), 97–112 (2002)
3. Chan, Y.E., Reich, B.H.: IT alignment: what have we learned? J. Inf. Technol. **22**(4), 297–315 (2007)
4. Luftman, J., Lyytinen, K., Zvi, T.B.: Enhancing the measurement of information technology (IT) business alignment and its influence on company performance. J. Inf. Technol. **32**(1), 26–46 (2017)
5. Kappelman, L., Torres, R., McLean, E., Maurer, C., Johnson, V., Kim, K.: The 2018 SIM IT issues and trends study. MIS Q. Exec. **18**(1), 51–84 (2019)
6. Jonathan, G.M., Rusu, L.: IT governance in public organizations: a systematic literature review. Int. J. IT/Bus. Alignment Gov. (IJITBAG) **9**(2), 30–52 (2018)
7. Karpovsky, A., Galliers, R.D.: Aligning in practice: from current cases to a new agenda. J. Inf. Technol. **30**(2), 136–160 (2015)

8. Rusu, L., Jonathan, G.M.: IT alignment in public organizations: a systematic literature review. In: Rusu, L., Viscusi, G. (eds.) Information Technology Governance in Public Organizations. ISIS, vol. 38, pp. 27–57. Springer, Cham (2017). https://doi.org/10.1007/978-3-319-58978-7_2

9. Caudle, S.L., Gorr, W.L., Newcomer, K.E.: Key information systems management issues for the public sector. MIS Q. **15**(2), 171–188 (1991)

10. Meijer, A., Thaens, M.: Alignment 2.0: strategic use of new internet technologies in government. Gov. Inf. Q. **27**(2), 113–121 (2010)

11. Fonstad, N.O., Subramani, M.: Building enterprise alignment: a case study. MIS Q. Exec. **8**(1), 496–505 (2009)

12. Venkatraman, N., Henderson, J.: Strategic alignment: leveraging information technology for transforming organizations. IBM Syst. J. **32**(1), 4–16 (1993)

13. Reich, B.H., Benbasat, I.: Measuring the linkage between business and information technology objectives. MIS Q. **20**(1), 55–81 (1996)

14. Gutierrez, A., Lycett, M.: IS alignment factors: dynamic relationships at strategic, tactical and operational level. In: Proceedings of the UK Academy for Information Systems Conference, pp. 11605–11616 (2011)

15. Mintzberg, H.: The structuring of organizations. In: Asch, D., Bowman, C. (eds.) Readings in Strategic Management. Palgrave, London (1989). https://doi.org/10.1007/978-1-349-20317-8_23

16. Dalton, D.R., Todor, W.D., Spendolini, M.J., Fielding, G.J., Porter, L.W.: Organization structure and performance: a critical review. Acad. Manag. Rev. **5**(1), 49–64 (1980)

17. Molina, J.L.: The informal organizational chart in organizations: an approach from the social network analysis. Connections **24**(1), 78–91 (2001)

18. Weber, M.: Economy and Society: An Outline of Interpretive Sociology, vol. 1. University of California Press, Berkeley (1969)

19. Simon, H.: Administrative behavior; A study of decision-making processes in administrative organization-3. Free Press, New York (1976)

20. Zenger, T.R., Lazzarini, S.G., Poppo, L.: Informal and formal organization in new institutional economics. In: Ingram, P., Silverman, B.S. (eds.) The New Institutionalism in Strategic Management, pp. 277–305. Emerald Group Publishing Limited, Bingley (2000)

21. Farris, G.F.: The effect of individual roles on performance in innovative groups. R&D Manag. **3**(1), 23–28 (1972)

22. Zenger, T.R., Lawrence, B.S.: Organizational demography: the differential effects of age and tenure distributions on technical communication. Acad. Manag. J. **32**(2), 353–376 (1989)

23. Krackhardt, D., Hanson, J.R.: Informal networks. Harv. Bus. Rev. **71**(4), 104–111 (1993)

24. Tushman, M., Nadler, D.: Organizing for innovation. Calif. Manag. Rev. **28**(3), 74–92 (1986)

25. Gulati, R., Puranam, P.: Renewal through reorganization: the value of inconsistencies between formal and informal organization. Organ. Sci. **20**(2), 422–440 (2009)

26. Zolper, K., Beimborn, D., Weitzel, T.: The effect of social network structures at the business/IT interface on IT application change effectiveness. J. Inf. Technol. **29**(2), 148–169 (2014)

27. Scott, R.W.: Organizations: Rational, Natural, and Open Systems. Prentice Hall, Englewood Cliffs (1981)

28. Selznick, P.: Foundations of the theory of organization. Am. Sociol. Rev. **13**(1), 25–35 (1948)

29. Dickson, W.J., Roethlisberger, F.J.: Management and the Worker. Routledge, London (2004)

30. Jonathan, G.M.: Influence of organizational structure on business-IT alignment: what we do (not) know. In: Proceedings of the 17th International Conference Perspectives in Business Informatics Research (BIR 2018), Stockholm, Sweden. pp. 375–386. CEUR-WS. org (2018)
31. Currie, W.: Organizational structure and the use of information technology: preliminary findings of a survey in the private and public sector. Int. J. Inf. Manag. **16**(1), 51–64 (1996)
32. Leifer, R.: Matching computer-based information systems with organizational structures. MIS Q. **12**(1), 63–73 (1988)
33. Lincoln, J.R.: Intra-(and inter-) organizational networks. Res. Sociol. Organ. **1**(1), 1–38 (1982)
34. Yin, R.K.: Case Study Research and Applications: Design and Methods. SAGE, Thousand Oaks (2017)
35. Benbasat, I., Goldstein, D.K., Mead, M.: The case research strategy in studies of information systems. MIS Q. **11**, 369–386 (1987)
36. Oates, B.J.: Researching information systems and computing. SAGE, Thousand Oaks (2005)
37. Atkins, C., Sampson, J.: Critical appraisal guidelines for single case study research. In: ECIS 2002 Proceedings, p. 15 (2002)
38. Siggelkow, N.: Persuasion with case studies. Acad. Manag. J. **50**(1), 20–24 (2007)
39. Dyer Jr., W.G., Wilkins, A.L.: Better stories, not better constructs, to generate better theory: a rejoinder to eisenhardt. Acad. Manag. Rev. **16**(3), 613–619 (1991)
40. Hu, Q., Huang, C.D.: Using the balanced scorecard to achieve sustained IT-business alignment: a case study. Commun. Assoc. Inf. Syst. **17**(1), 8 (2006)
41. Denscombe, M.: The Good Research Guide: For Small-Scale Social Research Projects. McGraw-Hill Education, London (2014)
42. Braun, V., Clarke, V.: Using thematic analysis in psychology. Qual. Res. Psychol. **3**(2), 77–101 (2006)
43. Soda, G., Zaheer, A.: A network perspective on organizational architecture: performance effects of the interplay of formal and informal organization. Strateg. Manag. J. **33**(6), 751–771 (2012)
44. Pfeffer, J., Leblebici, H.: Information technology and organizational structure. Pac. Sociol. Rev. **20**(2), 241–261 (1977)

Factors for Successful IT Outsourcing Relationships in Large Companies in Sweden: A Service Buyer's Perspective

Georg Hodosi, Alexander Stark, Eric van Beers, and Lazar Rusu[✉]

Department of Computer and Systems Sciences, Stockholm University,
Borgarfjordsgatan 12, 164 07 Kista, Sweden
{hodosi, lrusu}@dsv.su.se, coola.alle@hotmail.com,
eric.vanbeers@telia.com

Abstract. Relationship management in IT Outsourcing (ITO) is widely accepted as a prerequisite for a successful ITO. However, there is still a need for understanding the important factors that contribute to a successful ITO relationship in large companies in Sweden. Therefore, this study wants to address this knowledge gap. The studied companies are the largest ones regarding turnover in Sweden and are present in the "Large Cap" segment at Nasdaq Stockholm Exchange. The results of this research are compared with a previous study done in 2012 in large companies in Sweden. The findings show that the most important factors (from a buyer's perspective) for a successful ITO relationship are communication; conflict and conflict resolution; trust; commitment; cooperation; and internal competence. The identified relational factors in this study contribute to ITO research and can help ITO decision-makers in large companies to have successful ITO relationships and improve their ITO.

Keywords: IT outsourcing relationships · Factors · Communication · Trust · Commitment · Conflict resolution · Cooperation · Internal competence · Sweden

1 Introduction

The highly competitive business environment determines companies in turning progressively towards IT outsourcing (ITO) [1]. Nowadays, approximately every Fortune 500 company and many large governmental institutions have outsourced a notable portion of their IT services, and industry spread around the world has evolved around ITO, with a yearly increase rate of approximately 10% [2]. According to Leimeister [3, pp. 21–22] ITO is defined as: "handing over to one or more third party vendors (i.e., legally independent) the provision of some or all of an organization's IS functions such as, e.g., IT assets, activities, people, processes, or services for a contractually agreed monetary fee and period of time". As we could see, a relationship between the service buyer and provider is established already as the first contact between the parties and this relationship can develop in different directions, from developing to a long-time

© Springer Nature Switzerland AG 2020
M. Themistocleous and M. Papadaki (Eds.): EMCIS 2019, LNBIP 381, pp. 486–497, 2020.
https://doi.org/10.1007/978-3-030-44322-1_36

contract, or, no contacts, or everything in between these two pools. The research we have conducted have looked at the state when a contract is considered, or when an ITO contract has been established. More formally, a relationship is defined as "The state of being connected or related; the mutual dealings, connections, or feeling that exists between the two parties" [4, p. 3]. In this research study, by "relationship" or "relationships", it is meant the relationship(s) between the service buyer and service provider, in an IT outsourcing arrangement. In the same way, when in this research study, service delivery is mentioned, then it is always the IT service delivered by the provider that is addressed in the ITO arrangement. In opinion of Cullen et al. [5] ITO relationship is a prerequisite for a successful ITO that has additionally demonstrated that relationship management is significantly more expensive that ITO managers have estimated. More-over, Jahner et al. [6, p. 2] noticed that "Many deals do not fail because of the inability of the vendor to negotiate a contract, nor the inability to deliver IT services. Part of the failures of outsourcing relationships can be traced back to a lack of flexibility and evolution in these relationships". Furthermore, a study by Schmidt and Menth [7] shows that 60% of client organizations did not meet their predefined ITO goals and possibly as much as the majority of outsourcing deals either fail or do very badly [8]. On the other hand, researchers that have specifically looked at conflict resolution have found that there is "considerable evidence of large-scale outsourcing both enabling and also disabling the execution of business strategies" [9, p. 81]. The attributes of a successful ITO relationship are used by many researchers such as Alborz et al. [10], Sargent [11], and Goo and Nam [12], but no research studies define them, rather using them as success factors. For example, "trust" (the service buyer can trust its ITO provider) is a success factor, and a lack of trust could pose a threat to the working relationship. Despite of previous research and the long-term importance of ITO, many organizations still experience substantial problems with managing ITO relationships. The attention paid by both researchers and practitioners on ITO relationships has evolved because of the high rate of unsuccessful IT outsourcing arrangements, according to Jahner et al. [6]. There is also mentioned that a substantial number of IT outsourcing is unsuccessful in large companies [13] and that ITO relationships affects the success of ITO [14–16]. Moreover, unsuccessful ITO could cause, not fully functioning IT, with delivery delays and loss of customer confidence, but also considerable costs rising and inconveniences. Therefore, there is a need to understand what are the main factors that contribute to a successfully ITO relationship as a prerequisite for ITO success in large companies [13]. To address this lack of knowledge concerning the factors that contribute to a successful ITO relationship, we have formulated the following research question: "What factors contribute to successful ITO relationships in large companies in Sweden from a buyer's perspective?". The selected unit of analyses are the large companies in Sweden listed on the Nasdaq Stockholm stock exchange categorized as "Large Cap" segment by Nasdaq. In order to be listed as a "Large Cap" company, a company needs to meet a list of criteria set by Nasdaq, that includes, for example, a size of revenue of at least one billion euros as well as achieving certain financial stability [17].

2 Research Background

IT outsourcing arrangements are multidisciplinary, including IT management, strategic procurement, organizational, social, legal and economic theory. This accumulation of disciplines, "together with many interdependent IT tasks and projects, makes ITO very complicated. Therefore, the extensive use of IT within companies demands successful ITO relationships, as IT is involved in nearly all business operations and therefore needs to run smoothly and reliably in these companies" [16]. The theories and concepts used in this research for studying ITO relationships are presented below.

2.1 Incomplete Contract Theory (ICT)

The Royal Swedish Academy of Sciences awarded in 2016 to Oliver Hart, the Sveriges Riksbank Prize in Economic Sciences in Memory of Alfred Nobel for the contributions to contract theory. Hart [18] has defined an incomplete contract as: "… an incomplete contract has gaps, missing provisions, or ambiguities, and so situations will occur in which some aspects of the uses of nonhuman assets are not specified" [18, p. 29]. This incompleteness can lead to several problems, like, provider has no capacity for the unplanned activity, or, the price for the extra work can be high, or simply, the parties cannot agree on if and how to perform the not specified task, or, courts do not know how to interpret the situation. It is a consensus between the researchers that contracts cannot specify all possible scenarios or future contingencies [18–20].

2.2 Transaction Cost Theory (TCT)

Transaction Cost Theory (TCT) "adopts a comparative contractual approach to the study of economic organization in which the transaction is made the basic unit of analysis and the details of governance structures and human actors are brought under review" [21, p. 66]. Adapted to the ITO arrangements, TCT can be used to analyze which organization form is better to be used like: (1) keep it in-house; (2) outsource all IT; and (3) all possible forms between the pools (1) and (2). A transaction cost is a cost for a company in the exchange of services or goods and is covering all costs, both ex-ante and ex-post. The ex-ante costs are (1) costs for searching, like find provider; (2) information costs, like information about the product, service; and (3) negotiation costs like the costs for the buyer and seller to negotiate the price, deliverables and all the other conditions. The ex-post transaction costs are the followings: (1) decision costs; (2) delivery costs for the buyer to check the delivery; (3) legal and adaptation costs; and (4) time and/or inconvenience [22]. The main concern of the TCT is contracting [22] where contracting involves first a complete understanding of the asset and the service included and then the negotiation and rephrasing of clauses.

2.3 IT Outsourcing Relationships

Research in ITO relationships has been done in different fields, like, building conceptual models [23–26] or searching for success factors, important factors, key factors, dimensions, concepts, just to mention some expressions used similarly [27, 28] or exploring how to measure the ITO relationship quality [15, 29].

Many researchers have identified the factors that, by implementing them, the ITO relationships could be improved [26, 27, 30–33]. One of the most detailed ITO relationship models has been developed by Kern and Willcocks [24] describing the most important exchanges and contexts between the service buyer and provider(s). It is based on three major dimensions: (1) the context; (2) the interaction between the outsourcing parties; and (3) the behavioral attributes. The model provides a better understanding of the relationship complexity; however, for the use in practice, it is too well detailed. Therefore, in this research, we have used relationship factors that support ITO success of Hodosi et al. [26] and which are based on Transaction Cost Theory and Perrin and Pervan's model [25] and shown in Fig. 1.

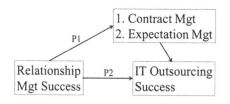

Fig. 1. The relationship factors that support ITO success [26]

In Fig. 1, are shown the general factors for a successful IT outsourcing entitled here ITO success (like Contract Management and Expectation Management), illustrated in the left half of the Fig. 1, and Relationship Factors, that are described in the right half of Fig. 1 [26]. The idea is that the general factor "Relationship Management" directly influences ITO success, but also indirectly through the influence on the other general factors, consisting of "Contract Management" as well as "Expectation Management". The "Contract Management" is done in most of the cases by IT or service management personnel and then lawyers verify the contract. The reason for this is that when managing these contracts, it is required to have a high level of competence of the specific service being outsourced, and how it is supposed to operate. The description of the service is the part of the contract management that most often encounter misinterpretations from both sides. This indicates a way of dealing with the complexity and bounded rationality by using a combination of expertise to achieve the best possible contract [34]. The relationship between the parties is described as a major factor that influences the efficiency when solving these misinterpretations. Furthermore, the relationship is described as an important factor in solving issues regarding any events that the contract does not cover. This can directly be linked to Williamson's [34] idea of the incomplete- ness of contracts, meaning that the relationship plays a major part in managing all the parts of the contract that makes it incomplete. Regarding "Expectation Management", we assume that by working towards the same goal, this will create the expectation that the other party (the service provider) works towards that same goal. A good, healthy relationship between the parties (service buyer and service provider) enables energetic management of activities important to the IT service itself. Actions that deal with eventual conflicts, deliveries and changes, expected or unexpected, will be managed, and conducted, in a more effective manner, and will therefore likely have a more effective result, thus contributing to a more successful ITO relationship, according to Hodosi et al. [26]. Therefore, the expectation management depends on a functioning communication which shares expectations and clarifies the parties' differences, to prevent conflicts [26].

Concerning the general factor entitled "Relationship Management Success", this is subdivided into the relationship factors, consisting of Communication, Conflict & Conflict Resolution, Trust, Commitment and Cooperation. These relationship factors contributing to ITO success shown in Fig. 1, are ranked according to the importance, with "Communication" being ranked as the most important one [26] are described below.

Communication. The communication between parties is vital for the success of the ITO relationship and must, in order to be effective, be open, honest, timely and accurate. Additionally, the communication needs to be meaningful to make sure that the contract's objectives are reached, which also help to avoid potential conflicts. According to Perrin and Pervan [25] there are also two types of reporting requirements, formal and informal communication. Informal is more ad-hoc, whereas formal communication is stricter and more scheduled [25]. Nowadays, there are several tools facilitating communication, which are recommended to be used.

Conflict and Conflict Resolution. ITO inevitably brings conflict because of differences in goals, procedures, cost estimation, or personal relationships together with cultural or other distances and differences between the parties [35]. Noordveld [35] points out that "25 per cent of all outsourcing projects fail due to the complexity of the outsourcing relationship" and therefore, the author recommends to take the conflict resolution process seriously [35, p. 249]. Conflict resolution refers to all type of issues, on all working levels and cause disagreements that occur between the IT outsourcing parties. These have to be solved immediately, preferably on the place where it happened, if not possible, then it has to be escalated. The conflicts can differ in size and consequence and most cases could include disagreements about objectives, like responsibilities, contract-related issues and mismatch of expectations [36, 37]. Consequently, it is critical to recognize that conflicts should be managed and resolved together and that involved parties agree on the solution [38].

Trust. "Trust is a subjective expectation of one entity about another within a specific context at a given time" [39, p. 1]. More specific to ITO, trust can be described as a firm's belief that the partner firm will behave in ways that will benefit the firm and its faith that the partner will not act opportunistically or otherwise take advantage of the relationship [23]. Detailed contracts reduce the level of risk and therefore promote a more trusting and long term relationship [22, 25, 26]. On the other hand, high levels of trust, together with well-functioning cooperation between the ITO parties could act as a replacement for complete and formal contracts [22, 25]. Moreover, high levels of trust in a relationship are positively correlated with the success of the relationship [25, 40].

Commitment. Commitment in a business relationship comprises the willingness of the parties to work together for accomplishing specific objectives and reach the agreed tar- gets. In the perspective of the service buyer, it is the willingness and capacity of the provider to deliver in time with the right quality the agreed IT service. However, in many cases, the provider has to be well informed about all details, and also supported by the service buyer to enable ITO success. Therefore, a level of commitment that is high from both parties could provide a mutually beneficial ITO relationship. It also indicates to the parties that it is a wish to continue the relationship [29, 38].

Cooperation. In ITO relationships, the term cooperation refers to how the service buyer and service provider are working together to the same end [23]. Perrin and Pervan [25] have observed that higher levels of trust in an ITO arrangement will result in a more cooperative behavior because the parties had better know how each of them would react. Cooperation in a relationship is beneficial for both parties and facilitates an environment where trust can be built up and the sharing of information will be improved. It also provides some measure of flexibility to deal with uncertainty and issues not covered in the contract in a non-adversarial manner [25].

3   Research Methodology

The research strategy used in this study is surveys strategy that has as advantages that is focus on empirical data, can collect both quantitative and qualitative data, is wide and inclusive coverage [41] and this properties are fitting well to address the research problem. The study's purpose was to ensure wide and broad coverage of the factors for successfully ITO relationships in large companies of the "Large-Cap" list on Nasdaq Stock Exchange, Stockholm. The non-probability sampling was used as an exploratory sample and those selected as respondents are having expertise and experience in the research issue we have investigated [41]. To collect qualitative data in the studied organizations and from this exploratory sample we have used interviews with partic- ipants that have knowledge about IT outsourcing in their organizations. The use of surveys strategy gave the research information about the current states of ITO rela- tionships in the studied companies. The data collection has been performed through semi-structured face-to-face interviews in six large companies in Sweden. All inter- views were recorded and conducted in a semi-structured way, which enabled the researchers to ask follow-up questions to otherwise previously structured questions [41]. The study has looked to identify the factors that contribute to a successful ITO relationship in these large companies from the service buyer's perspective. The interview questions were based upon the findings of [24, 26, 34]. The interview questions were sent in advance to the participants, so that they could prepare for the interviews. The participants in this research are from large companies in Sweden, have management positions, and are involved in the ITO in their companies. Before starting the interviews, the anonymity has been clarified and all the participants and their companies have required full anonymity. This means that this study cannot present the real number of employees, turnover, business sector, and their exact titles. In Table 1, are presented the generic roles of the interviewees in the six large companies, in order to avoid the risk of identifying them or their companies.

Table 1. Company number, generic role of the interviewees in large companies in Sweden, IT experience and the duration of the interviews

Company no.	Generic role of the interviewees in the large companies in Sweden	IT experience	Duration of the interviews
1	Global IT coordinator	20 years	45 min
2	Chief information officer	20 years	52 min
3	Chief information officer	30 years	40 min
4	IS vendor manager	25 years	50 min
5	Head of business systems	15 years	45 min
6	Head of IT sourcing	25 years	46 min

As we can see in Table 1, the respondents are actively working with IT and their competence varies from 15 to 30 years, and their the roles in the companies shows that the interviewees have responsibilities at the higher level of companies' management. As was mentioned before these companies are classified as large companies and have a large IT organization, and are operating in different business sectors. The data collected through interviews have been recorded, transcribed and analyzed with the NVivo software (a qualitative data analyzing software) and a word frequency analysis was conducted for data analysis to find out the most frequently used words that were relevant to the study. The contexts of the chosen words were compared to find the relevant themes. After that, the produced themes were compared with the themes identified in the research study of Hodosi et al. [26] that has done a similar research study in 2012 in large companies in Sweden. In this way, by re-using the factors identified by Hodosi et al. [26] and contrasting the data sources we have achieved data triangulation by comparing the findings in this study with the findings obtained by other researchers [42].

4   Results and Analyses

4.1   Relationship Management in Large Companies in Sweden

Concerning the relationship management, the findings of this study support the findings of Hodosi et al. [26] concerning the relationships between the ITO party's (service buyer and provider) through contract management that is influenced by communication and cooperation between the parties. The findings also strengthen that a successful relationship, as well as a working cooperation, leads to a good expectation and contract management [26]. Furthermore, the expectation management also depends on a functioning communication, which shares expectations and clarifies the parties' differences, to prevent conflicts. If the communication has failed and the expectations are not the same, between for an example, the operational and strategic level of operations, the cooperation might deteriorate. Therefore, expectation management seems also to be very important for ITO success.

4.2 Relationship Factors that Contribute to ITO Success in Large Companies in Sweden

The identified relationship factors that contribute to ITO success in large companies in Sweden are discussed below.

Communication. This is a prerequisite for all inter-personal understanding, and therefore, it is vital for the relationship. The interviewees emphasized that communication (like a relationship, described above) must work on all levels, for all teams. All of them explained the gap between (1) the strategic and operational level and (2) service buyer's operational level and the providers one. For the last one, they encounter obstacles in the form of resistance from employees along the way. Communication is a key for a successful ITO relationship and also for all activities in the ITO life-cycle. It is also a prerequisite for all the ITO relationship factors. It seems that there is a belief that communication can solve or avoid most of the problems and these explored companies are actively working to facilitate communication. Moreover, communication was identified in this study as the most important relational factor. The result is supported by other researchers [25, 26, 43].

Conflict and Conflict Resolution. All the interviewees had procedures for conflict resolutions, covering emerging and escalating situations. All the respondents acknowledge that conflicts arise and should be handled immediately. However, escalating the problem should be done first when on the level where it occurred, the thorough actions to resolve the problem have not solved the problem. The respondents also claim that communication and commitment are vital for successful management of conflicts. The results show that this factor seems not to be a critical issue, in the sense of that all the interviewed companies have in place instrument and practice for handling conflicts. Compared to previous findings of Hodosi et al. [26], the priority of this factor is much lower. It can be argued that these large companies (as flagships companies in Sweden) have well-working processes for conflict handling and resolution and therefore, the priority of this relational factor is lower.

Trust. The results show trust as an important relational factor. As they trust their providers, no special activities are performed to improve trust. They considered that providers in all cases, want to help if anything unexpected occurs. Of course, there is always some miscommunication; however, independent on the source for it, the providers endeavor to eliminate the problems. Therefore, it can be argued that these large companies, with a lot of experience in ITO, try to avoid challenging their providers outside the providers optimal working range, like complexity, workload, just to mention some factors. That is done to avoid risks, select solutions with the lowest risks, which is precisely what the Transaction Cost Theory recommends [22]. This could explain the high trust level.

Commitment. The importance of commitment towards the relationship and ITO success has also been found in this study. The providers have delivered what has been contractually negotiated. Problems occurred through misunderstandings have a high priority to be resolved. The participants see commitment as a prerequisite for trust building and relationship because commitment means that the provider delivers what has been agreed. It could mean contract but could also cover undocumented agreements. It is understood that in a commitment, the delivery quality and delivery time are also considered. Even if the participants did not have a negative experience with a commitment, a lack of it would lead to a loss of trust, which would be difficult (or more or less impossible) to rebuild it. Additionally, a lack of commitment would trigger conflict management with severe consequences. Finally, a strong commitment is a factor that could increase the length of the contract because the service buyer is satisfied with the provider's performance [26].

Cooperation. The study shows that cooperation is strongly related to contract management. Therefore, the result of this study varies on how much cooperation is included. It is less about the intention to help, or cultural factors; it is more the fact that the provider has to plan for this activity and therefore, it is contractually safeguarded. Nowadays, innovation in ITO is getting more and more critical and cooperation has been clearly specified as a relational factor by other researchers too [44, 45].

Internal Competence. The internal competence is a new factor that was identified in this study and is defined as the buyer's internal competence of contract management and business needs in relation to IT services. This competence stretches into the contract management, that is, the ability to understand the company's needs, and reflect those in an effective way within the contract. Moreover, because there is a shift towards cloud services and SaaS (Software as a Service) in these large companies in Sweden there is a move towards services that are more standard and the reduction of services customized for each customer. Therefore this shift emphases the importance of internal competence, like the ability to communicate the customers' needs and managing service description to the supplier, by recognizing the companies' needs and choosing a standard service proposal accordingly. Nevertheless, internal competence is an important relationship factor (e.g., by improving the competence in contracting) in ITO success. Several large companies in Sweden let consultants companies perform the ITO sourcing and contracting. Therefore, contracting competence remains at the consultant's company. On the other hand, it might also be so that this work is interdisciplinary (IT, sourcing, contracting) and is not recognized by the management as an essential issue. This research study has identified six factors that contribute to successful ITO relationships, and which are communication; conflict and conflict resolution; trust; commitment; cooperation; and internal competence. Apart from the first five factors mentioned before that were also identified in a previous study of Hodosi et al. [26] this study has identified a new relationship factor entitled "internal competence" that is important for successful ITO relationships.

5 Conclusion

The previous research has shown that the relationship between the parties (service buyer and service provider), as well as contract management, are important factors for ITO success [26]. Earlier research has also shown that the market trends are very much dependent upon the conditions of the service provider and buyer [46] as well as the local and global governance. In this context, there is a need to understand IT outsourcing relationships like the factors for successful IT outsourcing relationships. Therefore the objective of this research is to answer the research question: "What factors contribute to successful IT outsourcing relationships in large companies in Sweden from a buyer's perspective?". By finding the answer to this research question we could address the need of further knowledge about how to perform ITO relationships, which could reduce the number of not sufficiently functioning IT, like, delivery delays causing loss of customer confidence and also considerable costs escalating and inconveniences. The findings of this research are a number of six factors for a successful ITO relationship in large companies in Sweden (from a buyer's perspective and without having a priority order of the factors), and which are the followings: communication; conflict and conflict resolution: trust: commitment; cooperation; and internal competence (as a new factor compared to a previous research done by Hodosi et al. [26]). The results presented in this research contribute to ITO research and could help ITO decision-makers in large companies to consider these important factors in having successful ITO relationships and improve their ITO.

References

1. Diirr, B., Cappelli, C.: A systematic literature review to understand cross-organizational relationship. In: Proceedings of 51st Hawaii International Conference on System Sciences. Association for Information Systems (2018)
2. Könning, M., Westner, M., Strahringer, S.: A systematic review of recent developments in IT outsourcing research. Inf. Syst. Manag. **36**(1), 78–96 (2019)
3. Leimeister, S.: IT Outsourcing Governance: Client Types and their Management Strategies. Springer, Heidelberg (2010). https://doi.org/10.1007/978-3-8349-6303-1
4. Kern, T., Willcocks, L.: Exploring relationships in information technology outsourcing: the interaction approach. Eur. J. Inf. Syst. **11**(1), 3–19 (2002)
5. Cullen, S., Shanks, G., Willcocks, L.: A framework for relationships in outsourcing: contract management. In: Proceedings of the 50th Hawaii International Conference on System Sciences, pp. 5380–5389. IEEE (2017)
6. Jahner, S., Böhmann, T., Krcmar, H.: Anticipating and considering customers' flexibility demands in is outsourcing relationships. In: ECIS 2006 Proceedings. Association for Information Systems (2006)
7. Schmidt, N., Menth, L.: Establishing information technology outsourcing relationship quality: a comparative repertory grid study. In: ECIS 2016 Proceedings, Research Paper 160. Association for Information Systems (2016)
8. Ditmore, J.: Why IT outsourcing often fails. InformationWeek Global CIO. http://www.informationweek.com/global-cio/interviews/why-it-outsourcing-often-fails/240003659. Accessed 01 June 2019

9. Lacity, L., Willcocks, L.: Conflict resolution in business services outsourcing. J. Strat. Inf. Syst. **26**(2), 80–100 (2017)
10. Alborz, S., Seddon, P., Scheepers, R.: The quality-of-relationship construct in IT outsourcing. In: PACIS 2005 Proceedings, Paper 93. Association for Information Systems (2005)
11. Sargent, A.: Outsourcing relationship literature: an examination and implications for future research. In: Proceedings of the 2006 ACM SIGMIS CPR Conference on Computer Personnel Research: Forty-Four Years of Computer Personnel Research: Achievements, Challenges & the Future, pp. 280–287. Association for Computing Machinery (2006)
12. Goo, J., Nam, K.: Contract as a source of trust-commitment in successful IT outsourcing relationship: an empirical study. In: Proceedings of the 40th Annual Hawaii International Conference on System Sciences, pp. 1–10. IEEE (2007)
13. Hodosi, G., Rusu, L.: Risks, Relationships, and Success Factors in IT Outsourcing: A Study in Large Companies. Springer, Heidelberg (2019). https://doi.org/10.1007/978-3-030-05925-5
14. Aubert, B., Patry, M., Rivard, S., Smith, H.: IT outsourcing risk management at British Petroleum. In: Proceedings of 34th Annual Hawaii International Conference on System Sciences (HICSS-34). IEEE (2001)
15. Beimborn, D.: Considering the relative importance of outsourcing relationship quality. In: European Conference on Information Systems (ECIS) Proceedings, Paper 123. Association for Information Systems (2012)
16. Hodosi, G.: Information technology outsourcing in large companies in Sweden: a perspective on risks, relationships and success factors. Ph.D. thesis, Stockholm University (2017)
17. Granström, E.: Market cap segment review at Nasdaq Nordic exchange. https://business.nasdaq.com/mediacenter/pressreleases/1660396/market-cap-segment-review-at-nasdaq-nordic-exchanges. Accessed 30 June 2019
18. Hart, O.: Firms, Contracts, and Financial Structure. Clarendon Press, Oxford (1995)
19. Grossman, S., Hart, O.: The costs and benefits of ownership: a theory of vertical and lateral integration. J. Polit. Econ. **94**(4), 691–719 (1986)
20. Hart, O., Moore, J.: Foundations of incomplete contracts. Rev. Econ. Stud. **66**(1), 115–138 (1999)
21. Williamson, O.: The logic of economic organization. J. Law Econ. Organ. **4**(1), 65–93 (1988)
22. Williamson, O.: The Economic Institutions of Capitalism: Firms, Markets, Relational Contracting. The Free Press, London (1985)
23. Klepper, R.: The management of partnering development in I/S outsourcing. J. Inf. Technol. **10**(4), 249–258 (1995)
24. Kern, T., Willcocks, L.: Exploring information technology outsourcing relationships: theory and practice. J. Strat. Inf. Syst. **9**(4), 321–350 (2000)
25. Perrin, B., Pervan, G.: IT outsourcing relationship management and performance measurement system effectiveness. In: Proceedings of 16th Australasian Conference on Information Systems. Association for Information Systems (2005)
26. Hodosi, G., Rembisch, J., Rickmo, R., Rusu, L.: Important factors in IT outsourcing relationship, a model development and verification in major national companies. In: Americas Conference on Information Systems (AMCIS) 2012 Proceedings, Paper 5. Association for Information Systems (2012)
27. Kim, S., Chung, Y.: Critical success factors for is outsourcing implementation from an interorganizational relationship perspective. J. Comput. Inf. Syst. **43**(4), 81–90 (2003)

28. Schmidt, N., Müller, M., Rosenkranz, C.: Identifying the giants: a social network analysis of the literature on information technology outsourcing relationships. In: Proceedings of Twenty-Third European Conference on Information Systems (ECIS), Association for Information Systems (2015)
29. Lee, J., Kim, Y.: Effect of partnership quality on IS outsourcing success: conceptual framework and empirical validation. J. Manag. Inf. Syst. 15(4), 29–61 (1999)
30. Lyons, P., Brennan, L.: A typology and meta-analysis of outsourcing relationship frame works. Strat. Outsourcing Int. J. 7(2), 135–172 (2014)
31. Blijleven, V., Gong, Y., Mehrsai, A., Koelemeijer, K.: Critical success factors for Lean implementation in IT outsourcing relationships: a multiple case study. Inf. Technol. People 32(3), 715–730 (2018)
32. Rhodes, J., Lok, P., Loh, W., Cheng, V.: Critical success factors in relationship management for services outsourcing. Serv. Bus. 10(1), 59–86 (2016)
33. Hodosi, G., Rusu, L., Choo, S.: Relationship for large multinational companies: a service buyer perspective. Int. J. Soc. Organ. Dyn. IT 2(3), 29–47 (2012)
34. Williamson, O.E.: Transaction cost economics. In: Schmalensee, R., Willig, R. (eds.) Handbook of Industrial Organization, vol. 1, pp. 135–182. Elsevier, Amsterdam, The Netherlands (1989)
35. Noordveld, P.: Conflict resolution in outsourcing. In: Jansen, S., Brinkkemper S., Collaboration in outsourcing. In: Technology, Work and Globalization. Palgrave Macmillan, London (2012)
36. Dwyer, F., Schurr, P., Sejo, O.: Developing buyer-seller relationships. J. Mark. 51(2), 11–27 (1987)
37. Goles, T.: The impact of the client-vendor relationship on information systems outsourcing success. Unpublished Ph.D. thesis. University of Houston, Houston (2001)
38. Mohr, J., Spekman, R.: Characteristics of partnership success: partnership attributes, communication behavior, and conflict resolution techniques. Strat. Manag. J. 15(2), 135–152 (1994)
39. Raghebi, Z., Hashemi, M.: A new trust evaluation method based on reliability of customer feedback for cloud computing. In: 10th International ISC Conference on Information Security and Cryptology (ISCISC), pp. 1–6. IEEE (2013)
40. Kern, T.: The gestalt of an information technology outsourcing relationship: an exploratory analysis. In: Proceedings of Eighteenth International Conference on Information Systems, pp. 37–58. Association for Information Systems (1997)
41. Denscombe, M.: The Good Research Guide: For Small-Scale Social Research Projects. McGraw-Hill Education, New York (2014)
42. Yin, R.: Case Study Research Design and Methods, 4th edn. Sage Publications Inc., Thousand Oaks (2009)
43. Park, J., Lee, J., Lee, H., Truex, D.: Exploring the impact of communication effectiveness on service quality, trust and relationship commitment in IT services. Int. J. Inf. Manag. 32(5), 459–468 (2012)
44. Oshri, I., Kotlarsky, J., Gerbasi, A.: Strategic innovation through outsourcing: the role of relational and contractual governance. J. Strat. Inf. Syst. 24(3), 203–216 (2015)
45. Linden, R., Schmidt, N., Rosenkranz, C.: Outsourcing 2.0: towards an innovation-driven process model for client-vendor relationships in information technology outsourcing. In: Oshri, I., Kotlarsky, J., Willcocks, L.P. (eds.) Global Sourcing 2017. LNBIP, vol. 306, pp. 39–64. Springer, Cham (2017). https://doi.org/10.1007/978-3-319-70305-3_3
46. Lacity, M.C., Willcocks, L.P., Rottman, J.W.: Global outsourcing of back office services: lessons, trends, and enduring challenges. Strat. Outsourcing Int. J. 1(1), 13–34 (2008)

Barriers in Business-IT Alignment in the Banking Sector in a Developing Country: A Case Study of Commercial Banks in the Gambia

Ebrima Jobarteh, Neha Agrawal, and Lazar Rusu[(✉)]

Department of Computer and Systems Sciences,
Stockholm University, Borgarfjordsgatan 12, 164 07 Kista, Sweden
ejobarteh5@gmail.com, corp.neha@gmail.com,
lrusu@dsv.su.se

Abstract. Business-IT Alignment (BITA) is still one of the top management concerns in many organizations due to its strategic benefits. Researchers have highlighted the importance of understanding the significance of BITA in improving organizational performance and gaining competitive advantage. BITA is a dynamic process, and organizations need to adjust it continuously. Moreover, there is still a need for new knowledge on the barriers in BITA in different organizations, like e.g., those from developing countries where were done a few research studies. Therefore, this research has focused on organizations from the banking sectors of The Gambia to identify the barriers in BITA. The research strategy used was survey research and the data was collected through semi-structured interviews combine with internal documents of the studied organizations and analyzed using thematic analysis. The study has identified in total 26 barriers in BITA from which eight are new barriers in BITA in the banking sector organizations of The Gambia. The results of the study contribute to BITA research and can help business and IT managers in attaining and sustaining business-IT alignment and improving their organizational performance.

Keywords: Business-IT alignment · Barriers · Banking sector · Developing country · Strategic alignment maturity model · The Gambia

1 Introduction

The survey on IT issues and trends, done by Society for Information Management in 2018, has found business-IT alignment (BITA) to be still a top management concern [1]. According to Luftman et al. [2, p. 69], "Business-IT alignment refers to applying Information Technology in an appropriate and timely way, in harmony with business strategies, goals and needs". In the opinion of Colton et al. [3, p. 94], there is still "a continuing need for researchers to adapt and extend our knowledge of what it means for IT to be aligned with business". The use of information and communications technologies (ICT) within the organization have enabled a high dependence on them and the need for it to be aligned with business strategy to gain maximum efficiency of the

M. Themistocleous and M. Papadaki (Eds.): EMCIS 2019, LNBIP 381, pp. 498–511, 2020.
https://doi.org/10.1007/978-3-030-44322-1_37

tool [4]. In this way, the organizations will maximize their profit on their IT expenditures. As the business environment is dynamic, to maintain and sustain competitive advantage among the competitors, companies need to modify their goals and strategies to adapt to the business environment. This requires proper and dynamic alignment of business and IT strategy to achieve the changing goals of the business. Therefore, it is needed to keep the changing needs of business organizations and IT aligned [1]. Furthermore, according to Peppard and Ward [5], today's organizations are significantly dependent on their information systems; and effective application of IT resources that serve a crucial role in industries that are highly dependent on it. The integration of IT is becoming an expected method of not only conducting business developments but additionally introducing opportunities for achieving competitive advantage [5]. Thus, business-IT alignment is the foremost requirement for the organization to focus on to gain competitive advantage among the competitors and to improve the performance of the organization operations. There are many barriers in business-IT alignment in organizations that have been addressed in the previous research studies [6–11]. However, it cannot be said that these are the only barriers in BITA that need to be handle and improve organizational performance in a dynamic business environment. Accordingly, the knowledge of IT and its tools are changing continuously [12], and it is said that business-IT alignment change over time and organizations must adjust to new IT innovation to maintain BITA [13, 14]. Therefore, BITA requires new research studies to add new knowledge, because the organizational and technological conditions constantly change [15] like e.g., the barriers in business-IT alignment in organizations from developing countries where were done a few research studies. To address this lack of knowledge this research study has looked to answer to the following research question "What are the barriers in business-IT alignment in the banking sector organizations of a developing country?", focusing on The Gambia.

2 Research Background

2.1 Importance of Business-IT Alignment in Organizations

In an annotated bibliography of Chan and Reich [16], the authors have identified 150 papers produced over more than twenty-five years about business-IT alignment. This shows that business-IT alignment becomes a necessity for organizations to achieve and maintain their position in the market and shows the strategic benefits [16–18]. The business and IT performance implications of alignment have been demonstrated empirically and through case studies, e.g. [16, 17]. It can be said, that the results support the hypothesis that those organizations successfully aligning their business strategy with the IT strategy will perform better than those that do not [16]. The BITA topic and executive roles have been well researched. Many reasons have come up to be responsible for the failure of business-IT alignment. Major reasons for business-IT alignment failure as related to executive roles include the incapability to maintain internal and external business/IT relationships, failure to execute change, lack of senior management support, and a culture that refuses to shift [19]. BITA is a condition that can be described as an optimized relation between business and IT to optimize the value of IT. However, for today's modern and dynamic organizations, the important question is not "why alignment is important?" but rather "how it can be achieved and measured" [7].

2.2   Barriers in Business-IT Alignment

Alignment of business-IT has focused on the strategic alignment by some researchers [8, 20, 21], however, there are different dimensions towards determining the business-IT alignment. There are previous research studies done on business-IT alignment addressing the operational alignment [22] as well strategic alignment, and tactical alignment [7] in which these researchers have mentioned the barriers in BITA at different organizational levels like Operational, Tactical, and Strategic.

Strategic Alignment Barriers. The strategic alignment of business-IT refers to the degree to which the business plans and strategy and IT plans and strategy complement each other to gain a competitive advantage [16]. The strategic alignment contains an identification of a technology portfolio that facilitates the business process in a way that it can gain a competitive advantage and increase revenue and reduce cycle time [16].

Tactical Alignment Barriers. Alignment context at the tactical level that is the "functional integration" between the IT side (IT architecture, IT management processes, and IT skill) and the business side (administrative infrastructure, processes and skills) for effective deployment of IT applications has been recognized to be very important [23]. In fact, when IT does not understand the business environment, IT will not be able to support and drive business in a successful manner.

Operational Alignment Barriers. There is a need to be a fit between IT resources and business to create business value from IT. Although most practices and researches have focused on strategic alignment to create a synchronization between IT and business plans among the executive team. According to Wagner and Weitzel [22], operational alignment is the bringing of strategic plans into everyday life and creating value from the daily operation is operational alignment [22]. Moreover, operational alignment is considered by Wagner and Weitzel [22] a very important aspect of BITA and translates the strategic alignment to actions in the form of daily routines, activities.

Barriers in Business-IT Alignment Identified in the Research Literature. In this research, the previously identified barriers and mention by researchers like [7, 22, 24] are classified at the strategic, tactical and operational levels and classified according to the six different criteria of Strategic Alignment Maturity Model (SAMM) of Luftman [25] and shown in Table 1.

Table 1. Barriers in business-IT alignment identified in the research literature

Organizational level	Previous researches of barriers in business-IT alignment	Luftman [25] criteria	Authors
Strategic	IT lacks the support of senior business executive	Communications	[7]
Tactical	The channels of communication not clear (formal and informal networks)		
Tactical	Communication goes through informal networks		[7]
Strategical	Lack of cross-business-unit interaction		[7]
Operational	Limited or lack of shared knowledge across departments		[22]
Operational	Cross-business-unit interaction is not available		[22]
Strategic	The value of IT is demonstrated poorly	Competency/Value Measurement	[7]
Tactical	There are not enough links between metrics and objectives of both IT and business		[7]
Tactical	Business sees the value of IT low		[7]
Tactical	Different systems cannot well optimize to use together		[7]
Tactical	Ambiguous understanding between espoused strategies, strategies use, and managerial actions		[7]
Strategic	Business and IT has lack of joint strategic planning and IT governance	Governance	[7]
Strategic	Insufficient input from IT in business strategic planning		[7]
Tactical	Governance is separated, and IT project is not well prioritized		[7]
Strategic	IT is not considered a strategic partner and the relationship is from one side	Partnership	[7]
Strategic	The relationship between business and IT has tense in some areas		[7]
Tactical	Uncertain roles of business and IT staff and expectation		[7]
Strategic	IT architecture provides high adaptability to business process but there is no integration at high levels	Scope and Architecture	[7]
Tactical	IT architecture and explanation of infrastructure unmatched		[7]
Tactical	Insufficient understanding of IT architecture at business		[7]
Tactical	IT architecture is not flexible		[7]
Strategic	Business people influence issues related to career development, changing decision and leading	Skills	[7]
Tactical	Lack of information feedback between business and IT		[7]
Operational	Lack of mutual trust and understanding between business and IT		[22]

The barriers in BITA presented in Table 1 are those that will form the basis for setting the questions for conducting the interviews in this research.

3 Research Methodology

According to Denscombe [26] surveys strategy is focusing on empirical data and can be used to collect both quantitative and qualitative data. To answer the research question, we have used survey strategy because we have looked to identify the barriers in business-IT alignment at different organizational levels, in three commercial banks (that were selected based on their availability to participate in this research) in The Gambia. The non-probability sampling was used as an exploratory sample and those selected as respondents are having expertise and experience in the research issue we have investigated [26]. To collect qualitative data in the studied organizations and from this exploratory sample we have used interviews with participants that have knowledge about business-IT alignment in their organizations. The data collection was done through online interviews that were conducted with different business and IT managers in these three commercial banks that are involved in their organizations at the decision making level in IT and business. The previous research concerning barriers in BITA in different organizations has been used to define the interview questions that were grouped on the six criteria of SAMM [25] (Communications; Competency/Value measurements; Governance; Partnership; Scope and Architecture; and Skills) and on the organizational levels as are shown in Table 1. The interviews had followed a semistructured format with open-ended questions to allow the respondents to talk about issues related to business-IT alignment. In total seven interviews were conducted with business and IT managers in three organizations of the banking sector in the Gambia (Bank A, Bank B and Bank C). Apart from the data collected through interviews, we have used different internal documents (like public reports that were available from these banks) in order to have multiple sources of evidence and assure data triangulation [27]. The information about the participants in the interviews, their position in the studied organization, date of the interviews and duration of the interviews are presented in Table 2.

Table 2. Information about participants, their position in the studied organization, date of the interviews and duration of the interviews

Participant	Position	Organization	Date of interview	Duration of interview
Interviewee 1	Assistant CFO	Bank A	18th April 2019	72 min
Interviewee 2	IT Manager	Bank B	19th April 2019	62 min
Interviewee 3	Head of E-Business	Bank B	23rd April 2019	52 min
Interviewee 4	Marketing Manager	Bank B	24th April 2019	47 min
Interviewee 5	Marketing Manager	Bank C	24th April 2019	58 min
Interviewee 6	Assistant Head of Business Development	Bank C	25th April 2019	47 min
Interviewee 7	IT Manager	Bank A	24th April 2019	49 min

In order to comply with the consent form that the respondents have signed before the interviews the name of the studied organizations as well other information that ca reveal the name of these organizations are not provided in this paper. The data collected in the studied organizations was analyzed by using thematic analysis [28]. The transcripts of the interviews have been coded and grouped in sub-themes and themes by classifying the relationship between codes, sub-themes, and themes based on the similarity, differences, and variations and finally generate the thematic map that is shown in Fig. 1.

4 Results and Discussion

The results of this research study are shown in the thematic map from Fig. 1, with the identified barriers in BITA in the banking sector organizations in The Gambia as a developing country. The research has identified 26 barriers in BITA that are represented by the sub-themes shown in Fig. 1 and divided under the six themes that are the criteria of SAMM model [25]. Some of these barriers are similar to the barriers in BITA identified in the previous studies (a number of 18 barriers in BITA) therefore these barriers will not be discussed in this paper only the new ones in number of eight which are shown in grey color in Fig. 1.

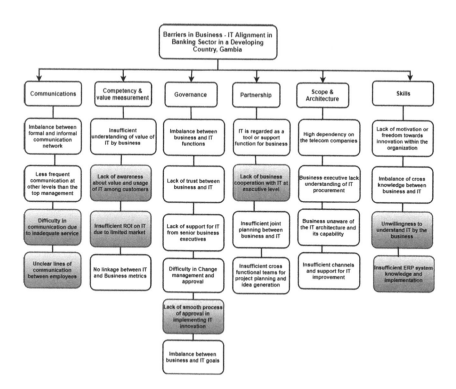

Fig. 1. Thematic map of the barriers in BITA in the banking sector of a developing country, The Gambia

The findings of this research are in total 26 barriers (from which we have eight new barriers) in BITA in the banking sector organizations of The Gambia. In Table 3 are presented the 26 barriers in BITA placed under the six main themes, and classified on the strategic, tactical and operational level, including the 8 new barriers in BITA that are highlighted in bold.

Table 3. Operational, strategic and tactical barriers in business-IT alignment identified in this research

Themes	Barriers in business-IT alignment	Organizational levels
Communications	Imbalance between formal and informal communication network	Tactical
	Less frequent communication at other levels than the top management	Strategic
	Difficulty in communication due to inadequate service	Tactical
	Unclear lines of communication between employees	Operational
	Insufficient understanding of value of IT by business	Tactical
Competency/Value Measurements	**Lack of awareness about value and usage of IT among customers**	Strategic
	Insufficient ROI on IT due to limited market	Operational
	No linkage between IT and Business Metrics	Strategic
Governance	Imbalance between business and IT functions	Tactical
	Lack of trust between business and IT	Operational
	Lack of support for IT from senior business executives	Strategic
	Difficulty in change management and approval	Tactical
	Lack of smooth process of approval in implementing IT innovation	Strategic
	Imbalance between business and IT goals	Tactical
Partnership	IT is regarded as a tool or support function for business	Strategic
	Lack of business cooperation with IT at executive level	Tactical
	Insufficient joint planning between business and IT	Strategic
	Insufficient cross functional teams for project planning and idea generation	Tactical
Scope & Architecture	High dependency on the telecom companies	Operational
	Business executive lack understanding of IT procurement	Tactical
	Insufficient channels and support for IT improvement	Strategic

(continued)

Table 3. (*continued*)

Themes	Barriers in business-IT alignment	Organizational levels
Skills	Lack of motivation or freedom towards innovation within the organization	Strategic
	Imbalance of cross knowledge between business and IT	Tactical
	Unwillingness to understand IT by the business	Operational
	Insufficient ERP system knowledge and implementation	Operational

The eight new barriers in BITA identified in the banking sector organizations of a developing country, like The Gambia are discussed below under the six themes.

In Communications theme, "*Difficulty in communication due to inadequate service*", is consider an operational barrier because interruption in communication within the organization as well as externally with the customers is affecting the business operations. The communication between staff using the service is a daily routine that supposedly converts the strategy into a daily routine [22], thus this barrier in BITA is at the operational level. If the formal network of communication gets affected because of interrupted service provided by the service provider than it would be even difficult to manage the day to day work and it must be working 24x7, otherwise will act as an operational barrier in BITA. Managing the service providers and make them provide uninterrupted service is a challenge for the business according to interviewee 5 and interviewee 7 and this a factor that hinders BITA.

"Internally the challenges we are facing will be if there is poor connectivity from our service providers. It hinders our process, […]" (Interviewee 5).

"… if those services are not efficient it might have an impact on the business because if you now have implement a solution and deliver it to the customers in many attempts they start having disruptions and the service due to poor internet services it can also create some issues." (Interviewee 7).

The strategy to overcome this barrier should be to maintain and create synchronization with the service provider, so the organization should make sure that the selected service provider would assure the proper service.

"*Unclear lines of communication between employees*", is consider a tactical barrier in BITA. This affects the cooperation between the staff, therefore, is consider a barrier in BITA at the tactical level [23]. If there is no clear communication among different level of organization, then there is a possibility of miscommunication among the staff, and it can lead to improper assignment and alignment of the task. According to interviewees 1 and 7 there is an unclear line of communication between fragmented units, and this a factor that hinders BITA.

"[…] is the responsibility of these managers to disseminate the information to their respective units. So, whether they do it or not, I don't know that…." (Interviewee 1).

"[...] So, it is not structured. Sometimes I call the head, sometimes I call the last person in the IT. Yeah. So, It is not structured is base [...] who is available there and who I think can solve that particular problem [...] I can call anyone." (Interviewee 1).

"... go around all the units to at least learn the way they run their business. It might not be sufficient [...] So it will be difficult to understand fully the way they operate." (Interviewee 7).

The strategy to overcome this barrier could be defining a proper communication line which is transparent for all the employees so that there will be no chance of miscommunication or misinterpretation among the employees at different levels.

In Competency/Value Measurements theme, *"lack of awareness about value and usage of IT among customers"* is consider a strategic barrier in BITA because the organization fails to make aware the customers about the innovations, their benefits, etc. thus the organization business strategy and IT strategy are failed to complement each other [16]. In the banking sector of The Gambia, one of the problems is customer's unawareness about the innovation according to interviewees 3, 5 and 7 and this hinders IT to grow and is a barrier in BITA.

"You can have a lot of IT products but if you don't know how to sell them is another thing. So people are queueing because they don't know that there is something very simple that they can do for them and they can use the IT products to save their time [...] We also have a mobile application, if you want to pay, and once you have your account details" (Interviewee 3).

"The level of illiteracy in The Gambia is very high, so most of the bank customers are not acquainted with technology and it's a challenge for them to use the App to do their transactions. Therefore, they embark more on the manual things for example coming to the bank for withdrawal money and buying things." (Interviewee 5).

In opinion of interviewee 7, the lack of awareness among customers demotivates the employees of the bank to present new innovative ideas and hinders the growth of the organization.

"...when you look at the number of people that are banking its ratio is very low. So, there are certain role off, if you want to role out now you must look at the number of people that might be using that. If the number is low than it might stop that project from being successful." (Interviewee 7).

The strategy to overcome this could be that the banks should organize some programs where the representative of the bank will spread awareness about the usage of new IT products and make them aware about the benefits of using those products.

"Insufficient ROI on IT due to limited market" is consider an operational barrier because IT is consider as a cost factor for the organization. When the IT strategy is known, there is a cooperation between staff; however, there is a lack of return in the daily operations of the IT investments [22]. It has been found that there are fewer opportunities for the expansion of IT because the introduction of a new IT product will be considered as cost factor instead of growth opportunity for the business. The IT investments should be consider as a long-term investment to get advantage from it and not to consider IT as cost that hinder BITA. The statements in the interviews depict these experiences among the IT managers and business managers as follows:

"They only see us as we are always spending money, we are always upgrading stuffs. For them we are wasting money." (Interviewee 1).

"Today in this country it's like more than 50% or 60% of the people don't have a bank account. Imagine people who do not have a bank account, you think they know anything about Internet banking or debit machine. They do not know that. Therefore, when you roll out the product you have to educate people why they should use the product in the first place, how will it benefit them and so forth. It's a constant challenge in this business." (Interviewee 6).

For this, the banks needs to understand that investments in new IT products will return all the IT investments, and also define new ways to attract their customers to use these IT products.

In Governance theme, *"Lack of smooth process of approval in implementing IT innovation"* is consider as a strategic barrier in BITA in getting the approval for implementing an innovative idea in the organization become of a tedious and lengthy process at the strategic level [16]. It has been found in this research that the banks follow a long process to get approval for a new idea to innovate from the executives. The implementation of the innovative idea is quite complicated. It is not a smooth line of communication between the senior management and general staff in motivating the staff to innovate in the way they work. The interviewees feel that the process of approving an innovative idea is hinder by the organization standard operating procedures (SOP) that is a barrier in BITA. Here are some statements from the interviewees.

"[…] personally, I have experienced it and they will say that no and this is how we do here, you have to follow the standard operation procedures (SOP). Existing organization SOP can be an obstacle to innovation…" (Interviewee 1).

"The freedom of innovation is there but it cannot come like that, it has to be reviewed and look into for details." (Interviewee 3).

For solving this, the banks should change its approval process concerning the new innovative ideas and their importance for their organizations.

In Partnership theme, *"Lack of business cooperation with IT at executive level"* is consider a tactical barrier because there is an imbalance between the IT and business staff at the executive level to manage the strategies of the organization [16]. According to this research, mostly, there are business executives at the top level, and therefore IT feels neglected at the executive level in the decision process. This result is distrust and no cooperation between business and IT, which work as a barrier in BITA. Here are some statements from the interviewees:

"Yes, we communicate with the IT department. Especially when we feel we need the IT team to implement the ideas, we have to communicate the ideas and make them know about the ideas." (Interviewee 6).

"… most of the senior managers come from accounting. Therefore, when an IT guy come with a product and we tell you this can make things easier […] (Interviewee 2).

"Yeah, they do involve us at a certain level when maybe they want to introduce something, but then they will go all the way to the implementation stage." (Interviewee 2).

To overcome this, the banking sector should give opportunities to IT to be present at the executive level and be equally as the business ate the top level of organization. This can facilitate cooperation between business and IT executives at the top level of organizations.

In Skills theme, *"Insufficient ERP system knowledge and its implementation"* is consider an operational barrier in BITA due to the fact the business grows in terms of innovation and customers and the daily routine of IT systems operations remains the same [22]. With the increase in IT products and customers, the data within the organization will also increase and then if the organization is not maintaining an ERP system, then it became difficult to align business and IT. An ERP system is a potential enabler of business-IT alignment that enable benefits like cost reduction, process standardization, productivity enhancement, workflow improvement, enhanced communication across departments, implementation of new business strategies in quick time responding to competitive dynamics, etc., for their organization and customers [29]. Here are some statements from the interviewees:

"No, we don't have ERP system." "[…] we don't have a separate system called ERP, that you are mentioning." (Interviewee 2).

"We have our internal systems it is... Our ATM we have a special unit that is controlling that system, they are in charge of that and they make sure that all the systems are working fine, we call them ATM custodians." (Interviewee 3).

"Unwillingness to understand IT by the business" is considered an operational barrier in BITA because of the lack of knowledge of business about IT that affects the functioning of the business [22]. The study been found that due to the lack of basic knowledge about IT, the business sometimes fails to serve the customers and they look towards IT only to solve this issue. The business units are not willing to learn about IT, because they believe that this is a technical issue and is the responsibility only of the IT department. An interviewee said that there is an unwillingness among the business staff to learn about IT even when they are forced to attend cross-functional trainings in IT:

"... if you don't have keen interest in it, you can't get anything on that. So, you must have keen interest." (Interviewee 4).

One of the IT managers said although he has advised his staff to teach the business unit about some of the IT functions and IT architecture but the business staff are not willing to learn about the IT function because they believe this is too technical.

"... It's like a brick wall. They don't want to know anything to do with IT." (Interviewee 2).

To overcome this, the business executives should involve their staff in more collaboration with IT department and continue to do the IT training of their business employees to acquire knowledge and keep themselves up to date in IT.

5   Conclusion

Business-IT alignment continues to be a top management concern among the executives in spite of the fact that organizations have difficulties in achieving BITA. Moreover, the lack of alignment between business and IT are among the reasons why organizations failed to maximize their return from IT investments. According to Chan & Reich [16], the presence of wide variety of variables that could influence BITA makes it important to carry out studies in different organizational and business environment settings. Therefore, it is still a need for new knowledge to identify the barriers in business-IT alignment in organizations from developing countries, where were done a few research studies.

Moreover, business-IT alignment requires a continuous adjustment to IT innovation and to both internal and external business environmental factors [30], and achieving business-IT alignment in these organizations requires maximizing the enablers and minimizing the inhibitors [24]. The research question that this research study has looked to address is *"What are the barriers in business-IT alignment in the banking sector organizations of a developing country?"* focusing on The Gambia. In this study, we have identified a number of 26 barriers in BITA in the banking sector organizations of a developing country like The Gambia including 8 new barriers like "Difficulty in communication due to inadequate service", "Unclear lines of communication between employees"; "Lack of awareness about value and usage of IT among customers"; "Insufficient ROI on IT due to limited market"; "Lack of business cooperation with IT at executive level"; "Lack of smooth process of approval in implementing IT innovation"; "Unwillingness to understand IT by the business"; and "Insufficient ERP system knowledge and implementation". In opinion of Luftman [31, p. 37] the evaluation of BITA status is "a fundamental step for an organization in identifying actions necessary for enhancing the congruent relationship between business and IT, and to ensure that IT is being leveraged to provide value to the business". On the other hand the process of business-IT alignment is continuous, and for an organization to achieve and sustain BITA there is a need for continuous adjustment of strategic, tactical, and operational alignment practices. Therefore, this research has looked to categorize the identified barriers in BITA at the strategic, tactical and operational level. The results of this study contribute to BITA research and can help business and IT managers to focus their efforts at different organizational levels in addressing the alignment gap, which will due to an improvement of their organizational performance.

Acknowledgements. The first author of this paper had a Swedish Institute scholarship that gave him the opportunity and support to do this research work during his master studies at Stockholm University.

References

1. Kappelman, L., Torres, R., McLean, E., Maurer, C., Johnson, V., Kim, K.: The 2018 SIM IT issues and trends study. MIS Q. Exec. **18**(1), 51–84 (2019)
2. Luftman, J.N., Bullen, C.V., Liao, D., Nash, E., Neumann, C.: Managing the Information Technology Resource: Leadership in the Information Age. Pearson/Prentice Hall, Upper Saddle River (2004)
3. Colton, T., Tallon, P., Sharma, R., Queiroz, M.: Strategic IT alignment: twenty five years on. J. Inf. Technol. **30**(2), 91–100 (2015)
4. Belalcázar, A., Díaz, J., Ron, M., Molinari, L.: Towards a strategic resilience of applications through the NIST cybersecurity framework and the strategic alignment model (SAM). In: Proceedings of 2017 International Conference on Information Systems and Computer Science, pp. 181–187. IEEE (2017)
5. Peppard, J., Ward, J.: The Strategic Management of Information Systems: Building a Digital Strategy, 4th edn. Wiley, Chichester (2016)

6. Gutierrez, A., Orozco, J., Serrano, A., Serrano, A.: Using tactical and operational factors to assess strategic alignment: an SME study. In: Proceedings of European and Mediterranean Conference on Information Systems (EMCIS), pp. 23–33. Association for Information Systems (2006)

7. El-Mekawy, M., Rusu, L., Perjons, E., Sedvall, K.-J.: Strategic and tactical business-IT alignment barriers in organizations acting in Sweden. Int. J. IT/Bus. Align. Gov. 6(2), 31–55 (2015)

8. Hiekkanen, K., Pekkala, A., Collin, J.: Improving strategic alignment: a case study. Inf. Resour. Manag. J. 28(4), 19–37 (2015)

9. Gbangou, L.P., Rusu, L.: Factors hindering business-IT alignment in the banking sector of a developing country. Procedia Comput. Sci. 100, 280–288 (2016)

10. Wang, J., Rusu, L.: Factors hindering business-IT alignment in small and medium enterprises in China. Procedia Comput. Sci. 138, 425–432 (2018)

11. Jonathan, G.M., Abdul-Salaam, A., Oluwasanmi, O., Rusu, L.: Business-IT alignment barriers in a public organisation: the case of federal inland revenue service of Nigeria. Int. J. Innov. Digit. Econ. (IJIDE) 9(1), 1–13 (2018)

12. Chege, S., Nyamboga, C., Wanyembi, G.: The relationship between the business-IT alignment maturity and the business performance for the banking industry in Kenya. Int. J. Technol. Syst. 3(1), 1–22 (2018)

13. Luftman, J.: Competing in the Information Age: Align in the Sand, 2nd edn. Oxford University Press, New York (2003)

14. Luftman, J., Lyytinen, K., Zvi, T.B.: Enhancing the measurement of IT business alignment and its influence on company performance. J. Inf. Technol. 32(1), 26–46 (2017)

15. Parappallil, J.J., Zarvic, N., Thomas, O.: A context and content reflection on business-IT alignment research. Int. J. IT/Bus. Align. Gov. (IJITBAG) 3(2), 21–37 (2012)

16. Chan, Y.E., Reich, B.H.: IT alignment: what have we learned? J. Inf. Technol. 22(4), 297–315 (2007)

17. Kearns, G.S., Lederer, A.L.: A resource-based view of strategic IT alignment: how knowledge sharing creates competitive advantage. Decis. Sci. 34(1), 1–29 (2003)

18. Leonard, J., Seddon, P.: A meta-model of alignment. Commun. Assoc. Inf. Syst. 31(11), 230–259 (2012)

19. Weiss, J.W., Anderson, D.: Aligning technology and business strategy: issues & frameworks, a field study of 15 companies. In: Proceedings of the 37th Hawaii International Conference on System Sciences, pp. 1–10. IEEE (2004)

20. Henderson, J.C., Venkatraman, H.: Strategic alignment: leveraging information technology for transforming organizations. IBM Syst. J. 32(1), 472–484 (1993)

21. Kurti, I., Barolli, E., Sevrani, K.: Critical success factors for business – IT alignment: a review of current research. Rom. Econ. Bus. Rev. 8(3), 79–97 (2017)

22. Wagner, H.-T., Weitzel, T.: How to achieve operational business-IT alignment: insights from a global aerospace firm. MIS Q. Exec. 11(1), 25–36 (2012)

23. Tarafdar, M., Qrunfleh, S.: IT-business alignment: a two-level analysis. Inf. Syst. Manag. 26(4), 338–349 (2014)

24. Tarafdar, M., Qrunfleh, S.: Examining tactical information technology-business alignment. J. Comput. Inf. Syst. 50(4), 107–116 (2010)

25. Luftman, J.: Assessing business-IT alignment maturity. Commun. Assoc. Inf. Syst. 4(14), 1–51 (2000)

26. Denscombe, M.: The Good Research Guide: For Small-Scale Social Research Projects. Open University Press, Maidenhead (2014)
27. Yin, R.: Case Study Research Design and Methods, 4th edn. Sage Publications Inc, Thousand Oaks (2009)
28. Braun, V., Clarke, V.: Using thematic analysis in psychology. Qual. Res. Psychol. 3(2), 77–101 (2006)
29. Kanna, K.: How an ERP system helps align IT with business strategy. https://www.3i-infotech.com/erp-system-helps-align-business-strategy/. Accessed 15 May 2019
30. Luftman, J., Brier, T.: Achieving and sustaining business-IT alignment. Calif. Manag. Rev. 42(1), 109–122 (1999)
31. Luftman, J., Lyytinen, K., Zvi, T.: Enhancing the measurement of information technology (IT) business alignment and its influence on company performance. J. Inf. Technol. 32(1), 26–46 (2017)

The Impact of Knowledge Sharing and Innovation Performance on the Organization – Moderating by Innovation Awards

Amal Alhassani and Khalid Almarri[✉]

Faculty of Business and Law, The British University in Dubai, Dubai, UAE
Khalid.almarri@buid.ac.ae

Abstract. Purpose - This study examines the relationship between knowledge sharing, innovation performance and achievement of the organizations that moderated by innovation awards. Design/methodology/approach - Appropriate quantitative techniques used to analyze the subject. The samples include qualified online - questionnaires panel respondents from employees working at project management departments in different organizations in the United Arab Emirates (UAE). The SPSS has been used to analysis the data. Knowledge sharing has been considered as the dependent variable, innovation awards is the moderator variable, and both innovation and firm are the independent variables findings. The results of the study show the significant effect of the moderator variable "innovation award" in the development and performance of the firm. The clarification of the regression analysis considers an advanced level of the variability in knowledge sharing as a dependent variable once involving the mediator variable "in the firm model. Thus, the firms can consider the innovation awards, since it is a valid and effective factor for development. Research limitations/implications - Include only governmental sector. Practical implications - The study results will be of immense benefit to develop the culture of knowledge sharing for the company in the market. Thus, adaptation of innovative techniques is also important for the satisfaction of the employees especially if they are in different projects. Originality/value - This paper is an effort to start studying the impact of innovation awards in the organizations which is not so rich in the academic literature. This study provides an applied data to the comparatively unexplored research area.

Keywords: Knowledge sharing · Innovation · Innovation awards · Firm performance

1 Introduction

Knowledge is extremely necessary as one of a major subject of the strategic resource for the businesses and firms within the market [1]. However, knowledge sharing is a standout amongst the most critical constructs in the firms because it's the heart of organization performance and employees are the main driver of knowledge and information [2].

© Springer Nature Switzerland AG 2020
M. Themistocleous and M. Papadaki (Eds.): EMCIS 2019, LNBIP 381, pp. 512–523, 2020.
https://doi.org/10.1007/978-3-030-44322-1_38

Sharing of knowledge have both opportunities and challenges to any counties plan to transition from the nature resources base to new creation system focusing on technology and innovation. The study of [3] pointed out, learning economy is very important specially if its focus on learning the process of knowledge and higher education can play a big role on that because the higher the level of knowledge among students in universities will simply discover the matter within the early stage to resolved.

The purpose of this paper is examining the relationship between knowledge sharing, innovation and the performance of the organizations that moderated by innovation awards or prizes. The quantitative approach was implemented in this research and an electronic survey has been used to distributing the questions. The sample of the study was chosen from a different organization and the employees are working at project management departments. The SPSS program has been selected to analyze the data collection for this study.

In the section of literature review, a four core concepts have been adopted to explain the significant relationship between knowledge sharing process, innovation award, innovation performance and organization achievement. The section also includes the hypotheses depend on the research model that design for this study.

There are some objectives that need to be highlighted as following:

- Implementing a clear sharing knowledge process in the organizations as an important factor.
- The need of having innovation services in operation process in the firms.
- Understanding the connection between sharing knowledge, innovation, and organization.
- Identify the importance of having innovation award.

In conclusion, the study will examine the impact of implementing some award or prizes competition in the organizations such as excellence or innovation awards and the advantage of winning on employees. However, using innovation service to implement this kind of environment with an awareness of the importance of knowledge sharing will raise some challenges in the firm. Furthermore, the results of the study show a significant effect of the moderator variable "innovation award" in the development and performance of the firm. The clarification of the regression analysis considers an advanced level of the variability in knowledge sharing as a dependent variable once involving the mediator variable in the firm model. Thus, the firms can consider the innovation awards, since it is a valid and effective factor for development.

2 Literature Review and Hypothesis Development

2.1 The Relationship Between Knowledge Sharing, Innovation Performance, and Innovation Awards

Knowledge is extremely necessary as one of a major subject of the strategic resource for the businesses and firms within the market [1] and there are many explanations in the literature for sharing knowledge. For instance, [4–6] clarify the meaning of knowledge sharing as the familiar communication process or the social culture that includes the sharing of the information between the employees in the workplace which is a very important resource that help to improve the productivity of the firms. In this vein [2], the activities of sharing knowledge process between employees can be an opportunity for the firm to progressing better to meet the customers' needs which is priority for the organizational performance. Those activists can also become an advantage for the organization because it is creating a lot of solutions that can help to improve the level of competition in the market.

The culture of the organization is very significant to recognize the way of using the knowledge sharing internal or external between the employees. According to [7], P., 2009, the newly research on organizational knowledge leaning found that the cultural characteristic of the employees affects the way of knowledge sharing. At the same time, changing the organizational environment become very important for the performance and that could happen easily if the organizations rise the level of the knowledge and learning in the work process [8].

Many scholars studied the sharing knowledge process like [6, 9–11]. They mention that Knowledge sharing process including two main concepts, the internal and external knowledge. The internal knowledge (donating) as bringing knowledge within the organization and its related to employees sharing their experience and activities with their colleagues such as solving problem and decision making. While, the external knowledge (collecting) is a getting or receiving new knowledge from the community, other organizations or strategic partners in the firm. Those concepts support and increase the innovation performance and innovation capability of the organization.

According to the above literature, there are many theories to support and test the connection among knowledge sharing and innovation performance [6, 11]. For example, a study of [12] found that its required to have a professional knowledge sharing for the innovation performance need in the organization. Moreover, a strong construction between innovation performance and knowledge sharing can happened when the organizations have a trust relationship between each other in the business market. In a related vein, there is a noteworthy impact with the following three contents: sharing knowledge, innovation and firm performance [13].

Recently, most of the governments and organizations are adopting the system of awarding the work process to improve their performance or achievement in the market. The awards and prizes have been designing to fit different criteria that manly created for certain department or unit in the organization. Each organization have a target from this award such as aiming to increase the revenue, or improving the quality standard of the work method, or improving the products and service. From this point view, the award program can prepare the firms and the country to be ready for the future knowledge cities as there is a clear vision of the relationship between the innovation awards and the innovation performance [14].

Based on [15] research study, there is a concern of implementing the innovation awards or prizes in the organization even sometime there is a significant requirement to have this kinds of prizes as a part of strategic planning or a target that need to be achieved for development the performance of the organization. The concern is how to involve the employees to participate in and succeed. To make this clear, there is a positive and negative impact of the awards in the organization which most of the staff are aware of it and its related to innovation environment of the firm.

Accordingly, the more participating of the staff in a culture of sharing knowledge process and supported by innovation awards, the more disposed to innovation performance will be found. This thinking prompts the following hypotheses:

H1. The Internal knowledge sharing process (Collecting Knowledge) on the organization will have a significant positive effect on innovation performance.

H1a. The positive influence of internal knowledge on innovation performance is moderated by innovation awards that lead the organization to be more successful.

H2: The External knowledge sharing process (Donating Knowledge) on the organization will have a significant positive effect on innovation performance.

H2a. The positive influence of external knowledge on innovation performance is moderated by innovation awards that lead the organization to be more successful.

2.2   The Relationship Between Innovation Performance and Company Achievement (Performance, Value and Growth)

The concept of innovation becomes one of the required elements that closely linked with sharing and creative knowledge in the firm. Moreover, innovation provides better and high growth performance that strongly supports competitiveness [16]. Furthermore, the innovation can generate a new thing for the firms or modified existence thing too [10]. In this vein, a study by [6] and [17] agree with the importation of having both knowledge sharing and innovation in the organization otherwise, there is no growth or competitiveness process will happen in this organization.

According to [18] and [19], the important section for the organization and leads to business performance is an open innovation which has five states process and knowledge is one of them. Furthermore, the innovation performance is the outcome of all the process in enterprise and it helps to understand the achievement of the organization through this performance For instance, a study by [20] was highlighting the significant influence of network competency on knowledge sharing at the organization and it can increase the innovation performance as well.

Based on [21] the organization prefers to hire knowledge people with a good qualification to have a successful firm. Thus, understanding the organizational culture that related to knowledge sharing is very importation for the firms and employees. The impact of vision and goals of the organization can lead to a clear and trust relationship between the employees and positive effect on sharing knowledge capabilities [2].

On the other hand, a study by [22] found a various organizational operation factor supporting knowledge sharing in the firms and it's important to know to understand the effect of each factors such as top managers support (leadership support), communication support (internal or external) and continuous learning for employees (learning and training support).

Many scholars contribute to studying the link between the age or experience of the organization and innovation performance such as [23] and [24]. Thus, the older firm can have more advantage to achieve better knowledge, innovation process and performance of the organizations, while the new or younger firms will need more experiences to know to use the innovation in a better way as the oldest firms. In fact, the more innovation performance and knowledge sharing used in the organization, the high growth and performance will be achieved for the firms in the business market.

Following the research study of [25], it was a provide the positive outcome of innovation award on the firm's achievement. Thus, there is a link between innovation award, growth and value through innovation performance.

Base on the above explanations, the proposed hypothesis innovation performance below created to assist as a mediator between knowledge sharing that supported with the award, and the organization achievements (organization value, organization performance, organization growth):

H3. The innovation performance that supported by excellence/innovation awards will have a significant positive effect on organization value.

H4. The innovation performance that supported by excellence/innovation awards will have a significant positive effect on organization performance.

H5. The innovation performance that supported by excellence/innovation awards will have a significant positive effect on organization growth.

3   Research Methodology

3.1   Sample and Data Collection

To investigate the connection between three concepts; knowledge sharing, innovation, and organizational achievement through innovation awards. This study implemented a quantitative approach by using a questionnaire that managed through online system (Google Form) during two months, from June to July 2018 (Appendix 1). The population that has been targeted are all employees working in project management departments in different organizations in the governmental sector in the UAE. It's mainly based on a study of knowledge and innovation of a population of 10,000 people who are working in the field of project management departments. It is not feasible to conduct a study of 10,000 people by considering each of their responses. This will give rise to both time and money constraints. Thus, a sample of 370 people has been considered for the study. A survey questionnaire was prepared and distributed to 370 people selected randomly out of which 152 responses were returned. The analysis in this case will be performed based on these 152 responses. The questionnaire as mention above, was distributed to 370 employees as a sample size with Confidence Level 95% and Margin of Error is 5%. Therefore, only 152 from the total sample size are accepted and responded to this survey. The arrangement of this questionnaire includes the main contact of the research study, for example its cover knowledge sharing, awards (innovation or excellence), the innovation performance and achievement of the organizations such as growth, value, and performance. The questionnaire of this study containing 38 questions consisting of 6 questions for demographic and occupational variables, while the remaining 32 questions covered the core variables of the conceptual model of the study. The variables were measured in the dependent and independent variables by using the five-point Likert scales that ranging from 1 (strongly disagree) to 5 (5 = strongly agree) for the questions. The demographic items were exception from this scale. The information was collected on the demographic profile of the respondents and additionally on other attributes such as knowledge sharing (both internal and external), innovation awards, innovation performance and firm performance. Knowledge sharing has been considered as the dependent variable, innovation awards are the moderator variable and innovation performance and firm performance are the independent variables. Several questions were asked to the selected employees under each of the variable names specified. Thus, in order to consider each of the variables, a median of the scores given by the respondents have been considered. For the independent variable, knowledge sharing, the sum of internal knowledge sharing, and external knowledge sharing has been considered.

3.2   Research Constructs

Base on the above literature review, a suitable measure for the construction is presented in the conceptual model as Fig. 1. This model is valid and with a success utilized in previous studies were acknowledged and adapted for this study which will help to answer the research queries as well as analyzing the hypotheses. Also, the theoretical model below is displaying the impact of the connection among to knowledge sharing, innovation performance and the achievement of the organizations (growth, performance, and value) that moderated by innovation awards.

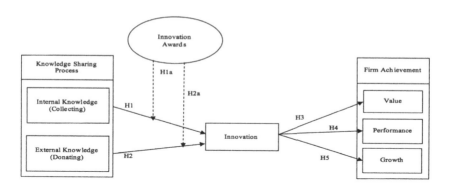

Fig. 1. Conceptual framework

4   Analysis and Findings

This section will be presenting the result of the data collection that has been analyzed by using IBM Statistical Package for Social Sciences (SPSS software) and aims to answer if there is an impact of knowledge sharing that moderated by innovation awards on the innovation and organization performances. There is some statistical test has been used in this paper such as descriptive statistics, reliability test (Cronbach's Alpha) and regression analysis test.

4.1 Descriptive Statistics

The demographic factors of the 152 includes their gender, nationality, age, education, the category of the job and the experiences years. Among the participating 152 respondents, 90 were male and 62 were female. Thus, there are 59.2% responses from the male and 40.8 responses from the females. Moreover, most of the employees in the government sectors are from the UAE followed by Egypt, Syria and India. There are also employees belonging to other nations but to a very less number. On the opposite hand, the age of most staff is between 20 to 39 years old. Most of them are completed their bachelor's degree and just a few of them completed masters' degree. Moreover, most of the staff are working in a senior position with experience range between 9 to 15 years.

Additionally, the descriptive analysis has been performed on the independent variables, dependent variable and the moderator variable. As it can be seen from the analysis that all the variables have a mean rating score close to each other and which is quite high. The standard deviation for the scores is quite close to one which indicates that the scores given by the respondents on the chosen issues are quite close to the average value. Thus, it can be said that most of the employees have given very high ratings. 50% of the people have rated 4 or higher in each of the aspects and most of the people have rated 4 at the aspects.

The next analysis that will be performed is the correlation analysis between all the selected variables (Table 1). The variable knowledge sharing has a strong association with the other variables, moderator, firm value, performance and growth. Thus, these factors can be considered for predicting the knowledge sharing between the employees.

Table 1. Correlations

		Moderator	Value	Performance	Growth	Knowledge_Sharing
Moderator	Pearson correlation	1	.732**	.566**	.643**	.774**
	Sig. (2-tailed)		.000	.000	.000	.000
	N	152	152	152	152	152
Value	Pearson correlation	.732**	1	.612**	.680**	.718**
	Sig. (2-tailed)	.000		.000	.000	.000
	N	152	152	152	152	152
Performance	Pearson correlation	.566**	.612**	1	.592**	.600**
	Sig. (2-tailed)	.000	.000		.000	.000
	N	152	152	152	152	152
Growth	Pearson correlation	.643**	.680**	.592**	1	.640**
	Sig. (2-tailed)	.000	.000	.000		.000
	N	152	152	152	152	152
Knowledge_Sharing	Pearson correlation	.774**	.718**	.600**	.640**	1
	Sig. (2-tailed)	.000	.000	.000	.000	
	N	152	152	152	152	152

**Correlation is significant at the 0.01 level (2-tailed).

4.2   Regression Analysis

The regression analysis has been finalized in this paper to investigate the relationship between the three main variables; knowledge sharing, innovation award, and firm performance. The following null and alternative hypothesis can be framed in order to run the analysis.

> *Alternate Hypothesis (H1):* Innovation award toward knowledge sharing will influence the firm performance.
> *Null Hypothesis (H0):* Innovation award toward knowledge sharing has no influence on the firm performance.

The multiple regression equation that can show the relationship of the knowledge sharing with growth, performance and value of the firm in the presence and the absence of the moderator variable (Innovation awards) are given as follows:

> *Knowledge Sharing = 1.310 + (0.883 * Value) + (0.320 * Performance)*
> *+ (0.398 * Growth)*
> *Knowledge Sharing = 1.120 + (0.426 * Value) + (0.226 * Performance)*
> *+ (0.205 * Growth) + (0.806 * Innovation Awards).*

The coefficient of R^2 (Coefficient of determination) for the first model, in the absence of the moderator variable has been found to be 0.580. This factor explained 58% of the variability in the knowledge sharing in the absence of the moderator variable innovation awards. On the other hand, the coefficient of R^2 (Coefficient of determination) for the second model, in the presence of the moderator variable has been found to be 0.670. This factor explained 67% of the variability in the knowledge sharing in the presence of the moderator variable innovation awards. Thus, the second model will be considered as a much better model in the prediction of knowledge sharing.

From the ANOVA in Table 2 and the model summary in Table 3, the significance value obtained is well below the stated 5% level. Thus, it can be said that the models are useful enough in predicting the response. Thus, the null hypothesis stated previously is rejected. Moving to the value of the VIF (Variance Inflation Factor), it can be seen clearly that the value lies within 5, which indicates that there is no problem of multicollinearity in the problem. The 95% of the confidence intervals for the slopes, β i, of the population in the regression line that refer to innovation awards have been obtained and provided in Table 3.

Table 2. ANOVA

Model		Sum of squares	df	Mean square	F	Sig.
1	Regression	349.302	3	116.434	68.087	.000[b]
	Residual	253.093	148	1.1710		
	Total	602.395	151			
2	Regression	403.333	4	100.833	74.462	.000[c]
	Residual	199.062	147	1.354		
	Total	602.395	151			

[a]Dependent Variable: Knowledge Sharing
[b]Predictors: (Constant), Growth, Performance, Value
[c]Predictors: (Constant), Growth, Performance, Value, Moderator.

Table 3. Coefficients[a]

Model		Unstandardized coefficients		Standardized coefficients	t	Sig.	95.0% confidence interval for B		Collinearity statistics	
		B	Std. error	Beta			Lower bound	Upper bound	Tolerance	VIF
1	(Constant)	1.310	.429		3.055	.003	.463	2.157		
	Value	.883	.153	.449	5.785	.000	.582	1.185	.470	2.216
	Performance	.320	.117	.194	2.744	.007	.090	.551	.567	1.762
	Growth	.398	.138	.220	2.886	.004	.125	.670	.488	2.047
2	(Constant)	1.120	.383		2.927	.004	.364	1.877		
	Value	.426	.154	.217	2.766	.006	.122	.730	.366	2.730
	Performance	.226	.105	.137	2.157	.033	.019	.433	.566	1.798
	Growth	.205	.126	.113	1.620	.107	−.045	.454	.460	2.175
	Moderator	.806	.128	.464	6.317	.000	.554	1.058	.416	2.405

[a]Dependent Variable: Knowledge_Sharing

5 Discussion

In order to conduct this research, at first, descriptive analysis of the variables has been conducted. This has been important as the validity of the data is important to evaluate. The analysis needs to be conducted with valid data. Thus, for the test of validity of the data, the descriptive analysis has been conducted to understand the shape and distribution of the data. The results have shown that there is no reason to identify the data as invalid.

The variables that are mostly considered for the analysis are innovation awards (Moderator variable), knowledge sharing (dependent variable) and independent variables such as value, performance and growth of the firm. The association of the variables with the dependent variable is the most important event that must be checked. If there is no relationship connotation among an independent variable and a dependent variable, then no need to consider that variable in the prediction model. In this matter, the knowledge sharing as an independent variable has a positive correlation with the independent variables as well as with the moderator variable. Thus, all the variables are important to be considered for testing the impact of knowledge sharing on the firm's performance.

It's seen that the high loadings variables in factor 1 are seen to be related to the understanding the need and initiative to facilitate in nurturing innovation. Thus, one factor could be related with the Recognizing need for innovation. The second factor seems to be related to variables which come together to represent the attitude towards culturing innovative solutions through knowledge sharing and seeking out competent employees and partnerships through Internal Knowledge Sharing. The third factor seems to consist of variables with high factor loadings which together seem to speak about inter and intra organizational communication to facilitate external knowledge sharing. The fourth factor consists of variables that speak about whether and how practicing innovativeness could lead to better products, services, and solutions Innovative Solutions. The fifth and final factor seems to have consisted of variables with high factor loadings which together seem to speak about the encouragement of innovation and its role in strategy formation Strategic commitment.

The condition of the firm is represented by the value of the firm, the achievement of the firm as well as with the growth of the firm. As an external factor and moderator variable in the model, the innovation award is expected to force an influence in development of the firm. From the regression analysis of the both the models, with the mediator and without the mediator, it has been observed that the explanation of variability in the dependent variable knowledge sharing is much higher when the mediator variable is involved in the model. Thus, it can be said that, innovation award is a very important factor. This factor should also be considered for development for the development of a firm. Thus, the preparedness of the employees to participating in sharing work, sharing knowledge and gathering it from others has a significant relationship with the innovation capability of a firm.

Practical Implication
There are sensible implications of the results obtained in this paper. These results can be useful to different companies as with the help of these results, the companies can develop the culture of sharing of knowledge. The factors that are mainly responsible for the enhancement of the innovation capability by sharing of knowledge of a company must have complete focus on. This will also be helpful in increasing the shares of a company in the market and will also enhance the performance of the company. There should be an arrangement of platforms by the organizations in which the employees will be having complete freedom in sharing the expertise they possess, their thoughts, views, and opinions about the companies. The employees might also have some important information at times that can be responsible for the growth of the individual as well as the company. The opportunity of conducting interactive sessions with the employees is also important. In these sessions, the authority can bring more confidence in the employees by sharing motivational thoughts and encouraging them.

6   Conclusion

This analysis acknowledges that few studies have examined the impact of innovation awards or prizes within the organization. Indeed, this research discovered the relationship between knowledge sharing process, innovation performance and firm achievement that moderated by innovation awards or prizes. The research confirms that innovation awards and knowledge sharing process contribute to firm's achievement through the awards

The results obtained from this study have shown that all the processes performed by the individuals have an association with the process of knowledge sharing. The behaviour in sharing knowledge has been influenced by the enjoyment that is obtained by providing help to others. The enjoyment of the employees leads to their job satisfaction and it has been observed that this satisfaction has a positive influence towards the knowledge sharing. Thus, the managers need to keep in mind that the enjoyment of the employees must be maintained and increased. The happier the employees are, the more they will be interested in helping others with the problems they face. This will be helpful for the growth of the organization. Adaptation of innovative techniques are also important for the satisfaction of the employees. While performing any work, the workload of the employees can be reduced if newer technologies are adopted by the companies.

The most updated software will reduce the workload of the employees and make the process faster. The employee can work on more projects if the work spent on each is reduced. This will be satisfactory for the employees as they will not have to sit with one work for a longer time and can work on various tasks. This will also be beneficial for the company as more work will be done within a lesser time. This will increase the productivity of the companies. The employees should be given proper training to develop their skills. Idea of awareness should also be incorporated in them. Moreover, sharing of these knowledges are very important for the organization especially if its supported by innovation awards.

In conclusion, in a company there are multiple departments and a lot of employees work in each of the departments. The employees in other departments might also have some ideas for the development of the departments in which they do not work for. These ideas might also be effective for the development of departments in an organization. Thus, knowledge sharing is extremely important for an organization and therefore the factors that are known to be influencing the knowledge sharing must be acknowledged by the organizations.

References

1. Hadad, S.: Strategies for developing knowledge economy in Romania. Manag. Mark. **12**(3), 416–430 (2017). http://dx.doi.org.ezproxy.uaeu.ac.ae/10.1515/mmcks-2017-0025
2. Kim, S., Lee, H.: The Impact of organizational context and information technology on employee knowledge-sharing capabilities. Pub. Adm. Rev. **66**(3), 370–385 (2006). https://doi.org/10.1111/j.1540-6210.2006.00595.x
3. Paunica, M., et al.: The role of higher education in a dynamic knowledge-driven economy. Econ. Manag. Finan. Mark. **6**(1), 414–419 (2011)
4. Teh, P., Sun, H.: Knowledge sharing, job attitudes and organisational citizenship behaviour. Ind. Manag. Data Syst. **112**(1), 64–82 (2012). https://doi.org/10.1108/02635571211193644
5. Wang, Z., Wang, N.: Knowledge sharing, innovation and firm performance. Expert Syst. Appl. **39**(10), 8899–8908 (2012). https://doi.org/10.1016/j.eswa.2012.02.017
6. Yeşil, S., et al.: Knowledge sharing process, innovation capability and innovation performance: an empirical study. Procedia – Soc. Behav. Sci. **75**, 217–225 (2013). https://doi.org/10.1016/j.sbspro.2013.04.025
7. Alothman, F.A., Busch, P.: Development of a critical factors model for the knowledge economy in Saudi Arabia. In: Australian Information Security Management Conference, p. 15 (2009)
8. Harrison, R.T., Leitch, C.M.: Learning and organization in the knowledge-based information economy: initial findings from a participatory action research case study. Br. J. Manag. **11**(2), 103–119 (2003). https://doi.org/10.1111/1467-8551.00154
9. Lin, H.: Knowledge sharing and firm innovation capability: an empirical study. Int. J. Manpow. **28**(3/4), 315–332 (2007). https://doi.org/10.1108/01437720710755272
10. Moon, H., Lee, C.: The mediating effect of knowledge-sharing processes on organizational cultural factors and knowledge management effectiveness. Perform. Improv. Q. **26**(4), 25–52 (2014). https://doi.org/10.1002/piq.21161

11. Bulutlar, F., Kamaşak, R.: The influence of knowledge sharing on innovation. Eur. Bus. Rev. **22**(3), 306–317 (2010). https://doi.org/10.1108/09555341011040994

12. Han, Y., Chen, G.: The relationship between knowledge sharing capability and innovation performance within industrial clusters: evidence from China. J. Chin. Econ. Foreign Trade Stud. **11**(1), 32–48 (2017). https://doi.org/10.1108/JCEFTS-06-2017-0018

13. Wang, Z., et al.: From knowledge sharing to firm performance: a predictive model comparison. J. Bus. Res. **69**(10), 4650–4658 (2016). https://doi.org/10.1016/j.jbusres.2016.03.055

14. Makkonen, T., Inkinen, T.: Innovation quality in knowledge cities: empirical evidence of innovation award competitions in Finland. Expert Syst. Appl. **41**(12), 5597–5604 (2014). https://doi.org/10.1016/j.eswa.2014.02.010

15. Rosenblatt, M.: The use of innovation awards in the public sector: individual and organizational perspectives. Innov. Manag. Pol. Pract. **13**(2), 207–219 (2011)

16. Aramburu, N., et al.: Knowledge sharing and innovation performance: a comparison between high-tech and low-tech companies. J. Intellect. Cap. **10**(1), 22–36 (2009). https://doi.org/10.1007/s40685-016-0032-9

17. Kamasak, R., et al.: Is the relationship between innovation performance and knowledge management contingent on environmental dynamism and learning capability? Evidence from a turbulent market. Bus. Res. **9**(2), 229–253 (2016). https://doi.org/10.1007/s40685-016-0032-9

18. Hadad, S.: Knowledge economy: characteristics and dimensions. Manag. Dyn. Knowl. Econ. **5**(2), 203–225 (2017). http://dx.doi.org.ezproxy.uaeu.ac.ae/10.25019/MDKE/5.2.03

19. Hagedoorn, J., Cloodt, M.: Measuring innovative performance: is there an advantage in using multiple indicators? Res. Pol. **32**(8), 1365–1379 (2003). https://doi.org/10.1016/S0048-7333(02)00137-3

20. Jian, Z., Wang, C.: The impacts of network competence, knowledge sharing on service innovation performance: moderating role of relationship quality. J. Ind. Eng. Manag. **6**(1). http://dx.doi.org.ezproxy.uaeu.ac.ae/10.3926/jiem.659

21. Jasimuddin, S.M., Zhang, Z. (Justin): Knowledge management strategy and organizational culture. J. Oper. Res. Soc. **65**(10), 1490–1500 (2014). http://dx.doi.org.ezproxy.uaeu.ac.ae/10.1057/jors.2013.101

22. Oyemomi, O., et al.: How knowledge sharing and business process contribute to organizational performance: using the fsQCA approach. J. Bus. Res. **69**(11), 5222–5227 (2016). https://doi.org/10.1016/j.jbusres.2016.04.116

23. Coad, A., et al.: Innovation and firm growth: does firm age play a role? - ScienceDirect (2015). https://www.sciencedirect.com/science/article/pii/S0048733315001687. Accessed 27 June 2018

24. Price, D.P., et al.: The relationship between innovation, knowledge, and performance in family and non-family firms: an analysis of SMEs. J. Innov. Entrep. **2**, 14 (2013). https://doi.org/10.1186/2192-5372-2-14

25. Nicolau, J.L., Santa-María, M.J.: Communicating excellence in innovation. Econ. Lett. **118**(1), 87–90 (2013). https://doi.org/10.1016/j.econlet.2012.09.025

The Impact of Cognitive Process Types on the Success of Exploratory Projects

Nahed Aldhaheri and Khalid Almarri[✉]

Faculty of Business and Law, The British University in Dubai, Dubai, UAE
Khalid.almarri@buid.ac.ae

Abstract. The purpose of this study was to understand the type of cognitive process used in exploratory projects. To achieve the study objective, the study relied on exploratory research design with a focus on historical case studies; the Manhattan Project and the Polaris Project. The study findings revealed that management of innovative projects relies on different aspects. It was also observed that design theory remains to be an essential tool in successful project management. The concept is perceived to be a necessary instrument, as it helps in creation of new knowledge while enabling project stakeholders to learn new aspects.

Keywords: Project · Project management · Rethinking project management · Classical project management · Design theory and innovation

1 Introduction

Projects are perceived to play an important role in our daily life. Furthermore, they are used to execute and sustain organizational goals. It is imperative to appreciate that projects should be considered as the engine that can be used towards achieving tomorrow's innovation, and in implementing strategic change in organizations. However, there are concerns that although implemented, most projects often fail to achieve their desired objective, an issue that has been cited by different scholars (Midler et al. 2016).

Project management is thus considered to have numerous economic benefits and contributes to achieving dramatic growth in the various sectors of the economy and across countries (Nutcache 2018). Besides, projects are perceived as an effective way through which organizations are able to structure their work, more so, in the current global setting, where innovation is a necessity (Ben et al. 2016). Nonetheless, despite the significant role played by projects, the base models and methodologies embraced in project management are perceived to have remained static for decades. Moreover, there are concerns that project managers have for years relied on rationalistic and technocratic approaches which have been criticized for their effectiveness in achieving project goals as they are linked to having a range of shortcomings that ought to be addressed.

To address the concern, scholars are shifting towards a new approach of project management as they are moving away from the classical approach that has been associated with lots of shortcomings. The trend has contributed towards the development of new insights. For instance, instead of considering projects as a tool, the

© Springer Nature Switzerland AG 2020
M. Themistocleous and M. Papadaki (Eds.): EMCIS 2019, LNBIP 381, pp. 524–533, 2020.
https://doi.org/10.1007/978-3-030-44322-1_39

schemes are perceived as a temporary organization of events structured towards achieving a business purpose. With the new thinking, a project should be considered as a holistic approach that can be embraced towards achieving organizational innovation, effectiveness, and efficiency. Besides, the concept of rethinking project management has transformed significantly in the recent past, an aspect that has helped project managers to come up with more effective strategies for managing projects. It is worth appreciating that good project management plays an essential role towards achieving project success. However, critics have indicated that despite using good project management practices, projects are still prone to failure (Blomquist et al. 2012). Therefore, embracing effective and innovative project management approaches do not guarantee the achievement of project goals. However, successful implementation of the innovative project as well as the complexity of the innovative project to be deployed is necessary. It is, therefore, necessary for the concerned stakeholders to evaluate the extent to which the respective organizations should implement the schemes.

To help address the issue of project failure in the modern setting, it is necessary to explore design theory to effectively understand its relevance in project management with a focus on innovative design. Some of the important case studies that will be reviewed in the study include the Polaris Project and the Manhattan Project, which have been instrumental in project management literature. Nonetheless, it is important to recognize that the proponent of the first case is renowned for the PERT technique as a project management tool, an aspect that is employed in the traditional project management. The case of Manhattan, on the other hand, will be used to reveal the concept of radical innovation, a field that has gained increased recognition in the recent past. Some of the important aspects discussed in the case include selectionism, a concept that is often employed in exploratory projects (Lenfle 2012).

The paper is arranged as follows: the next part present the literature review on PM and innovation, then research methodology which include summary about two case studies, and design theory, after that the results and analysis, and the final section represents the conclusion and research limitation.

2   Literature Review

Project management involves a wide range of activities which range from implementation, knowledge development and adoption of appropriate tools to achieve the organizational goals. Effective implementation of the set activities has a significant influence in determining project success or failure. However, failure in project management makes organizations to lose a lot of money, an aspect that is likely to affect a firm's profitability. For instance, in the US alone, project failure has made organizations lose over 150 billion in 2011 (Lenfle 2008). Moreover, failure probability is perceived to be high in a complex project that is associated with a high degree of innovation. When choosing an appropriate project management tool, it is, therefore, necessary for the project team to consider the degree of complexity. Besides, some of the important variables affected in the process include project monitoring, development times, evaluation and control among other important aspects. Flexibility is thus considered as an important attribute to be incorporated in the project management model.

According to Lenfle (2008), an innovative project is an ideal example of projects with a high degree of complexity. Such projects, therefore, demand for adoption of flexible strategies in the planning phase. However, because of the increased flexibility in the process, the decision-making process is considered to be more difficult. Different theories have been proposed to help resolve the challenges experienced in project management.

Stage-gate is among some of the recognized project management approaches used in the administration of innovating project management. Different scholars have suggested some of the milestones that ought to be evaluated to help determine if a project should continue or not. Therefore, based on the evaluation results, the set project should be carried out in phases. Based on the evaluation template, the score given will help the concerned stakeholders make informed stakeholders on whether the project is going on as desired or should be modified to control uncertainties associated with the set projects. Unlike other models, the Stage-Gate models take different aspects into consideration which is not the case in other models used in project management. Agile methodology is another technique that is often used in the implementation of innovative projects. The main reason as to why the above techniques are used in the management of innovative projects is because they give the management team an opportunity to conduct rapid testing of the projects to evaluate progress. Besides, the process helps the project management team to adapt to the changes, thus generating more flexibility which is required in resolving project complexity (Cicmil et al. 2006). Nonetheless, although the set methodologies are appreciated in the management of innovative projects because of the associated flexibility, they often lack the capability to help in the decision-making process an aspect that might compromise achievement of project goals. It is worth appreciating that project management process relies on different practices, an aspect that is known to contribute towards project success. This literature review will, therefore, seek to identify possible initiatives that can be used to help enhance the project management process. To achieve the study objective, the reviews from different scholars will be evaluated to identify some of the best practices that have been used in the past and how they can help streamline the process of project management. According to Claire and colleagues (2014), uncertainty, the lack of adequate knowledge on the innovative process and learning process are some of the important attributes contribute towards project failure, more so in the case of complex schemes. Thus, for innovative projects to be successfully implemented, the project team has to embrace a flexible approach.

However, based on the standard innovation management, organizational management has to be conducted at two levels. This includes strategic and operational management process which has been perceived to be effective. Some of the suggested steps in the process include project formulation, development, and launching and feasibility analysis.

Given a wide range of innovative projects to select from, scholars such as Mitchell and colleagues (2014) have indicated their concerns that different factors need to be embraced when selecting an appropriate project. Some of the important attributes considered in the process include the project feasibility and potential opportunities attained from the same. Feasibility attributes include aspects such as technology and organizational culture. Therefore, the various dimensions embrace different project management tools to ensure that the set objective is attained.

It is imperative to appreciate that the success of innovative projects is dependent on the quality of operational management as well as the capability of an organization. Some of the important attributes considered include financial structure, project team, market, project process and the nature of the organization.

Project team – implies the capability of the project manager administers the scheme to achieve the desired project deliverables.

Financial structure – this refers to the various financial attributes taken into consideration during the project implementation process.

Project process – this refers to the information flow process.

Company – refers to the impact of the scheme on the set organization Market – conditions to market access.

Project management as a field can be traced back to 2000 BC during the construction of the Egyptian Pyramids. Nevertheless, the issue of modern project management can only be traced to the 1950s. Studies examining the concept have indicated that project management can be divided into three major stages based on the historical development of the process. Critics, however, indicate that prior to the period, project management was never recognized. However, in the recent past, different tools and techniques to support the concept of project management have been developed (Gillier et al. 2015).

3   Research Methodology

The research methodology was done on the study relied on an exploratory design which is based on a historical case study; the Manhattan project and the Polaris Project. It is imperative to appreciate that this study targeted literature on project management with a focus on the case of innovative project management as for the case of Manhattan Project and the Polaris Project. The main purpose for using the case study is demonstrating the aspect of radical innovation and uncertainties associated to project management. This helped analyze how project managers achieve a successful implementation of the process. It is imperative to appreciate that descriptive research design is perceived as an essential approach. The study helps in the conducting studies with lots of uncertainties surrounding the research question. The approach is thus necessary for understanding topics that are not clearly understood (Stebbins 2001). Furthermore, the approach is very flexible and does not have to embrace a formal structure. The main reason for selecting these case studies were (Lenfle et al. 2016): both described as radical innovation project which is matching with exploratory projects, the cases exists in the same industrial field, same condition of skills, teams, and socio- professional levels, they have been widely studies and the historical materials were available, moreover one case described as PERT model and the other shown to be different in using managerial strategy.

3.1   Design Theory

Design theory is technique used to improve models of designers' cognitive, demonstrating and the relationship between the knowledge and innovation modelling the interaction between knowledge and innovation which generate tools than can shape the design procedure (Le Masson et al. 2011).

The important of design theory are:

1. It is used in the innovative design procedures because of their properties to explore the knowledge and concept (Le Masson et al. 2011).
2. The output of design theories exceeds producing the relation in known elements but also define new elements and relation between them which help analyze the projects (Lenfle et al. 2016).
3. It is shown successful in innovation process in serval studies (Lenfle et al. 2016).

One type of design theory is C-K design theory as shown in Fig. 1.

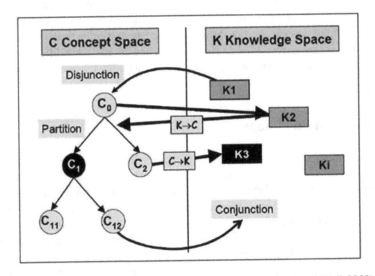

Fig. 1. The General pattern of C-K Design Theory (Hatchuel and Weil 2009).

3.2   The Polaris Project Case

In the US between (1953–1961) through Eisenhower management the Polaris project was established due to the situation that occurred from the issue of a 'missile gap' (Lenfle et al. 2016). During that time a lot of projects was started to improve the first thermonuclear intercontinental ballistic missiles (ICBM) and to protect the resources from other entities (Lenfle et al. 2016). The Polaris project was start in 1956 by UN Navy and the scope of it was to improve the first submarine- launched ballistic missiles (SLBM) to carry thermonuclear weapons (Lenfle et al. 2016). These missiles have unique characteristic due to difficulty in tracing or terminating it. Also, Polaris project is used PERT method to run the project but concentrated more on strategic options

(Lenfle et al. 2016). The main problem with the project was no previous designed missile for this type of work exit. The innovation issues around this project were (Lenfle et al. 2016):

1. Subsystems of the missile in the project.
2. Combination between the missiles and submarines.

Simply, the design strategy for the Polaris Project shows that (Lenfle et al. 2016):

1. The Knowledge foundation was existing from prior projects.
2. The theoretical evaluation process was significant for the project.
3. The team proposed many options for each item.
4. The skills were accessible from the contractors that work with the Navy.
5. The number of uncertainties was low, and the main one was the time required to finish each task.

Managerial Consequences
Two managerial innovation were created to run the project (Lenfle et al. 2016):

1. Constructing committed association was the main key point to run the innovation of this project, so Special Projects Office (SPO) was establish to overwhelmed the issues occur during the project and fasten the processes.
2. Using PERT technique to plan the project and improving that technique through the project which help to complete the design phase and observe the work performance in compare to schedule.

3.3   The Manhattan Project Case

It was established by Enric Fermi in 1942 and was built on the concept of the self-sustained nuclear chain reaction (Lenfle et al. 2016). It was start from the idea of simple model pile at the University of Chicago to create this weapon (Lenfle et al. 2016). The main issues of this project were: the manufacturing the materials and the design of the weapon (Lenfle et al. 2016). Also, the time was make the issue more worse because the Nazi Germany was built also the bomb (Lenfle et al. 2016). The challenges faced through this project despite materials, design and time were unknown there were no model had been build, no tests were performed (Lenfle et al. 2016).

Managerial Consequences
The uncertainties of this project were high because most of the knowledge was not exist so the design condition was different from the Polaris Project (Lenfle et al. 2016). Because of no knowledge foundation of this project it was difficult to guess how the project would clarify Project (Lenfle et al. 2016). So, to overcome this issue, it was starting to dealing synchronized improvement of many technologies. Because the items of this project were low in technology readiness level so how to deal with it was now clear to improve in which way. So, it was important to work on design strategy in order to expect the design procedure and managing the unknowing (Lenfle et al. 2016).

Design Strategy

The strategy was designed to create large knowledge so two main choices were made (Lenfle et al. 2016):

1. Splitting the materials manufacturing from bomb design. The objective of this separation was to prevent studying predefined numbers of materials that would lead to nowhere.
2. Due to high number of uncertainties and the time was critical factor, they managed to discover and apply many options for the manufacturing of materials and design the bomb.

From this strategy the outputs were:

1. To Change from one material to other.
2. To create new separation procedure for the martials and joining many procedures to get to the required level.
3. To adjust a strategy for concentrate tests.
4. To create flexible process to achieve the final stage in short time.

4   Results

Based on the research findings, it was evident that the management of innovative projects relies on different aspects. While some of the project management tends to stick to their initial product architectures, others change to adapt to the project uncertainties. The study also identified that to stick to the initial project approach, the project management has to embrace PERT and the traditional project management techniques. However, for the case of projects that adapt to existing situations, there is limited knowledge on how such schemes can be managed.

From the study findings, it is evident that most projects have limited information concerning combinative capabilities, which is required in the management of innovative projects. It was revealed that when the project concept lacks adequate understanding, the project has to rely on combinative capabilities to achieve splitting.

The case study demonstrated the concept in different ways. For instance, when dealing with non-architectural and innovative schemes to achieve knowledge creation, combinative capabilities have to remain unchanged. Nonetheless, the process does not imply the creation of new combinations as the existing ones are still considered relevant. However, when planning effective architectural innovations, there is a need to generate non-determinism and non-modularity. It thus implies that for the project to succeed, two important aspects have to be considered. Firstly, there is a need that project management has to create alternatives for achieving project goals. Secondly, the project has to engage in an exploration of mutual interactions.

It is thus evident that to achieve radical innovation in project management, it is not possible to rely on a single architecture, but to rely on multiple strategies as in the case of the Manhattan project. Prior to selecting the final strategy to embrace in the project, numerous alternatives were generated.

The research findings also demonstrated how project stakeholders can effectively manage architectural and non-architectural schemes. This shows the various strategies that project stakeholders can use to maintain combinative abilities, an attribute that helps in generating new knowledge. It was further revealed that non-architectural innovation demand for effective organization of various project activities, an aspect that portrays a traditional approach to project management. It thus revealed that new knowledge can only be created by developing appropriate project management practices which are perceived to be effective.

The study also revealed that when project managers embrace change, the project stakeholders have to develop alternative solutions for achieving the project deliverable. However, the main challenge in such a situation is how to come up with the alternative strategies that will help in achieving project goals. The identified alternatives have to be evaluated for relevance and how they can adapt to the change. Besides, the aspect is used to demonstrate the difference amid the Polaris and Manhattan project. Although both projects were complex and evolving, the Polaris project was certain while the Manhattan project was faced with lots of uncertainties. This shows that adapting to change in project management is a crucial attribute as it helps in the helps the project managers to explore different paths that they can employ to settle the business goal.

5 Analysis

It is worth recognizing that this study has contributed towards bridging the literature on project management with a focus on the recent innovative strategies. From the study, it is important to conclude that the design theory can help project managers to overcome the various challenges faced when using traditional project management tools. This will help reduce the issue of project failures, thus saving organizations a lot of resources and time. Based on the case study, both Polaris and Manhattan projects are ideal examples of radical innovation. Besides, both projects, as revealed, were complex in nature, hence the need for best practices to successfully implement them. Although the Polaris project seemed to be risky, it had limited uncertainties. This is the main reason as to why it embraced the non-splitting approach.

However, the Manhattan project, on the other hand, had a lot of uncertainties and limited information on the path to use to achieve the project goals. This shows that the scheme had to rely on knowledge creation, an aspect that demands the suggestion of Alternative paths to use in resolving the challenge. It thus implies that the project team has to find effective strategies on how to manage the unknown as well as taking the time to learn the problem.

From the findings, it is therefore imperative to acknowledge that design theory is a more effective strategy that can be used in the implementation of complex projects as compared to the traditional strategies of project management. Therefore, an effective understanding of architectural innovation contributes significantly towards the development of an ideal design process. While non-architectural innovations support the idea of using validation tools, the architectural innovation, on the hand, favors exploration. Some of the important attributes incorporated in the process include engaging all project stakeholders, use project scenarios and embracing new discussions based on the existing path.

To achieve project success, it is necessary for the project managers to link the concept to project management. The process helps in the exploration to help identify effective tools that can be used in project management to reduce incidents of project failure in the future (Soderlünd and Lenfle 2013). This implies that a rational approach should seek to define the problem as well as the appreciation of the alternative strategies that can be employed in advance. The concept is well demonstrated through the review of the Polaris project. However, for the case of innovative design where projects have a lot of uncertainties, traditional tools of project management should be considered inadequate.

Furthermore, the Manhattan project is necessary to help demonstrate the need for embracing new managerial approaches which incorporate flexibility. Moreover, from the scheme, it was evident that the project team was able to learn and engage in the development of new knowledge to resolve the unknowns. However, given a list of alternative solutions, project managers have to select the best alternative (Loch et al. 2006). Therefore, despite the existence of many unknowns, with the design theory, the project management team will be able to resolve the problem.

6   Conclusion

Project management remains to be an important attribute in any society. The main idea driven by the innovative project management is the incorporation of flexibility in the process from the early stages of development to implementation to help organizations to achieve their set goals. Therefore, with the approach, it is possible for the project team to evaluate the success of a new project and find alternative paths on how the set objectives can be achieved.

From the study findings, it was evident that there is no single strategy that fits all projects, hence the need to embrace different tools to help address existing challenges in project management. While some of the projects are straightforward, others are complex with lots of uncertainties. Based on the Manhattan project, linking project management and design theory remains to be an ideal strategy through which project stakeholders can rely upon to reach their set goals in the most efficient way possible. Besides, in the current competitive setting, the project faces sudden changes, an aspect that poses more risks and uncertainties. Therefore, more vigilant strategies should be developed to address such concerns, an aspect that will help enhance project success in the future. Moreover, project failure is a costly thing and needs to be addressed with the urgency that it deserves. Additionally, the main reason as to why the design strategy should rely upon project management is because the concept allows the project team to generate new knowledge and learn from the process, hence the participants are able to resolve the unknowns.

Research Limitations and Further Study

Nonetheless, the knowledge created in the above study relied on two major case studies. There is a need therefore for more research to be conducted in the future to gain a deeper insight into the link between project management and design theory, an area that has gained increased recognition in exploratory studies. Besides, with more studies, it is will be possible to develop innovative strategies that can be used in the project management process. In summary, the design theory has proved effective in developing new ways of managing the exploratory projects, which is an ideal area of the study.

References

Ben, M., Jouini, S., Midler, C., Silberzahn, P.: Contributions of design thinking to project management in an innovation context. Proj. Manag. J. **47**(2), 144–156 (2016)

Blomquist, T., Hallgren, M., Nilsson, A., Soderholm, A.: Project-as-practice: in search of project management research that matters. IEEE Eng. Manag. Rev. **40**(3), 88 (2012)

Cicmil, S., Williams, T., Thomas, J., Hodgson, D.: Rethinking project management: researching the actuality of projects. Int. J. Proj. Manag. **24**(8), 675–686 (2006)

Claire, J., Galvez, D., Boly, V., Camargo, M., Moselle, J.C.: A new innovation project maturity assessment methodology based on innovation degree. In: 2014 International ICE Conference on Engineering, Technology and Innovation (ICE), pp. 1–8, June 2014

Gillier, T., Hooge, S., Piat, G.: Framing value management for creative projects: an expansive perspective. Int. J. Proj. Manag. **33**(4), 947–960 (2015)

Lenfle, S.: Exploration, project evaluation and design theory: a rereading of the Manhattan case. Int. J. Manag. Proj. Bus. **5**(3), 486–507 (2012)

Midler, C., Killen, C.P., Kock, A.: Project and innovation management: bridging contemporary trends in theory and practice. Proj. Manag. J. **47**(2), 3–7 (2016)

Lenfle, S.: Exploration and project management. Int. J. Proj. Manag. **26**(5), 469–478 (2008)

Loch, C., DeMeyer, A., Pich, M.: Managing the Unknown. A New Approach to Managing High Uncertainty and Risks in Projects. Wiley, Hoboken (2006)

Mitchell, R., Phaal, R., Athanassopoulou, N.: Scoring methods for prioritizing and selecting innovation projects. In: 2014 Portland International Conference on Management of Engineering & Technology (PICMET), pp. 907–920, July 2014

Nutcache, N.: Project Management Evolution: What the Pyramids of Egypt Tell Us About the History of Project Management (Infographic) (2018). https://www.nutcache.com/blog/project-management-evolution/

Soderlünd, J., Lenfle, S.: Making project history: revisiting the past, creating the future. Int. J. Proj. Manag. **31**, 653–662 (2013)

Stebbins, R.A.: Exploratory Research in the Social Sciences, vol. 48. Sage (2001)

Lenfle, S., Le Masson, P., Weil, B.: When project management meets design theory: revisiting the Manhattan and Polaris projects to characterize 'radical innovation' and its managerial implications. Creat. Innov. Manag. **25**(3), 378–395 (2016)

Hatchuel, A., Weil, B.: C-K design theory: an advanced formulation. Res. Eng. Des. **19**, 181–192 (2009). https://doi.org/10.1007/s00163-008-0043-4

Management and Organizational Issues
in Information Systems

Facilitating ICT Adoption for Older Workers: Lessons Learned from Enterprise System Practitioners

Ewa Soja[1](✉) and Piotr Soja[2]

[1] Department of Statistics, Cracow University of Economics, Kraków, Poland
Ewa.Soja@uek.krakow.pl
[2] Department of Informatics, Cracow University of Economics, Kraków, Poland
Piotr.Soja@uek.krakow.pl

Abstract. The current study seeks is to investigate the role of employees' age in improving ICT implementation projects in organizations. The study draws from the opinions of 75 ES practitioners gathered during an exploratory research conducted in Poland. The discovered recommendations for improving ICT adoptions were analyzed following the data-driven, grounded theory-based approach, employing open and axial coding. Next, the distribution of respondent opinions among different age groups was analyzed. Then, the discovered recommendations were discussed from the perspective of strengths and weaknesses of older employees. The main findings imply that older employees mainly recommend improvement in preparatory and training-related activities, while the middle-aged employees emphasize the importance of implementation project run. The youngest workers, in turn, particularly highlighted the need for improvement in technology-related considerations.

Keywords: Enterprise systems · ICT adoption · Older workers · Age-diverse workforce · Ageing · Poland

1 Introduction

Nowadays, population ageing is a demographic phenomenon that affects the vast majority of countries and, as forecasted by demographers, will be progressing in the future [6, 17]. One of the consequences of population ageing is the process of labor force shrinking and ageing [10]. As a result, older adults in the workforce are and will be working until later ages [6, 8]. Prior research in the field of work psychology and organizational behavior suggests that workforce ageing is associated with numerous considerations. These include decrease of cognitive and physical capacities as people age [34], age-related changes in psychological characteristics affecting organizational outcomes such as work attitudes [40], and intergenerational differences in values and attitudes, which can contribute to conflict in the workplace [35]. In consequence, organizations have to focus on an effective management of an age-diverse workforce [34]. In particular, managers should aim at accommodating and leveraging age differences, for instance by considering job design from a lifespan perspective to improve work attitudes such as job satisfaction and involvement [34, 40].

© Springer Nature Switzerland AG 2020
M. Themistocleous and M. Papadaki (Eds.): EMCIS 2019, LNBIP 381, pp. 537–550, 2020.
https://doi.org/10.1007/978-3-030-44322-1_40

Contemporary businesses more and more rely on information and communication technology (ICT) and its use becomes obligatory for their employees. An example of a widely used technology whose usage is mandatory within organizations are enterprise systems (ES) [12]. ES are designed to support management and integration of the whole company and offer inter-organizational integration with company's clients and suppliers [37]. ES implementation and use involves many stakeholders and usually is a lengthy process which is risky and is experiencing various impediments [29], which indicates a need to conduct investigations into the improvement to such endeavors. Prior research suggests that ES adoption might be determined by various factors, including considerations related to both technology and employees' involvement [9, 29]. In consequence, improvements to such projects should be carried out in various areas. However, in light of workforce ageing, considering the fact that work ability may depend on age [14] and that employees' attitudes towards computers are becoming more negative with age [38], it appears important to examine to what extent the perceptions of possibilities to improve ES adoptions depend on employee age. Therefore, we formulated the following research question which guided our exploratory study: *What is the role of employee age in perceiving areas for improvement in ES adoption projects?*

The paper is organized as follows. In the next section, we present research background focusing on implications of workforce ageing and discussing the main considerations of ES adoptions reported by prior research. Next we reveal our research method and present our results. We then discuss our findings, explain implications, and discuss limitations and avenues for future research. The study ends with concluding remarks.

2   Background

Ageing of the population is inevitable and will deepen in the future. This is due to the changes in fertility and mortality in the past and the continuance of these trends in the future. The fertility rates remaining below the natural replacement level and the continuing projected gains in life expectancy related to decrease in mortality fundamentally change the age structures of populations and lead to demographic ageing [e.g. 10, 17].

Demographic projections also reveal that ageing of the population has an influence on the number and the structure of potential labor force. According to the European Commission's report [6] total labor supply is projected to decline by 9 percentage points between 2015 and 2070. At the same time, the total employment rate of the older people (55–64) will increase about 12.6% due to the projected impact of pension reforms. This means that in the future labor force will not only shrink but also gradually age.

To alleviate foreseen changes in labor resources appropriate strategies are needed. These should enable and promote longer working lives through life long training, education and skills updating, and the provision of appropriate working environments for older [10]. There is also a need to overcome stereotypical views about the older workers revealed by employers in European countries [39]. Similarly, problems with professional activity of older people associated with negative stereotypes about the abilities and productivity of older workers as compared with younger employees should be addressed [21].

Prior research indicates that several characteristics of employees change with age and it is possible to distinguish strengths and weaknesses of older workers, or in other words, strong and weak points [24]. As regards strong points, prior research indicates that ageing employees are associated with greater soft skills, reliability, considerable experience, and loyalty to the organization [14, 24, 36]. With respect to weak points, older workers are associated with lower flexibility as compared to younger work-mates, decreased perception and work pace, lower endurance, and lower level of education and new technology skills [14, 21, 24, 36]. There are also mixed findings with respect to some characteristics of older workers, such as attitudes to trainings and control of life. In addition, some characteristics, such as lower innovativeness, appear to be negative stereotypes not based on accumulated empirical evidence [22].

Extant research suggests that as age increases, attitudes toward computers tend to be more negative [38] and technology anxiety increases [18]. Therefore, since ICT solutions are widely used by today's businesses, in light of an ageing workforce, implementation of mandatory advanced ICT solutions might pose a challenge to adopting organizations. This especially applies to the process of ES adoption in an organization, which provides new conditions with a multitude of impacts. In particular, ES influences the behaviors of people, which in turn changes how systems are used, or not used in the case of user resistance and workarounds. Therefore, communication, change management, education, and user involvement are critical for the successful use of the ES, and to successfully guide ES adaptation and evolution in later phases [9].

Research into critical success factors (CSFs) for ES adoption suggests that many issues during the implementation and use of ES are related to the characteristics and attitudes of employees and activities aimed at shaping the appropriate attitudes of employees during the change process. For example, the most cited CSFs in the ranking prepared by Finney and Corbett [7] include top management commitment and support, change management, training and job redesign, project team composition, consultant selection and relationship, and project champion. In turn, issues related to technology were not listed among the 10 most cited CSFs out of the 26 items analyzed. As suggested by Awa and Ojiabo [2], technology-related issues might affect smaller companies to a greater extent than larger organizations.

Research in the area of ES acceptance suggests a number of issues that seem important from the point of view of older workers and might be associated with strengths and weaknesses of older employees. In particular, prior studies illustrate the important role of perceived compatibility/fit of the new ES [3, 20], which might be important for older workers due to their specific requirements associated with limited cognitive abilities and reduced work pace. The next important issues, attitude toward ES [1, 20, 27] and readiness for change [15, 27], appear important in the light of negative attitudes towards change and technology revealed by older employees. Other significant issues, communication and trainings [1, 16], are fundamental mechanisms of change management and their role appears evident for older workers in order to help them to accept organizational change associated with ES adoption. Finally, education level [3] appears important in the context of relatively lower level of education of older workers as compared to younger colleagues.

A major shortcoming of previous ES acceptance-related studies is that they do not perform age related analyzes and only few of them report age structure of their respondents [e.g. 3, 15, 16]. In addition, those few studies revealing age structure practically do not enquire older employees. Lack of emphasis on age-based analysis seems a problem not only among ES acceptance-related studies but also in ES field in general. Few studies in this field suggest that employee age may play a significant role in the perception of determinants of successful ES adoption [28], impediments [29] and threats [30] to ES adoption success. In this context, while perceiving solutions to the problems encountered, older employees put a greater emphasis on people-related solutions; while younger workers emphasize system-related solutions [31]. In the same vein, younger employees appear to place greater emphasis on technology - related determinants, while older employees seem to perceive process-related determinants to a greater extent [28]. We believe that in the light of global demographic changes an in-depth analysis of the role of employee age in the perception of improvements to successful adoption and use of mandatory business software such as enterprise systems is an interesting and worth investigating research topic.

3   Method

In order to answer our research question, associated with the role of employee age in perceiving areas for improvement in ES adoption projects, we adopted a qualitative research approach and we turned to practitioners to learn what are their views concerning the issues in question. The respondents were asked an open-ended question related to their perception of the most important issues that might help to improve ES implementation projects. The respondents were asked to provide recommendations on the basis of their prior experience and participation in ES implementation projects. We employed such a data-driven approach in order to gather a broad range of respondent opinions without imposing a predefined set of possible answers, allowing us to perform an in-depth investigation of the recommendations for improvement.

In consequence of the data gathering process, respondent opinions expressed in natural language have been collected. Next, following the grounded theory approach [5], we performed the process of open and axial coding. In the first step, during the process of open coding, we analyzed and compared the respondent opinions in search of similarities and differences, and, as a result, conceptual labels were assigned to the respondent statements. In the next step, the process of axial coding was performed, during which the relationships between the previously defined categories and subcategories were tested against data and verified. In consequence, the categorization of recommendations for improvement was elaborated and agreed upon by the authors.

In the next stage of the data analysis, the distribution of recommendations and recommendation categories across different respondent age ranges has been worked out.

The purpose of such an examination was to investigate the role of employee age in perceiving recommendations for improvement in ES adoptions. While defining the age groups, we used the idea of chronological age, which is determined by the calendar and is associated with predictable changes across a number of domains that include health, work, family, and life changes [4].

While defining older workers, we adopted the age cutoff of 50 years because most organizational decision markers in Poland refer to older workers as 50 years and older [32, 33]. A similar definition of older employee was employed by van Dalen et al. [36] in their research into potential of ageing workers. In addition, van Dalen et al. defined younger workers as those not older than 35 years. We also followed this idea and, in consequence, the following age groups were defined: Age 1 – less than 35 years (Younger), Age 2 – between 35 and 49 years (Middle-aged), and Age 3–50+ years (Older).

Table 1. Research sample demographics

	Total	Younger*	Middle-aged*	Older*
Median age				
Chronological age	40	31	40	55
Organizational age**	8	4	10	19
Role in the implementation process				
Member of the project team	20	7	7	6
None	15	5	4	6
Supervisor/Steering Committee	13	4	5	4
Project manager	12	4	4	4
Provider's representative/consultant	9	3	3	3
User	6	2	2	2
Organizational position				
Specialist	26	10	8	8
Manager	24	10	7	7
Director	15	3	6	6
Top management	10	2	4	4

Notes: *Younger – less than 35 years, Middle-aged – between 35 and 49 years, Older – 50 + years; **length of career stage in the current workplace

As a result of the data gathering process, in total, 75 respondents expressed their opinions as regards perceived recommendations for improvement to ES adoptions. During data gathering we made an effort to access respondents holding various organizational positions and playing different roles in the ES adoption projects. We also made an attempt to achieve a balanced representation of the defined age groups. The distribution of respondents by age groups and their organizational age, i.e. the length of career stage in the current workplace, is presented in Table 1. The table also illustrates the distribution of respondents by role in the implementation process and organizational position.

4 Data Analysis and Results

On the basis of data analysis four main categories of recommendations for improvement were extracted. These include recommendations associated with various aspects related to implementation project preparation (category "Project preparation"), suggestions related to the improvement in trainings (category "Training"), advice related to the implementation process run (category "Implementation process"), and recommendations associated with the enterprise system being implemented (category "System"). Recommendation categories and individual recommendations are presented in Table 2 together with their perceptions by age groups. The following subsections include the general presentation of recommendations without discussing the role of respondent age, which is performed in the separate section.

4.1 Category "Project Preparation"

The recommendations associated with the project preparation first and foremost relate to activities associated with company analysis prior to the implementation project start and project schedule definition, postulating more effort devoted to these activities. The preparatory activities should involve many stakeholders such as company's employees, system users, and department managers. More attention should be paid to the preparation of the project schedule and to the planned project time, which often requires extension. Other recommendations for improvement include evaluation of the total costs of the implemented system and its expansion (i.e. hardware, new sys- tem cost). It is also suggested to ensure better preparation of the company employees for the project and evaluation of their readiness and attitudes towards changes imposed by the implementation project. In addition, adequate employees' ICT skills needed during the project should be secured. The company's organizational structure and processes should be improved and its financial standing should be particularly taken into consideration.

4.2 Category "Training"

The training-related recommendations in general concentrate on the training participants and schedule. It is recommended that the company should ensure the proper training of its employees and their preparation for the new ES use. It is advised to pay more attention to the choice of the trainings' participants, allocate more time for trainings, and pay more attention to trainings' timing. In particular, often the trainings should be organized earlier and extended in time. It is suggested to organize more training sessions, including preliminary trainings on new processes. It is also recommended to pay more attention to the level of trainers' preparation for the trainings.

4.3 Category "Implementation Process"

The recommendations for improvement associated with the implementation process run refer first and foremost to project team composition and project management. In particular, the respondents recommend paying more attention to the project team composition and ensuring that the selected people represent all company's business areas affected by the implementation project. Special attention should be paid to effective project management, focusing on timeliness and cost control. The respondents also advise that good communication should start during the early stages of the project involving employees from company's various departments. The company's employees should be informed of the adoption project and its consequences and benefits. Other pieces of advice include better cooperation with the implementation services provider, focusing on clear definition of roles in the project and provider consultants' availability and preparation for the consulting sessions. The respondents also recommended ensuring appropriate time for system testing.

4.4   Category "System"

The system-related recommendations mainly relate to fit between the system and company needs, system functionality, infrastructure, and the process of system choice. Specifically, it is suggested that the system should satisfy the company needs and requirements, with an emphasis put on system fit to the company organization. Special attention should be paid to the system functionality. An appropriate IT infrastructure meeting the new system's requirements should be ensured. The company should also pay more attention and allocate more time to the process of the enterprise system choice. It is also advised to take into consideration company's legacy systems and evaluate their compatibility with the new enterprise system.

4.5   Improvement Recommendations by Age

The results of data analysis from the employee age perspective are presented in Table 2. The table displays the distribution of reported recommendations across the three age groups. The symbols in the table were defined on the basis of the percentage of responses provided by the respondents from an individual age group declaring a given recommendation. While presenting the data we followed the suggestions of Miles and Huberman [19] and we used the symbols ● ◕ ◑   ◔ for very high, high, medium, and low importance of perceived recommendations.

The category "Project preparation" has been reported by all respondents, with a special emphasis put by the oldest employees. The oldest pointed to all individual improvements within the category, emphasizing the importance of project schedule, compared to other groups of respondents. They uniquely declared BPR-related improvements and IT skills. The youngest, in turn, attached special importance to need definition. The middle-aged specially emphasized the role of detailed analysis and employee preparation.

The category "Training" has been declared first and foremost by the oldest employees, then by the youngest, while the middle-aged reported this category to a significantly lesser extent. The oldest especially emphasized the role of time and the need for organizing more trainings. The middle-aged do not perceive the need for improving employee trainings, which is an improvement emphasized by the youngest respondents. Nevertheless, it appears that the perception of the importance of trainers' quality clearly increases with age.

Table 2. Recommendations and recommendation categories by respondent age group

Improvement \ Age group	Younger	Middle-aged	Older
Project preparation	▬	▬	▬
need definition	●	◑	◑
schedule	◑	◑	◕
detailed analysis	◑	◕	◑
cost estimation	◔	◔	◑
employee preparation	◔	◑	◔
BPR			◑
finances		◔	◔
IT skills			◑
Training	▪	▪	▬
employees	◕		◑
time	◔	◔	●
more training	◔	◔	◑
trainers' quality		◔	◑
Implementation process	▪	▬	▪
team composition		◕	◔
project management	◔	◑	
communication		◔	◑
cooperation with provider	◔	◔	◔
testing		◑	
System	▬	▪	▪
fit to company needs	◑	◔	
functionality	◑	◔	
infrastructure	◔	◔	◔
choice	◔	◔	◔
fit to legacy systems	◔		

Note: ● – high, ◕ – medium, ◑ – low, ◔ – very low level of importance

"Implementation process" is a category reported first and foremost by the middle - aged employees, then by the oldest, and finally by the youngest workers. The middle - aged emphasize the importance of the project team composition and project management, and uniquely declare the improvements related to system testing. The youngest only to a limited extent declare the need for improvement in project management and cooperation with provider. The oldest report the improvements related to project team composition and cooperation with provider. They also emphasize the importance of communication improvements, whose perception appears to increase with age.

The perception of the category "System" appears to clearly decrease with age. The youngest perceive this category to the fullest extent, emphasizing the importance of system fit to company needs and system functionality. The middle-aged, in turn, indicate the importance of the majority of improvements in the category "System", except for fit to legacy systems. The oldest employees only point to the importance of good system choice and report basic improvements related to system (i.e. infrastructure).

5 Discussion of Findings

5.1 Strengths and Weaknesses of Older Workers

During the analysis we investigated which strong and weak points of the older workers allowed them to perceive (or not to perceive) recommendations for ES adoption projects improvement. To each reported recommendation we assigned those characteristics of older workers which, in our opinion, might have determined the reporting of this recommendation by the enquired respondents. For instance, a strong emphasis placed on the need to perform cost estimation and detailed analysis prior to ES implementation might have been caused by reliability and experience of older workers, which are some of the strong points of older employees. On the other hand, declaration of recommendations related to schedule and too short implementation time might have been caused by, from one hand, employees' experience, however, on the other hand, it might have been related to older workers' limitations (i.e. weak points) such as decreased work pace and limited endurance. In the same vein, lack of perception of system-related recommendations, such as improvement in system functionality, might primarily result from older respondents' limitations associated with outdated skills and lower level of technology-related education and skills.

Among strong and weak points of older workers highlighted by prior research, experience seems to play the most significant role. Experience appears to help older workers to perceive the need for improvements in each of the four categories, with a special emphasis put on project preparation. The second most important strong point of the older workers is awareness of one's own limitations, which is mainly manifested in the categories "Project preparation" and "Training". Next, there is a strong point related to soft interpersonal skills, which seems to be helpful in perceiving improvements associated with implementation process and, to a lesser extent, with project preparation and trainings. Finally, characteristics related to loyalty, reliability and collaboration skills of older workers might also be visible; however, to a small extent. Summing up the weak points of older workers, it appears that the most important role is played by their lower level of education or partially obsolete knowledge. The role of education-related issues is demonstrated in all categories and mainly results in lack of perception of the need for improvement in more detailed considerations of ES implementation process and more advanced system-related issues. Next, we might notice the important role of outdated technology-related skills, which are demonstrated in the system-related category of improvements and then in the category associated with project preparation. Then, the role of decreased work pace and limited endurance might be recognized, which seems to be associated with improvements related to trainings and project preparation.

It should be emphasized that perception (or lack of perception) of a number of improvements illustrate a disputable role of some characteristics of older workers. This refers first and foremost to the older employees' reluctance to participate in trainings, a characteristic inconsistently reported by prior research [14, 21]. It appears that this characteristic should have been demonstrated in the negative attitudes of older workers towards trainings. Meanwhile, it turns out that older workers do not avoid trainings and, moreover, they perceive the need for preparatory and additional trainings, which appears to deny this rule. Investigation if such attitudes are associated with a mandatory character of ES is an interesting research idea.

Other characteristics of older works whose role is disputable to a certain extent in the context of ES adoption are lower level of education and limited flexibility. The former should have prevented older employees from declaring improvements related to cooperation with provider and BPR. The latter, in turn, should have lead older employees to declare improvements related to system fit to company needs and prevent them from reporting BPR-related improvements. There is also a disputable role of experience, which should have lead older employees to declare improvements related to system fit to company needs.

5.2   Implications

The current study brings a number of insights into the role of employee age in the process of ES implementations and other comprehensive ICT-related initiatives involving mandatory system use. The propositions suggest some implications for team building during the project and include suggestions for employee preparation and organization of trainings, which are especially adequate for ageing workforce. We also propose recommendations useful in fostering cooperation between the youngest and older generations of employees in the context of technological change. Our suggestions are formulated for the purpose of better using potential of employees at various ages and overcoming stereotypes associated with older employees. While formulating our recommendations, we took into consideration important factors contributing to the successfulness of ES implementations.

In the case of team building, our study sheds some new light on the idea of balanced team composition, a well-known issue in the ES field [26]. Our results suggest that it is important not only to balance the team with respect to business areas of team members, but also to take into consideration age of participants, both adopters and providers. It appears necessary to recruit older employees into the project team, who might be excluded due to stereotypical perceptions of older workers and their attitudes towards changes. In fact, older people often reveal shortcomings in new technology knowledge; however, they appear to understand the necessity of adapting oneself to changes in mandatory settings. Their experience, awareness of one's own limitations (especially with regard to ICT) and interpersonal skills should allow them to properly diagnose employees' attitudes towards changes and contribute to developing solutions which are adequate for an organization in the context of ageing work force and continuously changing technology.

With respect to employee preparation, our findings suggest that it is important to involve older workers early in the project, during the planning stage, in order to adjust various preparatory activities to company age structure and achieve employee buy-in. It should be emphasized that building proper attitudes and motivations of employees within the change management program is an important success factor for ES implementation [e.g. 1, 7]. Hur [13] indicates that elderly empowerment is not a matter of social or ICT skills, but is more likely to result from their being interested in ICT and ICT-based activities. In a similar vein, Hill and colleagues [11] suggest that older people need to be properly motivated in order to become involved in new technologies. In the case of older people it appears necessary to demonstrate tangible benefits from using technology in everyday life. These might include strengthening the position on the job market by increasing computer self-efficacy, possibility of part time job at older age, personal empowerment, social connectedness, and independent living [10, 11, 34, 38, 39].

As regards the project schedule definition and adjusting training programs to employee age, it is important to take into consideration that the pace of project tasks should be slower for older employees, which is associated with a reduced rate of learning. However, as suggested by prior research, the ability to learn is not impaired with age [25]. Older employees would benefit from the organization of hands-on trainings on IT skills, which should be adequately long and organized early, preceding the actual implementation process. In order to increase training efficiency for older workers, it appears valuable to involve older employees as trainers or consultants. This would be an additional incentive to overcome mental impediments among the elderly, such as reluctance or fear of changes, as older workers might perceive such trainers as a demonstration of familiarity with new technology at a later age.

In the light of constant technological progress and ageing workforce it appears necessary to pay attention to cooperation between employees and the way of using their strong points. However, younger employees, generally possessing better ICT skills and multitasking capabilities (e.g. fast and parallel information processing [8, 34]), preferring learning by doing and revealing preference of instant gratifications, might experience difficulties in understanding and cooperation with older generations of workers [23]. It appears that middle-aged employees, with their understanding of organizational issues and project-intensive organization of work and revealing substantial experience and up-to-date knowledge of IT, might be a group linking the youngest with the oldest workers. Their activities might embrace both planning and coordinating such a youngest-oldest cooperation.

5.3   Limitations and Future Research

The main limitation of the current analysis stems from the fact that the study was based on the data gathered in one country, i.e. Poland. Therefore, the application of the current study's findings to other countries should be done with caution. However, as similar changes in population and workforce structure are taking place in other European Union countries [6], the current study's results might be applied, to a certain extent, to other countries within the EU.

Promising directions for future research, suggested by the current study's limitations, include a cross-country European research into ICT-related considerations for an ageing workforce. The particularly interesting research issues in this area include a cross-country data analysis and elaborating ICT adoption models aligned to country-specific considerations. Other directions for future studies include investigation into work-family balance in the digital economy and how mandatory nature of ES is shaping employees' attitudes towards training.

6　Conclusion

The current study investigated the role of employee age in improving ICT implementation projects, building on the experience of ES practitioners from Poland. Using a data-driven approach, the discovered recommendations for improvement were divided into four main categories: Project preparation, Training, Implementation process, and System. The analysis of improvement recommendations by respondent age allows us to conclude that in order to improve ICT implementation projects, work capacity of employees at various age should be taken into consideration. The results imply that, for older workers, preparatory activities are the most favorable stage of the implementation project, when they are able to make use of their strengths and compensate for their weaknesses. In particular, older employees' experience and ability to comprehend the whole help them to compensate for their weaknesses through project schedule and training alignment, leading to early skills building. The results achieved might help practitioners to leverage employees' potential and work out change management programs adapted to the age-diverse workforce in the organization. With this respect, our findings suggest that, for older workers, the most critical areas of change management are system- and implementation process-related considerations. The current study's results should also be valuable for researchers, encouraging them to incorporate age diversity in their future investigations.

Acknowledgments. This publication has been financed by the subsidy granted to Cracow University of Economics, Poland.

References

1. Amoako-Gyampah, K., Salam, A.F.: An extension of the technology acceptance model in an ERP implementation environment. Inf. Manag. **41**, 731–745 (2004)
2. Awa, H.O., Ojiabo, O.U.: A model of adoption determinants of ERP within T-O-E frame - work. Inf. Technol. People **29**(4), 901–930 (2016)
3. Calisir, F., Gumussoy, C.A., Bayram, A.: Predicting the behavioral intention to use enterprise resource planning systems: an exploratory extension of the technology acceptance model. Manag. Res. News **32**(7), 597–613 (2009)
4. Cleveland, J.N., Hanscom, M.: What is old at work? Moving past chronological age. In: Parry, E., McCarthy, J. (eds.) The Palgrave Handbook of Age Diversity and Work, pp. 17–46. Palgrave Macmillan, London (2017)

5. Corbin, J.M., Strauss, A.: Grounded theory research procedures, canons, and evaluative criteria. Qual. Sociol. **13**(1), 3–21 (1990). https://doi.org/10.1007/BF00988593
6. European Commission: The 2018 Ageing Report. Underlying Assumptions and Projection Methodologies. European Economy, Institutional Paper 065, November 2017 (2017). https://doi.org/10.2765/286359
7. Finney, S., Corbett, M.: ERP implementation: a compilation and analysis of critical success factors. Bus. Process Manag. J. **13**(3), 329–347 (2007)
8. Fisher, G.G., Chaffee, D.S., Tetrick, L.E., Davalos, D.B., Potter, G.G.: Cognitive functioning, aging, and work: a review and recommendations for research and practice. J. Occup. Health Psychol. **22**(3), 314–339 (2017)
9. Grabski, S.V., Leech, S.A., Schmidt, P.J.: A review of ERP research: a future agenda for accounting information systems. J. Inf. Syst. **25**(1), 37–78 (2011)
10. Harper, S.: Economic and social implications of aging societies. Science **346**(6209), 587–591 (2014)
11. Hill, R., Beynon-Davies, P., Williams, M.D.: Older people and internet engagement: acknowledging social moderators of internet adoption, access and use. Inf. Technol. People **21**(3), 244–266 (2008)
12. Holsapple, C.W., Wang, Y.-M., Wu, J.-H.: Empirically testing user characteristics and fitness factors in enterprise resource planning success. Int. J. Hum. – Comput. Interact. **19**(3), 323–342 (2005)
13. Hur, M.H.: Empowering the elderly population through ICT-based activities: an empirical study of older adults in Korea. Inf. Technol. People **29**(2), 318–333 (2016)
14. Ilmarinen, J.: Ageing workers. Occup. Environ. Med. **58**, 546–552 (2001)
15. Kwahk, K.-Y., Lee, J.-N.: The role of readiness for change in ERP implementation: theoretical bases and empirical validation. Inf. Manag. **45**, 474–481 (2008)
16. Lee, D., Lee, S.M., Olson, D.L., Chung, S.H.: The effect of organizational support on ERP implementation. Ind. Manag. Data Syst. **110**(2), 269–283 (2010)
17. Lutz, W., Sanderson, W., Scherbov, S.: The coming acceleration of global population ageing. Nature **451**, 716–719 (2008)
18. Meuter, M.L., Ostrom, A., Bitner, M.J., Roundtree, R.: The influence of technology anxiety on consumer use and experiences with self service technologies. J. Bus. Res. **56**, 899–906 (2003)
19. Miles, M.B., Huberman, A.M.: Qualitative Data Analysis: An Expanded Sourcebook. Sage Publications, Newbury Park (1994)
20. Nah, F., Tan, X., Teh, S.H.: An empirical investigation on end-user's acceptance of enterprise systems. Inf. Resour. Manag. J. **17**(3), 32–53 (2004)
21. Ng, T.W.H., Feldman, D.C.: Evaluating six common stereotypes about older workers with meta-analytical data. Pers. Psychol. **65**(4), 821–858 (2012)
22. Ng, T.W.H., Feldman, D.C.: A meta-analysis of the relationships of age and tenure with innovation-related behaviour. J. Occup. Organ. Psychol. **86**(4), 585–616 (2013)
23. Parry, E., Strohmeier, S.: HRM in the digital age – digital changes and challenges of the HR profession. Empl. Relat. **36**(4) (2014). https://doi.org/10.1108/ER-03-2014-0032
24. Reday-Mulvey, G.: Working Beyond 60: Key Policies and Practices in Europe. Palgrave Macmillan, London (2005)
25. Renaud, K., Ramsay, J.: Now what was that password again? A more flexible way of identifying and authenticating our seniors. Behav. Inf. Technol. **26**(4), 309–322 (2007)
26. Rothenberger, M.A., Srite, M., Jones-Graham, K.: The impact of project team attributes on ERP system implementations: a positivist field investigation. Inf. Technol. People **23**(1), 80–109 (2010)

27. Shivers-Blackwell, S.L., Charles, A.C.: Ready, set, go: examining student readiness to use ERP technology. J. Manag. Dev. **25**(8), 795–805 (2006)

28. Soja, E., Soja, P.: Exploring determinants of enterprise system adoption success in light of an ageing workforce. In: Themistocleous, M., Rupino da Cunha, P. (eds.) EMCIS 2018. LNBIP, vol. 341, pp. 419–432. Springer, Cham (2019). https://doi.org/10.1007/978-3-030-11395-7_32

29. Soja, E., Soja, P.: Exploring root problems in enterprise system adoption from an employee age perspective: a people-process-technology framework. Inf. Syst. Manag. **34**(4), 333–346 (2017)

30. Soja, E., Soja, P.: Investigating enterprise system adoption failure factors from an employee age perspective. In: Wrycza, S., Maślankowski, J. (eds.) SIGSAND/PLAIS 2017. LNBIP, vol. 300, pp. 124–135. Springer, Cham (2017). https://doi.org/10.1007/978-3-319-66996-0_9

31. Soja, E., Soja, P., Paliwoda-Pękosz, G.: Solving problems during an enterprise system adoption: does employees' age matter? In: Wrycza, S. (ed.) SIGSAND/PLAIS 2016. LNBIP, vol. 264, pp. 131–143. Springer, Cham (2016). https://doi.org/10.1007/978-3-319-46642-2_9

32. Soja, E., Stonawski, M.: Zmiany demograficzne a starsi pracownicy w Polsce z perspektywy podmiotów gospodarczych. In: Kurkiewicz, J. (ed.) Demograficzne uwarunkowania i wybrane społeczno-ekonomiczne konsekwencje starzenia się ludności w krajach europejskich, pp. 173–210. Wydawnictwo Uniwersytetu Ekonomicznego w Krakowie, Kraków (2012)

33. Stypińska, J.: Starszy pracownik na rynku pracy w Polsce: 40+? 50+? Czy tylko "plus"? Studia Socjologiczne **217**(2), 143–165 (2015)

34. Truxillo, D.M., Cadiz, D.M., Hammer, L.B.: Supporting the aging workforce: a review and recommendations for workplace intervention research. Ann. Rev. Organ. Psychol. Organ. Behav. **2**, 351–381 (2015)

35. Urick, M.J., Hollensbe, E.C., Masterson, S.S., Lyons, S.T.: Understanding and managing intergenerational conflict: an examination of influences and strategies. Work Aging Retire. **3**(2), 166–185 (2016)

36. Van Dalen, H.P., Henkens, K., Schippers, J.: Productivity of older workers: perceptions of employers and employees. Popul. Dev. Rev. **36**(3), 309–330 (2010)

37. Volkoff, O., Strong, D.M., Elmes, M.: Understanding enterprise systems-enabled integration. Eur. J. Inf. Syst. **14**, 110–120 (2005)

38. Wagner, N., Hassanein, K., Head, M.: Computer use by older adults: a multi-disciplinary review. Comput. Hum. Behav. **26**, 870–882 (2010)

39. Walker, A., Maltby, T.: Active ageing: a strategic policy solution to demographic ageing in the European Union. Int. J. Soc. Welfare **21**(1), 117–130 (2012)

40. Wille, B., Hofmans, J., Feys, M., De Fruyt, F.: Maturation of work attitudes: correlated change with big five personality traits and reciprocal effects over 15 years. J. Organ. Behav. **35**(4), 507–529 (2014)

Adoption of Digital Technology in Corporate R&D Context

Chao Li⬤, Nikolay Mehandjiev$^{(\boxtimes)}$⬤, Andrew James,
Azar Shahgholian⬤, Joseph Lampel⬤, and Matthew Allen⬤

Alliance Manchester Business School, University of Manchester,
Manchester M15 6PB, UK
n.mehandjiev@manchester.ac.uk

Abstract. Achieving tangible benefits from digitalization often requires changes in processes, culture and reward systems. This need is especially acute in research and development, yet the attitudes and skills of R&D staff may impede their use of automation. We examine the ongoing digitalization of R&D activities at Unilever. Using thematic analysis, we analyze in-depth interviews to uncover attitudes towards, and experiences with, digitalization of R&D using robots. We build on these findings and conduct sequence analysis to extract a number of within-interview sequential associations between themes. These associations have been mapped onto patterns aligned with four established models of digitalization and IT adoption: the Technology Acceptance Model, Resistance to Change, Task Technology Fit and Process Virtualization.

Keywords: Digitalization uptake · R&D automation

1 Research Context

The digitalization of industry, along with new developments such as the Internet of Things and Smart Factories, is likely to bring disruptive changes to businesses (Oks et al. 2016). The adoption of automation and digital technologies in manufacturing companies will lead to better efficiency and innovation performance (Kroll et al. 2018). In particular, in manufacturing, research has focused on the digitalization of manufacturing processes, for instance the application of big data analytics, advanced manufacturing technologies with sensors, advanced robotics and advanced tracking and tracing technologies, and the impacts of these digital technologies on the production management, such as supply chain management and smart operations in factories (Fazili et al. 2017; Ivanov et al. 2019; Nguyen et al. 2018). The emerging discussion on robotic process automation (RPA) among practitioners reveals the concerns and issues for the advanced digital technology adoption. Debrusk proposed five risks for organizations to execute pilots with robots across operations, including standardization issues, adherence to underlying systems, jeopardized success, the lack of process owner incentives and elimination of rethinking capabilities (DeBrusk 2017).

 Digitalization and automation are argued to represent potential sources of disruption to corporate R&D that may lead to better, faster and cheaper R&D (Schimpf 2016). R&D staff are usually recruited following advanced scientific training that

© Springer Nature Switzerland AG 2020
M. Themistocleous and M. Papadaki (Eds.): EMCIS 2019, LNBIP 381, pp. 551–566, 2020.
https://doi.org/10.1007/978-3-030-44322-1_41

confers occupational identity with strong emphasis on autonomy. Traditionally, this was consistent with the needs of corporate R&D. Thus, the corporation accorded R&D staff considerable autonomy - since the autonomy that R&D enjoys compared to other function is strategically crucial for innovation. The implementation of automation and digitalization in R&D gives rise to potential tension between the corporate strategic need to make full use of the benefits of the new technologies associated with automation and digitalization, and the occupational autonomy that R&D staff expect and have traditionally been given within the R&D function. This paper presents an exploratory case study on the technology adoption issues in the corporate R&D digitalization process and examines the underlying factors for accepting technology. This case study is focused on the fast moving consumer goods company Unilever and its ongoing digitalization R&D activities. Unilever produces a wide range of personal care, home care and food products many of whom are based on formulation chemistry. A formulation is a mixture of chemicals that do not react chemically but are designed to produce a final product with desirable characteristics (e.g. a hair shampoo or a domestic cleaning product). Digitalization of R&D has been adopted most rapidly in the pharmaceutical, aerospace and automotive industries, while companies in the formulation industries have been slower to adopt. Nonetheless, over the last decade, large companies in the formulation industries such as household and personal care, food, agrochemicals and coatings have been slowly incorporating modelling and automated high-throughput experimentation processes into their R&D activities (Chemistry Innovation and Intelligent Formulation 2011).

Unilever is making significant investments in automation and digitalization in its newly established R&D facility, the Material Innovation Factory (MIF), opened in 2017. MIF is a public-private research partnership between the University of Liverpool, Unilever and the Higher Education Funding Council for England (HEFCE). It focuses on materials chemistry, soft solids and complex mixtures. The MIF includes a dedicated floor for Unilever research groups to work on internal R&D programmes, and this floor represents the single largest concentration of robotic experimental and test equipment in Unilever. Some robots were relocated from Unilever's Port Sunlight R&D centre, yet most are newly designed and built as part of the investment in the MIF.

This paper makes two contributions to knowledge: Firstly, we establish the relevance of four established models of technology adoption to digitalisation in professional R&D context. We thus set the foundation of an adoption framework to reflect the distinct characteristics of R&D professionals in the context of advanced technology adoption, for example a stronger focus on performance, rather than ease of use and learning costs. Secondly, we use mixed methods approach, thus providing methodological insights for future case study research. We use qualitative approach (thematic analysis) combined with quantitative approach (sequence analysis), to analyze the data collected via semistructured interviews. Thematic analysis helps the researchers to get a comprehensive understanding of the research context and research questions, whilst the sequence analysis supports the researchers to identify association links between constructs.

2 Theoretical Background

Digital transformation is seen as a fundamental and disruptive change to all aspects of business, differentiated from the impacts of automation on manufacturing and processing environment. Therefore the introduction of robots and digital technologies in highly knowledge-intensive professional functions is expected to generate significant impact. This paper focuses on the introduction of robotics and digitalization in industrial R&D. The Industrial Research Institute (US) reports on a project on Digitalization and R&D Management, exploring a range of issues relevant to the digitalization of R&D, including virtual experimentation and simulation; the use of digitalization as a tool for internal and external collaboration; and Big Data (Chemistry Innovation and Intelligent Formulation 2011). Digitalization is reported to shape R&D and R&D management, in the form of virtualization, artificial intelligence, and other technologies (The Industrial Research Institute 2017). However, there is a lack of research examining the organizational and behavioral issues that arise in the adoption of these new technologies by industrial R&D professionals (Euchner 2017). This digital transformation may have a profound impact on the innovation process and the R&D function within large companies. Research has identified that professional workers, such as R&D staff, differ from other workers in the production process, in terms of professional identify and the acceptance of standardization and routinization process caused by digitalization (Susskind and Susskind 2017). R&D departments in large firms, as the highly knowledge intensive department and the core creators of new technologies and innovation, could be affected by the automation and digitalization process differently.

Given the lack of research focused on R&D digitalization in process industries, this paper considers a wider field of theories and frameworks of Information Systems (IS) technology adoption, including the Technology Adoption Model (TAM), the Theory of Planned Behaviour (TPB) and the Theory of Reasoned Action (TRA). Theory of Reasoned Action (TRA) (Fishbein and Ajzen 1975) seeks to explain and understand why people accept or reject computers, from the perspective of their intentions. The key construct described in TRA includes behavioral intention - defined as the strength of an individual to pursue a particular behavior which in turn is influenced by attitude and subjective norms; behavioral attitude - an individual's positive or negative feelings about performing the specific behavior, and subjective norms - an individual's perception that most people that are important to them think that they should or should not perform the behavior. Theory of Planned Behavior (TPB) (Ajzen 1991) is built on the TRA and extended the TRA by adding the construct of perceived behavioral control, which is defined as an individual's perception of the ease or difficulty of performing the behavior. The model has been applied to the understanding of adoption of many different technologies and in various industries (Harrison et al. 1997; Mathieson 1991; Pavlou and Fygenson 2006). The Technology Acceptance Model (TAM) (Davis 1989) extends the TPB by focusing particular attention on the role in adoption of the perceived usefulness and perceived ease of use of the innovation. In this model, attitude to use and intention to use are based on the definitions used in the TRA/TPB. For instance, perceived usefulness is defined as the degree to which a person believes that using a particular innovation will enhance their job performance, while perceived ease of use is defined as the degree to which a person believes that using a particular innovation would be free from effort.

These models offer differing but complementary insights into the process of innovation adoption (Solbraa Bay 2016). In particular, in highlighting the importance of Attitude – all three models have at their core an emphasis on the importance of individuals' beliefs or perceptions as key independent variables for adoption behavior; Ease of use and complexity – the TAM emphasizes perceived ease of use as an important factor in the adoption decision; and the Usefulness and relative advantage – the TAM highlights perceptions of usefulness or relative advantage in the intention to adopt an innovation.

3   Research Methodology

The aim to explore the automation and digitalization process of R&D activities and to understand the factors and conditions which determine success of the robotics uptake in an industrial context motivates our adopting the exploratory case study methodology (Yin 2009). This methodology has been widely used in social science fields like sociology, industrial relations and innovation studies (Lundvall 2007; Motohashi and Yun 2007; Xibao 2007). It is considered as a research strategy concerning how and why questions and allowing investigation of contextual realities and the differences between what was planned and what actually happened. It is also used as an empirical inquiry that investigates a contemporary phenomenon within real-life context (Yin 2009) and probes an area of interest in depth which enable the researcher to understand the complex real-life activities (Noor 2008). The case study approach enables researchers to go into the field, acting as an observer while collecting data for analysis and theory building, understanding the conditions, constraints and challenges of the research topic in the practical environment.

Within the scope of the explorative case study, semi-structured interviews were undertaken to conduct data collection and mixed methods (qualitative and quantitative methods) were adopted to conduct data analysis, in order to uncover the research context with a holistic view and explore the research question through multiple lens. Especially, this research adopts 18 semi-structured interviews with management team and engineers/scientists working with the automatic and digital tools for the data collection process. Different data analysis methods are adopted to analyze data collected via various approaches. The qualitative data collected via semi-structured interviews is analyzed using thematic analysis. The resultant list of themes and sub-themes is then analyzed using sequence analysis in order to identify patterns and relationships between themes and subthemes.

Figure 1 shows the methodological pathway of the research, including data collection and analysis methods used. The remainder of this section will introduce the rationale for selecting these methods and present the results from this selection.

A research protocol to guide the semi-structured interview was developed based on the understanding of research context and the study of existing literature on adoption of technology. Protocols were developed with the above factors in mind and related to the business context – to understand the progress and issues with the newly opened R&D

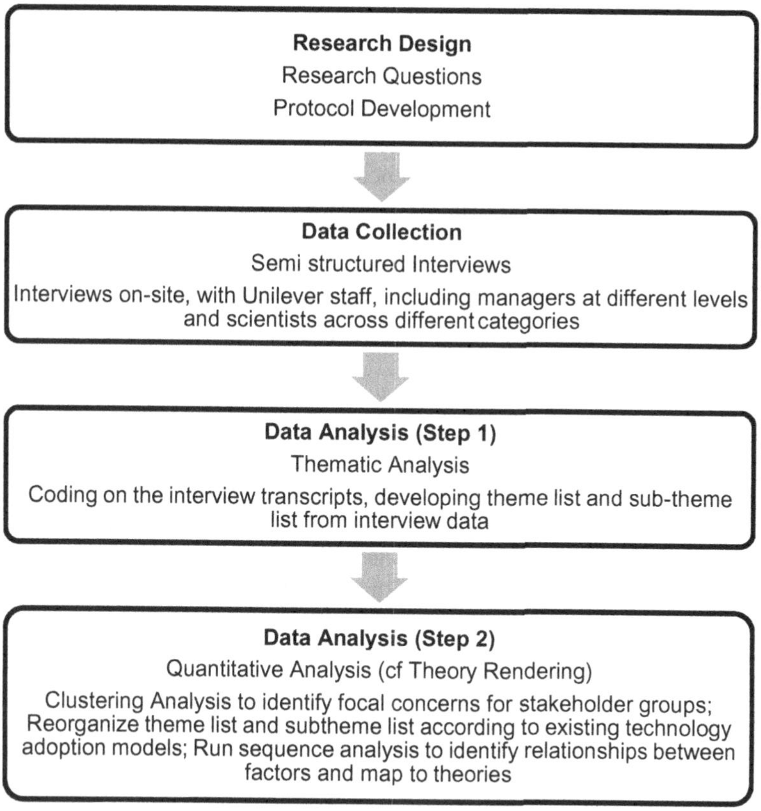

Research Design
Research Questions
Protocol Development

Data Collection
Semi structured Interviews
Interviews on-site, with Unilever staff, including managers at different levels and scientists across different categories

Data Analysis (Step 1)
Thematic Analysis
Coding on the interview transcripts, developing theme list and sub-theme list from interview data

Data Analysis (Step 2)
Quantitative Analysis (cf Theory Rendering)
Clustering Analysis to identify focal concerns for stakeholder groups; Reorganize theme list and subtheme list according to existing technology adoption models; Run sequence analysis to identify relationships between factors and map to theories

Fig. 1. Methodological pathway

facilities aiming for automatic and digital transformation. Semi-structured interviews were then conducted following the guidance of the above protocols. Both managers and R&D scientists related to MIF were approached for interviews in order to collect information of the research context and understand the research question from various angles. All the interviews were conducted by at least two professionally trained researchers from the research group, using interview protocols that were designed especially for interviews with managers and scientists.

The protocols act as guidelines of the interview and also give researches authority to vary and expand the conversation based on the interviewee's experience and responses. This allows the researcher to gather information from various perspectives and gain deeper understanding of research questions. Through interviews with managers and scientists with the two different sets of questions, the researchers were enabled a chance to understand the context of Unilever's digital strategy from a top-down perspective and to explore the conditions of acceptance and adoption of digital technologies from a bottom-up perspective. In total, 18 interviews were conducted from November 2017 to May 2018, including 5 interviews with senior and middle management, 7 interviews with team leader scientists and 6 interviews with scientists and technicians.

The analysis followed a mixed methods approach, where a qualitative thematic analysis established a number of relevant factors impacting attitudes and implementation of the digitalization process, and this was followed by quantitative analysis which aimed to profile concerns according to different types of stakeholders and to establish relationships between different factors and attitudes to technology uptake.

The qualitative analysis worked in inductive mode to extract the themes and subthemes discussed at interviews, then we proceeded in quantitative mode using clustering to profile concerns against stakeholder groups. This was followed by abductive qualitative analysis to align the derived codes with well-known factors from technology acceptance theories and finally we applied sequence analysis techniques to uncover any relationships between factors, and to map these to relationships from existing technology acceptance models.

The data collected via semi-structured interviews was analyzed using thematic analysis method, which is a well-used method in qualitative research focusing on examining themes, identifying, analyzing and reporting patterns based on interview data (Braun and Clarke 2006). (Guest et al. 2012) claim that thematic analysis goes beyond simply counting phrases or words in a text but moves on to identifying implicit and explicit ideas within data. The researchers start working on coding, which is the primary process for developing themes within raw data. Coding allows researchers to recognize important moments in the data and encode it prior to interpretation. In this research, all interview transcriptions were analyzed using thematic analysis and carefully coded by at least 2 researchers.

The thematic analysis of the semi-structured interview data strictly follows the standard process. For the first step, the researchers were assigned to read the transcriptions and note down the patterns shown in the data and potential themes emerged, when different researchers came up with an independent list of key themes that they picked up from the data. A discussion meeting was organized for all the researchers to explain the key theme list they generated for mutual understanding and therefore an integrated list of themes was agreed. The integrated list of themes was then used to analyze a few more interviews to test the robustness of the themes.

After continuous discussions and refinement, the coding system including the key themes and sub-themes was developed. The key themes emerged from the thematic analysis that indicating the conditions of the firm's digitalization process, includes characterization of digitalization, vision of the future, reasons for digitalization, attitude towards digitalization, impact on day to day work, behavioral influences on adoption, organizational influences and technological influences on adoption, and change management process. Within each theme, a series of subthemes are identified, illustrating in details how the key themes are constructed and represents the different thoughts among the informants.

4   Research Findings

4.1   Key Factors Influencing Digital Technology Adoption of Corporate R&D

The primary findings also show that there are several factors that could affect the introduction of digitalization into the R&D process, especially, behavioral, organizational and technological influences.

Vision, Understanding and Attitude of Digitalization. The analysis identifies although staff holding promising vision and understanding the reasons of digitalization, such as improving efficiency, creating new approach to research, utilizing big data and modelling, there are still different attitude towards the transformation from traditional approach to digital approach. While understanding the reason behind the introduction of digitalization, including growing competitive threats, developing better experimentation in terms of new possibilities improved efficiency, accuracy and standardization, as well as achieving better financial performance via better productivity, there are still mixed attitudes among the interviewed staff. While some staff are quite positive and highly engaged, there are a large number of employees who are hesitate and resistant to the change, or even fearful to the change. The reasons why there are these attitudes could be linked to the different aspects, for instance, the perceptions of how digitalization impacts on their work, the behavioral, organizational and technological factors.

Impact of Digitalization on Day to Day Work. Interviewee's perception of the actual or potential impact of digitalization on the content of her/his work, how s/he carries out that work, how and with whom s/he communicates, and her/his responsibilities (include here both formal and informal aspects) reflects on their attitudes towards the adoption of the digital technologies. For instance, some employees are concerned about the management of relationships with team members and the lost control of their work content, time and data generated from the new experimental approaches. They would also have to change work habits and change experimental methods to adapt to the change. These impacts of digitalization on day to day work have are mentioned as concerns in the process of digital technology adoption.

Organizational Influences of Technology Adoption. The organizational factors include elements like the organizational structure of Unilever, management style, global labs, prior experience of ICT implementation and MIF enabling networking, which represents what types of organizational structures and behaviors that could affect the digital technology adoption within the company. For instance, different categories and functions within the company might have different programs of the technology introduction, which could lead to different work progress and acceptance level among employees on using the new technologies. Another organizational factor is the networking effect within and across organizations that generated during digitalization. While utilizing digital tools, more opportunities for networking and sharing data/experimentation across research teams, as well as with collaborators outside the company, are generated. According to some informants, the benefit acquired from networking encourages them to engage in the digitalization process and make them more likely to adopt digital technologies.

Technological Influences of Technology Adoption. The technological factors covers aspects such like commissioning and validating robots, data quality/trust in robot generated data, ICT infrastructure, inappropriate expectations of the technology, learning/new skill sets, perceived unreliability of the technology, etc. For instance, while the digital technology was introduced into the traditional system, it requires new working approaches which lead to learning of new techniques and new skills of employees. The new techniques learning is different from existing knowledge base and requires more effort, which is identified as an important factor that hinders the adoption of digital technology. Meanwhile, having been working on bench for decades, it is not easy for scientists and engineers to believe that the data produced from robot-run experiments are as solid as that from bench experiments. In the initial process of robot commissioning and validation, the perceived unreliability of the technology is also an important factor influencing the adoption. While the pressure of individual/team performance exists in the organization, it is essential that individual scientists and teams could get access to technologies that have been established and could produce trustful information.

Change Management and Management Commitment. Besides the above factors identified in the coding system from behavioral, organizational and technological perspectives, the thematic analysis also discovered impacts from firm change management activities, in terms of what has been done (or what is planned) to prepare and support individuals, teams, and the company as a whole in making the change towards digitalization. Within the change management scope, communication and consultation from management is identifies as a critical factor that influences the adoption process. Management commitment is another important factor. For instance, the interviews uncover the expectation from employees to receive strong and clear message from top management and middle management and to understand how the transformation could benefit their individual work. Otherwise, if the message is not conveyed effectively, it is hard for employees to figure out how the digital transformation relates to their individual and team work responsibilities. Financial compensation and incentives, trainings sessions and other supporting programs are identified as good approaches to facilitate the digital transformation process, as they could take out some obvious obstacles for some employees.

4.2 New Technology Acceptance Model for Corporate R&D Digitalization

In order to further identify the focal points of concern for different types of stakeholders and to identify relationships between the different factors, we have used a data mining technique, the sequence analysis. Before applying sequence analysis, the codes identified from the thematic analysis were reorganized into a new structure, which links to existing technology adoption theories. The codes are reclassified into different constructs according to the primary sequence analysis results and a reconsideration of the constructs relating to existing theories, a technique borrowed from the palette of grounded theory analysis but fully aligned with the exploratory nature of our case study research. For instance, relative change management activities such as change in vision and language used to communicate and management communications are classified into the new group labelled as communication quality, while the change management activities such as financial compensation for extra travel and incentives are classified into the new group of facilitating conditions. Using the restructured codes, sequence analysis was applied to explore potential linkages among the constructs considering the order in which they appear in the text. The analysis was run on 1429 lines of codes.

Table 1 shows the association rules identified between the constructs Task Characteristics (TaC), Technology Characteristics (TeC), Perceived Compatibility (PC), Perceived Usefulness (PU), and Intention to Use (ItU). The results shows that TaC and PU appear together in 2/3rds of our interviews and that in 41.6% of the cases the mention of TaC is shortly followed by discussion of PU. Overall, the derived rules suggest that the characteristics of technology and task and how people perceive the compatibility of the technology to the task are very important for their perception of usefulness of the technology.

Table 1. Association rules related to perceived usefulness.

If antecedent then consequent	Support %	Confidence %
If task characteristics *then* perceived usefulness	66.6	41.6
If technology characteristics *then* perceived usefulness	100	38.8
If Perceived Compatibility *then* Perceived Usefulness	83.3	46.6
If Perceived Usefulness *then* Intention to use	94.4	23.5

Meanwhile, another rule identified in the analysis is the link between PU and ItU, which also appear frequently together. The result indicates that when our respondents discussed the usefulness of the technology, they also discussed their intention to use and adopt the technology. In the next section we describe how the association rules identified between the task and technology characteristics and perceived usefulness indicate the relevance of the Task-Technology fit model (Goodhue and Thompson 1995) and the process virtualization theory (Overby 2012) for our focal context of R&D digitalization.

Table 2 shows the association rules identified between the constructs Facilitating Conditions (FC), Perceived Ease of Use (PEoU) and Intention to Use (ItU). According to the sequence analysis, interview participants discuss frequently FC and PEoU in close sequence, and also PEoU and ItU are often discussed together. The results show that the facilitating conditions such as training and supports for adoption activities are essential for people's perception of ease of use of the technology and therefore affects people's intention of use and the technology adoption performance. In the next section we explain why the interplay between perceived ease of use, facilitating conditions and intention to use depicted in Table 2 is indicative of the relevance of the UTAUT (Venkatesh et al. 2016) to our focal context.

Table 2. Association rules related to perceived ease of use.

If antecedent then consequent	Support %	Confidence %
If facilitating conditions *then* perceived ease of use	83.3	46.6
If perceived ease of use *then* intention to use	72.2	30.7

Table 3 shows the rules related to Resistance to Change (RtC) and some organizational characteristics, including Organizational Factors (OF), Communication Quality (CQ), Job Security (JS), and Employee-Management Relationships (EMR). The first a few rules shows that OF and CQ are linked to RtC, with RtC as consequent. The following rules shows that RtC is linked with PU, while RtC is identified as antecedent and PU is identified as consequent. The relationship shows that the organizational characteristics and communication between management and employees have influence on employee's resistant attitude to accept the change, which further impacts on their perception of usefulness of the technology. In the next section, we demonstrate how the links between constructs identified in Table 3 indicate the relevance of the Resistance to Change model (Amarantou et al. 2018) to our context and suggests ways in which its constructs interact with variables from the UTAUT (Venkatesh et al. 2016) and TTF (Goodhue and Thompson 1995).

Table 3. Association rules related to perceived usefulness.

If antecedent then consequent	Support %	Confidence %
If organizational factors *then* resistance to change	100	22.2
If communication quality *then* resistance to change	94.4	29.4
If (resistance to change > resistance to change) *then*	33.3	66.6
Perceived usefulness	38.8	57.14
If job security *then* perceived usefulness		
If employee-management relationship *then* perceived usefulness	38.8	57.14

5 Proposing a Technology Adoption Theory Within the Context of Digitizing Research and Development Activities

The results from our exploratory study of Unilever's digital technology transformation project provide a rich insight into factors which impact the digitalization of research and development work in corporate context. Considering the widely accepted models of technology adoption, we have found sufficient evidence to consider the following shortlist of models relevant to our focal context: UTAUT (Venkatesh et al. 2016), TTF (Goodhue and Thompson 1995) and Resistance to Change (Amarantou et al. 2018). The association rules also implicate specific ways of linking the elements of these three models.

First of all, the research results are aligned with conventional technology adoption models, by identifying that perceived usefulness and perceived ease of use are two main factors that affect user's intention to use and adopt the technology (see Tables 1 and 2 in the previous section). The Technology Acceptance Model (Davis 1989) extended the Theory of Planned Behavior by focusing particular attention on the role in adoption of the perceived usefulness and perceived ease of use of the innovation. Perceived usefulness is defined as the degree to which a person believes that using a particular innovation will enhance her or his job performance and perceived ease of use is defined as the degree to which a person believes that using a particular innovation would be free from effort. Our findings from the thematic analysis and sequence analysis are consistent with Yi et al. (2006) study of information technology acceptance in the US healthcare sector, demonstrating that perceived usefulness plays the most important role in determining physicians' intentions to accept a technology.

Furthermore, the analysis in the previous section also demonstrates the importance of antecedents of perceived usefulness and perceived ease of use found in the task-technology fit model (Goodhue and Thompson 1995), and, to a lesser extent, the process virtualization model (Overby 2012), with the key antecedents of perceived compatibility and task-technology fit (Table 1), and facilitating conditions (Table 2). Our association rules also identify how these constructs could be integrated into the traditional technology adoption model within our focal context. Facilitating conditions, which refer to the organizational and technological support that the organization provides to employees in to adopt the new technology, are identified as important antecedent of perceived ease of use. Agarwal and Prasad (2000) examined the adoption of new software development process innovations by systems developers and found that certain beliefs about the attributes of target technologies, including the perception of relative advantage, ease of use and compatibility, played a part as did external factors such as organizational tenure, prior technical knowledge, training experiences and perceived job insecurity (Agarwal and Prasad 2000). In addition, the research emphasizes that structured training is highly beneficial for professionals to integrate the new technology into their work.

The task characteristics and the technology characteristics are aligned with the task-technology fit model, which explains that when the capabilities of the technology match the tasks which users' perform, is this likely to have a positive impact on the performance of adopters (Goodhue and Thompson 1995). The task-technology fit model emphasizes that technology has to match tasks and the requirement of users. In this model, the research identifies that interviewees pay attention to the technology characteristics and how the adoption of certain technologies could support their achievement of every work and job tasks. In particular, this concern links to their perception of usefulness of the technology and leads to their different levels of intention to use the technology.

The perceived compatibility, which has been identified also as an antecedent of perceived usefulness (PU), could be sourced back to the process virtualization theory (Overby 2012). The process virtualization theory focuses on how the introduction of digital technology leads the transition of traditional physical activities into virtual processes. According to the interviews, the transition process from physical activities to automatic and digital techniques is sometimes questioned by employees since there might be missing parts/tacit knowledge/experience during the transition. Therefore, the transformation from traditional working approaches to digital methods needs to concern the perceived compatibility and make sure that the new technologies comply with and represent the traditional approach in order to win user's trust and gain higher level of perceived usefulness.

Finally, the research results in Table 3 indicate that a set of organizational and psychological factors may also affect user's perception of technology usefulness and thus impact on user's intention to use. In particular, resisting change could be affected by the communication quality between management team and employees and a set of other organizational factors (see Table 3) which are not common in the technology acceptance literature. The resistance to change model (Amarantou et al. 2018) can thus act as a source of guidance towards reducing problems associated with organization change. This findings suggests that management team of an organization which seeks to achieve technology transition, should pay attention to the communication and language shared with employees to reduce their resistance attitude and increase their perceived usefulness of the technology.

6 Summary and Conclusion

This paper presents an exploratory case study capturing the digital transformation of Research and Development activities within a multi-national company, connected with a migration to a new facility and increased use of robots for experimentation and testing. We have used semi-structured interviews to gather detailed information about the considerations and perceptions of a number of experts and their managers regarding this transformation. We have analyzed the transcribed interviews to extract themes related to technology adoption using thematic analysis followed by sequence analysis. This resulted in a set of association rules between themes related to four existing technology adoption models. The association rules also indicated ways in which elements may interact within and between models. Thus our mixed methods study gave rise to an innovative emergent model of technology adoption in the context of digitalization of R&D activities in a multi-national corporation.

Appendix 1: Managerial Questions

Managerial questions
(General questions to Managers to get context to Unilever digitization/automation)
1. The term "digitization" is widely used today, both within Unilever and elsewhere. What does digitization mean to you? How do your colleagues interpret the term? Does their interpretation differ significantly from yours? If so, in what way?
2. In your opinion, what are the MAIN reasons UNILEVER is introducing digitization?
3. How far have you progressed with digitization?
4. What have been the challenges? What have been the challenges for others do you think?
5. Have the working practices of staff changed as a result of digitization?
6. How do you see the introduction of digitization in the near to medium future?

Appendix 2: Questions for MIF R&D Scientists

Managerial questions
(General questions to Managers to get context to Unilever digitization/automation)
1. What part does the MIF play in your role?
2. What were your expectations of the MIF before you began working here?
3. What does MIF mean for the way that you work?
4. What training have you received for MIF?
5. How long did it take you to feel mastery of the work process?
6. What are the main challenges that you've faced?
7. How has your experience compared to that of your colleagues?
8. More widely, do you have any views about the introduction of digitization in Unilever?

Appendix 3: Reclassification of Codes

Reclassification of codes	
Communication quality	Includes codes Change in vision and language used to communicate change Management commitment; Relationship management; Top management awareness
Employee-management relationship	Consultation; Management style; Performance measurement and Incentives
Facilitating Conditions	Financial compensation for extra travel; Support for adoption; Training; Incentives
Intention to use	Engaging; Excited; Positive
Job security	Fearful
Organizational factors	Differences between categories; Different levels of staff access to MIF; Lack of formal change management process; Role of champions; Resource allocation;
Perceived compatibility	Work habits; Inappropriate expectations of the technology; The need for new skill sets; Previous experience using robots

(continued)

(continued)

Reclassification of codes	
Perceived ease of use	Travel to work; Location change; Learning of new skills
Perceived usefulness	High expectation; Data sharing; Productivity; Better experimentation - data utilization; Better experimentation - new possibilities; Better experimentation - standardization; Collaboration; Competitive threats; Efficiency/accuracy/repeatability; Supplier specification; Disrupt through digital; Efficiency/added value; Global R&D/internal sharing; New approach to research
Resistance to change	Hesitate; Negative; Resistant; Sceptical; Established work habits
Task characteristics	Experimental methods; Time management
Technology characteristics	Logistics; Commissioning and validating robots; Data quality; ICT infrastructure; Perceived unreliability of the technology; Standardization; Technical limits of automation - measuring intangible aspects; Translating physical to automated processes; Trust in robot generated data

References

Agarwal, R., Prasad, J.: A field study of the adoption of software process innovations by information systems professionals. IEEE Trans. Eng. Manag. **47**(3), 295–308 (2000)

Amarantou, V., Kazakopoulou, S., Chatzoudes, D., Chatzoglou, P.: Resistance to change, an empirical investigation of its antecedents. J. Organ. Change Manag. **31**(2), 426–450 (2018). https://doi.org/10.1108/JOCM-05-2017-0196

Ajzen, I.: The theory of planned behavior. Organ. Behav. Hum. Decis. Process. **50**(2), 179–211 (1991)

Braun, V., Clarke, V.: Using thematic analysis in psychology. Qual. Res. Psychol. **3**(2), 77–101 (2006)

Chemistry Innovation and Intelligent Formulation: Smart formulation: the use of modelling and high throughput experimentation (HTe) to revolutionise formulation development in the UK, UK (2011)

Davis, F.D.: Perceived usefulness, perceived ease of use, and user acceptance of information technology. Manag. Inf. Syst. Q. **13**(3), 319–340 (1989)

DeBrusk, C.: Five robotic process automation risks to avoid. MIT Sloan Manag. Rev. (2017). https://sloanreview.mit.edu/article/five-robotic-process-automation-risks-to-avoid/. Accessed 13 Mar 2020

Euchner, J.: Navigating the digitalization of R&D. Res.-Technol. Manag. **60**(5), 10–11 (2017). https://doi.org/10.1080/08956308.2017.1348123

Fazili, M., Venkatadri, U., Cyrus, P., Tajbakhsh, M.: Physical Internet, conventional and hybrid logistic systems: a routing optimisation-based comparison using the Eastern Canada road network case study. Int. J. Prod. Res. **55**(9), 2703–2730 (2017)

Fishbein, M., Ajzen, I.: Belief, Attitude, Intention and Behavior: An Introduction to Theory and Research. Addison-Wesley, Reading (1975)

Goodhue, D.L., Thompson, R.L.: Task-technology fit and individual performance. Manag. Inf. Syst. Q. **19**(2), 213–236 (1995)

Guest, G., Macqueen, K.M., Namey, E.: Applied Thematic Analysis. Sage, Thousand Oaks (2012)

Harrison, D.A., Mykytyn, Peter P., Riemenschneider, C.K.: Executive decisions about adoption of information technology in small business: theory and empirical tests. Inf. Syst. Res. **8**(2), 171–195 (1997)

Ivanov, D., Dolgui, A., Sokolov, B.: The impact of digital technology and Industry on the ripple effect and supply chain risk analytics. Int. J. Prod. Res. **57**(3), 829–846 (2019)

Kroll, H., Horvat, D., Jäger, A.: Effects of automatisation and digitalisation on manufacturing companies' production efficiency and innovation performance. Discussion Papers- Innovation Systems and Policy Analysis: 58 (2018)

Lundvall, B.Å.: National innovation systems—analytical concept and development tool. Ind. Innov. **14**(1), 95–119 (2007)

Mathieson, K.: Predicting user intentions: comparing the technology acceptance model with the theory of planned behavior. Inf. Syst. Res. **2**(3), 173–191 (1991)

Motohashi, K., Yun, X.: China's innovation system reform and growing industry and science linkages. Res. Policy **36**(8), 1251–1260 (2007)

Nguyen, T., Zhou, L., Spiegler, V., Ieromonachou, P., Lin, Y.: Big data analytics in supply chain management: a state-of-the-art literature review. Comput. Oper. Res. **98**, 254–264 (2018)

Noor, K.B.M.: Case study: a strategic research methodology. Am. J. Appl. Sci. **5**(11), 1602–1604 (2008)

Oks, S.J., Fritzsche, A., Lehmann, C.: The digitalisation of industry from a strategic perspective. In: R&D Management Conference, Cambridge, UK (2016)

Overby, E.: Migrating processes from physical to virtual environments: process virtual- ization theory. In: Dwivedi, Y., Wade, M., Schneberger, S. (eds.) Information Systems Theory. ISI, vol. 28, pp. 107–124. Springer, New York (2012). https://doi.org/10.1007/978-1-4419-6108-2_6

Pavlou, P.A., Fygenson, M.: Understanding and predicting electronic commerce adoption: an extension of the theory of planned behavior. Manag. Inf. Syst. Q. **30**(1), 115–143 (2006)

Schimpf, S.: Crowdsourcing, digitisation and acceleration: is corporate R&D disrupting itself? In: R&D Management Conference 2016 "From Science to Society: Innovation and Value Creation", Cambridge, UK (2016)

Solbraa Bay, T.: Innovation adoption in robotics: consumer intentions to use autonomous vehicles. Norwegian School of Economics (2016)

Susskind, R., Susskind, D.: The future of the professions: how technology will transform the work of human experts. J. Nurs. Regul. **8**(2), 52 (2017)

The Industrial Research Institute: Digitalization and its implications for R&D management. Res.-Technol. Manag. **60**(5), 22–23 (2017)

Venkatesh, V., Thong, J.Y.L., Xu, X.: Unified theory of acceptance and use of technology: a synthesis and the road ahead. J. Assoc. Inf. Syst. **17**(5), 328–376 (2016). Article 1

WEF: White Paper - Digital Transformation Initiative Chemistry and Advanced Materials Industry. Switzerland (2017)

Xibao, L.: A case study on the changes in the innovation capability of China's regions: a concept based on the innovation system. Manag. World **12**, 18–30 (2007)

Yi, M.Y., Jackson, J.D., Park, J.S., Probst, J.C.: Understanding information technology acceptance by individual professionals: toward an integrative view. Inf. Manag. **43**(3), 350–363 (2006)

Yin, R.: Case Study Research: Design and Methods, four edn. Sage, Thousand Oaks (2009)

ERP Implementation: Requirements Engineering for ERP Product Customization

Tarik Kraljić(✉) and Adnan Kraljić

Ghent University, Ghent, Belgium
{tarik.kraljic,adnan.kraljic}@ugent.be

Abstract. Requirements Engineering (RE) is the basis for efficient software implementation and quality management. Tools which support RE in general are numerous nowadays; however, the task of providing a tool that specializes in RE for dynamic, customizable service-centric systems (like ERP systems) has been addressed rarely. According to this we proposed an artifact in a form of software functionalities list derived from performing literature review and through intensive discussion with our industry partners. Relevance of proposed application functionalities were discussed with experts in a form of interviews and those are presented in this research paper. A support application for collaborative requirements engineering and software artifacts traceability, with focus on ERP product customization will be developed and presented in further research work.

Keywords: Collaborative requirements engineering · Enterprise Resource Planning · ERP implementation · Customizable software (ERP) products

1 Introduction

For at least a decade, documentation and negotiation of the requirements for systems based on commercial off-the-shelf (COTS) components have been regarded as an important sub- area of Requirements Engineering (RE). An important example of a project dealing with COTS-based system is the implementation of an enterprise solution based on packaged software, or the widely called Enterprise Resource Planning (ERP) [1].

ERP, a term coined by Gartner Research Group in 1992, is a type of Commercial - off-the- Shelf (COTS) software that should provide an integrated optimized solution as a bundle for businesses to take care of functions including all internal and external operations required.

The role of Enterprise Resource Planning (ERP) systems in managing business processes has expanded significantly over the past decade from an emphasis on specific business areas such as sales, manufacturing or purchasing, to broader use throughout the company.

By the definition, ERP systems come with best practice (an in-built process suggestion) of how a business should work and how data should flow within the organization. While the built-in processes in an ERP often can be considered best practices, there is no guarantee that they will work better than the current processes in an organization [2].

© Springer Nature Switzerland AG 2020
M. Themistocleous and M. Papadaki (Eds.): EMCIS 2019, LNBIP 381, pp. 567–581, 2020.
https://doi.org/10.1007/978-3-030-44322-1_42

Instead of making a system completely adapted to the company's processes, an ERP system offers a set of processes for the organization to follow [3]. While the main job of the system is to improve the flow of information in an organization, it's inevitable that the business processes are affected as well [3]. In fact, using an ERP as a solution to solve operational problems such as ineffective business processes is frequently stated as motivation for the implementation [4]. But, we are witness of high numbers ERP projects which do not satisfies initial customer expectations. As Fig. 1 shows, less than 50% of implementations achieve expected benefits, while only 17% of the companies experienced more than eighty percent of their projected benefits.

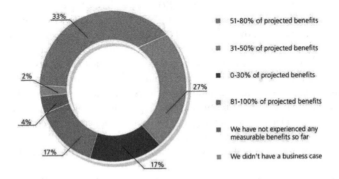

Fig. 1. Project expected benefits

Research done by the consulting group Panorama Consulting Solutions shows that one of the reasons that ERP implementations take longer than expected or fail to achieve their expected benefits can be attributed to the high degree of code customization used to tailor ERP systems to business requirements (business process requirements) (see Fig. 2). The research shows that 60% of companies perform some degree of customization which can contribute to longer implementation times and higher costs (Panorama Consulting Solutions Report 2012).

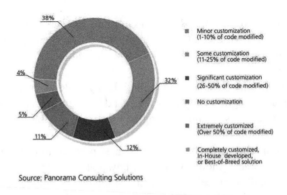

Fig. 2. Levels of ERP customization

As we see in Fig. 2. ERP systems implementations tend to be conservative, regarding the scope of customization and change. And this is the issue for the most customers – they are not satisfied with the extend of system modification in favor of their own business processes.

This paper rests on previous work in ERP RE [4, 5] and the experiences published by [6, 7]. Our research also builds on the works of Davenport [8, 9], Hong and Kim [10], Gattiket and Goodhue [11], Markus [12], and Soh et al. [13] in analyzing the alignment perspective in ERP projects. Although the ERP literature highlight the issue of misalignments in ERP projects, the mere assertion that they arise from unmet organizational requirements masks the variety of sources of misalignments.

> In order to better manage and improve business processes by implementing one type of COTS based system (ERP), company has to set clear functional requirements which are derivate from Requirements Engineering process.

2 Requirements Engineering and ERP Software

The requirements for ERP concern the business processes and the data flows that the ERP system. These requirements reflect the needs of organizational units in one or more companies for a system that helps solve management and cooperation problems related to processing, for example, a purchase order, a good receipt, a sales order or managing human resources. RE for ERP is about composition and reconciliation of conflicting demands [14]. The RE process usually starts with a general set of business process and data requirements, then helps explore standard ERP-package functionality to see how closely it matches the ERP adopting organization's process and data needs [15].

This typically happens in an iterative fashion and includes:

- Mapping each partner company's organizational structure into the ERP- package's predefined organization units;
- Defining a scope for business process standardization using standard application modules;
- Creating business process and data architectures specific to the extended enterprise based on predefined reusable package-specific process and data models;
- Specifying data conversion, reporting, and interface requirements.

Currently, vendors of business software packages and their consulting partners provide standard RE processes for ERP projects. In addition, a number of creative solutions were proposed by researchers and practitioners to further reduce the cost of RE -for- ERP by avoiding scope definition problems, involving the right stakeholders, assigning sufficient resources, adopting goal-directed project management practices, and enlisting the vendors' and consultants' support to those problems [4]. Despite these efforts, it is still very difficult to find a match between the flexibility often required by the business and the rigidity usually imposed by the ERP-package modules [16].

Case studies and experience reports about ERP implementations are now being published by companies in nearly any industry sector. Furthermore, there is much bigger awareness of the importance of good ERP practices and their adoption.

To demonstrate the surge of RE publication on ERP systems, we did a brief search of literature sources in a few prominent bibliographic databases (IEEE Explore, ACM Digital Library, Springer link), which produced Fig. 3.

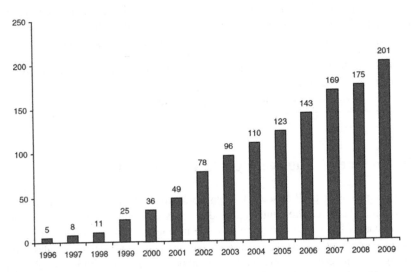

Fig. 3. Number of publications in three bibliographic databases in the last 15 years

3 Activates in Requirements Engineering Process

The activities involved in requirements engineering vary widely, depending on the type of system being developed and the specific practices of the organization(s) involved. These may include:

1. *Requirements inception or requirements elicitation* - Developers and stakeholders meet, the latter are inquired concerning their needs and wants regarding the software product.
2. *Requirements analysis and negotiation* - Requirements are identified (including new ones if the development is iterative) and conflicts with stakeholders are solved. Both written and graphical tools (the latter commonly used in the design phase but some find them helpful at this stage, too) are successfully used as aids. Examples of written analysis tools: use cases and user stories. Examples of graphical tools: UML [8] and LML.

3. *System modeling* - Some Engineering fields (or specific situations) require the product to be completely designed and modeled before its construction or fabrication starts and, therefore, the design phase must be performed in advance. For instance, blueprints for a building must be elaborated before any contract can be approved and signed. Many fields might derive models of the system with the Lifecycle Modeling Language, whereas others, might use UML. Note: In many fields, such as Software Engineering, most modeling activities are classified as design activities and not as requirement engineering activities.

4. *Requirements specification* - Requirements are documented in a formal artifact called Requirements Specification (RS). Nevertheless, it will become official only after validation. A RS can contain both written and graphical (models) information if necessary. Example: Software requirements specification (SRS).

5. *Requirements validation* - Checking that the documented requirements and models are consistent and meet the needs of the stakeholder. Only if the final draft passes the validation process, the RS becomes official.

6. *Requirements management* - Managing all the activities related to the requirements since inception, supervising as the system is developed and, even until after it is put into use (e.g., changes, extensions, etc.)

In the next paragraphs we will discuss one of the most common Requirements engineering framework/tool introduced by the biggest ERP vendors (SAP and Oracle). It is widely known as Fit Gap Analysis.

4 Fit Gap Analysis

The ERP implementation process consists of the following phases: a fit and gap analysis (FGA) to identify business processes and customization requirements, which act as the principal decision making phase for customization needs; system design and development; data conversions from legacy system; testing of the new system; training of the super-users and end users; and deployment. These activities may vary with the nature of the project based on if it is an upgrade or merger. ERP is generally distributed in two forms [17]: Generic or Preconfigured. Generic ERP software targets a variety of businesses and industries, and therefore must be configured early. Preconfigured ERP software is tailored to a specific industrial sector. However, both forms need customizations.

During requirements elicitation, interviews with users during various phases of a project are a necessity. At project initiation, stakeholders are interviewed to determine scope, rationale and core gaps in requirements. During analysis, meeting users help discover and document requirements for enhancements, customizations and reengineering needs. Sessions with stakeholders throughout the testing phase helps to validate and verify that gaps have been closed. In agile development, these activities are iterative and incremental, and therefore fit - gap analysis (FGA) represents a plausible solution.

In FGA, we deal with two domains. The first is the domain that already exists, which is the source domain of the business needs and basic non-functional requirements. This is commonly termed as the legacy system. The second domain is the demonstrative ERP solution. The ERP demo environment is the target domain which will be customized and adjusted with required configuration. At the beginning, a high-end workable prototype is placed for analysis. Analysts can therefore choose to work on different modules of functionalities to: identify the fitting business functions, discard obsolete legacy features, suppress additional ERP features, and/or prescribe necessary customizations.

The principal goals of FGA include: creating a workable prototype of the target domain; assigning legacy experts and domain consultants for business areas; engaging associated technical experts of both legacy and target domain in analysis; documenting and specifying functional needs for each requirement; and iteratively refactoring specifications according to an agile development life-cycle. Non-functional requirements such as the minimum hardware and platform vary based on the vendor software and release version.

SAP Solution Manager in SAP Activate on-premise project

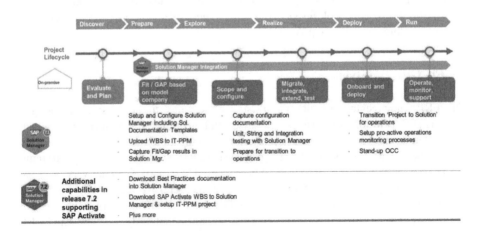

5 Challenges for Requirements Engineering in the Context of Customizable Software (ERP) Products

Unfortunately, the ERP implementations failure rate keeps high [18]. Therefore, many studies have been conducted in order to find and categorize all the challenges that ERP system implementation projects face. In this section we address the challenges to the requirements engineering in the context of (ERP) product customization and implementation, with additional focus on collaborative aspect of various involved stakeholders—specifically: business analyst (often called ERP consultant), the representative of the ERP vendor who discusses requirements for customized product with the customer and has to identify the collection of requirements which both satisfy the needs of the customer and makes the implementation efficient (thus, business analyst is usually a requirements engineer); product manager, who is responsible for development of the software product and plans its releases; project manager, who is responsible for the implementation of the customized product; customer, who purchases the ERP system implementation; developer, who develops the system and sometimes customizes it to specific needs of the customer; and finally tester, who develops test cases with aim to check the functionality and proper alignment of the product to specific needs and requirements. These challenges are result of our extensive literature review, and were additionally filtered through intensive discussions with our industry experts (7 SAP consultants). We have identified some of these challenges and took them into consideration while designing our approach and framework.

1. *Collaborative requirements knowledge management*
   One of the challenges for RE is to bring various forms and representations of knowledge about requirements into well-defined and documented business requirements blueprint. On one hand, information about requirements can be held in more or less (un)structured textual form, like office documents; such documents are usually result of requirements negotiation between business analyst and customer. On the other hand, project and product managers, as well as developers and testers, need more concise and strict representation of requirements and knowledge about software product (e.g. in form of models or class diagrams), in order to perform their tasks in satisfying manner.

2. *Software artifacts traceability and Change management*
   For achieving successful product customization and implementation, as well as efficient quality management/control, stakeholders need the ability to trace changes in requirements and their various interdependencies with other software artifacts (issues and customer requests, tests, risks), as well as their realization (e.g. request release, branch-specific product) and state (implemented, under customization/ development, deprecated). This tracing ability is also a basis for effective change management, since it helps with tracking changes (e.g. in standard product, requirements, other artifacts) and propagating them further (e.g. change of requirement needs to be reflected in the product implementation) in order to maintain actuality of requirements.

3. *Quality of requirements*
   Besides the consistency of product functionality with requirements, mentioned in previous challenge, quality attributes (e.g. completeness, stability, verifiability, comprehensibility) are also crucial for efficient requirements reuse. Only when these quality attributes are met, the requirements quality will be sufficient for successful requirements knowledge management. There are several approaches to model quality assessment which can be used to assess the quality of requirements (e.g. [18] for model-based requirements and [19] for textual requirements).

4. *Problems related to products and services*

New challenges are emerging lately as a result of introduction of services in the cloud, increasing the need for the flexibility of the customization process. Similarly, customer-specific services demand for more flexible composition as well. These services may have many variants (e.g. for different industries) or are even customer-specific, which makes the requirements management an even more complicated task.

Also we faced with more generic challenges such as:

1. Functional Challenges

   Integrators of ERP product line software are faced with the task of analyzing the portability of existing legacy functionalities, which have already met the users' satisfaction criteria, and mapping them to corresponding ERP features that should also meet client needs and expectations. If the approach to tackling this problem is not exercised during the preparation phase, financial expenditure may arise or the project life cycle may cross the originally planned timeline [20].

   Some aspects of the legacy functionality that may make attaining the same (or greater) level of satisfaction in ERP difficult can be if the desired feature is: operating smoothly; heavily cross-linked and distributed; flexible and extensible to cheaper COTS; 100% compatible and requires no/minimal support and maintenance; capable of achieving a very high level of user satisfaction [20]. In the research problem under investigation, the targeted functionality is performing satisfactorily, and we address the question of how requirements engineering can be used to support porting this functionality to a new product line implementation while satisfying all business and data constraints.

2. Data Challenges

   Another aspect of the research problem is determining how the variations of data in the current system will be represented in ERP. ERP implementations already have their own underlying database, which is well-defined for most of the known modules of the target business function(s). Beside interconnection and embedded data operations fulfilling generic requirements, almost all implementation projects will end up specifying a handful of customizations that must be synchronized among the systems implemented. This increases complexity during version control, upgrades, new acquisitions and significant change management operations [21].

   ERP systems contain two sets of data: (1) setup data, and (2) transactional data. Setup data represents system constants and universal data, e.g., department identifiers or position numbers. Transactional data is the data that gets newly inserted, modified, discarded, batched and accessed on a daily basis for business operations, e.g., employee benefit premium, accounts receivables encumbrance value. Experience indicates that communication alone is insufficient for a precise gap estimate in the data requirements if representative or actual data is not utilized.

Finally, integrity constraints must be defined to ensure that there is no data loss or corruption, thereby allowing every piece of required information to be accurately transferred to the new system. For instance, if human resources already passed big bang adoption and financials is on transition, to receive a valid ledger for the business we will still need payroll and related information from the new system. Furthermore, the legacy system needs to be simultaneously operating to avoid errors in the budget year.

6 Artifect Proposal - Framework for Requirements Engineering in the Context of ERP Systems

In order to get valuable feedback regarding problem and artifact relevance, we have proposed mock up solution for Requirements Engineering software application in the context of customizable service-centric systems such as ERP system. In next paragraphs we outlined functionalities of our supporting software application, which is addressing the challenges mentioned in previous sections. In the following paragraphs, we explain the Requirements Engineering software application in more detail.

The application has been mocked up in discussion with experts from our industry partners in this project. Our primary focus was to support collaboration of various stakeholders, so our application was focused to provide a front-end for these stakeholders to create and manage requirements artifacts. We took into account that a product like an enterprise resource management system today is a complex network of services. These services may have many branch or industry-oriented versions (variants) or are even customer -specific.

Typical scenarios we decided to consider are:

Consultants authoring customer-specific requirements, looking for similar requirements having been implemented for other customers.
Product managers planning releases and variants on the basis of various internal and external requests.

After thorough discussion and literature research our concept has included the following aspects:

A Requirements Knowledge Base describing a business oriented view of the product as a base of interrelated requirements
Support for traceability among artifacts related with product requirements like issues (e.g. customer requests, bugs), test cases and the product components
A change-driven lifecycle model where every data element (like a requirement, a product component or an issue) has an associated lifecycle state which may change over time (e.g. a requirement being productive or deprecated)
An evaluation-controlled process by systematic assessment of data elements (e.g. attaching requirements, test cases and product components with risk categories and risk values)

To provide each stakeholder with the appropriate view on the Requirements

Knowledge Base to support the stakeholders tasks (following the principles of view- based software engineering); this e.g. means that consultants are provided with interfaces where text can be easily edited, product managers get graphical charts to bundle and abstract requirements, whereas developers interact based on textually described models

The support users of the system by recommendations derived from the central Requirements Knowledge Base (e.g. proposing links between artifacts). In the following we describe the current status of the tool prototype, followed by an outlook on next steps.

The tool development and related research (e.g. comparison with tools available on the market, literature study) showed us the huge potential of the concept.

7 Tool Functionality

The functionality of the current prototype can be shortly summarized as follows:

Change-driven refinement process guiding the requirements engineer through the engineering phase, as well as involving various stakeholders into the process of ERP product customization. This allows flexible alignment with the dynamic business, architectural and technical requirements put in front of the specific ERP implementation.

Support for creation and description of use cases, business processes, requirements and services, in web forms supporting both structured data in the background (e.g. Use cases attached with external files) and informal, unstructured, wiki-kind text editing facilities.

Enhanced stakeholder collaboration (different types of stakeholders, their improved involvement and faster and more efficient interaction among them).

Framework is optimized for processing large numbers of requirements.

Support for all kinds of software artifacts and linking among them (linking among all types of artifacts in a repeatable process) - it provides tight coupling of requirements and other artifacts.

Suitable/customized visualizations (trees, graphs, tables, diagrams, charts, matrices) of requirements and their prioritization, traceability links, tests results, risks and change impact - in order to support analysis, decision/strategy making and tracking of evolutionary change aspect.

Support for issues - capability for importing issues from external Issue tracker systems and linking them to requirements.

Support for test cases - capability for importing tests from external Test suites and linking them to requirements.

Risk assessment support - with implemented risk assessment model.

Portability - the tool can easily be adapted to various platforms (e.g. different operating systems, different RDBMS) by doing simple modifications (Fig. 4).

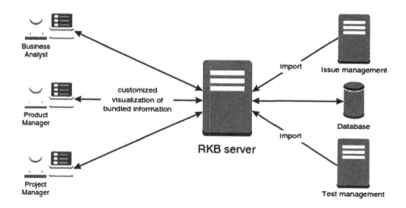

Fig. 4. Prototype software architecture

8 Interviews with ERP Experts from Two Consulting Companies

As mentioned earlier, our research was done in cooperation with large consulting company which specializes in SAP ERP systems for SMEs. The experts from our ERP consulting company, in charge of the overall cooperation with us, expressed satisfaction with our proposed application and its functionalities, particularly with the proposed web-based user interface, as well as with Knowledge Base functionality to support the different stakeholders. Some improvements were proposed; these proposals for improvement will certainly be taken into careful consideration during advanced phases of the tool development.

Company A: Acron Turkey
ACRON is an information technologies consultancy firm established to become a stronger and global IT brand that is shaping the international market for consultancy services and applications to meet the expectations of today's world and future. With over 350 consultants in its 400 people team and further enriched service content and custom package solutions, ACRON is one of the best known brands of information technologies in Turkey. It has received "Best Performance Award" among SAP Business Partners and greatest number of SAP consultants, certified consultants, and "SAP Business Analytics" consultants in Turkey. Providing added-value services such as process consultancy, quality assurance department and the like, ACRON is a business partner that has competent service for over 200 customers.

Company B: Actual Slovenia
Actual is the leading regional SAP consulting company with the head office in Koper and since April 2001 it has been a SAP partner for Croatia, Slovenia, Bosnia and Herzegovina, Serbia and Montenegro, Albania, Romania and Slovakia. Actual has around +200 employees and more than +120 consultants with rich business and IT experience gained and proven by numerous SAP implementations in Slovenia and in the region. Actual belongs to the elite society of Slovenian "knowledge exporters".

We chose 3 participants from both companies. All participants are the ERP consultants, with over 7 years of experience in SAP ERP implantations. Also, they are all Manager levels in their companies (started as junior consultants and become SAP modules mangers) which should indicate solid knowledge in both technical and process aspects.

9 Discussion on Interviews with Expert from Company A and Company B

Some might argue that there are many Requirements engineering tools on market, but interviews with experts showed us limited usability in practice.

However, by looking at the our concepts and functionalities, 5 out of 6 interviewed experts found change-driven refinement process guiding the requirements engineer through the engineering phase particularly helpful.

Company B experts also highly valued functionalities that support creation and description of use cases, business processes, requirements and services, in web forms supporting both structured data in the background (e.g. use cases attached with external files) and informal, unstructured, wiki-kind text editing facilities.

All experts from both companies agreed upon critical need of enhanced stakeholder collaboration (different types of stakeholders, their improved involvement and faster and more efficient interaction among them).

Company A experts stated that currently they do not have centralized application which support all kinds of project artifacts and link among them (link among all types of artifacts in a repeatable process). As they claimed the software should provide tight connection between ERP requirements and all other artifacts such as data migration, validation etc.

All experts agreed that visualization falls short in current tools they used. 5 of 6 experts rated functionality which provides suitable/customized visualizations (trees, graphs, tables, diagrams, charts, matrices) of requirements and their prioritization, traceability links, tests results, risks and change impact—as one the most important functionality they currently miss. Also all experts from both companies highly valued proposed functionalities such as:

Support for issues—capability for importing issues from external Issue tracker systems and linking them to requirements.

Support for test cases—capability for importing tests from external Test suites and linking them to requirements.

Risk assessment support—with implemented risk assessment model.

Technical experts valued proposed portability of the application, as it is critical that application could be easily adapted to various platforms (e.g. different operating systems, different RDBMS) by doing simple modifications. It is achieved using Java Spring Framework.

Other functionality such as change-driven lifecycle model where every data element (like a requirement, a product component) has an associated lifecycle state which may change over time (e.g. a requirement being productive or deprecated) is listed as something that we could adopt from other solutions that they are already using.

In company B, all experts suggested that solution should be a web based application in order to enable easy collaboration among stakeholders from various devices, such as laptops, smart phones, tablets. We decided to develop a web-based application; the tool that can be accessed by any stakeholder through a web browser. The application will allow multi-user access and will be protected through role-based access control.

10 Limitations and Future Work

The greatest limitation of the research presented in this paper is that the proposed RE supporting application functionalities would be implemented within a proof-of-concept prototype that does not in its breadth match the scope of a real ERP system.

Building a application which would be fully ready for integration with different ERP systems such as SAP ERP and Oracle ERP would be rather expensive and probably not suitable for academic research funding. Our mission would be to find a proper industry partner which would developed application to full extension which would be fully ready for real projects and environments.

11 Conclusion and Future Work

This paper presented challenges and our proposed RE support application mock up for collaborative requirements engineering in the environment of customizable service-centric systems, more specifically ERP systems. Our application functionalities will support the collaboration of various success-critical stakeholders such requirements engineers, project and product managers, business analysts, customers, etc., in the context of ERP system development and, particularly, product customization. The mock up of support RE application have been presented and discussed with 6 experts from 2 relevant ERP consulting companies for small and medium-sized enterprises. Interviews clearly *showed tremendous space in market for such RE supporting tool which should help ERP implementation process*. The current software application developed in the RE community in the past decade might only partly serve the needs of the ERP projects embracing the current market trends and complexity of implementation.

The implementation phase of building application will our next step and prototype would be evaluated by more experts following the theoretically supported by Design Science research framework.

References

1. Daneva, M., Wieringa, R.: Requirements engineering for enterprise systems: what we know and what we don't know? In: Nurcan, S., Salinesi, C., Souveyet, C., Ralyté, J. (eds.) Intentional Perspectives on Information Systems Engineering. Springer, Heidelberg (2010). https://doi.org/10.1007/978-3-642-12544-7_7
2. Shang, S., Seddon, P.B.: Managing process deficiencies with enterprise systems. Bus. Process Manag. J. **13**(3), 405–416 (2007)
3. Somers, T.M., Nelson, K.G.: A taxonomy of players and activities across the ERP project life cycle. Inf. Manag. **41**, 257–278 (2004)
4. Daneva, M.: ERP requirements engineering practice: lessons learnt. IEEE Softw. **21**(2), 26–33 (2004)
5. Daneva, M.: Patterns of success and failure in ERP requirements engineering. In: Proceedings of 12th International Workshop on Software Metrics, Shaker, Aachen, pp. 527–546 (2004)
6. Alvares, R., Urla, J.: Tell me a good story: using narrative analysis to examine information requirements interviews during an ERP implementation. DATA BASE Adv. IS **33**(1), 38–52 (2002)
7. Arinze, B., Anandarajan, M.: A framework for using OO mapping methods to rapidly configure ERP systems. Commun. ACM **46**(2), 61–65 (2003)
8. Davenport, T.: The future of enterprise system-enabled organizations. Inf. Syst. Front. **2**(2), 163–180 (2000)
9. Davenport, T.: Mission Critical: Realizing the Promise of Enterprise Systems. HBS Press, Boston (2000)
10. Hong, K.-K., Kim, Y.-G.: The critical success factors for ERP implementation: an organizational fit perspective. Inf. Manag. **40**, 25–40 (2000)
11. Gattiker, T.F., Goodhue, D.L.: Understanding the local-level costs and benefits of ERP through organizational information processing theory. Inf. Manag. **41**, 431–443 (2004)
12. Markus, M.L., Tanis, C., van Fenema, P.C.: Multisite ERP implementations. Commun. ACM **43**(4), 42–87 (2000)
13. Soh, C., Sia, S.K., Boh, W.F., Tang, M.: Misalignments in ERP implementations: a dialectic perspective. Int. J. Hum.-Comput. Interact., 81–100 (2009)
14. Ross, J.W., Vitale, M.R.: The ERP revolution: surviving vs. thriving. Inf. Syst. Front. **2**(2), 233–241 (2000). https://doi.org/10.1023/A:1026500224101
15. Parr, A., Shanks, G.: A model of ERP project implementation. J. Inf. Technol. **15**, 289–303 (2000)
16. Daneva, M., Wieringa, R.: Cost estimation for cross-organizational ERP projects: research perspectives. Softw. Qual. J. **16**(3), 459–481 (2008). https://doi.org/10.1007/s11219-008-9045-8
17. Maiden, N.A., Ncube, C.: Acquiring COTS software selection requirements. IEEE Softw. **15**(2), 46–56 (1998)
18. Chimiak-Opoka, J.: Measuring UML models using metrics defined in OCL within the SQUAM framework. In: Whittle, J., Clark, T., Kühne, T. (eds.) MODELS 2011. LNCS, vol. 6981, pp. 47–61. Springer, Heidelberg (2011). https://doi.org/10.1007/978-3-642-24485-8_5
19. Gervasi, V., Nuseibeh, B.: Lightweight validation of natural language requirements. Softw: Pract. Exp. **32**(2), 113–133 (2002)

20. Etien, A., Rolland, C.: Measuring the fitness relationship. Requir. Eng. **10**(3), 184–197 (2005)
21. Klaus, H., Rosemann, M., Gable, G.G.: What is ERP? Inf. Syst. Front. **2**, 141–162 (2000). https://doi.org/10.1023/A:1026543906354

Conceptualizing IT Project Portfolio Management in Terms of Organisational State-Transition Approach

Hamed Sarbazhosseini[✉]

University of Canberra, Canberra, Australia
Hamed.sarbazhosseini@canberra.edu.au

Abstract. IT Project Portfolio Management (IT PPM) is an area of organizational activity that attempts to assist in aligning business goals with an organization's strategic goals. This paper aims to investigate IT PPM from an Information Systems perspective whereby Organizational State-Transition Approach (OSTA) has been evaluated to determine how and why IT PPM solutions are being used in an organizational context. The OSTA was developed with the purpose that it might bring structure to this area of organizational activity. Therefore, the OSTA has been investigated based on literature and the methodology was formulated to collect and analyze data. The results of data have been to evaluate and explore how it might contribute to theory and practice in the future. It concludes by discussing several identified themes regarding how and why organizations benefit from using IT PPM. In addition, it reflects on the use of OSTA in this field.

Keywords: IT Project Portfolio Management · Conceptualization of PPM · Organizational State-Transition Approach

1 Background

The past two decades have seen rapid growth to the project management community and project management approaches are increasingly being integrated into organizational processes [1, 2]. IT PPM is being adopted as a method to align projects with organizational strategy [3, 4]. And according to various analyses, PPM and its performance have been suggested to be assessed at the project, portfolio and organizational levels [5], with an effective PPM required to promote an organization's overall goals [6].

IT PPM is a holistic approach that selects and prioritizes projects and/or programs, optimizes benefits, and aligns them with organizational strategy [4, 7–9]. The importance of PPM can be seen throughout recent literature conducted in this specific field. Clegg et al. [10] studied practices, projects and portfolios in current research trends, aiming to provide a future practice-based research agenda. The research identified numerous areas for further consideration in PPM such as performativity of PPM's discursive practices; how practice is made intelligible across different PPM contexts and what dynamic capabilities require developing for successful PPM. Danesh et al. [6]

M. Themistocleous and M. Papadaki (Eds.): EMCIS 2019, LNBIP 381, pp. 582–593, 2020.
https://doi.org/10.1007/978-3-030-44322-1_43

looks at the literature review of PPM from the perspective of decision making. Martinsuo [11] has studied PPM in practice and in context and suggests that PPM be used when uncertainties and complexities arise within a business environment to assist with negotiations and bargaining. Killen et al. [12] has also undertaken a comprehensive literature review in the PPM field.

IT PPM has been studied from many different perspectives and while this is not the purpose of this paper, it is important to acknowledge the increased attention that PPM is receiving and the recent topics that surround it. The study of IT PPM has prominently focused on various fields including, uncertainties within a management environment [13, 14], strategy implementation [15], business strategy [9], innovation and new product development [16], agile portfolio management [17], PPM office [18], decision making [6, 19] and dependencies between projects or programs and PPM [20, 21], maturity models [22] and even studies that try to enhance the knowledge of competency standards in PPM [23]. Bredillet et al. [24] has developed a conceptual framework where PPM is considered an organizational capability and a collection of routines in the project management office. A study of Hadjinicolaou and Dumrak [25] has investigated association of benefits and barriers in PPM to project success through a questionnaire survey.

The above background represents the diverse and increased attention in IT PPM in recent years. This research has been motivated by McDonald and Sarbazhosseini [26] where they suggested that the PPM domain has aspects that make research in it difficult and considered that the use of OSTA as a conceptual framework to provide a coherent structure to the field would be beneficial. Therefore, this study reflects on PPM from an IS perspective investigating how the organizational state-transition approach (STA) can be evaluated in terms of PPM.

This paper proceeds as follow: first, the OSTA has been discussed and the literature have been analyzed from this perspective; second, the research has been formulated in terms of OSTA to collect and analyze data; third, the results of OSTA in PPM have been discussed in different case studies to present the themes which requires organization's attention in implementation of PPM; and finally, the issues in current practice of PPM have been discussed in terms of OSTA.

2   The OSTA

The nature of OSTA is coming from state-transition approach where it has been validated in different disciplines such as Object-Oriented Systems [27], the health domain [28], the ecological studies [29]. It is the ongoing, continuous nature of systems that makes the STA useful in looking at organizational state, change and responsiveness [30].

The issues for OSTA as a way of describing systems and their change are (a) to determine and represent the current state of complex systems, (b) to express desired states in terms of systems indicators and (c) to frame action that changes the system in a way that it produces the desired change to state indicators without damaging other states of the system. Figure 1 shows the general form of OSTA. The cloud is the organizational system whose state and transition are the focus of attention. From the critical realist perspective, the system in itself is knowable only through the phenomena it presents to an observer. These phenomena are its state indicators and the dotted lines represent the instantiations of these indicators by extraction of information from the system, often achieved through business intelligence systems (BI) and management information systems (MIS). The desired state of these indicators constitutes a vision of how the system ought to be. This vision is motivated by economic and business values, and by psychological, social, aesthetic, political and other values. Transitions are the actions taken to change the system such that the indicators will move from the current to the desired state. These transitions may comprise methods, techniques and tools including software [26].

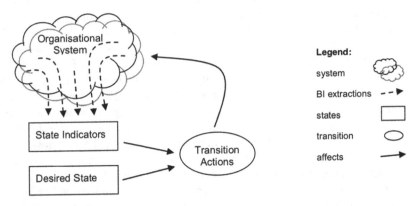

Fig. 1. General form of OSTA (adopted from McDonald and Sarbazhosseini [26])

The academic literature was collected and initially analyzed thematically and temporally. The variety of constructs was very broad with a range of overlapping 'takes' on the domain so the literature review was re-analyzed to attempt to classify the constructs into the categories of OSTA and to review some of the diversity in the literature.

To summarize, the literature was reviewed thematically then re-examined using OSTA in an attempt to ground it in actual systems indicators and transitions. This analysis was able to separate out those parts of the management jargon that related to actual states, desired states and the justification for why those states are desired. That said, it is an extensive literature, and when analyzed provided a less than extensive set of well-formed attributes in OSTA terms.

3   Research Design

Given the conceptual structure of the PPM domain as seen through the OSTA lens, the next issue for the research was how to formulate questions and collect empirical data from different cases that might address them. Because of the nature of the literature, the original thematic review produced a very varied set of constructs. An ends-means type research framework would suggest research questions like Why do organizations apply PPM? What kind of actions do organizations take in order to achieve goals? etc. From an OSTA perspective, suggested research questions revolve more around: What are the indicators of state and how are these evaluated? How are desired states determined? How do we know? We contend that OSTA style questions reveal more about the domain than the ends-means style.

The seven case-studies were selected randomly. Initially five government departments were contacted and after they agreed to participate another group of five organizations were contacted and then more organizations were contacted until enough data were collected to analyses. The researcher conducted 24 interviews with portfolio managers and reviewed more than 12 documents such as P3M3 assessments or documents that described the organizations strategic goals and objectives.

Interviewees were recruited from the portfolio management offices of the government agencies.

The four major criteria for judging the quality of case study research design are construct validity, internal validity, external validity and reliability [31, 32]. Construct validity was addressed through using multiple sources of evidence such as interview notes and transcripts and document reviews and establishing a chain of evidence. Internal validity was provided by following Thematic and Comparative coding techniques [33, p2–12] where data was analyzed and checked with a second researcher to make sure that the data are coded consistently [33, 34]. External validity was ensured through use of replication logic with multiple case studies. Reliability was managed by using a case study protocol and developing case study database. In this research, a pilot study was undertaken to attest the case study protocol and ensure that data could be collected to meet the research purpose.

The collected data was coded and analyzed following Saldaña [32 p. 139]. The data was transcribed and preliminary reviewed and prepared in word documents and the categorized in NVIVO based on interview questions. The data was then analyzed in different cycles to make sure that all themes were analyzed and explored through this investigation. A data analysis protocol was undertaken. In this process, thematic analysis was used to develop themes from interview transcripts and notes. These themes represent the most common keywords and discussion that interviewees discussed during the interviews.

In the following section, the findings of the data analysis are provided by explaining the themes discovered in this research. It should be noted that some parts of these themes were tested through academic publications [26] and results were peer-reviewed with the researchers involved in this project in different cycles to ensure the internal and external validity of the data.

4   Conceptualizing IT PPM in Terms of the OSTA

The Fig. 2 has been developed as a result of the data analyses in terms of the OSTA. The themes were discovered as a result of the thematic analysis in each state.

The following themes were found across the organizations represented in the study in terms of OSTA.

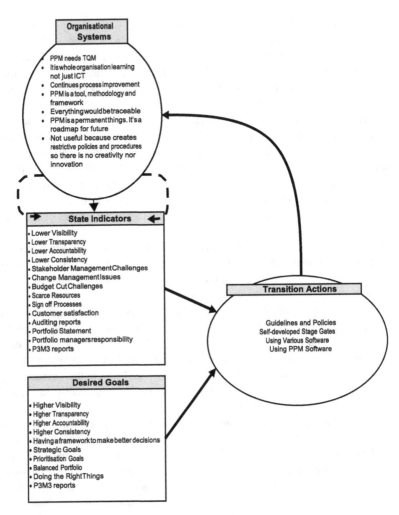

Fig. 2. Conceptualising IT PPM in terms of OSTA presenting discovered themes in each state [26, 35]

4.1   State Indicators

Organizations commonly had low levels of visibility, transparency, accountability and consistency. By applying PPM, they wished to achieve a better state. The studied cases had issues with stakeholder management, change management and budget cuts. These issues were said to be contributing to or leading to cultural issues within the organizations, particularly when there are interconnections and interrelationships among projects in a portfolio. The state indicators also show that having limited resources and managing them in the portfolio is a challenge.

4.2 Desired State

The organizations which were investigated wish to achieve higher visibility, transparency, accountability and consistency. The organizations believed that with use of PPM, they will have consistent decision-making processes because PPM frames their actions and processes. For the same reason, PPM helps them to increase the level of visibility, transparency, accountability and consistency in organizations.

In addition, organizations desired to achieve strategic goals in order to deliver what they have been asked. The organizations believed that they needed PPM in order to be able to prioritize their jobs and to make the right decisions based on their priorities. In addition, one of the objectives was to achieve a balanced portfolio by reducing risk and allocating resources efficiently among projects. The P3M3 reports indicated that organizations, in order to target a new level, need bigger budgets, however, they wish to improve their levels by considering different issues.

4.3 Transitions

Analyzing the transition actions indicate that government organizations had followed the guidelines and procedures. It was also discovered that organizations commonly developed stage gates based on PRINCE2. These Stage Gates have been a key element in guiding and advising organizational decision-making processes and actions. Using the software for government cases seems to be a major challenge in managing projects as different tools are used.

4.4 Summary

Figure 2 has been developed based on the empirical finding in terms of OSTA. By considering State Indicators, Transition Actions, and the Desired State from the empirical study, it can be seen that there is disharmony between actions and goals. This shows that there is no evidence to suggest that the transition actions that organizations take lead to the desired state. While the transition actions discussed in literature can lead to goals based on academic literature, this cannot be found from empirical analyses. Furthermore, this study was not aimed to find if those actions lead to goals.

The analysis shows that organizations commonly wanted to have higher visibility, transparency, accountability and consistency. The organizations believed that with the use of PPM, they will have consistent decision-making processes because PPM frames their actions and processes. For the same reason, PPM helps them to increase the level of visibility, transparency, accountability and consistency in organizations.

The organizations believed that they needed PPM to be able to prioritize their jobs and to make the right decisions based on their priorities. In addition, one of the objectives was to achieve a balanced portfolio by reducing risk and allocating resources efficiently among projects. The P3M3 document reviews indicated that organizations, to target a new level, need bigger budgets, however, they wish to improve their levels by considering different issues.

One of the main findings of this empirical research was that organizations were unclear about what strategy means for them. Some of them interpreted strategic alignment with achieving government's initiatives and delivering portfolio on-time and on-budget and with an appropriate resource allocation.

5   Inconsistencies Between Transition Actions and Desired State

Transition actions found in this study show that there is no clear evidence that these actions lead to a desired state. Although the PPM literature explains the processes or tools an organization has to take to achieve a goal, it appears that organizations do not have enough control to manage actions or processes to do so.

It was discovered from the literature that each of the desired actions identified has a particular set of actions that leads to achievement of goals. However, it was not evident that organizations that were studied know exactly what actions would help them to achieve their goals.

Looking at transition actions organizations take to achieve a goal does not provide the evidence to assist them in meeting future goals. It is clear that the organizations studied do not have a clear understanding of strategic goals and the actions taken to deliver them. The actions by the cases can be categorized mainly as guidelines and policies, self-developed stage-gates and using software, but they cannot ensure achievement of their set goals.

The transition actions made by organizations demonstrate there is a gap between desired goals and the actions taken to achieve these goals. This comparison was raised when looking at the different actions taken by government cases.

It was clear from the literature review that organizations take different actions in order to meet their objectives, however, it was discovered that Stage Gates were the most commonly used framework. Guidelines and policies were also a commonly used tool although it was discussed that organizations felt this limited creativity and innovation in government organizations.

6   Conclusion

In this study, the OSTA was evaluated to better understand PPM in organizations with the aim of brining a structure to this knowledge area. The comparison of themes from the literature and the empirical study represented a valuable discussion on organizations that implemented PPM in different ways from what it is discussed in literature.

The state indicators show that organizations have lower visibility, transparency, consistency and accountability. These criteria have never been developed or emphasized in the PPM literature. It also seems that organizations have issues with managing stakeholders when there is a lack of consistency and a need for a change. It seems that these issues lead to cultural issues, particularly when project managers follow a management style that is not based on policies and procedures or organizational guidelines. In addition, the comparison of state indicators as described in the literature and demonstrated by the study shows that organizations find their current state differently to what is described in the literature.

Discussion around desired state discovered that organizations implement PPM differently because their state indicators are different from what it is mentioned in the literature. Organizations want to deliver goals in a way that improves their state indicator. For example, they want to achieve higher visibility or consistency throughout their organization so as to better control the finance and progress of projects in a portfolio.

From a transition actions perspective, the study shows that there is a lack of information about whether these transition actions would lead to the desired state. It shows that organizations that do not use PPM software have different objectives compared to those that have PPM software in their organization. The study also shows that perhaps those organizations that use PPM software can better focus on their strategic goals.

6.1 Reflection on the OSTA

This research contributes to the theory by reflecting on the OSTA used. The OSTA was applied and evaluated in PPM to better understand the phenomena. The OSTA introduces a new approach to apply to PPM as its on-going and dynamic characteristic. In addition, the framework's clarity and completeness was discussed as major reason that OSTA was useful in PPM. Furthermore, it reflects by revealing the ignorance of gap between transition actions and the desired state by analyzing states identified through populated framework in Fig. 2.

6.2 New Approach

This study contributes to knowledge by developing a version of the state-transition approach. This reliable approach has been well established and used in different fields such as clinical, ecological studies, computer sciences and software engineering (discussed in McDonald and Sarbazhosseini [26]. With the on-going and dynamic environment of PPM, the OSTA is developed and applied to PPM as a research frame.

In this regard, the OSTA was first validated in PPM literature. The interview questions, data collection, as well as analysis methods, were developed through the OSTA. The summary of data found from the study is presented in terms of the OSTA. This assisted to better understand the data. Last themes from the empirical study derived from applying the OSTA are discussed. The OSTA is used to compare the findings from the empirical study and literature review. This comparison helps to better understand the PPM theory by discussing the interrelationship among states of the OSTA and the themes which were discovered.

The new approach used in this study has led to a new understanding of PPM. It is the OSTA simplicity and clarity as well as on-going and dynamic advantage that is useful for understanding PPM phenomena in organizations.

The OSTA reflected theory by identifying the gaps between actions that organizations took and the goals that they wanted to achieve. This study has discovered the relationship between actions and goals in the PPM literature, meaning that particular actions lead to achievement of certain goals. However, there was no evidence to identify this relationship between the actions and goals from the findings. Now the big uncertainty is whether these organizations achieve their goals based on the actions that they take.

Organizations can take advantage of the OSTA to assess and clarify the steps that they follow to reduce the risk of failures and to assist the stakeholders to make right decisions at the right times. It is essential for organizations to first understand their capabilities and their desired state and then apply the OSTA to assist them to better understand the required actions they need to take to achieve their goals.

It was found that government cases do not use PPM software. Instead they use a variety of tools in different sections due to limited budget or lack of personnel training. Perhaps this is the reason that these organizations are looking for other criteria such as higher visibility in their processes. Using appropriate PPM software assists organizations establish a consistency in their decision-making and accountability processes.

6.3   Strength of the Research

This research's strength is in the evaluation of a reliable, well-established version of the state-transition approach. The OSTA was used in PPM to better frame the literature. The OSTA assisted in the formulation of the research and collection of data to address the questions. In order to address the research objectives, well-designed research was deployed. The interview protocol involved a set of procedures and instruments to enable interaction between the researcher and study participants including designs for participant contact, an interview data collection instrument, the interview scripts and analysis techniques. The protocol was desk-checked by the researcher before use. The interview script included items from PPM and the OSTA perspectives. In parallel, document analyses were conducted in order to strengthen the findings from interviews. This research considered a number of cases to address the research questions.

To conclude, the OSTA was used to frame the phases of the research project into PPM. The research offers a structure within which to frame the literature, research questions and to collect and assess the case data. The use of OSTA was conducted in parallel with a comparison of PPM literature and case data.

6.4   Limitations of the Research

It should be noted that while PPM is a wide field used in different disciplines it was challenging to determine exactly what PPM delivers to organizations by investigating it in the literature.

During interviews, it was discovered that interviewee responses were sometimes biased and the researchers' interview technique needed to be modified to allow elaboration of questions. In order to better engage in the interviews, a version of OSTA was presented during interviews. This helped the interviewees to track the questions and the structure of questions in terms of the OSTA. In addition, visualizing the OSTA helped the researcher to take notes based on the OSTA. However, it should be acknowledged that providing the OSTA diagram could also stimulate biased response from interview participants (i.e., they attempt to interpret what the researcher might be looking for in the questions response rather than responding in more natural and immediate manner while the interviewer attempted to use his skills to communicate well with the participants to solve the issue.)

6.5   Future Work

It was discovered that there is a lack of evidence to show that actions organizations take can lead to goals. For this reason, future research could test the actions based on the OSTA and discover if those actions lead to portfolio goals (i.e. linkage/relationships between actions and goals).

This study applied one-iteration of the OSTA. The suggestion for future research is to apply the OSTA in different circumstances to better understand the theories. For organizations to better manage changes and successes, it is suggested they implement the OSTA in different settings or circumstances to maximize their portfolio success.

When organizations wish to use OSTA, or apply PPM, they need to consider the new criteria found in this research. Adaptation of the OSTA can be useful for an organization to enhance their PPM processes and achievements.

It is clear that there is no existing formula or process for determining the success rates of PPM. By comparing state indicators to the desired state this research proved the OSTA to be a successful tool for organizations to assess success rates.

This paper concludes that "Project Portfolio Management is a great regime that assists organizations to achieve their strategic goals; however, there is still a lot to be learnt about this phenomenon."

Acknowledgements. The authors would like to acknowledge that this research was part of the main author's PhD project.

References

1. Killen, C.P., Kjaer, C.: Understanding project interdependencies: the role of visual representation, culture and process. Int. J. Proj. Manag. 30(5), 554–566 (2012)
2. PMI: The High Cost of Low Performance How will you improve business results? PMI's PULSE of the PROFESSION, 8th Global Project Management Survey (2016)
3. Crawford, L., Hobbs, J.B., Turner, J.R.: Aligning capability with strategy: Categorizing projects to do the right projects and to do them right. Proj. Manag. J. 37(2), 38–50 (2006)
4. Niknazar, P., Bourgault, M.: Theories for classification vs. classification as theory: implications of classification and typology for the development of project management theories. Int. J. Proj. Manag. 35(2), 191–203 (2017)
5. Müller, R., Martinsuo, M., Blomquist, T.: Project portfolio control and portfolio management performance in different contexts. Proj. Manag. J. 39(3), 28–42 (2008)
6. Danesh, D., Ryan, M.J., Abbasi, A.: Multi-criteria decision-making methods for project portfolio management: a literature review. Int. J. Manag. Decis. Making 17(1), 75–94 (2018)
7. Kendall, G., Rollins, S.: Advanced Project Portfolio Management and the PMO: Multiplying ROI at Warp Speed. International Institute for Learning Inc. and J. Ross Publishing, Inc., Florida (2003)
8. Archer, N., Ghasemzadeh, F.: Project portfolio selection and management. In: The Wiley Guide to Managing Projects, pp. 237–255 (2004)
9. Meskendahl, S.: The influence of business strategy on project portfolio management and its success—A conceptual framework. Int. J. Proj. Manag. 28, 807–817 (2010)
10. Clegg, S., Killen, C.P., Biesenthal, C., Sankaran, S.: Practices, projects and portfolios: current research trends and new directions. Int. J. Proj. Manag. 36, 762–772 (2018)

11. Martinsuo, M.: Project portfolio management in practice and in context. Int. J. Proj. Manag. **31**, 794–803 (2013)

12. Killen, C., Hunt, R., Kleinschmidt, E.: Managing the new product development project portfolio: a review of the literature and empirical evidence. In: PICMET Proceedings, Porland, Oregon (2007)

13. Petit, Y.: Project portfolios in dynamic environments: organizing for uncertainty. Int. J. Proj. Manag. **30**, 539–553 (2012)

14. Martinsuo, M., Korhonen, T., Laine, T.: Identifying, framing and managing uncertainties in project portfolios. Int. J. Proj. Manag. **32**, 732–746 (2014)

15. Hyväri, I.: Project portfolio management in a company strategy implementation, a case study. Proc. – Soc. Behav. Sci. **119**, 229–236 (2014)

16. Jugend, D., da Silva, S.L., Salgado, M.H., Miguel, P.A.C.: Product portfolio management and performance: evidence from a survey of innovative Brazilian companies. J. Bus. Res. **69**, 5095–5100 (2016)

17. Stettina, C.J., Offerman, T., de Mooij, B., Sidhu, I.: Gaming for agility: using serious games to enable agile project & portfolio management capabilities in practice. In: IEEE International Conference on Engineering, Technology and Innovation (2018)

18. Unger, B.N., Gemunden, H.G., Aubry, M.: The three roles of a project portfolio management office: their impact on portfolio management execution and success. Int. J. Proj. Manag. **30**, 608–620 (2012)

19. Baptestone, R., Rabechini Jr., R.: Influence of portfolio management in decision-making. J. Ind. Eng. Manag. **11**(3), 406–428 (2018)

20. Pajaresa, J., López, A.: New methodological approaches to project portfolio management: the role of interactions within projects and portfolios. Proc. – Soc. Behav. Sci. **119**, 645–652 (2014)

21. Bilgin, G., Eken, G., Ozyurt, B., Dikmen, I., Birgonul, M.T., Ozorhon, B.: Handling project dependencies in portfolio management. Proc. Comput. Sci. **121**, 356–363 (2017)

22. Nikkhou, S., Taghizadeh, K., Hajiyakhchali, S.: Designing a portfolio management maturity model (Elena). Proc. – Soc. Behav. Sci. **226**, 318–325 (2016)

23. Young, M., Conboy, K.: Contemporary project portfolio management: reflections on the development of an Australian Competency Standard for Project Portfolio Management. Int. J. Proj. Manag. **31**, 1089–1100 (2013)

24. Bredillet, C., Tywoniak, S., Tootoonchy, M.: Exploring the dynamics of project management office and portfolio management co-evolution: a routine lens. Int. J. Proj. Manag. **36**, 27–42 (2018)

25. Hadjinicolaou, N., Dumrak, J.: Investigating association of benefits and barriers in project portfolio management to project success. In: 7th International Conference on Engineering, Project, and Production Management, pp. 274–281 (2017)

26. McDonald, C., Sarbazhosseini, H.: A state transition approach to conceptualizing research: the project portfolio management domain. In: 24th Australian Conference in Information Systems, Melbourne (2013)

27. UML: Getting Started with UML. Object Management Group (1997). http://www.uml.org/. Accessed 1 Aug 2018

28. Siebert, U., et al.: State-transition modeling: a report of the ISPOR-SMDM modeling good research practices task force–3. Med. Decis. Making **32**(5), 690–700 (2012)

29. Stringham, T.K., Krueger, W.C., Shaver, P.L.: State and transition modelling: an ecological process approach. J. Range Manag. **56**, 106–113 (2003)

30. Yin, R.K.: Case study Research: Design and Methods, 5th edn. Sage, Thousand Oaks (2014)

31. Trochim, W.M.K.: Five Big Words. Web Centre for Social Research Methods (2018). http://www.socialresearchmethods.net/kb/naturres.php. Accessed Oct 2018

32. Saldaña, J.: The Coding Manual for Qualitative Researchers. Sage Publications Ltd., London (2012)
33. Yin, R.K.: Case study research: Design and methods, 4th edn. Sage Publications, USA (2009)
34. Yin, R.K.: Case Study Research and Applications Design and Methods, 6th edn. Sage Publications, Thousand Oaks (2018)
35. Sarbazhosseini, H., Banihashemi, S., Adikari, S.: Human-centered framework for managing IT project portfolio. In: Nah, F.H., Siau, K. (eds.) HCII 2019. LNCS, vol. 11589, pp. 432–442. Springer, Cham (2019). https://doi.org/10.1007/978-3-030-22338-0_35

The Effect of Big Data Analytics Capability on Firm Performance: A Pilot Study in China

(Claude) Chien-Hung Liu$^{(\boxtimes)}$ and Nikolay Mehandjiev

Alliance Manchester Business School, The University of Manchester,
Manchester, UK
chienhung.liu@postgrad.manchester.ac.uk,
n.mehandjiev@manchester.ac.uk

Abstract. Big data analytics (BDA) becomes a critical phenomenon today that brings revolution to firms in different ways, yet how firms create BDA capability that reflects on firm performance (FPER) in specific industry sectors is not yet clear, with the majority of existing studies taking cross-sector perspectives. This study addresses this gap by focusing on Consumer-Packaged Goods (CPG) & Retail industries in China, drawing on the resource-based view (RBV), and BDA literature. This paper presents the first pilot stage of the study, using a limited sample to derive an initial model of the relationship between BDAC and FPER, hypothesizing that it is partially mediated by the Digital Dynamic Capability (DDC). Apart from laying the foundation for the second stage of a more focused study by validating a measurement model, the analysis of the hypothesized structural model confirms some of the initial hypotheses. The results of our studies will benefit executives who face decision making before and after BDA investment. The insights from this study may help firms avoid unnecessary mistakes, and provides immediate contributions in developing and configuring firm-specific BDAC for enhancing firm performance.

Keywords: Big data · Big data analytics capability · Dynamic capability · Firm performance

1 Introduction

Big data analytics (BDA) has been ranked among the top agenda of the senior executive [18]. "BDA is now considered as a game-changer enabling improved business efficiency and effectiveness because of its high operational and strategic potential" [17, p. 357]. However, given this growing importance, it seems that not every organization has found its way to unlock the potential of its BDA investment, reflecting on firm performance yet [49].

A few studies start to understand this big data phenomenon through exploring the BDA capability, and firm performance (BDAC - FPER) relationship as big data analytics (BDA) is broadly considered a critical phenomenon today that brings revolution to firms in different ways [14]. The current BDA studies mainly focus on exploring BDAC-FPER relationship across different types of industries [3, 17, 21], and there is a little industry-specific empirical study in this research stream, especially in China. To fill these research

© Springer Nature Switzerland AG 2020
M. Themistocleous and M. Papadaki (Eds.): EMCIS 2019, LNBIP 381, pp. 594–608, 2020.
https://doi.org/10.1007/978-3-030-44322-1_44

gaps and to better understand this big data phenomenon, this study, therefore, drawing on resource-based view (RBV), and BDA literature, aims to explore what BDA capabilities should a firm possess and how they impact on firm performance with a focus on the Consumer-Packaged Goods (CPG) & Retail industries in China.

This research aims to achieve the following purposes:

(1) To benefit executives who face decision making before and after BDA investment. The insights from this study are expected to help firms avoid unnecessary mistakes and develop and configuring firm-specific BDAC for enhancing firm performance.
(2) To advance BDA research by addressing this gap by considering big data challenges in the development of the BDAC model and by providing new understanding in the validation of BDAC-FPER relationship and its interaction with DDC.
(3) To enrich the BDA research in IS and Strategy disciplines by providing more empirical evidence in China.

Scholars from strategy and management discipline believe that the resource-based view (RBV) is a compelling theory in exploring the relationship between capabilities and firm performance [6, 32]. For example, Barney [5] argues that how firms achieve a competitive advantage rely on whether they are capable of owning resources that are valuable, rare, inimitable, and non-substitutable or VRIN resource for short. Firms need a certain kind of ability to integrate and drive the use of these resources for results, which is defined as capability [29]. Also, recent BDA research has provided evidence supporting that BDA is a kind of a VRIN resource that can shape BDA capabilities (BDAC) that may lead to superior firm performance [3, 17, 21, 27].

In the context of BDAC, IS scholars begin to explore how BDA capability (BDAC) may impacts on firm performance through the lens of resource-based view (RBV), and the attentions on this BDA research stream have been growing. Previous IS research indicates that firms may combine and deploy several firm-level resources to form capabilities for competitive advantage by [7, 20]. Additional findings from recent BDA research [3, 21] suggest that BDAC is such a distinct capability of a firm that can create a competitive advantage. However, many firms implementing BDA are still puzzled and have little knowledge about how they should start by building big data analytics (BDA) capabilities [21]. "The evolution of BDA is still in its early stage" [18, p. 7], and thus this research believes that BDAC is an emerging subject for both business practitioners and academia and is worth being explored and researched.

This study aims to explore big data phenomena through the lens of the RBV framework with a focus on the CPG and Retail industries in China by proposing the research questions (RQs) below:

RQ: How can firm performance (FPER) be enhanced through big data analytics capabilities (BDAC)?

2   Relevant Literature

The existing research discussing how BDAC may bring an impact on firm performance (FPER) primarily focuses on anecdotal evidence [2, 3, 31]. Lack of empirical evidence supporting extant literature remains a gap that needs further addressed [1, 15]. The results of reviewing the primary BDA papers from the past three years are presented in Table 1, highlighting the main contributions, scopes, sample sizes and sources, and derives related research gaps and opportunities.

Table 1. Relevant BDAC-FPER research (2016–2019)

Author	Contribution	Region/sector	Research gap & opportunity
[21]	Developed a theoretical framework of BDAC model with constructs and survey instruments and validated the relationship of BDAC-Market Performance and BDAC-Operation Performance.	The U.S. Broad sectors N = 108	No industry-specific BDA Research Lack of business users (Non-IT) as respondents
[17]	Validated BDAC-Firm Performance relationship and its mediating effect of process-oriented dynamic capability	China Broad sectors N = 225	No industry-specific BDA Research
[3]	Validated BDAC-Firm performance relationship with its moderator effect of analytics capability-business alignment (ACBSA)	The U.S. Broad sectors N-152	Lack of business users (Non-IT) as respondents

For example, Gupta and George [21] contribute a theoretical framework of BDAC model that is made up by a three-order construct model, and they provide a survey instrument with good validity and reliability. Their research suggests that positive relationships exist between BDAC and market performance (MP) and between BDAC and operational performance (OP). Wamba et al. [17] confirms that BDAC might directly affect firm performance (FPER) and be mediated by process-oriented dynamic capability. Akter et al. [3] confirm the positive relationship between BDAC and firm performance mediated by the process-oriented dynamic capably. These studies do not focus on specific industries and solicit views from IT and analytics professionals mainly. This engenders research gaps and opportunities open for industry-specific BDA research and research, including the opinions from Non-IT business users. Indeed, these users are the final consumer of the BDA value chain and help to realize the value of big data through customer interactions.

3 Relationships Between BDAC and FPER

Drawing on the RBV [5, 20] and BDAC-FPER studies [3, 17, 21], this study argues that to achieve a firm's superior performance, a firm needs to have BDAC, a type of VRIN resources, that consist of tangible BDA resources, intangible BDA resources and human BDA resources [20]. Accordingly, the study proposes the hypothesis below:

> *H1. Big data analytics capabilities (BDAC) has a positive and significant effect on firm performance (FPER)*

In the digital era, big data are mostly collected, processed and stored through numerous and varied forms of digital objects that connect us [11]. Digital data are at the very foundation of this big data trend [45] where digital data are generated every day in many forms such as tweets, clicks, videos and sensor data from a mobile device [24]. Brynjofsson [9] suggest that digitalization may impact on firm performance. The more digital adoption a firm has in its business processes may result in higher performance benefits [9].

Accordingly, this research suggests that digital dynamic capability (DDC) may play a mediator role between BDAC-FPER relationship. Thus, the second and third hypotheses are formulated below:

> *H2. Big data analytics capabilities (BDAC) has a positive and significant effect on digital dynamic capabilities (DDC)*
> *H3. Digital dynamic capability (DDC) will mediate the relationship between BDAC-FPER*

Motivated by this emerging big data phenomenon, this study aims to advance this BDA research steam by exploring BDAC-FPER relationship and its mediating effect of digital dynamic capacity (DDC) with a focus on the CPG & Retail industries in China. Based on the strategy and information systems (IS) literature, this study proposes the research model with defined constructs using the resource-based view, dynamic capability view, and relevant BDA capability studies. Thus, the research model and construct definitions are presented below (Table 2) (Fig. 1):

4 Research Design

4.1 Method

This study uses the questionnaire as a survey method to collect data as it attains the causal relationship between constructs and helps research become more generalizable [34]. Recent BDA studies choose questionnaire-based survey as research methods [3, 17, 21]. This study considers the questionnaire-based survey a suitable research method and thus adopts the same approach.

To increase the research rigor, this study has reviewed extant BDAC-FPER literature first. Then this study adopts research design approach from [17, 21], and organizes survey research into two studies: (1) Study I: a pilot study; (2) Study II: the main study. The current study is the pilot study component of the two-phase study. In the pilot study

Table 2. Construct definition

Construct	Definition	Source
Big Data Analytics Capability (BDAC)	A firm's organization ability to utilize big data asset in combination with tangible, intangible and human capability to create competitive advantages	[18, 21]
Tangible Resource	Resources that can be sold or bought in a market, such as data, technology, and basic resources of the firm	[21, 41]
Intangible Resource	Resources that are not tradable and making a firm highly heterogeneous across firms	[21, 41]
Human Skills Resource	Resources that consist of its employees' experience, knowledge, business acumen, problem-solving abilities, leadership qualities, and relationships with others pertaining to the big data resource, including technical and managerial skills of a firm's human big data resource	[17]
Firm performance (FPER)	The extent to which a firm generates superior performance for its competitors and are best measured relative to the competition	[37, 38]
Digital dynamic capability	Capabilities that can "continuously look for, acquire, assimilate, apply, effective use of a firm's unique digital and big data analytics in a changing environment	[8, 42, 43]

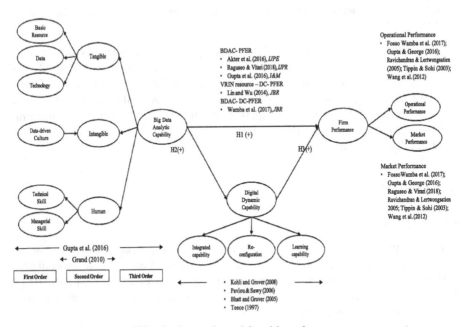

Fig. 1. Research model and hypotheses

phase, Akter et al. [3] suggest using experienced experts as questionnaire evaluators to conduct the content validity of the survey. This study selected three industry practitioners as questionnaire evaluators to ensure that the content, meaning, translation and question flows are explicit. This study chooses three experts based on the roles of the big data value chain - big data integration, data analytics, and big data consumer: BDA IT: 1 person, BDA analytics: 1 person, and BDA business users: 1 person. This is followed by the limited distribution of the questionnaire to validate the measurement model and make limited conclusions about the hypothesized structural model. The questionnaire is presented at Appendix: Table 5.

4.2 Sample

Snowballing (Non-parametric sampling) is chosen as a sampling method as no universal panel data is existing in China that list out all companies investing in BDA. SurveyMonkey, a cloud-based mobile survey system based in the U.S., which is similar to the Qualtrics platform, was used. Referring to relevant BDA study, [3] and [17] have a sample size of 61 and 41, respectively, for their pilot studies. Thus, the expected minimum sample size of this study was set to 50. For the pilot study purpose, the questionnaires were sent to desired respondent groups in CPG and retail industries in China during 9th February 2019 and 20th February 2019. 79 responses were received, and 54 of them were completed, leading to a response rate of 68.3%.

Of the respondents, 67% were female, and 53% were BDA analysts, 55% were middle managers, 73% worked with local private enterprise, 60% worked with an organization more than 10,000 persons, and the majority (69%) had a postgraduate qualification or above. Table 6 showed the respondents' profiles and features of their employers.

5 Analysis and Results

Data collected from the online questionnaire platform was downloaded and coded into Excel and transformed into CSV format. The missing values were checked before the data were ready for SEM analysis using SmartPLS 3.0. There were no missed values in the collected data set. To assess the proposed research model, this study used structural equation modelling (SEM) to estimate the parameters in the models. Wetzels et al. [47, p. 178] indicate that "partial least squares (PLS) can allow for more theoretical parsimony and reduce model complexity'. Relevant BDA scholars [3, p. 121] provides evidence showing that "PLS is more suitable for estimating a hierarchical model than covariance-based SEM (CB-SEM)". Thus, this study chose SmartPLS 3.0 as an SEM analytics tool to assess the model [3, 39]. SEM is a two-step process: (1) confirmatory factor analysis (CFA) was used for measurement model confirmation, and (2) structural model was confirmed while hypothesized relationships were confirmed. This study applied SEM-PLS with a path weighting scheme as structural model weighting scheme [17] and nonparametric bootstrapping [12, 17] with 5000 interactions to calculate the estimates [17, 23].

5.1 Measurement Model

This pilot study tested and examined measurement model against data, as represented by the samples collected [22]. The measurement model was designed on SmartPLS 3.0, and the proposed research model was represented as an inner and outer models' diagram. Construct validity and reliability, and discernment validity are examined. Following [3] on BDA study, item loadings, average variance extracted (AVE) and composite reliability (CR) are the criteria used to check the construct validity of the measurement model. The results of the examination are discussed by critical quality criteria as follows:

First, the results (Table 3) confirm that all outer loadings in the measurement models are highly significant (P < 0.001) as required for convergent validity. The results of outer factor loading indicate that all 44 items have factor loadings higher than 0.5, the minimum thresholds. 38 items have factor loadings exceeding a high threshold of 0.7 for factor loadings [22].

Table 3. Assessment of first-order, reflective model.

Constructs	Items	Loading	CR	AVE	Constructs	Items	Loading	CR	AVE
BDACT-BS	BS1	0.85	0.81	0.69	BDACH-MS	MS1	0.95	0.97	0.84
	BS2	0.8				MS2	0.96		
BDACT-DT	DT1	0.64	0.77	0.54		MS3	0.95		
	DT2	0.77				MS4	0.78		
	DT3	0.77				MS5	0.9		
BDACT-TG	TG1	0.72	0.82	0.49		MS6	0.93		
	TG2	0.72			DDC-DIC	DIC1	0.87	0.87	0.78
	TG3	0.63				DIC2	0.88		
	TG4	0.66			DDC-DLC	DLC1	0.91	0.96	0.83
	TG5	0.75				DLC2	0.89		
BDACI-DDC	DD1	0.70	0.89	0.62		DLC3	0.94		
	DD2	0.86				DLC4	0.93		
	DD3	0.74				DLC5	0.87		
	DD4	0.86			DDC-DRC	DRC1	0.92	0.91	0.83
	DD5	0.76				DRC2	0.90		
BDACH-TS	TS1	0.69	0.96	0.80	FPER-MP	MP1	0.60	0.77	0.47
	TS2	0.86				MP2	0.57		
	TS3	0.95				MP3	0.73		
	TS4	0.93				MP4	0.80		
	TS5	0.95			FPER-OP	OP1	0.96	0.89	0.67
	TS6	0.95				OP2	0.80		
						OP3	0.70		
						OP4	0.80		

Second, the AVE values for first-order constructs, second-order and third-order constructs were calculated as shown in Table 3, respectively. Among first-order constructs, 9 out 11 constructs have AVE values higher than 0.5, exceeding the 50% rule of thumb [22], excepting technology construct (TG) of 49% and market performance construct (MP) of 47%. Among second-order constructs and third-order constructs, all six constructs have AVEs higher than 0.5 of threshold [22].

Third, the composite reliability (CR) estimates of all 11 first-order constructs exceed 0.7, the threshold for adequate reliability. The composite reliability (CR) estimates as for second-order-constructs, and third-order constructs all exceed 0.7 of threshold [22].

5.2   Structural Model

The analysis also estimates three constructs relationships: BDAC and FPER, BDAC and DDC, and DDC and FPER. The results (Table 4) show that the hypothesized relationship (H1) of BDAC → FPER is statistically significant at the 0.05 level (P = 0.000 < 0.05) and hypothesized relationship (H2) of BDAC → DDC is statistically significant at the 0.05 level as well since both T statistics are above 1.96. However, the hypothesized (H3) of DDC → FPER is not statistically significant within the currently limited sample as its T statistics is 0.658, which is less than 1.96 at the level of 0.05.

This study further examines the path estimates of BDAC → FPER and of BDAC → DDC. The path estimates (Table 4) show that BDAC enhanced FPER with a path coefficient of 0.644 (p < 0.05), explaining 64.4% of the variance, thus supporting H1. Besides, BDAC enhanced DDC, with a path coefficient of 0.809 (p < 0.05), explaining 80.9% of the variance, thus supporting H2. In addition, both BDAC and DDC impact FPER, explaining 54.5% of its variance, while BDAC impacts DDC, explaining 65.5% of its variance.

Table 4. Path Coefficients

	Original sample (O)	Sample mean (M)	Standard deviation (STDEV)	T statistics (|O/STDEV|)	P values
BDAC -> BDAC-Human (BDACH)	0.968	0.968	0.009	105.101	0.000
BDAC -> BDAC-Intangible (BDACI)	0.716	0.706	0.11	6.499	0.000
BDAC -> BDAC-Tangible (BDACT)	0.922	0.919	0.026	34.853	0.000
BDAC -> DDC	0.809	0.8	0.072	11.207	0.000
BDAC -> FPER	0.644	0.62	0.179	3.597	0.000

(continued)

Table 4. (*continued*)

	Original sample (O)	Sample mean (M)	Standard deviation (STDEV)	T statistics (|O/STDEV|)	P values
BDAC-Human (BDACH) -> BDACH-Mgnt Skill	0.97	0.968	0.012	79.187	0.000
BDAC-Human (BDACH) -> BDACH-Tech skills	0.967	0.965	0.014	68.944	0.000
BDAC-Intangible (BDACI) -> BDACI-Data-driven culture	1	1	0	6,854.46	0.000
BDAC-Tangible (BDACT) -> BDACT-Basic Resource	0.804	0.8	0.059	13.637	0.000
BDAC-Tangible (BDACT) -> BDACT-Data	0.925	0.926	0.02	45.895	0.000
BDAC-Tangible (BDACT) -> BDACT-Technology	0.952	0.951	0.017	57.175	0.000
DDC -> DDC-DIC	0.87	0.866	0.043	20.241	0.000
DDC -> DDC-DLC	0.968	0.968	0.009	104.566	0.000
DDC -> DDC-DRC	0.803	0.797	0.074	10.833	0.000
DDC -> FPER	0.114	0.121	0.173	0.658	0.511
FPER -> FPER-MP	0.904	0.91	0.023	39.05	0.000
FPER -> FPER-OP	0.901	0.901	0.045	19.999	0.000

6 Conclusions

6.1 Summary and Expected Future Contribution

Overall, this pilot study (study I) aims to bring more empirical studies in the limited development of extant BDA research, and fill up research gaps that industry-specific BDA research, BDA study from China, and digital dynamic capability are limited. Results of this study (Study I) provide empirical evidence to support the feasibility of future main study (study II). The expected contributions of the main study will be threefold:

First, the insights generated by this study will benefit executives who face decision making before and after BDA investment. The insights from this study may make immediate contributions in developing and configuring firm-specific BDAC for enhancing firm performance.

Second, the nature of and challenges from big data have gone beyond the prior IS discussions on IT capability and its relationship with firm performance. Consequently, this study advances existent BDAC research by addressing this gap by considering big data challenges in the development of the BDAC model.

Third, limited studies have addressed big data in the strategy literature. This study enriches the BDA Strategy research by providing more empirical evidence.

Fourth, this study is among the earliest BDA studies in China that have industry specific focus.

Overall, this study contributes to information system (IS) and strategy disciplines by exploring what resources, beyond technology, may help create BDAC and bringing in new empirical evidence of validating BDAC-FPER relationship and mediating effects of DDC on BDAC-FPER relationship. Despite its limited sample, the current pilot study has validated the measurement model and two of the hypotheses underpinning the structural model representing the relationship between BDAC, DDE and FPER, and thus it already engenders some of the managerial implications expected from the full study.

6.2 Limitations and Work to Be Completed

However, this study is not without its limitations. First, this study is the pilot study (Study I) of two-phase research, and thus the sample size is still relatively small at this stage. The sample size will be expected to increase substantially in the next phase of the study (Study II), which will expand to other industries in China. Finally, as Bhatt and Grover observed about BDA study, this steam is still in its early stage and will be keeping evolving as technology advances [8], and thus it is impossible and feasible to include all possible BDA dimensions when this study finishes. Future research may continue to improve the BDAC model by identifying new big data resources, and a more extensive study from China would be necessary to verify the model from this study.

A Appendix

See Table 5.

Table 5. Survey measures

1st-order construct	Code	Items	Source
Data	DT1	My organization has enabled us to approach very large, unstructured, or fast-moving data for analysis	[13, 21]
	DT2	My organization has consolidated data from multiple internal sources at a data hub (i.e. Data Lake, EDW, data-mart, etc.)	[13, 21]
	DT3	My organization has integrated external and internal data supporting business analytics	[13, 21]

(continued)

Table 5. (*continued*)

1st-order construct	Code	Items	Source
Technology	TG1	My organization uses parallel computing supporting big data (i.e., Hadoop, etc.)	[13, 21]
	TG2	My organization has data visualization tools	[13, 21]
	TG3	My organization uses cloud-based services for data process and analytics (i.e. GoogleML, Amazon AWS, etc.)	[13, 21]
	TG4	My organization uses open-source software for big data analytics (i.e. R, Python, etc.)	[13, 21]
	TG5	My organization uses non-structured databases (i.e. NoSQL, MongoDB, etc.) for database management.	[13, 19, 21]
Basic resource	BS1	My organization has an adequate budget for big data analytics projects	[13, 21, 48]
	BS2	My organization provides sufficient time to big data analytics projects	[13, 21, 40]
Technical skills	TS1	My organization provides employees with training in big data analytics in any form (online, offline or mixed)	[21, 30]
	TS2	My organization recruits new talents for big data analytics	[21, 30]
	TS3	The big data analytics team in my organization have the right skills to perform their jobs	[10, 21, 40]
	TS4	The big data analytics team in my organization have the right education to perform their jobs	[10, 21]
	TS5	The big data analytics team in my organization have the right experience to perform their jobs	[10, 21]
	TS6	The big data analytics team in my organization are well trained	[10, 21]
Managerial skills	MS1	The big data analytics managers in my organization understand business needs from functional managers	[21, 30]
	MS2	The big data analytics managers in my organization can work with functional managers to identify big data application in my business	[13, 21, 30]
	MS3	The big data analytics managers in my organization can support other functional managers through big data activities	[21, 30]
	MS4	The big data analytics managers in my organization can foresee the future needs from functional managers	[21, 30]
	MS5	The big data analytics managers in my organization can apply big data to the right scenarios	[13, 21]
	MS6	The big data analytics managers can know thoroughly and find the value of output from big data	[4, 30]
Data-driven culture	DD1	My organization always considers data a tangible asset	[26, 30]
	DD2	My organization always use data, not instinct, for decision making	[10, 30, 40]
	DD3	My organization always listens to big data insights when data is contrary to our positions.	[28, 30]
	DD4	My organization always uses insights extracted from data to improve business	[10, 30, 40]
	DD5	My organization always encourages employees to use data for reaching decisions.	[10, 30, 40]

(*continued*)

Table 5. (*continued*)

1st-order construct	Code	Items	Source
Market performance	MP1	My organization has entered new markets more quickly than our competitors	[17, 21, 35, 36, 44, 46]
	MP2	My organization has introduced new products or services to the market faster than our competitors	[17, 21, 35, 36, 44, 46]
	MP3	Our success rate of new products or services has been higher than our competitors	[17, 21, 35, 36, 44, 46]
	MP4	Our market share has exceeded that of our competitors	[17, 21, 35, 36, 44, 46]
Operational performance	OP1	Our productivity has exceeded that of our competitors	[17, 21, 36, 44, 46]
	OP2	Our profit rate has exceeded that of our competitors	[17, 21, 36, 44, 46]
	OP3	Our return on investment (ROI) has exceeded that of our competitors	[17, 21, 36, 44, 46]
	OP4	Our sales revenue has exceeded that of our competitors	[17, 21, 36, 44, 46]
Digital dynamic integration capability	DIC1	Facing the changing digital landscape (i.e. EC, social media, data technology, AI, etc.), my organization is flexible and fast to changes in the organizational process when needed.	[25, 43]
	DIC2	Facing the changing digital landscape (i.e. EC, social media, data technology, AI, etc.), my organization can respond to changing environments through coordinate internal and external competencies.	[25, 43]
Digital dynamic reconfiguration capability	DRC1	When digital data generation methods must evolve in our organization (e.g. in-sights from big data, SFA, Mobile App), personnel can successfully manage their evolution.	[33, 43, 45]
	DRC2	When digital data generation methods must evolve (e.g., insights from big data, SFA, Mobile App) in our organization, personnel can effectively direct their reorganization.	[33, 43, 45]
Digital dynamic learning capability	DLC1	My organization always looks for updated knowledge in digitalisation and big data analytics development.	[8, 43]
	DLC2	My organization always acquires new and relevant knowledge in digital and big data analytics.	[8, 43]
	DLC3	My organization always assimilates relevant knowledge of digital and big data analytics.	[8, 43]
	DLC4	My organization always applies relevant knowledge in digital and big data analytics.	[8, 43]
	DLC5	My organization has made effective use of existing competencies and new knowledge in digital and big data analytics	[8, 43]

Table 6. Profile of Respondents

Dimension	Frequency	Percent	Dimension	Frequency	Percent
Sex			*Job Level*		
Female	37	67%	Senior executive	13	24%
Male	18	33%	Middle manager	30	55%
Total	55	100%	Employee	12	22%
			Total	55	100%
Type of Organization					
Foreign Private	12	22%	*Size of the organisation*		
Local Private	40	73%	0–19	0	0%
State Owned	3	5%	20–99	2	4%
Total	55	100%	100–249	1	2%
			250–499	0	0%
Total Work Experience			500–999	1	2%
1–5 Yr	11	20%	1000–2499	6	11%
11–15 Yr	14	25%	2500–4999	6	11%
16–20 Yr	11	20%	5000–9999	6	11%
20 Yr+	4	7%	10000–24999	11	20%
6–10 Yr	15	27%	25000–49999	6	11%
Total	55	100%	50000–99999	11	20%
			100000+	5	9%
Age				55	100%
18–25	3	5%			
26–33	20	36%	*Education*		
34–41	19	35%	Postgraduate degree (Master/Ph.D.)	38	69%
42–49	13	24%	Undergraduate	17	31%
Total	55	100%	Total	55	100%

References

1. Abbasi, A., Sarker, S., Chiang, R.H.L.: Big data research in information systems: toward an inclusive research agenda. J. Assoc. Inf. Syst. **17**, 1–32 (2016)
2. Agarwal, R., Dhar, V.: Editorial—Big data, data science, and analytics: the opportunity and challenge for is research. Inf. Syst. Res. **25**, 443–448 (2014)
3. Akter, S., Wamba, S.F., Gunasekaran, A., Dubey, R., Childe, S.J.: How to improve firm performance using big data analytics capability and business strategy alignment? Int. J. Prod. Econ. **182**, 113–131 (2016)
4. Athey, S., Toole, K.O.: How big data changes business management. News. Graduate, September 2013

5. Barney, J.: Firm resources and sustained competitive advantage. J. Manag. **17**(1), 99–120 (1991)
6. Barney, J.B., Clark, D.N.: Resource-Based Theory: Creating and Sustaining Competitive Advantage. Oxford University Press on Demand, Oxford (2007)
7. Bharadwaj, A.S.: A resource-based perspective on information technology capability and firm performance: an empirical investigation. MIS Q. **24**(1), 169–196 (2000)
8. Bhatt, G.D., Grover, V.: Types of information technology capabilities and their role in competitive advantage: an empirical study. J. Manag. Inf. Syst. **22**(2), 253–277 (2005)
9. Brynjolfsson, E., Yang, S.: The intangible benefits and costs of investments: evidence from financial markets. In: Proceedings of the Eighteenth International Conference on Information Systems, p. 147. Association for Information Systems (1997)
10. Carmeli, A., Tishler, A.: The relationships between intangible organizational elements and organizational performance. Strateg. Manag. J. **25**(13), 1257–1278 (2004)
11. Chamoux, J.P. (ed.): The Digital Era 1: Big Data Stakes. Wiley, Hoboken (2018)
12. Chin, W.W.: How to write up and report PLS analyses. In: Esposito Vinzi, V., Chin, W.W., Henseler, J., Wang, H. (eds.) Handbook of Partial Least Squares. SHCS, pp. 655–690. Springer, Germany (2010). https://doi.org/10.1007/978-3-540-32827-8_29
13. Davenport, T.: Big Data at Work: Dispelling the Myths. Uncovering the Opportunities. Harvard Business Review Press, Boston (2014)
14. Davenport, T.H., Harris, J.G.: Competing on Analytics: The New Science of Winning. Harvard Business School Press, Boston (2007)
15. Davenport, T.H., Barth, P., Bean, R.: How big data is different. MIT Sloan Manag. Rev. **54**(1), 43–46 (2012)
16. Fornell, C., Larcker, D.F.: Evaluating structural equation models with unobservable variables and measurement error. J. Mark. Res. **18**, 39–50 (1981)
17. Wamba, S.F., Gunasekaran, A., Akter, S., Ren, S.J.-F., Dubey, R., Childe, S.J.: Big data analytics and firm performance: effects of dynamic capabilities. J. Bus. Res. **70**, 356–365 (2017)
18. Garmaki, M., Boughzala, I., Wamba, S.F.: The effect of big data analytics capability on firm performance. In: PACIS, p. 301 (2016)
19. Gordon, K.: Principles of Data Management. BCS Learning & Development Limited, Swindon (2007). ISBN 13: 9781902505848
20. Grant, R.M.: The resource-based theory of competitive advantage. In: Faulkner, D. (ed.) Strategy: Critical Perspectives on Business and Management, vol. 135, pp. 122–148 (2002)
21. Gupta, M., George, J.F.: Toward the development of a big data analytics capability. Inf. Manag. **53**(8), 1049–1064 (2016)
22. Hair, J.F., Black, W.C., Babin, B.J., Anderson, R.E.: Multivariate Data Analysis: Pearson New International Edition. Pearson Education Limited, Essex (2014)
23. Hair, J.F., Ringle, C.M., Sarstedt, M.: PLS-SEM: indeed a silver bullet. J. Mark. Theory Pract. **19**(2), 139–152 (2011)
24. Kietzmann, J., Plangger, K., Eaton, B., Heilgenberg, K., Pitt, L., Berthon, P.: Mobility at work: a typology of mobile communities of practice and contextual ambidexterity. J. Strateg. Inf. Syst. **22**(4), 282–297 (2013)
25. Kohli, R., Grover, V.: Business value of IT: an essay on expanding research directions to keep up with the times. J. Assoc. Inf. Syst. **9**(1), 1 (2008)
26. Laney, D.: 3D data management: controlling data volume. Velocity and variety (2001)
27. Lin, Y., Wu, L.Y.: Exploring the role of dynamic capabilities in firm performance under the resource-based view framework. J. Bus. Res. **67**(3), 407–413 (2014)
28. McAfee, A., Brynjolfsson, E., Davenport, T.H., Patil, D.J., Barton, D.: Big data: the management revolution. Harvard Bus. Rev. **90**(10), 60–68 (2012)

29. Makadok, R.: Toward a synthesis of the resource-based and dynamic capability views of rent creation. Strateg. Manag. J. **22**(5), 387–401 (2001)
30. Mata, F.J., Fuerst, W.L., Barney, J.B.: Information technology and sustained competitive advantage: a resource-based analysis. MIS Q. **19**, 487–505 (1995)
31. Mithas, S., Lee, M.R., Earley, S., Murugesan, S., Djavanshir, R.: Leveraging big data and business analytics. IT Prof. **15**(6), 18–20 (2013)
32. Newbert, S.L.: Empirical research on the resource-based view of the firm: an assessment and suggestions for future research. Strateg. Manag. J. **28**(2), 121–146 (2007)
33. Pavlou, P.A., El Sawy, O.A.: From IT leveraging competence to competitive advantage in turbulent environments: the case of new product development. Inf. Syst. Res. **17**(3), 198–227 (2006)
34. Pinsonneault, A., Kraemer, K.L.: Survey research methodology in management information systems: an assessment. J. Manag. Inf. Syst. **10**, 75–105 (1993)
35. Raguseo, E., Vitari, C.: Investments in big data analytics and firm performance: an empirical investigation of direct and mediating effects. Int. J. Prod. Res. **56**(15), 5206–5221 (2018)
36. Ravichandran, T., Lertwongsatien, C., Lertwongsatien, C.: Effect of information systems resources and capabilities on firm performance: a resource-based perspective. J. Manag. Inf. Syst. **21**(4), 237–276 (2005)
37. Rai, A., Patnayakuni, R., Seth, N.: Firm performance impacts of digitally enabled supply chain integration capabilities. MIS Q. **30**, 225–246 (2006)
38. Rai, A., Tang, X.: Leveraging IT capabilities and competitive process capabilities for the management of interorganizational relationship portfolios. Inf. Syst. Res. **21**(3), 516–542 (2010)
39. Ringle, C.M., Wede, S., Becker, J.M.: SmartPLS 3. SmartPLS (2014)
40. Ross, J.W., Beath, C.M., Quaadgras, A.: You may not need big data after all. Harvard Bus. Rev. **91**(12), 90+ (2013)
41. Teece, D.J.: Intangible assets and a theory of heterogeneous firms. In: Bounfour, A., Miyagawa, T. (eds.) Intangibles, Market Failure and Innovation Performance, pp. 217–239. Springer, Cham (2015). https://doi.org/10.1007/978-3-319-07533-4_9
42. Teece, D.J.: Explicating dynamic capabilities: the nature and micro-foundations of (sustainable) enterprise performance. Strateg. Manag. J. **28**(13), 1319–1350 (2007)
43. Teece, D.J., Pisano, G., Shuen, A.: Dynamic capabilities and strategic management. Strateg. Manag. J. **18**(7), 509–533 (1997)
44. Tippins, M.J., Sohi, R.S.: IT competency and firm performance: is organizational learning a missing link? Strateg. Manag. J. **24**(8), 745–761 (2003)
45. Vitari, C., Raguseo, E.: Digital data, dynamic capability and financial performance: an empirical investigation in the era of big data. Systemes d'Information Manag. **21**(3), 63–92 (2016)
46. Wang, N., Liang, H., Zhong, W., Xue, Y., Xiao, J.: Resource structuring or capability building? An empirical study of the business value of information technology. J. Manag. Inf. Syst. **29**(2), 325–367 (2012)
47. Wetzels, M., Odekerken-Schroder, G., Van Oppen, C.: Using PLS path modelling for assessing hierarchical construct models: guidelines and empirical illustration. MIS Q. **22**, 177 (2009)
48. Wixom, B.H., Watson, H.J.: An empirical investigation of the factors affecting data warehousing success. MIS Q. **25**, 17–41 (2001)
49. Woerner, S.L., Wixom, B.H.: Big data: extending the business strategy toolbox. J. Inf. Technol. **30**(1), 60–62 (2015)

Digital Services for Industry 4.0: Assessing Collaborative Technology Readiness

Asia Ramzan[1], Sonia Cisneros-Cabrera[1(✉)], Pedro Sampaio[1],
Nikolay Mehandjiev[1], and Nikolai Kazantsev[1,2]

[1] Alliance Manchester Business School,
The University of Manchester, Manchester, UK
{asia.ramzan, sonia.cisneroscabrera,
P.sampaio, n.mehandjiev}@manchester.ac.uk,
nikolai.kazantsev@postgrad.manchester.ac.uk
[2] National Research University "Higher School of Economics", Moscow, Russia

Abstract. Collaborative technologies, such as peer-to-peer (P2P) communication systems, information sharing technologies, and online team meeting facilities have long been available to support the daily operation of businesses. We investigate how collaborative technologies can adapt to further underpin emerging business paradigms, namely the "Industry 4.0" trend. Our purpose is to contribute to the understanding of what characteristics would maintain a collaborative technology current and ready to be part of the digital services available to support the fourth industrial revolution demands. To fulfil this purpose, we propose a taxonomic solution for assessment of collaborative technologies readiness for Industry 4.0; the analysis obtained using this classification scheme serves as an indicator to elicitate what is required to be addressed to meet Industry 4.0 goals. We also present details about the taxonomy development and validation using a benchmarking approach. Finally, we exemplify how our taxonomy can be applied to assess a collaborative technology.

Keywords: Digital services · Collaborative technologies · Industry 4.0 · Technology readiness

1 Introduction

Industry 4.0 (I4.0) refers to an emerging trend which revolutionises the way manufacturing domains carry out their operations. I4.0 involves use of cyber-physical systems and transdisciplinary approaches to automate processes and enable services innovation fostering an agile business environment [1–3]. Approaches underpinning the I4.0 revolution include the digitalisation of processes to enable agility and costs reduction, new models of business collaborations and the development and implementation of Information and Communication Technologies (ICTs) to support operations [4, 5]. In these approaches, collaboration appears as a core enabler [6, 7]. Digital services supporting collaboration provide the process "glue" that enable cross- organizational links across the supply chains that are core to the I4.0 paradigm.

© Springer Nature Switzerland AG 2020
M. Themistocleous and M. Papadaki (Eds.): EMCIS 2019, LNBIP 381, pp. 609–622, 2020.
https://doi.org/10.1007/978-3-030-44322-1_45

Despite recent advances in the understanding of enablers for I4.0 [8, 9], there are still limitations towards assessing processes, technology features, use cases, functional capabilities, standards, and data security features of current collaborative technologies. There is also limited guidance on how these technologies align with the I4.0 vision [5].

We contribute to bridging this gap by specifying what characteristics would enable a collaborative technology to support the operations of businesses towards the fourth industrial revolution, guided by the following research questions:

1. What are the key features and capabilities supported by collaborative technologies in the digital services domain?
2. What are the existing gaps in existing domain-specific collaborative technologies towards enabling the Industry 4.0 vision?

We present the specification of these key features and capabilities in a taxonomic solution that also enables the assessment of collaborative technologies readiness to support I4.0 goals and principles, such as interoperability, modularity, service orientation and information transparency [10]. The taxonomy proposed is applicable to available digital services which offer collaborative technologies in the form of applications, systems and tools, and is a first step towards the development of a comprehensive I4.0 digital services readiness assessment framework, focused on the collaborative technologies service offering.

The remainder of this paper is structured as follows: Sect. 2 presents the background information on collaborative technologies within digital services. Section 3 details the research method used for taxonomy development for collaborative technologies assessment. Section 4 presents the taxonomy developed, and Sect. 5 specifies the validation approach. Section 6 illustrates how to use the taxonomy with a sample of real-world domain-specific digital services with collaborative technologies functionalities. Finally, Sect. 7 presents conclusions and future directions of the research.

2 Collaborative Technologies Overview

The existing classification of collaborative technologies includes the division into two main categories: Horizontal and Vertical [7, 11]. Horizontal collaborative technologies usage includes personal, educational and business communications [11]. They can be further divided into four sub-categories: (1) peer-to-peer (P2P) communication systems, (2) social media tools, (3) information sharing and (4) team meeting support [11]. On the second classification, vertical collaborative technologies are relevant to a specific industry domain to which such digital services are specifically designed [11]; an example of this is the AirSupply[1] Tool specifically supporting the aerospace industry by providing communication services that are secure and traceable between companies in the Aerospace supply chain. Another example is the FREIGHTQUOTE[2] tool which is used mainly to support processes of logistics to reduce freight costs by optimisation approaches.

---

[1] https://www.boostaerospace.com/airsupply/.

[2] https://www.freightquote.com/define/what-is-transportation-management-system-tms.

The number of users and industries also serve as criteria to differentiate vertical and horizontal collaborative technologies [7]. For example, a social media tool such as Twitter[3] can be considered a horizontal domain-independent digital communication technology used for broadcasting and one to one interactions for both personal and commercial purposes. In contrast, AirCollab[4] is a domain-specific communication technology used for collaboration in the aerospace industry on a "many-to-many" approach.

Our work further classifies the collaborative technologies. We aim to systematise the variety of concepts through a taxonomy classification by unifying terminologies and characteristics of collaborative technologies into a single structure. As a basis for developing the initial structure of the taxonomy, we departed from the European Union's I4.0 vision articulated in the Horizon 2020 (H2020) vision document [12]. The next section presents the development of a taxonomy of collaborative technologies supporting I4.0 capabilities.

3 Taxonomy Development Methodology: Collaborative Technologies for Industry 4.0

The taxonomy development method adopted for this research is based on Nickerson's method [13]. Nickerson et al. presented a comprehensive literature review of existing methods to develop a taxonomy in different domains; the method proposed focuses on taxonomy development applicable in Information Systems research (IS) based on the design science paradigm [14]. The method follows a three-level measurement model [15] with some modifications and also considers meta-characteristics and ending conditions for taxonomy development. Nickerson's method employs two approaches for the development of taxonomies: (1) inductive and (2) deductive. This approach also guides the logic for conceiving new dimensions or uses of collaborative technologies. The method also prescribes the interleaving application of inductive and deductive approaches, which we used for understanding and organising the concepts associated with the term "collaborative technology".

The steps followed in the development included the selection of a convenience sample of collaborative technologies available in the literature [14] from which we extracted its potential applications. We identified the characteristics of user interaction from the extracted applications (e.g. the application of collaborative technology for audio or video communications involves the user in audio and video conferencing). We also determined the multiplicity dimension of the features such as a sole company user and a group of companies of users who can have privileges to use the application. In this activity, we employed the deductive approach to ensure alternative perspectives were considered and represented in the taxonomy. For example, some collaborative technologies (e.g. Microsoft Lync[5]) are designed to support general interactions between people.

---

[3] https://twitter.com.

[4] http://www.boostaerospace.com/aircollab/.

[5] https://products.office.com/en-us/microsoft-lync-2013.

In contrast, certain collaborative technologies (e.g. AirSupply) are developed for individuals who work for a given company. Similarly, some collaborative technologies cannot be used in certain locations of the world; for example, some countries have blocked Skype services due to security threats [16]. Our deductive approach, thus, leads us to identify the former feature as access rights of using the application and the latter feature as user location identification characteristics. In the following section, we present the taxonomy developed using this approach.

4   The Industry 4.0 Collaborative Technologies Taxonomy

The taxonomy depicted in Fig. 1 illustrates the broad range of conceptual constructs to classify collaborative technologies offering digital services enabling I4.0. The key features and capabilities concepts present the novelty in the designed taxonomy; both supported in defining a concept of "collaborative technology". The designed taxonomy encompasses six major categories (i.e. Industries, Types, Uses, Applications, Features and Services) and many sub-categories. We start by presenting the different industries for which such digital service can be available, from the heavy machinery manufacturing industries, such as aerospace, railway and automotive domains, to healthcare industries. Secondly, we conceptualise the different roles a collaboration technology can take within an organisation, e.g. to support decision making, as an e-commerce platform, or to support e-learning. Next, we classify the concepts of horizontal and vertical collaborative technologies (see the details in Sect. 2), and also the different uses a collaborative technology can take: business- to-business (B2B), business-to-consumer (B2C) or consumer-to-consumer (C2C). In the fifth branch of the collaborative technologies taxonomy, we present the features that make a collaborative technology, which includes conferencing, screen-sharing, document-sharing, information-sharing, audio and video coordination, online communication, web browsing and multiple language support.

On the conferencing feature, for example, we consider the use of calendars for conferences or meetings, with invite features, reminders, and alert functionalities. The time tracker functionality, for example, helps to interact with others on an exact given time (e.g. a German user needs to consider the time zone of other users living in the United Kingdom while inviting to an online meeting). Finally, we present the core capabilities for I4.0 that a collaborative technology may present. These capabilities are access-control, production planning[6], matchmaking[7], team creation[8], governance rules

---

[6] Production planning service is used to plan products, materials and resources [23].

[7] Matchmaking is a service that provides suggestions of best potential partners for a given business opportunity [24].

[8] Team creation is a kind of temporary alliance that is developed for short-term to share skills or core competencies and resources in order to better respond to business opportunities [24, 25].

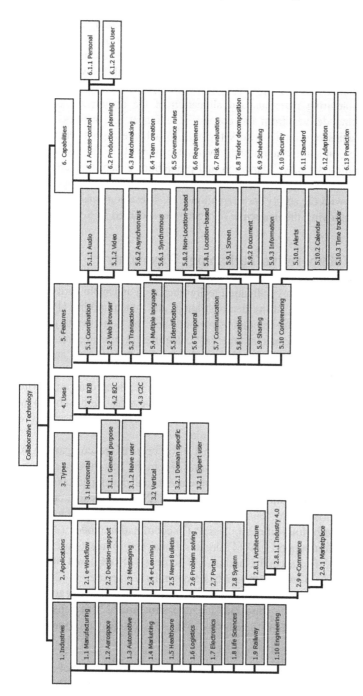

Fig. 1. Collaborative technology taxonomy towards Industry 4.0 support

support, requirements analysis[9], risk evaluation[10], tender-decomposition[11], scheduling, security, adaptation and predictions. In this branch, we also present the access control capability of the application, which determines that the services may be of use for business or personal purposes. Following this branch of core capabilities, we also have the production planning and scheduling capabilities to support the planning of the production and manufacturing materials and allocation of the resources. Also, the concept of matchmaking derives from the context of alliances, or business teams, where different companies or suppliers work together to achieve a goal where their selection is made based on some criteria and governance rules [17]. The risk evaluation, tender-decomposition security, adaptation and predictions capabilities are added to the taxonomy to test if a collaborative technology can support secure interoperability across the supply chain with the ability for adaptation [10]. These concepts were added to the taxonomy by employing the deductive approach, as specified in Sect. 3 above.

5 Validation of Collaborative Technology Taxonomy

There are various types of taxonomy validation techniques such as Delphi card sorting [18], orthogonality demonstration, utility demonstration, and benchmarking [19]. The Delphi card sorting is an in-person validating method, and the participants need to organise and label artefacts or concepts into relevant categories. A typical card-sorting exercise consists of four different states named planning, preparing, sorting and analysis. We have not employed this method due to limited resources. The orthogonality technique is used to extend the existing or base taxonomy by defining categories with clear classification criteria. The utility demonstration technique is also applicable to an extended taxonomy. We have not extended any taxonomy; therefore, both techniques are not suitable to validate our classification scheme.

We utilised benchmarking as an approach that also supports the comparison of taxonomies with other related classification structures. From the literature, we identified three taxonomical structures with a similar structure to our developed taxonomy: Mentzas [20], Nickerson [21] and Bafoutsou and Mentzas [22]; we compared our work with those. In the comparison, we found that the first classification structure [20] categorised group software in four different classes: (1) coordination model, (2) information sharing, (3) decision support and (4) organisational environment (user roles: centralised, decentralised). The second classification scheme [21] explored nine different categories, out of which two characteristics are similar to the ones in [20]. The "characteristics" category groups other six categories, and "application" category lists "workflow management" only. The third classification structure [22] organises collaborative systems in 24 different categories with 17 classes recognised as

---

[9] These are customers' requirement analysis that can be in the form of tracing individual customer order specification from the shop floor and monitoring their order execution and may involve forecasting item delivery and evaluating customer satisfaction [26].

[10] Risk evaluation is a process to compare the estimated risk against the given risk criteria [27].

[11] Tender-decomposition is a business opportunity that supports tenders breakdown into sub-tenders [28].

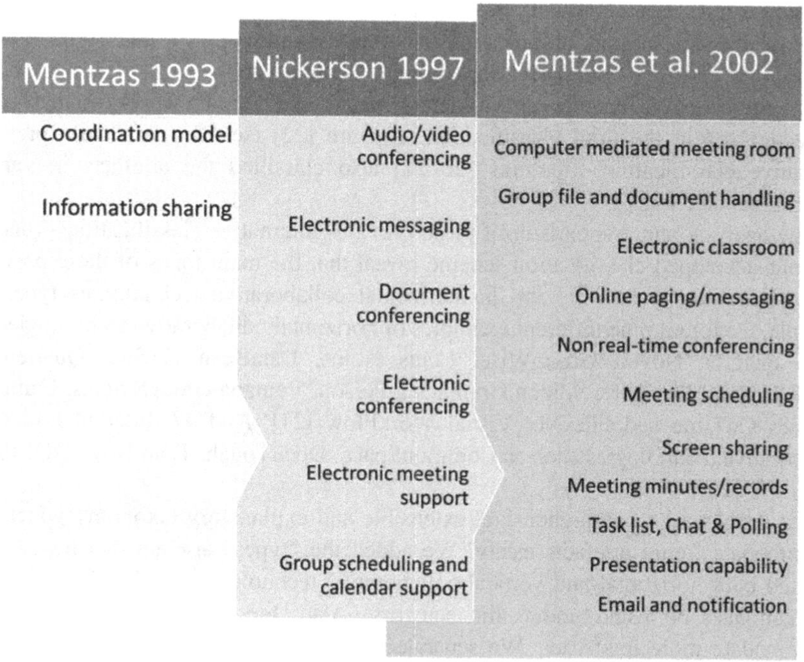

Mentzas 1993	Nickerson 1997	Mentzas et al. 2002
Coordination model	Audio/video conferencing	Computer mediated meeting room
Information sharing		Group file and document handling
	Electronic messaging	Electronic classroom
	Document conferencing	Online paging/messaging
		Non real-time conferencing
	Electronic conferencing	Meeting scheduling
		Screen sharing
	Electronic meeting support	Meeting minutes/records
		Task list, Chat & Polling
	Group scheduling and calendar support	Presentation capability
		Email and notification

Fig. 2. Similar collaborative technology taxonomies – Characteristics

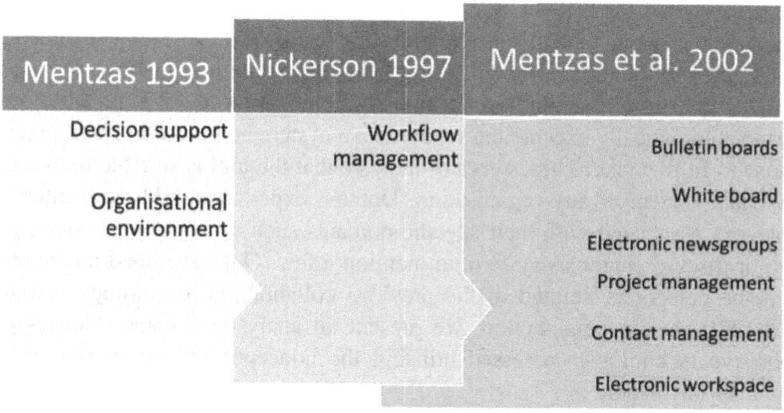

Mentzas 1993	Nickerson 1997	Mentzas et al. 2002
Decision support	Workflow management	Bulletin boards
Organisational environment		White board
		Electronic newsgroups
		Project management
		Contact management
		Electronic workspace

Fig. 3. Similar collaborative technology taxonomies - Applications

"characteristics". Four out of 17 categories were already present in the previous taxonomies, and 13 new categories were added as "characteristics". Figure 2 depicts the similarities found. Figure 3 presents the other seven similar categories identified as applications of collaborative technologies.

In the similarities identified, in comparison to the taxonomy we present in Fig. 1, we found decision support, organisation environment and workflow management under applications category. Similarly, the bulletin boards, whiteboard, electronic newsgroups, project management, contact management and electronic workspace categories are recognised in the third classification structure [22] (see Fig. 3). These previous alternative classification structures [20–22] also classified the artefacts in various applications (see Fig. 3).

The analysis and comparison of these previous alternative classification structures with our developed classification scheme reveal that the main focus of these previous structures seems to be only on the horizontal collaborative technologies type. For example, we found nine different examples of horizontal collaborative technologies are listed such as Novell GroupWise, Lotus Notes, DataBean FarSite, Quarterdeck WebTalk, Intel ProShare, Silicon Graphics InPerson, Ventana GroupSytems, Campbell Services OnTime and FilesNet Visual WorkFlow [21]. And 47 different horizontal collaborative technologies such as CommonSpace, DocuTouch, TeamNow, DOLPHIN and CVW [22].

We developed a comprehensive, extensible and explanatory taxonomy which can accommodate future artefacts easily. We added the "types" artefact that has accommodated both horizontal and vertical collaborative technologies, and in future, a new type can also be listed under this category. Also, the "industries" category can accommodate more industries. We separated the application and characteristics categories in such a way it can differentiate that a collaborative technology has specific features for using some applications (e.g. decision making and problem - solving). The designed classification scheme also assists the user in the selection of a suitable tool by introducing the "uses" of an artefact which informs, for example, whether the tool should be designed for B2B or B2C activities.

The novelty in our developed taxonomy is the inclusion of the "capability" category that keeps unique artefacts which highlights the strength of the tool. For instance, tender-decomposition, machine-to-machine communication and VE creation services support to automatically execute the supply chain system and assist in creating a virtual enterprise to fulfil a task. These services indicate that the tool is suitable to execute the supply chain system of any organisation. Domain experts can add capabilities under this category associated with their specific domains such as inventory system, payroll system, or disease diagnosis system, to mention a few. Our developed taxonomy also covered the categories defined in the previous collaborative technology taxonomies (see [20–22]). In the next section, we present an analysis of some domain-specific collaborative technologies assessed utilising the concepts defined in the taxonomy presented in this paper.

6 Assessing Collaborative Technologies: Representative Example

In this section, we present an example of use for the taxonomy of collaborative technologies. We assessed 10 domain-specific collaborative applications. For our analysis, we selected the following platforms: BoostAerospace[12], SAP Ariba[13], SupplyOn[14], KINAXIS[15], Quintiq[16], Generix group[17], ARTS[18], iQluster[19], Tradcloud[20] and Exostar[21]. The selection criteria included the consideration of digital services that offer collaborative technologies for supply chains and those which present information about their features, capabilities, functionalities and tools. These platforms were analysed with regards to their applications in supply chain system and capabilities to support an I4.0 solution utilising the collaborative technology taxonomy presented in Fig. 1. Table 1 presents the results of the readiness assessment where the columns of the table represent the analysed domain-specific collaborative technology, and the rows of the table represent the information about the technologies' applications in different industries, features and capabilities, linked to Fig. 1.

The analysis we carried out supports the identification that collaborative technologies are designed to facilitate supply chain systems of different industries but are not yet providing services (such as matchmaking and tender-decomposition) needed for an I4.0 support. Moreover, team selection and matchmaking services in these analysed tools have limited functionality and therefore provide only partial support. The collaborative team creation and governance services are also designed with limited functionalities in existing collaborative technologies consequently partially supported. For example, the Aircollab (a sub-system of Boostaerospace) platform has partial support in virtual collaboration of internal and external partners. Similarly, Boostaerospace has partial support in governance with founders, customers and service providers.

The majority of the analysed technologies do not have the capability to provide certain services (e.g. production planning and risk evaluation) and only a few tools provide full support, for example, the Quintiq platform renders full support to the production planning service, however, ARTS provides partial support and none of the other selected tools presents complete coverage regarding this service. Similarly, the KINAXIS tool supplies complete support in risk evaluation activity and SAP Ariba, SupplyOn and Exostar provide partial aid in this regard. The rest of the other six tools

---

[12] https://www.boostaerospace.com/.

[13] https://www.ariba.com/.

[14] http://www.supplyon.com/.

[15] http://www.kinaxis.com/en/.

[16] http://www.quintiq.com/.

[17] https://www.generixgroup.com/en.

[18] https://www.arts.aero/references.

[19] https://valuechain.com/supply-chain-intelligence/iQluster/

[20] https://www.tradecloud1.com/blog/topic/collaboration.

[21] https://www.exostar.com/.

Table 1. Existing collaborative technologies and their readiness to support Industry 4.0 Principles. The numbered items on the table are references to the categories and subcategories of the collaborative technologies taxonomy presented in Fig. 1. The notation of the analysed technologies is as follows: BoostAerospace = BA, SAP Ariba = SA, SupplyOn = SO, KINAXIS = KX, Quintiq = QN, Generix group = GX, ARTS = AS, iQluster = iQ, Tradcloud = TC and Exostar = EX. ✓ means the indicated characteristic is fully supported, P means partial support and X means the reviewed platform provides no support on the given characteristic.

Analysed Collaborative Technologies

No.				BA	SA	SO	KX	QN	GX	AS	iQ	TC	EX
1 Industries	1.1 Manufacturing			X	X	X	X	✓	X	X	✓	✓	✓
	1.2 Aerospace			✓	✓	✓	✓	✓	X	✓	X	X	✓
	1.3 Automotive			X	X	✓	✓	✓	X	✓	X	X	✓
	1.4 Marketing			✓	✓	✓	✓	✓	✓	✓	✓	✓	✓
	1.5 Healthcare			X	X	X	X	✓	X	X	X	X	✓
	1.6 Logistics			✓	✓	✓	✓	✓	✓	✓	✓	✓	✓
	1.7 Electronics			X	X	X	✓	X	X	X	X	X	X
	1.8 Life Sciences			X	X	X	✓	X	X	X	X	X	✓
	1.9 Railway			X	X	✓	X	X	X	X	X	X	X
	1.10 Engineering			X	X	✓	X	X	X	X	X	X	X
2 Applications	2.1 E-workflow			X	X	X	X	X	X	X	X	X	X
	2.2 Decision-support			X	X	X	X	X	X	X	X	X	X
	2.3 Messaging			✓	✓	✓	✓	✓	✓	✓	✓	✓	✓
	2.4 E-learning			X	X	X	X	X	X	X	X	X	X
	2.5 News bulletin			✓	✓	✓	✓	✓	✓	✓	✓	✓	✓
	2.6 Problem-solving			✓	✓	✓	✓	✓	✓	✓	✓	✓	✓
	2.7 Portal			✓	✓	✓	✓	✓	✓	✓	✓	✓	✓
	2.8 System	2.8.1 Architecture	2.8.1.1 Industry 4.0	X	X	✓	X	X	X	X	X	X	X
	2.9 e-Commerce	2.9.1 Marketplace		X	X	X	X	P	X	X	X	X	X
3 Types	3.1 Horizontal	3.1.1 General purpose		X	X	X	X	X	X	X	X	X	X
		3.1.2 Naïve user		X	X	X	X	X	X	X	X	X	X
	3.2 Vertical	3.2.1 Domain specific		✓	✓	✓	✓	✓	✓	✓	✓	✓	✓
		3.2.2 Expert user		✓	✓	✓	✓	✓	✓	✓	✓	✓	✓
4 Uses	4.1 Business-to-business			✓	✓	✓	✓	✓	✓	✓	✓	✓	✓
	4.2 Business-to-consumer			✓	✓	✓	✓	✓	✓	✓	✓	✓	✓
	4.3 Consumer-to-consumer			X	X	X	X	X	X	X	X	X	X
5 Features	5.1 Coordination	5.1.1 Audio		X	X	X	X	X	X	X	X	X	X
		5.1.2 Video		X	X	X	X	X	X	X	X	X	X
	5.2 Web browser			✓	✓	✓	✓	✓	✓	✓	✓	✓	✓
	5.3 Transaction			✓	✓	✓	✓	✓	✓	✓	✓	✓	✓
	5.4 Multiple languages			X	✓	✓	✓	X	✓	✓	X	X	X
	5.5 Identification			✓	✓	✓	✓	✓	✓	✓	✓	✓	✓
	5.6 Temporal	5.6.1 Synchronous		✓	✓	✓	✓	✓	✓	✓	✓	✓	✓
		5.6.2 Asynchronous		✓	✓	✓	✓	✓	✓	✓	✓	✓	✓

(continued)

Table 1. (*continued*)

No.			B A	S A	S O	K X	Q N	G X	A S	i Q	T C	E X
	5.7 Communication		✓	✓	✓	✓	✓	✓	✓		✓	✓
	5.8 Location	5.8.1 Location- based	✓	✓	✓	✓	✓	✓	✓	✓	✓	✓
		5.8.2 Non-location based	✓	✓	✓	✓	✓	✓	✓	✓	✓	✓
	5.9 Sharing	5.9.1 Screen	P	P	P	P	P	P	P	P	P	P
		5.9.2 Document	P	P	P	P	P	P	P	P	P	P
		5.9.3 Information	P	P	P	P	P	P	P	P	P	P
	5.10 Conferencing	5.10.1 Alerts	X	X	X	X	X	X	X	X	X	X
		5.10.2 Calendar	X	X	X	X	X	X	X	X	X	X
		5.10.3 Time Tracker	X	X	X	X	X	X	X	X	X	X
	5.10 Conferencing		✓	✓	✓	✓	✓	✓	✓	✓	✓	✓
6 Capabilities	6.1 Access control	6.1.1 Personal	X	X	X	X	X	X	X	X	X	X
		6.1.2 Public	✓	✓	✓	✓	✓	✓	✓	✓	✓	✓
	6.2 Production planning		X	X	X	X	✓	X	P	X	X	X
	6.3 Matchmaking		X	X	X	X	X	X	X	X	X	X
	6.4 VE creation		P	X	X	X	X	X	X	X	X	X
	6.5 Governance rules		P	X	X	X	X	X	X	X	X	X
	6.6 Requirements		P	P	P	P	P	P	P	P	P	P
	6.7 Risk evaluation		X	P	P	✓	X	X	X	X	X	P
	6.8 Tender decomposition		X	X	X	X	X	X	X	X	X	X
	6.9 Scheduling		X	X	X	P	✓	✓	X	P	X	X
	6.10 Security		✓	✓	✓	✓	✓	✓	✓	✓	✓	✓
	6.11 Standard		X	X	✓	X	X	X	X	X	X	X
	6.12 Adaptation		X	X	X	X	X	X	X	X	X	X
	6.13 Prediction		X	X	X	X	X	X	X	X	X	X

are not capable of measuring the risk against the given risk criteria. The management of the scheduling service has similar issues as production planning, and risk evaluation services have in the existing tools. Quintiq and Generix group fully helps in scheduling of resources and services involved in supply chain system; however, KINAXIS and iQluster have partial support and none of the rest of the tools has designed and managed such service.

All existing collaborative technologies are designed to connect and communicate with business communities, and customer requirements are dealt with by human experts which means that these systems are not capable of auto-analysing (parse, build internal representations and semantically understand) customer requirements and produce a workflow design accordingly. All analysed domain-specific collaborative technologies provide some level of support to communication, sharing, transaction execution, web-browsing, temporal and security features. However, remote conference calling is not possible with users needing to use ad-hoc applications for this purpose. For example, SupplyOn and Quintiq technology users use Webinar (a horizontal collaborative technology) for remote conferencing.

These analysed technologies are also used as bulletin boards to announce physical conferences, events and venues such as BoostAerospace used ISC (International Supplier Centre) Berlin and SAP Ariba conferences held at Las Vegas, Prague and Sydney in 2017 for customers and supplier's connections. Similarly, the sharing feature is partially implemented in all analysed digital services. These technologies support only information sharing where their users need to employ some other platforms for the documents and screen sharing. The adaptability, coordination, and predicting features are missing in all of the analysed collaborative technologies.

7   Conclusions

In this paper we specified key features and capabilities supported by collaborative technologies in the digital services arena and categorised them into a taxonomy of what forms a collaborative technology using Nickerson's methodology [13], particularly adding a category of capabilities that support the I4.0 goals. We identified the existing gaps in a sample of domain-specific collaborative technologies towards enabling the I4.0 vision utilising the taxonomy of collaborative technologies as an assessment tool. With this taxonomy, we contribute to the understanding of what characteristics collaborative technologies should address to support the fourth industrial revolution demands, and through its usage example, we presented a contribution to, for example, Research & Development (R&D) projects in the area of collaboration through technologies, where practitioners can utilise our taxonomy to systematically identify what characteristics should be developed towards an I4.0 project implementation. Finally, we also propose our work to be an initial step towards a more comprehensive I4.0 digital services readiness assessment framework.

Acknowledgements. The work presented has received funding from the European Commission under the European Union's Horizon 2020 research and innovation programme (grant agreement n° 723336). Financial support has been provided from the National Council of Science and Technology (abbreviated CONACYT) to Sonia Cisneros-Cabrera (agreement n° 461338).

References

1. Möller, D.P.F.: Digital manufacturing/Industry 4.0. Guide to Computing Fundamentals in Cyber-Physical Systems. CCN, pp. 307–375. Springer, Cham (2016). https://doi.org/10.1007/978-3-319-25178-3_7
2. Oesterreich, T.D., Teuteberg, F.: Understanding the implications of digitisation and automation in the context of Industry 4.0: a triangulation approach and elements of a research agenda for the construction industry. Comput. Ind. **83**, 121–139 (2016). https://doi.org/10.1016/j.compind.2016.09.006
3. Almada-Lobo, F.: The Industry 4.0 revolution and the future of manufacturing execution systems (MES). J. Innov. Manag. (2015). https://doi.org/10.24840/2183-0606_003.004_0003
4. Cisneros-Cabrera, S., Ramzan, A., Sampaio, P., Mehandjiev, N.: Digital marketplaces for Industry 4.0: a survey and gap analysis. In: Camarinha-Matos, L.M., Afsarmanesh, H., Fornasiero, R. (eds.) PRO-VE 2017. IAICT, vol. 506, pp. 18–27. Springer, Cham (2017). https://doi.org/10.1007/978-3-319-65151-4_2

5. Heng, S.: Industry 4.0: upgrading of Germany's industrial capabilities on the horizon, April 2014
6. Camarinha-Matos, L.M., Fornasiero, R., Afsarmanesh, H.: Collaborative networks as a core enabler of Industry 4.0. In: Camarinha-Matos, L.M., Afsarmanesh, H., Fornasiero, R. (eds.) PRO-VE 2017. IAICT, vol. 506, pp. 3–17. Springer, Cham (2017). https://doi.org/10.1007/978-3-319-65151-4_1
7. Shih, H.-p., Lai, K.-h., Cheng, T.C.E.: Examining structural, perceptual, and attitudinal influences on the quality of information sharing in collaborative technology use. Inf. Syst. Front. **17**(2), 455–470 (2013). https://doi.org/10.1007/s10796-013-9429-6
8. Havle, C.A., Ucler, C.: Enablers for Industry 4.0. In: Proceedings of ISMSIT 2018 - 2nd International Symposium on Multidisciplinary Studies and Innovative Technologies (2018). https://doi.org/10.1109/ismsit.2018.8567293
9. Trotta, D., Garengo, P.: Industry 4.0 key research topics: a bibliometric review. In: 2018 7th International Conference on Industrial Technology and Management, ICITM 2018 (2018). https://doi.org/10.1109/icitm.2018.8333930
10. Hermann, M., Pentek, T., Otto, B.: Design principles for Industrie 4.0 scenarios. In: 2016 49th Hawaii International Conference on System Sciences (HICSS), pp. 3928–3937. IEEE (2016). https://doi.org/10.1109/hicss.2016.488
11. Erhun, F., Keskinocak, P.: Collaborative supply chain management. In: Kempf, K.G., Keskinocak, P., Uzsoy, R. (eds.) Planning Production and Inventories in the Extended Enterprise. ISORMS, vol. 151, pp. 233–268. Springer, New York (2011). https://doi.org/10.1007/978-1-4419-6485-4_11
12. European Commission: Digital Automation. Research & Innovation Opportunities (2015). http://ec.europa.eu/research/participants/portal/desktop/en/opportunities/h2020/topics/fof-11-2016.html. Accessed 21 Nov 2018
13. Nickerson, R.C., Varshney, U., Muntermann, J.: A method for taxonomy development and its application in information systems. Eur. J. Inf. Syst. (2013). https://doi.org/10.1057/ejis.2012.26
14. Rummler, S., Ng, K.B.: Collaborative technologies and applications for interactive information design: emerging trends in user experiences (2009). https://doi.org/10.4018/978-1-60566-727-0
15. Bailey, K.D.: A three-level measurement model. Qual. Quant. **18**, 225–245 (1984). https://doi.org/10.1007/BF00156457
16. Green, E.: What to do if Skype is blocked in your country—NordVPN. NordVPN (2018). https://nordvpn.com/blog/why-is-skype-blocked-in-certain-countries/. Accessed 04 Nov 2019
17. Petersen, S.A.: Virtual enterprise formation and partner selection: an analysis using case studies. Int. J. Netw. Virtual Organ. **4**(2), 201–215 (2007). https://doi.org/10.1504/IJNVO.2007.013544
18. Soranzo, A., Cooksey, D.: Testing taxonomies: beyond card sorting. Bull. Assoc. Inf. Sci. Technol. (2015). https://doi.org/10.1002/bult.2015.1720410509
19. Usman, M., Britto, R., Börstler, J., Mendes, E.: Taxonomies in software engineering: a systematic mapping study and a revised taxonomy development method. Inf. Softw. Technol., 43–59 (2017). https://doi.org/10.1016/j.infsof.2017.01.006
20. Mentzas, G.N.: Coordination of joint tasks in organizational processes. J. Inf. Technol. **8**, 139–150 (1993). https://doi.org/10.1057/jit.1993.20
21. Nickerson, R.C.: A taxonomy of collaborative applications. In: Proceedings of the {AIS} 1997 Americas Conference on Information Systems (1997)
22. Bafoutsou, G., Mentzas, G.: Review and functional classification of collaborative systems. Int. J. Inf. Manag. (2002). https://doi.org/10.1016/s0268-4012(02)00013-0

23. Jiru, F., Harcuba, O.: Main Processes and Their Requirements in the DigiCor Platform (2017)
24. Kazantsev, N., Pishchulov, G., Mehandjiev, N., Sampaio, P.: Formation of demand-driven collaborations between suppliers in Industry 4.0 production networks. In: Grubbström, R. W., Hinterhuber, H.H., Lundquist, J. (eds.) 20th International Working Seminar on Production Economics, Innsbruck, Austria, vol. 3, pp. 255–266 (2018)
25. Camarinha-Matos, L.M., Afsarmanesh, H.: The virtual enterprise concept. In: Camarinha-Matos, L.M., Afsarmanesh, H. (eds.) PRO-VE 1999. ITIFIP, vol. 27, pp. 3–14. Springer, Boston, MA (1999). https://doi.org/10.1007/978-0-387-35577-1_1
26. Maguire, M., Bevan, N.: User requirements analysis. In: Hammond, J., Gross, T., Wesson, J. (eds.) Usability. ITIFIP, vol. 99, pp. 133–148. Springer, Boston, MA (2002). https://doi.org/10.1007/978-0-387-35610-5_9
27. Refsdal, A., Solhaug, B., Stølen, K.: Risk evaluation. Cyber-Risk Management. SCS, pp. 91–96. Springer, Cham (2015). https://doi.org/10.1007/978-3-319-23570-7_9
28. Cisneros-Cabrera, S., Sampaio, P., Mehandjiev, N.: A B2B team formation microservice for collaborative manufacturing in Industry 4.0. In: 2018 IEEE World Congress on Services (SERVICES). IEEE, San Francisco (2018). https://doi.org/10.1109/services.2018.00032

An Online Platform for 'Black Swan' Event Management in the Hospitality Industry

Angelika Kokkinaki[1(✉)], Styliani Kleanthous[2], Fotini Zioga[3],
Chrisostomi Maria Kirillou[1], and Maria Papadaki[4]

[1] University of Nicosia, Nicosia, Cyprus
kokkinaki.a@unic.ac.cy
[2] University of Cyprus, Nicosia, Cyprus
styliani.kleanthous@ouc.ac.cy
[3] Open University of Cyprus, Latsia, Cyprus
zioga.f@ouc.ac.cy
[4] Faculty of Business and Law, British University of Dubai, Dubai, UAE
maria.papadaki@buid.ac.ae

Abstract. Black swan Events or Low Probability High Impact Events (LoPHIEs), like wildfires, earthquakes and volcanic eruptions have significant and multifaceted implications in every economic sector of the area affected; among them, the hospitality and travel industry may be at the frontier of those affected in terms of span and impact. This paper outlines a vivid demonstration of the complexity of involved business processes and their interconnections through a case study. Appropriate preparations for hospitality and travel SMEs to such events have been identified and implemented through a purpose specific information system. To design this online platform, we followed a requirements analysis methodology. The main elements from the implementation of this platform have also been included, whereas elements of an initial usability evaluation have also been presented.

Keywords: Crisis management · Black swan events · Hospitality · Tourism

1 Introduction and Research Background

Black swan events, or low probability, high impact events (LoPHIEs), which include crises, disasters or emergencies, have significant implications upon the operation of involved and affected organizations (Hergert 2004); the hospitality and tourism industry is directly affected by LoPHIEs. Wildfires, earthquakes and volcanic eruptions demonstrate the complexity of interconnections between organizations involved in or affected by LoPHIEs. Appropriate preparations to such events may make the difference between a major disruption of operations in the affected organizations or their resilience and survival (Coombs and Holladay 2010; Halder 2015). Organizations' preparedness to LoPHIEs is usually distinguished by three phases, namely methods that prepare the organization BEFORE the event, methods that are initiated DURING the event to limit damage and methods that examine the aftermath (Bernstein 2011; Coombs 2007; Coombs and Holladay 2010).

© Springer Nature Switzerland AG 2020
M. Themistocleous and M. Papadaki (Eds.): EMCIS 2019, LNBIP 381, pp. 623–634, 2020.
https://doi.org/10.1007/978-3-030-44322-1_46

Such approaches exhibit some fundamental limitations (Diakou and Kokkinaki 2013). The most common limitation in these approaches is the biases raised in judgment or decision-making that usually have a huge impact in the quantification of probability, uncertainty and risk (e.g., Armstrong 2006; Berg et al. 2009; Fildes et al. 2009; Goodwin and Wright 2010; Jakoubi and Tjoa 2007; Onkal and Gonul 2007; Pennock et al. 2001). This proved to be especially important when an event occurs and has an impact on a specific business sector, for example the travel industry. Consequently, we need to understand the procedures and needs of this sector and how they currently respond to possible crises, like the eruption of Eyjafjallajökull in Iceland.

The paper is structured as follows: Sect. 2 will describe the requirements analysis methodology for designing the online platform for black swan events management, Sect. 3 will give information and description of the online platform and Sect. 3.1 will provide an initial usability evaluation of the platform. Section 4 will conclude this paper.

2 Methodological Procedure for Requirements Analysis

The purpose of this study was to understand how a company in the hospitality and tourism industry handles the effects of LoPHIEs and through this to identify the requirements for a web information system that can be used in such situations by small businesses in the tourism industry and specifically by tourist accommodations.

We followed a qualitative approach that involved semi-structured interviews with different people working in a market-leader travel company to understand what they know about black swan events, and what measures the company took when they had to deal with such an event in the past.

This empirical research was performed at a company in Europe, specializing in tourist lodging and accommodation services. One of the basic services of the company is its customer service and support, available in over 40 languages, along with support for the hotel/accommodation owners who are using the platform on a daily basis for updating accommodation availability. The company has shown rapid growth in recent years in response to serving travellers and accommodation providers, and has continuously optimized its online platform to better serve the users.

The choice of this company was based on its worldwide impact and its active presence during one of the most prominent black swan events. It also combines experienced staff in both technology and administration. All the above, combined with the easy access we had to this company led us to choose it as an environment of our research.

2.1 Instruments and Procedures

To select the sample of employees from the aforementioned, who would be involved in the survey, a sampling frame was created based on specific criteria. These predetermined criteria are intended to give us as accurate results as possible.

More specifically, the introduction of the above criteria includes:

Employment Time: This criteria depends on how long they have been working for the company and if they have faced different events that they could consider as black swan events. They can report/outline these events and analyze what they themselves perceive as more important.

Field of Specialization: An employees specialization is of great importance for how s/he perceives, events and what information s/he can provide about black swan events.

Department: We get information from the department to which the employee belongs about the collective reaction of the department to that event, as well as the changes that the department has applied to address black swan phenomena in the future.

The sample of the research was targeted and carefully selected to provide answers to the questions of this research. This approach helped to collect information about what is considered a black swan event in different parts of the company and to triangulate the collected data within the company's various departments. According to the criteria established, the sample of the survey is presented in the Table 1 below.

Table 1. Interviews undertaken with employees

Code no.	Position/Department	Position/Department during the event	Employment time
E1	Senior Coordinator/Marketing	Global Support Coordinator/Hotels Department	6
E2	Global PR Coordinator/Personal Relationships	Content Editor/Content Department	5
E3	Team Leader Long Tail Support/Strategic Partnerships	Project manager/Customer Support	11
E4	Account Manager XML/IT	Senior Customer Care/Customer Support	10
E5	Senior Team Leader/IT	Back-end Developer/IT	10
E6	Product Owner/Marketing	Technical Coordinator/ Strategic Partnerships	8

After we selected the sample for this research, we followed a mandatory procedure to comply with the ethical considerations of the research and the company's protocols. We first informed the human resource department that gave permission to the primary investigator to perform the study within the company and to use the specific sample. Then, the selected employees were contacted via email to invite them to take part in the study, provided them with details about the purpose of the study, the procedures that would be followed, and the duration of the interviews, and asked their permission to use a recording device during the interview. Most of the participants agreed to the interview recordings, and, for those who did not agree, we have only used written notes taken at the time of the interview.

2.2   Case Selection - Eyjafjallajökull Volcano Eruption

This section aims to present the findings of the primary data collection phase conducted at a well- known accommodation provider regarding black swan events. More specifically, the section provides a description and analysis of the data collected through interviews with the company's employees regarding their perception of which events are considered black swan events, who were called to deal with these events upon their occurrence, how the corporation reacted to them and finally how its organizational structures could be affected.

The sample of this study was selected in such a way as to effectively achieve disparity across different departments within the company and responsibilities of the employees. The objective was to collect as much information as possible about what is considered as a black swan event, from different sections of the company. Initially we needed to investigate the familiarity of the participants and employees in the company with black swan events and their experiences with such events.

Through the analysis of the data gathered, it can be concluded that only one employee in the company was familiar with the term black swan when describing an event. In the course of the interviews, however, it turned out that, while there have been several events experienced by the employees that meet the characteristics of black swan events, the term is not used within the company to describe them. During the interviews, most of the respondents reported different events that occurred during the time of their employment in the company and that had the characteristics of a black swan. After free and open communication between the researcher and the respondents, the eruption of the Icelandic volcano, *Eyjafjallajökull*, which took place in March 2010, was considered a representative example of a black swan event that most of the employees were familiar with, and consequently, it was selected for further analysis.

The eruption of the Eyjafjallajökull volcano led to the gradual closure of Europe's airspace for six days in order to avoid airplane crashes. European cities were, therefore, left with closed airports and all passengers traveling to destinations outside Europe, with intermediate stops at European airports, were also affected. Based on statistics, it is estimated that the event affected 105,000 flights in total and 7 million passengers in many different countries for almost one month (21 March to 24 April). In addition, the economic impact of the volcanic eruption was extremely high: airspace closure, loss in tourism revenue and decline in productivity ended up costing $5 billion. Based on estimations, the explosion caused damages to insured property amounting to $98 million, ranking it as the sixth most devastating explosion.

2.2.1   Implications of the Event

As expected, such an event affected the industry stakeholders (customers and hospitality providers), as well as intermediators between hotel tenants and hoteliers. According to respondents, the crisis that the company had to deal with is summarized in the following points:

- A large number of accommodation cancellations were made by passengers who could not reach their destination.
- Passengers had to extend their accommodation stay due to the closure of airports.
- Company employees could not return to their base.

As a result of the above points, the number of requests for amendments and cancellations of reservations increased dramatically. Initially, the Customer Service Department was the division directly affected by the situation, due to the insufficient number of employees to manage effectively the significant increase in the call volume and online requests.

2.2.2 Addressing the Event

Based on the Eyjafjallajökull volcano eruption, the following sub-sections describe a series of actions for addressing the event, as emerged through interviews with company employees and aim to form the foundations of a consolidated action plan for dealing with Black swan events within the tourism industry.

2.2.3 Impact Group

In this chaotic situation, action was required to stabilize it and resolve problems of inefficiency. As respondents reported, one of the first steps taken was to set up an impact group for coordinating actions and regulating the situation both internally and externally. This group was attended by individuals from each department. From an organizational point of view, the impact group consisted of people who either had managerial posts, acted as project managers, or were team leaders or technicians.

The way the impact team worked was critical for decision-making. Group meetings were scheduled every two hours (approximately) during the day. Initially, each unit that was represented in the impact group provided information on the evolution of the events, the problems they were facing and what they had successfully resolved. Then, there was an open discussion and effort to solve problems using brainstorming.

It is noteworthy that the company maintained a powerful IT department that could provide solutions to address this crisis by building new components in the IT systems. That is why the use of computer technology in the impact group meetings was critical for several reasons. Indicatively, they could respond at the same time to what configurations were feasible and let others know how much time would be required for implementing those configurations, as well as suggest a different approach if they felt it necessary.

Subsequently, the participants in the impact group communicated the decisions taken to the other employees of the departments by calling brief meetings and sending emails. The procedure described above was repeated until a relative stability occurred.

2.2.4 First Line of Communication

The impact group established an emergency communication line; representatives handling calls through this line could make decisions to address minor issues. The representatives would forward complicated issues to another dedicated communication line. All personnel were updated and were asked if they wanted to join the emergency communication line. The second line of communication was handled by employees in the Customer Service department.

Until the instantiation of this specific LoPHIE, only customer service employees were trained on the procedures to follow in emergency situations. In order to gain competencies addressing customers' requests effectively, one had to attend a thorough training session which lasted a month. Due to time constraints, the Personnel Training

Department had to reconsider and parameterize the educational material focusing only on typical procedures and create short intensive training seminars for employees serving the front-end emergency line of communication.

For optimal implementation of the emergency line initiative, in-house chat rooms were created where employees could ask more experienced personnel for clarifications about the case they were handling. This enabled the speedy exchange of formal and tacit knowledge between novice and experienced customer representatives. In addition, call tracking systems were further developed in the company's call centre which record the volume of calls received by each group. This made it easier to locate overloaded support lines, and call forwarding could be then activated. During this crisis, all employees involved in resolving and restoring stability had to work overtime.

2.2.5   Extending Customer Service

Despite the immediate mobilization of the company to help the Customer Service department, the volume of requests was too high and additional measures were needed to cope with the emergency. The company carried out a mass recruitment for the Customer Service department. Within one day, 100 people were hired on a monthly contract and started to work the next day. To enable the newly recruited employees to handle their duties so quickly, the Personnel Training Department created a second round of high-speed training seminars. One of the objectives of these training seminars was also to ensure the new employees understood the philosophy of the company before taking part in the crisis management.

2.2.6   Negotiations with Hotels

A special weight in the management of this crisis was the negotiations that took place with the hotels regarding cancellations of reservations made through the company's website without any cancellation costs. Excellent cooperation between hotels and the company was reported, and there was no intention for any party to exploit the situation. In most cases, cancellations were made free of charge and, where this was not possible, hoteliers offered the tenants the option of rescheduling their booking for another time in the same or another hotel of the same standards with which they were collaborating.

2.2.7   Contacting Hotel Tenants

According to the respondents, the company was not active in social media network at the time of the event, which made it difficult to connect and communicate instructions to hotel occupants who had not yet contacted the Customer Services department. In cooperation with the IT department, an extra space was created on the homepage of the website, where instructions were posted to hotel tenants regarding what they should do if their reservations were affected by the volcano eruption.

Essentially, it was defined and advised that the arrival of the tenants was considered 'urgent' if it was within the next 45 h, where priority was given to settling the cancellation or extending their stay. In this way, an initial routing of the communication was established, and additional calls could be avoided.

2.3   Organizational Structures of the Company After the Event

Responses determining the recovery time were found to be indistinguishable, and differed depending on the respondents' department and position held. The departments that took longer to return to normal work were the Customer Service and the Hotel Support departments, as these were the departments most affected by the crisis. The recovery period was reported to range from 2 to 5 weeks.

According to the same respondents, the additional components of the information systems created only to support this event had to be re-implemented to be included as core functions in the systems, which was quite time-consuming.

The results are presented in more detail in the Table 2 below.

Table 2. Recovery timeout

Department	Reset time (weeks)
Marketing	2
Customer service	4–5
Hotel support	4
Content	2

The participants in the study pointed out that this was an extreme, unpredictable event and that the company was not ready to deal with it. Nonetheless, it is encouraging that the company was organized; the departments involved worked in coordination and reacted quickly to the situation, thus achieving to provide support to both tenants and hotel owners.

When the situation was stabilized, meetings were held in order to evaluate the way the company reacted and what could be done differently if such a situation happened again in the future. A common conclusion from these meetings was the need to establish emergency procedures. In addition, one further conclusion was that the information systems used within the company should be scalable and more flexible.

Part of the procedures established after the eruption of the volcano were concerned with the other departments creating the first communication lines to provide support to the Customer Service department in cases of unusually increased number of calls (i.e., high season demand in the summer months). In achieving this, the way in which staff training is carried out has been restructured. Furthermore, the IT department had to set up the appropriate infrastructure to enable calls and call centre support requests to be routed to the rest of the departments.

The Eyjafjallajökull crisis helped the company redefine how customer service is managed. Over the next years, more emphasis has been put on enhancing the company's customer-centric philosophy. Customer Service department has been restructured; new roles have been identified to improve communication and new processes have been implemented to enable settlement of similar events more effectively in the future.

3 Online Platform for Black Swan Event Management

Based on the insights outlined in the previous section, it appears that certain functional specifications are considered important for the organization to be able to handle a black swan event. This is linked to both the immediate reaction of employees as well as the direct parameterization of information systems that are used to make it easier to deal with the situation right away. Our goal is to develop an online management application that small-sized hotel units can be use, which, apart from the basic functionality, will be enriched with additional black swan events management mechanisms.

For the purpose of demonstrating the proposed Event Management Services for black swan events, basic hotel management mechanisms were also implemented. Through the online application, owners or administrators will be able to manage the reservations and the hotel's availability, as well as to access the guests' details so as to have further communication with them. The additional black swan events management mechanisms enable managers of the hotel unit to follow simple procedures that can face a potential crisis, without the need for additional technical support. Since any additional technical support for information systems in small businesses is not covered by their own employees, but instead by external partners, this online application aims to address issues with minimal response time to any LoPHIE.

The application consists of the following:

Back-end, which contains the management part of the application, e.g., room availability, and the management of additional procedures related to Black swan events.

Front-end, which consists of the public space of the application that can be used by customers for booking a room and getting additional information on the hotel and the surrounding area.

3.1 Back-End Implementation Based on Requirements

For the development of an online platform that could be employed to address LoPHIs, we used the Drupal CMS. In this paper we will focus only on the design and implementation of the back-end features that also contain the tools for black swan events management.

3.1.1 Hiding the Room Search Mechanism

To implement the mechanism that will hide the search engine from the public site during emergencies, the Emergency module is used. This module allows the website's public space to be adapted during a crisis (Fig. 1). It gives the flexibility of creating multiple emergency levels according to the situation. For this application, we created two levels (Medium and Low), which are both related to the search for availability.

3.1.2 Implementation of Alert Messages

The site Alert (Fig. 1) module has been used for implementing alert messages that would appear in case of an emergency. This module allows for setting the timeframe for the alert messages to appear and disappear after the time frame ends (Fig. 2).

Fig. 1. Emergency module for hiding room search

Fig. 2. Alert messages

3.1.3 Update Messages from Relevant Parties

Updates from stakeholders are made using the Drupal open-source content management software (Wunderground weather module and Feed Aggregator see Fig. 1), which are projected at the management panel through block structures. The manager of the hotel unit can customize the sources' updates by creating and adding new feeds (Fig. 3).

3.1.4 Mass Customer Message Updates

Using this functionality, the unit manager can inform a group of customers about a specific situation that affects their bookings. In this way, we ensure that all interested customers will be informed even if they do not enter the website. Similarly, the manager does not have to inform each interested customer, one by one.

Fig. 3. Update messages

3.2 Front-End Design of the Online Application

The basic function of the public section of the application is to demonstrate how users can, through the search engine, search and book available hotel rooms. Apart from that, they can also find information about the services offered by the hotel and the contact form.

As we can see in Fig. 4, the availability search engine is found only on the homepage of the site. In order to make the reservation, the user is asked to provide his/her personal details and email address. The payment method is added to the app and indicates what the hotel accepts as a payment for the duration of the residence. After the user has completed the reservation, he/she receives a confirmation message via email with the details of the reservation.

Fig. 4. Interface for searching and booking accommodation

3.2.1 Bookings Management

In the booking management part (Fig. 5), the manager can inform the customers about any updates regarding their reservation, manage the procedures for black swan events, and send mass or individual messages to the customers.

Fig. 5. Booking management form

4 Conclusion

Black swan events or Low Probability High Impact Events (LoPHIEs), like wildfires, earthquakes and volcanic eruptions, have significant implications to the hospitality and travel industry; a vivid demonstration of the complexity of interconnections between organizational units involved in or affected by LoPHIEs are outlined in this paper through a case study. Appropriate preparations for hospitality and travel SMES to such events have been identified and implemented through a purpose specific information system. To design this platform, we followed a requirements analysis methodology. The main elements from the implementation of this platform have also been included, and elements of an initial usability evaluation have also been presented.

For future development, it is foreseen that novel technological methods and tools that have the potential to handle large volumes of information, fuse heterogeneous data from multiple sensing systems and take fast decisions at critical turning points must be examined in more detail.

References

Armstrong, J.S.: Findings from evidence-based forecasting: methods for reducing forecast error. Int. J. Forecast. **22**(3), 583–598 (2006)

Berg, J.E., Neumann, G.R., Rietz, T.A.: Searching for Google's value: using prediction markets to forecast market capitalization prior to an initial public offering. Manag. Sci. **55**(3), 348–361 (2009)

Coombs, W.T.: Ongoing Crisis Communication: Planning, Managing, and Responding, 2nd edn. Sage, Los Angeles (2007)

Coombs, W.T., Holladay, J.S.: PR Strategy and Application: Managing Influence. Blackwell, Chichester (2010)

Diakou, C.-M., Kokkinaki, A.I.: Enabling sustainable development through networks of collective intelligence. In: 4th Conference of the IDRiM Society, 4–6 September 2013. Northumbria University, Newcastle (2013)

Fildes, R., Goodwin, P., Lawrence, M., Nikolopoulos, K.: Effective forecasting and judgmental adjustments: an empirical evaluation and strategies for improvement in supply-chain planning. Int. J. Forecast. **25**(1), 3–23 (2009). https://doi.org/10.1016/j.ijforecast.2008.11.010

Goodwin, P., Wright, G.: The limits of forecasting methods in anticipating rare events. Technol. Forecast. Soc. Change **77**, 355–368 (2010)

Halder, B.: Approaches of Humanitarian Crisis Management - Associated Risks with the ICT-based Crowdsourcing Paradigm (2015). Available at SSRN: http://ssrn.com/abstract= 2568233 or http://dx.doi.org/10.2139/ssrn.2568233

Hergert, M.: The effect of terrorist attacks on shareholder value: a study of United States international firms. Int. J. Manag. **21**(1), 25–28 (2004)

Jakoubi, S., Tjoa, S., Quirchmayr, G.: Rope: a methodology for enabling the risk-aware modelling and simulation of business processes. In: ECIS 2007 Proceedings (2007). Paper 47

Onkal, D., Gonul, M.S.: Judgmental adjustment: a challenge to providers and users of forecasts. Foresight **2**, 13–17 (2007)

Author Index